Electronic Discovery and Records Management Guide: Rules, Checklists, and Forms

2009 Edition

Jay E. Grenig
Browning E. Marean
Mary Pat Poteet

Mat #40714877

e-mail copyright.west@thomsonreuters.com or fax (651) 687-7551

ISBN 978-0-314-98736-5

About the Authors

Jay E. Grenig is a Professor of Law at Marquette University Law School. He has taught at Pepperdine University School of Law, Willamette University College of Law, Vermont Law School, Cornell University School of Industrial and Labor Relations, the University of Southern California Graduate School of Public Administration, Golden Gate University, and Chapman College. Prof. Grenig practiced law in the San Francisco Bay Area for several years. He received a B.A. from Willamette University and a J.D. from the University of California, Hastings College of the Law.

Prof. Grenig is the author or coauthor of numerous books and articles, including *Handbook of Federal Civil Discovery and Disclosure* (with Kinsler), *Virginia Practice: Civil Discovery* (with others), *Illinois Practice: Civil Discovery* (with others), *eDiscovery and Digital Evidence* (with Gleisner), *West's Federal Jury Practice and Instructions* (with others), *Alternative Dispute Resolution*, and *West's Federal Forms: District Court*. He is managing editor of *Electronic Discovery and Records Management Quarterly*.

Prof. Grenig is Reporter for the Local Rules Committee for the U.S. District Court for the Eastern District of Wisconsin and a member of the Wisconsin Judicial Council. He is a member of the American Law Institute, the Working Group on Electronic Document Retention and Production of the Sedona Conference, the College of Labor and Employment Lawyers, ARMA International, AIIM, and the Order of the Coif. He was selected as one of the Wisconsin Leaders in the Law in 2008.

Browning E. Marean is a partner in DLA Piper's San Diego office. He is a member of the firm's Litigation Group and is co-chair of the firm's Electronic Discovery Readiness and Response Group. Mr. Marean specializes in the areas of complex business litigation, technology matters, professional responsibility, and knowledge management. He is admitted to practice in California and Texas.

Mr. Marean joined the firm (then Gray Cary Ames & Frye) in 1969. He is a member of DLA Piper's Technology Committee, and is an emeritus member of the California State Bar Law Practice Management Committee. He is a member of the San Diego County Bar Association Ethics Committee and the Sedona Conference.

Mr. Marean is a nationally known teacher and lecturer on various topics including electronic discovery, records retention, knowledge management, and computer technology Mr. Marean received his law degree from the University of California, Hastings College of the Law, and his undergraduate degree from Stanford University.

Mary Pat Poteet is the Director of Litigation Support for DLA Piper US LLP and is based in San Diego. She is a member of the firm's Electronic Discovery Readiness and Response Group and manages a team of litigation support professionals throughout the country. Ms. Poteet provides consultation services on various litigation support issues, including complex litigation, data management and electronic evidence handling and processing. She speaks and writes frequently on electronic discovery topics and is a contributing author of the *California Civil Discovery Practice*, 4th ed.

Ms. Poteet joined the firm 2005. She is the Litigation Support Peer Group Vice President for the International Legal Technology Association and is on the Editorial Board of the *Litigation Today* magazine. She is a founding member of the Electronic Discovery Reference Model and she graduated from San Diego State University.

Preface

The rapidity with which electronic discovery is becoming commonplace in federal and state courts, and in all types of cases, is breathtaking. It is estimated that more than 93% of all communications are digital. Ninety-eight percent of all business records are now electronic, and 80% of them are never converted to paper or any other tangible form. The increased use of electronically stored information is reflected in the 2006 amendments to the Federal Rules of Civil Procedure, the adoption by the National Conference of Commissioners on Uniform State Laws of the Uniform Rules Relating to the Discovery of Electronically Stored Information, the multi-year project of the Working Group on Electronic Document Retention and Production of the influential Sedona Conference to develop The Sedona Principles (Second) Best Practices Recommendations & Principles for Addressing Electronic Document Production, and the American Bar Association's publication of standards relating to electronic discovery. In addition, the Federal Judicial Center has published Managing Discovery of Electronic Information: A Pocket Guide for Judges, and the Conference of Chief Justices has issued guidelines for state trial courts to use in dealing with discovery of electronically stored information.

This book provides a comprehensive guide to all aspects of electronic discovery—from records management to spoliation. While reference is made to applicable rules of the Federal Rules of Civil Procedure, the book is intended to provide guidance for discovery in state courts, as well.

Part I examines the nature and sources of electronically stored information. Rules of procedure and best practices applicable to electronically stored information are identified. Additionally, the need to protect electronically stored information and to establish policies governing use of computers are explored in Part I. Part I also includes a section on ethical issues.

Given the explosive growth in the amount of electronically stored information, a proper records management program is essential to reducing the expense and disruption that can be caused by electronic discovery. Part II examines the various aspects of records management, including developing a program, records retention, records destruction, and litigation holds.

Discovery and disclosure are examined from the perspectives of both the discovering party and the responding party in Part III and Part IV. Part III emphasizes the importance of the discovery conference in controlling costs and obtaining the best result for all parties. Keeping in mind that all the discovery rules of civil procedure, not just the rules specifically referencing electronic discovery, apply to electronic discovery, Part III addresses depositions, interrogatories, requests for production and inspection, and requests for admission. The issues relating to obtaining electronic discovery from third-parties are also addressed in Part III.

Part IV looks at electronic discovery from the perspective of the responding party. The critical issues of privilege and spoliation are discussed. Dealing with "not reasonably accessible electronically stored information" and cost-shifting are also addressed in Part IV.

The book features more than 50 checklists and over 100 electronic discovery forms. In addition, the book includes the text (including Advisory Committee Notes) for the 2006 and 2007 amendments to the discovery rules of the Federal Rules of Civil Procedure. It also contains the 2007 edition of the Sedona Principles Best Practices Recommendations & Principles for Addressing Electronic Document Production, and an examination of the proposed new Rule 502 of the Federal Rules of Evidence governing privilege waiver.

Readers who have suggestions or comments are encouraged to contact the authors at Marquette University Law School, P.O. Box 1881, Milwaukee, WI 53201-1881 (jgrenig@earthlink.net).

Jay E. Grenig
Browning E. Marean
Mary Pat Poteet

Milwaukee, Wisconsin
September 2008

Table of Contents

PART I. INTRODUCTION

CHAPTER 1. ELECTRONICALLY STORED INFORMATION

I. GUIDELINES

II. CHECKLISTS

III. FORMS

CHAPTER 2. RULES OF PROCEDURE AND BEST PRACTICES

I. GUIDELINES

II. CHECKLISTS

III. RULES

CHAPTER 3. PROTECTING ELECTRONICALLY STORED INFORMATION

I. GUIDELINES

II. CHECKLISTS

III. FORMS

PART II. RECORDS MANAGEMENT

CHAPTER 4. RECORDS MANAGEMENT PROGRAMS

I. GUIDELINES

II. CHECKLISTS

III. FORMS

CHAPTER 5. RECORDS RETENTION

I. GUIDELINES

II. CHECKLISTS

III. FORMS

CHAPTER 6. DESTRUCTION OF ELECTRONICALLY STORED INFORMATION

I. GUIDELINES

II. CHECKLISTS

III. FORMS

CHAPTER 7. LITIGATION HOLDS

I. GUIDELINES

II. CHECKLISTS

III. FORMS

PART III. OBTAINING DISCOVERY OF ELECTRONICALLY STORED INFORMATION

CHAPTER 8. DISCOVERY AND DISCLOSURE

I. GUIDELINES

II. CHECKLISTS

III. FORMS

CHAPTER 9. DISCOVERY CONFERENCE

I. GUIDELINES

II. CHECKLISTS

III. FORMS

CHAPTER 10. DEPOSITIONS

I. GUIDELINES

II. CHECKLISTS

III. FORMS

CHAPTER 11. INTERROGATORIES

I. GUIDELINES

II. CHECKLISTS

III. FORMS

CHAPTER 12. REQUESTS FOR PRODUCTION AND INSPECTION

I. GUIDELINES

II. CHECKLISTS

III. FORMS

CHAPTER 13. REQUESTS FOR ADMISSIONS

I. GUIDELINES

II. CHECKLISTS

III. FORMS

CHAPTER 14. DISCOVERY FROM NON-PARTIES OF ELECTRONICALLY STORED INFORMATION

I. GUIDELINES

II. CHECKLISTS

III. FORMS

PART IV. RESPONDING TO DISCOVERY OF ELECTRONICALLY STORED INFORMATION

CHAPTER 15. RESPONDING TO DISCOVERY

I. GUIDELINES

II. CHECKLISTS

III. FORMS

CHAPTER 16. PRIVILEGE AND PRIVACY

I. GUIDELINES

II. CHECKLISTS

III. FORMS

CHAPTER 17. SPOLIATION

I. GUIDELINES

II. CHECKLISTS

III. FORMS

CHAPTER 18. NOT REASONABLY ACCESSIBLE ELECTRONICALLY STORED INFORMATION

I. GUIDELINES

II. CHECKLISTS

III. FORMS

CHAPTER 19. MOTIONS AND PROTECTIVE ORDERS

I. GUIDELINES

II. CHECKLISTS

III. FORMS

Part I

INTRODUCTION

Chapter 1

Electronically Stored Information

I. GUIDELINES

II. CHECKLISTS

III. FORMS

Research References

Additional References

Eisner, A New Year's Resolution to Save on Discovery Costs, Elec. Disc. & Records Mgt. Q., Spring 2008, at 22

O'Connor, Pumping Up the Volume on Audio Discovery, Elec. Disc. & Records Mgt. Q., Spring 2008, at 28

Schlueter, Making the Case for Audio in Litigation & Compliance, Elec. Disc. & Records Mgt. Q., Winter 2007, at 18

Skapik & Rogers, Budgeting for eDiscovery: Cost and Containment Considerations, Elec. Disc. & Records Mgt. Q., Spring 2008, at 3

A.L.R. Library

Admissibility of computerized private business records, 7 A.L.R. 4th 8

Treatises and Practice Aids

eDiscovery & Digital Evidence §§ 6:10 to 6:12

Grenig and Kinsler, Federal Civil Discovery and Disclosure §§ 13.1 to 13.6 (2d ed.)

Trial Strategy

Recovery and Reconstruction of Electronic Mail as Evidence, 41 Am. Jur Proof of Facts 3d 1

Computer Technology in Civil Litigation, 71 Am. Jur Trials 111

Law Reviews and Other Periodicals

Brownstone, Preserve or Perish: Destroy or Drown—eDiscovery Morphs into Electronic Information Management, 8 N.C. J. L. & Tech 1 (2006)

Coyle, "Metadata" Mining Vexes Lawyers, Bars—Invisible Document Data a Big Problem, Nat'l L.J., Feb. 18, 2008, at 1

Davis, Am I My Client's Keeper in Discovery Situations?, Nat'l L. J., May 5, 2008, at 3

Note, The Requirement for Metadata Production under Williams v. Sprint/United Management Co.: An Unnecessary Burden for Litigants Engaged in Electronic Discovery, 93 Cornell L. Rev. 221 (2007)

Paul & Baron, Information Inflation: Can the Legal System Adapt, 13 Rich. J.L. Tech. 10 (2007)

Williams & Wenker, Qualcomm Ruling Shakes Up the Litigation World: The Hefty Sanctions Underscore Attorneys' E-Discovery Duties, Nat'l L. J., March 10, 2008, at S3

Additional References

Ball, When Out-of-Box Means Out-of-Luck, LegalTechnology, May 29, 2008, at http://www.law.com/tech

Gaasbeck, Danger on the Road: How to Challenge a Black Box Report, Trial, Feb. 2007, at 50

Grenig, Growing Use and Expense of Electronic Discovery IS Driven by the Increased Use of Electronically Stored Information, in Instant Awareness: An Immediate Look at the Legal, Governmental, and Economic Ramifications of the amendments to the Federal Rules of Civil Procedure and Electronic Discovery 23 (Aspatore 2008)

Keane, E-Discovery Changes and Costs, in Instant Awareness: An Immediate Look at the Legal, Governmental, and Economic Ramifications of the Amendments to the Federal Rules of Civil Procedure and Electronic Discovery 53 (Aspatore 2008)

Paskach, Predictability and Consistency in eDiscovery, Metropolitan Corporate Counsel, Mar. 2007

ABA Discovery Standards, http://www.abanet.org/litigation/discoverystandards/2005civildiscoverystandards.pdf

Electronic Discovery Reference Model Project, http://www.edrm.net

EMC Corp., http://www.emc.com

The Sedona Conference, http://www.thesedonaconference.org

TechTarget, Inc., http://www.searchstorage.com

KeyCite®: Cases and other legal materials listed in KeyCite Scope can be researched through the KeyCite service on Westlaw®. Use KeyCite to check citations for form, parallel references, prior and later history, and comprehensive citator information, including citations to other decisions and secondary materials.

I. GUIDELINES

§ 1:1 Generally

Today, most documents are in electronic form. The growth in electronically stored information and the variety of systems or devices for creating and storing such information has been dramatic. This creates new issues for discovery as electronically stored information may exist in dynamic databases and other forms very different from static paper.[1] Of considerable significance is the overwhelming volume of electronically stored information. New technologies and judicial and regulatory requirements have also created new concerns.

Discovery of electronically stored information has been significant in a number of high-profile cases. In more and more state and federal cases, lawyers and state and federal judges must focus on preserving, gathering, reviewing and producing electronically stored information.

Discovery and disclosure of electronically stored information pose many of the same problems as discovery and disclosure of paper documents but they also pose additional problems. The volume, number of storage locations, and data volatility of electronically stored information are significantly greater than those of paper documents. Electronically stored information contains nontraditional types of data including metadata, system data, and deleted data. Furthermore, the costs of locating, reviewing, and preparing electronically stored information for production may be much greater than in conventional discovery proceedings.

Computer-based discovery also has advantages over paper-based discovery. Costs of photocopying and transport can be much lower, and frequently nonexistent in electronic discovery. Reviewing and organizing evidence using various forms of computer manipulation can be less expensive than in paper-based discovery. The cost of using a litigation support system is greatly reduced if the documents are in electronic form from the beginning.

This guide takes a proactive approach to discovery of electronically stored information—proper planning in advance of possible discovery can greatly reduce the costs

---

[Section 1:1]

[1]See Ball, Piecing Together the E-Discovery Plan, Trial, June 2008 ("The problem is, e-discovery is not simple. It's complex, technical, and tricky. There are no shortcuts—no form, checklist, or script that's going to get the defendant to find the relevant information and turn it over in a reasonably usable way.").

and burden of complying with discovery requests. Thus, initial emphasis is given to records management. Records management is important for both plaintiffs and defendants. While discovery is frequently thought of (and written about) as though it is the plaintiff that is discovering information in the possession of the defendant, in actual practice plaintiffs can also be the target of discovery requests by defendants.

This guide also recognizes that issues relating to the discovery of electronically stored information arise in state and federal court, as well as administrative proceedings. While specific references are made to the 2006 amendments to the Federal Rules of Civil Procedure, the discussion in this guide includes state and federal courts.

§ 1:2 Electronically stored information

"Electronically stored information" has a very broad meaning. The Uniform Rules Relating to the Discovery of Electronically Stored Information states that "electronically stored information" is "information that is stored in an electronic medium and is retrievable in perceivable form." Electronically stored information comprises all current types of computer-based information, and it encompasses future changes and developments. Electronically stored information may be found in databases that do not correspond to hard copy materials.

The ordinary operation of computers—including turning a computer on and off or accessing a particular file—can alter or destroy electronically stored information, and computer systems automatically discard or overwrite as part of their routine operation. Computers can create information without the operator's direction or awareness, a feature with no direct counterpart in hard copy materials. Although electronically stored information may be deleted, it continues to exist, but in forms often difficult to locate, retrieve or search. Electronically stored information may be incomprehensible when it is separated from the system creating it. These distinctive features of electronic discovery can often increase the expense and burden of discovery.

In *Zubulake v. UBS Warburg LLC*,[1] District Judge Scheindlin divided electronically stored information into two broad categories:

1. Data kept in an accessible format, broken down into three subcategories, listed in order from most accessible to least accessible:
   a. Active, online data, such as hard drives
   b. Near-line data, such as optical disks
   c. Offline storage/archives lacking the coordinated control of an intelligent disk subsystem
2. Electronic data that are relatively inaccessible, broken down into two subcategories, ranked in order of accessibility:
   a. Backup tapes
   b. Erased, fragmented or damaged data

§ 1:3 Locations and sources of electronically stored information

Electronically stored information can be found in a wide range of locations, including individual desktop computers, laptop computers, network hard drives, removable media, servers, backup tapes or other storage media, personal digital assistants, cellular telephones, Internet data, paging devices, GPS navigation systems, thumb drives, MP3 players, and audio systems such as voice mail.[1] Even automobiles may contain "black boxes" with electronically stored information.

[Section 1:2]

[1]Zubulake v. UBS Warburg LLC, 217 F.R.D. 309, 324, 91 Fair Empl. Prac. Cas. (BNA) 1574 (S.D. N.Y. 2003).

[Section 1:3]

[1]See Smith v. Cafe Asia, 246 F.R.D. 19, 102 Fair Empl. Prac. Cas. (BNA) 155, 90 Empl. Prac. Dec. (CCH) P 43044 (D.D.C. 2007) (ordering plaintiff to preserve graphic images stored on cell phone).

§ 1:4 Volume and duplicability of electronically stored information

Not only is there more electronically stored information than paper documents, electronically stored information is created at much greater rates than paper documents. Consequently, the amount of information available for potential discovery has greatly increased with the advent of electronically stored information.

§ 1:5 Persistence of electronically stored information

Electronically stored information is more difficult to dispose of than paper documents. While a shredded paper is usually irretrievably lost, disposal of electronically stored information is much different. Deleting electronically stored information normally does not actually erase the information from the computer's storage devices; deleting simply finds the information's entry in the disk director and changes it to a "not used" status. When electronically stored information is deleted, the computer can write over the deleted information. Until the computer writes over the deleted information, the information can be recovered by searching the disk itself rather than the disk's directory. Electronically stored information may be recoverable long after the information has been deleted.

§ 1:6 Dynamic nature of electronically stored information

Unlike paper documents, electronically stored information has dynamic content likely to change over time, even without human intervention. Workflow systems automatically update files and transfer electronically stored information from one location to another. Web pages are constantly updated with information fed from other applications. E-mail systems reorganize and remove electronically stored information automatically. Even the act of merely accessing or moving digital electronically stored information can change it.

§ 1:7 Electronically stored information and metadata

Unlike paper, electronically stored information contains metadata. Metadata are information about the document or file recorded by the computer to assist the computer, and often the user, in storing and retrieving the document or file at a later date. Metadata may be useful for the system administration, as they provide information regarding the generation, handling, transfer, and store of the electronically stored information.

"System metadata" are data that a computer's operating system compiles about a file's name, size, and location, as well as its last modified, accessed, and created dates and time stamps. "Application metadata" are information embedded in documents, including user comments and tracked changes. System metadata can facilitate searching and sorting data chronologically, and suggesting whether the data can be trusted. System metadata present little potential for disclosure of privileged or confidential information should be routinely preserved and produced. Robocopy, a free download from Microsoft, can preserve system metadata, but it cannot restore data already corrupted. Robocopy can also be difficult to use.

Metadata may show:

- Who may have opened the file
- On what dates and times persons accessed the file
- When modifications, including additions, deletions, or revisions, were made to the file
- To whom files were distributed or forwarded
- Who made additions, deletions, or revisions to the file

Descriptive metadata describe a resource for purposes such as discovery and identification. It can include such elements as author, title, and abstract. Structural metadata indicate how compound objects are put together. They identify data format, media format, or the type of data representation and file types, hardware and software needed to render the data, and the compression method and encryption algorithms used, if any. Administrative metadata provide information to help manage a resource, such as when and how it was created, file type and other technical information, and who can access it.

Generally, the computer creates the metadata automatically with time, date, and user stamps. Users can add layers of metadata. For example, when using the "track changes" on a document, the editor identifies the editor's fingerprint on the document and leaves evidence of every character added or deleted. Metadata can also show the relations documents have with other portions of documents, showing what has been cut, copied, and pasted into other materials.

§ 1:8 Environmental dependence and obsolescence of electronically stored information

Electronically stored information, unlike paper data, may be incomprehensible when separated from its environment. If the raw data in a data based are produced without the underlying structure, the raw data will appear as a long list of undefined numbers of characters. To make sense of the raw data, the viewer needs the context including labels, columns, report formats, and other information.

§ 1:9 Dispersal and searchability of electronically stored information

While paper documents will often be consolidated in a handful of boxes or filing cabinets, electronically stored information can reside in numerous locations, such as desktop hard drives, laptop computers, network servers, floppy disks, backup tapes, flash drives, and thumb drives. In many cases, it may be much easier and less expensive to copy electronically stored information. It may also be easier to search and organize electronically stored information compared with the manual alternatives.[1]

§ 1:10 Ethics and sanctions

Attorneys and their clients have significant responsibilities for properly identifying, searching for, collecting and producing electronically stored information in compliance with the Federal Rules of Civil Procedure. For the discovery system to function, attorneys and clients must work together to ensure that both understand how and where electronic documents, records, and e-mails are maintained and to determine how best to locate, review, and produce responsive documents. The courts will not accept ignorance on the part of either as an excuse.[1] Various types of discovery abuse have resulted in sanctions imposed on parties and their attorneys.[2] Sanctions have been imposed using a number of theories, including negligence,[3] intentional deception,[4] purposeful sluggishness,[5] gross negligence,[6] and reckless disregard.[7]

Federal Rules of Civil Procedure 11, 26(g) and 37

[Section 1:9]

[1]See, e.g., In re Bristol-Myers Squibb Securities Litigation, 205 F.R.D. 437, 51 Fed. R. Serv. 3d 1212 (D.N.J. 2002). See also MANUAL FOR COMPLEX LITIG. (FOURTH) § 11.446.

[Section 1:10]

[1]Qualcomm Inc. v. Broadcom Corp., 2008 WL 66932 (S.D. Cal. 2008), vacated in part, 2008 WL 638108 (S.D. Cal. 2008); Phoenix Four, Inc. v. Strategic Resources Corp., 2006 WL 1409413 (S.D. N.Y. 2006).

[2]See, e.g., Metropolitan Opera Ass'n, Inc. v. Local 100, Hotel Employees and Restaurant Employees Intern. Union, 212 F.R.D. 178, 171 L.R.R.M. (BNA) 2897 (S.D. N.Y. 2003), adhered to on reconsideration, 175 L.R.R.M. (BNA) 2870, 2004 WL 1943099 (S.D. N.Y. 2004) (imposing sanctions for defendant's various and serious failings during discovery relating to electronic records).

[3]See, e.g., Finley v. Hartford Life and Acc. Ins. Co., 249 F.R.D. 329 (N.D. Cal. 2008) (defendant's failure to make initial disclosure of full version of surveillance video subject to sanction; sanctioning defendant's attorneys for failure to make reasonable inquiry concerning missing portion of surveillance video requested by plaintiff not warranted).

provide for sanctions under specified conditions. In addition, has inherent power to assess sanctions. In order to assess attorney's fees pursuant to its inherent power, a district court must find a party or attorney "acted in bad faith, vexatiously, wantonly, or for oppressive reasons."[8] There is a split among the circuits as to whether sanctions, other than attorney's fees, may be imposed against attorneys or parties under the inherent-powers doctrine in the absence of bad faith.[9] The court in *Qualcomm* relied on a "reckless" standard in concluding sanctions were appropriate under the court's inherent power.[10]

---

[4]See Qualcomm Inc. v. Broadcom Corp., 2008 WL 66932 (S.D. Cal. 2008), vacated in part, 2008 WL 638108 (S.D. Cal. 2008).

[5]In re Seroquel Products Liability Litigation, 244 F.R.D. 650 (M.D. Fla. 2007) (sanctions imposed on drug manufacturer for failing to meet its own commitments regarding electronic discovery in multi-district products liability suit).

[6]Phoenix Four, Inc. v. Strategic Resources Corp., 2006 WL 1409413 (S.D. N.Y. 2006) (imposing sanctions on defendants' counsel for failure to search computer workstations for relevant electronic records and for late production of documents).

[7]United Medical Supply Co., Inc. v. U.S., 77 Fed. Cl. 257 (2007) (sanctions against government were warranted where government repeatedly violated its obligation to maintain relevant records after it had knowledge of contractor's claim, and misrepresented its efforts to locate responsive documents and to prevent further spoliation).

[8]Chambers v. NASCO, Inc., 501 U.S. 32, 45–46, 111 S. Ct. 2123, 115 L. Ed. 2d 27, 19 Fed. R. Serv. 3d 817 (1991).

[9]Bad faith required: Youn v. Track, Inc., 324 F.3d 409, 55 Fed. R. Serv. 3d 611, 2003 FED App. 0087P (6th Cir. 2003); In re Mroz, 65 F.3d 1567, Bankr. L. Rep. (CCH) P 76678, 32 Fed. R. Serv. 3d 1244 (11th Cir. 1995). Bad faith not required: Republic of Philippines v. Westinghouse Elec. Corp., 43 F.3d 65 (3d Cir. 1994); Harlan v. Lewis, 982 F.2d 1255 (8th Cir. 1993). See also U.S. v. Seltzer, 227 F.3d 36 (2d Cir. 2000) (distinguishing between misconduct undertaken as a zealous advocate on behalf of a client, which requires showing of bad faith before sanctions may be imposed, and misconduct undertaken merely as an officer of the court but not on behalf of client.

[10]See Fink v. Gomez, 239 F.3d 989 (9th Cir. 2001).

In *Qualcomm, Inc. v. Broadcom, Corp.*,[11] a magistrate judge imposed sanctions of $8,568,633 against Qualcomm based on Qualcomm's intentional failure to produce over 46,000 responsive e-mails and other discovery misconduct, ordered certain in-house and former outside counsel to participate in comprehensive "Case Review and Enforcement of Discovery Obligations" program to create a case management protocol that would serve as a model for future litigants, and referred investigation of possible ethical violations to California State Bar. Rejecting a claim of inadvertence, the magistrate judge found that Qualcomm had failed to conduct basic searches for electronic documents.

Pointing out that Rule 26(g) imposes a duty of good faith and reasonable inquiry on all attorneys involved in litigation who rely on discovery responses executed by another attorney, the magistrate judge faulted the outside counsel for accepting unsubstantiated assurances of the client that searches for documents had been sufficient, particularly in light of warning signs to the contrary. Because the California Rules of Professional Conduct (unlike those in many other states) do not permit lawyers to reveal client confidences and secrets even in order to protect themselves against accusations of wrongdoing, the lawyers were not permitted to reveal their side of the story regarding their dealings with Qualcomm during discovery.

The magistrate judge noted a number of warning signs that signaled Qualcomm's failure to comply with its obligation to search for and produce all responsive documents. Qualcomm did not search the computers of the corporate representatives who were selected for Rule 30(b)(6) depositions or take reasonable steps to be sure that those representatives had Qualcomm's knowledge about the matter in dispute. Qualcomm ignored the significance of a distribution list indicating that one of its employees was a member of a group working on a key matter.

Qualcomm accepted and paid the $8,568,633.24 in sanc-

---

[11]Qualcomm Inc. v. Broadcom Corp., 2008 WL 66932 (S.D. Cal. 2008), vacated in part, 2008 WL 638108 (S.D. Cal. 2008).

tions ordered by the magistrate judge. A district judge vacated and remanded that portion of the magistrate judge's January 7 order imposing sanctions against Qualcomm's six outside counsel. The judge instructed that, in any future hearing held by the magistrate judge, the attorneys be allowed to defend their conduct by any and all means, and not be prevented from doing so by Qualcomm's attorney-client privilege.

While *Qualcomm* presents an extreme case involving the concealment of a large quantity of electronically stored information and the implausibility of a claim that a reasonable search could have missed this much material, the case sends a message to attorneys: attorneys must exercise reasonable diligence to assure themselves that a client has searched for all relevant information; they must heed and act upon warning signs. Clients must also be made aware of the consequences of the failure to comply with discovery requests.

Qualcomm illustrates the importance of performing a thorough factual investigation before filing suit.[12] It also demonstrates the importance of having a records management and litigation protocol in place before suit is filed (or before being sued). Law firms must develop practice management systems insuring that clients are properly advised at the beginning of litigation about the scope of discovery obligations, their likely cost, and the nature of the attorneys' obligations to the court to insure compliance by the client. Law firms may be reluctant to agree to represent a client if the client is unwilling to give the attorneys full access to the information the lawyers deem necessary to comply with discovery requests. Once litigation begins, firms should have in place oversight systems to assure that individual attorneys are complying with their responsibilities to oversee the discovery process. In

---

[12]See, e.g., Atmel Corp. v. Authentec Inc., 2008 WL 276393 (N.D. Cal. 2008) (plaintiff's attorney acknowledged not doing any investigation to determine how negotiations and discussions about the covenant not to sue were carried out without leaving any paper or electronic trail of responsive documents).

response to these issues, some law firms have established special units within their litigation practice groups to assist firm lawyers with electronic discovery issues and to ensure compliance with obligations imposed by the courts and the Federal Rules of Civil Procedure.

II. CHECKLISTS

§ 1:11 Checklist of types of electronically stored information

☐ E-mail and e-mail attachments

☐ Word processing documents such as those produced in MS Word or in WordPerfect

☐ Spreadsheets including Excel

☐ Presentation documents such as PowerPoint

☐ Graphics

☐ Animations

☐ Images

☐ Audio, video and audiovisual recordings

☐ Voice mail

☐ Electronic calendars or scheduling systems

☐ Proprietary software files

☐ Internet browsing applications, including bookmarks, cookies, and history logs

☐ Computer programs evincing a particular process, incorporating specific information, or demonstrating the use of proprietary methodologies

☐ Computer operation logs containing usage information

☐ Logs and text of electronic messages or e-mails, including trashed or deleted messages, message drafts, or mailing lists

☐ Electronic messaging records for messages within a specific company's network or across a wider network, such as the Internet

☐ Manufacturer's specifications for a computer

☐ Source codes for computer programs

§ 1:12 Checklist of locations of electronically stored information

- ☐ Individual desktop or laptop computers
- ☐ Mainframe computer systems
- ☐ Network hard drives
- ☐ Removable media, including discs, cartridges, tapes, and other storage media
- ☐ Servers
- ☐ Archival data on backup tapes or other storage media onsite and offsite
- ☐ Personal digital assistants
- ☐ Cellular telephones and other handheld wireless devices
- ☐ Internet data, including instant messaging
- ☐ Paging devices
- ☐ Audio systems, including voice mail
- ☐ GPS navigation systems
- ☐ MP3 players
- ☐ Thumb or flash drives

§ 1:13 Checklist for cost-effective discovery

- ☐ Take a broad view of discovery and pinpoint discovery needs.
  - ☐ What is really needed to win case?
  - ☐ Who will electronically stored information help your case?
  - ☐ Can you get the same result using less expensive traditional discovery?
  - ☐ Is it cost-effective to have a computer forensics expert collect electronically stored information and perform labor intensive procedures to obtain information?
- ☐ Become educated on the various methods and formats of electronically stored information.
  - ☐ How the information stored?
  - ☐ In what format is the information stored?

- ☐ What methods are available for searching the electronically stored information?
- ☐ How is the information backed up? Archived?

☐ Find a local, affordable computer expert. A local person, such as an academic, a graduate student, or a freelance IT person may share his or her practical knowledge and expertise to assist you in obtaining the information needed. Use the IT person to evaluate the opposing party's computer system.

☐ Hire a computer systems forensics expert. after you understand the information systems involved, a competent computer forensic expert can save time and money. The complexity of electronic discovery requires retention of an expert at the early stages of litigation. The forensic expert can be helpful in crafting requests for production with the requisite specificity.

☐ Early in the case determine what you need to win the case and avoid chasing unnecessary electronically stored information. Consultation with the computer forensics expert can be very helpful at this stage.

☐ Use the meet and confer process to narrow issues and learn about the opposing party's position on discovery of electronically stored information. The discussion should include the opponent's preservation of evidence, description of backup systems, types of computer systems, and production formats.

☐ Specify the production format that will the best results for your case.

☐ When a responding party designates a source of information as not reasonably accessible, it may take limited discovery, including sampling, to determine whether the sources are not reasonably accessible. Sampling may provide knowledge that can help you decide whether the sources contain useful information. The limited discovery may include:

- ☐ Sampling information contained on sources identified as not reasonably accessible
- ☐ Inspection of sources

☐ Depositions of witnesses knowledgeable about the responding party's information systems

Comment

This checklist is adapted from *Gonzalez & Montoya, Ten Tips Leading to Efficient and Effective eDiscovery for the Small Law Firm*, GP/Solo, April 2007.

III. FORMS

§ 1:14 Discovery project management template

Discovery Project Management Template				
Case Name: ________________				
Client Matter Number: ________________				
Item	**Task**	**Re-spon-sible**	**Date Due**	**Notes**
1	Initial discussions with client re status to date			
2	Conduct litigation hold strategy meeting			
3	Determine scope of hold			
4	Determine recipients of hold			
5	Coordinate with HR re incoming/departing employees subject to hold			
6	Determine if third parties have relevant data			
7	Determine if computer forensics implicated			
8	Issue litigation hold communication			
9	Schedule periodic follow-up reminders re litigation hold			
10	Send opposition appropriate preservation demand			
11	Receive confirmation of hold instructions from recipients			
12	Develop outline of legal and factual issues			
13	Prepare and interview IT staff re systems, backups, etc.			
14	Identify sources of data and possible 30(B)(6) witness(es)			
15	Determine relative accessibility of data sources			
16	Determine if backup tapes are implicated			
17	Determine if ongoing conduct implicated			
18	Consider taking snapshot of system			
19	Develop plan for gathering electronic data			
20	Develop plan for dealing with databases			
21	Develop plan for gathering paper documents			
22	Contact US-LitSupport for vendor recommendations/bids			
23	Select outside vendors if required			

Discovery Project Management Template				
Case Name: _______________				
Client Matter Number: _______________				
Item	**Task**	**Re-spon-sible**	**Date Due**	**Notes**
24	Select platform for hosting data			
25	Develop initial budget for discovery			
26	Prepare custodian interview questions			
27	Prepare 30(B)(6) witness(es)			
28	Perform interviews of custodians			
29	Meet and confer with opposition			
30	Negotiate and obtain appropriate protective order re data			
31	Determine desired production format(s)			
32	Negotiate production format(s) with opposition			
33	Negotiate timetable for production(s)			
34	Negotiate timetable for receiving production(s)			
32	Create tracking log for gathering, processing, review and production			
33	Gather electronic data			
34	Gather paper data			
35	Determine OCR strategy for paper			
36	Determine extent of coding required for paper			
37	Develop estimate of amount of data			
38	Determine review platform and process			
39	Determine culling strategies; keyword list; date range limitations			
40	Determine review team composition			
41	Train review team			
42	Intensive review of key custodian(s) data			
43	Develop budget estimate for discovery			
44	Load data for review			
45	Review data for relevance and privilege			
46	Create privilege log			
47	Determine disposition of data post litigation			

Roles

IT = Client IT staff

IC = Inside Counsel

OC = Outside Counsel

LS = Outside Counsel's Litigation Support Team

V = Outside Vendor

Chapter 2

Rules of Procedure and Best Practices

I. GUIDELINES

II. CHECKLISTS

III. RULES

Research References

Treatises and Practice Aids

eDiscovery & Digital Evidence §§ 6:10 to 6:12
Grenig and Kinsler, Federal Civil Discovery and Disclosure §§ 13.1 to 13.6 (2d ed.)

Law Reviews and Other Periodicals

Rogers, A Search for Balance in the Discovery of ESI Since December 1, 2006, 14 Rich. J.L. & Tech. 8 (2008)

Rosenthal, A Few Thoughts on Electronic Discovery after December 1, 2006, 116 Yale L.J. Pocket Part 167 (2006)

Additional References

Baicker-McKee, Rewriting the E-Discovery Rules—The 2006 Amendments, in Instant Awareness: An Immediate Look at the Legal, Governmental, and Economic Ramifications of the amendments to the Federal Rules of Civil Procedure and Electronic Discovery 5 (Aspatore 2008)

Ballard, Living with, and Learning, the New Rules Governing Electronic Discovery, in Instant Awareness: An Immediate Look at the Legal, Governmental, and Economic Ramifications of the amendments to the Federal Rules of Civil Procedure and Electronic Discovery 13 (Aspatore 2008)

Burney, Mining E-Discovery Stateside, L.Tech. News, Jan. 18, 2008

Carpenter, Making the amended Federal Rules of Civil Procedure Your Best Friend, Elec. Disc. & Records Mgt. Q., summer 2007, at 11

Grenig, It's Not Just the Fed—States Consider & Adopt E-Discovery Rules and Guidelines, Elec. Disc. & Records Mgt. Q., summer 2007, at 26

Simon, One Year Later: The Impact of the Electronic Discovery Amendments to the Federal Rules of Civil Procedure, in Instant Awareness: An Immediate Look at the Legal, Governmental, and Economic Ramifications of the amendments to the Federal Rules of Civil Procedure and Electronic Discovery 45 (Aspatore 2008)

ABA Discovery Standards, http://www.abanet.org/litigation/discoverystandards/2005civildiscoverystandards.pdf

The Sedona Conference, http://www.thesedonaconference.org

KeyCite®: Cases and other legal materials listed in KeyCite Scope can be researched through the KeyCite service on Westlaw®. Use KeyCite to check citations for form, parallel references, prior and later history, and comprehensive citator information, including citations to other decisions and secondary materials.

I. GUIDELINES

§ 2:1 Generally

The discovery of electronically stored information has changed the face of litigation. Increasingly, cases of all types in state and federal court involve documents created by word processing, databases, spreadsheets, e-mails, text messages, and records of Internet activity.

Because of the rapidly growing importance of discovery of electronically stored information, in 2006 the Federal Rules of Civil Procedure were amended to address the discovery of electronically stored information, state procedure rules relating to electronically stored information are being or have been amended. Uniform Rules Relating to the Discovery of Electronically Stored Information are being considered.

§ 2:2 Federal Rules of Civil Procedure

In 2006 significant amendments relating to discovery of electronic information were made to the Federal Rules of Civil Procedure. Amended Rule 26(b)(2) provides that a party is not required to produce electronically stored information that is not "reasonably accessible" because of "undue burden or cost." The plaintiff has the burden of going to court and showing why it is entitled to the information. The amendment attempts to codify *Zubulake v. UBS Warburg*[1] with respect to shifting costs.

Amended Rule 26(b)(5) contains a "clawback" provision, allowing a party that has produced evidence it claims is protected by the attorney-client privilege or the work-product doctrine to notify the receiving party of its claim and provide a basis for the claim. After receiving notification, the receiving party must return, sequester, or destroy the information and may not disclose it to third parties. In the alternative, the receiving party has the option of submitting the information to the court for a decision on whether the information is protected and whether a waiver has taken place. The clawback provision can be superseded by the parties' agreement.

Under the amendment to Rule 16(b), a pretrial confer-

[Section 2:2]

[1]Zubulake v. UBS Warburg LLC, 217 F.R.D. 309, 322, 91 Fair Empl. Prac. Cas. (BNA) 1574 (S.D. N.Y. 2003).

ence includes discussion of issues relating to electronically stored information, including the form of producing electronically stored information, preservation of data, and approaches to asserting claims of privilege or work-product protection after inadvertent production in discovery.

Amended Rule 33(d) allows a party to produce electronically stored information in response to interrogatories. Rule 34(a) provides a definition of electronically stored information. This clearly indicates that electronically stored information is subject to production and discovery. Amended Rule 34(b) provides that, when a production format is not specified, a responding party should produce documents in the format in which the information is "ordinarily maintained" or in a form that is reasonably usable.

Amended Rule 37(f) provides a safe harbor, providing that "a party shall not be sanctioned for loss of electronically stored information if the loss occurs, absent exceptional circumstances, a court may not impose sanctions under these rules on a party for failing to provide electronically stored information lost as a result of the routine, good faith operation of an electronic information system."

A number of federal courts have also established local rules, guidelines, or protocols dealing with the discovery of electronically stored information.[2]

[2]Alaska, Arizona, Eastern and Western Districts of Arkansas, Northern District of California, Colorado, Connecticut, Delaware, Middle District and Southern Districts of Florida, Southern District of Georgia, Central District of Illinois, Southern and Northern Districts of Indiana, Northern and Southern Districts of Iowa, Kansas, Maryland, Eastern District of Missouri, New Jersey, Southern District of New York, Western District of North Carolina, Northern and Southern Districts of Ohio, Eastern, Middle and Western Districts of Pennsylvania, Eastern, Middle, and Western Districts of Tennessee, Eastern, Northern, and Southern Districts of Texas, Utah, Vermont, Southern District of West Virginia, and Wyoming.

§ 2:3 Uniform Rules Relating to the Discovery of Electronically Stored Information

In 2006, a committee of the National Conference of Commissioners on Uniform State Laws held its initial meeting to discuss uniform rules relating to the discovery of electronically stored information. The drafting committee's determined that the significant issues relating to the discovery of information in electronic form had been vetted during the Federal Rules amendment process. It has drafted uniform rules that mirror the spirit and direction of the amendments to the Federal Rules of Civil Procedure. The committee has adopted, often verbatim, language from both the Federal Rules and comments that it deemed valuable. The rules have been modified, where necessary, to accommodate the varying state procedures and are presented in a form that permits their adoption as a discrete set of rules applicable to discovery of electronically stored information.[1]

§ 2:4 State rules of civil procedure

Although considerable attention has been directed toward the changes in the Federal Rules of Civil Procedure, several states have adopted court rules addressing discovery of electronically stored information.[1]

§ 2:5 The Sedona Principles

The Sedona Conference Working Group on Best Practices for Electronic Document Retention & Production has promulgated fourteen principles regarding discovery of electronically stored information, entitled THE SEDONA PRINCIPLES (SECOND) BEST PRACTICES RECOMMENDATIONS &

[Section 2:3]

[1]See http://www.law.upenn.edu/bll/archives/ulc

[Section 2:4]

[1]See, e.g., Arizona, California, Connecticut, Idaho, Illinois, Indiana, Louisiana, Minnesota, Mississippi, Montana, New Hampshire, New Jersey, New York, North Carolina, Texas, and Utah.

PRINCIPLES FOR ADDRESSING ELECTRONIC DOCUMENT PRODUCTION SEDONA PRINCIPLES.[1] While not law, the principles are definitely persuasive authority of the first order. The fourteen principles are:

1. Electronically stored information is potentially discoverable under Fed. R. Civ. P. 34 or its state equivalents. Organizations must properly preserve electronically stored information that can reasonably be anticipated to be relevant to litigation.
2. When balancing the cost, burden, and need for electronically stored information, courts and parties should apply the proportionality standard embodied in Fed. R. Civ. P. 26(b)(2)(C) and its state equivalents, which require consideration of the technological feasibility and realistic costs of preserving, retrieving, reviewing, and producing electronically stored information, as well as the nature of the litigation and the amount in controversy.
3. Parties should confer early in discovery regarding the preservation and production of electronically stored information when these matters are at issue in the litigation and seek to agree on the scope of each party's rights and responsibilities.
4. Discovery requests for electronically stored information should he as clear as possible, while responses and objections to discovery should disclose the scope and limits of the production.
5. The obligation to preserve electronically stored information requires reasonable and good faith efforts to retain information that may be relevant to pending or threatened litigation. However, it is unreasonable to expect parties to take every conceivable

[Section 2:5]

[1]http://www.thesedonaconference.org/; THE SEDONA PRINCIPLES (SECOND) BEST PRACTICES RECOMMENDATIONS & PRINCIPLES FOR ADDRESSING ELECTRONIC DOCUMENT PRODUCTION is the product of the Sedona Conference Working Group on Best Practices for Electronic Document Retention & Production. Copyright 2007 by the Sedona Conference. Reprinted with permission.

step to preserve all potentially relevant electronically stored information.

6. Responding parties are best situated to evaluate the procedures, methodologies, and technologies appropriate for preserving and producing their own electronically stored information.
7. The requesting party has the burden on a motion to compel to show that the responding party's steps to preserve and produce relevant electronically stored information were inadequate.
8. The primary source of electronically stored information for production should be active data and information. Resort to disaster recovery backup tapes and other sources of electronically stored information that are not reasonably accessible requires the requesting party to demonstrate need and relevance that outweigh the costs and burdens of retrieving and processing the electronically stored information from such sources, including the disruption of business and information management activities.
9. Absent a showing of special need and relevance, a responding party should not be required to preserve, review, or produce deleted, shadowed, fragmented, or residual electronically stored information.
10. A responding party should follow reasonable procedures to protect privileges and objections in connection with the production of electronically stored information.
11. A responding party may satisfy its good faith obligation to preserve and produce relevant electronically stored information by using electronic tools and processes, such as data sampling, searching, or the use of selection criteria, to identify data reasonably likely to contain relevant information.
12. Absent party agreement or court order specifying the form or forms of production, production should be made in the form or forms in which the information is ordinarily maintained or in a reasonably usable form, taking into account the need to produce

reasonably accessible metadata that will enable the receiving party to have the same ability to access, search, and display the information as the producing party where appropriate or necessary in light of the nature of the information and the needs of the case.

13. Absent a specific objection, party agreement or court order, the reasonable costs of retrieving and reviewing electronically stored information should be borne by the responding party, unless the information sought is not reasonably available to the responding party in the ordinary course of business. If the information sought is not reasonably available to the responding party in the ordinary course of business, then, absent special circumstances, the costs of retrieving and reviewing such electronic information may be shared by or shifted to the requesting party.
14. Sanctions, including spoliation findings, should be considered by the court only if it finds that there was a clear duty to preserve, a culpable failure to preserve and produce relevant electronically stored information, and a reasonable probability that the loss of the evidence has materially prejudiced the adverse party.

§ 2:6 Electronic Discovery Reference Model Project (EDRM)

Launched in May 2005, the Electronic Discovery Reference Model (EDRM) Project was created to address the lack of standards and guidelines in the electronic discovery market—a problem identified in the 2003 and 2004 Socha-Gelbmann Electronic Discovery Surveys as a major concern for vendors and consumers alike. The completed reference model provides a common, flexible and extensible framework for the development, selection, evaluation and use of electronic discovery products and services. The completed model was placed in the public domain in May 2006.[1]

§ 2:7 ABA eDiscovery Standards

In August 2004, the American Bar Association added electronic discovery to the ABA's Civil Discovery Standards.[1] The ABA Standards include five specific standards relating to electronic discovery. The first standard addresses preserving and producing electronic information, and includes a list of the places electronic documents can be found. It also contains a list of factors courts should consider when deciding how to allocate the costs of discovery.

The second standard provides that, in appropriate cases, some or all discovery materials should be converted to electronic format. The third standard describes the need to confer about electronic discovery at the initial discovery conference. The fourth standard examines how attorney-client privilege and attorney work product material can be protected. The fifth standard acknowledges that in the future new storage media may not be electronic and suggests that existing discovery standards be consulted when data is stored in a new form.

§ 2:8 Managing Discovery of Electronic Information: A Pocket Guide for Judges

The Federal Judicial Center has published a pocket guide for federal judges suggesting how the discovery of electronically stored information should be managed. The Pocket Guide encourages judges to actively manage cases involving electronically stored information, raising points

---

[Section 2:6]

[1]The reference model can be found at http://www.edrm.net

[Section 2:7]

[1]The Standards can be downloaded from http://www.abanet.org/litigation/discoverystandards/2004civildiscoverystandards.pdf.

for the parties' consideration rather than awaiting the parties' identification and argument of the points.[1]

§ 2:9 Guidelines for State Trial Courts Regarding Discovery of Electronically-Stored Information

The Conference of Chief Justices has issued guidelines for state trial courts to use in dealing with discovery of electronically stored information. They have been drafted to offer guidance to judges faced with addressing practical problems the created by the discovery of electronically stored information.[1]

II. CHECKLISTS

§ 2:10 Checklist of common electronic discovery mistakes

- ☐ Failing to have a discovery plan ready to implement at the first sign of impending litigation
- ☐ Neglecting to implement a backup policy or a document retention policy
- ☐ Declining to cease document destruction practices once there is a preservation duty
- ☐ Conducting do-it-yourself collection of electronically stored information rather than using individuals properly trained in handling digital data
- ☐ Ignoring key locations of electronically stored information and important file types
- ☐ Overlooking metadata preservation
- ☐ Failing to recognize that delete does not mean delete
- ☐ Assuming the information technology department can shoulder the electronic discovery burden alone

---

[Section 2:8]

[1]The Guide can be downloaded at http://www.fjc.gov/library/fjc_catalog.nsf.

[Section 2:9]

[1]The Guidelines can be downloaded at http://www.ncsconline.org/images/EDiscCCJGuidelinesFinal.pdf.

- ☐ Neglecting to chose carefully an electronic evidence expert
- ☐ Failing to use an online repository tool for paper and electronic document review

Comment

This checklist is adapted from a paper prepared by Jonathan Sachs, Legal Consultant for Kroll Ontrack.

III. RULES

§ 2:11 Federal Rules of Civil Procedure relating to discovery of electronically stored information*

III. PLEADINGS AND MOTIONS

Rule 16. Pretrial Conferences; Scheduling; Management

IV. DEPOSITIONS AND DISCOVERY

Rule 26. General Provisions Governing Discovery; Duty of Disclosure
Rule 33. Interrogatories to Parties
Rule 34. Production of Documents, Electronically Stored Information, and Things and Entry Upon Land for Inspection and Other Purposes
Rule 37. Failure to Make Disclosures or Cooperate in Discovery; Sanctions

VI. TRIALS

Rule 45. Subpoena

[Section 2:11]

*The 2007 amendments to the Federal Rules of Civil Procedure are effective December 1, 2007, absent contrary Congressional action.

III. PLEADINGS AND MOTIONS

* * *

Rule 16. Pretrial Conferences; Scheduling; Management

(a) Purposes of a Pretrial Conference. In any action, the court may order the attorneys and any unrepresented parties to appear for one or more pretrial conferences for such purposes as:

(1) expediting disposition of the action;

(2) establishing early and continuing control so that the case will not be protracted because of lack of management;

(3) discouraging wasteful pretrial activities;

(4) improving the quality of the trial through more thorough preparation; and

(5) facilitating settlement.

(b) Scheduling.

(1) *Scheduling Order.* Except in categories of actions exempted by local rule, the district judge—or a magistrate judge when authorized by local rule—must issue a scheduling order:

(A) after receiving the parties' report under Rule 26(f); or

(B) after consulting with the parties' attorneys and any unrepresented parties at a scheduling conference or by telephone, mail, or other means.

(2) *Time to Issue.* The judge must issue the scheduling order as soon as practicable, but in any event within the earlier of 120 days after any defendant has been served with the complaint or 90 days after any defendant has appeared.

(3) *Contents of the Order.*

(A) Required Contents. The scheduling order must limit the time to join other parties, amend the pleadings, complete discovery, and file motions.

(B) Permitted Contents. The scheduling order may:

(i) modify the timing of disclosures under Rules 26(a) and 26(e)(1);

(ii) modify the extent of discovery;

(iii) provide for disclosure or discovery of electronically stored information;

(iv) include any agreements the parties reach for asserting claims of privilege or of protection as trial-preparation material after information is produced;

(v) set dates for pretrial conferences and for trial; and

(vi) include other appropriate matters.

(4) *Modifying a Schedule.* A schedule may be modified only for good cause and with the judge's consent.

(c) Attendance and Matters for Consideration at a Pretrial Conference.

(1) *Attendance.* A represented party must authorize at least one of its attorneys to make stipulations and admissions about all matters that can reasonably be anticipated for discussion at a pretrial conference. If appropriate, the court may require that a party or its representative be present or reasonably available by other means to consider possible settlement.

(2) *Matters for Consideration.* At any pretrial conference, the court may consider and take appropriate action on the following matters:

(A) formulating and simplifying the issues, and eliminating frivolous claims or defenses;

(B) amending the pleadings if necessary or desirable;

(C) obtaining admissions and stipulations about facts and documents to avoid unnecessary proof, and ruling in advance on the admissibility of evidence;

(D) avoiding unnecessary proof and cumulative evidence, and limiting the use of testimony under Federal Rule of Evidence 702;

(E) determining the appropriateness and timing of summary adjudication under Rule 56;

(F) controlling and scheduling discovery, including orders affecting disclosures and discovery under Rule 26 and Rules 29 through 37;

(G) identifying witnesses and documents, scheduling the filing and exchange of any pretrial briefs, and setting dates for further conferences and for trial;

(H) referring matters to a magistrate judge or a master;

(I) settling the case and using special procedures to assist in resolving the dispute when authorized by statute or local rule;

(J) determining the form and content of the pretrial order;

(K) disposing of pending motions;

(L) adopting special procedures for managing potentially difficult or protracted actions that may involve complex issues, multiple parties, difficult legal questions, or unusual proof problems;

(M) ordering a separate trial under Rule 42(b) of a claim, counterclaim, cross-claim, third-party claim, or particular issue;

(N) ordering the presentation of evidence early in the trial on a manageable issue that might, on the evidence, be the basis for a judgment as a matter of law under Rule 50(a) or a judgment on partial findings under Rule 52(c);

(O) establishing a reasonable limit on the time allowed to present evidence; and

(P) facilitating in other ways the just, speedy, and inexpensive disposition of the action.

(d) Pretrial Orders. After any conference under this rule, the court should issue an order reciting the action taken. This order controls the course of the action unless the court modifies it.

(e) Final Pretrial Conference and Orders. The court may hold a final pretrial conference to formulate a trial plan, including a plan to facilitate the admission of evidence. The conference must be held as close to the start of trial as is reasonable, and must be attended by at least one attorney who will conduct the trial for each party and by any unrepresented party. The court may modify the order issued after a final pretrial conference only to prevent manifest injustice.

(f) Sanctions.

(1) *In General.* On motion or on its own, the court may issue any just orders, including those authorized by Rule 37(b)(2)(A)(ii)–(vii), if a party or its attorney:

(A) fails to appear at a scheduling or other pretrial conference;

(B) is substantially unprepared to participate—or does not participate in good faith—in the conference; or

(C) fails to obey a scheduling or other pretrial order.

(2) *Imposing Fees and Costs.* Instead of or in addition to any other sanction, the court must order the party, its attorney, or both to pay the reasonable expenses—including attorney's fees—incurred because of any noncompliance with this rule, unless the noncompliance was substantially justified or other circumstances make an award of expenses unjust.

[As amended Apr. 12, 2006, eff. Dec. 1, 2006; April 30, 2007, eff. Dec. 1, 2007.]

Committee Note to 2006 Amendment

The amendment to Rule 16(b) is designed to alert the court to the possible need to address the handling of discovery of electronically stored information early in the litigation if such discovery is expected to occur. Rule 26(f) is amended to direct the parties to discuss discovery of electronically stored information if such discovery is contemplated in the action. Form 35 is amended to call for a report to the court about the results of this discussion. In many instances, the court's involvement early in the litigation will help avoid difficulties that might otherwise arise.

Rule 16(b) is also amended to include among the topics that may be addressed in the scheduling order any agreements that the parties reach to facilitate discovery by minimizing the risk of waiver of privilege or work-product protection. Rule 26(f) is amended to add to the discovery plan the parties' proposal for the court to enter a case-management or other order adopting such an agreement. The parties may agree to various arrangements. For example, they may agree to initial provision of requested materials without waiver of privilege or protection to enable the party seeking production to designate the materials desired or protection for actual production, with the privilege review of only those materials to follow. Alternatively, they may agree that if privileged or protected information is inadvertently produced, the producing party may by timely notice assert the privilege or protection and obtain return of the materials without waiver. Other arrangements are possible. In most circumstances, a party who receives information under such an arrangement cannot assert that production of the information waived a claim of privilege or of protection as trial-preparation material.

An order that includes the parties' agreement may be helpful in avoiding delay and excessive cost in discovery. *See Manual for Complex Litigation* (4th) § 11.446. Rule 16(b)(6) recognizes the propriety of including such agreements in the court's order. The rule does not provide the court with authority to enter such a case-management or other order without party agreement, or limit the court's authority to act on motion.

Committee Note to 2007 Amendment

The language of Rule 16 has been amended as part of the general restyling of the Civil Rules to make them more easily understood and to make style and terminology consistent throughout the rules. These changes are intended to be stylistic only.

When a party or its representative is not present, it is enough to be reasonably available by any suitable means, whether telephone or other communication device.

* * *

IV. DEPOSITIONS AND DISCOVERY

Rule 26. Duty to Disclose; General Provisions Governing Discovery

(a) Required Disclosures.

(1) Initial Disclosure.

(A) In General. Except as exempted by Rule 26(a)(1)(B) or as otherwise stipulated or ordered by the court, a party must, without awaiting a discovery request, provide to the other parties:

(i) the name and, if known, the address and telephone number of each individual likely to have discoverable information—along with the subjects of that information—that the disclosing party may use to support its claims or defenses, unless the use would be solely for impeachment;

(ii) a copy—or a description by category and location—of all documents, electronically stored information, and tangible things that the disclosing party has in its possession, custody, or control and may use to support its claims or defenses, unless the use would be solely for impeachment;

(iii) a computation of each category of damages claimed by the disclosing party—who must also make available for inspection and copying as under Rule 34 the documents or other evidentiary material, unless privileged or protected from disclosure, on which each computation is based, including materials bearing on the nature and extent of injuries suffered; and

(iv) for inspection and copying as under Rule 34, any insurance agreement under which an insurance business may be liable to satisfy all or part of a possible judgment in the action or to indemnify or reimburse for payments made to satisfy the judgment.

(B) Proceedings Exempt from Initial Disclosure. The following proceedings are exempt from initial disclosure:

(i) an action for review on an administrative record;

(ii) a forfeiture action in rem arising from a federal statute;

(iii) a petition for habeas corpus or any other proceeding to challenge a criminal conviction or sentence;

(iv) an action brought without an attorney by a person in the custody of the United States, a state, or a state subdivision;

(v) an action to enforce or quash an administrative summons or subpoena;

(vi) an action by the United States to recover benefit payments;

(vii) an action by the United States to collect on a student loan guaranteed by the United States;

(viii) a proceeding ancillary to a proceeding in another court; and

(ix) an action to enforce an arbitration award.

(C) Time for Initial Disclosures—In General. A party must make the initial disclosures at or within 14 days after the parties' Rule 26(f) conference unless a different time is set by stipulation or court order, or unless a party objects during the conference that initial disclosures are not appropriate in this action and states the objection in the proposed discovery plan. In ruling on the objection, the court must determine what disclosures, if any, are to be made and must set the time for disclosure.

(D) Time for Initial Disclosures—For Parties Served or Joined Later. A party that is first served or otherwise joined after the Rule 26(f) conference must make the initial disclosures within 30 days after being served or joined, unless a different time is set by stipulation or court order.

(E) Basis for Initial Disclosure; Unacceptable Excuses. A party must make its initial disclosures based on the information then reasonably available to it. A party is not excused from making its disclosures because it has not fully investigated the case or because it challenges the sufficiency of another party's disclosures or because another party has not made its disclosures.

(2) *Disclosure of Expert Testimony.*

(A) In General. In addition to the disclosures required by Rule 26(a)(1), a party must disclose to the other parties the identity of any witness it may use at trial to present evidence under Federal Rule of Evidence 702, 703, or 705.

(B) Written Report. Unless otherwise stipulated or ordered by the court, this disclosure must be accompanied by a written report—prepared and signed by the witness—if the witness is one retained or specially employed to provide expert testimony in the case or one whose duties as the party's employee regularly involve giving expert testimony. The report must contain:

(i) a complete statement of all opinions the witness will express and the basis and reasons for them;

(ii) the data or other information considered by the witness in forming them;

(iii) any exhibits that will be used to summarize or support them;

(iv) the witness's qualifications, including a list of all publications authored in the previous ten years;

(v) a list of all other cases in which, during the previous four years, the witness testified as an expert at trial or by deposition; and

(vi) a statement of the compensation to be paid for the study and testimony in the case.

(C) Time to Disclose Expert Testimony. A party must make these disclosures at the times and in the sequence that the court orders. Absent a stipulation or a court order, the disclosures must be made:

(i) at least 90 days before the date set for trial or for the case to be ready for trial; or

(ii) if the evidence is intended solely to contradict or rebut evidence on the same subject matter identified by another party under Rule 26(a)(2)(B), within 30 days after the other party's disclosure.

(D) Supplementing the Disclosure. The parties must supplement these disclosures when required under Rule 26(e).

(3) *Pretrial Disclosures.*

(A) In General. In addition to the disclosures required by Rule 26(a)(1) and (2), a party must provide to the other parties and promptly file the following information about the evidence that it may present at trial other than solely for impeachment:

(i) the name and, if not previously provided, the address and telephone number of each witness—separately identifying those the party expects to present and those it may call if the need arises;

(ii) the designation of those witnesses whose testimony the party expects to present by deposition and, if not taken stenographically, a transcript of the pertinent parts of the deposition; and

(iii) an identification of each document or other exhibit, including summaries of other evidence—separately identifying those items the party expects to offer and those it may offer if the need arises.

(B) Time for Pretrial Disclosures; Objections. Unless the court orders otherwise, these disclosures must be made at least 30 days before trial. Within 14 days after they are made, unless the court sets a different time, a party may serve and promptly file a list of the following objections: any objections to the use under Rule 32(a) of a deposition designated by another party under Rule 26(a)(3)(A)(ii); and any objection, together with the grounds for it, that may be made to the admissibility of materials identified under Rule 26(a)(3)(A)(iii). An objection not so made—except for one under Federal Rule of Evidence 402 or 403—is waived unless excused by the court for good cause.

(4) *Form of Disclosures.* Unless the court orders otherwise, all disclosures under Rule 26(a) must be in writing, signed, and served.

(b) Discovery Scope and Limits.

(1) *Scope in General.* Unless otherwise limited by court order, the scope of discovery is as follows:

Parties may obtain discovery regarding any nonprivileged matter that is relevant to any party's claim or defense—including the existence, description, nature, custody, condition, and location of any documents or other tangible things and the identity and location of persons who know of any discoverable matter. For good cause, the court may order discovery of any matter relevant to the subject matter involved in the action. Relevant information need not be admissible at the trial if the discovery appears reasonably calculated to lead to the discovery of admissible evidence. All discovery is subject to the limitations imposed by Rule 26(b)(2)(C).

(2) *Limitations on Frequency and Extent.*

(A) When Permitted. By order, the court may alter the limits in these rules on the number of depositions and interrogatories or on the length of depositions under Rule 30. By order or local rule, the court may also limit the number of requests under Rule 36.

(B) Specific Limitations on Electronically Stored Information. A party need not provide discovery of electronically stored information from sources that the party identifies as not reasonably accessible because of undue burden or cost. On motion to compel discovery or for a protective order, the party from whom discovery is sought must show that the information is not reasonably accessible because of undue burden or cost. If that showing is made, the court may nonetheless order discovery from such sources if the requesting party shows good cause, considering the limitations of Rule 26(b)(2)(C). The court may specify conditions for the discovery.

(C) When Required. On motion or on its own, the court must limit the frequency or extent of discovery otherwise allowed by these rules or by local rule if it determines that:

(i) the discovery sought is unreasonably cumulative or duplicative, or can be obtained from some other source that is more convenient, less burdensome, or less expensive;

(ii) the party seeking discovery has had ample opportunity to obtain the information by discovery in the action; or

(iii) the burden or expense of the proposed discovery outweighs its likely benefit, considering the needs of the case, the amount in controversy, the parties' resources, the importance of the issues at stake in the action, and the importance of the discovery in resolving the issues.

(3) *Trial Preparation: Materials.*

(A) Documents and Tangible Things. Ordinarily, a party may not discover documents and tangible things that are prepared in anticipation of litigation or for trial by or for another party or its representative (including the other party's attorney, consultant, surety, indemnitor, insurer, or agent). But, subject to Rule 26(b)(4), those materials may be discovered if:

(i) they are otherwise discoverable under Rule 26(b)(1); and

(ii) the party shows that it has substantial need for the materials to prepare its case and cannot, without undue hardship, obtain their substantial equivalent by other means.

(B) Protection Against Disclosure. If the court orders discovery of those materials, it must protect against disclosure of the mental impressions, conclusions, opinions, or legal theories of a party's attorney or other representative concerning the litigation.

(C) Previous Statement. Any party or other person may, on request and without the required showing, obtain the person's own previous statement about the action or its subject matter. If the request is refused, the person may move for a court order, and Rule 37(a)(5) applies to the award of expenses. A previous statement is either:

(i) a written statement that the person has signed or otherwise adopted or approved; or

(ii) a contemporaneous stenographic, mechanical, electrical, or other recording—or a transcription of it—that recites substantially verbatim the person's oral statement.

(4) *Trial Preparation: Experts.*

(A) Expert Who May Testify. A party may depose any person who has been identified as an expert whose opinions may be presented at trial. If Rule 26(a)(2)(B) requires a report from the expert, the deposition may be conducted only after the report is provided.

(B) Expert Employed Only for Trial Preparation. Ordinarily, a party may not, by interrogatories or deposition, discover facts known or opinions held by an expert who has been retained or specially employed by another party in anticipation of litigation or to prepare for trial and who is not expected to be called as a witness at trial. But a party may do so only:

(i) as provided in Rule 35(b); or

(ii) on showing exceptional circumstances under which it is impracticable for the party to obtain facts or opinions on the same subject by other means.

(C) Payment. Unless manifest injustice would result, the court must require that the party seeking discovery:

(i) pay the expert a reasonable fee for time spent in responding to discovery under Rule 26(b)(4)(A) or (B); and

(ii) for discovery under (B), also pay the other party a fair portion of the fees and expenses it reasonably incurred in obtaining the expert's facts and opinions.

(5) *Claiming Privilege or Protecting Trial-Preparation Materials.*

(A) Information Withheld. When a party withholds information otherwise discoverable by claiming that the information is privileged or subject to protection as trial-preparation material, the party must:

(i) expressly make the claim; and

(ii) describe the nature of the documents, communications, or tangible things not produced or disclosed—and do so in a manner that, without revealing information itself privileged or protected, will enable other parties to assess the claim.

(B) Information Produced. If information produced in discovery is subject to a claim of privilege or of protection as trial preparation material, the party making the claim may notify any party that received the information of the claim and the basis for it. After being notified, a party must promptly return, sequester, or destroy the specified information and any copies it has; must not use or disclose the information until the claim is resolved; must take reasonable steps to retrieve the information if the party disclosed it before being notified; and may promptly present the information to the court under seal for a determination of the claim. The producing party must preserve the information until the claim is resolved.

(c) Protective Orders.

(1) *In General.* A party or any person from whom discovery is sought may move for a protective order in the court where the action is pending—or as an alternative on matters relating to a deposition, in the court for the district where the deposition will be taken. The motion must include a certification that the movant has in good faith conferred or attempted to confer with other affected parties in an effort to resolve the dispute without court action. The court may, for good cause, issue an order to protect a party or person from annoyance, embarrassment, oppression, or undue burden or expense, including one or more of the following:

(A) forbidding the disclosure or discovery;

(B) specifying terms, including time and place, for the disclosure or discovery;

(C) prescribing a discovery method other than the one selected by the party seeking discovery;

(D) forbidding inquiry into certain matters, or limiting the scope of disclosure or discovery to certain matters;

(E) designating the persons who may be present while the discovery is conducted;

(F) requiring that a deposition be sealed and opened only on court order;

(G) requiring that a trade secret or other confidential research, development, or commercial information not be revealed or be revealed only in a specified way; and

(H) requiring that the parties simultaneously file specified documents or information in sealed envelopes, to be opened as the court directs.

(2) *Ordering Discovery.* If a motion for a protective order is wholly or partly denied, the court may, on just terms, order that any party or person provide or permit discovery.

(3) *Awarding Expenses.* Rule 37(a)(5) applies to the award of expenses.

(d) Timing and Sequence of Discovery.

(1) *Timing.* A party may not seek discovery from any source before the parties have conferred as required by Rule 26(f), except in a proceeding exempted from initial disclosure under Rule 26(a)(1)(B), or when authorized by these rules, by stipulation, or by court order.

(2) *Sequence.* Unless, on motion, the court orders otherwise for the parties' and witnesses' convenience and in the interests of justice:

(A) methods of discovery may be used in any sequence; and

(B) discovery by one party does not require any other party to delay its discovery.

(e) Supplementing Disclosures and Responses.

(1) *In General.* A party who has made a disclosure under Rule 26(a)—or who has responded to an interrogatory, request for production, or request for admission—must supplement or correct its disclosure or response:

(A) in a timely manner if the party learns that in some material respect the disclosure or response is incomplete or incorrect, and if the additional or corrective information has not otherwise been made known to the other parties during the discovery process or in writing; or

(B) as ordered by the court.

(2) *Expert Witness.* For an expert whose report must be disclosed under Rule 26(a)(2)(B), the party's duty to supplement extends both to information included in the report and to information given during the expert's deposition. Any additions or changes to this information must be disclosed by the time the party's pretrial disclosures under Rule 26(a)(3) are due.

(f) Conference of the Parties; Planning for Discovery.

(1) *Conference Timing.* Except in a proceeding exempted from initial disclosure under Rule 26(a)(1)(B) or when the court orders otherwise, the parties must confer as soon as practicable—and in any event at least 21 days before a scheduling conference is to be held or a scheduling order is due under Rule 16(b).

(2) *Conference Content; Parties' Responsibilities.* In conferring, the parties must consider the nature and basis of their claims and defenses and the possibilities for promptly settling or resolving the case; make or arrange for the disclosures required by Rule 26(a)(1); discuss any issues about preserving discoverable information; and develop a proposed discovery plan. The attorneys of record and all unrepresented parties that have appeared in the case are jointly responsible for arranging the conference, for attempting in good faith to agree on the proposed discovery plan, and for submitting to the court within 14 days after the conference a written report outlining the plan. The court may order the parties or attorneys to attend the conference in person.

(3) *Discovery Plan.* A discovery plan must state the parties' views and proposals on:

(A) what changes should be made in the timing, form, or requirement for disclosures under Rule 26(a), including a statement of when initial disclosures were made or will be made;

(B) the subjects on which discovery may be needed, when discovery should be completed, and whether discovery should be conducted in phases or be limited to or focused on particular issues;

(C) any issues about disclosure or discovery of electronically stored information, including the form or forms in which it should be produced;

(D) any issues about claims of privilege or of protection as trial-preparation materials, including—if the parties agree on a procedure to assert these claims after production—whether to ask the court to include their agreement in an order;

(E) what changes should be made in the limitations on discovery imposed under these rules or by local rule, and what other limitations should be imposed; and

(F) any other orders that the court should issue under Rule 26(c) or under Rule 16(b) and (c).

(4) *Expedited Schedule.* If necessary to comply with its expedited schedule for Rule 16(b) conferences, a court may by local rule:

(A) require the parties' conference to occur less than 21 days before the scheduling conference is held or a scheduling order is due under Rule 16(b); and

(B) require the written report outlining the discovery plan to be filed less than 14 days after the parties' conference, or excuse the parties from submitting a written report and permit them to report orally on their discovery plan at the Rule 16(b) conference.

(g) Signing Disclosures and Discovery Requests, Responses, and Objections.

(1) *Signature Required; Effect of Signature.* Every disclosure under Rule 26(a)(1) or (a)(3) and every discovery request, response, or objection must be signed by at least one attorney of record in the attorney's own name—or by the party personally, if unrepresented—and must state the signer's address, e-mail address, and telephone number. By signing, an attorney or party certifies that to the best of the

person's knowledge, information, and belief formed after a reasonable inquiry:

(A) with respect to a disclosure, it is complete and correct as of the time it is made; and

(B) with respect to a discovery request, response, or objection, it is:

(i) consistent with these rules and warranted by existing law or by a nonfrivolous argument for extending, modifying, or reversing existing law, or for establishing new law;

(ii) not interposed for any improper purpose, such as to harass, cause unnecessary delay, or needlessly increase the cost of litigation; and

(iii) neither unreasonable nor unduly burdensome or expensive, considering the needs of the case, prior discovery in the case, the amount in controversy, and the importance of the issues at stake in the action.

(2) *Failure to Sign.* Other parties have no duty to act on an unsigned disclosure, request, response, or objection until it is signed, and the court must strike it unless a signature is promptly supplied after the omission is called to the attorney's or party's attention.

(3) *Sanction for Improper Certification.* If a certification violates this rule without substantial justification, the court, on motion or on its own, must impose an appropriate sanction on the signer, the party on whose behalf the signer was acting, or both. The sanction may include an order to pay the reasonable expenses, including attorney's fees, caused by the violation.

[As amended Apr. 12, 2006, eff. Dec. 1, 2006; April 30, 2007, eff. Dec. 1, 2007.]

Committee Note to 2006 Amendment

Subdivision (a). Rule 26(a)(1)(B) is amended to parallel Rule 34(a) by recognizing that a party must disclose electronically stored information as well as documents that it may use to support its claims or defenses. The term "electronically stored information" has the same broad meaning in Rule 26(a)(1) as in Rule 34(a). This amendment is consistent with the 1993 addition of Rule 26(a)(1)(B). The term "data compilations" is deleted as unnecessary because it is a subset of both documents and electronically stored information.

Subdivision (b)(2). The amendment to Rule 26(b)(2) is designed to address issues raised by difficulties in locating, retrieving, and providing discovery of some electronically stored information. Electronic storage systems often make it easier to locate and retrieve information. These advantages are properly taken into account in determining the reasonable scope of discovery in a particular case. But some sources of electronically stored information can be accessed only with substantial burden and cost. In a particular case, these burdens and costs may make the information on such sources not reasonably accessible.

It is not possible to define in a rule the different types of technological features that may affect the burdens and costs of accessing electronically stored information. Information systems are designed to provide ready access to information used in regular ongoing activities. They also may be designed so as to provide ready access to information that is not regularly used. But a system may retain information on sources that are accessible only by incurring substantial burdens or costs. Subparagraph (B) is added to regulate discovery from such sources.

Under this rule, a responding party should produce electronically stored information that is relevant, not privileged, and reasonably accessible, subject to the (b)(2)(C) limitations that apply to all discovery. The responding party must also identify, by category or type, the sources containing potentially responsive information that it is neither searching nor producing. The identification should, to the extent possible, provide enough detail to enable the requesting party to evaluate the burdens and costs of providing the discovery and the likelihood of finding responsive information on the identified sources.

A party's identification of sources of electronically stored information as not reasonably accessible does not relieve the party of its common-law or statutory duties to preserve evidence. Whether a responding party is required to preserve unsearched sources of potentially responsive information that it believes are not reasonably accessible depends on the circumstances of each case. It is often useful for the parties to discuss this issue early in discovery.

The volume of—and the ability to search—much electronically stored information means that in many cases the responding party will be able to produce information from reasonably accessible sources that will fully satisfy the parties' discovery needs. In many circumstances the requesting party should obtain and evaluate the information from such sources before insisting that the responding party search and produce information contained on sources that are not reasonably accessible. If the requesting party continues to seek discovery of information from sources identified as not reasonably accessible, the parties should discuss the burdens and costs of accessing and retrieving the information, the needs that may establish good cause for requiring all or part of the requested discovery even if the information sought is not reasonably accessible, and conditions on obtaining and producing the information that may be appropriate.

If the parties cannot agree whether, or on what terms, sources identified as not reasonably accessible should be searched and discoverable information produced, the issue may be raised either by a motion to compel discovery or by a motion for a protective order. The parties must confer before bringing either motion. If the parties do not resolve the issue and the court must decide, the responding party must show that the identified sources of information are not reasonably accessible because of undue burden or cost. The requesting party may need discovery to test this assertion. Such discovery might take the form of requiring the responding party to conduct a sampling of information contained on the sources identified as not reasonably accessible; allowing some form of inspection of such sources; or taking depositions of witnesses knowledgeable about the responding party's information systems.

Once it is shown that a source of electronically stored information is not reasonably accessible, the requesting party may still obtain discovery by showing good cause, considering the limitations of Rule 26(b)(2)(C) that balance the costs and potential benefits of discovery. The decision whether to require a responding party to search for and produce information that is not reasonably accessible depends not only on the burdens and costs of doing so, but also on whether those burdens and costs can be justified in the circumstances of the case. Appropriate considerations may include: (1) the specificity of the discovery request; (2) the quantity of information available from other and more easily accessed sources; (3) the failure to produce relevant information that seems likely to have existed but is no longer available on more easily accessed sources; (4) the likelihood of finding relevant, responsive information that cannot be obtained from other, more easily accessed sources; (5) predictions as to the importance and usefulness of the further information; (6) the importance of the issues at stake in the litigation; and (7) the parties' resources.

The responding party has the burden as to one aspect of the inquiry—whether the identified sources are not reasonably accessible in light of the burdens and costs required to search for, retrieve, and produce whatever responsive information may be found. The requesting party has the burden of showing that its need for the discovery outweighs the burdens and costs of locating, retrieving, and producing the information. In some cases, the court will be able to determine whether the identified sources are not reasonably accessible and whether the requesting party has shown good cause for some or all of the discovery, consistent with the limitations of Rule 26(b)(2)(C), through a single proceeding or presentation. The good-cause determination, however, may be complicated because the court and parties may know little about what information the sources identified as not reasonably accessible might contain, whether it is relevant, or how valuable it may be to the litigation. In such cases, the parties may need some focused discovery, which may include sampling of the sources, to learn more about what burdens and costs are involved in accessing the information, what the information consists of, and how valuable it is for the litigation in light of information that can be obtained by exhausting other opportunities for discovery.

The good-cause inquiry and consideration of the Rule 26(b)(2)(C) limitations are coupled with the authority to set conditions for discovery. The conditions may take the form of limits on the amount, type, or sources of information required to be accessed and produced. The conditions may also include payment by the requesting party of part or all of the reasonable costs of obtaining information from sources that are not reasonably accessible. A requesting party's willingness to share or bear the access costs may be weighed by the court in determining whether there is good cause. But the producing party's burdens in reviewing the information for relevance and privilege may weigh against permitting the requested discovery.

The limitations of Rule 26(b)(2)(C) continue to apply to all discovery of electronically stored information, including that stored on reasonably accessible electronic sources.

Subdivision (b)(5). The Committee has repeatedly been advised that the risk of privilege waiver, and the work necessary to avoid it, add to the costs and delay of discovery. When the review is of electronically stored information, the risk of waiver, and the time and effort required to avoid it, can increase substantially because of the volume of electronically stored information and the difficulty in ensuring that all information to be produced has in fact been reviewed. Rule 26(b)(5)(A) provides a procedure for a party that has withheld information on the basis of privilege or protection as trial-preparation material to make the claim so that the requesting party can decide whether to contest the claim and the court can resolve the dispute. Rule 26(b)(5)(B) is added to provide a procedure for a party to assert a claim of privilege or trial-preparation material protection after information is produced in discovery in the action and, if the claim is contested, permit any party that received the information to present the matter to the court for resolution.

Rule 26(b)(5)(B) does not address whether the privilege or protection that is asserted after production was waived by the production. The courts have developed principles to determine whether, and under what circumstances, waiver results from inadvertent production of privileged or protected information. Rule 26(b)(5)(B) provides a procedure for presenting and addressing these issues. Rule 26(b)(5)(B) works in tandem with Rule 26(f), which is amended to direct the parties to discuss privilege issues in preparing their discovery plan, and which, with amended Rule 16(b), allows the parties to ask the court to include in an order any agreements the parties reach regarding issues of privilege or trial-preparation material protection. Agreements reached under Rule 26(f)(4) and orders including such agreements entered under Rule 16(b)(6) may be considered when a court determines whether a waiver has occurred. Such agreements and orders ordinarily control if they adopt procedures different from those in Rule 26(b)(5)(B).

A party asserting a claim of privilege or protection after production must give notice to the receiving party. That notice should be in writing unless the circumstances preclude it. Such circumstances could include the assertion of the claim during a deposition. The notice should be as specific as possible in identifying the information and stating the basis for the claim. Because the receiving party must decide whether to challenge the claim and may sequester the information and submit it to the court for a ruling on whether the claimed privilege or protection applies and whether it has been waived, the notice should be sufficiently detailed so as to enable the receiving party and the court to understand the basis for the claim and to determine whether waiver has occurred. Courts will continue to examine whether a claim of privilege or protection was made at a reasonable time when delay is part of the waiver determination under the governing law.

After receiving notice, each party that received the information must promptly return, sequester, or destroy the information and any copies it has. The option of sequestering or destroying the information is included in part because the receiving party may have incorporated the information in protected trial-preparation materials. No receiving party may use or disclose the information pending resolution of the privilege claim. The receiving party may present to the court the questions whether the information is privileged or protected as trial-preparation material, and whether the privilege or protection has been waived. If it does so, it must provide the court with the grounds for the privilege or protection specified in the producing party's notice, and serve all parties. In presenting the question, the party may use the content of the information only to the extent permitted by the applicable law of privilege, protection for trial-preparation material, and professional responsibility.

If a party disclosed the information to nonparties before receiving notice of a claim of privilege or protection as trial-preparation material, it must take reasonable steps to retrieve the information and to return it, sequester it until the claim is resolved, or destroy it.

Whether the information is returned or not, the producing party must preserve the information pending the court's ruling on whether the claim of privilege or of protection is properly asserted and whether it was waived. As with claims made under Rule 26(b)(5)(A), there may be no ruling if the other parties do not contest the claim.

Subdivision (f). Rule 26(f) is amended to direct the parties to discuss discovery of electronically stored information during their discovery-planning conference. The rule focuses on "issues relating to disclosure or discovery of electronically stored information"; the discussion is not required in cases not involving electronic discovery, and the amendment imposes no additional requirements in those cases. When the parties do anticipate disclosure or discovery of electronically stored information, discussion at the outset may avoid later difficulties or ease their resolution.

When a case involves discovery of electronically stored information, the issues to be addressed during the Rule 26(f) conference depend on the nature and extent of the contemplated discovery and of the parties' information systems. It may be important for the parties to discuss those systems, and accordingly important for counsel to become familiar with those systems before the conference. With that information, the parties can develop a discovery plan that takes into account the capabilities of their computer systems. In appropriate cases identification of, and early discovery from, individuals with special knowledge of a party's computer systems may be helpful.

The particular issues regarding electronically stored information that deserve attention during the discovery planning stage depend on the specifics of the given case. *See Manual for Complex Litigation (4th)* § 40.25(2) (listing topics for discussion in a proposed order regarding meet-and-confer sessions). For example, the parties may specify the topics for such discovery and the time period for which discovery will be sought. They may identify the various sources of such information within a party's control that should be searched for electronically stored information. They may discuss whether the information is reasonably accessible to the party that has it, including the burden or cost of retrieving and reviewing the information. *See* Rule 26(b)(2)(B). Rule 26 (f)(3) explicitly directs the parties to discuss the form or forms in which electronically stored information might be produced. The parties may be able to reach agreement on the forms of production, making discovery more efficient. Rule 34(b) is amended to permit a requesting party to specify the form or forms in which it wants electronically stored information produced. If the requesting party does not specify a form, Rule 34(b) directs the responding party to state the forms it intends to use in the production. Early discussion of the forms of production may facilitate the application of Rule 34(b) by allowing the parties to determine what forms of production will meet both parties' needs. Early identification of disputes over the forms of production may help avoid the expense and delay of searches or productions using inappropriate forms.

Rule 26(f) is also amended to direct the parties to discuss any issues regarding preservation of discoverable information during their conference as they develop a discovery plan. This provision applies to all sorts of discoverable information, but can be particularly important with regard to electronically stored information. The volume and dynamic nature of electronically stored information may complicate preservation obligations. The ordinary operation of computers involves both the automatic creation and the automatic deletion or overwriting of certain information. Failure to address preservation issues early in the litigation increases uncertainty and raises a risk of disputes.

The parties' discussion should pay particular attention to the balance between the competing needs to preserve relevant evidence and to continue routine operations critical to ongoing activities. Complete or broad cessation of a party's routine computer operations could paralyze the party's activities. *Cf. Manual for Complex Litigation (4th)* § 11.422 ("A blanket preservation order may be prohibitively expensive and unduly burdensome for parties dependent on computer systems for their day-to-day operations.") The parties should take account of these considerations in their discussions, with the goal of agreeing on reasonable preservation steps.

The requirement that the parties discuss preservation does not imply that courts should routinely enter preservation orders. A preservation order entered over objections should be narrowly tailored. Ex parte preservation orders should issue only in exceptional circumstances.

Rule 26(f) is also amended to provide that the parties should discuss any issues relating to assertions of privilege or of protection as trial-preparation materials, including whether the parties can facilitate discovery by agreeing on procedures for asserting claims of privilege or protection after production and whether to ask the court to enter an order that includes any agreement the parties reach. The Committee has repeatedly been advised about the discovery difficulties that can result from efforts to guard against waiver of privilege and work-product protection. Frequently parties find it necessary to spend large amounts of time reviewing materials requested through discovery to avoid waiving privilege. These efforts are necessary because materials subject to a claim of privilege or protection are often difficult to identify. A failure to withhold even one such item may result in an argument that there has been a waiver of privilege as to all other privileged materials on that subject matter. Efforts to avoid the risk of waiver can impose substantial costs on the party producing the material and the time required for the privilege review can substantially delay access for the party seeking discovery.

These problems often become more acute when discovery of electronically stored information is sought. The volume of such data, and the informality that attends use of e-mail and some other types of electronically stored information, may make privilege determinations more difficult, and privilege review correspondingly more expensive and time consuming. Other aspects of electronically stored information pose particular difficulties for privilege review. For example, production may be sought of information automatically included in electronic files but not apparent to the creator or to readers. Computer programs may retain draft language, editorial comments, and other deleted matter (sometimes referred to as "embedded data" or "embedded edits") in an electronic file but not make them apparent to the reader. Information describing the history, tracking, or management of an electronic file (sometimes called "metadata") is usually not apparent to the reader viewing a hard copy or a screen image. Whether this information should be produced may be among the topics discussed in the Rule 26(f) conference. If it is, it may need to be reviewed to ensure that no privileged information is included, further complicating the task of privilege review.

Parties may attempt to minimize these costs and delays by agreeing to protocols that minimize the risk of waiver. They may agree that the responding party will provide certain requested materials for initial examination without waiving any privilege or protection — sometimes known as a "quick peek." The requesting party then designates the documents it wishes to have actually produced. This designation is the Rule 34 request. The responding party then responds in the usual course, screening only those documents actually requested for formal production and asserting privilege claims as provided in Rule 26(b)(5)(A). On other occasions, parties enter agreements—sometimes called "clawback agreements"—that production without intent to waive privilege or protection should not be a waiver so long as the responding party identifies the documents mistakenly produced, and that the documents should be returned under those circumstances. Other voluntary arrangements may be appropriate depending on the circumstances of each litigation. In most circumstances, a party who receives information under such an arrangement cannot assert that production of the information waived a claim of privilege or of protection as trial-preparation material.

Although these agreements may not be appropriate for all cases, in certain cases they can facilitate prompt and economical discovery by reducing delay before the discovering party obtains access to documents, and by reducing the cost and burden of review by the producing party. A case-management or other order including such agreements may further facilitate the discovery process. Form 35 is amended to include a report to the court about any agreement regarding protections against inadvertent forfeiture or waiver of privilege or protection that the parties have reached, and Rule 16(b) is amended to recognize that the court may include such an agreement in a case-management or other order. If the parties agree to entry of such an order, their proposal should be included in the report to the court.

Rule 26(b)(5)(B) is added to establish a parallel procedure to assert privilege or protection as trial-preparation material after production, leaving the question of waiver to later determination by the court.

Committee Note to 2007 Amendment

The language of Rule 26 has been amended as part of the general restyling of the Civil Rules to make them more easily understood and to make style and terminology consistent throughout the rules. These changes are intended to be stylistic only.

Former Rule 26(a)(5) served as an index of the discovery methods provided by later rules. It was deleted as redundant. Deletion does not affect the right to pursue discovery in addition to disclosure.

Former Rule 26(b)(1) began with a general statement of the scope of discovery that appeared to function as a preface to each of the five numbered paragraphs that followed. This preface has been shifted to the text of paragraph (1) because it does not accurately reflect the limits embodied in paragraphs (2), (3), or (4), and because paragraph (5) does not address the 'scope of discovery.

The reference to discovery of "books" in former Rule 26(b)(1) was deleted to achieve consistent expression throughout the discovery rules. Books remain a proper subject of discovery.

Amended Rule 26(b)(3) states that a party may obtain a copy of the party's own previous statement "on request." Former Rule 26(b)(3) expressly made the request procedure available to a nonparty witness, but did not describe the procedure to be used by a party. This apparent gap is closed by adopting the request procedure, which ensures that a party need not invoke Rule 34 to obtain a copy of the party's own statement.

Rule 26(e) stated the duty to supplement or correct a disclosure or discovery response "to include information thereafter acquired." This apparent limit is not reflected in practice; parties recognize the duty to supplement or correct by providing information that was not originally provided although it was available at the time of the initial disclosure or response. These words are deleted to reflect the actual meaning of the present rule.

Former Rule 26(e) used different phrases to describe the time to supplement or correct a disclosure or discovery response. Disclosures were to be supplemented "at appropriate intervals." A prior discovery response must be "seasonably * * * amend[ed]." The fine distinction between these phrases has not been observed in practice. Amended Rule 26(e)(1)(A) uses the same phrase for disclosures and discovery responses. The party must supplement or correct "in a timely manner."

Former Rule 26(g)(1) did not call for striking an unsigned disclosure. The omission was an obvious drafting oversight. Amended Rule 26(g)(2) includes disclosures in the list of matters that the court must strike unless a signature is provided "promptly * * * after being called to the attorney's or party's attention."

Former Rule 26(b)(2)(A) referred to a "good faith" argument to extend existing law. Amended Rule 26(b)(1)(B)(i) changes this reference to a "nonfrivolous" argument to achieve consistency with Rule 11 (b)(2).

As with the Rule 11 signature on a pleading, written motion, or other paper, disclosure and discovery signatures should include not only a postal address but also a telephone number and electronic-mail address. A signer who lacks one or more of those addresses need not supply a nonexistent item.

Rule 11(b)(2) recognizes that it is legitimate to argue for establishing new law. An argument to establish new law is equally legitimate in conducting discovery.

* * *

Rule 33. Interrogatories to Parties

(a) In General.

(1) *Number.* Unless otherwise stipulated or ordered by the court, a party may serve on any other party no more than 25 written interrogatories, including all discrete subparts. Leave to serve additional interrogatories may be granted to the extent consistent with Rule 26(b)(2).

(2) *Scope.* An interrogatory may relate to any matter that may be inquired into under Rule 26(b). An interrogatory is not objectionable merely because it asks for an opinion or contention that relates to fact or the application of law to fact, but the court may order that the interrogatory need not be answered until designated discovery is complete, or until a pretrial conference or some other time.

(b) Answers and Objections.

(1) *Responding Party.* The interrogatories must be answered:

(A) by the party to whom they are directed; or

(B) if that party is a public or private corporation, a partnership, an association, or a governmental agency, by any officer or agent, who must furnish the information available to the party.

(2) *Time to Respond.* The responding party must serve its answers and any objections within 30 days after being served with the interrogatories. A shorter or longer time may be stipulated to under Rule 29 or be ordered by the court.

(3) *Answering Each Interrogatory.* Each interrogatory must, to the extent it is not objected to, be answered separately and fully in writing under oath.

(4) *Objections.* The grounds for objecting to an interrogatory must be stated with specificity. Any ground not stated in a timely objection is waived unless the court, for good cause, excuses the failure.

(5) *Signature.* The person who makes the answers must sign them, and the attorney who objects must sign any objections.

(c) Use. An answer to an interrogatory may be used to the extent allowed by the Federal Rules of Evidence.

(d) Option to Produce Business Records. If the answer to an interrogatory may be determined by examining, auditing, compiling, abstracting, or summarizing a party's business records (including electronically stored information), and if the burden of deriving or ascertaining the answer will be substantially the same for either party, the responding party may answer by:

(1) specifying the records that must be reviewed, in sufficient detail to enable the interrogating party to locate and identify them as readily as the responding party could; and

(2) giving the interrogating party a reasonable opportunity to examine and audit the records and to make copies, compilations, abstracts, or summaries.

[As amended Apr. 12, 2006, eff. Dec. 1, 2006; April 30, 2007, eff. Dec. 1, 2007.]

Committee Note to 2006 Amendment

Rule 33(d) is amended to parallel Rule 34(a) by recognizing the importance of electronically stored information. The term "electronically stored information" has the same broad meaning in Rule 33(d) as in Rule 34(a). Much business information is stored only in electronic form; the Rule 33(d) option should be available with respect to such records as well.

Special difficulties may arise in using electronically stored information, either due to its form or because it is dependent on a particular computer system. Rule 33(d) allows a responding party to substitute access to documents or electronically stored information for an answer only if the burden of deriving the answer will be substantially the same for either party. Rule 33(d) states that a party electing to respond to an interrogatory by providing electronically stored information must ensure that the interrogating party can locate and identify it "as readily as can the party served," and that the responding party must give the interrogating party a "reasonable opportunity to examine, audit, or inspect" the information. Depending on the circumstances, satisfying these provisions with regard to electronically stored information may require the responding party to provide some combination of technical support, information on application software, or other assistance. The key question is whether such support enables the interrogating party to derive or ascertain the answer from the electronically stored information as readily as the responding party. A party that wishes to invoke Rule 33(d) by specifying electronically stored information may be required to provide direct access to its electronic information system, but only if that is necessary to afford the requesting party an adequate opportunity to derive or ascertain the answer to the interrogatory. In that situation, the responding party's need to protect sensitive interests of confidentiality or privacy may mean that it must derive or ascertain and provide the answer itself rather than invoke Rule 33(d).

Committee Note to 2007 Amendment

The language of Rule 33 has been amended as part of the general restyling of the Civil Rules to make them more easily understood and to make style and terminology consistent throughout the rules. These changes are intended to be stylistic only.

The final sentence of former Rule 33(a) was a redundant cross-reference to the discovery moratorium provisions of Rule 26(d). Rule 26(d) is now familiar, obviating any need to carry forward the redundant cross-reference.

Former Rule 33(b)(5) was a redundant reminder of Rule 37(a) procedure and is omitted as no longer useful.

Former Rule 33(c) stated that an interrogatory "is not necessarily objectionable merely because an answer * * * involves an opinion or contention * * *." "[I]s not necessarily" seemed to imply that the interrogatory might be objectionable merely for this reason. This implication has been ignored in practice. Opinion and contention interrogatories are used routinely. Amended Rule 33(a)(2) embodies the current meaning of Rule 33 by omitting "necessarily."

Rule 34. Producing Documents, Electronically Stored Information, and Tangible Things, or Entering Onto Land, for Inspection and Other Purposes

(a) In General. A party may serve on any other party a request within the scope of Rule 26(b):

(1) to produce and permit the requesting party or its representative to inspect, copy, test, or sample the following items in the responding party's possession, custody, or control:

(A) any designated documents or electronically stored information—including writings, drawings, graphs, charts, photographs, sound recordings, images, and other data or data compilations—stored in any medium from which information can be obtained either directly or, if necessary, after translation by the responding party into a reasonably usable form; or

(B) any designated tangible things; or

(2) to permit entry onto designated land or other property possessed or controlled by the responding party, so that the requesting party may inspect, measure, survey, photograph, test, or sample the property or any designated object or operation on it.

(b) Procedure.

(1) *Contents of the Request.* The request:

(A) must describe with reasonable particularity each item or category of items to be inspected;

(B) must specify a reasonable time, place, and manner for the inspection and for performing the related acts; and

(C) may specify the form or forms in which electronically stored information is to be produced.

(2) *Responses and Objections.*

(A) Time to Respond. The party to whom the

request is directed must respond in writing within 30 days after being served. A shorter or longer time may be stipulated to under Rule 29 or be ordered by the court.

(B) Responding to Each Item. For each item or category, the response must either state that inspection and related activities will be permitted as requested or state an objection to the request, including the reasons.

(C) Objections. An objection to part of a request must specify the part and permit inspection of the rest.

(D) Responding to a Request for Production of Electronically Stored Information. The response may state an objection to a requested form for producing electronically stored information. If the responding party objects to a requested form—or if no form was specified in the request—the party must state the form or forms it intends to use.

(E) Producing the Documents or Electronically Stored Information. Unless otherwise stipulated or ordered by the court, these procedures apply to producing documents or electronically stored information:

(i) A party must produce documents as they are kept in the usual course of business or must organize and label them to correspond to the categories in the request;

(ii) If a request does not specify a form for producing electronically stored information, a party must produce it in a form or forms in which it is ordinarily maintained or in a reasonably usable form or forms; and

(iii) A party need not produce the same electronically stored information in more than one form.

(c) Nonparties. As provided in Rule 45, a nonparty may be compelled to produce documents and tangible things or to permit an inspection.

[As amended Apr. 12, 2006, eff. Dec. 1, 2006; April 30, 2007, eff. Dec. 1, 2007.]

Committee Note to 2006 Amendment

Subdivision (a). As originally adopted, Rule 34 focused on discovery of "documents" and "things." In 1970, Rule 34(a) was amended to include discovery of data compilations, anticipating that the use of computerized information would increase. Since then, the growth in electronically stored information and in the variety of systems for creating and storing such information has been dramatic. Lawyers and judges interpreted the term "documents" to include electronically stored information because it was obviously improper to allow a party to evade discovery obligations on the basis that the label had not kept pace with changes in information technology. But it has become increasingly difficult to say that all forms of electronically stored information, many dynamic in nature, fit within the traditional concept of a "document." Electronically stored information may exist in dynamic databases and other forms far different from fixed expression on paper. Rule 34(a) is amended to confirm that discovery of electronically stored information stands on equal footing with discovery of paper documents. The change clarifies that Rule 34 applies to information that is fixed in a tangible form and to information that is stored in a medium from which it can be retrieved and examined. At the same time, a Rule 34 request for production of "documents" should be understood to encompass, and the response should include, electronically stored information unless discovery in the action has clearly distinguished between electronically stored information and "documents."

Discoverable information often exists in both paper and electronic form, and the same or similar information might exist in both. The items listed in Rule 34(a) show different ways in which information may be recorded or stored. Images, for example, might be hard-copy documents or electronically stored information. The wide variety of computer systems currently in use, and the rapidity of technological change, counsel against a limiting or precise definition of electronically stored information. Rule 34(a)(1) is expansive and includes any type of information that is stored electronically. A common example often sought in discovery is electronic communications, such as e-mail. The rule covers—either as documents or as electronically stored information—information "stored in any medium," to encompass future developments in computer technology. Rule 34(a)(1) is intended to be broad enough to cover all current types of computer-based information, and flexible enough to encompass future changes and developments.

References elsewhere in the rules to "electronically stored information" should be understood to invoke this expansive approach. A companion change is made to Rule 33(d), making it explicit that parties choosing to respond to an interrogatory by permitting access to responsive records may do so by providing access to electronically stored information. More generally, the term used in Rule 34(a)(1) appears in a number of other amendments, such as those to Rules 26(a)(1), 26(b)(2), 26(b)(5)(B), 26(f), 34(b), 37(f), and 45. In each of these rules, electronically stored information has the same broad meaning it has under Rule 34(a)(1). References to "documents" appear in discovery rules that are not amended, including Rules 30(f), 36(a), and 37(c)(2). These references should be interpreted to include electronically stored information as circumstances warrant.

The term "electronically stored information" is broad, but whether material that falls within this term should be produced, and in what form, are separate questions that must be addressed under Rules 26(b), 26(c), and 34(b).

The Rule 34(a) requirement that, if necessary, a party producing electronically stored information translate it into reasonably usable form does not address the issue of translating from one human language to another. *See* In re Puerto Rico Elec. Power Authority, 687 F.2d 501, 504, 34 Fed. R. Serv. 2d 1119 (1st Cir. 1982).

Rule 34(a)(1) is also amended to make clear that parties may request an opportunity to test or sample materials sought under the rule in addition to inspecting and copying them. That opportunity may be important for both electronically stored information and hard-copy materials. The current rule is not clear that such testing or sampling is authorized; the amendment expressly permits it. As with any other form of discovery, issues of burden and intrusiveness raised by requests to test or sample can be addressed under Rules 26(b)(2) and 26(c). Inspection or testing of certain types of electronically stored information or of a responding party's electronic information system may raise issues of confidentiality or privacy. The addition of testing and sampling to Rule 34(a) with regard to documents and electronically stored information is not meant to create a routine right of direct access to a party's electronic information system, although such access might be justified in some circumstances. Courts should guard against undue intrusiveness resulting from inspecting or testing such systems.

Rule 34(a)(1) is further amended to make clear that tangible things must—like documents and land sought to be examined—be designated in the request.

Subdivision (b). Rule 34(b) provides that a party must produce documents as they are kept in the usual course of business or must organize and label them to correspond with the categories in the discovery request. The production of electronically stored information should be subject to comparable requirements to protect against deliberate or inadvertent production in ways that raise unnecessary obstacles for the requesting party. Rule 34(b) is amended to ensure similar protection for electronically stored information.

The amendment to Rule 34(b) permits the requesting party to designate the form or forms in which it wants electronically stored information produced. The form of production is more important to the exchange of electronically stored information than of hard-copy materials, although a party might specify hard copy as the requested form. Specification of the desired form or forms may facilitate the orderly, efficient, and cost-effective discovery of electronically stored information. The rule recognizes that different forms of production may be appropriate for different types of electronically stored information. Using current technology, for example, a party might be called upon to produce word processing documents, e-mail messages, electronic spreadsheets, different image or sound files, and material from databases. Requiring that such diverse types of electronically stored information all be produced in the same form could prove impossible, and even if possible could increase the cost and burdens of producing and using the information. The rule therefore provides that the requesting party may ask for different forms of production for different types of electronically stored information.

The rule does not require that the requesting party choose a form or forms of production. The requesting party may not have a preference. In some cases, the requesting party may not know what form the producing party uses to maintain its electronically stored information, although Rule 26(f)(3) is amended to call for discussion of the form of production in the parties' prediscovery conference.

The responding party also is involved in determining the form of production. In the written response to the production request that Rule 34 requires, the responding party must state the form it intends to use for producing electronically stored information if the requesting party does not specify a form or if the responding party objects to a form that the requesting party specifies. Stating the intended form before the production occurs may permit the parties to identify and seek to resolve disputes before the expense and work of the production occurs. A party that responds to a discovery request by simply producing electronically stored information in a form of its choice, without identifying that form in advance of the production in the response required by Rule 34(b), runs a risk that the requesting party can show that the produced form is not reasonably usable and that it is entitled to production of some or all of the information in an additional form. Additional time might be required to permit a responding party to assess the appropriate form or forms of production.

If the requesting party is not satisfied with the form stated by the responding party, or if the responding party has objected to the form specified by the requesting party, the parties must meet and confer under Rule 37(a) (2) (B) in an effort to resolve the matter before the requesting party can file a motion to compel. If they cannot agree and the court resolves the dispute, the court is not limited to the forms initially chosen by the requesting party, stated by the responding party, or specified in this rule for situations in which there is no court order or party agreement.

If the form of production is not specified by party agreement or court order, the responding party must produce electronically stored information either in a form or forms in which it is ordinarily maintained or in a form or forms that are reasonably usable. Rule 34(a) requires that, if necessary, a responding party "translate" information it produces into a "reasonably usable" form. Under some circumstances, the responding party may need to provide some reasonable amount of technical support, information on application software, or other reasonable assistance to enable the requesting party to use the information. The rule does not require a party to produce electronically stored information in the form it which it is ordinarily maintained, as long as it is produced in a reasonably usable form. But the option to produce in a reasonably usable form does not mean that a responding party is free to convert electronically stored information from the form in which it is ordinarily maintained to a different form that makes it more difficult or burdensome for the requesting party to use the information efficiently in the litigation. If the responding party ordinarily maintains the information it is producing in a way that makes it searchable by electronic means, the information should not be produced in a form that removes or significantly degrades this feature.

Some electronically stored information may be ordinarily maintained in a form that is not reasonably usable by any party. One example is "legacy" data that can be used only by superseded systems. The questions whether a producing party should be required to convert such information to a more usable form, or should be required to produce it at all, should be addressed under Rule 26(b)(2)(B).

Whether or not the requesting party specified the form of production, Rule 34(b) provides that the same electronically stored information ordinarily need be produced in only one form.

Committee Note to 2007 Amendment

The language of Rule 34 has been amended as part of the general restyling of the Civil Rules to make them more easily understood and to make style and terminology consistent throughout the rules. These changes are intended to be stylistic only.

The final sentence in the first paragraph of former Rule 34(b) was a redundant cross-reference to the discovery moratorium provisions of Rule 26(d). Rule 26(d) is now familiar, obviating any need to carry forward the redundant cross-reference.

The redundant reminder of Rule 37(a) procedure in the second paragraph of former Rule 34(b) is omitted as no longer useful.

* * *

Rule 37. Failure to Make Disclosures or to Cooperate in Discovery; Sanctions

(a) Motion for an Order Compelling Disclosure or Discovery.

(1) *In General.* On notice to other parties and all affected persons, a party may move for an order compelling disclosure or discovery. The motion must include a certification that the movant has in good faith conferred or attempted to confer with the person or party failing to make disclosure or discovery in an effort to obtain it without court action.

(2) *Appropriate Court.* A motion for an order to a

party must be made in the court where the action is pending. A motion for an order to a nonparty must be made in the court where the discovery is or will be taken.

(3) *Specific Motions.*

(A) To Compel Disclosure. If a party fails to make a disclosure required by Rule 26(a), any other party may move to compel disclosure and for appropriate sanctions.

(B) To Compel a Discovery Response. A party seeking discovery may move for an order compelling an answer, designation, production, or inspection. This motion may be made if:

(i) a deponent fails to answer a question asked under Rule 30 or 31;

(ii) a corporation or other entity fails to make a designation under Rule 30(b)(6) or 31(a)(4);

(iii) a party fails to answer an interrogatory submitted under Rule 33; or

(iv) a party fails to respond that inspection will be permitted—or fails to permit inspection—as requested under Rule 34.

(C) Related to a Deposition. When taking an oral deposition, the party asking a question may complete or adjourn the examination before moving for an order.

(4) *Evasive or Incomplete Disclosure, Answer, or Response.* For purposes of this subdivision (a), an evasive or incomplete disclosure, answer, or response must be treated as a failure to disclose, answer, or respond.

(5) *Payment of Expenses; Protective Orders.*

(A) If the Motion Is Granted (or Disclosure or Discovery Is Provided After Filing). If the motion is granted—or if the disclosure or requested discovery is provided after the motion was filed—the court must, after giving an opportunity to be heard, require the party or deponent whose conduct necessitated the motion, the party or attorney advising that conduct, or both to pay the movant's reasonable expenses incurred in making the motion, including attorney's fees. But the court must not order this payment if:

(i) the movant filed the motion before attempting in good faith to obtain the disclosure or discovery without court action;

(ii) the opposing party's nondisclosure, response, or objection was substantially justified; or

(iii) other circumstances make an award of expenses unjust.

(B) If the Motion Is Denied. If the motion is denied, the court may issue any protective order authorized under Rule 26(c) and must, after giving an opportunity to be heard, require the movant, the attorney filing the motion, or both to pay the party or deponent who opposed the motion its reasonable expenses incurred in opposing the motion, including attorney's fees. But the court must not order this payment if the motion was substantially justified or other circumstances make an award of expenses unjust.

(C) If the Motion Is Granted in Part and Denied in Part. If the motion is granted in part and denied in part, the court may issue any protective order authorized under Rule 26(c) and may, after giving an opportunity to be heard, apportion the reasonable expenses for the motion.

(b) Failure to Comply with a Court Order.

(1) *Sanctions in the District Where the Deposition Is Taken.* If the court where the discovery is taken orders a deponent to be sworn or to answer a question and the deponent fails to obey, the failure may be treated as contempt of court.

(2) *Sanctions in the District Where the Action Is Pending.*

(A) For Not Obeying a Discovery Order. If a party or a party's officer, director, or managing agent—or a witness designated under Rule 30(b)(6) or 31(a)(4)—fails to obey an order to provide or permit discovery, including an order under Rule 26(f), 35, or 37(a), the court where the action is pending may issue further just orders. They may include the following:

(i) directing that the matters embraced in the order or other designated facts be taken as established for purposes of the action, as the prevailing party claims;

(ii) prohibiting the disobedient party from supporting or opposing designated claims or defenses, or from introducing designated matters in evidence;

(iii) striking pleadings in whole or in part;

(iv) staying further proceedings until the order is obeyed;

(v) dismissing the action or proceeding in whole or in part;

(vi) rendering a default judgment against the disobedient party; or

(vii) treating as contempt of court the failure to obey any order except an order to submit to a physical or mental examination.

(B) For Not Producing a Person for Examination. If a party fails to comply with an order under Rule 35(a) requiring it to produce another person for examination, the court may issue any of the orders listed in Rule 37(b)(2)(A)(i)–(vi), unless the disobedient party shows that it cannot produce the other person.

(C) Payment of Expenses. Instead of or in addition to the orders above, the court must order the disobedient party, the attorney advising that party, or both to pay the reasonable expenses, including attorney's fees, caused by the failure, unless the failure was substantially justified or other circumstances make an award of expenses unjust.

(c) Failure to Disclose, to Supplement an Earlier Response, or to Admit.

(1) *Failure to Disclose or Supplement.* If a party fails to provide information or identify a witness as required by Rule 26(a) or (e), the party is not allowed to use that information or witness to supply evidence on a motion, at a hearing, or at a trial, unless the failure was substantially justified or is harmless. In addition to or instead of this sanction, the court, on motion and after giving an opportunity to be heard:

(A) may order payment of the reasonable expenses, including attorney's fees, caused by the failure;

(B) may inform the jury of the party's failure; and

(C) may impose other appropriate sanctions, including any of the orders listed in Rule 37(b)(2)(A)(i)–(vi).

(2) *Failure to Admit.* If a party fails to admit what is requested under Rule 36 and if the requesting party later proves a document to be genuine or the matter true, the requesting party may move that the party who failed to admit pay the reasonable expenses, including attorney's fees, incurred in making that proof. The court must so order unless:

(A) the request was held objectionable under Rule 36(a);

(B) the admission sought was of no substantial importance;

(C) the party failing to admit had a reasonable ground to believe that it might prevail on the matter; or

(D) there was other good reason for the failure to admit.

(d) Party's Failure to Attend Its Own Deposition, Serve Answers to Interrogatories, or Respond to a Request for Inspection.

(1) *In General.*

(A) Motion; Grounds for Sanctions. The court where the action is pending may, on motion, order sanctions if:

(i) a party or a party's officer, director, or

managing agent—or a person designated under Rule 30(b)(6) or 31(a)(4)—fails, after being served with proper notice, to appear for that person's deposition; or

(ii) a party, after being properly served with interrogatories under Rule 33 or a request for inspection under Rule 34, fails to serve its answers, objections, or written response.

(B) Certification. A motion for sanctions for failing to answer or respond must include a certification that the movant has in good faith conferred or attempted to confer with the party failing to act in an effort to obtain the answer or response without court action.

(2) *Unacceptable Excuse for Failing to Act.* A failure described in Rule 37(d)(1)(A) is not excused on the ground that the discovery sought was objectionable, unless the party failing to act has a pending motion for a protective order under Rule 26(c).

(3) *Types of Sanctions.* Sanctions may include any of the orders listed in Rule 37(b)(2)(A)(i)–(vi). Instead of or in addition to these sanctions, the court must require the party failing to act, the attorney advising that party, or both to pay the reasonable expenses, including attorney's fees, caused by the failure, unless the failure was substantially justified or other circumstances make an award of expenses unjust.

(e) Failure to Provide Electronically Stored Information. Absent exceptional circumstances, a court may not impose sanctions under these rules on a party for failing to provide electronically stored information lost as a result of the routine, good-faith operation of an electronic information system.

(f) Failure to Participate in Framing a Discovery Plan. If a party or its attorney fails to participate in good faith in developing and submitting a proposed discovery plan as required by Rule 26(f), the court may, after giving an opportunity to be heard, require that party or attorney to pay to any other party the reasonable expenses, including attorney's fees, caused by the failure.

[As amended Apr. 12, 2006, eff. Dec. 1, 2006; April 30, 2007, eff. Dec. 1, 2007.]

Committee Note to 2006 Amendment

Subdivision (f). Subdivision (f) is new. It focuses on a distinctive feature of computer operations, the routine alteration and deletion of information that attends ordinary use. Many steps essential to computer operation may alter or destroy information, for reasons that have nothing to do with how that information might relate to litigation. As a result, the ordinary operation of computer systems creates a risk that a party may lose potentially discoverable information without culpable conduct on its part. Under Rule 37(f), absent exceptional circumstances, sanctions cannot be imposed for loss of electronically stored information resulting from the routine, good-faith operation of an electronic information system.

Rule 37(f) applies only to information lost due to the "routine operation of an electronic information system"—the ways in which such systems are generally designed, programmed, and implemented to meet the party's technical and business needs. The "routine operation" of computer systems includes the alteration and overwriting of information, often without the operator's specific direction or awareness, a feature with no direct counterpart in hard-copy documents. Such features are essential to the operation of electronic information systems.

Rule 37(f) applies to information lost due to the routine operation of an information system only if the operation was in good faith. Good faith in the routine operation of an information system may involve a party's intervention to modify or suspend certain features of that routine operation to prevent the loss of information, if that information is subject to a preservation obligation. A preservation obligation may arise from many sources, including common law, statutes, regulations, or a court order in the case. The good faith requirement of Rule 37(f) means that a party is not permitted to exploit the routine operation of an information system to thwart discovery obligations by allowing that operation to continue in order to destroy specific stored information that it is required to preserve. When a party is under a duty to preserve information because of pending or reasonably anticipated litigation, intervention in the routine operation of an information system is one aspect of what is often called a "litigation hold." Among the factors that bear on a party's good faith in the routine operation of an information system are the steps the party took to comply with a court order in the case or party agreement requiring preservation of specific electronically stored information.

Whether good faith would call for steps to prevent the loss of information on sources that the party believes are not reasonably accessible under Rule 26(b)(2) depends on the circumstances of each case. One factor is whether the party reasonably believes that the information on such sources is likely to be discoverable and not available from reasonably accessible sources.

The protection provided by Rule 37(f) applies only to sanctions "under these rules." It does not affect other sources of authority to impose sanctions or rules of professional responsibility.

This rule restricts the imposition of "sanctions." It does not prevent a court from making the kinds of adjustments frequently used in managing discovery if a party is unable to provide relevant responsive information. For example, a court could order the responding party to produce an additional witness for deposition, respond to additional interrogatories, or make similar attempts to provide substitutes or alternatives for some or all of the lost information.

Committee Note to 2007 Amendment

The language of Rule 37 has been amended as part of the general restyling of the Civil Rules to make them more easily understood and to make style and terminology consistent throughout the rules. These changes are intended to be stylistic only.

* * *

VI. TRIALS

* * *

Rule 45. Subpoena

(a) In General.

(1) *Form and Contents.*

(A) Requirements—In General. Every subpoena must:

(i) state the court from which it issued;

(ii) state the title of the action, the court in which it is pending, and its civil-action number;

(iii) command each person to whom it is directed to do the following at a specified time and place: attend and testify; produce designated documents, electronically stored information, or tangible things in that person's possession, custody, or control; or permit the inspection of premises; and

(iv) set out the text of Rule 45(c) and (d).

(B) Command to Attend a Deposition—Notice of the Recording Method. A subpoena commanding attendance at a deposition must state the method for recording the testimony.

(C) Combining or Separating a Command to Produce or to Permit Inspection; Specifying the Form for Electronically Stored Information. A command to produce documents, electronically stored information, or tangible things or to permit the inspection of premises may be included in a subpoena commanding attendance at a deposition, hearing, or trial, or may be set out in a separate subpoena. A subpoena may specify the form or forms in which electronically stored information is to be produced.

(D) Command to Produce; Included Obligations. A command in a subpoena to produce documents, electronically stored information, or tangible things requires the responding party to permit inspection, copying, testing, or sampling of the materials.

(2) *Issued from Which Court.* A subpoena must issue as follows:

(A) for attendance at a hearing or trial, from the court for the district where the hearing or trial is to be held;

(B) for attendance at a deposition, from the court for the district where the deposition is to be taken; and

(C) for production or inspection, if separate from a subpoena commanding a person's attendance, from the court for the district where the production or inspection is to be made.

(3) *Issued by Whom.* The clerk must issue a subpoena, signed but otherwise in blank, to a party who requests it. That party must complete it before service. An attorney also may issue and sign a subpoena as an officer of:

(A) a court in which the attorney is authorized to practice; or

(B) a court for a district where a deposition is to be taken or production is to be made, if the attorney is authorized to practice in the court where the action is pending.

(b) Service.

(1) *By Whom; Tendering Fees; Serving a Copy of Certain Subpoenas.* Any person who is at least 18 years old and not a party may serve a subpoena. Serving a subpoena requires delivering a copy to the

named person and, if the subpoena requires that person's attendance, tendering the fees for 1 day's attendance and the mileage allowed by law. Fees and mileage need not be tendered when the subpoena issues on behalf of the United States or any of its officers or agencies. If the subpoena commands the production of documents, electronically stored information, or tangible things or the inspection of premises before trial, then before it is served, a notice must be served on each party.

(2) *Service in the United States.* Subject to Rule 45(c)(3)(A)(ii), a subpoena may be served at any place:

(A) within the district of the issuing court;

(B) outside that district but within 100 miles of the place specified for the deposition, hearing, trial, production, or inspection;

(C) within the state of the issuing court if a state statute or court rule allows service at that place of a subpoena issued by a state court of general jurisdiction sitting in the place specified for the deposition, hearing, trial, production, or inspection; or

(D) that the court authorizes on motion and for good cause, if a federal statute so provides.

(3) *Service in a Foreign Country.* 28 U.S.C. § 1783 governs issuing and serving a subpoena directed to a United States national or resident who is in a foreign country.

(4) *Proof of Service.* Proving service, when necessary, requires filing with the issuing court a statement showing the date and manner of service and the names of the persons served. The statement must be certified by the server.

(c) Protecting a Person Subject to a Subpoena.

(1) *Avoiding Undue Burden or Expense; Sanctions.* A party or attorney responsible for issuing and serving a subpoena must take reasonable steps to avoid imposing undue burden or expense on a person subject to the subpoena. The issuing court must enforce this duty and impose an appropriate sanction—which may

include lost earnings and reasonable attorney's fees—on a party or attorney who fails to comply.

(2) *Command to Produce Materials or Permit Inspection.*

(A) Appearance Not Required. A person commanded to produce documents, electronically stored information, or tangible things, or to permit the inspection of premises, need not appear in person at the place of production or inspection unless also commanded to appear for a deposition, hearing, or trial.

(B) Objections. A person commanded to produce documents or tangible things or to permit inspection may serve on the party or attorney designated in the subpoena a written objection to inspecting, copying, testing or sampling any or all of the materials or to inspecting the premises—or to producing electronically stored information in the form or forms requested. The objection must be served before the earlier of the time specified for compliance or 14 days after the subpoena is served. If an objection is made, the following rules apply:

(i) At any time, on notice to the commanded person, the serving party may move the issuing court for an order compelling production or inspection.

(ii) These acts may be required only as directed in the order, and the order must protect a person who is neither a party nor a party's officer from significant expense resulting from compliance.

(3) *Quashing or Modifying a Subpoena.*

(A) When Required. On timely motion, the issuing court must quash or modify a subpoena that:

(i) fails to allow a reasonable time to comply;

(ii) requires a person who is neither a party nor a party's officer to travel more than 100 miles from where that person resides, is employed, or regularly transacts business in person—except that, subject to Rule 45(c)(3)(B)(iii), the person may be commanded to attend a trial by traveling from any such place within the state where the trial is held;

(iii) requires disclosure of privileged or other protected matter, if no exception or waiver applies; or

(iv) subjects a person to undue burden.

(B) When Permitted. To protect a person subject to or affected by a subpoena, the issuing court may, on motion, quash or modify the subpoena if it requires:

(i) disclosing a trade secret or other confidential research, development, or commercial information;

(ii) disclosing an unretained expert's opinion or information that does not describe specific occurrences in dispute and results from the expert's study that was not requested by a party; or

(iii) a person who is neither a party nor a party's officer to incur substantial expense to travel more than 100 miles to attend trial.

(C) Specifying Conditions as an Alternative. In the circumstances described in Rule 45(c)(3)(B), the court may, instead of quashing or modifying a subpoena, order appearance or production under specified conditions if the serving party:

(i) shows a substantial need for the testimony or material that cannot be otherwise met without undue hardship; and

(ii) ensures that the subpoenaed person will be reasonably compensated.

(d) Duties in Responding to a Subpoena.

(1) *Producing Documents or Electronically Stored Information.* These procedures apply to producing documents or electronically stored information:

(A) Documents. A person responding to a subpoena to produce documents must produce them as they are kept in the ordinary course of business or must organize and label them to correspond to the categories in the demand.

(B) Form for Producing Electronically Stored Information Not Specified. If a subpoena does not specify a form for producing electronically stored information, the person responding must produce it in a form or forms in which it is ordinarily maintained or in a reasonably usable form or forms.

(C) Electronically Stored Information Produced in Only One Form. The person responding need not produce the same electronically stored information in more than one form.

(D) Inaccessible Electronically Stored Information. The person responding need not provide discovery of electronically stored information from sources that the person identifies as not reasonably accessible because of undue burden or cost. On motion to compel discovery or for a protective order, the person responding must show that the information is not reasonably accessible because of undue burden or cost. If that showing is made, the court may nonetheless order discovery from such sources if the requesting party shows good cause, considering the limitations of Rule 26(b)(2)(C). The court may specify conditions for the discovery.

(2) *Claiming Privilege or Protection.*

(A) Information Withheld. A person withholding subpoenaed information under a claim that it is privileged or subject to protection as trial-preparation material must:

(i) expressly make the claim; and

(ii) describe the nature of the withheld documents, communications, or tangible things in a manner that, without revealing information itself privileged or protected, will enable the parties to assess the claim.

(B) Information Produced. If information produced in response to a subpoena is subject to a claim of privilege or of protection as trial-preparation material, the person making the claim may notify any party that received the information of the claim and the basis for it. After being notified, a party must promptly return, sequester, or destroy the specified information and any copies it has; must not use or disclose the information until the claim is resolved; must take reasonable steps to retrieve the information if the party disclosed it before being notified; and may promptly present the information to the court under seal for a determination of the claim. The person who produced the information must preserve the information until the claim is resolved.

(e) Contempt. The issuing court may hold in contempt a person who, having been served, fails without adequate excuse to obey the subpoena. A nonparty's failure to obey must be excused if the subpoena purports to require the nonparty to attend or produce at a place outside the limits of Rule 45(c)(3)(A)(ii).

[As amended Apr. 12, 2006, eff. Dec. 1, 2006; April 30, 2007, eff. Dec. 1, 2007.]

Committee Note to 2006 Amendments

Rule 45 is amended to conform the provisions for subpoenas to changes in other discovery rules, largely related to discovery of electronically stored information. Rule 34 is amended to provide in greater detail for the production of electronically stored information. Rule 45(a)(1)(C) is amended to recognize that electronically stored information, as defined in Rule 34(a), can also be sought by subpoena. Like Rule 34(b), Rule 45(a)(1) is amended to provide that the subpoena can designate a form or forms for production of electronic data. Rule 45(c)(2) is amended, like Rule 34(b), to authorize the person served with a subpoena to object to the requested form or forms. In addition, as under Rule 34(b), Rule 45(d)(1)(B) is amended to provide that if the subpoena does not specify the form or forms for electronically stored information, the person served with the subpoena must produce electronically stored information in a form or forms in which it is usually maintained or in a form or forms that are reasonably usable. Rule 45(d)(1)(C) is added to provide that the person producing electronically stored information should not have to produce the same information in more than one form unless so ordered by the court for good cause.

As with discovery of electronically stored information from parties, complying with a subpoena for such information may impose burdens on the responding person. Rule 45(c) provides protection against undue impositions on nonparties. For example, Rule 45(c)(1) directs that a party serving a subpoena "shall take reasonable steps to avoid imposing undue burden or expense on a person subject to the subpoena," and

Rule 45(c)(2)(B) permits the person served with the subpoena to object to it and directs that an order requiring compliance "shall protect a person who is neither a party nor a party's officer from significant expense resulting from" compliance. Rule 45(d)(1)(D) is added to provide that the responding person need not provide discovery of electronically stored information from sources the party identifies as not reasonably accessible, unless the court orders such discovery for good cause, considering the limitations of Rule 26(b)(2)(C), on terms that protect a nonparty against significant expense. A parallel provision is added to Rule 26(b)(2).

Rule 45(a)(1)(B) is also amended, as is Rule 34(a), to provide that a subpoena is available to permit testing and sampling as well as inspection and copying. As in Rule 34, this change recognizes that on occasion the opportunity to perform testing or sampling may be important, both for documents and for electronically stored information. Because testing or sampling may present particular issues of burden or intrusion for the person served with the subpoena, however, the protective provisions of Rule 45(c) should be enforced with vigilance when such demands are made. Inspection or testing of certain types of electronically stored information or of a person's electronic information system may raise issues of confidentiality or privacy. The addition of sampling and testing to Rule 45(a) with regard to documents and electronically stored information is not meant to create a routine right of direct access to a person's electronic information system, although such access might be justified in some circumstances. Courts should guard against undue intrusiveness resulting from inspecting or testing such systems.

Rule 45(d)(2) is amended, as is Rule 26(b)(5), to add a procedure for assertion of privilege or of protection as trial-preparation materials after production. The receiving party may submit the information to the court for resolution of the privilege claim, as under Rule 26(b)(5)(B).

Other minor amendments are made to conform the rule to the changes described above.

Committee Note to 2007 Amendment

The language of Rule 45 has been amended as part of the general restyling of the Civil Rules to make them more easily understood and to make style and terminology consistent throughout the rules. These changes are intended to be stylistic only.

The reference to discovery of "books" in former Rule 45(a)(l)(C) was deleted to achieve consistent expression throughout the discovery rules. Books remain a proper subject of discovery.

Former Rule 45(b)(l) required "prior notice" to each party of any commanded production of documents and things or inspection of premises. Courts have agreed that notice must be given "prior" to the return date, and have tended to converge on an interpretation that requires notice to the parties before the subpoena is served on the person commanded to produce or permit inspection. That interpretation is adopted in amended Rule 45(b)(1) to give clear notice of general present practice.

The language of former Rule 45(d)(2) addressing the manner of asserting privilege is replaced by adopting the wording of Rule 26(b)(5).

The same meaning is better expressed in the same words.

Chapter 3

Protecting Electronically Stored Information

I. GUIDELINES

II. CHECKLISTS

III. FORMS

Research References

Treatises and Practice Aids

eDiscovery and Digital Evidence §§ 10:1 to 10:20
Grenig and Kinsler, Federal Civil Discovery and Disclosure §§ 13.1 to 13.6 (2d ed.)

Trial Strategy

Computer Technology in Civil Litigation, 71 Am. Jur Trials 111

Law Reviews and Other Periodicals

Brownstone, Preserve or Perish: Destroy or Drown—eDiscovery Morphs into Electronic Information Management, 8 N.C. J. L. & Tech 1 (2006)

Gergacz, Employees' Use of Employer Computers to Communicate with Their Own Attorneys and the Attorney-Client Privilege, 10 Computer L.R. & Tech. J. 269 (2006)

Juhnke, Under the Radar: Unauthorized Software is Sneaking into the Workplace, and Creating Discovery Nightmares, Nat'l L.J., Aug. 20, 2007, at S1.

Additional References

Protecting Privacy and Security of Electronically Stored Information, Elec. Disc. & Records Mgt. Q. summer 2007

KeyCite®: Cases and other legal materials listed in KeyCite Scope can be researched through the KeyCite service on Westlaw®. Use KeyCite to check citations for form, parallel references, prior and later history, and comprehensive citator information, including citations to other decisions and secondary materials.

I. GUIDELINES

§ 3:1 Generally

Policies regarding computer use are an important of a records management program. Because an unprotected computer can quickly be infected or hacked after connecting to the Internet, it is essential to protect electronically stored information. The use of computers and the Internet by members or employees can open an organization to liability for infringement of intellectual property rights, copyright violations, unfair competition, defamation, sexual harassment, wrongful termination, fraud, and invasion of privacy. In addition, connection to the Internet means exposure to computer hackers, viruses, and industrial espionage.

Organizations allowing use of computers and particularly the Internet by its employees should have a computer use policy in place to limit exposure to liability and to protect electronically stored information. A computer use policy should set forth an objective standard for employees to apply when using electronic media and services. It should describe appropriate uses of the Internet and make clear that employees are using the organization's equipment. Users should understand that there is no privacy expectation in the use of computers and that e-mail and Internet usage may be monitored. In-house counsel should be proactive in educating employees on the best practices regarding e-mail and other digital information

Shadow information technology (sometimes referred to as rogue IT or consumer IT) may operate outside an organization's information technology department. There are three categories of shadow IT: storage of convenience, tools of convenience, and applications of convenience. Storage of convenience include thumb drives, jump drives, and Internet-based storage. Tools of convenience include communication platforms, utilities, hardware and software applications, MySpace, Facebook, Voice over Internet Protocol (VOIP), and Internet service provider mail such as Yahoo! or Gmail. An application of convenience is based on a corporate standard but is used in an unconventional way or instead of existing enterprise programs. Organizations that do not limit shadow IT may create a number of problems, including serious problems in ensuring that all potentially relevant sources of data are located in response to discovery requests.

§ 3:2 Updates

It is normally prudent to install the latest updates of applications in order to reduce security vulnerabilities. However, because the installation of updates can interfere with the operation of the computer or peripherals, it is important to back up data before installing updates.

§ 3:3 Passwords

It is essential to use passwords and keep them safe. If it is necessary to write down a password, it should be written in a code so that only the password owner can figure out the password. No one should be told a password. Any compromised password should be changed immediately. The same password should not be used for everything. One should not allow Web sites to remember a password and one should not let the Web browser remember Web site passwords. A password should be at least eight characters long, contain at least one upper case letter, one lower case letter, one number, and one symbol. A password should be significantly different than previously used passwords.

Because laptops and personal data assistants are easily lost or stolen, the built-in password protection on these devices should be enabled. However, this will probably not prevent someone with specialized knowledge from bypassing this protection. Employees and staff should also be warned about the danger of accessing the Internet on public computers. They may be leaving behind passwords, surfing history, data in temporary files, cookies, and other personal information.

§ 3:4 Computer viruses

A computer virus is a normally undetectable program within a program that causes the computer to function in an abnormal manner. There is no excuse for not regularly using antivirus software, keeping it up to date, and using it properly. An antivirus scan should be run on the entire hard disk at least once a week and preferably daily.

Even where antivirus software has been installed, employees and staff should be instructed that e-mail attachments should be opened cautiously. No one should open an attachment that is unexpected, even if the message appears to be from a known source. Employees and staff should also be instructed not to download programs without first checking with the information systems administrator.

Consideration should be given to prohibiting the connection of MP3 players such as iPods to computers. MP3 players can accidentally put a virus on a network. In addition, MP3 players, which are nothing more than external storage with a music player built in, can be used to take information off a computer network.

§ 3:5 Spyware and firewalls

Because information can flow both ways when connected

to the Internet, a firewall is necessary to prevent unauthorized access to computers and networks. Hardware firewalls are also available to protect networks. Spyware and adware can be avoided by using an anti-spyware or anti-adware programs These programs should be run weekly and updated regularly.

§ 3:6 Backup storage

It is important to have a computer backup storage system. Backups should be done daily. Hardware is available for automatic backups. A specific individual should be assigned responsibility for backups. The backup log should reviewed on a regular basis to determine whether backups are being made as required. In addition, the backup system should be tested periodically to ensure the backup system is working.

§ 3:7 Technology use policy

It is important to implement a technology use policy, informing all persons using computers of what they can and cannot do when using e-mail, surfing the Internet, and using computers and other digital systems. Employees must be educated about the necessity of protecting confidential information.

Access to servers, routers, phone switches, and individual computers should be restricted. Something as simple as putting a password on a screensaver can prevent unauthorized users from using a computer that has been inadvertently left on. Because high-capacity USB drives or thumb drives are compact, easy to use, and can store huge amounts of information, they can be used to quickly steal data. It may be appropriate to disable USB ports on computers. Consideration should be given to using technology controlling anything that connects to a USB port including thumb drives and iPods. Employees should avoid using a home computer for work purposes if the computer is used by others.

Employees and staff should be warned about e-mails appearing to come from legitimate companies. (This is referred to as "phishing.") These fake e-mails attempt to trick people into revealing confidential information, thinking they are replying to their bank, credit card company, or Internet service provider. Legitimate companies should not send e-mails asking that personal information be updated. The Web links in e-mails should be used with great care. It is safer to access the Web site of an e-mail sender through the browser rather than the hyperlink.

A technology use policy should describe the extent of usage allowed, specifically stating the restrictions on the use of e-mail and the Internet. The policy should inform employees that the organization's computer, technology, and communications system, including e-mail and the Internet, are the sole property of the organization. It is important to inform employees that no e-mail message is considered private, and that employees should not expect their messages will remain private.[1] The policy should state that the organization reserves the right to monitor usage of e-mail and the Internet in the ordinary course of business.[2]

A technology policy should prohibit the use of e-mail or

[Section 3:7]

[1]See Scott v. Beth Israel Medical Center Inc., 17 Misc. 3d 934, 847 N.Y.S.2d 436 (Sup 2007) (e-mails physician sent to his personal attorney by computer system owned by physician's employer were not protected by attorney-client privilege where hospital had e-mail policy mandating that computer and e-mail systems could be used solely for business purposes and warning that employees had no expectation of privacy in any communication created, received, saved, or sent using hospital's computers). See also In re Asia Global Crossing, Ltd., 322 B.R. 247 (Bankr. S.D. N.Y. 2005); Long v. Marubeni America Corp., 2006 WL 2998671 (S.D. N.Y. 2006). But see Sims v. Lakeside School, 2007 WL 2745367 (W.D. Wash. 2007) (policy dictates that communications to one's spouse or lawyer be protected to preserve sanctity of communications made in confidence); Curto v. Medical World Communications, Inc., 99 Fair Empl. Prac. Cas. (BNA) 298, 2006 WL 1318387 (E.D. N.Y. 2006) (inconsistent or sporadic enforcement of computer-policy insufficient to destroy employee's reasonable expectation of privacy as to e-mails at issue).

[2]But see U.S. v. Ziegler, 474 F.3d 1184, 153, 153 Lab. Cas. (CCH) P 60340 (9th Cir. 2007), cert. denied, 128 S. Ct. 879, 169 L. Ed. 2d 738 (U.S. 2008) (government search had to comply with Fourth Amend-

the Internet to communicate harassing, offensive, defamatory, or sensitive messages, including, but not limited to messages inappropriate under the organization's sexual harassment policy. The policy should prohibit soliciting or proselytizing for charitable, religious, political, or other nonbusiness purposes. It should also prohibit the transmission of trade secrets, confidential or privileged communications; unauthorized copying and distributing of copyrighted material; and uses such as chain mail that degrade system performance

II. CHECKLISTS

§ 3:8 Computer use policy checklist

- ☐ **Compliance with Intellectual Property Laws**
  - ☐ Shareware properly licensed.
  - ☐ Software licenses.
  - ☐ Copyrighted material.
  - ☐ Proper use of trademarks and service marks.
  - ☐ Determine reasonable efforts to be made to avoid disclosure and consequent loss of trade secret status.
- ☐ **Authorized Computer Use**
  - ☐ Business communications.
  - ☐ Limited personal use.
- ☐ **Unauthorized Computer Use; Types of Prohibited Material**
  - ☐ Fraudulent.
  - ☐ Harassing.
  - ☐ Intimidating.
  - ☐ Sexually explicit.
  - ☐ Political.
  - ☐ Commercial.
- ☐ **Uses in Violation of U.S. Export Restrictions**

---

ment where employee had reasonable expectation of privacy over personal items saved on workplace computer when computer terminal was in private, locked office).

- ☐ **Installation of Unauthorized Software Including Encryption Software**
- ☐ **Maintaining confidentiality of attorney-client communications**
- ☐ **Virus detection and avoidance**
- ☐ **Identify individual(s) authorized to install and use encryption software**
- ☐ **Employee privacy**
  - ☐ Require written employee consent to management review of material created, stored, and disseminated using company's computers and networks.
  - ☐ Acknowledgment of no expectation of privacy.
- ☐ **Employees must maintain secrecy of their passwords and understand that they will be held liable for all transactions conducted with their passwords**

III. FORMS

§ 3:9 Computer use policy—Personal use prohibited

COMPUTER USE POLICY

Section One
Purpose

This document describes the policies and guidelines for use of the computer and telecommunications resources of *[[name of organization]/[owner of computer system]]* ("Employer"). All computer users employed by Employer have the responsibility to use these resources in a professional, ethical, and lawful manner. The computers and computer accounts provided to employees by Employer are to assist them in the performance of their jobs. The computer and telecommunications system belong to Employer and may only be used for authorized business purposes.

Section Two
Waiver of Privacy

Employees waive their right of privacy in anything they

create, store, send, or receive on Employer's computer or telecommunications system. Employees consent to management or supervisory personnel of Employer accessing and reviewing all material employees create, store, send, or receive on the computer or telecommunications system.

Section Three
Prohibited Use

Use of Employer's computer or telecommunications system for any of the following activities is strictly prohibited:

1. Sending, receiving, displaying, printing, or otherwise disseminating material that is fraudulent, harassing, embarrassing, sexually explicit, obscene, intimidating, or defamatory;
2. Sending, receiving, displaying, printing, or otherwise disseminating confidential, proprietary business information or trade secrets in violation of Employer policy or proprietary agreements;
3. Transmitting, storing, or otherwise disseminating commercial or personal advertisements, solicitations, promotions, destructive programs (for example, viruses or self-replicating code), or political material;
4. Violating any state, federal, or international law governing intellectual property (for example, copyright, trademark, and patent laws) and online activities; and
5. Violating any license governing the use of software.

Section Four
Violations

Violations of this policy may result in disciplinary action, including possible termination of employment, legal action, and criminal liability.

Section Five
Employee Acknowledgment

I have read, understand, and agree to comply with the

foregoing policies, rules, and conditions governing the use of Employer's computer and telecommunications equipment and services.

Dated: *[Date of signing]*

Signature: ________________
Printed name of employee: ________________
[Computer account of employee]

Comment

This is basic computer-use policy restricting use of computer and telecommunications equipment to official purpose only. Personal use by employees is prohibited. Some employers may be reluctant to adopt such a policy for fear of an employee backlash. This is a particular concern in the educational environment where students and faculty generally oppose restrictions on computer use. In such cases, a simple, one-page policy can address most of the major concerns surrounding the use of computer and telecommunications equipment and resources. This form is a useful starting point for developing a more streamlined policy. Any computer use policy should require that employees acknowledge in writing that they understand the policy.

§ 3:10 Computer use policy—Personal use restricted

COMPUTER USE POLICY

Section One
Purpose

A. To remain competitive, better serve our customers and provide our employees with the best tools to do their jobs, *[[Name of business]/[Owner of computer system]]* makes available to our workforce access to one or more forms of electronic media and services, including computers, e-mail, telephones, voicemail, fax machines, external electronic bulletin boards, wire services, online services, intranet, Internet, and the World Wide Web.

B. *[[name of business]/[owner of computer system]]* encourages the use of these media and associated services because they can make communication more efficient and effective and because they are valuable sources of information about vendors, customers, technology, and new products and services. However, all employees and everyone connected with the organization should remember that electronic media and services provided by the company are company property and their purpose is to facilitate and support company business. All computer users have the responsibility to use these resources in a professional, ethical, and lawful manner.

C. To ensure that all employees are responsible, the following guidelines have been established for using e-mail and the Internet. No policy can lay down rules to cover every possible situation. Instead, it is designed to express *[[name of business]/[owner of computer system]]* philosophy and set forth general principles when using electronic media and services.

Section Two
Prohibited Communications

Digital or electronic media cannot be used for knowingly transmitting, retrieving, or storing any communication that is:

1. Discriminatory or harassing;
2. Derogatory to any individual or group;
3. Obscene, sexually explicit or pornographic;
4. Defamatory or threatening;
5. In violation of any license governing the use of software; or
6. Engaged in for any purpose that is illegal or contrary to *[[name of business]/[owner of computer system]]* policy or business interests.

Section Three
Personal Use

The computers, digital or electronic media and services provided by *[[name of business]/[owner of computer sys-*

tem]] are primarily for business use to assist employees in the performance of their jobs. Limited, occasional, or incidental use of digital or electronic media (sending or receiving) for personal, nonbusiness purposes is understandable and acceptable, and all such use should be done in a manner that does not negatively affect the systems' use for their business purposes. However, employees are expected to demonstrate a sense of responsibility and not abuse this privilege.

Section Four
Access to Employee Communications

A. Generally, digital or electronic information created and/or communicated by an employee using e-mail, word processing, utility programs, spreadsheets, voicemail, telephones, Internet and bulletin board system access, and similar electronic media is not reviewed by the company. However, the following conditions should be noted. *[[Name of business]]/[Owner of computer system]]* routinely gathers logs for most digital or electronic activities or monitor employee communications directly, for example, telephone numbers dialed, sites accessed, call length, and time at which calls are made, for the following purposes:
   1. Cost analysis;
   2. Resource allocation;
   3. Optimum technical management of information resources; and
   4. Detecting patterns of use that indicate employees are violating company policies or engaging in illegal activity.

B. *[[Name of business]]/[Owner of computer system]]* reserves the right, at its discretion, to review any employee's digital or electronic files and messages to the extent necessary to ensure electronic media and services are being used in compliance with the law, this policy and other company policies.

C. Employees should not assume digital or electronic

communications are completely private. Accordingly, if they have sensitive information to transmit, they should use other means.

Section Five
Software

To prevent computer viruses from being transmitted through the company's computer system, unauthorized downloading of any unauthorized software is strictly prohibited. Only software registered through *[[name of business]]/[owner of computer system]]* may be downloaded. Employees should contact the system administrator if they have any questions.

Section Six
Security/Appropriate Use

A. Employees must respect the confidentiality of other individuals' digital or electronic communications. Except in cases in which explicit authorization has been granted by company management, employees are prohibited from engaging in, or attempting to engage in:
   1. Monitoring or intercepting the files or electronic communications of other employees or third parties;
   2. Hacking or obtaining access to systems or accounts they are not authorized to use;
   3. Using other people's log-ins or passwords; and
   4. Breaching, testing, or monitoring computer or network security measures.

B. No e-mail or other digital or electronic communications can be sent that attempt to hide the identity of the sender or represent the sender as someone else.

C. Digital or electronic media and services should not be used in a manner likely to cause network congestion or significantly hamper the ability of other people to access and use the system.

D. Anyone obtaining digital or electronic access to other

companies' or individuals' materials must respect all copyrights and cannot copy, retrieve, modify, or forward copyrighted materials except as permitted by the copyright owner.

Section Seven
Encryption

Employees can use encryption software supplied to them by the systems administrator for purposes of safeguarding sensitive or confidential business information. Employees who use encryption on files stored on a company computer must provide their supervisor with a sealed hard copy record (to be retained in a secure location) of all of the passwords and/or encryption keys necessary to access the files.

Section Eight
Participation in Online Forums

A. Employees should remember that any messages or information sent on company-provided facilities to one or more individuals via an electronic or digital network—for example, Internet mailing lists, bulletin boards, and online services—are statements identifiable and attributable to *[[name of business]/[owner of computer system]]*.

B. *[[Name of business]/[Owner of computer system]]* recognizes that participation in some forums might be important to the performance of an employee's job. For instance, an employee might find the answer to a technical problem by consulting members of a news group devoted to the technical area.

Section Nine
Violations

Any employee who abuses the privilege of their access to e-mail or the Internet in violation of this policy will be subject to corrective action, including possible termination of employment, legal action, and criminal liability.

Section Ten
Employee Agreement on Use of E-mail and the Internet

I have read, understand, and agree to comply with the foregoing policies, rules, and conditions governing the use of the Company's computer and telecommunications equipment and services. I understand that I have no expectation of privacy when I use any of the telecommunication equipment or services. I am aware that violations of this guideline on appropriate use of the e-mail and Internet systems may subject me to disciplinary action, including termination from employment, legal action and criminal liability. I further understand that my use of the e-mail and Internet may reflect on the image of *[[name of business]/[owner of computer system]]* to our customers, competitors and suppliers and that I have responsibility to maintain a positive representation of the company. Furthermore, I understand that this policy can be amended at any time.

Dated: *[Date of signing]*

Signature: ________________
Printed name of employee: ________________
[Computer account of employee]

Comment

A written computer use policy adopted by a business should include statements that excessive personal use could subject an employee to disciplinary actions; that there is no expectation of privacy in anything created or stored using the office computer systems; and that management may review files and e-mail. The policy should also require employees to acknowledge in writing that they understand the policy.

§ 3:11 Computer use policy—Educational institution

COMPUTER NETWORK AND INTERNET ACCESS AND USE

Faculty, staff and student access to the *[name of institution]* ("School") Network and/or Internet is consistent with and beneficial to the educational mission of School. The Network/Internet refers to the global network of computers created by the interfacing of smaller contributing networks. Its services are intended to support curriculum, instruction, and open educational inquiry and research.

In this document, "Network/Internet Access" refers to all information accessed through the use of School equipment and resources for connection to and use of the Network/Internet online services, e-mail, bulletin board, network system, etc. Access to the Network/Internet serves as a natural extension of the educational lessons learned within the classroom by providing access to educational resources and reference materials. Such access reinforces the specific subject matter taught by requiring the use of critical thinking skills, by promoting tolerance for diverse views, and by teaching socially appropriate forms of civil discourse and expression. Therefore, faculty, staff and students shall be allowed access to both School Computer Network and the Internet consistent with School's curriculum, educational mission, and this Policy and implementing procedures.

Nevertheless, School has a duty to insure that the manner in which the Network/Internet is used does not conflict with the basic educational mission of School. Use of the Network and/or Internet may be restricted in light of the maturity level of students involved and the special characteristics of the school environment. Therefore, School will not permit student use of the Network/Internet which: (a) causes substantial disruption of the proper and orderly operation of School or School activities; (b) violates the rights of others; (c) is socially inappropriate or inappropriate due to the maturity level of the students; (d) is primarily intended as an immediate solicitation of funds; or (e) constitutes gross disobedience or misconduct.

Comment

Organizations and businesses that allow use of the Internet by its members and employees should have a computer use policy in place to limit exposure to liability. The use of computers and the Internet by members or employees can open an organization to liability for infringement of intellectual property rights, copyright violations, unfair competition, defamation, sexual harassment, wrongful termination, fraud, and invasion of privacy. In addition, connection to the Internet means exposure to computer hackers, viruses, and industrial espionage.

The policy should set forth an objective standard for members and employees to apply when using electronic media and services. It should set out appropriate use of the Internet and make clear that members and employees are using the organization's equipment. Users should understand that there is no privacy expectation in the use of computers and that e-mail and Internet usage may be monitored.

Part II

RECORDS MANAGEMENT

Chapter 4

Records Management Programs

I. GUIDELINES

II. CHECKLISTS

III. FORMS

Research References

Additional References

Carpenter, Using Automated E-mail Filing to Escape "Inbox Hell," Elec. Disc. & Records Mgt. Q., fall 2007, at 28

Wilkins, Technologies for Managing E-mail, ARMA International's Hot Topics, 2008, at 2

Treatises and Practice Aids

eDiscovery & Digital Evidence § 5:15

Grenig and Kinsler, Federal Civil Discovery and Disclosure §§ 13.1 to 13.6 (2d ed.)

Trial Strategy

Computer Technology in Civil Litigation, 71 Am. Jur Trials 111

Law Reviews and Other Periodicals

Brownstone, Preserve or Perish: Destroy or Drown—eDiscovery Morphs into Electronic Information Management, 8 N.C. J. L. & Tech 1 (2006)

Additional References

Andolsen, Does Your RIM Program Need a Strategic Alignment?, Information Mgt. J., July/Aug. 2007, at 35

Fitzpatrick, The Cost of Prevention in E-Discovery, in Instant Awareness: An Immediate Look at the Legal, Governmental, and Economic Ramifications of the amendments to the Federal Rules of Civil Procedure and Electronic Discovery 5 (Aspatore 2008)

Isaza, Determining the Scope of Legal Holds: Waypoints for Navigating the Road Ahead, Information Mgt. J., March/Apr. 2008, at 34

Kahn & Silverberg, Eight Steps for Keeping Information management and E-Discovery on Target, Information Mgt. J., May/June 2008, at 48
Making a Molehill out of a Mountain: Pre-culling Reduces Data Pool—and Related Costs—Prior to E-discovery, eMag Link, May 2007, www.emaglink.com/newsletter
ABA Discovery Standards, http://www.abanet.org/litigation/discoverystandards/2005civildiscoverystandards.pdf
ARMA, http://www.arma.org
eDirect Impact, Inc., http://www.edirectimpact.com
Electronic Discovery Reference Model Project, http://www.edrm.net
EMC Corp., http://www.emc.com
The Sedona Conference, http://www.thesedonaconference.org
TechTarget, Inc., http://www.searchstorage.com

I. GUIDELINES

§ 4:1 Generally

Records management programs are fundamental tools addressing the creation, retention and disposition of records—including electronically stored information. Because of the huge volume of electronically stored information, some of which is saved on hard drives or backup tapes and often stored offsite, an organization can be overwhelmed when it receives a request to produce electronically stored information in discovery. A proper records management program can control expenses, limit harm to the organization's public image, and increase efficiency.

A records management program enables an organization to dispose of worthless records in order to free physical or digital storage space, to reduce requirements for handling and managing the records, and to make retrieval of information more efficient and economical. A records management program ensures that legally required records are preserved and protected, protecting the organization in the event of litigation or government investigation.

A records management program may become part of the underwriting decision of an organization's insurance carrier. If those programs are not adequate, that may affect the cost of or the ability to obtain insurance. Insurance costs can be reduced if an organization is willing to develop a records management program before it becomes a party to a lawsuit.

Typically, the destruction of electronically stored information does not result in sanctions or raise an adverse inference of spoliation if the destruction is done in accordance with a departmental records retention policy without knowledge the document is relevant to any party in litigation. Because of the expense of responding to government investigations or civil discovery, organizations have an incentive to establish records management programs disposing of records that no longer must be maintained for legal or other purposes. If a records management program limits how long information is kept, the organization will have less information to search and review.

An appropriate records management program can also aid an organization in establishing what electronically stored information is not reasonably accessible because of undue burden or cost.[1] In addition, the "safe harbor" provision in Rule 37(f) of the Federal Rules of Civil Procedure provides: "Absent exceptional circumstances, a court may not impose sanctions under these rules for failing to provide electronically stored information lost as a result of the routine good-faith operation of an electronic information system."

Before a records management program can be developed, it is essential to know the following:

- What record types the organization generates and retains

[Section 4:1]

[1]See Fed. R. Civ. P. 26(b)(2)(B).

- Where the records are located
- Who controls each type of record
- When records may be destroyed

Finally, in developing a records management program, it should never be forgotten that an organization's information primarily exists to permit the organization to do business. The organization's need for information should be a significant factor in structuring its retention program.

§ 4:2 Compared with litigation holds

Records management programs are not the same as litigation holds. At times, it may be necessary to suspend records management programs in order to insure compliance with a preservation letter, preservation order, or litigation hold to ensure that discoverable electronically stored information is not destroyed in the course of the routine destruction of information. However, the destruction of electronically stored information pursuant to a bona fide records management program where no litigation is anticipated or no preservation letter or order has been received normally will be acceptable.

§ 4:3 Developing a records management program—Generally

An appropriate records management program should focus on the life cycles of the records. It should have a central classification system defining record types and determining life expectancies. A records information management team should be established and be responsible for ensuring compliance and providing guidance. The organization's legal department should be responsible for advising the team.

A records management program must be systematically developed in the ordinary course of business. Consideration must be given to the values of various records. All retention requirements, such as regulatory, statutory, taxation, administrative, research, and historical, must be considered. Development of the program should be documented, and it must be approved by appropriate persons in the organizations.

The retention periods for records should be determined only after thorough legal research of applicable statutes, regulations, and case law. In addition to complying with legal requirements, the retention periods should be consistent for comparable records. A reasonable records retention period reflects reasonable industry practices and prudent business judgment.

Whenever development of a records management program is undertaken, the program should be neutral and involve considerations such as:

- Disaster recovery
- Business necessity and continuity
- Government regulations requiring the retention of certain documents and the routine discarding of others

Proper development of the records management program demonstrates that it was conceived and executed over a period of time, and was not developed for the purpose of destroying documentary evidence before litigation or a government investigation.

§ 4:4 Developing a records management program—Attorney-client privilege

Should the appropriateness of a records management program come into question, a court may determine there has been a subject-matter waiver of the attorney-client privilege with respect to any advice counsel gave in implementing the program.[1] Retaining and consulting a lawyer to develop a document records management program, if done in anticipation of litigation, may invoke the crime/fraud exception to the attorney-client privilege.[2]

If counsel is contacted after litigation is anticipated, it

[Section 4:4]

[1]Cf. Zubulake v. UBS Warburg LLC, 220 F.R.D. 212, 216, 92 Fair Empl. Prac. Cas. (BNA) 1539 (S.D. N.Y. 2003) (referring to attorney's directive regarding litigation hold).

[2]See Antidote Intern. Films, Inc. v. Bloomsbury Publishing, PLC, 242 F.R.D. 248, 250 (S.D. N.Y. 2007) (e-mail fell within crime/fraud

is too late to begin a document retention plan. Instead, it is time to talk about a preservation plan. Even if a valid retention plan is in effect, an organization must ordinarily take steps to suspend its normal retention plan. Particularly in the case of electronically stored information evidence, once a party reasonably anticipates litigation, the party should suspend its routine document retention/ destruction policy and put in place a litigation hold to ensure preservation of relevant documents.[3]

§ 4:5 Developing a records management program—The team

While records management programs are supported and maintained by information technology personnel, records management programs are collaboratively designed to meet corporate record classification and retention schedule standards. A properly developed and maintained records management program can be helpful in showing that any lost electronically stored information that was lost as the result of the routine, good-faith operation of an electronic information system.[1]

Developing and implementing an effective records management program is a complicated, time-consuming task that may require a team of professionals who fully understand the organization and the types of records created by the organization. Of course, the persons involved will vary depending upon the size and nature of the organization. Senior personnel from key units within the

---

exception); Rambus, Inc. v. Infineon Technologies AG, 220 F.R.D. 264 (E.D. Va. 2004), subsequent determination, 222 F.R.D. 280 (E.D. Va. 2004) (crime/fraud exception to attorney-client privilege and work-product doctrine applies when client was engaged in or planning a fraudulent or criminal scheme when it sought advice of counsel and documents involved bear close relationship to the fraudulent or criminal scheme).

[3]Zubulake v. UBS Warburg LLC, 220 F.R.D. 212, 218, 92 Fair Empl. Prac. Cas. (BNA) 1539 (S.D. N.Y. 2003).

[Section 4:5]

[1]See Fed. R. Civ. P. 37(f).

organization knowledgeable of the types of documents that are created within the organization must be involved. The team should include records retention specialists possessing the necessary skill sets for managing the process. The team should also include information technology personnel familiar with the types of electronically stored information the organization creates and receives, know where the electronically stored information is stored and how to locate it, and understand the technological capabilities of the organization. Lawyers and regulatory specialists familiar with the legal requirements for document retention should also be involved.

Before beginning, the team members should clearly define their individual roles and responsibilities within the project. The goal of the team should be to develop a concise policy clearly defining the record type, applicable retention period, and the source of the retention requirement (whether business, statutory, or regulatory). The team should document and retain records outlining how the program was developed and implemented to be able to demonstrate it used best efforts to comply with document retention requirements.

§ 4:6 Developing a records management program—Determining organizational needs

The record retention needs of different parts of an organization may vary. This fact must be taken into account when creating a records management program. Different parties create and use records in different ways. In order to be effective, the retention program must accommodate different uses and needs.

Record values affect a records management program. Legal requirements dictate what an organization must do. Legal considerations suggest what an organization may want to do. In considering litigation, government investigations, and audits, the records management program recognizes that records that should exist, do exist. The program also recognizes that records that should not exist do not exist.

§ 4:7 Developing a records management program—Threatened or pending litigation

Before implementing a document records management program, the team should undertake an inventory of threatened and pending litigation or government investigations. The team must take steps, in consultation with counsel, to ensure that all potentially responsive documents are preserved.

§ 4:8 Developing a records management program—Training and publicizing

After taking steps to ensure that the program meets all legal requirements, training of all employees should be conducted. The program should be well-publicized within the organization, and employees should be advised of where to direct questions. It is essential that all employees comply with a records management program in order for it to succeed. The wide variety of employees an organization has should be considered in planning and implementing a records management program. Consultants, contract personnel, and vendors all require clear instruction regarding records.

§ 4:9 Elements of a records management program—Generally

A records management program must address more issues than the preserving records for the amount of time required by state or federal law. A records management program should address a number of matters, including the retention and destruction of all records regardless of the media; destruction schedules; program controls; procedures for suspending records destruction in case of foreseeable, pending, or actual litigation or governmental investigation; and records management program record keeping.

§ 4:10 Elements of a records management program—Coverage

A records management program should address all types

of business records, regardless of medium. The program should not distinguish between paper and electronically stored information. A records management program should recognize that most organizational electronically stored information can be found in different repositories, such as individual hard drives or file shares. Because some organizations microfilm original records and then destroy the original records, it is especially important the records management program include microfilm records.

A records management program must cover all records, including reproductions or copies. Records management programs that apply only to originals or record copies are inadequate. Under the Uniform Photographic Copies of Business and Public Records as Evidence Act, reproductions or photocopies of records have the same legal significance as the original and may be used in place of the original for all purposes. Where a records management program does not cover copies, such as information copies or personal copies of records, those copies may be discovered or subpoenaed even though the original records were properly destroyed under the records management program.

§ 4:11 Elements of a records management program—Written approval

The records retention schedule must be reviewed and approved in writing by the manager responsible for the records, legal counsel, and, where appropriate, the tax manager. In addition, the entire records manage program must be approved in writing by the organization's chief executive officer, legal counsel, and the tax manager. These written approvals demonstrate that the program was developed in the ordinary course of business instead of in anticipation of litigation or a government investigation. Copies of the written approvals should be maintained indefinitely.

In determining the legal requirements for a records management program, thorough research of the legal issues involved should be conducted. If the research is done by a non-lawyer, the research should be reviewed by a lawyer. The researcher should determine which regulatory agencies should be consulted to determine retention requirements. Relevant statutes, regulations, and guidelines should be reviewed and documented. The legal requirements should be related to the specific records or categories of records of the organization. After the records retention schedule is prepared, the proposed schedule, and list of legal requirements, and copies of applicable statutes, regulations, and cases should be presented to counsel for review.

§ 4:12 Elements of a records management program—Disposition of records

With respect to backup systems, a records management program should indicate the purpose of backing up records, including e-mails, is for disaster recovery. Backup tapes created for disaster may not be subject to a litigation hold unless they are accessible.[1]

Backup for purposes of disaster recovery should be distinguished from off-line storage of long-term, low access information. Off-line storage, such as annual accounting records, should be treated separately from backup. Backup of information with short-term retention, such as e-mails, should be segregated from other records.

After a records management program is approved, records should be destroyed in accordance with the records retention schedule in the program. Where electronically stored information is inconsistently destroyed, a court

[Section 4:12]

[1]Zubulake v. UBS Warburg LLC, 220 F.R.D. 212, 218, 92 Fair Empl. Prac. Cas. (BNA) 1539 (S.D. N.Y. 2003) (while e-mail backup tapes created for disaster recovery not subject to litigation hold unless they are accessible, if a company can locate the information of "key players," that information should be preserved even if it exists in the form of disaster recovery backup tapes).

may find this inconsistency to be evidence that the destruction was done in bad faith.[2]

Some records management programs specify that the records manager will provide legal counsel, department managers, and the tax manager with a list of records that can be destroyed. After review, records, other than those relating to litigation or government investigation, or that are still needed by the organization, can be destroyed at the designated time.

Destruction of records in a selective manner, even if permitted by the retention schedule, may create the impression that the records management program has not been properly implemented. Improper destruction of records may be considered as suggesting guilt or liability. Improper destruction may also be found to be obstruction of justice.

§ 4:13 Elements of a records management program—E-mail

A limit on the storage space available to individual e-mail users is a common feature of e-mail management programs. Users are typically given a warning before e-mail is deleted. An e-mail management program may also provide for automatic deletion of user mailbox contents.

Some organizations do not limit the size or duration of individual mailboxes, but focus on providing extended capacity for certain classes of employees. Some classifications, such as executives and accountants, may have all their e-mail saved for substantial periods of time as their information will probably be subject to litigation or regulatory inquiry.

---

[2]See, e.g., In re Prudential Ins. Co. of America Sales Practices Litigation, 169 F.R.D. 598, 615, 36 Fed. R. Serv. 3d 767 (D.N.J. 1997) (adverse inference from destruction of relevant computer records because document retention policy was haphazard and uncoordinated).

§ 4:14 Elements of a records management program—Establishing retention periods

In determining records retention periods, the organization must first determine which electronically stored information is deemed to be a record. Next, it must determine what retention periods are required by state or federal law, or by organizational needs. The default retention period for many public records is permanent, and only a schedule can authorize its destruction. Determining the retention schedule for public records requires careful review of applicable statutes, regulations, and ordinances.

§ 4:15 Elements of a records management program—Documentation

The organization must keep and maintain documentation relating to the development and implementation of the records management program, including legal research, program approvals, retention schedules, and program modifications. These records can be of critical importance in establishing that the records management program was developed and implemented in the ordinary course of business. Legal research records can be help in showing the organization has used its best efforts to comply with any records retention requirements.

§ 4:16 Elements of a records management program—Suspension of destruction of records

The routine destruction of electronically stored information may lead to severe sanctions once an organization is on notice of potential litigation. A records management program must provide for the suspension of records destruction and the preservation of records in the case of foreseeable, pending, or actual litigation or government investigation. In such event, records destruction must cease immediately. The records program should provide that any employee who receives any information regarding potential litigation or government investigation immediately inform the legal counsel or chief executive officer.

§ 4:17 Elements of a records management program—Monitoring and managing

A records management program must be rigorously enforced. Employees must be trained and educated about the program and the consequences of not following it. The program must be easy to follow, periodically reviewed, and regularly audited.

Monitoring and managing a records management program can be made difficult because of the number of records controlled by employees. A records management program that is not easy to understand and implement can also be a serious problem.

An organization must actively audit and enforce its records management program. At least one person in the organization must be designated to manage and monitor the records management program. That person is responsible for ensuring that the program is up-to-date and that retention and destruction is being conducted in accordance with the records management program. The responsible person must be familiar enough with the records management program and its operation to be able to testify in court about the program.

§ 4:18 Records management software

Software that can systematically control records within an organization is now available. What software if appropriate for an organization depends on such factors as the size and complexity of the organization, knowing what the organization needs and how the software will be used, and the cost of acquiring and maintaining the software.

The first step in selecting records management software is identifying records management needs by conducting a records inventory. An inventory will determine the quantity of records, their physical and environmental condition, how often they are referenced, and where they are located. It provides a survey of the existing records situation, determines storage needs, identifies vital and archival records, improves recordkeeping habits, and provides a foundation for a records management plan.

After inventory is complete, an organization should determine records management software needs by investigating what records management functions the software will support, what general functions the software must possess, and what performance criteria the software must meet. Records management functions include destruction notification, destruction of electronic records, request processing, file and box tracking, file management, and document management. General functions include help features, menus and commands, speed and accuracy, generation of standard reports, ease of use, ability to manage records in all formats, and security classification and access privileges. Minimum performance criteria to look for include the ability to perform on a current computer system and the inclusion of vendor-supplied support, maintenance, and training.

There are many types of software products available to meet particular needs, such as indexing and searching products, document management software, and records management applications (RMAs). There are many commercial off-the-shelf software products immediately available providing such benefits as proven reliability, lower cost, availability of user manuals and online tutorials. Some organizations develop applications using commercially available database management software packages such as Microsoft Access or Lotus Approach. Others have a customized application written tailored to the organization's particular needs.

It is essential to carefully evaluate and test available records management software packages, as well as investigate of vendors before purchasing records management software. Knowledge of what is included in the price of the software can create a more productive and efficient records management program.

II. CHECKLISTS

§ 4:19 Checklist for establishing records management program

☐ Senior management must support the policy.

- ☐ Employees should be required to notify the records information management team whenever important or significant amounts of electronically stored information are transferred away from the normal storage places for any reason.
- ☐ Electronically stored information must be identified and classified.
- ☐ A records management program should set a time after which employees should not retain individual types of electronically stored information.
- ☐ The records management program should be in writing.
- ☐ Each employee should sign a receipt acknowledge the employee's reading of the policy.
- ☐ Appropriate technology should be used to manage and monitor the retention program.
- ☐ Specific persons should be assigned to monitor and audit the retention program on a regular basis.
- ☐ Development of the policy should be developed in coordination with information technology personnel.
- ☐ The records management program must embrace the entire organization.
- ☐ The records management program must ensure that all needed electronically stored information is retained.
- ☐ The records management program must ensure that all electronically stored information required to be retained are retained for the appropriate period of time.
- ☐ The records management program must provide that all authorized users can access the electronically stored information records efficiently and economically.
- ☐ The records management program must ensure that all electronically stored information can be read and used.
- ☐ The records management program must ensure that all electronically stored information will be regarded as authentic once located and retrieved.

- ☐ The records management program should provide for litigation hold procedures to ensure that potentially responsive electronically stored information is not destroyed once litigation or a government investigation is reasonably anticipated.
- ☐ The records management program should establish procedures for the timely destruction of appropriate documents as their respective retention periods expire.

Comment

See Melnitzer, *Keeping Track of the Invisible Paper Trail: What Legal Departments Can Learn from Boeing's Experience*, CORPORATE LEGAL TIMES, Feb. 2003, at 15.

§ 4:20 Checklist for establishing collaborative records management system

- ☐ Build a collaborative foundation for the records management system, involving customers, clients, employees, and suppliers.
- ☐ Create business process workflows—knowing where the "knowledge" resides and how it gets there, including identifying duplicate information or redundant processes.
- ☐ Choose easily improvable processes and teams with the flexibility to try new things.
- ☐ Change the view of systems from vertical to horizontal, allowing entry or retrieval from multiple applications on one screen or in multiple portals.
- ☐ Understand the current portals include not only web applications, but the ability to enter and retrieve information in word processing documents, e-mail applications, and other places.

Comment

This form is adapted from Grote, *Five Things You're Doing Right*, at http://www.edirectimpact.com.

§ 4:21 Checklist for e-mail retention policy

- ☐ Effective date of policy

- ☐ Last change date and changes made
- ☐ Person or department responsible for policy
- ☐ Scope or coverage of policy
- ☐ Purpose of policy
- ☐ Policy statement
    - ☐ Reasons for complying with policy
    - ☐ Importance of complying with policy
- ☐ Definitions
- ☐ Responsibilities
- ☐ Procedures
- ☐ Other retention policy guidelines
    - ☐ Duplicate copies
    - ☐ Convenience copies
- ☐ Litigation hold policy
- ☐ Consequences if policy not followed

Comment

This checklist is adapted from Tolson, *E-mail Retention Policy: A Step-by-Step Approach,*.

III. FORMS

§ 4:22 Records management policy statement

Policy Purpose: To provide guidelines for properly establishing a records and information management (RIM) program and assisting those departments that require long-term records retention and procedures for implementing an effective RIM program. Records and information management includes areas such as inactive records, vital records, microfilming, and records retention.

Policy

1. Records and information management (RIM) is the systematic control of all records, regardless of media, from their creation or receipt, through their processing, distribution, organization, storage, and retrieval to their disposition. Information flows through the organization in the form of paper and electronic records

such as word processing documents, spreadsheets, e-mail, graphical images, and voice or data transmissions. Information can be stored on a variety of storage media, such as microfilm, microfiche, diskette, optical disk, CD-ROM, videotape, and paper.

2. This policy details the requirements and responsibilities to initiate a well-defined RIM program. The RIM program applies to those departments that require a long-term records-retention, -storage, and -destruction program.
   a. Ensure only essential records of continuing value are preserved. Records should be retained in the active office areas as long as they serve the immediate administrative, legal, or fiscal purpose for which they were created.
   b. Establish safeguards against the illegal removal, loss, or destruction of records. Records either should be disposed of in accordance with an approved records-retention schedule or transferred to the records-retention center until the prescribed retention period has expired.
   c. Management of records is the responsibility of the owner, or creator, of the record. The department director or the director's designated representative should contact the records manager to discuss initiating a records-management program or reviewing an existing records-management program to handle records properly from their creation through their destruction. Departments can be provided guidance on how records should be organized and stored to ensure timely and efficient retrieval.
   d. The records-retention schedule is the key tool for departments to use to manage their records effectively. Information is a valuable asset; however, if records that contain information cannot be retrieved efficiently or are retained beyond their legal, regulatory, or administrative retention period, they lose their value and may impose a liability to the organization.

3. The benefits of an effective RIM program include:
   a. Greater assurance of legal compliance to minimize liability and discovery impacts;
   b. Improved customer service with higher quality of service and faster retrieval of documents;
   c. Improved staff productivity with effective records-management systems;
   d. Reduced storage costs through elimination of unnecessary and duplicate documents;
   e. Ensured safety of vital organizational records; and
   f. Efficient, cost-effective records-retention and -disposal system.
4. The components of an effective RIM program that may be activated by the records manager include:
   a. Records-retention program;
   b. Vital records program;
   c. Inactive records-management program;
   d. Electronic records-management program;
   e. Records-management handbook/records liaisons' training;
   f. Micrographics (microfilming) program;
   g. Forms-management program (corporate communications);
   h. Active records-management program; and
   i. Copy and reprography program (purchasing).
5. Significant recurring activities initiated by the records manager include:
   a. Annual inventory of the records center: The records manager will annually inventory all records in the records center to confirm information in the records-retention tracking system.
   b. Annual review of the records-retention schedule: The records manager will have the records-retention schedule reviewed and validated annually for accuracy.
   c. Annual files purge program: The records manager will advertise and initiate an annual files purge by all departments. The purpose is to have individuals

review personal active file systems, as well as electronic document folders, and to purge documents that are no longer required. No original documents are to be destroyed.

Proponent

1. The vice president for information systems or his designee is the proponent for the RIM program.
2. All questions concerning compliance with this policy should be directed to the records manager unless otherwise indicated.

Roles and Responsibilities

1. The vice president of finance, vice president of legal affairs, and the chief information officer, as needed, will be requested to identify to the records manager the individual who can perform the following tasks:
   a. Review and provide functional approval of an updated or changed records-retention schedule, as required, for all departments.
   b. Become familiar with the purpose of the records-retention schedule.
2. Department directors who need to implement a records-management program should contact the records manager for guidance/assistance and will need to:
   a. Identify a records liaison and inform them of the duties of the records liaison;
   b. Review and update records-retention schedules annually;
   c. Review the records-management handbook, as needed; and
   d. Coordinate departmental activities that may impact records management with the records manager to include office consolidation, office closures, and approval of new or replacement, records storage, and file equipment as requested.
3. Departmental records liaisons are responsible for:

a. Obtaining records liaisons' overview training from the records manager;
b. Becoming familiar with and maintaining the records-management handbook;
c. Assisting in developing and enforcing the records-retention schedule for their department;
d. Managing the department's records; and
e. Attending quarterly or as otherwise required records liaisons' meetings.

4. Records manager is responsible for:
   a. Assisting in the design, development, implementation, and/or review of records-management programs to include the programs listed in paragraph 2, Policy, above;
   b. Managing the records-retention center for all departments to ensure safe storage, quick retrieval, records confidentiality, and appropriate records disposition;
   c. Developing and maintaining the records-retention schedule;
   d. Managing the microfilming of records as required;
   e. Issuing and updating the records-management handbook;
   f. Educating and training records liaisons;
   g. Approving records storage and retrieval equipment for departmental purchase as requested;
   h. Participating actively as a member of the following committees:
      i. Records Committee on an as-needed basis for retention issues;
      ii. Forms Approval Committee as a member on an as-needed basis;
   i. Presenting records and information management issues, as required, to the Information Systems Steering Committee or other appropriate forum; and
   j. Chairing quarterly Records Management Committee meeting with records liaison.

Procedures

Detailed procedures can be found in the records-management handbook. For the most frequent requirements, procedures are summarized below.

1. Records-Retention Schedules
   a. Each department is responsible for determining retention periods for records created. A record may be kept beyond the legal or regulatory retention period if it satisfies an administrative need based on business necessity, which is stated on the records-retention schedule. To create or update a records retention schedule:
      i. Contact the records manager to assist you;
      ii. Inventory all current records maintained, including all media types;
      iii. Create a master list of data and record types and draft preliminary retention schedule;
      iv. Determine retention periods based on legal, administrative, and historical value;
      v. Obtain approval for retention schedule from IS, Finance, and Legal;
      vi. Publish and implement the retention schedule; and
      vii. Review annually
   b. State, federal, and/or regulatory requirements prescribe minimum records-retention periods.
   c. Once the specific retention period for any paper or electronic record has been reached, the record will be destroyed consistent with appropriate procedures.
   d. Notwithstanding minimum retention periods, all records shall be maintained until all required audits are completed and shall be kept beyond the listed retention period if litigation is pending or in progress. Records manager must be notified of any litigation that would require retention of records beyond normal disposition.
   e. Destruction of records is permitted in accordance with the law only after expiration of the retention

periods stated on the approved departmental retention schedules.

2. Files Transferred to Records Center
   a. Files will be accepted throughout the year once the department has coordinated set patterns for retention with the records manager.
   b. The departmental records liaison will contact records manager via e-mail of a files transfer requirement.
   c. Storage boxes and Records Center Control Card Form must be obtained from records management.
   d. Files must be packed in approved storage boxes.
   e. A Records Center Control Card Form must accompany the boxes.
   f. Records management will provide instructions for proper packing and labeling of boxes in the records-management handbook.
   g. Pickup will be coordinated with records manager.
3. Request for Retrieving Files or Records
   a. Office wishing to retrieve records will contact the records-retention center.
   b. The departmental records liaison will provide information for locating the file from the Records Center Control Card.
   c. Telephone request should not exceed five (5) records per call. For more than five records, a written request should be mailed or e-mailed to records management.
   d. Retrieved records will be tagged with a Records Center Reference Request form. This form *must* be returned to allow prompt and accurate refiling.
   e. Notify records management if file is to be reactivated.
4. Microfilming Records
   a. Medical records will be microfilmed in records management and stored in the information services department for reference and retrieval.
   b. Other departmental records meeting certain specifications will be microfilmed and stored within the

department or in records management. This should be coordinated with the records manager.

5. Assistance in the Selection of Records Filing System Equipment
   a. All new records-management and filing equipment should be reviewed by the records manager, as requested, prior to purchase to ensure they are efficient and cost-effective in storage space.
   b. Existing file systems can be reviewed and recommendations provided for improvement.
6. Records-Retention Requirements for Automated Systems
   a. Systems and programming managers will contact the records manager who will assist the department that owns the data in determining records-retention requirements for the electronic data on new and existing systems.
   b. A valid retention schedule will be prepared for electronic records.
7. Vital Records Program

The implementation of a vital records program to protect and preserve records that contain information vital to the conduct of business in the event of a major disaster is crucial. These documents contain the information necessary to recreate the organization's legal and financial position. Vital records generally represent only a small portion of all records and information maintained by the organization. The records manager will review the vital records program annually. Areas of importance are financial records, employee records, insurance policy information, ownership records, major contracts and agreements, corporate records, and negotiable instruments.

Electronic Records Policy Statement

Each organization's e-mail policy should reflect its own culture and the legal and regulatory framework within which it operates. Developers of the policy must consider factors such as legal issues, records-management retention policies, and information management administration of the e-mail system, along with financial and regulatory issues.

Sample 1: The electronic-mail system is owned by the company, and it is to be used for company business. Occasional use of the system for messages of a personal nature will be treated like any other message. The company desires to respect the right to privacy of its employees and does not monitor electronic mail messages as a routine matter. It does, however, reserve the right to access them, view their contents, and track traffic patterns.

Sample 2: When using e-mail, the message created or used may or may not be a record. When it is designated as a record, it is subject to the records-retention policies of the company. Within the company, each person is responsible for controlling records according to the records-management policies, and when an e-mail message is considered a record, it falls into this category.

Sample 3: Before selecting e-mail as a means for communication or document transmission, users should consider the need for immediacy, formality, accountability, access, security, and permanence. E-mail differs from other forms of communication. It is immediate and informal, similar to a telephone conversation, yet it is more permanent. It is as irrevocable as a hard-copy document, yet easy to duplicate, alter, and distribute.

The City (organization, company, etc.) reserves the right to monitor employee use of e-mail by systems administrators or departmental supervisors. Employees are reminded that e-mail use is provided *primarily* for business purposes and not for personal purposes and that employees cannot expect protection of their personal or business-related e-mail correspondence under privacy laws and regulations.

The City will not monitor e-mail messages as a routine matter. The City will, however, respond to legal processes and fulfill its obligations to third parties. The City will inspect the contents of e-mail messages in the course of an investigation triggered by indications of impropriety or as necessary to locate substantive information that is not more readily available by other means.

Electronic Records Guideline

Retention periods are established for records according to departmental, fiscal, and legal requirements. Each record listed on a records-retention schedule specifies a specific period of time that the record is retained. *This retention applies whether the record is on paper or residing on magnetic or optical media (hard disk, floppy disk, tape, CD, etc.).* Once records have reached their designated time for destruction, they should be destroyed or eliminated from all storage media; that is, file cabinets, inactive storage, magnetic media, backups, etc.

Backup media should be stored in a different location than the computer equipment that is used to create them. Electronic records retained in a backup system follow the same retention as similar paper records listed on a retention schedule.

Drafts generally are not retained and should never be retained longer than the finalized version that becomes the record.

Databases are modified over time through the addition, deletion, or revision of information. Reports may be periodically generated to capture or record the information at a point in time. Records that are in databases may use a retention period until they are superseded. Once information has been superseded, it is generally lost unless provision is made to save it as a report. Historical data should be archived or deleted according to the department's retention schedule.

Comment

This form is adapted from a form provided by the American Records Management Association.

§ 4:23 Records management program

_______ Company

RECORDS MANAGEMENT PROGRAM

1.0. Records

The records of _______ Company ("Company") include

essentially all records produced by employees, whether in paper or electronic form. Records include, but are not limited to, e-mails, memoranda, calendars, appointment books, and expense records. All employees are expected to comply fully with all records-retention or records-destruction policies and schedules.

2.0. Legal Requirements

The law requires Company to maintain certain types of records for specified periods of time. Failure to retain records for the statutory periods may subject Company and employees to penalties and fines.

3.0. Destruction Schedules

Company has established retention or destruction schedules for specific categories of records. The minimum retention periods for the following categories of records set forth below.

3.1. Board and Board Committee Materials

Company should keep permanent copies of all Board of Director and Board committee meeting minutes in Company's minute book. Company should keep a copy of all Board and Board committee materials for no less than three years.

3.2. Legal Files

The Company Legal Department Legal counsel should be consulted to determine the retention period of particular legal files. Generally, Company should keep legal documents for ten years.

3.3. Tax Records

Tax records include, but are not limited to, documents relating to expenses, deductions, accounting procedures, payroll, and other documents concerning Company's revenues and expenses. Tax records should be retained for at least six years from the date of filing the applicable return.

3.3. Employment and Personnel Records

State and federal law requires Company to keep certain employment and personnel information, including employment applications. Company should keep personnel files reflecting performance reviews and any complaints brought against Company or individual employees under applicable state and federal statutes. Company should keep all final memoranda and correspondence reflecting performance reviews and actions taken by or against personnel in the employee's personnel file. Employment and personnel records should be retained for six years.

3.4. Intellectual Property

Company should keep permanently documents relating to intellectual property and development of intellectual property, such as copyrights or patents

3.5. Trade Secrets

Company should keep all documents designated as containing trade secret information for at least the life of the trade secret. Documents detailing the development process are often also of value to Company and are protected as a trade secret where Company derives independent economic value from the secrecy of the information, and Company has taken affirmative steps to keep the information confidential.

3.6. Public Filings

Company should retain permanent copies of all publicly filed documents.

3.7. Marketing and Sales Documents

Company should keep final copies of marketing and sales documents for the same period of time it keeps other corporate files—generally three years. Company should keep sales invoices, contracts, leases, licenses, and other legal documentation for at least three years beyond the life of the relevant agreement.

3.8. Contracts

Company should retain executed copies of all contracts entered into by Company should be retained for at least three years beyond the life of the agreement, and longer in the case of publicly filed contracts.

3.9. E-mail

E-mail that needs to be saved should be either printed in hard copy and kept in the appropriate file, or downloaded to a computer file and kept electronically or on disk as a separate file. The retention period for e-mail depends upon the subject matter of the e-mail, as covered elsewhere in this policy.

3.10. Press Releases

Company should retain permanent copies of all press releases.

4.0. Litigation or Potential Litigation

If an employee believes, or is informed by Company, that certain records are relevant to litigation, or potential litigation, the employee must preserve those records until the Company Legal Department determines the records are no longer needed.

4.1. Duty to Preserve

This duty to preserve supersedes any established destruction schedule for those records.

4.2. Questions Regarding Duty to Preserve

If an employee believe the duty to preserve may apply, or has any question regarding the possible applicability of the duty to preserve, the employee should contact the Company Legal Department.

5.0. Failure to Comply

An employee's failure to comply with this Document Retention Policy may result in disciplinary action, including suspension or termination. An employee should refer questions about this policy to [*name*], at [*telephone number*] or [*e-mail address*].

6.0. Acknowledgment

I have read and understand the Document Retention Policy.

Dated: ______

____

Employee Signature

____

Printed Employee Name

Comment

This basic retention policy can be modified depending upon the size of the organization, and whether the organization is required by state or federal law to keep documents for particular lengths of time.

§ 4:24 Electronically stored information guidelines for access, retention, destruction

Electronically Stored Information Guidelines for Access, Retention, Destruction

1. Introduction

2. Employee Responsibility
3. Word Processing Files
4. Administrative Databases
5. Electronic Spreadsheets
6. Schedules of Daily Activities
7. Tracking and Control Records
8. WWW Materials
9. E-mail
10. Optical Imaging
11. Migration
12. Records Destruction
13. Security
14. Changes to These Guidelines
15. For More Information

INTRODUCTION

Most employees at the University create and use electronic records every day. If you send or receive e-mail, exchange notices of meetings, or create word processing documents, then you are using electronic records. The informational content of electronic record systems constitutes an important part of the University's corporate memory and must be managed as a valuable University asset documenting functions and accountability.

[State] law defines public records as "all books, papers, maps, photographs, cards, tapes, disks, diskettes, recordings, and other documentary materials, regardless of physical form or characteristics, which are prepared, owned, used, in the possession of or retained by a public agency." *[Citation.]* The *[state]* Open Records Act mandates that "public records shall be open for inspection by any person, except as otherwise provided by *[statute]. [Citation.]*

Electronic records are subject to retention, destruction, and inspection under these laws just as if the record were stored on paper. Records management standards and principles apply to all forms of recorded information, from creation to final disposition. Guidance on records management issues, including electronic records matters, may be obtained from the University Archives and Records Center, which administers state and university policy concerning the management of university records. Feel free to call us at *[telephone number]*, e-mail us, or visit our Web site at *[URL]*.

EMPLOYEE RESPONSIBILITY

As noted above, University policy for management of University records is administered by the University Archives and Records Center. The Center's Director serves as the University's records manager. The Director works with departments to help them deal with records problems. However, the departments themselves—their administrators, staff, and faculty—are accountable for the day-to-day administration, control, preservation, access, and security of records within their custody in accordance with state and federal laws. It is ultimately the responsibility of the creators and users of electronic records to ensure that they are properly cared for.

In other words:

> University employees are responsible for maintaining the integrity of records whether stored electronically or in hard copy. Information in records systems must be maintained until the legal, fiscal, and administrative retention periods have been met.
>
> All employees must ensure that electronic records are maintained so that they are readily available for appropriate use, and so that established records management procedures, including disposition and/or destruction, can be carried out.
>
> Under no circumstances will employees permit the destruction or loss of records, in electronic or hard copy, if the employee has any reason to believe that the records are related to any current open records request, subpoena, litigation, investigation, audit, or other governmental proceeding.

Offices should use electronic information systems that maintain appropriate controls when creating records and which will support them in the context of their business purpose or the activity performed. Records that are vital in supporting the core activities of the University must be identified and scheduled for routine backup. However, while simply backing up a record is crucial, it is not the same as archiving a file. Hard copies, microfilm copies, or magnetic tapes of information systems or records systems, as appropriate, will provide preservation for documents requiring long term or permanent retention.

Consistent with the State University Model Schedule, most University records have a limited retention period. If an office retains records for the required length of time, on whatever medium it chooses, it is meeting legal requirements. Records required for audit purposes must be made available in hard copy or on a current computer system according to Internal Revenue procedures.

WORD PROCESSING FILES

Offices should take measures to protect permanent records produced by word processing software, either by printing the documents or preserving them in electronic form separately from materials of a non-permanent nature. This is to prevent accidental deletion or destruction with non-permanent records when the retention period for non-permanent records has expired. Non-permanent word processing files may be stored with other non-permanent electronic records and deleted with them at the end of their retention period.

Once a printed record copy is distributed, the electronic version may be deleted. If the official record copy is kept electronically, however, it must be retained for the retention period listed in the University Model Schedule.

Documents such as letters, messages, memoranda, reports, handbooks, policies and procedures, and manuals written on hard drives or diskettes are considered works in progress or drafts until the final draft is accepted as the official version. Creators may delete drafts and revisions once the record copy has been produced. The working copies should be retained only if they are used to document how decisions were reached in developing programs and policies of the office or unit, or aid in the interpretation or purpose of the final document (e.g. to explain why certain changes were made or to clarify intent.)

Some records are now created only in electronic form, whereas in years past they might have been hard copies. In these cases, the Model University Schedule that applied to the hard copy is still applicable to the current electronic version. If the retention period has been met and a hard copy would be destroyed, the electronic version may be deleted.

ADMINISTRATIVE DATABASES

Many offices use databases containing information fields arranged and secured so that the information can be maintained or removed for use for various purposes. Much of the utility of a database lies in its flexibility and dynamic character. They change often as information is added, deleted, or modified. Ultimately, from this body of raw information, many different distinct queries can produce different results.

Documents generated from selected information in databases are often produced in hard copy and distributed; however, the databases themselves are retained primarily in electronic format. Few records generated from databases are to be retained permanently. Record copies of reports and other documents generated from databases that document official policies should be printed for permanent retention. Records that are non-policy in nature and are used for informational purposes, or do not set official guidelines or procedures, may be deleted in accordance with the Model University Schedule.

If hard copy records produced from a database are maintained in the office files, and these hard copies have a limited retention period, the electronic files may be deleted when the information is superseded or no longer useful.

ELECTRONIC SPREADSHEETS

Spreadsheets in electronic format such as hard disks or

diskettes and used to produce a hard copy that is maintained in established files may be deleted when no longer useful. If the spreadsheet is kept electronically, it can be deleted when the authorized retention period is reached. If the electronic system contains several spreadsheets with different retention periods, and if the software does not easily allow deletion of individual records, delete the records after the longest retention period has been met.

SCHEDULES OF DAILY ACTIVITIES

Calendars, appointment books, and schedules documenting meetings, appointments, telephone calls, and other activities by university personnel are increasingly kept in electronic format. Calendars relating to the official activities of the president, provost, vice presidents, and deans must be retained permanently. These should be printed periodically and filed in the official records. Otherwise, calendars may be deleted at the discretion of the employee.

TRACKING AND CONTROL RECORDS

Logs, registers, and other records in electronic format used to track and document the status of correspondence, reports, or other records that are approved for destruction under the guidelines of the Model University Schedule may be deleted when no longer needed.

WEB SITE MATERIALS

University departments and schools are increasingly using the World Wide Web instead of or in conjunction with paper documents to publish information about their programs. Materials provided on University Web sites must be managed as other university records are. Documents that in hard copy format would qualify as official university records with permanent or long term value should be printed and retained. Web site documents that do not set or document official policies or procedures and are of a transitory nature may be deleted once their usefulness has ended.

E-MAIL

Electronic mail is a major factor in University offices since correspondence, memos, and reports are increasingly sent and stored electronically. E-mail does fall under the statutory definition of public records, and as such, *the e-mail issued by and received by University employees is subject to open records requests and can be discoverable under legal actions brought against the university.* Senders and recipients of e-mail must be aware that the legal standards for the retention and disposition of University records also apply to e-mail. E-mail categories include official and general, the same as that of hard copy office correspondence.

Official is defined as documenting the major functions, activities and programs of the university and important events in its history. E-mail that falls under this definition must be retained under the guidelines in the University Model Schedule. Employees should print and retain in department files or store in an accepted, retrievable electronic format e-mail that reflects the official position of the university or that documents the administrative, legal, and fiscal requirements of the institution. The University Archives and Records Center recommends printing these e-mails as the most reliable form of long-term preservation.

General e-mail correspondence which is non-policy in nature and not critical to administrative, fiscal, or legal requirements can be deleted in accordance with guidelines in the University Model Records Retention Schedule. Form letters, notices of meetings, duplicates and forwarded messages from other offices, spam, and other e-mail messages of a transient nature can be considered reference or information-only material and can be deleted at the discretion of the user. Disposition of electronic mail should take place on a regular and systematic basis in accordance with approved records retention guidelines.

Information Technology has developed default settings for the archiving capabilities of the University's GroupWise e-mail applications. However, it is important to understand that the GroupWise client cannot determine the relative significance of individual pieces of e-mail. Responsible management of e-mail, including determining which e-mails constitute important university records and which do not, *must* be the responsibility of the account user. The University Records Manager will provide advice and support on how to make these decisions, but *it is the department and its employees that will be held responsible in the event of a record being inappropriately retained or prematurely destroyed.*

As employees leave the University, e-mail accounts remain active for one month after the termination date before being deleted. Before a staff member leaves the unit, a supervisor should confer with the account owner to determine what e-mail must be retained, who within the unit should keep it, and to ensure that the e-mail is forwarded to the proper recipient(s) for appropriate retention. Likewise, any other electronic files maintained on a departing staff member's hard drive should be given a similar assessment. If that person also manages an e-mail service account, arrangements should be made to transfer control of the account to another person within the unit. If there are questions about what records should be retained and what may be deleted, please contact the University Archives. If there are other questions concerning the management of e-mail accounts or other electronic resources, please contact Information Technology.

OPTICAL IMAGING

Many offices now use scanners to render paper documents into computer-readable form, usually utilizing optical storage media such as CD-ROMs or DVDs. However, as of this writing, there are no nationally recognized records management standards concerning the longevity of any digital storage media. Considering that such formats as CD-ROMs have existed less than twenty-five years, it is difficult to make definite claims on their longevity over the many decades during which some university records must be preserved.

The Policy Memorandum on Optical Storage of Public Records issued by the *[name]* contains the following guideline on records to be converted from hard copy to electronic formats and stored on optical systems. "Public records which are either, (1) scheduled as permanent or, (2) whose vital retention status is ten years or greater, must have manual, eye-readable counterparts." This means that for records with a long retention period, a copy of the records must be maintained on a human readable format such as paper or microfilm. This is because the archival standards for permanence have not yet been met by electronic systems and optical disk media. For further information refer to the Policy Memorandum on Optical Storage or contact the University Archives at *[telephone number]* or e-mail us).

MIGRATION

Migration is a name for the conversion of files in obsolete formats and/or upon obsolete media into forms that may be more easily read by contemporary computers and software. (An example would be migrating old files from WordPerfect format on 5¼-inch floppy disks to Microsoft Word format on CD-ROMs.)

If records are migrated to new versions of software and/or new hardware or are otherwise altered when new hardware and/or software are implemented, an audit trail of any migrations and changes must be maintained. The new system must be able to read the records that the University Model Schedule requires the University to maintain.

University offices must develop procedures for system and data migration that identify which records will be migrated and the schedule for data backups and recopying, maintaining an audit trail of any migrations that are actually completed. The full migration plan should include backward compatibility in the new electronic records system or software. This means that change to a new system or software should include the conversion of records from the previous system for access in the new one, or it should provide a mechanism such that the records from the previous system can still be accessed. If not, it will be necessary to print the inactive electronic records to paper if the records have not reached the legal destruction period.

RECORDS DESTRUCTION

Although many of the same practices apply in the application of records schedules for both hard copy and electronic copies, the destruction of these records is different. Hard copy records are destroyed in labor intensive methods such as shredding or by sending them to the landfill. Although electronic records may be erased or written over, records containing confidential information can sometimes be recovered even if they have been erased or the media reformatted. Software that deletes records from a drive is available and destruction of confidential records using these programs is recommended. In some cases the hard drive should also be reformatted to protect the confidentiality of the records. This precaution should be taken if a computer is sent to the Inventory Control Warehouse as surplus property. It is also important that personnel responsible for electronic records maintain a record of destruction of records that are deleted from office systems. The audit trail will include information on disposition status of records and whether the records were destroyed or transferred to hard copy.

The ________ Office of Technology has published a set of best practices for the destruction of electronic records and sanitization of electronic media. This set of best practices can be found at *[URL]*.

For advice on how University can best comply with these best practices, please contact the University Information Technology Help Desk at *[URL]*.

SECURITY

Many university records contain confidential data. Unauthorized access to or disclosure of these records by university employees is prohibited. For further information on policies and procedures for computer security and computer accounts, contact Information Technology. If you have questions about privacy or confidentially, please contact the University Archives. University Archives will consult with University Counsel and/or the appropriate university office that executed the agreement regarding confidentiality restrictions as needed. If you have questions about the matter of open records requests, contact *[name]*, University's open records officer, by e-mail.

CHANGES TO THESE GUIDELINES

Because electronic technology changes quickly, the University Archives anticipates that these electronic records guidelines will require revision. We welcome any suggestions on the subject of the management and preservation of electronic records from university personnel. Contact *[name]*, University Records Manager.

FOR MORE INFORMATION

To learn more about the state's policies and best practices for electronic systems and records, see *[URL]*.

For University-specific inquiries, contact the University Archives by phone at *[number]*, or by e-mail, or visit our Web site at *[URL]*.

Comment

This form is adapted from one used by the University of Louisville. It can easily be adapted for use by other types of public entities. By deleting the provisions regarding public records, it can also be adapted for use by private organizations.

§ 4:25 Public records management policy

University of ______

Public Records Management Policy

1.0. POLICY

The policy of the University of ______ ("University") is

to ensure that public records are properly managed in compliance with relevant state and federal laws.

2.0. SCOPE

This public records management policy applies to all University institutions and departments.

3.0. PURPOSE

The purpose of this policy is to facilitate the transaction of business, ensure public accountability, and preserve the history of University institutions by fulfilling state and federal legal requirements for public records management.

4.0. PUBLIC RECORDS MANAGEMENT

4.1. Definition and Ownership of Public Records. Public records include all materials, regardless of physical form or characteristics, that employees create or receive in connection with the transaction of public business on behalf of the University. All public records that employees create, receive, or retain are owned by the University and State of ________.

4.2. Duties of the Chancellor. The *[title]* shall designate a public records and forms officer.

4.3. Duties of the Public Records and Forms Officers. The records officer shall

(1) develop and maintain a public records management program fulfilling state and federal legal requirements;

(2) provide records management training and assistance to University employees;

(3) upon request, provide special assistance to University legal counsel, legal custodians for public records requests, auditors, and archivists; and

(4) collaborate with University technology professionals in developing and maintaining information and

digitization systems that create, receive, store, destroy, and archive electronic public records in compliance with state and federal legal requirements.

4.4. Characteristics of Public Records Management Programs. Public records management programs facilitate ongoing business activities, ensure public accountability, and preserve the history of the University. In order to successfully perform these vital functions, public records management programs should be developed and maintained using a collaborative decision-making process involving University institutions and departments: records and forms officers, information technology professionals, legal counsel, legal custodians, auditors, and archivists. In some instances, this collaborative decision-making process should involve University employees from other professional fields, including but not limited to: business officers, administrators, faculty, staff, students, human resource managers, and registrars.

Public records management programs shall:

(1) ensure that public records are created, received, and retained in compliance with this policy and state and federal legal requirements;

(2) properly classify public records, so as to support University functions and ensure appropriate disposition of these records;

(3) obtain approval for disposition of public records from the State of ________ *[name of agency]*;

(4) ensure secure storage of public records throughout the life cycle of these records;

(5) ensure that expired public records are destroyed, paying special attention to the additional steps necessary to destroy expired electronic records; and

(6) preserve the history of the University by implementing archival processes ensuring the security,

accessibility, accuracy, authenticity, readability, and reliability of public records notwithstanding the passage of time.

4.5. **Treatment of Electronic Public Records.** Public records management programs shall ensure that throughout their life cycle, electronic public records are secure, accessible, accurate, authentic, legible, readable, and reliable. These programs shall also ensure that upon disposition, electronic public records are either properly destroyed or archived. Because some information technology systems may retain portions of deleted electronic records, public records management programs must ensure that expired electronic records are actually destroyed.

4.6. **Information and Digitization Systems and Business Tools.** University and University employees must not purchase, support, or utilize information and digitization systems, or business tools that fail to comply with this policy and state and federal legal requirements for public records management. The procurement, development, and maintenance of information and digitization systems should include public records management functions.

4.7. **Electronically-Stored Information.** Information and digitization systems routinely create electronically-stored information that, in many instances, comprise a public record. Therefore, University employees and the technology professionals who provide, support, and manage information and digitization systems must ensure that electronically-stored information is only created, received, or retained if it supports UW System institution business functions.

4.8. **Review of Public Records Management Programs.** The State of ________ Department of ________ has authority to periodically audit the public records management programs at University in order to evaluate legal compliance. In order to ensure the success of such an audit or to ensure compliance with this policy, the Public Records and Forms Officer may conduct periodic reviews of public records management programs.

5.0. PUBLIC RECORDS MANAGEMENT ROLES AND RESPONSIBILITIES

5.1. Employee Supervisors. Supervisors of University employees are responsible for ensuring that the employees under their supervision attend public records management training sessions and manage public records in compliance with this policy and state and federal legal requirements.

5.2. Employees. University employees are responsible and accountable for managing public records in compliance with this policy and state and federal legal requirements. Failure to do so may result in loss of access to University information and digitization systems and business tools, as well as appropriate disciplinary action.

5.3. Use of Business Tools. University employees must manage and retain public records using only information and digitization systems and business tools that are supported by the University.

5.4. Suspension of Public Records Retention Schedules. Record retention schedules must be suspended whenever University records are relevant to litigation, audit, or public records requests. Any suspension of retention schedules shall be carefully tailored to the scope of the litigation, audit, or public records request. Although University will suspend public records retention schedules when reasonably necessary, the University is not responsible for individual employees acting outside the scope of their authority, or in a manner inconsistent with the suspension of public records retention schedules.

Comment

This form is adapted from a policy used by the University of

Wisconsin System. It can be adapted for use by other public agencies that have public records.

§ 4:26 Records management certification

RECORDS MANAGEMENT CERTIFICATION FOR ELECTRONIC RECORDS FORM

This certifies that the records named below maintained in electronic format are usable and certifiable for the life of the electronic system. Furthermore, the electronic system which manages these records, meets the following:

- the records are managed uniformly and efficiently
- the records are accurate and reliable
- the records are accessible when needed
- the records and system are protected from unauthorized access
- the records are maintained/destroyed in accordance with the records retention and disposition schedules adopted pursuant to *[statute]*
- migration strategies standards implemented
- disaster recovery and backup systems standards implemented
- all items on the Electronic Document Management Checklist have been completed per the Records Management Guideline for Electronic Records

---

1. Record Series Title(s):

7. System Format:

2. Court/Office:

8. System Director/Head Representative:

3. Address:

4. Phone: (___) _______

9. Phone: (___) _______

5. Type or Print Name

10. Type or Print Name

6. Authorized Signature & Title

11. Authorized Signature & Title

Date: ________ **Date: ________**

Chapter 5

Records Retention

I. GUIDELINES

II. CHECKLISTS

III. FORMS

Research References

Additional References

ABA Discovery Standards, http://www.abanct.org/litigation/discoverystandards/2005civildiscoverystandards.pdf
ARMA, http://www.arma.org
Electronic Discovery Reference Model Project, http://www.edrm.net
eDirect Impact, Inc, http://www.edirectimpact.com
EMC Corp., http://www.emc.com
The Sedona Conference, http://www.thesedonaconference.org
TechTarget, Inc., http://www.searchstorage.com

Treatises and Practice Aids

eDiscovery & Digital Evidence §§ 8:9, 8:10

Grenig and Kinsler, Federal Civil Discovery and Disclosure §§ 13.1 to 13.6 (2d ed.)

Trial Strategy

Recovery and Reconstruction of Electronic Mail as Evidence, 41 Am. Jur Proof of Facts 3d 1

Computer Technology in Civil Litigation, 71 Am. Jur Trials 111

KeyCite®: Cases and other legal materials listed in KeyCite Scope can be researched through the KeyCite service on Westlaw®. Use KeyCite to check citations for form, parallel references, prior and later history, and comprehensive citator information, including citations to other decisions and secondary materials.

I. GUIDELINES

§ 5:1 Generally

After information is produced, employees must determine whether the information should be considered and retained as a "record" for purposes of the records management program. Each employee should be familiar with the definition of records from their records management training. The training should explain how records should be retained.

Employees should be trained to ask whether the electronically stored information reflects an activity by the organization. Does the electronically stored information reflect fiscal, operational, administrative, legal, vital, or historical value? If the information does, the information is a record, and proper steps must be taken to retain the information and its associated metadata.

§ 5:2 Definition of record

ISO 15489[1] defines a record as follows:

> A "record" is information created, received, and maintained as evidence by an organization or person in the trans-

[Section 5:2]

[1]The international standard for records management of the International Organization for Standardization.

action of business, or in the pursuance of legal obligations, "regardless of media."

A record includes information holding operational, legal, fiscal, vital or historical value. Examples of records are:

- A final draft of a contract
- Evaluation report of a current employee
- Insurance related documents
- Company charter

Information without operational, legal, fiscal, vital, or historical value is not a record. Additionally, duplicates and copies of existing records are not records. Examples include:

- Personal messages
- E-mail inviting staff to a party
- Routine notices

Duplicates and copies should be disposed of as soon as they are no longer of use or value. Retaining duplicates or copies beyond their use can increase the cost of discovery.

§ 5:3 Definition of vital records

Vital records are any records, regardless of archival value, essential to the functions of an organization during and after an emergency. Vital records also include records essential to the protection of the rights and interests of that organization and of the individuals for whose rights and interests it has responsibility. The loss of vital records during a disaster could result in the disruption of essential services, exposure to unplanned expenses, loss of revenue, increased vulnerability to litigation, or loss of productivity due to gaps in information. The length of retention of vital records may be mandated by internal company policy as well as by statute or regulation.

If an organization is anticipating or engaged in a legal or regulatory discovery request, or internal investigation, then records and documents associated with the matter become vital records. Documents deemed vital to discovery may include custodian files, e-mail and instant messages stored on servers, desktop computers, laptops, smart phones, and thumb drives. These documents must be identified and declared records for discovery purposes. They become vital records to the matter and should be managed as such. An existing vital record may be identified as relevant to a legal matter or internal investigation. In this case, the retention date for the record may have to be changed to meeting the overriding requirement of the legal matter.

§ 5:4 Record capture (metadata)

Upon the declaration that a document is a record, the document and its existing metadata must be captured. At this time, a new piece of metadata will be added—the records management classification of the record. The records management program might physically move the record into a separate repository, move it into a repository with all of the enterprise data (with slightly different metadata, like "Read Only" and the records management classification) or keep the document where it is, but record the metadata into the records management program.

There are several considerations to take into account within the confines of the records management program:

- How the record is going to be captured.
- When the record will be captured.
- What metadata will be captured.
- How the document declaration will be made.

The records management program will also need to account for different categories of electronic documents, like e-mail and Word or Excel files and databases.

A final consideration is what metadata must be captured by a records management system. The records management team might desire little other than the date, author and classification of a document. On the other hand, discovery users will need a great deal more.

§ 5:5 Document declaration

Document declaration requires an employee to decide which documents and communications are "records" and indicate that to the records management system. A document declaration step that is too intrusive risks not only hindering employee productivity, but might even result in records not being declared as employees avoid the burdens of the declaration process. On the other hand, a document declaration process is ineffective.

The timing of the declaration is important. Some file and e-mail systems allow for metadata modification, meaning that a declaration made after the document is sent or initially saved might include altered metadata. This may not cause concern in the records management, but could raise preservation concerns during discovery.

A records management program should prompt e-mail users to declare whether a message and its attachments are a record and determine where to file it when the message is sent or received. What qualifies as a record should be defined by the records management program.

Computer applications, such as Word, Excel, PowerPoint, or Visio may be integrated with a records management program so the user is prompted, whenever a "Save" or "Close" operation is executed, to declare whether the file is a record and, if so, where to store it. The user should have a standard set of files, defined and set up by the records management team at server levels, in which to store the document or message.

Voice mail, being brief, informal messages, presents similar issues as e-mails. The records management program should provide that voice mail, including backups, is automatically erased after a brief period such as 30 days. It is probably unnecessary to allow for the formalization of voice mail records.

The Internal Revenue Service considers computer records as recordkeeping under the Internal Revenue Code. The records management program must provide that records with tax implications be maintained from for the requisite period and must make the records available on a current computer system.[1]

Databases provide special problems as they may contain a number of files and fields of data used for a variety of purposes. The records management program may consider retaining a database as an official record until superseding. This reflects that only the current version of the data base must be maintained.

A records management program may wish to consider drafts of documents as nonrecords for retention purposes. The records management program could permit the drafts and original notes of many documents to be destroyed in a relatively short period of time after the final draft has been accepted. The records management program should consider the final draft to be a record. Some word processing files could be saved for longer periods to facilitate the revision of drafts.

§ 5:6 Web sites

A Web site may be a simple, static page listing the hours of operation and a contact phone number for an agency, or a Web site may be complex with multiple pages and interactive databases allowing remote users to change the site. Some Web sites are used for conducting business transactions and storing sensitive data such as credit card numbers or personal identification information.

Content on Web sites must be preserved, but this depends on factors, such as the type of information found on the site, and whether or not it exists in another place. Organizations should evaluate their Web sites and develop a strategy for documenting the site as information changes. This assessment is based on the type and amount of information found on the Web site and the level of risk to the organization (legal, fiscal, or administrative) if that information is lost or unavailable. This may mean that

[Section 5:5]

[1]See 26 C.F.R. § 601.105.

the organization retains periodic "snapshots" of the entire site, or captures individual pages or records on the site.

Materials provided on organization Web sites must be managed as other agency records are. Documents that would qualify as records with permanent or long-term value should be captured and retained (either in hard copy or electronically). This may apply to individual parts of the organization Web site or it may apply to the entire Web site. For example, if an organization places a publication on its Web site, and the publication is not available in any other form, then that publication is a record and should be captured and retained in some way. If the organization publishes a report on its Web site and has paper copies or the computer file that was used to create the report, then the copy on the Web site is a duplicate copy and probably does not need to be captured.

Additionally, if a Web site is being used to conduct a business transaction the Web pages associated with the activity are considered part of that transaction's legal documentation and must be retained in order to establish what the user saw when the order was placed.

§ 5:7 E-mail

Because e-mail rarely represents the official position of an organization, the records management program may provide that e-mail messages are automatically erased from the computer system after a short period of time such as 30 days. Backup tapes of e-mail messages may also be deleted after the same period. An automatic deletion program should be coupled with options so a user can move e-mail of significance to an appropriate storage location.

It may be advisable to have e-mail from or to such employees as executives, accountants, human resources representatives saved for substantial periods of time because such information may be subject to litigation or supervisory inquiry. Some types of e-mail content, such as e-mails relating to critical business records, trade secrets, contracts, and regulatory issues, may be important enough that dedicated content-management storage should be made available.

A management records program should provide for the creation and dissemination of litigation holds. Such provisions can include centralizing the issuance of litigation notices, providing for cessation or interruption of destruction procedures, identifying information, and lifting of litigation holds.[1]

II. CHECKLISTS

§ 5:8 Identification checklist

- ☐ Identify key witnesses and custodians
- ☐ Determine key time frames
- ☐ Compile keyword lists
- ☐ Identify potentially relevant document types
- ☐ Map the organization's information system
- ☐ Diagram the network
  - ☐ Document management systems
  - ☐ Data types
  - ☐ E-mail systems
  - ☐ Additional data sources
- ☐ Determine whether forensic data capture will be necessary
- ☐ Determine relevance of
  - ☐ Backup media
  - ☐ Retired hardware
  - ☐ Disaster recovery systems
- ☐ Identify
  - ☐ Legacy systems
  - ☐ Offsite and third-party systems

[Section 5:7]

[1]Zubulake v. UBS Warburg LLC, 229 F.R.D. 422, 94 Fair Empl. Prac. Cas. (BNA) 1, 85 Empl. Prac. Dec. (CCH) P 41728 (S.D. N.Y. 2004).

Comment

This form is adapted from the Electronic Discovery Reference Manual (http://www.edrm.net).

III. FORMS

§ 5:9 Records management and archives program

Records Management and Archives Program

[Organization] is required to create and retain certain records as more generally described below. These standards apply regardless of whether the record is created or maintained on paper or electronic format. Simply changing the medium does not change our obligation to create or store records.

The *[organization's]* Records Center provides a mandatory records retention and disposition program:

- Protect the interests of *[organization]* and its employees, customers, and clients.
- Reduce the *[organization's]* risk and liability in litigation, investigation or audit through compliance with applicable policy and law.
- Provide an efficient and effective records management program free of charge to all division of the *[organization]*.
- Expand availability of expensive office space by the transfer of inactive records to the records center for storage.
- Provide cost savings to the *[organization]* through the provision of centrally staffed records management.

What is a record?

Records are all books, papers, maps, photographs, electronic mail (e-mail) or other documentary materials, regardless of physical form or characteristics made or received by the *[organization]* and its employees in connection with the transaction of business and preserved or appropriate for preservation by the *[organization]* as evidence of the organization, functions, policies, decisions, procedures, operations, or other activities of the government, or because the informational and historical value of the data contained in it.

- Records as defined above, which include electronically stored information, are the property of the *[organization]*. They are in no sense personal property. They are not the property of a specific department or division of the *[organization]*.
- No one should assume that records include only paper materials. In the phrase "regardless of physical form or characteristics" establishes that records include e-mail, any type of electronic file or data, machine-readable output, still photographs, motion pictures, audio recordings, charts, maps, drawings, plans, video recordings, and micrographics, or any digitization magnetic tape or other electronic storage of any of these things.

An example of a paper record is the original of a multi-page form. This along with related attachments is the official record for the maximum retention period. Departments generating or controlling original records or designated "record copies" (multiple copies of the same document may each have record status, same as the original, if they serve a separate administrative purpose and are controlled under different filing systems).

- All records must be retained in a readable format, so employees must ensure that electronically stored information is retained in a manner so that the document remains readable regardless of changes in technology or equipment obsolescence. Printing out the documents and saving to a file system, maintaining the old equipment and software applications, or migrating the records to new technology, may meet this requirement. Employees must also assure that electronically stored information meets relevant audit or tracking requirements. If anyone has any questions regarding the status of records, the person should contact the *[organization's]* Records Center.

The storage of inactive paper records is centralized through the Records Center. The Records Center does not have an electronic data warehouse at this time so the storage and preservation of electronic records (e.g., business related e-mail) is the responsibility of each user in the department involved in the relevant function or transaction being documented. However, with proper documentation/metadata, the Records Center will accept electronic records on media for storage (e.g., disk, tape, etc.). The ability to read and retrieve information from these stored media rests with the owning department. If a person is involved in designing or purchasing new electronic systems that create or store electronic records, that persons should consult with the Records Center.

All departments or sub units considering the purchase of a microform or imaging system must obtain approval from *[name]*, *[title]* before purchasing it.

What is not considered a record for retention purposes (Non-record)

Materials not considered as records for retention scheduling purposes include *[list]*. In addition there may be other materials that are not records such as preliminary drafts not circulated for comment, some types of working papers, notes, personal e-mails created during incidental use and similar items that would normally be disposed of when superseded or no longer needed. When in doubt about the status or classification of a record, check with the staff at the Records Management Center. Use of "Instant Messenger" (IM) to conduct official business is at this time is not recommended for various reasons.

Using the example of the check request, the designated department copy or convenience copies of the form are not considered a record copy unless specifically designated as such and scheduled for retention with the Records Center. Therefore these convenience copies do not need to be retained for the period as assigned to the original record or other official records copies. *[These additional copies may be considered "public records" and subject to production in response to public records requests when still available.]*

Departmental convenience copies/non-records should be kept within the department no longer than necessary for reference and never exceed the retention period of the original. *[Department staff can destroy non-records without notifying the Records Center, unless the documents already or are expected to be subject to a public records request. In that case the non-record material may not be destroyed. This may include backup and "scratch" tapes.]*

Records Destruction

All records made or received by public employees of the *[organization]* fitting the legal definition of records are the property of the *[organization]*. Therefore their disposition must be approved by the *[organization]* before their destruction. Destruction of public records without authority is a disciplinable offense. The Director of the Records Center has the sole responsibility to authorize the destruction of *[organization]* records.

No *[organization]* records, either stored at the Records Center or active at departments, that are involved in or are expected to be involved in public records requests, grievances, litigation or other legal processes shall be transferred, destroyed or overwritten until they have been released for transfer, destruction or reuse by the relevant authority that is the source of the prohibition or restriction. This includes relevant non-record material such as convenience copies or relevant documents and backup system media.

COMMENT

This form is adapted from one used by the University of Arizona. It must be adapted to reflect the specific requirements and obligations of the organization for which it is prepared.

§ 5:10 Sample retention schedule

School Transportation Office Retention Schedule

This list is a records retention schedule designed specifically for the records of the district transportation office and should help the office manage its records more efficiently. By using this schedule conscientiously and by discarding and transferring records to the records center on an annual basis, the office should be able to control its records better. Comments indicate more specific retention actions that the office must make. The records are listed in order by series title, but some key words within the title are in bold face to make them easier to find.

SERIES	**OFFICE RETENTION**	**STORAGE RETENTION**	**SCHEDULE & NUMBER**
Bids, successful	2 years	+ 4 years	ED-1: 259
Comments: Keep in office two years for reference, then transfer to the records center.			
Bus driver handbook documenting policies and procedures	until separation	Permanent	ED-1: 9
Comments: Send one copy of handbook to records center when it is superseded.			
Bus driver qualification file, including driver training certificates and character references	1 year after separation	6 years after separation	ED-1: 303
Bus route schedule or diagram: GIS version	update annually	n/a	ED-1: 305a
Comments: These records are updated annually; keep GIS version for current schedules and diagrams; maintain paper records for extra six years.			
Bus route schedule or diagram: Paper printouts from GIS	2 years	+ 6 years	ED-1: 305a
Comments: Keep two years of paper versions in office for reference.			
District-wide consumption and dispensing records for vehicle fuel and oil	6 years	n/a	ED-1: 253
Comments: Since records are not voluminous, dispose from office.			
Driver's daily log report	2 years	+ 4 years	ED-1: 308
Employees' payroll report slips detailing sick, personal and other leave	1 year	+ 5 years	ED-1: 184
Employees' time cards / sheets	1 year	+ 5 years	ED-1: 183
Field trip report	1 year	+ 5 years	ED-1: 395
Grant program files	2 years	+ 8 years	ED-1: 13a&b

SERIES	OFFICE RETENTION	STORAGE RETENTION	SCHEDULE & NUMBER
Comments: Keep records in office for two years; then records center will keep records for six additional years, to ensure all files are kept at least "6 years after renewal or close of grant or denial of application" (as required in ED-1 schedule).			
Legal agreements, including contract, lease and release involving district vehicles	until expiration	+ 6 years	ED-1: 6
Comments: Keep records in office until expiration or final payment, then transfer to records center.			
Maintenance, testing, service and repair records for vehicles: Cumulative summary for vehicle	6 years after vehicle is no longer in use	n/a	ED-1: 250a
Comments: Records kept in office because of reference needs; segregate service records into files by year once they are superseded or become obsolete.			
Maintenance, testing, service and repair records for vehicles: Individual report when posted to summary report	1 year	6 years	ED-1: 250b
Maintenance, testing, service and repair records for vehicles	until log is filed	+ 6 years	ED-1: 250d
Transportation records, non-public schools, including parental requests and consents	3 years	n/a	ED-1: 309
Personnel case file, master summary record	6 years after separation	Permanent	ED-1: 199a
Comments: Personnel records should be segregated from the active personnel files once they become inactive and filed by the year they became inactive. See special personnel case file retention sheet for specifics about what records are considered part of the district's "master summary record."			
Personnel case file, other records	6 years after separation	n/a	ED-1: 199b
Comments: These non-permanent records should be weeded from the personnel files before forwarding the files to the records center. See special personnel case file retention sheet for specifics about which records should be weeded from the file.			
Purchase orders (duplicates)	2 years	n/a	ED-1: 19
Comments: Accounts payable maintains original for 6 years.			

SERIES	OFFICE RETENTION	STORAGE RETENTION	SCHEDULE & NUMBER
Report of theft, vandalism, arson, or property damage to bus garage or vehicles	6 years after vandalism	n/a	ED-1: 32
Comments: These records are uncommon, so maintain them in office until time to discard them.			
Request for use of vehicle (when a chargeback is involved)	3 years	+ 3 years	ED-1: 254a
Comments: Keep in office for three years, long enough to accumulate one full box of records.			
Request for use of vehicle (when no chargeback is involved)	1 year	n/a	ED-1: 254b
Seniority list ranking employees by length of service	3 years after superseded or obsolete	n/a	ED-1: 230
Comments: Office should segregate lists into files by year once they are superseded or become obsolete. Discard from office.			
Vendor listing printout	As updated	n/a	ED-1: 260
Warehouse requisition form for supplies (duplicates)	1 year	n/a	ED-1: 19
Comments: Warehouse maintains original for 6 years.			

Comment

This is a sample retention schedule suggested by the New York State Education Department.

§ 5:11 Guidelines for managing e-mail

Guidelines for Managing E-mail

I. Introduction

E-mail is an important communication tool for conducting business. Increasingly, *[organization]* employees use e-mail systems to distribute memos, circulate drafts, disseminate directives, transfer official documents, send external correspondence, and support various aspects of the *[organization's]* operations. Well-designed and properly managed e-mail systems expedite business communications, eliminate paperwork, and automate routine office tasks. More advanced office systems being contemplated will employ mail frameworks in more complex work flow and document management processes, and move more record keeping to online computerized systems.

Because of the dynamic and often informal nature of e-mail, many questions have arisen over the official and legal status of e-mail messages. For the *[organization]*, two policies: (1) "Status of E-mail as a Public Record" and (2) "Internet and E-mail Acceptable Use Policy," clarify the public record status of e-mail messages and set broad parameters for the management and acceptable use of e-mail in the *[organization]*. Since e-mail meets the statutory definition of a public record in *[state]*, it is subject to management requirements that may not be obvious. For example, e-mail may be subject to open records requests, yet its users may have inappropriate expectations of privacy and informality; e-mail may be destroyed inappropriately; or it may be accumulating in systems when it should have been destroyed after it no longer has value to the *[organization]*. Case law shows that electronic mail certainly is discoverable in civil litigation, and its inappropriate retention may bring risk.

II. Definitions

The very term "e-mail" may be confusing because it is used to mean both the e-mail system and the messages distributed by the system. It can also be used to describe the action of sending or receiving an e-mail message. For the purposes of this document, the word "e-mail" is distinguished by the following terms:

- **E-mail *systems*** are the applications that enable users to compose, transmit, receive, and manage, text and/or graphic e-mail messages and images across LAN and WAN networks and through gateways connecting the latter with the Internet. Within *[organization]*, the e-mail environment is almost exclusively Microsoft Exchange/Outlook-based.
- **E-mail *messages*** are any communication supported

by e-mail systems for the conduct of official agency business internally, between other state, local, and federal agencies, and externally with constituents, voters, vendors, clients, and others. This definition applies equally to the contents of the communication, the transactional information associated with each message, and any attachments to the body of the message.

- **E-mail *server*** is the hardware on which the application resides. For most *[organization]* departments this server is housed and physically managed by the *[specify]*. Messages stored on this server, however, belong to the department. **Any open records requests for messages stored on these servers will be handled by the department, not *[specify]*.** For proper records management, e-mail messages need to be moved off of this server and stored in a secure environment under the department's control.
- **Transactional information** is information about the e-mail message. It can include the name of the sender and all recipients, the date and time the message was created and sent, the host application that generated the message, and all of the systems and computers the message was routed through. Some or all of this metadata may or may not be a visible part of the message. The federal courts have ruled that this information is a vital part of the message itself, (Armstrong v. Executive Office of the President, Office of Admin., 1 F.3d 1274 (D.C. Cir. 1993)) and is an important consideration when storing e-mail messages.

III. Managing E-mail Messages as Public Records

E-mail messages are a form of business communication. They contain information about business activities which, like records in other formats, are subject to audit, open records requests, and legal processes such as discovery and subpoena. E-mail messages sent or received in the course of business transactions are government records and must be retained and managed for as long as they are needed for administrative, fiscal, legal, or historical requirements.

1. Identification of E-mail Messages

The first step after receiving a message is to determine if it was created or received as part of the business of *[organization]*, then establish what kind of record the message is. While the *[organization]* records officer should be the person coordinating the records management activities of the agency, the originator of the record, i.e., author of the message, or the recipient is usually the person who makes the initial retention decision based on the nature of the message within the scope of his or her responsibilities.

If the message was not created or received as part of the business of the *[organization]*, it is considered **non-record** material. Non-record material has nothing to do with the actions of the organization and should be deleted immediately. Examples may include:

Personal Messages are those received from friends or work colleagues which have nothing to do with agency business. Employees need to be reminded that the e-mail system is provided by the *[organization]* primarily for work use. While a certain amount of personal material maybe acceptable, abuse of the system can lead to disciplinary action and even dismissal. *[Organization]* departments should have an appropriate use policy that addresses the timely deletion of such messages.

"Spam" is the term for "junk" e-mail. It is similar to advertising mail received at home. It is completely unsolicited and, generally, unwanted. Some spam can be offensive in nature and sent by hackers as a way of disrupting normal business operations. Spam is a growing problem in government e-mail accounts. While there are tools and techniques for restricting the amount of spam received, there is currently no way to keep it out completely without interfering with the ability to receive important messages. Departments should contact their IT staff if they are receiving large amounts of spam.

Unsolicited e-mail refers to mail that may be

unwanted, but is somewhat business related, such as advertising from vendors. This could also include non-work related e-mail from coworkers such as jokes, miscellaneous news articles, non-work related announcements, etc. As with personal messages, an agency e-mail use policy should address the timely deletion of such non-work related e-mail.

If the message is business related, then the message recipient should determine what type of message it is and apply the proper retention period. This can be done by checking *[specify]*, available on line at *[URL]*, or by consulting with the *[organization's]* Records Officer.

2. Value and Retention of E-mail Records

All e-mail messages do not have the same value to the *[organization]*, and therefore do not have the same retention period. The information in the e-mail, the reason it was created, and the administrative, fiscal, legal, and/or historical value of the e-mail to the *[organization]* determine as with any other kind of record, what kind of record the message is. The majority of e-mail messages in most departments are minor administrative records having only brief convenience or reference value. However, e-mail is also used to transmit records having significant administrative, legal, research, or other value and may need to be retained long-term, and some may need to be retained permanently.

As public records, e-mail messages are subject to the same retention requirements as the same type of record in another format or medium. This means that e-mail messages must be retained and disposed of in the same manner as the *[organization's]* other records, according to records retention schedules approved by *[specify]*. Retention periods for e-mail records will vary according to the information the messages contain and the functions the messages perform. Just as the *[organization]* cannot schedule all paper or microfilm records together under a single retention period, the *[organization]* cannot simply schedule e-mail as a single record series.

No record, paper or electronic, should be destroyed if

it is the subject of an Open Records request and/or legal action (e.g., discovery motion, subpoena, court order). Even if the retention period for the record allows for its destruction, it must be retained until the Open Records request (including any and all appeals) and/or the legal action is completed. Departments should establish procedures for dealing with Open Records requests.

E-mail messages may have one of three different values depending on the content and function of the message to the agency.

(1) Informational and reference materials are transitory in nature. They have no meaningful value to an agency for documenting policy, establishing guidelines or procedures, or certifying transactions and may be destroyed as soon as they are no longer needed. Most e-mail messages fall into this category. Some examples of these types of messages are communications received from a professional listserv (not used for project development or creation of policy) or, general announcements received by all employees, such as news of an upcoming fire drill or impending building repair. These records can be disposed of when they are no longer needed as outlined in the schedule: *[specify]*.

(2) Temporary records have some documentary value to the agency, but do not need to be retained permanently. The retention period is determined by assessing their administrative, fiscal, or legal value. This time period may range from a few months to several years and should be defined in the *[organization's]* records schedule. These records must remain accessible for the entire retention period specified in the schedule. E-mail records in this category should be managed and maintained like the rest of the *[organization's]* temporary records. Some examples of temporary records are: *[specify]*.

(3) Permanent records are programmatic records of the *[organization]* having lasting historical value because they constitute evidence or document the *[organization's]*organizational functions, policies, decisions, procedures, and

essential transactions. Some examples of permanent records are:

- Official correspondence having enduring historical or legal value
- Annual or summary reports

All e-mail messages must be reviewed and classified in a timely manner to ensure good records management practice throughout the enterprise. All *[organization]* employees who use e-mail must be trained in using records retention schedules to identify the types of records they create and receive. **Non-business related and transitory e-mail messages should be removed from the e-mail system as soon as possible.** If this is done by the employee on a regular basis, then e-mail can be managed with relative ease. Departments may find it helpful to have "file clean-up" or "file management" days on a periodic basis. These are selected days where employees are encouraged to go through their e-mail folders and clean out messages that have passed their retention period. This can be coordinated with "file clean-up" for paper records as well.

3. Responsibility for Retention

Once it has been determined that an e-mail message is a record that needs to be retained, a decision needs to be made as to who in the *[organization]* is responsible for retaining it: the sender or the recipient. If the message comes from outside the *[organization]*, this record represents incoming correspondence and should be retained by the person in the agency who received the message and acted on it. An exception to this would occur if someone else (such as another department) in the *[organization]*is responsible for handling the action required to be dealt with in the e-mail. In these cases, the initial recipient may forward it to that person, who would be responsible for filing the message.

If the message is sent and received by personnel within the same department, not all staff need to retain a copy of the same message. If the message that was sent, was not altered in any way (responded to, edited, had attachments added, etc.) then the original sender has the responsibility for retaining the message. If a recipient made alterations to a message, then the recipient would be responsible for retaining the message. If there is a string of multiple replies between two or more people to the same message, then only the last reply needs to be saved **only if all of the replies and comments are captured in the final message.** This is done by ensuring that the "include original message text" feature is activated for any replies and forwards.

4. Filing Structures. Employees should be trained in using the organization's e-mail application to create folders for organizing their e-mail messages. An organized system of folders helps individuals in separating informational, temporary, and permanent records and can help ensure that important records are not accidentally lost or misplaced. Folders are more helpful if the individual's filing structure mirrors that of the agency, especially if the agency employs an electronic record keeping system. An electronic record keeping system is an electronic system that stores and organizes electronic files for enhanced distribution and access. It can also be referred as a document management system. Departments should develop a standardized system for naming files and folders to avoid confusion over the contents of a file.

This should be a location on the organization's network that is secure and backed-up on a regular basis. All departments need to establish logical and coherent filing structures and naming conventions for creating folders on the agency's network drive(s). Employees need to be trained in how to create folders in the e-mail application and where/how to place the folders on the network drive(s).

These folders **should not be located on the individual's workstation** (their "C" drive). This is not a secure location and is not backed-up to protect from accidental loss. The folders should also not be located in the application's "In-box." These folders should be located in the folders created for that individual located on the agency network or in an electronic record keeping system if the agency employs one. Departments should utilize their IT staff to assist with the proper placement of Outlook or other network folders.

5. Accessibility of E-mail Records. Because e-mail messages are public records, they are subject to the same Open Records requirements as any of the organization's other public records. The legal issues governing this access are frequently very complex. E-mail messages must be managed in such a way that departments can respond promptly to Open Records requests.

E-mail messages available for public inspection must remain accessible throughout their *entire* retention period and should be maintained in a manner permitting efficient and timely retrieval. Developing a standardized system of document naming, filing, indexing and retrieval (within the e-mail application or grouped together with other files in electronic record keeping systems), will assist a department in maintaining the accessibility of non-exempt e-mail messages throughout the required retention period.

Appropriate measures should be taken by the department's records custodian to insure that e-mail messages that are the subject of pending open records requests and/or litigation are not deleted from the e-mail, or other electronic record keeping system, before the request, and any appeals, are satisfied and completed. When the custodian is made aware of the request or litigation, agencies should generate a separate file that captures a complete copy of the appropriate e-mail message(s) and maintain that copy in a separate secure directory under the control of the designated records custodian for a period of 30 days or as long as the case is being litigated or appealed. Documentation of this procedure (date, time, and number of messages) should also be created and maintained as long as the file is maintained. Once a secure copy of the message(s) has been generated, the other copy can be handled according to the agency's records management procedures and the principles spelled out in these guidelines.

Having e-mail messages that are inaccessible, either through hardware/software obsolescence or because of faulty indexing schemes, can be as problematic as inappropriately destroying the records and could expose the organization to legal risk.

IV. Preservation of E-mail Records

Departments have responsibility for developing guidelines and procedures to incorporate e-mail messages into their overall record-keeping systems following policies approved by *[specify]*. Department administrators should also develop policies and systems designed to ensure that e-mail records are appropriately preserved, secured, and made accessible throughout their established retention periods. Procedures and systems configuration will vary according to the department's needs and particular hardware and software used.

Simply backing up the e-mail system onto tapes or other media or purging all messages after a set amount of time is not an appropriate strategy for managing e-mail.

Organization records of long-term value should not be stored on individual workstations. The records should be stored on a secure drive that has the proper security features to protect the records from alteration or destruction and to provide regular back-up. Offsite employees with laptops should download their messages to the organization's network drives on a regular schedule.

There are three ways to preserve e-mail messages: on-line, near-line, and off-line. All of the methods have advantages and disadvantages that must be considered before determining which is right for the agency.

1. On-line Storage

On-line storage maintains e-mail messages in the e-mail application itself. This is a good method for storing temporary and short-term records (less than five year's retention). Microsoft Outlook does have limited capability to carry out this approach which can be employed by using the "archiving" function in the application.

There are several advantages to storing e-mail messages in the e-mail application. The messages can be searched and retrieved quickly and easily with electronic indexing. The dynamic functionality of the messages can be retained, and the messages can be stored in their native format. Since the *[organization]* already has the e-mail application in place, the costs are less than running the e-mail application with a parallel system.

Messages must be moved off the main e-mail server and into a secure drive or the application will not respond properly and messages could be lost.

2. Near-line Storage

Near-line storage involves the transfer of the e-mail messages and transactional information into an electronic record keeping system, other than the e-mail system itself. For example, an e-mail message dealing with a particular project could be stored in a file on the agency's network drive with other electronic files dealing with the same project. The message still retains some of its functionality, including the ability to be indexed and retrieved electronically. If the agency stores other records in electronic format, then the e-mail messages can be integrated with other related project files.

Disadvantages to storing records near-line are the potential costs for the equipment, maintenance and service for the electronic record keeping system. The agency should consider the costs and benefits, and the compatibility of their e-mail application and the electronic record keeping system. Storing messages external to the e-mail application may mean converting the messages to a different format, which could result in the loss of important information. Records with retention periods of more than five years need to be migrated and possibly converted to new formats and systems as older ones become outdated. Finally, if a department still maintains many of its records in paper, then the two systems (paper filing system and the electronic system) must be integrated and work together.

3. Off-line (Paper) Systems

In some cases, especially for permanent and long-term (greater than ten to fifteen years) records, the best preservation solution may be to print the e-mail messages, and transactional information, onto paper. This solution makes sense if a department does not already have an electronic system in place that is designed for long-term records protection and accessibility or if a majority of its records are kept in paper form.

The biggest advantage to off-line storage is the stability of the medium. Departments do not have to worry about hardware and software becoming outdated and the records becoming irretrievable. E-mail messages can be filed with other records of the same type or series directly, making the retention and disposition process easier.

The disadvantage is that the e-mail messages lose their dynamic functionality as electronic documents. They cannot be searched and retrieved as quickly and efficiently as in a well-managed electronic system. Finally, with the pervasive use of e-mail applications in the course of government business, the volume of paper records will build up quickly.

Note: No matter what storage option a department chooses, transactional metadata *must* be properly captured and stored with the e-mail message for the full value of the document to be preserved. This task is usually easy in e-mail applications that readily display this information. Applications that do not display the metadata need to be configured so that the data stays with the message in whatever form the message is retained.

VI. Other Management Considerations for E-mail Systems

Electronic systems share some of the same management

concerns as off-line (paper) systems. Below are some considerations to help department managers with overall management of e-mail records.

Transactional information (metadata)

This data is the information about the e-mail message that accompanies the message for routing, tracking, and usage purposes. It can include the name of the sender and all recipients, the date the message was created and sent, information about the host application that generated the message, and a record of all of the systems and computers the message was routed through. In some e-mail applications, this metadata is a visible part of the message; in some applications, it is in the header; and in some other applications, the metadata is stored in a "properties" file. Transactional information is an important consideration in any information system for retention of e-mail and any legal use that may be made of an e-mail message.

Distribution lists

In a distribution list, groups of recipients are referenced under a common name. For instance, if an employee is a member of a planning committee, then a list can be created that contains the e-mail addresses of all of the members of that committee; to send a message to the entire committee, the list name is typed into the "To" line of the message, rather than each individual address. If such lists are used, then the names and addresses of all the list members need to be retained along with the message, if that information is important to the evidentiary value of the message. For example, knowing that a message was sent to "Budget Committee" but not knowing the names of the recipients omits part of a documentary function the message was intended to serve.

Back-ups and System Security

Electronic storage systems should be backed up

regularly to protect from system failures, unintentional deletions, or tampering. Routine back-up procedures are for emergency recovery purposes, however, and do not constitute a long-term record keeping solution for e-mail. Recovering messages from back-up tapes can be problematic and many tapes are re-used repeatedly.

Ad-hoc lists created in an individual's "Contacts" folder put the individual addresses in the message. However, lists that are on the global list in Exchange only put the name of the list on the message. One work around for this is for the sender to "BCC" themselves and they will receive a message with all of the addresses listed that can filed or record keeping purposes.

Departments should develop procedures to provide for the security of e-mail records so that they cannot be altered or deleted, intentionally or unintentionally. This security is important to ensure that the e-mail records remain reliable and authentic evidence of the department's activity, for regulatory, auditing and legal accountability. The department must document its procedures for handling and securing agency e-mail and who has access to the system. An audit trail should be maintained to track any alterations to messages in the system.

Deletion of E-mail Messages

Non-permanent records should be deleted when the proper retention period has expired. Simply deleting the message *does not* necessarily remove it from the hard drive or server, however. Utility programs can be purchased to make sure hard drives are wiped clean and the messages are completely removed. This will eliminate wasted storage space and help avoid legal consequences if deleted messages are recovered. As with any of these procedures, the destruction policy needs to be well documented and followed by all levels of the agency.

Expired messages should be removed from back-up tapes of both the e-mail server and from any other electronic record keeping system the agency may employ. Even if the e-mail messages have been properly deleted from the electronic files, messages on back-up tapes are still discoverable and could present legal liability to the *[organization]*.

Control of Copies

Because e-mail messages can be forwarded and routed to multiple addresses, copies of the messages could exist after the retention period has expired. All agency staff should be trained in identifying what constitutes the official, or "record" copy. In most cases, the author or creator and/or the principal recipient of the e-mail message is responsible for maintaining the record copy, but the retention for other copies is governed by the function the record plays in documenting the work of the recipient. Employees should be encouraged to delete unofficial copies of messages as soon as possible.

When an Employee Leaves

Any time an employee leaves the *[organization]*, the employee's e-mail messages need to be reviewed by the appropriate personnel to ensure that any records are properly classified and stored, and that any non-records are disposed of in the correct manner. **This should be done before the former employee's account is removed from the e-mail server.** Ideally, the employee would be doing this type of file management on a regular basis, just as they do with paper files. Employee exit procedures, however, should verify that records remaining in an e-mail account are appropriately transferred to others within the organization or deleted, as is dictated by retention schedules.

If the employee had personal messages on the e-mail system, the *[organization]* is under no obligation to retain that information. However, in cases where the employee was dismissed or demoted due to misuse of the e-mail system, these messages may be used as evidence by the *[organization]* or the employee in responding to the charges. While the *[organization]* is not obligated to retain non-business related material, it cannot destroy evidence, and may be required to allow the employee access to these messages in order to rebut the charges.

VII. Employee Training

All employees should be trained in using the records retention schedule to identify and classify the records they create. They should be aware of proper retention and disposition procedures and of who to contact when records need to be transferred out of their custody. Because individual employees have direct control over the creation and distribution of e-mail messages, departments should provide training for their employees on agency *[organization]* procedures. Depending on the type of e-mail and record keeping system a department uses, policies and procedures will vary.

In addition to those mentioned previously, the following issues should be addressed in any e-mail policy:

1. **Appropriate Usage of E-mail Systems.** The e-mail system is provided, at the *[organization's]* expense, to assist employees in carrying out government business. The e-mail system is property of the *[organization]*, and the *[organization]* has the right to monitor and review the use of the system. The courts have been fairly consistent about the use of computing resources at the workplace, especially the government workplace, for personal transactions: these transactions are not private, nor do they belong to the individual. E-mail should be used only to transmit business-related information. Every department should develop a written policy statement for its employees regarding appropriate usage of an e-mail system. The *[organization's]* "Internet and Electronic Mail Acceptable Use Policy" provides the minimum requirements for state agencies to follow and can serve as a model for local departments in developing their own use policy.

2. **E-mail Confidentiality/Privacy.** E-mail messages travel through several computers and networks and could be captured and viewed at any point along the way. E-mail communication should be used with the assumption that a message might be read by many people, not just the intended recipient. Sensitive, or confidential information should not be transmitted via e-mail unless the proper protocols have been followed to secure the message.

Because e-mail has become such a commonly used business communication tool, care needs to be taken to protect personal privacy rights of other co-workers (or any other third party). While information of a personal nature (Social Security Numbers, home phone numbers and addresses, medical conditions, etc.) should not be included in e-mail messages, it is unreasonable to expect staff not to use the benefits of the messaging system for this type of communication. While these messages are usually exempt from Open Records requests, they could be stored in an in-box with non-exempt messages and exposed inadvertently.

3. **Subject Lines.** Proper use of clear and concise subject lines helps identify the content of e-mail messages and helps index and retrieve e-mail messages stored in electronic record-keeping systems. Clear, concise subject lines are also a courtesy for the recipient in distinguishing important messages from the sea of unimportant junk, or "spam," mail that a person may receive. A good subject line should be as descriptive as possible about the content of the message. Here are some examples of good and bad subject lines:

Poor or Confusing Subject Lines	Good Subject Lines
"Report"	"Contact Info"
"Minutes"	"Quarterly Financial Report"

"Important"	"Jan 2007 Board Minutes"
"Today?"	"Revised Admin Procedures"
"News"	"Lunch Plans Today?"
"Helpful Info"	"New Human Resources Manager Appointed?"

4. **Viruses.** Government agencies and businesses are the most popular targets for people trying to disrupt computer systems. Many viruses can be attached to e-mail messages sent to recipients without the sender's knowledge. Employees may even receive viruses from someone they know and trust. Departments should establish policies regarding the opening of e-mail attachments and for system security.
5. **Encryption.** Because encryption can complicate long-term storage of e-mail, it should only be used when the function of the message dictates the need and when methods exist to decrypt. If used, the encryption method must follow established *[organization]* guidelines and procedures.

Comment

This form is adapted from Guidelines prepared by the Kentucky Department for Libraries and Archives. The Guidelines should be modified to meet the needs and structures of a particular organization.

Chapter 6

Destruction of Electronically Stored Information

I. GUIDELINES

II. CHECKLISTS

III. FORMS

Research References

Additional References

ABA Discovery Standards, http://www.abanet.org/litigation/discoverystandards/2005civildiscoverystandards.pdf
ARMA, http://www.arma.org
Electronic Discovery Reference Model Project, http://www.edrm.net
EMC Corp., http://www.emc.com

Information Requirements Clearinghouse, http://www.irch.com
The Sedona Conference, http://www.thesedonaconference.org
TechTarget, Inc., http://www.searchstorage.com

Treatises and Practice Aids

eDiscovery & Digital Evidence §§ 8:9, 8:10
Grenig and Kinsler, Federal Civil Discovery and Disclosure §§ 13.1 to 13.6 (2d ed.)

Trial Strategy

Recovery and Reconstruction of Electronic Mail as Evidence, 41 Am. Jur Proof of Facts 3d 1
Computer Technology in Civil Litigation, 71 Am. Jur Trials 111

KeyCite®: Cases and other legal materials listed in KeyCite Scope can be researched through the KeyCite service on Westlaw®. Use KeyCite to check citations for form, parallel references, prior and later history, and comprehensive citator information, including citations to other decisions and secondary materials.

I. GUIDELINES

§ 6:1 Generally

It would be unreasonable to require an organization to institute a records management program that in effect required it to routinely retain all possible evidence. However, if an organization routinely destroys electronically stored information that conceivably could be detrimental to the person or entity in some future litigation, this can result in an adverse court ruling.[1]

The issue often becomes whether an organization in adopting a records management program knew or should have known that litigation was imminent. In *Lewy v. Remington Arms Co.*,[2] the Eighth Circuit ruled:

In cases where a document records management program is

[Section 6:1]

[1]See, e.g., Carlucci v. Piper Aircraft Corp., 102 F.R.D. 472, 38 Fed. R. Serv. 2d 1654 (S.D. Fla. 1984).

[2]Lewy v. Remington Arms Co., Inc., 836 F.2d 1104, Prod. Liab. Rep. (CCH) P 11662, 24 Fed. R. Evid. Serv. 516 (8th Cir. 1988).

> instituted in order to limit damaging evidence available to potential plaintiffs, it may be proper to give an [adverse inference] instruction similar to the one requested by the Lewys. Similarly, even if the court finds the policy to be reasonable given the nature of the documents subject to the policy, the court may find that under the particular circumstances certain documents should have been retained notwithstanding the policy. For example, if the corporation knew or should have known that the documents would become material at some point in the future then such documents should have been preserved. Thus, a corporation cannot blindly destroy documents and expect to be shielded by a seemingly innocuous document records management program.

An effective records management program requires a comprehensive records retention policy, supporting record classification and retention schedule. There are a variety of rules, regulations and case law regarding the duty to preserve electronically stored information. In most circumstances, there are severe consequences for failing to do so.

Electronically stored information should be destroyed under a records retention program when it is no longer needed or is no longer required to be retained. Not only is it expensive to store electronically stored information when there is no need to store it, the consequences of storing electronically stored information when it no longer must be stored can be exceptionally expensive.

In the absence of a statute or regulation, it is not necessary to document disposition of electronically stored information. However, it is prudent to develop a records destruction authorization form to authorize and document records disposal. The authorization form should include series titles and dates, quantity of records, method of destruction, and authorization signatures. One or more of the following people should sign the form:

- The records management officer
- The manager of the office that "owns" the records
- The chief administrative official.

To certify destruction, the form should also include the dated signature of the witness.

§ 6:2 Statutes

Organizations subject to regulation by various governmental agencies charged with oversight often have heavy preservation obligations due to the nature of their industry. For example, those companies who have chosen to avail themselves of being licensed brokers of the sale and exchange of securities must comply with record retention requirements of SEC 17a-3 and SEC 17a-4 (requiring all communications with clients to be maintained for periods of three and six years).

A number of statutes should be considered with respect to when and how electronically stored information may be destroyed. These include:

- Health Insurance Portability and Accountability Act (HIPAA)[1]
- USA Patriot Act[2]
- Gramm-Leach-Bililey Act (Disclosure of Nonpublic Personal Information)[3]
- Sarbanes-Oxley Act (Public Company Accounting Reform and Investor Protection Act of 2002)[4]
- Fair and Accurate Credit TransactionsAct (FACTA)[5]

§ 6:3 Identification and review

The first step in destruction of electronically stored information is identification of the information to be destroyed in accordance with the records management program. Responsible persons or departments should be notified of the planned destruction and given an opportunity to halt the destruction. Destruction of specific documents or categories of documents should be halted

---

[Section 6:2]

[1]Pub.L. No. 104-191, Aug. 21, 1996, 110 Stat. 1936.

[2]Pub.L. No. 107-56, Oct. 26, 2001, 115 Stat. 272; Pub.L. No. 109-177, Mar. 9, 2006, 120 Stat. 192.

[3]15 U.S.C.A. §§ 6801 to 6809.

[4]Pub.L. No. 107-204, July 30, 2002, 116 Stat. 745.

[5]Pub.L. No. 108-159, Dec. 4, 2003, 117 Stat. 1952.

when litigation or a government investigation is foreseeable, or an audit is anticipated.

§ 6:4 Disposition of electronically stored information—Generally

A records management program should establish a formal disposition procedure regularly disposing of records at least once a year. An established disposition procedure safeguards against the accidental destruction of records that have not attained their minimum retention periods or that have met their retention periods but are needed for some other purpose, such as litigation or investigations.

§ 6:5 Disposition of electronically stored information—After microfilming or electronic imaging

The cost advantages and improved efficiency offered by microfilming or electronic imaging paper documents can only be realized if the original records are destroyed after microfilming or electronic imaging. When the original records are destroyed after reproduction in accordance with any applicable legal requirements, the records continue to exit. The reproduced documents preserve the information contained in the original record, but in a different form.

§ 6:6 Disposition of electronically stored information—E-mail

Records management programs relating to e-mail, including associated metadata, must comply with statutory, regulatory and business requires. The programs must also reflect the need to preserve and produce e-mails as a result of litigation or investigations.

§ 6:7 Disposition of electronically stored information—Duplicates

The ease with which electronically stored information can be duplicated creates serious records management problems. An effective records management program providing procedures for destruction of duplicate records can be helpful in reducing the burden of responding to discovery requests or implementing litigation holds.

§ 6:8 Destruction of electronically stored information

In selecting a method of destruction for electronically stored information, it is essential carefully to evaluate the records to be destroyed, local environmental restrictions, and the availability of equipment and staff resources. It is then necessary to determine the available destruction alternatives.

With electronically stored information, it is important to have procedures for the deletion of electronic files. It is possible to erase and reuse magnetic media, but for the best security it is better to erase all the information on the medium before reusing. Magnetic media can also be destroyed through incineration (which melts and deforms the media) or by shredding. Destruction of electronic records, however, can be very difficult, since copies of a single file may reside in numerous locations, some not accessible even by the organization's system administrator.

II. CHECKLISTS

§ 6:9 Records destruction checklist

- ☐ Are the records confidential?
- ☐ What is the quantity of records to be destroyed?
- ☐ How often will records destruction take place?
- ☐ What is the physical composition of the records?
- ☐ Do the records contain numerous fasteners, such as staples or paper clips?
- ☐ Are there restrictions on incineration or disposal in a landfill in your area?
- ☐ Do you have access to a vendor who provides bonded recycling?
- ☐ Do you have space and staff for an on-site destruction program?

- ☐ Can your equipment handle the bulk to be destroyed?
- ☐ Can your shredder handle non-paper records such as microfilm?
- ☐ Will you be able to contain the dust produced by a shredder?
- ☐ Is it more efficient and economical to use an outside vendor or facility?

III. FORMS

§ 6:10 Records destruction authorization form

RECORDS DESTRUCTION AUTHORIZATION FORM

Record Series	Dates of Records	Schedule Item	Retention

Destruction authorized by Records Management Officer

____

Date ______

Department Head

____

Date ______

Destruction certified by Witness

Record Series	**Dates of Re-cords**	**Sched-ule Item**	**Reten-tion**
______________________ Date ______			

§ 6:11 Certificate of records destruction

Instructions for Completing Certificate of Records Destruction

The *[form]* documents that records were destroyed properly and in accordance with the *[organization]* Records Management Program.

Before a state agency or locality can destroy public records:

- A Records Officer for your organization must be designated in writing by completing and filing a *[form]*.
- Records to be destroyed must be covered by an *[organization]*-approved general or agency-specific Records Retention and Disposition Schedule and the retention period for the records must have expired.
- All investigations, litigation, and required audits must be completed. Existing records cannot be destroyed if they are pertinent to an investigation (including requests under the *Freedom of Information Act*), litigation, or where a required audit has not been undertaken.
- The organization's designated Records Officer and an Approving Official must authorize records destruction by signing each *[form]*.

After a department has destroyed public records:

- The individual or company responsible for destroying the records must sign and date *[form]*. This final signature certifies the records have **actually been destroyed**.
- A copy of the *[form]* must be retained by the organization.

- The *[form]*, with all original signatures, must be delivered to *[place]* be retained for fifty years.

  Mail forms to: *[address]*

Instructions:

1. Enter full name of agency, locality or organization.
2. Enter name of division, department, and section.
3. Enter name of individual completing the form, preferably the individual responsible for or familiar with the records.
4. Enter address of the agency or locality completing the form.
5. Enter telephone number of the person completing the form including extension, if applicable.
6. Records to be destroyed:
   a) Enter both the retention schedule and series numbers that apply to the records to be destroyed. ENTER ONLY ONE SERIES NUMBER PER LINE.
   b) Enter the exact records series title as listed on the approved retention schedule. You may add detail to this title if it is important to identifying the records.
   c) Enter the date range of the records to be destroyed, from oldest to most recent. Indicate starting month/ year and ending month/year.
   d) Enter the location where the records are stored (optional).
   e) Enter the total volume or amount of records to be destroyed. Refer to the Volume Equivalency Table (available from the Archival and Records Management Services Division) to convert boxes or drawers of paper or microform records to their cubic foot equivalents. If destroying electronic records, enter the approximate size of the files by megabyte, type of media containing data, or number of files.
   f) Enter the method used to destroy the records, i.e., trash, shredding, recycling, landfill, burning, etc.
7. Printed name and signature of individual responsible for maintaining records or agency/locality head.

8. Printed name and signature of agency/locality Records Officer.
9. Enter name of individual or company that destroyed the records and the date they were destroyed.

If multiple *[forms]* are submitted, all three required signatures must be on each page.

EXAMPLES:

a) Schedule and Records Series Number	b) Records Series Title	c) Date Range (mo/yr)	d) Location	e) Volume	f) Destruction Method
	Garnishments	1/1960–12/1997	Basement	15 cu. ft.	Burned
	Payroll Records and Deduction Authorizations	7/2001–6/2002	Server 4	30 MB	Electronic Shredding
	Hospice Program Records	1/1999–12/2003		2 cu. ft.	Shredded by vendor
	Dairy Products Inspections Records	7/1995–6/2005	Rm. 504	52 cu. ft.	Shredded in-house

COMMENT

This form is adapted from one used by the Commonwealth of Virginia. It can be adapted for use by public or private organizations.

§ 6:12 Guidelines for sanitization of information technology equipment and electronic media

SANITIZATION OF INFORMATION TECHNOLOGY EQUIPMENT AND ELECTRONIC MEDIA

Policy: The purpose of this policy is to ensure secure and appropriate disposal of information technology (IT) equipment, devices, network components, operating systems, application software and storage media belonging to *[organization]* to prevent unauthorized use or misuse of state information. All IT equipment shall be properly sanitized prior to disposal or release and sanitization procedures shall be properly documented to prevent unauthorized release of sensitive and/or confidential information that may be stored on that equipment and other electronic media. This policy supports the Enterprise Architecture for security and privacy and outlines procedures that must be followed to protect the *[organization]*.

Policy Maintenance: The Office of the CIO has issued this Enterprise Policy. The *[organization]* Office of Technology (OT), Office of Infrastructure Services, is responsible for the maintenance of this policy. This policy shall be adhered to by all agencies and employees within the *[organization]*. However, departments may choose to add to this policy, in order to enforce more restrictive policies as appropriate. Therefore, employees are to refer to their department's internal policy, which may have additional information or clarification of this Enterprise Policy.

Responsibility for Compliance: Each department is responsible for assuring that appropriate employees within their organizational authority have been made aware of the provisions of this policy, that compliance by the employee is expected, and that unauthorized and/or neglectful release of computer equipment and/or related media, especially that which contain sensitive and/or confidential information, may result in disciplinary action pursuant to *[citation]* up to and including dismissal.

It is also each department manager's responsibility to enforce and manage this policy. Failure to comply may result in additional shared service charges to the department for OT's efforts to remediate issues related to lack of or improper sanitization of computer equipment and related media.

Definitions:

Clearing: The process of deleting the data on the media before the media is reused. It is important to note that clearing *will* allow for the retrieval of information if certain retrieval procedures are used and is not approved for computer equipment or media that contain sensitive and/or confidential data.

Coercivity: Magnetic media is divided into three types (I, II, III) based on their coercivity. Coercivity of magnetic media defines the magnetic field necessary to reduce a magnetically saturated material's magnetization to zero. The level of magnetic media coercivity must be ascertained before executing any degaussing procedure.

Degauss: Procedure that reduces the magnetic flux on media virtually to zero by applying a reverse magnetizing field. Properly applied, degaussing renders any previously stored data on magnetic media unreadable and may be used in the sanitization process. Degaussing is more effective than overwriting magnetic media.

Degausser: Device used to remove data from magnetic storage medium.

DoD Sanitization Standard (5520.22-M): US Department of Defense standard for clearing and sanitizing data on writable media.

Dynamic Random Access Memory (DRAM): The most common kind of random access memory (RAM) for personal computers and workstations. Unlike firmware chips (ROMs, PROMs, etc.) DRAM loses its content when the power is turned off.

Electronically Alterable PROM (EAPROM): A PROM whose contents can be changed.

Electronically Erasable PROM (EEPROM): User-modifiable read-only memory (ROM) that can be erased and reprogrammed (written to) repeatedly through the application of higher than normal electrical voltage. A special form of EEPROM is flash memory.

Erasable Programmable ROM (EPROM): Programmable read-only memory (programmable ROM) that can be erased and re-used. Erasure is caused by shining an intense ultraviolet light through a window that is designed into the memory chip.

Flash EPROM (FEPROM): Non-volatile device similar to EEPROM, but where erasing can only be done in blocks or the entire chip.

Programmable ROM (PROM): Read-only memory (ROM) that can be modified once by a user.

Magnetic Bubble Memory: A non-volatile memory device for computers that uses magnetic bubbles for recording bits. The technology was used in early 1980s but is obsolete today.

Magnetic Core Memory: Random access memory (RAM) system that was developed at MIT in 1951. Magnetic core memory replaced vacuum tubes and mercury delay lines with a much more compact and reliable technology. Semiconductor memories largely replaced magnetic cores in the 1970s.

Magnetic Plated Wire: Non-volatile memory created by Honeywell in 1960s. Magnetic plated wire consists of a copper conductor covered with a thin layer of highly magnetic material, over which a polyurethane insulating film is enameled.

Nonvolatile RAM (NOVRAM): Memory that does not lose its information while its power supply is turned off.

Oersteds: The unit of magnetic field strength in the centimeter-gram-second system.

Overwriting: A software process that replaces the data previously stored on magnetic storage media with a predetermined set of meaningless data. Overwriting is an acceptable method for clearing; however, the effectiveness of the overwrite procedure may be reduced by several factors, including: ineffectiveness of the overwrite procedures, equipment failure (e.g., misalignment of read/write heads), or inability to overwrite bad sectors or tracks or information in inter-record gaps.

Overwriting Procedure: The preferred method to clear magnetic disks is to overwrite all locations three (3) times (the first time with a random character, the second time with a specified character, the third time with the complement of that specified character).

Read Only Memory (ROM):: Built-in computer memory containing data that normally can only be read, not written to. The data in ROM is not lost when the computer power is turned off. The ROM is sustained by a small long-life battery in your computer.

Sanitizing: The process of removing the data on the media before the media is reused in an environment that does not provide an acceptable level of protection for the data. In general, laboratory techniques cannot retrieve data that has been sanitized/purged. Sanitizing may be accomplished by degaussing.

Static Random Access Memory (SRAM): Random access memory (RAM) that retains data bits in its memory as long as power is being supplied. SRAM is used for a computer's cache memory and as part of the random access memory digital-to-analog converter on a video card.

Procedures:

1.0. Sanitization of IT Equipment and Electronic Media

The sale, transfer, or disposal of computers, computer peripherals, and computer software or other IT devices can create information security risks for the *[organization].* These risks are related to potential violation of software license agreements, unauthorized release of sensitive and/or confidential information, and unauthorized disclosure of trade secrets, copyrights, and other intellectual property that might be stored on the hard disks and other storage media. It should be noted that computers containing sensitive and/or confidential data must have their hard drives securely erased as specified by the US Department of Defense (DoD) standards listed in section 1.4—Recommended DoD Sanitation Procedures.

The following procedures must be followed when a computer system is sold, transferred, or disposed of. This policy does not supersede specific policies, directives or standards required by federal or state agencies pertaining to the disposal of computer equipment. The following procedures also apply to contractor-supplied computers.

- Before a computer system is sold, transferred, or otherwise disposed of, all sensitive and/or confidential program or data files on any storage media must be completely erased or otherwise made unreadable in accordance with DoD standards (5220.22-M) unless there is specific intent to transfer the particular software or data to the purchaser/recipient.
- The computer system must be relocated to a desig-

nated, secure storage area until the data can be erased.

- Hard drives of surplus computer equipment must be securely erased within 60 days after replacement.
- Whenever licensed software is resident on any computer media being sold, transferred, or otherwise disposed of, the terms of the license agreement must be followed.

After the sanitization of the hard drive is complete, the process must be certified and a record maintained as specified by the agency's records retention schedule.

1.1. Sanitization of Hard Drives

The following section outlines the acceptable methods to expunge data from storage media. Sanitization must be performed on hard drives to ensure that information is removed from the hard drive in a matter that gives assurance that the information cannot be recovered. Before the sanitization process begins, the computer must be disconnected from any network to prevent accidental damage to the network operating system or other files on the network.

There are three acceptable methods to be used for the sanitization of hard drives:

- Overwriting
- Degaussing
- Physical Destruction

The method used for sanitization, depends upon the operability of the hard drive:

- Operable hard drives that will be reused must be overwritten prior to disposition. If the operable hard drive is to be removed from service completely, it must be physically destroyed or degaussed.
- If the hard drive is inoperable or has reached the end of its useful life, it must be physically destroyed or degaussed.

Clearing data (deleting files) removes information from

storage media in a manner that renders it unreadable unless special utility software or techniques are used to recover the cleared data. However, because the clearing process does not prevent data from being recovered by technical means, it is *not* an acceptable method of sanitizing state owned hard disk storage media.

1.1.1. Overwriting Specifications

Overwriting is an approved method for sanitization of hard disk drives. Overwriting of data means replacing previously stored data on a drive or disk with a predetermined pattern of meaningless information. This effectively renders the data unrecoverable. All software products and applications used for the overwriting process must meet the following specifications:

- The data must be properly overwritten with a pattern. OT requires overwriting with a pattern, and then its complement, and finally with a random pattern of 1s and 0s.
- Sanitization is not complete until three overwrite passes and a verification pass is completed.
- The software must have the capability to overwrite the entire hard disk drive, independent of any BIOS or firmware capacity limitation that the system may have, making it impossible to recover any meaningful data.
- The software must have the capability to overwrite using a minimum of three cycles of data patterns on all sectors, blocks, tracks, and any unused disk space on the entire hard disk medium.
- The software must have a method to verify that all data has been removed.
- Sectors not overwritten must be identified.

1.1.2. Degaussing Specifications

Degaussing is a process whereby the magnetic media is erased. Hard drives seldom can be used after degaussing. The degaussing method should only be used when the hard drive is inoperable and will not be used for further service.

Please note that extreme care should be used when using degaussers since this equipment can cause extreme damage to nearby telephones, monitors, and other electronic equipment. Also, the use of a degausser does not guarantee that all data on the hard drive will be destroyed. Degaussing efforts should be audited periodically to detect equipment or procedure failures.

The following standards and procedures must be followed when hard drives are degaussed:

- Follow the product manufacturer's directions carefully. It is essential to determine the appropriate rate of coercivity for degaussing.
- Shielding materials (cabinets, mounting brackets), which may interfere with the degausser's magnetic field, must be removed from the hard drive before degaussing.
- Hard disk platters must be in a horizontal direction during the degaussing process.

1.1.3. Physical Destruction

Hard drives must be destroyed when they are defective or cannot be repaired or sanitized for reuse. Physical destruction must be accomplished to an extent that precludes any possible further use of the hard drive. This can be attained by removing the hard drive from the cabinet and removing any steel shielding materials and/or mounting brackets and cutting the electrical connection to the hard drive unit. The hard drive should then be subjected to physical force (pounding with a sledge hammer) or extreme temperatures (incineration) that will disfigure, bend, mangle or otherwise mutilate the hard drive so it cannot be reinserted into a functioning computer.

1.2. Sanitization of Other Computer Media

If there is any risk of disclosure of sensitive data on media other than computer hard drives, the appropriate sanitization methods as outlined in the DoD recommended sanitization procedures should be followed. Particular attention should be paid to floppy disks, tapes, CDs, DVDs, and optical disks.

Memory components should also be sanitized before disposal or release. Memory components reside on boards, modules, and sub-assemblies. A board can be a module, or may consist of several modules and sub-assemblies.

Unlike magnetic media sanitization, clearing may be an acceptable method of sanitizing components for release. Memory components are categorized as either volatile or nonvolatile, as described below. DoD Sanitization Procedures should be followed as specified in section 1.4

Volatile memory components *do not* retain data after removal of all electrical power sources, and when reinserted into a similarly configured system do not contain residual data, i.e. SRAM, DRAM.

Nonvolatile memory components *do* retain data when all power sources are discontinued. Nonvolatile memory components include Read Only Memory (ROM), Programmable ROM (PROM), or Erasable PROM (EPROM) and their variants. Memory components that have been programmed at the vendor's commercial manufacturing facility and are considered unalterable in the field may be released; otherwise, DoD Sanitization Procedures must be followed.

1.3. **Certification of Sanitization**

Sanitization may be required in instances other than surplusing. It is recommended that a record is kept for all sanitization procedures, it is required when equipment is surplused. Prior to submitting surplus forms (B217-2: Declared Surplus) from *[department]* to the department's appropriate organizational unit, the sanitizing process must be documented on an additional form that explicitly outlines the method(s) used to expunge the data from the storage media, the type of equipment/media being sanitized, the name of the individual requesting sanitization, and the name of the person responsible for the sanitization A template for the form is attached at the end of this policy, *[organization]* Record of IT Equipment Sanitization. Its lower portion contains the elements required by the Division of Surplus Property. A completed record (including the top section) must be maintained in a central location designated by the agency. This information must be maintained as outlined by the *[organization department]* record retention schedule.

The *[organization]* requires a copy of the proof of sanitization accompany all hard drives earmarked for disposal. This proof may be a copy of the entire "Record of IT Equipment Sanitization" or of the lower portion of the form. In instances where attaching the paper form to the equipment is a poor method, a label containing the required information may be affixed to the hard drive(s), equipment case (e.g., CPU box) or appropriate surface. The label must contain the name and signature of the person performing the sanitization, equipment identification and sanitization method used as provided in the lower portion of the "Record of IT Equipment Sanitization."

For disposition other than to the *[department]*, it is highly recommended that an adhesive label be affixed to the equipment case to record the sanitization process before transfer. Questions remain about leased equipment and equipment maintained through a service agreement. Agencies must assess liability on a case by case review.

1.4. **Recommended DoD Sanitization Procedures**

Media	**Procedure(s)**
Magnetic Tape	
Type I*	a, b, or m
Type II**	b or m
Type III***	m
Magnetic Disk	
Bernoullis	m
Floppies	m
Non-Removable Rigid Disk	a, b, d, or m

Media	**Procedure(s)**
Magnetic Tape	
Removable Rigid Disk	a, b, d, or m
Optical Disk	
Read Many, Write Many	m
Read Only	m, n
Write Once, Read Many (WORM)	m, n
Memory	
Dynamic Random Access Memory (DRAM)	c, g, or m
Electronically Alterable PROM (EAPROM)	j or m
Electronically Erasable PROM (EEPROM)	h or m
Erasable Programmable ROM (EPROM)	l, then c or m
Flash EPROM (FEPROM)	c, then I or m
Programmable ROM (PROM)	m
Magnetic Bubble Memory	a, b, c, or m
Magnetic Core Memory	a, b, e, or m
Magnetic Plated Wire	c and f, or m
Magnetic Resistive Memory	m
Nonvolatile RAM (NOVRAM)	c, g, or m
Read Only Memory (ROM)	m
Static Random Access Memory (SRAM)	c and f, g, or m

Sanitization Procedure Key

a. Degauss with a Type I degausser.

b. Degauss with a Type II degausser.

c. Overwrite all addressable locations with a single character.

d. Overwrite all addressable locations with a character, its complement, then a random character and verify.

THIS METHOD IS NOT APPROVED FOR SANITIZING MEDIA THAT CONTAINS EXTREMELY CONFIDENTIAL OR SENSITIVE INFORMATION.

e. Overwrite all addressable locations with a character, its complement, and then a random character.

f. Each overwrite must reside in memory for a period longer than the classified data resided.

g. Remove all power to include battery power.

h. Overwrite all locations with a random pattern, all locations with binary zeros, all locations with binary ones.

i. Perform a full chip erase as per manufacturer's data sheets.

j. Perform i. above, then c. above, three times.

k. Perform an ultraviolet erase according to manufacturer's recommendation.

l. Perform k above, but increase time by a factor of three.

m. Destroy—disintegrate, incinerate, pulverize, shred, or melt.

n. Destruction required only if classified information is contained.

This information was extracted from the US Department of Defense 5220.22-M Clearing and Sanitization Matrix.

*Type 1 magnetic tape includes all tapes with a coercivity factor (amount of electrical force required to reduce the recorded magnetic strength to zero) not exceeding 350 oersteds.

**Type 2 magnetic tape includes all tapes with a coercivity factor between 350 and 750 oersteds.

***Type 3 magnetic tape commonly referred to as high-energy tape (4 or 8mm tape are examples), includes all tapes with a coercivity factor between 750 and 1700.

[*Organization*] Record of IT Equipment Sanitization

Date Requested: ________

Department:____

Person Submitting Request: ________________________

Equipment Serial Number: __________________________

Equipment Inventory Number: ____________________
Equipment Manufacturer/Model:____________________

Equipment/Media Type:

☐ Server
☐ Workstation: Assigned to (name of user): __________
☐ Magnetic Tape (Type I, II or III)
☐ Magnetic Disk (Bernoulli, floppy, non-removable rigid disk, removable rigid disk)
☐ Optical Disk (read many-write many, read only, write once-ready many (WORM)
☐ Memory (DRAM, PROM, EAPROM, EPROM, FEPROM, ROM, SRAM etc.)
☐ Cathode Ray Tube (CRT)
☐ Printer
☐ Other (describe) ____________________

Disposition:

☐ Transfer ☐ Surplus ☐ Donation ☐ Repair/maintenance
☐ Return to Contractor ☐ Other (explain)__________

Decommissioning provisions:

☐ Equipment/media has been kept in continuous physical protection until sanitization
☐ Information requiring archiving as public records identified and preserved
☐ Temporary backups made (e.g., for equipment scheduled for repair)
☐ OEM operating system and other software available for reload for repurposed equipment
☐ MARS Fixed Asset documents completed
☐ Agency asset management procedures completed
☐ ________ form completed (Finance & Administration: Declared Surplus)
☐ Compliant with procedures for disposal of hazardous waste if destroyed
☐ Other (describe) ____________________

***General* description of data residing on equipment/ media to be sanitized:**

____

____

____

Department: ________________
Person Performing Sanitization: ________________
Title: _______ Date Completed: _______
Equip. Inventory #: _______ Equip. Serial #: _______
Signature: _______________________

Sanitization Method Used:

- ☐ DoD-compliant Overwrite (list software used):______
- ☐ Type I Degausser
- ☐ Type II Degausser
- ☐ Full Chip Erase
- ☐ Ultraviolet Erase
- ☐ Physical Destruction (disintegrate, incinerate, pulverize, shred, melt)
- ☐ Other (describe) ______________________________

COMMENT

This form is adapted from one used by the Commonwealth of Kentucky.

Chapter 7

Litigation Holds

I. GUIDELINES

II. CHECKLISTS

III. FORMS

Research References

Treatises and Practice Aids

eDiscovery & Digital Evidence §§ 8:9, 8:10

Grenig and Kinsler, Federal Civil Discovery and Disclosure §§ 13.1 to 13.6 (2d ed.)

Trial Strategy

Recovery and Reconstruction of Electronic Mail as Evidence, 41 Am. Jur Proof of Facts 3d 1

Computer Technology in Civil Litigation, 71 Am. Jur Trials 111

Law Reviews and Other Periodicals

Allman, Managing Preservation Obligations after the 2006 Federal E-Discovery Amendments, 13 Rich. J.L. & Tech. 9 (2007)

Additional References

Ball, When Out-of-Box Means Out-of-Luck, LegalTechnology, May 29, 2008, at http://www.la.com/tech

Ball, The Perfect Preservation Letter, Trial, April 2007

Isaza, Legal Holds & Spoliation: Identifying a Checklist Considerations that Trigger the Duty to Preserve, http://www.armaed.foundation.org

Isaza, Braking for Legal Holds: How to Read the Signals, Information Mgt. J., Jan./Feb. 2008, at 36

Isaza, Determining the Scope of Legal Holds: Waypoints for Navigating the Road Ahead, Information Mgt. J. March/Apr 2008, at 34

Stio & Quigley, Getting a Grip on the Litigation Hold, e-Discovery, 2007, at 20

ABA Discovery Standards, http://www.abanet.org/litigation/discoverystandards/2005civildiscoverystandards.pdf

ARMA, http://www.arma.org

eDirect Impact, Inc., http://www.edirectimpact.com
Electronic Discovery Reference Model Project, http://www.edrm.net
EMC Corp., http://www.emc.com
The Sedona Conference, http://www.thesedonaconference.org

KeyCite®: Cases and other legal materials listed in KeyCite Scope can be researched through the KeyCite service on Westlaw®. Use KeyCite to check citations for form, parallel references, prior and later history, and comprehensive citator information, including citations to other decisions and secondary materials.

I. GUIDELINES

§ 7:1 Generally

One of the most common record-preservation mistakes is failing to cease document destruction procedures upon notice of suit or the likelihood of suit or investigation.[1] The destruction of electronically stored information during the routine implementation of a document retention policy in the usual course of business is normally acceptable. Once an organization reasonably anticipates litigation, it must suspend its routine document retention/destruction policy and put in place a "litigation hold."[2] This duty applies to both plaintiffs and defendants.

A litigation hold involves taking protective steps to protect electronically stored information for potential

[Section 7:1]

[1]See Broccoli v. Echostar Communications Corp., 229 F.R.D. 506, 62 Fed. R. Serv. 3d 817 (D. Md. 2005) (defendant had a duty to preserve employment and termination documents when its management learned of plaintiff's potential Title VII claim). See Sedona Principle 1 ("Electronically stored information is potentially discoverable under Fed. R. Civ. P. 34 or its state equivalents. Organizations must properly preserve electronically stored information that can reasonably be anticipated to be relevant to litigation.").

[2]Zubulake v. UBS Warburg LLC, 220 F.R.D. 212, 218, 92 Fair Empl. Prac. Cas. (BNA) 1539 (S.D. N.Y. 2003). See In re eBay Seller Antitrust Litigation, 2007 WL 2852364 (N.D. Cal. 2007) (litigation hold notices may be protected by attorney-client privilege and work product doctrine, but identities of employees receiving notices are not protected).

discovery or evidentiary purposes. A litigation hold can take many forms, from evidentiary copies prepared by a forensic professional to simply taking custody of a laptop or backup tapes.[3] It is important to preserve the integrity of the contents of electronically stored information. This includes formatting of the document, its metadata, and, where applicable, its revision history.

In implementing a litigation hold, counsel must evaluate the extent to which retention policies must be suspended because of the impending litigation. The best way to protect an organization is to be sure to halt immediately all electronically stored information handling policies that result in the recycling of backups or other electronically stored information destruction as soon as litigation is reasonably foreseeable. Software may assist in creating a cost effective litigation hold. However, the software can be very expensive.

§ 7:2 Foreseeablity of litigation

The duty to preserve potentially stored information and paper documents arise where litigation is "reasonably anticipated." Once this occurs, there is a duty to put in place a litigation hold to ensure the preservation of relevant documents.[1] Once the duty to preserve arises, the de-

---

[3]See Consolidated Aluminum Corp. v. Alcoa, Inc., 244 F.R.D. 335 (M.D. La. 2006) (as general rule, party's duty to place a litigation hold on evidence does not apply to inaccessible backup tapes for electronic evidence—those typically maintained solely for purpose of disaster recovery, which may continue to be recycled on the schedule set forth in party's policy, but if backup tapes are accessible (actively used for information retrieval), then such tapes would likely be subject to litigation hold).

[Section 7:2]

[1]See Rambus, Inc. v. Infineon Technologies AG, 222 F.R.D. 280, 288 (E.D. Va. 2004) (enforcing litigation hold by granting motion to compel production of documents and testimony relating to plaintiff's document retention, collection, and production).

struction of the information raises a presumption that disclosure of the materials would be damaging.[2]

The U.S. District Court for the Southern District of New York in *Zubulake v. UBS Warburg LLC*,[3] has described the obligation of a party who anticipates litigation to preserve electronically stored information evidence in the following terms:

> A party or anticipated party must retain all relevant documents (but not multiple identical copies) in existence at the time the duty to preserve attaches, and any relevant documents created thereafter. In recognition of the fact that there are many ways to manage electronic data, litigants are free to choose how this task is accomplished. For example, a litigant could choose to retain all then-existing backup tapes for the relevant personnel (if such tapes store data by individual or the contents can be identified in good faith and through reasonable effort), and to catalog any later-created documents in a separate electronic file. That, along with a mirror-image of the computer system taken at the time the duty to preserve attaches (to preserve documents in the state they existed at that time), creates a complete set of relevant documents. Presumably there are a multitude of other ways to achieve the same result.
>
> The scope of a party's preservation obligation can be described as follows: Once a party reasonably anticipates litigation, it must suspend its routine document retention/destruction policy and put in place a "litigation hold" to ensure the preservation of relevant documents. As a general rule, that litigation hold does not apply to inaccessible backup tapes (e.g., those typically maintained solely for the purpose of disaster recovery), which may continue to be recycled on the schedule set forth in the company's policy. On the other hand, if backup tapes are accessible (i.e., actively used for information retrieval), then such tapes *would* likely be subject to the litigation hold.

---

[2]See Arista Records, Inc. v. Sakfield Holding Co. S.L., 314 F. Supp. 2d 27, 34, 71 U.S.P.Q.2d 1035 (D.D.C. 2004) (defendant's destruction of electronically stored information precluded defendant from attacking plaintiff's analysis of existing electronic information and resulted in denial of defendant's motion to dismiss on grounds of lack of jurisdiction).

[3]Zubulake v. UBS Warburg LLC, 220 F.R.D. 212, 218, 92 Fair Empl. Prac. Cas. (BNA) 1539 (S.D. N.Y. 2003).

§ 7:3 Initial considerations

The crucial goal of a litigation hold is to prevent any alteration of the electronically stored information. As soon as the attorney knows that certain electronically stored information may be responsive to a discovery demand, the attorney should ensure that the information is properly preserved as soon as possible. Electronically stored information is volatile—easily deleted, modified, copied, or lost. The sooner the lawyer has it properly protected, the better.

Counsel faces a number of important considerations when it comes to deciding what electronically stored information to store and how. In deciding what electronically stored information to preserve, counsel should carefully research the subject. Counsel should not rely on counsel's own understanding of what constitutes electronically stored information or how it can be preserved. Counsel does not want to be in the position of becoming a witness if and when the question of electronically stored information preservation becomes an issue in litigation.

Most counsel are not in a position to determine:

- What metadata is and how it ought to be preserved, if at all.
- What the distinction is between backup and disaster tape systems.
- What backup or data storage sequences should be suspended.
- What steps should be taken to "image" hard drives.
- What steps should be taken to segregate business e-mail from personal e-mail or otherwise protect employee privacy or trade secret privileges.
- What must be done to distinguish between unique and duplicate electronically stored information.
- What steps should be taken to preserve web pages, intranet systems, or ASP data depositories.

§ 7:4 Scope of duty to preserve

An organization must retain all relevant documents (but

not multiple identical copies) in existence at the time the duty to preserve attaches, and any relevant documents created thereafter.[1] Organizations are free to choose how this task is accomplished.[2] The duty to preserve extends to those employees likely to have relevant information (the "key players" in the litigation).[3] Whether the party is required to preserve unsearched sources of potentially responsive information it believes are not reasonably accessible depends on the circumstances of each case.[4]

Communication between parties to a dispute can be a helpful in determining the scope of a duty to preserve electronically stored information. Rule 26(f) of the Federal Rules of Civil Procedure places considerable importance on the duty to confer. Rule 26(f) is intended to have the parties consider the nature and basis of their claims and defenses.

This may be helpful in determining the duty to preserve. For example, if a plaintiff in a product liability suit has already decided it will not be pursuing a defective design

---

[Section 7:4]

[1]Zubulake v. UBS Warburg LLC, 220 F.R.D. 212, 218, 92 Fair Empl. Prac. Cas. (BNA) 1539 (S.D. N.Y. 2003). See Sedona Principle 5 ("The obligation to preserve electronically stored information requires reasonable and good faith efforts to retain information that may be relevant to pending or threatened litigation. However, it is unreasonable to expect parties to take every conceivable step to preserve all potentially relevant electronically stored information.").

[2]Zubulake v. UBS Warburg LLC, 220 F.R.D. 212, 218, 92 Fair Empl. Prac. Cas. (BNA) 1539 (S.D. N.Y. 2003). See Sedona Principle 6 ("Responding parties are best situated to evaluate the procedures, methodologies, and technologies appropriate for preserving and producing their own electronically stored information.").

[3]See Consolidated Aluminum Corp. v. Alcoa, Inc., 244 F.R.D. 335 (M.D. La. 2006). See, also, In re NTL, Inc. Securities Litigation, 244 F.R.D. 179, 68, 68 Fed. R. Serv. 3d 1145 (S.D. N.Y. 2007), order aff'd, 2007 WL 1518632 (S.D. N.Y. 2007) (sanctions imposed for destruction of evidence including e-mails of approximately 44 of defendants' key players).

[4]Cf. Cache La Poudre Feeds, LLC v. Land O'Lakes, Inc., 244 F.R.D. 614, 68 Fed. R. Serv. 3d 1181 (D. Colo. 2007) ($5,000 sanction for defendants' failure to preserve hard drives of departed employees).

strategy, but will instead pursue a different strategy, the plaintiff might agree that certain electronically stored information need not be preserved, even though the legal standards might typically suggest it should be. Of course, it is ultimately the court that can approve or reject any proposed discovery plan.

Not all relevant electronically stored information will be on the organization's systems. Responsive electronically stored information may be in the possession of contractors, agents, vendors, clients, lawyers, accountants, consultants, experts, outside directors, and former employees. Nonparties over whom the organization has control or influence must be factored into the litigation hold.[5]

§ 7:5 Preservation plans

Every organization should adopt a formal, written records management program, including implementation protocols. The program must include an adequate litigation hold provision. In addition, it must not have been instituted or followed in bad faith. Bad faith may include suddenly following the destruction schedule to limit damaging evidence available to potential litigation adversaries.[1]

A written preservation plan focuses on preserving electronically stored information once litigation is

---

[5]Cf. John B. v. Goetz, Medicare & Medicaid 302216, 2007 WL 3012808 (M.D. Tenn. 2007), on reconsideration in part, 2007 WL 4014015 (M.D. Tenn. 2007), mandamus granted, order vacated in part, 531 F.3d 448 (6th Cir. 2008) (finding that records of contractors were in the possession custody and control of defendants, that contractors were agents of defendants, and that contractors' contracts with defendants required contractors to make their responsive records available, court ordered defendants to obtain information from contractors and to produce that information).

[Section 7:5]

[1]Rambus, Inc. v. Infineon Technologies AG, 222 F.R.D. 280, 288–89 (E.D. Va. 2004) (compelling production of documents and testimony relating to plaintiff's records management program).

foreseeable. The success of a preservation plan depends to a very large degree on an intimate knowledge on the part of counsel of the administrative controls and architecture of the client's computer system. For most attorneys, such knowledge can only be acquired by retaining technical assistance. This is especially important when it comes to devising workable preservation plans. Technical assistance is important for another reason. It is important to remember that clients, or their agents, may have reasons to be less than candid with their counsel, whether inside or outside of an organization.

Typically preservation should focus on preserving media—hard drives, floppy disks, and backup tapes, for example—rather than particular files, folders, or other forms of data. Preserving media, as opposed to preserving just the electronically stored information that appears responsive or interesting initially, preserves not only the potentially responsive data, but also files and other data that could become important as discovery progresses. Preserving media also preserves other information, such as metadata or deleted material, that could be later used to corroborate or authenticate the electronically stored information that is produced.

Counsel should give special consideration to archive media, such as backup systems. Frequently, system administrators will only maintain a limited quantity of backup media, and then reuse them on a scheduled cycle—known as tape rotation. Counsel should ensure that all relevant backup media are pulled out of service and stored in a safe place, preferably in the custody of someone who can later establish a chain of custody for authentication purposes.

§ 7:6 Preservation orders

In appropriate cases, a party may seek a preservation order from the court. Because preservation orders are burdensome and expensive, in the absence of a clear need preservation orders should not be entered without a particularized showing of a need.[1]

§ 7:7 Preservation letters—Generally

The preservation letter is a very important tool. At a minimum, it places the other party on notice with respect to its duties to avoid spoliation. It also serves as an excellent basis for seeking sanctions, if it is later discovered that spoliation did in fact occur.

A preservation letter is not a discovery request; it is simply a request that the other party preserve the party's electronically stored information so that it is not deleted or altered through intentional misconduct or the normal processes associated with the deletion of computer files due to the ongoing business of a party. A party can disregard the request to preserve, but once the request has formally been made and evidence disappears, a preservation letter may place the discovering party in a superior position to seek sanctions or other relief.

§ 7:8 Preservation letters—Timing

A preservation letter should be sent to the other party or the other party's attorney at the earliest possible moment, describing the electronically stored information to be preserved, and requesting a meeting to construct a mutually acceptable search and production protocol. A preservation letter should be sent before, or at the same time, as the commencement of litigation and well before any voluntary disclosures by a party under Rule 26 of the

---

[Section 7:6]

[1]Valdez v. Town of Brookhaven, 2007 WL 1988792 (E.D. N.Y. 2007); Treppel v. Biovail Corp., 233 F.R.D. 363 (S.D. N.Y. 2006).

Federal Rules of Civil Procedure, and before any discovery has occurred.[1]

§ 7:9 Preservation letters—Contents

The actual tenor and content of a preservation letter is to some extent a matter of supposition. However, the preservation letter does not have to be a matter of guesswork either. Basic investigative work should uncover appropriate points to include in a preservation letter. For example, much can be inferred about the nature of possible electronically stored information in the possession of a party and its location from the nature of the parties' relationship, the subject matter of the dispute, the party's government filings, and a party's own Web site.

At a minimum, a letter should begin with a general statement that the discovering party expects the party to preserve electronically stored information evidence that may be relevant to the issues in a case, or may lead to the discovery of such evidence. The preservation letter should include a request that the other party suspend its regular document retention policy pending discovery. The preservation letter should identify all possible locations where such evidence might conceivably reside.

The letter should inform the opposing party that a mere file backup of the hard drive is not adequate preservation. The party must be instructed to image hard drives in bit-stream copies, where all areas, used and unused, of the hard drive are copied. If a file is deleted before a backup is made, the deleted file will not be copied unless it is a bit-stream copy. The letter should also request that deleted files that are reasonably recoverable be immediately undeleted.

§ 7:10 Preservation letters—Consequences

Writing a preservation letter is not an idle gesture. A

[Section 7:8]

[1]See Grenig and Kinsler, Federal Civil Discovery and Disclosure §§ 1.20 to 1.25 (2d ed.).

party has the duty to protect and preserve evidence once it is on notice that it must do so. Courts have held that a party may be under a duty to prevent spoliation even if litigation is only reasonably anticipated. Serious sanctions may be imposed for failure to preserve.

§ 7:11 Consequences of preservation

Preservation does not mean that counsel must later agree to produce evidence. By preserving electronically stored information, counsel is only assuring that the electronically stored information will be available if the information is later determined to be relevant or discoverable.

§ 7:12 Consequences of failure to preserve

If it is later determined that counsel should have preserved electronically stored information but did not, counsel could face charges of complicity in evidence spoliation subjecting counsel and the client to serious penalties.[1]

§ 7:13 Implementing a litigation hold—Generally

A litigation hold involves eight steps:

- Identifying
- Preserving
- Collecting
- Processing
- Reviewing
- Analyzing
- Producing
- Presenting

An organization and its counsel must take all reason-

[Section 7:12]

[1]See Sedona Principle 7 ("The requesting party has the burden on a motion to compel to show that the responding party's steps to preserve and produce relevant electronically stored information were inadequate.").

able steps to locate and preserve all relevant electronically stored information and hardcopy information.[1] Outside counsel and in-house counsel are responsible for coordinating and overseeing the preservation and production process by:

- Instituting immediately, and periodically reissuing, a litigation hold on deletion or destruction of information
- Communicating immediately and directly with all key players
- Safeguarding all pertinent electronic archival and backup media[2]

Electronically stored information involves e-mail, file systems, and documents. Each type of information requires different review and production strategies.

§ 7:14 Implementing a litigation hold—Identifying

Identification involves determining the scope, breadth, and depth of electronically stored information that may be sought during discovery. The identification process should take into consideration any claims and defenses, preservation demands, disclosure requirements, and discovery demands. In identifying electronically stored information that might be pursued during discovery, it is helpful to start from a larger pool of potentially discoverable electronically stored information and then assess how much should be preserved and collected.

The organization and its counsel must determine if the current electronically stored environment is susceptible to a cost-efficient harvesting of information. There must be

---

[Section 7:13]

[1]See Sedona Principle 6 ("Responding parties are best situated to evaluate the procedures, methodologies, and technologies appropriate for preserving and producing their own electronically stored information.").

[2]Zubulake v. UBS Warburg LLC, 229 F.R.D. 422, 432–35, 94 Fair Empl. Prac. Cas. (BNA) 1, 85 Empl. Prac. Dec. (CCH) P 41728 (S.D. N.Y. 2004)

an analysis of where the content resides and their inclusion of responsive electronically stored information. In addition, counsel should determine whether the client organization has systems in place to identify electronically stored information that is potentially relevant.

Counsel can guide the organization to avoid a costly scenario of casting too big a net in a litigation hold. If organizations are not certain exactly where electronically stored information resides, the net may become large and hamper other natural courses that electronically stored information goes through as part of the document destruction or retention policy.

§ 7:15 Implementing a litigation hold—Preserving

If an organization can identify where particular employee documents are stored on electronic media, then the media storing the documents of "key players" to the existing or threatened litigation should be preserved if the information contained on the media is not otherwise available.[1]

After identifying key people, it is important to copy their e-mails, their desktop or notebook hard drives, and network folders where they store their files. The more important the person, the more thorough the preservation effort.

§ 7:16 Implementing a litigation hold—Collecting

It is essential to determine which collected materials are likely to be the most important, as well as which materials can be processed most expeditiously. In determining what to collect, it is helpful to evaluate the magnitude of the risk in the case. It may not make sense to spend more on collection than the case is worth.

[Section 7:15]

[1]Zubulake v. UBS Warburg LLC, 220 F.R.D. 212, 218, 92 Fair Empl. Prac. Cas. (BNA) 1539 (S.D. N.Y. 2003).

§ 7:17 Implementing a litigation hold—Processing

The overall set of data can be reduced by setting aside duplicate files. Consideration should also be given to setting aside files that it appears will not be relevant because of such factors as type, origin, or date. It can be helpful to convert the electronically stored information to a form that allows a more effective and efficient review.

§ 7:18 Implementing a litigation hold—Reviewing

Reviewing has two components: relevance and privilege. The reviewing process can be the most expensive part of electronic discovery.

§ 7:19 Implementing a litigation hold—Analyzing

Analysis involves the evaluation of a collection of electronic discovery materials to determine relevant summary information, such as key topics of the case, important people, specific vocabulary, and important individual documents. This information can help with early decisions and in improving the productivity of all remaining electronic discovery activities.

§ 7:20 Implementing a litigation hold—Producing

In determining what forms of production to use there are four basic choices:

- Native (for example, producing Excel spreadsheets as.xls files)
- Quasi-native (for example, extracting part of a data base, loading it into another data base, and producing that)
- Quasi-paper (for example, converting e-mail messages to TIFF or PDF formats)
- Paper

A "native data" file is a file in the file format in which it was created, such as Microsoft Word, or WordPerfect. A uniform or standard image format, such as TIFF or PDF, is a file format into which files, including native files, may be converted for review or production.

It may be better for a party to review or produce in native format. In other cases, electronic evidence discovery software may be more appropriate. Frequently, the parties agree to exchange electronically stored information in native format. When the parties cannot agree, the court may order production in native format.

Metadata are hidden data that can only be seen when a digital document is viewed in its native format using the program that originally produced the document. Often even the user of a program may not know it is there unless the user knows how to find it. When a document is created by a particular program (such as MS Word) there is hidden information (metadata) about that document that can only be viewed if the data are opened by that program. While metadata are discoverable, the production files with all associated metadata should be conditioned upon a showing of need or sharing expenses.[1]

Metadata are generally of more significance with respect to database applications, where the metadata are the key to showing the relationships among the data. It is of less importance with respect to word processing applications, where the metadata are not critical to understanding the substance of the document.

§ 7:21 Implementing a litigation hold—Presenting

Consideration must be given to how to present most effectively the electronically stored information at depositions, hearings, and trial. The question of whether paper production is sufficient has been litigated in a number of

---

[Section 7:20]

[1]Manual of Complex Litigation Fourth § 11.446. But see Williams v. Sprint/United Management Co., 230 F.R.D. 640, 96 Fair Empl. Prac. Cas. (BNA) 1775, 62 Fed. R. Serv. 3d 1052, 29 A.L.R.6th 701 (D. Kan. 2005) (absent a timely objection or a stipulation to the contrary, an order to produce in native format presumptively encompasses metadata, even if the request did not specifically refer to metadata).

cases.[1] Whether production must include metadata or whether it can be produced in a uniform image such as TIFF or PDF is also a frequent subject of dispute.

II. CHECKLISTS

§ 7:22 Checklist of facts triggering a litigation hold

- ☐ Written notice
  - ☐ Preservation letter
  - ☐ Service of complaint
  - ☐ Investigation notice
  - ☐ Discovery demands, including subpoenas
  - ☐ Court orders
- ☐ Pre-litigation discussions, demands and agreements
- ☐ Facts or circumstances that would put a reasonable person notice
  - ☐ Reasonably foreseeable litigation or investigation
  - ☐ Related lawsuits or investigations
  - ☐ Stated threats to sue
  - ☐ Knowledge of the organization, its agents, servants, and employees

§ 7:23 Checklist of steps in a litigation hold

- ☐ **Identifying**
  - ☐ Claims and defenses
  - ☐ Preservation demands
  - ☐ Disclosure requirements
  - ☐ Discovery demands
- ☐ **Preserving**
  - ☐ Key players

[Section 7:21]

[1]See, e.g., In re Honeywell Intern., Inc. Securities Litigation, 230 F.R.D. 293, 296–97 (S.D. N.Y. 2003) (electronic production ordered where third-party accounting firm had produced hard copies of work papers).

- ☐ Key documents
- ☐ **Collecting**
  - ☐ Importance of collected materials
  - ☐ Ease of processing
- ☐ **Processing**
  - ☐ Duplicate files
  - ☐ Irrelevant files?
- ☐ **Reviewing**
  - ☐ Relevance
  - ☐ Privilege
- ☐ **Analyzing**
  - ☐ Relevant summary information
    - ☐ Key topics
    - ☐ Important people
    - ☐ Vocabulary
    - ☐ Individual documents
- ☐ **Producing**
  - ☐ What forms of production are most sensible?
    - ☐ Native?
    - ☐ Quasi-native?
    - ☐ Quasi paper?
    - ☐ Paper?
- ☐ **Presenting**
  - ☐ How can electronically stored information be presented most effectively?

§ 7:24 Checklist of litigation hold actions

- ☐ Timely suspend document retention policies.
- ☐ Comply with preservation letters.
- ☐ Turn off digital devices only by unplugging.
- ☐ Request that information be preserved in native format whenever possible to preserve metadata.
- ☐ Quarantine digital media.
- ☐ Create bit-stream backups (imaging) of digital media.
- ☐ Avoid booting up suspect machines.
- ☐ Avoid redeploying machines unless the data they

contain are irrelevant to imminent or ongoing litigation.

- ☐ Forbid forensically naive network administrators or other members of the information technology department from checking out or otherwise investigating relevant devices.

Comment

This checklist is adapted from Van Buskirk, *Practical Strategies for Digital Discovery*, The Brief, Spring 2003, at 50, 54.

§ 7:25 Checklist for preservation letter

- ☐ A statement of the name, venue and basic elements of the litigation or investigation, with sufficient specificity to provide the non-party recipient an adequate understanding of its subject matter, scope, and relevant time period.
- ☐ A description of the legal or business relationship between the requesting party and the recipient creating the need for the recipient to take steps to preserve relevant material. If the relationship is such that the needed relevant material in the recipient's custody is, in reality, owned or within the control of the requesting party, this description should state this. To the extent known by the requesting party, this relationship description should include identification of the names, titles and locations of those persons within the non-party recipient's organization who are most likely to have been involved with the needed relevant material.
- ☐ A copy of or reference to any contract or agreement in effect during the relevant time period.
- ☐ Identification of the range of different types of material to be preserved, such as:
  - ☐ Paper and electronic documents
  - ☐ Voicemail
  - ☐ E-mail
  - ☐ Databases and other data

- ☐ Audio Files
- ☐ Video Files
- ☐ Photographs or image files
- ☐ Physical samples
- ☐ Other

☐ A statement that the recipient should suspend its normal retention schedule and disposition policies for all relevant material until further written notice, and that the recipient should not delete or destroy any relevant material, regardless of routine or automated practices in effect prior to the receipt of the Preservation Notice.

☐ A request that the recipient distribute the Preservation Notice to all persons within their organization, or within the control of their organization, who are known or suspected to have relevant material in their possession, custody or control.

☐ A request that the recipient track and obtain acknowledgment from all persons within their organization, or within the control of their organization, to whom the Preservation Notice was distributed, that such persons received and understood the Preservation Notice, and that such persons identify and categorize any relevant material within their possession, custody or control. Such request should also include an inquiry as to whether such persons know of others within the organization who may have relevant material, who should also receive a copy of the Preservation Notice.

☐ A request that the recipient direct any questions about the subject matter or scope of the Preservation Notice to a designated legal representative of the requesting party.

☐ A request that the recipient, and any of its employees or agents having possession, custody or control of relevant material, hold such material in suspense and safe from modification or destruction, until they are contacted by a legal representative of their own organization (or, of the requesting party's organization, if appropriate) to provide guidance on how such relevant material will be collected.

☐ A request that the recipient periodically reissue and refresh the Preservation Notice distributed to persons within their organization, or within the control of their organization, to remind persons having relevant material that the Preservation Notice is still in effect, until they are advised to the contrary.

☐ Written acknowledgement of receipt of notice; confirmation of intent to comply with preservation request.

§ 7:26 Checklist for preservation of e-mails upon dismissal of employee

☐ Determine how the dismissed employee's e-mail account will be handled. The messages could be stored on a secure folder on the organization's network drive, stored on a CD-ROM, etc.)

☐ Determine who will review the messages? This should be someone in the organization familiar with the records that could be in the employee's e-mail account, and who has the authority to make decisions about deleting records.

☐ Determine how long messages should be retained, taking into account such matters as the periods for appealing unemployment compensation denials, limitation periods for the employee's filing discrimination claims, and the statute of limitations for trade secret claims. Once a case has been filed, messages must be retained for the duration of any legal investigation, audit, lawsuit or administrative hearing. If no appeal is made in the appropriate time period, then the non-record messages may be deleted.

III. FORMS

§ 7:27 Preservation letter—To party

[date]

[name]
[address]

Subject: Preservation of electronically stored information

Please preserve all electronically stored information relating to *[describe]*, including hidden system files or metadata, presently located on or contained in a free standing computer or laptop, or on any part of a server, CPU or digital device that may contain data storage capabilities including, but not limited to hard disk drives, optical disk drives, removable media, such as floppy disk drives, CD-ROM and DVD drives, Zip drives, Jaz drives, Maxtor drives or snap drives, data processing cards, computer magnetic tapes, backup tapes, drum and disk storage devices or any other similar electronic storage media or system of whatever name or description.

Please also preserve all digital images relating to *[describe]* that may be stored on any type of hardware used to store or manipulate electronic images, including but not limited to microfilm, microfiche and their repositories and readers, or design or engineering computer systems and regardless of any digital image's format, including.jpg, .bmp, or some other advanced or proprietary form of digital image format, such as CAD layered drawings.

Please preserve all existing sources of electronically stored information relating to *[describe]* that may not presently be in use by your company or may have been deleted from your active systems, whether the source is a backup tape or disk, some other data retention system or some form of disaster recovery system.

Including the imaging of hard drives, please take all reasonable steps to preserve electronically stored information relating to *[describe]* that may have been deleted from your active files and which may not be readily recoverable from a backup medium, such as metadata.

Please also preserve electronically stored information relating to *[describe]* that is subject to your control regardless of where else it may be located on-site at your main offices, within the network infrastructure of your company or on or in one of your other computer support systems including those at your subsidiaries, predecessors, successors, assigns, joint venturers, partners, parents, agents or affiliates (in this country or throughout the world), including but not limited to the following locations:

a. Your LAN and WAN network systems, regardless of methods of connectivity (e.g., by T1, T3, or optical lines), domains, including PDCs, network OS (such as Novell, Microsoft, UNIX, Citrix, or some other similar type) or protocols, or your backup and disaster recovery hardware and media, regardless of the physical location of those electronic storage systems.
b. Your e-mail servers and any repository of your e-mail (including within the inbox, sent box, deleted box or some similar file of the computers of employees or management), or in any backup form whatsoever, regardless of whether you use Microsoft Exchange, Outlook, Outlook Express, Lotus Notes or some combination of e-mail management software or some alternative commercial or proprietary e-mail management software.
c. Your IS administrative offices, including backup and disaster recovery restoration repositories, data retention repositories, purge repositories, training repositories, or libraries of hardcopy materials of any description (regardless of where located) and online training and operation manuals that have been scanned to disk.
d. Your offsite technical and service bureau support systems, including but not limited to ASP (application service provider) support, scanning or data conversion support, offsite data storage or archive support.
e. Your web hosting and administration services, including intranet and extranet sites, regardless of whether they are now publicly posted or exist in English or some other language.

Please consider yourself under a continuing obligation to preserve electronically stored information relating to *[describe]* that may come into existence after the date of this letter, or that may exist now or in the future but of which you have no current knowledge.

Very truly yours,

[signature, etc.]

§ 7:28 Preservation letter—To client

[date]

[name 1]
[address]

Subject: *[Case Name]*
Data Preservation

Dear *[name 1]*:

Your assistance and cooperation are required with respect to preserving information in this case, including electronically stored information. Electronically stored information is an important and irreplaceable source of discovery and evidence.

This lawsuit requires that all employees preserve all information from *[organization's]* computer systems, removable electronic media, and other locations relating to *[describe]*. This includes, but is not limited to, e-mail and other electronic communication, word processing documents, spreadsheets, databases, calendars, telephone logs, contact manager information, Internet usage files, and network access information.

You must take every reasonable step to preserve this information until further notice from *[name 2]*. Failure to do so could result in extreme penalties against *[organization]* including dismissal of the case.

If you have any questions or need further information, please contact *[name 3]* at *[telephone number]*.

Sincerely,

[signature, etc.]

§ 7:29 Preservation letter—To client—Another form

[date]

[name 1]
[address]

Subject: *[Case Name]*
Preservation of Electronically Stored Information

Dear *[name 1]*:

The purpose of this letter is to inform you that the *[organization]* is involved in a litigation proceeding known as *[case name, case no., jurisdiction]* (the Case). As a result, *[organization]* may be required to produce certain documents, including electronically stored information, relating to the case. In an effort to ensure that *[organization]* is taking all reasonable steps to preserve and safeguard evidence relating to the case, the documents in the categories listed below, whether in hard copy or electronic form, cannot be altered, destroyed or discarded for any reason.

Documents subject to this requirement may be in paper or electronic form, including e-mails, instant text messages, memorandums, and all correspondence, whether in draft or final form. Documents also refer to handwritten and typewritten documents and nonidentical copies of the same documents.

Your failure to retain these documents or ignore the directive of this memorandum can result in severe consequences, including various forms of punishment imposed by a court of law.

Documents Covered:

Until further notice, please search for and then maintain any documents relating to the following topics:

Any and all documents relating to the *[describe]*, including, without limitation: *[list all potentially relevant documents]*

Any and all communications relating to, or stemming from, the *[describe]*.

Instructions:

Please instruct all personnel within the *[organization]* not to alter, destroy, discard, interfile, annotate, remove, rearrange or modify any documents identified for production in the case. Please also inform all appropriate personnel who are responsible for handling, or who have access to, the documents of the instructions conveyed in this letter. Additionally, please instruct such personnel that they must segregate and label all documents that may be produced in the *[describe]*.

Questions:

Any questions or concerns about this memorandum should be directed to *[name]* at *[telephone number]*. Thank you for your cooperation in this matter.

Very truly yours,

[signature, etc.]

§ 7:30 Preservation letter—To nonparty

[date]

[name 1]
[address]

Subject: *[Case Name]*
Data Preservation

Dear *[name 1]*:

Your assistance and cooperation are required with respect to preserving *[organization]* information in this case, including electronically stored information. Electronically stored information is an important and irreplaceable source of discovery and evidence.

You are requested to preserve all information from *[organization's]* computer systems, removable electronic media, and other locations relating to *[describe]*. This includes, but is not limited to, e-mail and other electronic communication, word processing documents, spreadsheets, databases, calendars, telephone logs, contact manager information, Internet usage files, and network access information.

You must take every reasonable step to preserve this information until further notice from *[name 2]*. Failure to do so could result in extreme penalties against *[organization]*.

If you have any questions or need further information, please contact *[name 3]* at *[telephone number]*.

Sincerely,

[signature, etc.]

§ 7:31 Interim preservation order

[Caption]

Interim Order Regarding Preservation

1. Order to Meet and Confer

To further the just, speedy, and economical management of discovery, the parties are ORDERED to confer as soon as practicable, no later than 30 days after the date of this order, to develop a plan for the preservation of documents, data, and tangible things reasonably anticipated to be subject to discovery in this action. The parties may conduct this conference as part of the discovery conference if it is scheduled to take place within 30 days of the date of this order. The resulting preservation plan may be submitted to this Court as a proposed order under *[rule]*.

2. Subjects for Consideration

The parties should attempt to reach agreement on all issues regarding the preservation of documents, data, and tangible things. These issues include, but are not necessarily limited to:

(a) the extent of the preservation obligation, identifying the types of material to be preserved, the subject matter, time frame, the authors and addressees, and key words to be used in identifying responsive materials;

(b) the identification of persons responsible for carrying out preservation obligations on behalf of each party;

(c) the form and method of providing notice of the duty to preserve to persons identified as custodians of documents, data, and tangible things;

(d) mechanisms for monitoring, certifying, or auditing custodian compliance with preservation obligations;

(e) whether preservation will require suspending or modifying any routine business processes or procedures, with special attention to document-management programs and the recycling of computer data storage media;

(f) the methods to preserve any volatile but potentially discoverable material, such as voicemail, active data in databases, or electronic messages;

(g) the anticipated costs of preservation and ways to reduce or share these costs; and

(h) a mechanism to review and modify the preservation obligation as discovery proceeds, eliminating or adding particular categories of documents, data, and tangible things.

3. Duty to Preserve

(a) Until the parties reach agreement on a preservation plan, all parties and their counsel are reminded of their duty to preserve evidence that may be relevant to this action. The duty extends to documents, data, and tangible things in the possession, custody and control of the parties to this action, and any employees, agents, contractors, carriers, bailees, or other nonparties who possess materials reasonably anticipated to be subject to discovery in this action. Counsel is under an obligation to exercise reasonable efforts to identify and notify such nonparties, including employees of corporate or institutional parties.

(b) "Documents, data, and tangible things" is to be interpreted broadly to include writings; records; files; correspondence; reports; memoranda; calendars; diaries; minutes; electronic messages; voicemail; e-mail; telephone message records or logs; computer and network activity logs; hard drives; backup data; removable computer storage media such as tapes, disks, and cards; printouts; document image files; Web pages; databases; spreadsheets; software; books; ledgers; journals; orders; invoices; bills; vouchers; checks; statements; worksheets; summaries; compilations; computations; charts; diagrams; graphic presentations; drawings; films; charts; digital or chemical process photographs; video, phonographic, tape, or digital recordings or transcripts thereof; drafts; jottings; and notes. Information that serves to identify, locate, or link such material, such as file inventories, file folders, indices, and metadata, is also included in this definition.

(c) "Preservation" is to be interpreted broadly to accomplish the goal of maintaining the integrity of all documents, data, and tangible things reasonably anticipated to be subject to discovery under *[rules]* in this action. Preservation includes taking reasonable steps to prevent the partial or full destruction, alteration, testing, deletion, shredding, incineration, wiping, relocation, migration, theft, or mutation of such material, as well as negligent or intentional handling that would make material incomplete or inaccessible.

(d) If the business practices of any party involve the routine destruction, recycling, relocation, or mutation of such materials, the party must, to the extent practicable for the pendency of this order, either

(1) halt such business processes;

(2) sequester or remove such material from the business process; or

(3) arrange for the preservation of complete and accurate duplicates or copies of such material, suitable for later discovery if requested.

(e) Before the conference to develop a preservation plan, a party may apply to the court for further instructions regarding the duty to preserve specific categories of documents, data, or tangible things. A party may seek permission to resume routine business processes relating to the storage or destruction of specific categories of documents, data, or tangible things, upon a showing of undue cost, burden, or overbreadth.

4. Procedure in the Event No Agreement Is Reached

If, after conferring to develop a preservation plan, counsel do not reach agreement on the subjects listed under paragraph 2 of this order or on other material aspects of preservation, the parties are to submit to the court within three days of the conference a statement of the unresolved issues together with each party's proposal for their resolution of the issues. In framing an order regarding the preservation of documents, data, and tangible things, the court will consider those statements as well as any statements made in any applications under paragraph 3(e) of this order.

Entered this date: ________

____

Judge

Comment

The purpose of this order is requiring the parties to confer and develop their own preservation plan. If the court determines such a conference is unnecessary or undesirable, the order may be modified to serve as a stand-alone preservation order.

§ 7:32 Preservation order halting routine destruction

[Caption]

ORDER

[Party] has moved for an order prohibiting the alteration or destruction of evidence during the pendency of this action. *[Party]* has filed papers opposing the motion.

Upon careful review of the papers submitted in support of and in opposition to the motion, the court has determined that (1) no hearing on the motion is necessary; (2) an order requiring the preservation of evidence is appropriate; and (3) an interim order shall forthwith enter requiring the parties to take steps to prevent the alteration or destruction of evidence as follows:

1. Until the issues in these proceedings can be further refined, the court reminds all parties of their duty to preserve evidence that may be relevant to this action. The duty extends to documents, data and tangible things in the possession, custody and control of the parties to this action, and any employees, agents, contractors, carriers, bailees or other nonparties who possess materials reasonably anticipated to be subject to discovery in this action. Counsel are under an obligation to exercise efforts to identify and notify such nonparties, including employees of corporate or institutional parties.

2. "Documents, data and tangible things" is to be interpreted broadly to include writings, records, files, correspondence, reports, memoranda, calendars, diaries, minutes, electronic messages, voicemail, e-mail, telephone message records or logs, computer and network activity logs, hard drives, backup data, removable computer storage media such as tapes, disks and cards, printouts, document image files, web pages, databases, spreadsheets,

software, books, ledgers, journals, orders, invoices, bills, vouchers, checks, statements, worksheets, summaries, compilations, computations, charts, diagrams, graphic presentations, drawings, films, digital or chemical process photographs, video, phonographic, tape or digital recordings or transcripts thereof, drafts, jottings and notes. Information that serves to identify, locate, or link such material, such as file inventories, file folders, indices and metadata, is also included in this definition.

3. "Preservation" is to be interpreted broadly to accomplish the goal of maintaining the integrity of all documents, data and tangible things reasonably anticipated to be subject to discovery under Fed. R. Civ. P. 45 and 56(e) in this action. Preservation includes taking reasonable steps to prevent the partial or full destruction, alteration, testing, deletion, shredding, incineration, wiping, relocation, migration, theft, or mutation of such material, as well as negligent or intentional handling that would make material incomplete or inaccessible.

4. Counsel are directed to inquire of their respective clients if the business practices of any party involve the routine destruction, recycling, relocation, or mutation on such materials and, if so, direct the party, to the extent practicable for the pendency of this order, either to

a. halt such business processes;

b. sequester or remove such material from the business process; or

c. arrange for the preservation of complete and accurate duplicates or copies of such material, suitable for later discovery if requested.

The most senior lawyer or lead trial counsel representing each party shall, not later than *[date]*, submit to the court under seal and pursuant to Fed. R. Civ. P. 11, a statement that the directive in paragraph 4, above, has been carried out.

Entered this date: ____

____

Judge

Comment

This form is adapted from an order in In re National Security Agency Telecommunications Records Litigation, 2007 WL 3306579 (N.D. Cal. 2007).

§ 7:33 Preservation protocol for electronically stored information

[Caption]

Electronically Stored Information Preservation Protocol

[Caption]

1. As used herein, the term "potentially discoverable electronic information" refers to Defendant's and Plaintiff's electronic "documents" that contain or potentially contain information relating to facts at issue in the litigation, where the term "documents" is used as it is defined in Fed. R. Civ. P. 34(a)

2. During the pendency of these actions, the Defendant and the Plaintiff shall securely maintain, to the extent that they currently exist and may contain potentially discoverable electronic information: (1) e-mail backup tapes and (2) network backup tapes (together, the "Backup Tapes") created in the ordinary course of business during the period from [start date] through [stop date]. The Defendant and the Plaintiff shall be obligated to retain only one day's Backup Tapes among all Backup Tapes created in the ordinary course during a given month, provided that such day's Backup Tapes represent a complete backup of the data contained on the subject servers on that day (as opposed to merely an incremental backup of the subject servers). If only incremental backup tapes have been retained for a given month, then all such incremental tapes shall be retained. All Backup Tapes other than those specifically required to be preserved pursuant to this paragraph and paragraph 3 below may be recycled, overwritten, or erased, as the case may be, pursuant to

Defendant's and Plaintiff's otherwise applicable retention schedule.

3. All electronic information or data archived or backed up during the period from *[date]*, as part of a special backup, i.e., a backup made other than in the ordinary course of business by Defendant or Plaintiff, whether due to system upgrade, transition planning, system migration, disaster recovery planning, or any other reason, that potentially contains potentially discoverable electronic information shall be securely retained, to the extent that they currently exist, for the remainder of the litigation.

4. All current or legacy software and hardware necessary to access, manipulate, print, etc., potentially discoverable electronic information that either is "live" or has been archived or backed up shall be securely retained, to the extent that they currently exist, for the remainder of the litigation.

5. Defendants and Plaintiff shall circulate retention notices designed to ensure the preservation of potentially discoverable electronic and other information to those employees potentially possessing such information. Thereafter, Defendant and Plaintiff shall quarterly re-notify their employees of their continuing obligation to preserve such information.

6. Defendant and Plaintiff shall take the following measures to secure and retain, to the extent that it exists, the potentially discoverable electronic information that is on the desktop and laptop hard drives of their respective employees. Either (1) hard drives containing potentially discoverable electronic data shall be retained with all potentially discoverable electronic data contained therein retained intact; or, (2) employees shall be instructed to copy all potentially discoverable electronic information to a secure, backed-up network storage device or backup medium for the remainder of the litigation, making all reasonable efforts to retain all metadata (file creation dates, modification dates, etc.) associated with the potentially discoverable electronic information at issue. The periodic retention notifications disseminated pursuant to paragraph 5 above shall advise employees poten-

tially possessing potentially discoverable electronic information of their obligation to store discoverable electronic information on a secure, backed-up network storage device or backup medium to ensure its preservation and instruct such employees in the manner of doing so in accordance with this paragraph.

7. Plaintiff, within 15 days of receiving the list of business units referred to below, shall identify by name, title, or departmental category, employees of Defendant for which the Defendant shall be responsible for maintaining the hard drive, or a mirror-image copy (i.e., a bit-by-bit copy) of such hard drive, during the pendency of this litigation. Defendant shall, within 15 days of receiving the list of business units referred to below identify by name, title, or departmental category, employees of Plaintiff for which the Plaintiff shall be responsible for maintaining the hard drive, or a mirror-image copy (i.e., a bit-by-bit copy) of such hard drive, during the pendency of this litigation. In no event shall the number of computers subject to the provisions of this paragraph be greater than [insert number] for Defendant and Plaintiff. The hard drives or image copies of such hard drives preserved pursuant to this paragraph shall be labeled to identify the employee who primarily used the computer associated with that hard drive. To facilitate the identification of the appropriate employees, the parties will provide to each other identification by business unit and positions the employees they reasonably believe could have potentially discoverable electronic information. The parties will meet and confer in good faith and exchange additional information as may be necessary to facilitate the identification, and limit the number, of employees for whom the provisions of this paragraph shall be applicable.

8. To the extent that Defendant or Plaintiff have implemented a system for the purpose of preserving external e-mails (e-mails sent to or received by Defendant's or Plaintiff's employees) in an easily accessible form, other than an e-mail server or the Backup Tapes identified in paragraph 2 or 3 above, all e-mails that were created during the period from [date range] that contain potentially

discoverable electronic information, and that are stored on any such system as of the date hereof, shall be preserved during the pendency of this litigation.

9. Within 45 days, Defendant and Plaintiff will provide written answers to the best of their ability to the questions concerning information system and electronic document retention practices set forth in attached Schedule C [omitted]. Should any party believe it cannot in good faith answer any of the questions as posed, the parties will confer to resolve any disputes and, if necessary, seek Court intervention.

10. By agreeing to preserve potentially discoverable electronic information in accordance with the terms hereof, Defendant and Plaintiff are not waiving any objection to the ultimate discoverability of such information at such point when discovery is authorized in these actions.

11. Nothing herein shall be deemed to affect the Defendant's and Plaintiff's obligations to preserve hardcopy documents pursuant to the Court's Case Management Order. If counsel learn that potentially discoverable hardcopy documents were destroyed by a party subsequent to being named as a party in, and receiving a copy of, a complaint pertaining to that public offering, counsel for such party shall notify opposing counsel in writing of such destruction within two weeks of learning so.

Part III

OBTAINING DISCOVERY OF ELECTRONICALLY STORED INFORMATION

Chapter 8

Discovery and Disclosure

I. GUIDELINES

II. CHECKLISTS

III. FORMS

Research References

Treatises and Practice Aids

eDiscovery & Digital Evidence §§ 7:1 to 7:22

Grenig and Kinsler, Federal Civil Discovery and Disclosure §§ 1.1 to 1.200 (2d ed.)

Trial Strategy

Recovery and Reconstruction of Electronic Mail as Evidence, 41 Am. Jur Proof of Facts 3d 1

Computer Technology in Civil Litigation, 71 Am. Jur Trials 111

Law Reviews and Other Periodicals

Llewellyn, Electronic Discovery Best Practices, 10 Rich. J.L. & Tech. 51 (2004)

Meyer & Wraspir, eDiscovery: Preparing Clients for (and Protecting Them Against) Discovery in the Electronic Information Age, 26 Wm. Mitchell L. Rev. 939 (2000)

Poirier et al., Computer-Based Litigation Support Systems: The Discoverability Issues, 54 U. Mo. K.C. L. Rev. 440 (1986)

Waxse, "Do I Really Have to Do That?" Rule 26(a)(1) Disclosures and Electronic Information, 10 Rich. J.L. & Tech. 50 (2004)

Additional References

Ball, Piecing Together the E-Discovery Plan, Trial, June 2008

Gonzalez & Montoya, Ten Tips Leading to Efficient and Effective eDiscovery for the Small Law Firm, GP/Solo, Apr. 2007

Kassis, Prepare Yourself to Confer Under the amended Federal Rules of Civil Procedure Before Conferring, Elec. Disc. & Records Mgt. Q., summer 2007, at 16

ABA Discovery Standards, http://www.abanet.org/litigation/discoverystandards/2005civildiscoverystandards.pdf

Electronic Discovery Reference Model Project, http://www.edrm.net

Federal Judicial Center, http://www.fjc.gov

The Sedona Conference, http://www.thesedonaconference.orge

KeyCite®: Cases and other legal materials listed in KeyCite Scope can be researched through the KeyCite service on Westlaw®. Use KeyCite to check citations for form, parallel references, prior and later history, and comprehensive citator information, including citations to other decisions and secondary materials.

I. GUIDELINES

§ 8:1 Generally

Discovery of electronically stored information can be useful in most civil suits. For example, in tort suits, computer records of accidents may used to support a claim that a particular product or place was dangerous. In marital dissolution cases, a home computer might show evidence of assets, such as on-line stock trading, or even evidence of infidelity. A personnel database may contain evidence of a pattern and practice of discrimination that will be helpful in an employment discrimination suit.

Basic discovery principles apply to discovery of electronically stored information. Discovery is proper if the information sought is not privileged and it meets the applicable relevancy standard. If the information is relevant, it need not be admissible at trial if the discovery appears reasonably calculated to lead to the discovery of admissible evidence.

The major issue in the discovery of electronically stored information is not whether electronically stored information is discoverable, but the scope of production permitted or required and the cost of discovery. While discovery of electronically stored information has sometimes been equated with traditional paper-based discovery, there are important differences, including the sheer volume of digital information.

Planning for discovery of electronically stored information should begin early in the litigation. As soon as litigation threatens, the opposing party should be put on notice to preserve all possibly related electronically stored information. In order to reduce the possibility of documents being deleted, parties should consider seeking a particularized preservation order ensuring that all sources, including primary, secondary or off-site computer files be preserved pending discovery.

§ 8:2 Producing and exchanging electronically stored information

There are several reasons for encouraging parties to produce and exchange electronically stored information in digital form:

- **Reducing need to recopy discovery responses.** Discovery requests may be transmitted in computer-accessible form. For example, interrogatories may be served on computer disks and answered using the same disk.
- **Reducing costs.** Production of electronically stored information on disks, CD-ROMs, or by file transfers can significantly reduce the costs of copying, transporting, storing, and managing documents. Protocols may be established by the parties facilitating the handling of electronically stored information, from initial production to use in depositions, and pretrial procedures to presentation at trial.
- **Ease of search.** Electronically stored information can be more easily searched, located, and organized than paper documents.
- **Document depository.** Electronically stored information may form the contents for a common document depository.

§ 8:3 Saving time and money

Expenditures made on electronic discovery, including preservation, collection and production can end up costing millions of dollars. The Manual for Complex Litigation Fourth suggests several ways to save time and money when discovery of digital information is involved:

- **Phased or sequenced discovery of computerized data.** Electronically stored information often is not accessible by date, author, addressee, or subject matter without costly review and indexing. Therefore, it may be appropriate for the court to phase or sequence discovery of electronically stored information by accessibility. At the outset, allowing discovery of relevant, non-privileged electronically stored information available to the respondent in the routine course of business is appropriate and should be treated as a conventional document request. If the requesting party requests more electronically stored information, consider additional sources in ascending order of cost and burden to the responding party, e.g., metadata or system data, archived data, backup data, and legacy data. The judge should encourage the parties to agree to phased discovery of electronically stored information as part of the discovery plan. But with or without a prior agreement, the judge may engage in benefit-and-burden analysis at each stage and enter an appropriate order, which may include cost sharing between the parties or cost shifting to the requesting party.

- **Computerized data produced in agreed-on formats.** Information subject to discovery increasingly exists in digital or computer-readable form. The judge should encourage counsel to produce requested electronically stored information in formats and on media that reduce transport and conversion costs, maximize the ability of all parties to organize and analyze the electronically stored information during pretrial preparation, and ensure usability at trial. Wholesale conversion of electronically stored information to paper form for production, only to be reconverted into computerized data by the receiving party, is costly and wasteful. Particularly in multiparty cases, data production on CD-ROM or by Internet-based data transfer can increase efficiency.
- **Sampling of computer data.** Parties may have vast collections of electronically stored information, such as stored e-mail messages or backup files containing routine business information kept for disaster recovery purposes. Unlike collections of paper documents,

electronically stored information is not normally organized for retrieval by date, author, addressee, or subject matter, and may be very costly and time-consuming to investigate thoroughly. Under such circumstances, judges have ordered that random samples of electronically stored information be restored and analyzed to determine if further discovery is warranted under benefit versus burden considerations.

§ 8:4 Types of discoverable electronically stored information

Electronically stored information can include anything from earlier versions and drafts to "deleted" information stored on backup media or user information saved with electronically stored information. Electronically stored information can be discoverable long after paper records have been destroyed.

Electronically stored information readily available and accessible from computers is called "active data." Active data may exist in the form of e-mail messages, word processing documents, spreadsheets, databases, or calendars. Unless privileged, this information is normally discoverable.

Documents that were never saved may still "exist" and be discoverable. This "replicant" data may be created when automatic backups occur, creating and storing a "file clone." Replicant data are normally saved to a user's hard drive and not a network server. Replicant data can frequently be found on backup media. Because backup media can potentially contain multiple copies of irrelevant documents, discovery of this information can be very expensive.

Because "deleting" information on a computer merely instructs the computer to write over the hard disk space containing that particular document, it may take some time to overwrite the space containing the "deleted" information. The deleted electronically stored information is invisible to the ordinary user system administrator, but a computer forensic expert may be able to recover parts of the document that have not yet been overwritten.

Electronically stored information also includes information on publicly available Web sites. A discovering party should download all publicly available information at the earliest possible moment.

§ 8:5 Discovery plan

There are a number of steps that will enhance the probability of uncovering relevant electronically stored information and forcing its discovery without breaking the bank. The following are some suggested steps that a discovering party's attorney may consider:

- Send out a letter before or immediately after a lawsuit is commenced, demanding that all electronically stored information be segregated and preserved. If there is reason to believe that it will not be done, seek a protective order.
- Preserve evidence existing on any Web site by downloading its contents to with Adobe Acrobat before the lawsuit is commenced.
- Early in a lawsuit, serve interrogatories that seek only information about the other party's computer systems. These interrogatories should seek to carefully define possible sources of electronically stored information, and inquire whether those sources exist on a computer system and where they are stored. Also inquire as to which software programs and operating systems are being used by the party (including all of the technical specifications), and get the user and administrator manuals used in connection with all relevant software and operating systems that are not available commercially.
- Learn who does the computer work for a party (e.g., its Management Information System or Information System administrators) by use of interrogatories or through a deposition. After discovering who did or does the computer work for a party, depose those individuals. If possible, use these people to start to

assemble a map of an adversary's computing infrastructure (servers, operating systems, databases, web servers, applications). If custom software is relevant, it may be useful to identify the persons (e.g., employees or consultants) who created it and may have knowledge of data sources, flows, storage, and replicas.

- Serve a second set of interrogatories that seeks disclosure of facts and evidence, and include in that set a separate section that specifically seeks disclosure of relevant digital evidence. When seeking discovery of electronically stored information, ask that any electronically stored information be provided just as it exists in the computer systems of the responding party. This may occasion a number of battles relating to format, metadata, privilege, convenience, and cost. It may be necessary to postpone insisting on productions in native format until after reviewing what the other party is willing to give without a battle. However, in the best of all worlds, insist that electronically stored information be provided in the native digital format if at all possible, instead of just accepting hardcopies, PDFs, or TIFFs.
- Review all electronically stored information received so that follow up requests for a native format production can be made if necessary. Use backup copies since you should have the originals provided by respondent safely locked away.
- Electronically stored information that is provided in PDF or TIFF format is a good start (and will provide a good deal of flexibility in dealing with digital evidence), if it is organized and labeled so that it can be imported into a text and file indexer, such as the DT-Search indexer. When electronically stored information is received in PDF or TIFF formats, it is necessary to review it quickly in order to determine: (1) if it is responsive to the discovery requests; and (2) if it is labeled in a manner that will enable meaningful indexing.
- If the case is important enough, do not settle for

e-mail productions in hardcopy or PDF format. Seek to get the "metadata" associated with e-mail productions. If you do not have the e-mail program used to send and receive the discovered e-mail, and, if it is not available commercially, make a demand for a copy of the software. Minimally, get the e-mails exported with the mail headers intact.

- Once discovery of electronically stored information is obtained, organize and manage it in order to easily search and retrieve information. Programs such as Concordance, Summation or Trial Director can be used to accomplish this task. DT-Search, a relatively inexpensive program, can also be used.
- If a credible demonstration can be made that crucial electronically stored information is being withheld, sanctions may be sought.
- If there is reason to believe that significant electronically stored information exists that is being withheld, consider retaining the services of a forensic computer expert to assist in pursuing more discovery. Such a move is expensive, and should only be considered if there is a reasonable belief that electronically stored information is being concealed.
- If the case is big enough, seek onsite inspection of the responding party's computer system and, possibly, the appointment of a special master or court-appointed expert witnesses who can independently inspect the responding party's system.

§ 8:6 Discovering who does computer work

Counsel should seek to learn who does the computer work for the responding party (for example, its Management Information System or Information System employees and software/systems consultants hired to develop and maintain in-house systems) by using interrogatories or depositions. It should not be assumed that the CIO (chief information officer) or department head is the most knowledgeable about the storage of electronically stored information in a company database or e-mail system. It may be a relatively low level administrator. After discovering who did, or does, the computer work for a responding party, the discovering party's counsel should depose those individuals.

One should not overlook the fact that a former employee may know a great deal and may have also separated on less than amicable terms from an organization. Such person may be a willing source of valuable information concerning the electronically stored information of a producing party.

§ 8:7 Disclosure

In federal court, the parties are required to disclose the description and location of relevant electronically stored information before a discovery request is submitted.[1] This imposes on the parties a duty to identify all sources and locations of digital data.[2] Rule 26(a)(2) also requires the parties to disclose the identities of their electronic discovery or forensic experts if they will be called at trial. After disclosure, more detailed information can be obtained by using traditional discovery tools such as interrogatories, depositions, and requests for production.

In *Kleiner v. Burns*,[3] the plaintiff moved to compel Yahoo! "to disclose all voice mail, electronic mail (email or e-mail), websites, web pages, and other digital data relevant to the above action." Relying on Rule 26(a)(1)(B) of the Federal Rules of Civil Procedure, the court ordered Yahoo! to disclose all data compilations in its possession, custody and control that were relevant to disputed facts alleged with particularity in the pleadings. The court went on to say that, under Rule 26(a)(1)(B), disclosures should:

[Section 8:7]

[1]See Fed.R.Civ.P. 26(a)(1)(B), requiring initial disclosure of "a copy of, or a description by category and location of all documents, electronically stored information, and tangible things that are in the possession, custody, or control of the party. . .."

[2]See Kleiner v. Burns, 48 Fed. R. Serv. 3d 644 (D. Kan. 2000).

[3]Kleiner v. Burns, 48 Fed. R. Serv. 3d 644 (D. Kan. 2000).

> Describe and categorize to the extent identified during the initial investigation, the nature and location of potentially relevant documents and records, including computerized data and other electronically-recorded information, sufficiently to enable opposing parties (1) to make an informed decision concerning which documents might need to be examined, at least, initially, and (2) to frame their document requests in a manner likely to avoid squabbles resulting from the words of the requests.[4]

The court held that computerized data and other digitally-recorded information

> includes, but is not limited to: voice mail messages and files, backup voice mail files, e-mail messages and files, backup e-mail files, deleted e-mails, data files, program files, backup and archival tapes, temporary files, system history files, web site information stored in textual, graphical or audio format, web site log files, cache files, cookies, and other electronically-recorded information.[5]

§ 8:8 Seeking expert assistance

Parties are often forced to litigate on a limited budget, and thus are tempted to forego technical assistance unless it is absolutely necessary. This means that many times the focus is placed on the experts needed for trial. Parties assume they can obtain enough evidence during discovery to provide those experts the information they require. When it comes to discovery of electronically stored information, this can be a very costly mistake.

Using an expert may pay dividends when the responding party resists production. The expert can participate in meetings with the responding party's information technology staff, write memoranda to educate the court about technology issues, and testify at hearings as to the need for electronically stored information. Retaining this expert can save hours that would otherwise be spent in depositions and preparation to understand the technology and where to find the electronically stored information.

---

[4]Kleiner v. Burns, 48 Fed. R. Serv. 3d 644 (D. Kan. 2000). See also Theofel v. Farey-Jones, 359 F.3d 1066, 1078–79 (9th Cir. 2004) (overbroad e-mail subpoena exposed lawyer and client to liability).

[5]Kleiner v. Burns, 48 Fed. R. Serv. 3d 644 (D. Kan. 2000).

II. CHECKLISTS

§ 8:9 Checklist for approaching discovery of electronically stored information

☐ **Make sure the party you represent has a rational, transparent and defensible policy on the retention and destruction of electronically stored information.** The success or failure of arguments about sanctions and cost-shifting will turn on the defensibility of a party's document retention and destruction policy. If a party does not have a written policy concerning document retention and destruction that is rational, defensible and transparent, it enters any dispute about the discovery of electronically stored information with a tremendous handicap.

☐ **Raise issues relating to the preservation and production of electronically stored information immediately with opposing counsel.** Counsel should confer early and often about the preservation and production of electronically stored information. Those conferences should begin as soon as the parties anticipate that litigation may ensue. From the discovering party's standpoint, it is critical that these discussions take place to make sure that no relevant data are destroyed. From the responding party's standpoint, it is critical that these discussions take place to minimize the possibility that sanctions may later be imposed and also to facilitate preservation and production.

☐ **Make sure that preservation and production issues are part of the discovery conference agenda.** The discovery conference is an appropriate time to finalize any issues relating to the preservation and production of digital materials. Issues that cannot be resolved can then be presented to the court at the scheduling conference.

☐ **The goal should be to resolve preservation and production issues without the court's intervention. If the court's help is needed in resolving preservation and production issues, it**

should be sought immediately. As with all other types of discovery disputes, the parties should do everything that they can to resolve discovery disputes without the necessity for court intervention. This is particularly true when the issues involve discovery of electronically stored information. The parties and their counsel are in the best position to resolve issues about preservation and production. However, if they must seek court intervention, delay is fatal. If there is a problem a party should seek immediate intervention. If a problem still exists at the time of the scheduling conference, a party should make sure that the issue is raised at that time.

☐ **Help the court resolve preservation and production issues.** Most courts will not be as conversant with technology issues as the parties and their counsel. The parties should do everything possible to educate the court and to help the court understand the discovery of electronically stored information issues. If expert testimony is presented, it is important to make sure the testimony is in understandable and useful form.

☐ **Use a focused discovery approach and be ready to justify your requests.** "Fishing expeditions" in the area of electronically stored information are doomed to failure. The approach to the discovery of electronically stored information must be focused. The discovering party must also be able to support its discovery requests with more than conjecture. The discovering party must be able to point to objective sources to support arguments about what the discovery of backup tapes may show in order to have the court require sampling.

☐ **All things being equal, documents should be requested in digital form.** No rule fits absolutely in every situation. Generally, however, it makes sense to request electronically stored information in digital form. Electronically stored information in that form will generally provide more useful information than the same data in paper format.

☐ **Counsel must rigorously communicate with their clients, particularly with the computer systems people.** It is essential that there be good communication between in house counsel, retained counsel and the systems technology people. It is essential that the lawyer know more about the clients' computer systems and their document destruction and retention policy than any other person. Bad things will happen to the lawyer and the client if the lawyer does not know everything about the digital assets of the client.

☐ **Communicate with opposing counsel and the court.** The key to successful resolution of preservation and production issues involving electronically stored information in digital form is communication—communication with opposing counsel to resolve issues and, where court intervention is necessary, communication with the court. The communication must be candid. Sanctions have often been imposed because counsel was not candid with the court and opposing counsel until it was too late.

☐ **Be reasonable.** More so than with any other area of discovery, the court is looking for reasonableness on both sides. On the discovering party's side, the court wants reasonable and focused discovery requests. On the responding party's side, the court expects a reasonable approach to the preservation and production of digital documents. The court also expects the parties to create reasonable solutions.

§ 8:10 Checklist for subjects to be explored during discovery

☐ Overall network configuration

☐ Employee computer use

- ☐ Do employees use computers at work?
- ☐ Do employees use computers at home?
- ☐ Do employees use laptops?
- ☐ Do employees use personal digital assistants?

    - ☐ Is the equipment owned by the responding party and returned when employees leave the job?
    - ☐ Do employees store documents on network drives or on local hard drives?
- ☐ User manuals
    - ☐ Do manuals exist?
    - ☐ Where are the manuals kept?
- ☐ E-mail systems
    - ☐ Who uses the e-mail systems?
    - ☐ Where is e-mail stored?
    - ☐ How long are messages retained?
- ☐ Computer and server network logs
- ☐ Archiving procedures
    - ☐ How often does the responding party backup data?
    - ☐ What media and software are used?
    - ☐ Where are removable media kept?
    - ☐ How is such information indexed?
- ☐ Organizational policies
    - ☐ What are the responding party's policies for document retention and encryption?
    - ☐ How is such information indexed?
- ☐ Servers
    - ☐ Where are the servers located?
    - ☐ Who has access to the servers?
- ☐ Locations of old or replaced computers and hard drives
- ☐ Deletions
    - ☐ Have data been erased or deleted recently?
- ☐ Party's Web site
- ☐ Who decides the content of the responding party's Web site?

§ 8:11 Discovery checklist

- ☐ Request that the electronically stored information be submitted in computer-readable form, allowing for complete key word searches to locate relevant information and to reformat the information in a preferred form, such as a table or list.

- ☐ Determine how the costs for obtaining and handling the electronically stored information will be borne.
- ☐ Discuss with opposing counsel the sharing of costs.
- ☐ Identify potentially relevant electronically stored information and in what format it might be stored, such as e-mail, graphics files, or word processing files.
- ☐ Determine the discovery methods to use to discover electronically stored information, such as interrogatories, depositions, and requests for documents.
- ☐ Discuss with a computer expert technology issues such as the framing of discovery questions, the specific computer systems involved in the litigation, and the potential need for computer forensics assistance to recover electronically stored information.
- ☐ Consult with another computer expert who may act as a witness at trial.
- ☐ Consider obtaining a protective order for certain electronically stored information, such as information that contains trade secrets or is computer source code.
- ☐ Use discovery to obtain information on the computer system used by the opposing party, including the type of hardware, operating systems, and applications used.
- ☐ Determine how counsel will process and use the electronically stored information that is discovered. Processing may involve searching through the information; use of the information may involve the production of trial exhibits

Comment

This is a checklist of considerations to be addressed by the practitioner planning the discovery of electronically stored information. These items are useful in the formulation of discovery requests, such as interrogatories.

§ 8:12 Checklist for drafting discovery requests

- ☐ **Correct Names.** Make sure that to identify correctly

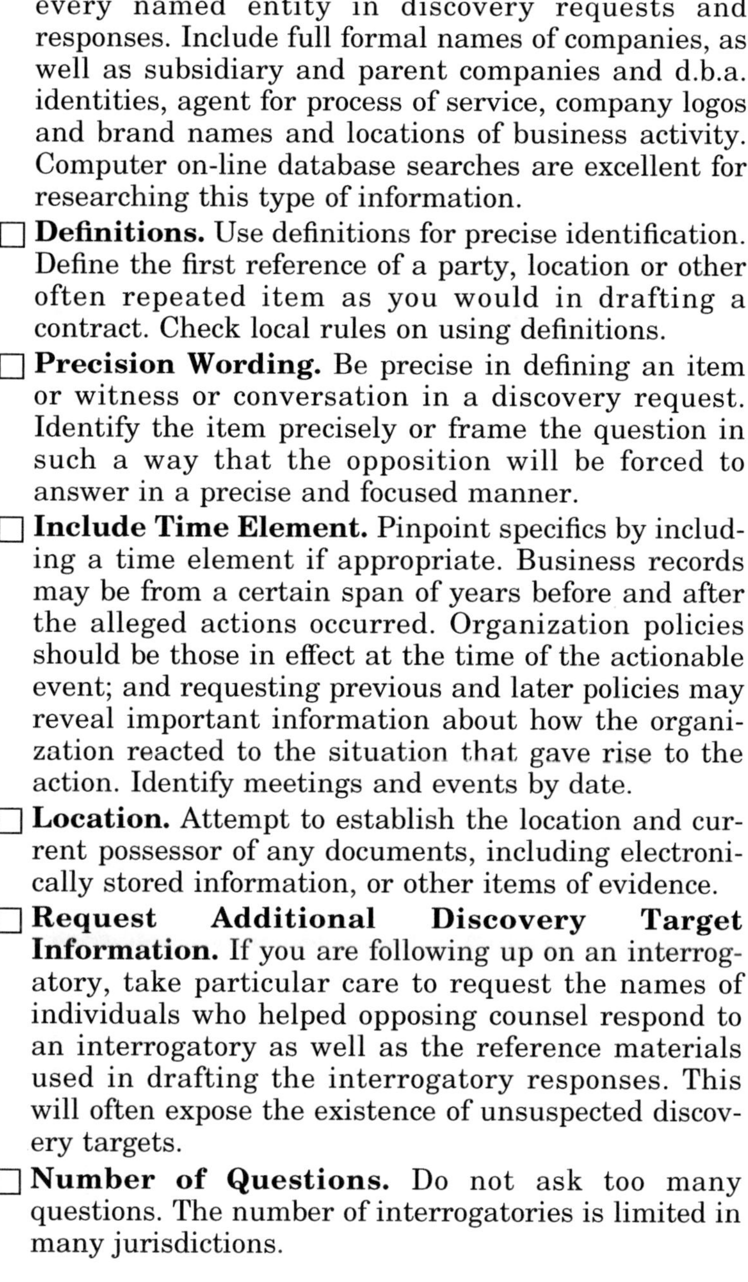

every named entity in discovery requests and responses. Include full formal names of companies, as well as subsidiary and parent companies and d.b.a. identities, agent for process of service, company logos and brand names and locations of business activity. Computer on-line database searches are excellent for researching this type of information.

☐ **Definitions.** Use definitions for precise identification. Define the first reference of a party, location or other often repeated item as you would in drafting a contract. Check local rules on using definitions.

☐ **Precision Wording.** Be precise in defining an item or witness or conversation in a discovery request. Identify the item precisely or frame the question in such a way that the opposition will be forced to answer in a precise and focused manner.

☐ **Include Time Element.** Pinpoint specifics by including a time element if appropriate. Business records may be from a certain span of years before and after the alleged actions occurred. Organization policies should be those in effect at the time of the actionable event; and requesting previous and later policies may reveal important information about how the organization reacted to the situation that gave rise to the action. Identify meetings and events by date.

☐ **Location.** Attempt to establish the location and current possessor of any documents, including electronically stored information, or other items of evidence.

☐ **Request Additional Discovery Target Information.** If you are following up on an interrogatory, take particular care to request the names of individuals who helped opposing counsel respond to an interrogatory as well as the reference materials used in drafting the interrogatory responses. This will often expose the existence of unsuspected discovery targets.

☐ **Number of Questions.** Do not ask too many questions. The number of interrogatories is limited in many jurisdictions.

☐ **Eliminate Vague Wording.** Eliminate vagueness from questions.

III. FORMS

§ 8:13 Guidelines for discovery of electronically stored information

1. Existence of electronically stored information

A. Before the discovery conference, counsel should become knowledgeable about their clients' information management systems and their operation, including how electronically stored information is stored and retrieved.

B. Counsel should make a reasonable attempt to review their clients' electronically stored information to ascertain the contents, including archival, backup, and legacy data (outdated formats or media)

2. Duty to disclose

A. Disclosures pursuant to *[rule]* must include any electronically stored information the disclosing party may use to support its claims or defenses, unless used solely for impeachment.

B. To determine what information must be disclosed pursuant to this rule, counsel should review, with their clients, the clients' electronically stored information files, including current, backup, archival, and legacy computer files.

C. Counsel should be aware that documents in paper form may have been generated by the client's information system; thus, there may be electronically stored information related to a paper document.

D. If any party intends to disclose electronically stored information, counsel should identify those individuals with knowledge of their clients' electronic information systems who can facilitate the location and identification of discoverable electronically stored information before the discovery conference

3. Duty to notify

A. A party seeking discovery of electronically stored information should notify the opposing party of that fact immediately,

B. If known at the time of the discovery conference, should identify as clearly as possible the categories of electronically stored information that may be sought

C. Parties and counsel are reminded that, under *[rule]* if the requesting party has not designated a form of production in its request,

D. If the responding party objects to the designated form, then the responding party must state in its written response the form it intends to use for producing electronically stored information.

4. Duty to confer regarding electronically stored information

During the discovery conference, the parties should confer regarding the following matters:

A. Electronically stored information in general

Counsel should attempt to agree on steps the parties will take to segregate and preserve electronically stored information in order to avoid accusations of spoliation.

B. E-mail information

Counsel should attempt to agree on the scope of e-mail discovery and e-mail search protocol.

C. Deleted information

Counsel should attempt to agree on whether responsive deleted information still exists, the extent to which restoration of deleted information is needed, and who will bear the costs of restoration.

D. Embedded data and metadata.

"Embedded data" typically refers to draft language, editorial comments, and other deleted matter retained by computer programs.

"Metadata" typically refers to information describing the history, tracking, or management of an electronic file.

The parties should discuss at the discovery conference whether embedded data and metadata exist, whether it will be requested or should be produced, and how to handle determinations regarding privilege or protection of trial preparation materials.

E. Backup and archival data.

Counsel should attempt to agree on whether responsive backup and archival data exist, the extent to which backup and archival data are needed, and who will bear the cost of obtaining such electronically stored information.

F. Format and media.

Counsel should attempt to agree on the format and media to be used in the production of electronically stored information.

G. Reasonably accessible information and costs.

1. The volume of, and ability to search, electronically stored information means that most parties' discovery needs will be satisfied from reasonably accessible sources.
2. Counsel should attempt to determine if any responsive electronically stored information is not reasonably accessible, i.e., information that is only accessible by incurring undue burdens or costs.
3. If the responding party is not searching or does not plan to search sources containing potentially responsive information, it should identify the category or type of such information.
4. If the requesting party intends to seek discovery of electronically stored information from sources identified as not reasonably accessible, the parties should discuss:
5. The burdens and costs of accessing and retrieving the information
6. The needs that may establish good cause for requiring production of all or part of the information, even if the information sought is not reasonably accessible

7. Conditions on obtaining and producing this information such as scope, time, and allocation of cost.

H. Privileged or trial preparation materials.

1. Counsel should attempt to reach an agreement regarding what will happen in the event privileged or trial preparation materials are inadvertently disclosed.
2. If the disclosing party inadvertently produces privileged or trial preparation materials, it must notify the requesting party of such disclosure.
3. After the requesting party is notified, it must return, sequester, or destroy all information and copies and may not use or disclose this information until the claim of privilege or protection as trial preparation materials is resolved.
4. The parties may agree to provide a quick peek, whereby the responding party provides certain requested materials for initial examination without waiving any privilege or protection.
   a. The parties may also establish a clawback agreement, whereby materials that are disclosed without intent to waive privilege or protection are not waived and are returned to the responding party, so long as the responding party identifies the materials mistakenly produced.
   b. Other voluntary agreements should be considered as appropriate. The parties should be aware that there is an issue of whether such agreements bind third parties who are not parties to the agreements.

5. Duty to confer when requesting electronically stored information from non-parties

Parties issuing requests for electronically stored information from non-parties should attempt to informally confer with the non-party (or counsel, if represented). During this meeting, counsel should discuss the same issues with regard to requests for electronically stored information that they would with opposing counsel as set forth in paragraph 4 above.

Comment

This form is adapted from Guidelines used in the U.S. District Court for the District of Kansas.

§ 8:14 Default standard for discovery of electronically stored information

DEFAULT STANDARD FOR DISCOVERY OF ELECTRONICALLY STORED INFORMATION

1. **Introduction.** It is expected that parties to a case will cooperatively reach agreement on how to conduct e-discovery. In the event that such agreement has not been reached by the scheduling conference, however, the following default standards shall apply until such time, if ever, the parties conduct electronic discovery on a consensual basis.
2. **Discovery conference.** Parties shall discuss the parameters of their anticipated electronic discovery at the discovery conference, as well as at the scheduling conference with the court, consistent with the concerns outlined below. More specifically, before the discovery conference, the parties shall exchange the following information:
   a. A list of the most likely custodians of relevant electronic materials, including a brief description of each person's title and responsibilities.
   b. A list of each relevant electronic system that has been in place at all relevant times and a general description of each system, including the nature, scope, character, organization, and formats employed in each system. The parties should also include other pertinent information about their electronic documents and whether those electronic documents are of limited accessibility. Electronic documents of limited accessibility may include those created or used by electronic media no longer in use, maintained in redundant electronic storage media, or for which retrieval involves substantial cost.
   c. The name of the individual responsible for that party's electronic document retention policies ("the

retention coordinator"), as well as a general description of the party's electronic document retention policies for the systems identified above.

d. The name of the individual who shall serve as that party's electronic discovery liaison.

e. Provide notice of any problems reasonably anticipated to arise in connection with e-discovery.

To the extent that the state of the pleadings does not permit a meaningful discussion of the above by the time of the discovery conference, the parties shall either agree on a date by which this information will be mutually exchanged or submit the issue for resolution by the court at the scheduling conference.

3. **Electronic discovery liaison.** In order to promote communication and cooperation between the parties, each party to a case shall designate a single individual through which all electronic discovery requests and responses are made ("electronic discovery liaison"). Regardless of whether the electronic discovery liaison is an attorney (in-house or outside counsel), a third party consultant, or an employee of the party, the liaison must be:

a. Familiar with the party's electronic systems and capabilities in order to explain these systems and answer relevant questions.

b. Knowledgeable about the technical aspects of electronic discovery, including electronic document storage, organization, and format issues.

c. Prepared to participate in electronic discovery dispute resolution.

The court notes that, at all times, the attorneys of record shall be responsible for compliance with electronic discovery requests. However, the electronic discovery liaisons shall be responsible for organizing each party's c-discovery efforts to insure consistency and thoroughness and, generally, to facilitate the electronic discovery process.

4. **Timing of electronic discovery.** Discovery of electronic documents shall proceed in a sequenced fashion.

a. After receiving requests for document production, the parties shall search their documents, other than those identified as limited accessibility electronic documents, and produce responsive electronic documents in accordance with *[rule]*.
b. Electronic searches of documents identified as of limited accessibility shall not be conducted until the initial electronic document search has been completed. Requests for information expected to be found in limited accessibility documents must be narrowly focused with some basis in fact supporting the request.
c. On-site inspections of electronic media under *[rule]* shall not be permitted absent exceptional circumstances, where good cause and specific need have been demonstrated.

5. **Search methodology.** If the parties intend to employ an electronic search to locate relevant electronic documents, the parties shall disclose any restrictions as to scope and method which might affect their ability to conduct a complete electronic search of the electronic documents. The parties shall reach agreement as to the method of searching, and the words, terms, and phrases to be searched with the assistance of the respective c-discovery liaisons, who are charged with familiarity with the parties' respective systems. The parties also shall reach agreement as to the timing and conditions of any additional searches which may become necessary in the normal course of discovery. To minimize the expense, the parties may consider limiting the scope of the electronic search (e.g., time frames, fields, document types).
6. **Format.** If, during the course of the discovery conference, the parties cannot agree to the format for document production, electronic documents shall be produced to the requesting party as image files (e.g., PDF or TIFF), When the image file is produced, the producing party must preserve the integrity of the electronic document's contents, i.e., the original formatting of the document, its metadata and, where applicable, its revi-

sion history. After initial production in image file format is complete, a party must demonstrate particularized need for production of electronic documents in their native format.

7. **Retention.** Within the first 30 days of discovery, the parties should work towards an agreement outlining the steps each party shall take to segregate and preserve the integrity of all relevant electronic documents. In order to avoid later accusations of spoliation, a deposition of each party's retention coordinator may be appropriate.

   The retention coordinators shall:

   a. Take steps to ensure that e-mail of identified custodians shall not be permanently deleted in the ordinary course of business and that electronic documents maintained by the individual custodians shall not be altered.
   b. Provide notice as to the criteria used for spam and/or virus filtering of e-mail and attachments; e-mails and attachments filtered out by such systems shall be deemed non- responsive so long as the criteria underlying the filtering are reasonable.

   Within seven days of identifying the relevant document custodians, the retention coordinators shall implement the above procedures and each party's counsel shall file a statement of compliance as such with the court.

8. **Privilege.** Electronic documents that containing privileged information or attorney work product shall be immediately returned if the documents appear on their face to have been inadvertently produced or if there is notice of the inadvertent production within 30 days of such.
9. **Costs.** Generally, the costs of discovery shall be borne by each party. However, the court will apportion the costs of electronic discovery upon a showing of good cause.
10. **Discovery disputes and trial presentation,** At this time, discovery disputes shall be resolved and trial presentations shall be conducted consistent with each individual judge's guidelines.

§ 8:15 Protocol for discovery of electronically stored information

SUGGESTED PROTOCOL FOR DISCOVERY OF ELECTRONICALLY STORED INFORMATION

1. On December 1, 2006, amendments to Fed.R.Civ.P. 16, 26, 33, 34, 37, and 45, and Form 35, became effective, creating a comprehensive set of rules governing discovery of electronically stored information.

Given these rule changes, it is advisable to establish a suggested protocol regarding, and a basic format implementing, only those portions of the amendments that refer to electronically stored information. The purpose of this Suggested Protocol for Discovery of Electronically Stored Information (the "Protocol") is to facilitate the just, speedy, and inexpensive conduct of discovery involving electronically stored information in civil cases, am to promote, whenever possible, the resolution of disputes regarding the discovery of electronically stored information without Court intervention.

While this Protocol is intended to provide the parties with a comprehensive framework to address and resolve a wide range of electronically stored information, it is not intended to be an inflexible checklist. The Court expects the parties will consider the nature of the claim, the amount in controversy agreements of the parties, the relative ability of the parties to conduct discovery of electronically stored information, and such other factors as may be relevant under the circumstances. Therefore not all aspects of this Protocol may be applicable or practical for a particular matter, and indeed, if the parties to do not intend to seek discovery of electronically stored information it may be entirely inapplicable to a particular case. The Court encourages the parties to use this Protocol in cases in which there will be discovery of electronically stored information, and to resolve electronically stored information issues informally and without Court supervision whenever possible. In this regard, compliance with this Protocol may be considered by the Court in resolving discovery disputes, including whether sanctions should be awarded.

SCOPE

2. This Protocol applies to the electronically stored information provisions of Fed.R.Civ.P. 16, 26, 33, 34, or 37, and, insofar as it relates to electronically stored information, this Protocol applies to Fed.R.Civ.P. 45 in all instances where the provisions of Fed.R.Civ.P. 45 are the same as, or substantially similar to, Fed.R.Civ.P. 16, 26, 33, 34, or 37. In such circumstances, if a Conference pursuant to Fed.R.Civ.P. 26(f) is held, it may include all parties, as well as the person or entity served with the subpoena, if the Conference has not yet been conducted. If the Conference has been conducted, upon written request of any party or the person or entity served with the subpoena, a similar conference may be conducted regarding production of ESI pursuant to the subpoena. As used herein, the words "party" or "parties" include any person or entity that is served with a subpoena pursuant to Fed.R.Civ.P. 45. Nothing contained herein modifies Fed.R.Civ.P. 45 and, specifically, the provision of Rule 45(c)(2)(B) regarding the effect of a written objection to inspection or copying of any or all of the designated materials or premises.
3. In this Protocol, the following terms have the following meanings:
   A. "Metadata" means: (i) information embedded in a native file that is not by the operation of a computer or other information technology system whet a native file is created, modified, transmitted, deleted or otherwise manipulated by a user of such system. Metadata are a subset of electronically stored information.
   B. "Native file(s)" means electronically stored information in the electronic format of the application it which such electronically stored information is normally created, viewed and/or modified. Native files are a subset of electronically stored information.
   C. "Static image(s)" means a representation of electronically stored information produced by converting na-

tive file into a standard image format capable of being viewed and printed on standard computer systems. In the absence of agreement of the parties or order of Court, a static image should be provided in either Tagged Image File Format (TIFF, or.TIF files) or Portable Document Format (PDF). I load files were created in the process of converting native files to static images, or if load files may be created without undue burden or cost, load files should be produced together with Static Images.

CONFERENCE OF PARTIES AND REPORT

4. The parties are encouraged to consider conducting a Conference of Parties to discuss discovery of electronically stored information ESI regardless of whether such a Conference is ordered by the Court. The Conference of Parties should be conducted in person whenever practicable. Within 10 calendar days thereafter the parties may wish to file, or the Court may order them to file, a joint report regarding the results of the conference. This process is also encouraged if applicable in connection with a subpoena for electronically stored information under Fed.R.Civ.P. 45. The report may state that the parties do not desire discovery of electronically stored information in which event Paragraphs 4A and B are inapplicable.
   A. The report should, without limitation, state in the section captioned "Disclosure or discovery of electronically stored information should be handled as follows," the following:
      (1) Any areas on which the parties have reached agreement and, if any, on which the parties request Court approval of that agreement;
      (2) Any areas on which the parties are in disagreement and request intervention of the Court.
   B. The report should, without limitation, if it proposes a "clawback" agreement, "quick peek," or testing or sampling, specify the proposed treatment of privileged information and work product. On-site inspec-

tions of electronically stored information under Fed.R.Civ.P. 34(b) should only be permitted in circumstances where good cause and specific need have been demonstrated by the party seeking disclosure of electronically stored information ("Requesting Party"), or by agreement of the parties. In appropriate circumstances the Court may condition on-site inspections of electronically stored information to be performed by independent third-party experts, or set such other conditions as are agreed by the parties or deemed appropriate by the court.

C. Unless otherwise agreed by the parties, the report described by this provision should be filed with the Court prior to the commencement of discovery of electronically stored information.

NEED FOR PRIOR PLANNING

5. Insofar as it relates to electronically stored information, before planning and preparation is essential for a Conference of Parties pursuant to Fed.R.Civ.P. 16, 26(f), and this Protocol. Counsel for the Requesting Party and Counsel for the party producing, opposing, or seeking to limit disclosure of electronically stored information ("Producing Party") bear the primary responsibility for taking the planning actions. Failure to reasonably comply with the planning requirements in good faith may be a factor considered by the Court in imposing sanctions.

EXCHANGE OF INFORMATION BEFORE RULE 26(f) CONFERENCE

6. Insofar as it relates to electronically stored information, in order to have a meaningful Conference of Parties, it may be necessary for parties to exchange information prior to the Fed.R.Civ.P. 26(f) Conference of Parties. Parties are encouraged to take the steps described in ¶ 7 of this Protocol and agree on a date that is prior to the Fed.R.Civ.P. 26(f) Conference of Parties, on which agreed date they will discuss by

telephone whether it is necessary or convenient to exchange information about electronically stored information before the conference.

A. A reasonable request for prior exchange of information may include information relating to network design, the types of databases, database dictionaries, the access control list and security access logs and rights of individuals to access the system and specific files and applications, the electronically stored information document retention policy, organizational chart for information system personnel, or the backup and systems recovery routines, including, but not limited to, tape rotation and destruction/overwrite policy.

B. An unreasonable request for a prior exchange of information should not be made.

C. A reasonable request for a prior exchange of information should not be denied.

D. To the extent practicable, the parties should, prior to the Fed.R.Civ.P. 26(f) Conference of Parties, discuss the scope of discovery of electronically stored information, including whether the time parameters of discoverable electronically stored information, or for subsets of electronically stored information, be narrower than the parameters for other discovery.

E. Prior to the Fed.R.Civ.P. 26(f) Conference of Parties, Counsel should discuss with their clients and each other who will participate in the Fed.R.Civ.P 26(f) Conference of Parties. This discussion should specifically include whether one or more participants should have an electronically stored information coordinator (see Paragraph 7.B) participate in the Conference. If one participant believes the other should have an electronically stored information coordinator participate, and the other disagrees, the Requesting Party should state its reasons in a writing sent to all other parties within a reasonable time before the Rule 26(f) Conference. If the Court subsequently determines the Conference was not productive due to the absence of an electronically stored information coordinator, it may consider the letter in conjunction with any request for sanctions under Fed.R.Civ.P. 37.

PREPARATION FOR RULE 26(f) CONFERENCE

7. Before the Fed.R.Civ.P. 26(f) Conference of Parties, Counsel for the parties should:
   A. Take such steps as are necessary to advise their respective clients, including, but not limited to, "key persons" with respect to the facts underlying the litigation, and information systems personnel, of the substantive principles governing the preservation of relevant or discoverable electronically stored information while the lawsuit is pending. As a general principle to guide the discussion regarding litigation hold policies, Counsel should consider the following criteria:
      (1) Scope of the litigation hold, including:
         (a) A determination of the categories of potentially discoverable information to be segregated and preserved;
         (b) Discussion of the nature of issues in the case, as per Fed.R.Civ.P. 26(b)(1);
            (i) Whether electronically stored information is relevant to only some or all claims and defenses in the litigation;
            (ii) Whether electronically stored information is relevant to the subject matter involved in the action;
         (c) Identification of "key persons" and likely witnesses and persons with knowledge regarding relevant events;
         (d) The relevant time period for the litigation hold;
      (2) Analysis of what needs to be preserved, including:
         (a) The nature of specific types of electronically stored information, including, e-mail and attachments, word processing documents, spreadsheets graphics and presentation documents,

images, text files, hart drives, databases, instant messages, transaction logs, audit and video files, voicemail, Internet data, computer logs, text messages, or backup materials, and native files, and how it should be preserved;

(b) the extent to which metadata, deleted data, or fragmented data, will be subject to litigation hold;

(c) paper documents that are exact duplicates of electronically stored information;

(d) any preservation of electronically stored information that has been deleted but not purged;

(3) Determination of where electronically stored information subject to the litigation hold is maintained, including:

(a) format, location, structure, and accessibility of active storage backup, and archives;

(i) servers;

(ii) computer systems, including legacy systems;

(iii) remote and third-party locations;

(iv) backup media (for disasters) vs. backup media for archival purposes or record retention laws;

(b) network, intranet, and shared areas (public folders, discussion databases, departmental drives, and shared network folders)

(c) desktop computers and workstations;

(d) portable media; laptops; personal computers; PDAs; paging devices; mobile telephones; and flash drives;

(e) tapes, discs, drives, cartridges and other storage media;

(f) home computers (to the extent, if any, they are used for business purposes);

(g) paper documents that represent electronically stored information.

(4) Distribution of the notification of the litigation hold:

(a) to parties and potential witnesses;

(b) to persons with records that are potentially discoverable;

(c) to persons with control over discoverable information including:

(i) IT personnel/director of network services;

(ii) custodian of records;

(iii) key administrative assistants:

(d) third parties (contractors and vendors who provide IT services)

(5) Instructions to be contained in a litigation hold notice, including that:

(a) there will be no deletion, modification, alteration of electronically stored information subject to the litigation hold;

(b) the recipient should advise whether specific categories of electronically stored information subject to the litigation hold require particular actions (e.g., printing paper copies of e-mail and attachments) or transfer into "read only" media;

(c) loading of new software that materially impacts electronically stored information subject to the hold may occur only upon prior written approval from designated personnel;

(d) where metadata, or data that has been deleted but not purged, is to be preserved, either a method to preserve such data before running compression, disk defragmentation or other computer optimization or automated maintenance programs or scripts of any kind ("File and System Maintenance Procedures"), or the termination of all File and System Maintenance Procedures during the pendency of the litigation hold in respect of Native Files subject to preservation;

(e) reasonably safeguarding and preserving all portable or removable electronic storage media containing potentially relevant electronically stored information;

(f) maintaining hardware that has been removed

from active production, if such hardware contains legacy systems with relevant electronically stored information and there is no reasonably available alternative that preserves access to the native files on such hardware.

(6) Monitoring compliance with the notification of litigation hold, including:

(a) identifying contact person who will address questions regarding preservation duties;

(b) identifying personnel with responsibility to confirm that compliance requirements are met;

(c) determining whether data of "key persons" requires special handling (e.g., imaging/cloning hard drives);

(d) periodic checks of logs or memoranda detailing compliance;

(e) issuance of periodic reminders that the litigation hold is still in effect.

B. Notify one or more information technology or information systems personnel to act as the electronically stored information coordinator and discuss electronically stored information with that person;

C. Identify those personnel who may be considered "key persons" by the events placed in issue by the lawsuit and determine their electronically stored information practices, including those matters set forth in Paragraph 7.D, below. The term "key persons" is intended to refer to both the natural person or persons who is/are a "key person(s)" with regard to the facts that underlie the litigation, and any applicable clerical or support personnel who directly prepare, store, or modify electronically stored information for that key person or persons, including, but not limited to, the network administrator, custodian of records or records management personnel, and an administrative assistant or personal secretary;

D. Become reasonably familiar with their respective clients' current and relevant past electronically stored information, if any, or alternatively, identify a person who can participate in the Fed.R.Civ.P. 26(f) Conference of Parties and who is familiar with at least the following:

(1) E-mail systems; blogs; instant messaging; Short Message Service (SMS) systems; word processing systems; spreadsheet and database systems; system history files, cache files, and cookies; graphics, animation, or document presentation systems; calendar systems; voice mail systems, including specifically, whether such systems include electronically stored information; data files; program files; internet systems; and, internet systems. This Protocol may include information concerning the specific version of software programs and may include information stored on electronic bulletin boards, regardless of whether they are maintained by the party, authorized by the party, or officially sponsored by the party; provided however, this Protocol extends only to the information to the extent such information is in the possession, custody, or control of such party. To the extent reasonably possible, this includes the database program used over the relevant time, its database dictionary, and the manner in which such program records transactional history in respect to deleted records.

(2) Storage systems, including whether electronically stored information is stored on servers, individual hard drives, home computers, "laptop" or "notebook" computers, personal digital assistants, pagers, mobile telephones, or removable/portable storage devices, such as CD-Roms, DVDs, "floppy" disks, zip drives, tape drives, external hard drives, flash, thumb or "key" drives, or external service providers.

(3) Backup and archival systems, including those that are onsite, offsite, or maintained using one or more third-party vendors. This Protocol may include a reasonable inquiry into the backup routine, application, and process and location of storage

media, and requires inquiry into whether electronically stored information is reasonably accessible without undue burden or cost, whether it is compressed, encrypted, and the type of device on which it is recorded (e.g., whether it uses sequential or random access), and whether software that is capable of rendering it into usable form without undue expense is within the client's possession, custody, or control.

(4) Obsolete or "legacy" systems containing electronically stored information and the extent, if any, to which such electronically stored information was copied or transferred to new or replacement systems.

(5) Current and historical Web site information, including any potentially relevant or discoverable statements contained on that or those site(s), as well as systems to backup, archive, store, or retain superseded, deleted, or removed web pages, and policies regarding allowing third parties' sites to archive client Web site data.

(6) Event data records automatically created by the operation, usage, or polling of software or hardware (such as recorded by a motor vehicle's GPS or other internal computer prior to an occurrence), if any and if applicable, in automobiles, trucks, aircraft, vessels, or vehicles or equipment.

(7) Communication systems, if any and if applicable, such as electronically stored information records of radio transmissions, telephones, personal digital assistants, or GPS systems.

(8) Electronically stored information erasure, modification, or recovery mechanisms, such as metadata scrubbers or programs that repeatedly overwrite portions of storage media in order to preclude data recovery, and policies regarding the use of such processes and software, as well as recovery programs that can defeat scrubbing, thereby recovering deleted, but inadvertently produced electronically stored information, that, in some cases, may even include privileged information.

(9) Policies regarding records management, including the retention or destruction of electronically stored information prior to the client receiving knowledge that a claim is reasonably anticipated.
(10) "Litigation hold" policies that are instituted when a claim is reasonably anticipated, including all such policies that have been instituted, and the date on which they were instituted.
(11) The identity of custodians of key electronically stored information, including "key persons" and related staff members, and the information technology or information systems personnel, vendors, or subcontractors who are best able to describe the client's information technology system.
(12) The identity of vendors or subcontractors who store electronically stored information for, or provide services or applications to, the client or a key person; the nature, amount, and a description of the electronically stored information stored by those vendors or subcontractors; contractual or other agreements that permit the client to impose a "litigation hold" on such electronically stored information, and, if not, why not

E. Negotiation of an agreement that outlines what steps each party will take to segregate and preserve the integrity of relevant or discoverable electronically stored information. This agreement may provide for depositions of information system personnel on issues related to preservation, steps taken to ensure that electronically stored information is not deleted in the ordinary course of business, steps taken to avoid alteration of discoverable electronically stored information, and criteria regarding the operation of spam or virus filters and the destruction of filtered electronically stored information.

TOPICS TO DISCUSS AT RULE 26(f) CONFERENCE

8. The following topics, if applicable, should be discussed at the Fed.R.Civ.P. 26(f) Conference of Parties:
   A. The anticipated scope of requests for, and objections to, production of electronically stored information, as well as the form of production of electronically stored information and, specifically, but without limitation, whether production will be of the native file, static image, or other searchable or non-searchable formats.
      (1) If the parties are unable to reach agreement on the format for production, electronically stored information should be produced to the Requesting Party as static images. When the static image is produced, the Producing Party should maintain a separate file as a native file and, in that separate file, it should not modify the native File in a manner that materially changes the file and the metadata. After initial production in static images is complete, a party seeking production of native file electronically stored information should demonstrate particularized need for that production.
      (2) The parties should discuss whether production of some or all electronically stored information in paper format is agreeable in lieu of production in electronic format. When parties have agreed or the Court has ordered the parties to exchange all or some documents as electronic files in native file format in connection with discovery, the parties should collect and produce said relevant files in native file formats in a manner that preserves the integrity of the files, including, but not limited to, the contents of the file, the metadata (including system metadata, substantive metadata, and embedded metadata, as more fully described in Paragraph 11 of this Protocol) related to the file, and the file's creation date and time. The general process to preserve the data integrity of a file may include one or more of the following procedures: (a) duplication of responsive files in the file system (i.e., creating a forensic copy, including a bit image copy, of the file system or pertinent portion),

(b) performing a routine copy of the files while preserving metadata (including, but not limited to, creation date and time), and/or (c) using reasonable measures to prevent a file from being, or indicate that a file has been, modified, either intentionally or unintentionally, since the collection or production date of the files. If any party desires to redact contents of a native file for privilege, trade secret, or other purposes (including, but not limited to, metadata), then the Producing Party should indicate that the file has been redacted, and an original, unmodified file should be retained at least during the pendency of the case.

B. Whether metadata are requested for some or all electronically stored information and, if so, the volume and costs of producing and reviewing the electronically stored information.

C. Preservation of electronically stored information during the pendency of the lawsuit, specifically, but without limitation, applicability of the safe harbor provision of Fed.R.Civ.P. 37, preservation of metadata, preservation of deleted electronically stored information electronically stored information backup or archival electronically stored information, electronically stored information contained in dynamic systems, electronically stored information destroyed or overwritten by the routine operation of systems, and, offsite and offline electronically stored information (including electronically stored information stored on home or personal computers). A dynamic system is a system remaining in use during the pendency of the litigation and in which the electronically stored information changes on a routine and regular basis, including the automatic deletion or overwriting of such electronically stored information. This discussion should include whether the parties can agree on methods of review of electronically stored information by the responding party in a manner that does not unacceptably change metadata.

(1) If Counsel are able to agree, the terms of an agreed-upon preservation order may be submitted to the Court;

(2) If Counsel are unable to agree, they should attempt to reach agreement on the manner in which each party should submit a narrowly tailored, proposed preservation order to the Court for its consideration.

D. Post-production assertion, and preservation or waiver of, the attorney-client privilege, work product doctrine, and/or other privileges in light of clawback, quick peek, or testing or sampling procedures, and submission of a proposed order. If metadata are to be produced, Counsel may agree, and should discuss any agreement, that metadata not be reviewed by the recipient and the terms of submission of a proposed order encompassing that agreement to the Court. Counsel should also discuss procedures under which electronically stored information that contains privileged information or attorney work product should be immediately returned to the Producing Party if the electronically stored information appears on its face to have been inadvertently produced or if there is prompt written notice of inadvertent production by the Producing Party. The Producing Party should maintain unaltered copies of all such returned materials under the control of counsel of record. This provision is procedural and return of materials pursuant to this Protocol is without prejudice to any substantive right to assert, or oppose, waiver of any protection against disclosure.

E. Identification of electronically stored information that is or is not reasonably accessible without undue burden or cost, specifically, and without limitation, the identity of such sources and the reasons for a contention that the electronically stored information is or is not reasonably accessible without undue burden or cost, the methods of storing and retrieving that electronically stored information, and the anticipated costs and efforts involved in retrieving that electronically stored information. The party asserting that electronically stored information is not reasonably accessible without undue burden or cost should be prepared to discuss in reasonable detail, the information described in Paragraph 10 of this Protocol.

F. Because identifying information may not be placed on electronically stored information as easily as bates-stamping paper documents, methods of identifying pages or segments of electronically stored information produced in discovery should be discussed, and, specifically, and without limitation, the following alternatives may be considered by the parties electronically paginating native file electronically stored information pursuant to a stipulated agreement that the alteration does not affect admissibility; renaming native files using bates-type numbering systems, e.g., ABC0001, ABC0002, ABC0003, with some method of referring to unnumbered pages within each file, using software that produces "hash marks" or "hash values" for each native file; placing pagination on static images; or any other practicable method. The parties are encouraged to discuss the use of a digital notary for producing native files.

G. The method and manner of redacting information from electronically stored information if only part of the electronically stored information is discoverable. As set forth in Paragraph 11.D, if metadata are redacted from a file, written notice of such redaction, and the scope of that redaction, should be provided.

H. The nature of information systems used by the party or person or entity served with a subpoena requesting electronically stored information, including those systems described in Paragraph 7.D above. This Protocol may suggest that Counsel be prepared to list the types of information systems used by the client and the varying accessibility, if any, of each system. It may suggest that Counsel be prepared to identify the electronically stored information custodians, for example, by name, title, and job responsibility. It also may suggest that, unless impracticable, Counsel be able to identify the software (including the version) used in the ordinary course of business to access the electronically stored information, and the file formats of such electronically stored information.

I. Specific facts related to the costs and burdens of preservation, retrieval, and use of electronically stored information.

J. Cost sharing for the preservation, retrieval and/or production of electronically stored information, including any discovery database, differentiating between electronically stored information that is reasonably accessible and electronically stored information that is not reasonably accessible; provided however that absent a contrary showing of good cause, e.g., Fed.R.Civ.P. 26(b)(2)(C), the parties should generally presume that the Producing Party bears all costs as to reasonably accessible electronically stored information and, provided further, the parties should generally presume that there will be cost sharing or cost shifting as to electronically stored information that is not reasonably accessible. The parties may choose to discuss the use of an Application Service Provider that is capable of establishing a central repository of electronically stored information for all parties.

K. Search methodologies for retrieving or reviewing electronically stored information such as identification of the systems to be searched; identification of systems that will not be searched; restrictions or limitations on the search; factors that limit the ability to search; the use of key word searches, with an agreement on the words or terms to be searched; using sampling to search rather than searching all of the records; limitations on the time frame of electronically stored information to be searched; limitations on the fields or document types to be searched; limitations regarding whether backup, archival, legacy or deleted electronically stored information is to be searched; the number of hours that must be expended by the searching party or person in conducting the search and compiling and reviewing electronically stored information; and the amount of pre-production review that is reasonable for the Producing Party to undertake in light of the considerations set forth in Fed.R.Civ.P. 26(b)(2)(C).

L. Preliminary depositions of information systems personnel, and limits on the scope of such depositions. Counsel should specifically consider whether limitations on the scope of such depositions should be submitted to the Court with a proposed order that, if entered, would permit Counsel to instruct a witness not to answer questions beyond the scope of the limitation, pursuant to Fed.R.Civ.P. 30(d)(1).

M. The need for two-tier or staged discovery of electronically stored information, considering whether electronically stored information initially can be produced in a manner that is more cost-effective, while reserving the right to request or to oppose additional more comprehensive production in a later stage or stages. Absent agreement or good cause shown, discovery of electronically stored information should proceed in the following sequence: 1) after receiving requests for production of electronically stored information, the parties should search their electronically stored information other than that identified as not reasonably accessible without undue burden or cost, and produce responsive electronically stored information within the parameters of Fed.R.Civ.P 26(b)(2)(C); 2) searches of or for electronically stored information identified as not reasonably accessible should not be conducted until the prior step has been completed; and, 3 requests for information expected to be found in or among electronically stored information that was identified as not reasonably accessible should be narrowly focused, with factual basis supporting each request.

N. The need for any protective orders or confidentiality orders, in conformance with the Local Rules and substantive principles governing such orders.

O. Any request for sampling or testing of electronically stored information; the parameters of such requests; the time, manner, scope, and place limitations that will voluntarily or by Court order be placed on such processes; the persons to be involved; and the dispute resolution mechanism, if any, agreed-upon by the parties.

P. Any agreement concerning retention of an agreed-upon Court expert, retained at the cost of the parties, to assist in the resolution of technical issues presented by electronically stored information.

PARTICIPANTS

9. The following people:

A. Should, absent good cause, participate in the Fed.R.Civ.P. 26(f) Conference of Parties: lead counsel and at least one representative of each party.

B. May participate in the Fed.R.Civ.P. 26(f) Conference of Parties: clients or representatives of clients or the entity served with a subpoena; the designated electronically stored information coordinator for the party; forensic experts; and in-house information system personnel. Identification of an expert for use in a Fed.R.Civ.P. 26(f) Conference of Parties does not, in and of itself, identify that person as an expert whose opinions may be presented at trial within the meaning of Fed.R.Civ.P. 26(b)(4)(A), (B).

C. If a party is not reasonably prepared for the Fed.R.Civ.P. 26(f) Conference used to support a motion for sanctions by the opposing party for the costs incurred in connection with that Conference.

REASONABLY ACCESSIBLE

10. No party should object to the discovery of electronically stored information pursuant to Fed.R.Civ.P. 26(b)(2)(B) on the basis that it is not reasonably accessible because of undue burden or cost unless the objection has been stated with particularity, and not in

conclusory or boilerplate language. Wherever the term "reasonably accessible" is used in this Protocol, the party asserting that electronically stored information is not reasonably accessible should be prepared to specify facts that support its contention.

PRINCIPLES RE METADATA

11. The production of metadata apart from its native file may impose substantial costs, either in the extraction of such metadata from the native files, or in its review for purposes of redacting non-discoverable information contained in such metadata. The persons involved in the discovery process are expected to be cognizant of those costs in light of the various factors established in Fed.R.Civ.P. 26(b)(2)(C). The following principles should be utilized in determining whether metadata may be discovered:
    A. Metadata are part of electronically stored information. Such metadata, however, may not be relevant to the issues presented or, if relevant, not be reasonably subject to discovery given the Rule 26(b)(2)(C) cost-benefit factors. Therefore, it may be subject to cost-shifting under Fed.R.Civ.P. 26(b)(2)(C).
    B. Metadata may generally be viewed as either system Meta-Data, substantive metadata, or embedded metadata. System metadata are data that are automatically generated by a computer system. For example, system metadata often include information such as the author, date and time of creation, and the date a document was modified. Substantive metadata are data that reflects the substantive changes made to the document by the user. For example, it may include the text of actual changes to a document. While no generalization is universally applicable, system metadata are less likely to involve issues of work product and/or privilege.
    C. Except as otherwise provided in sub-paragraph E, below, metadata, especially substantive metadata,

need not be routinely produced, except upon agreement of the requesting and producing litigants, or upon a showing of good cause in a motion filed by the Requesting Party in accordance with the procedures set forth in the Local Rules of this Court. Consideration should be given to the production of system metadata and its production is encouraged in instances where it will not unnecessarily or unreasonably increase costs or burdens. As set forth above, upon agreement of the parties the Court will consider entry of an order approving an agreement that a part: may produce metadata in native files upon the representation of the recipient that the recipient will neither access nor review such data. This Protocol does not address the substantive issue of the duty to preserve such metadata, or its admissibility into evidence or use in the course of depositions or other discovery.

D. If a Producing Party produces electronically stored information without some or all of the metadata was contained in the electronically stored information, the Producing Party should inform all other of this fact, in writing, at or before the time of production.

E. Some native files contain, in addition to substantive metadata, system metadata, embedded metadata, which for purposes of this Protocol, means the text, numbers, content, data, or other information directly or indirectly inputted into a native file by a user and which typically visible to the user viewing the output display of the native file screen or as a print out. Examples of embedded metadata include, but are not limited to, spreadsheet formulas (which display as the result formula operation), hidden columns, externally or internally linked file: sound files in PowerPoint presentations), references to external file content (e.g., hyperlinks to HTML files or URLs), references and fields the field codes for an auto-numbered document), and certain database information if the data is part of a database (e.g., a date field in a database will display as a formatted date, but its actual value is typically a long integer). Subject to the other provisions of this Protocol related to the and benefits of preserving and producing metadata (see generally Paragraph 8), subject to potential redaction of substantive metadata, and substantive metadata and subject to reducing the scope of production of embedded metadata, embedded metadata is generally discoverable and in appropriate cases, see Fed.R.Civ.P. 26(b)(2)(C), should be produced as a matter of course. If the parties determine to produce embedded metadata, either in connection wit a native file production or in connection with static image production in lieu of native file production, the parties should normally discuss and agree on use of appropriate tools and methods to remove other metadata, but preserve the embedded metadata, prior to such production.

Comment

This form is adapted from a Protocol developed by the U.S. District Court for the District of Maryland. It can be adapted for use in other courts, including state courts, and also adapted to fit the circumstances of a particular case.

§ 8:16 Initial disclosure

[Caption]

In accordance with Rule 26(a)(1) of the Federal Rules of Civil Procedure, *[plaintiff] [defendant]* makes its mandatory disclosure as follows:

A. Witnesses

1. *[Name]* at *[address]* is likely to have discoverable information relevant to disputed facts alleged with particularity in the pleadings including *[describe]*.
2. *[Name]* at *[address]* is likely to have discoverable information relevant to disputed facts alleged with particularity in the pleadings including *[describe]*.
3. *[Name]* at *[address]* is likely to have discoverable information relevant to disputed facts alleged with particularity in the pleadings including *[describe]*.

B. Documents and Electronically Stored Information
   1. Contract between *[name]* and *[name]* dated *[date]*.
   2. Correspondence between *[name]* and *[name]* dated *[date]*.
   3. Memorandum from *[name]* to *[name]* dated *[date]*.
   4. *[Description by category and location of electronically stored information]*

C. Computation of Damages
   1. Explanation

   [Explain how any category of claimed damages has been calculated.]

   2. Documents Upon Which Computation Based
      a. Medical bill from *[name]* dated *[date]*.
      b. Automobile repair invoice from *[name]* dated *[date]*.

   D. Insurance Agreements
   1. Insurance Policy No. issued by *[name of insurer]* on *[date]*.
   2. Insurance Policy No. issued by *[name of insurer]* on *[date]*.

Dated: ________

[signature etc.]

§ 8:17 Order for appointment of special master

[Caption]

ORDER FOR APPOINTMENT OF SPECIAL MASTER

The stipulation of the parties for the appointment of a special master for discovery is approved, and

IT IS HEREBY ORDERED that *[name]* is appointed special master for discovery in the above-entitled action to serve at the pleasure of the court and in accordance with the terms of the parties' stipulation for appointment of a special master; and

IT IS FURTHER ORDERED that the parties shall abide by the terms and conditions of the stipulation for the duration of the pendency of this action or until further order of the court.

Dated: ________

____
Judge

Chapter 9

Discovery Conference

I. GUIDELINES

II. CHECKLISTS

III. FORMS

Research References

Treatises and Practice Aids

eDiscovery & Digital Evidence §§ 6:1 to 6:19

Grenig and Kinsler, Federal Civil Discovery and Disclosure §§ 1.186 to 1.189 (2d ed.)

Trial Strategy

Recovery and Reconstruction of Electronic Mail as Evidence, 41 Am. Jur Proof of Facts 3d 1
Computer Technology in Civil Litigation, 71 Am. Jur Trials 111

Additional References

Kassis, Prepare Yourself to Confer Under the amended Federal Rules of Civil Procedure Before Conferring, Elec. Discovery & Records Mgt. Q., Summer 2007, at 16
ABA Discovery Standards, http://www.abanet.org/litigation/discoverystandards/2005civildiscoverystandards.pdf
Electronic Discovery Reference Model Project, http://www.edrm.net
Federal Judicial Center, http://www.fjc.gov
The Sedona Conference, http://www.thesedonaconference.org

KeyCite®: Cases and other legal materials listed in KeyCite Scope can be researched through the KeyCite service on Westlaw®. Use KeyCite to check citations for form, parallel references, prior and later history, and comprehensive citator information, including citations to other decisions and secondary materials.

I. GUIDELINES

§ 9:1 Generally

The Manual for Complex Litigation Fourth § 11.446 emphasizes the importance of a conference as follows:

> The judge should encourage the parties to discuss the scope of proposed computer-based discovery early in the case, particularly any discovery of data beyond that available to the responding parties in the ordinary course of business. The requesting parties should identify the information they require as narrowly and precisely as possible, and the responding parties should be forthcoming and explicit in identifying what data are available from what sources, to allow formulation of a realistic computer-based discovery plan.

Under Rule 26(f) of the Federal Rules of Civil Procedure, parties must confer and develop a discovery plan at least 21 days before the Rule 16(b) scheduling and planning conference to plan for discovery.[1] By local rule, a court may provide a different time frame. The attorneys of record and all unrepresented parties that have appeared in the case are jointly responsible for arranging the conference, for attempting in good faith to agree on the proposed discovery plan, and for submitting to the court within 14 days after the conference a written report outlining the plan.

The duty to confer is mandatory and the substantive communications between counsel may later be considered by a court in deciding issues regarding a particular side's good faith. Even in states without a similar requirement, a conference to plan for discovery can be helpful to both sides.

Because organizations must quickly identify what sources exist, the conference is an excellent opportunity for a determination as to what electronically stored information is regularly being deleted, what data systems are no longer being used, and what electronically stored information is in a remote or third party location.

A successful Rule 26(f) conference depends upon cooperation and candor. There can be benefits from collaborating with the opposing party regarding criteria to be used in identifying information to be retained. On the other hand, the traditional adversarial approach may result in inefficiencies with resultant delays and increased costs.

§ 9:2 Preparing for the conference

Counsel's thorough preparation for the conference will usually result in a productive and beneficial result. Counsel should be familiar with all the components of a client's information technology infrastructure. There will

---

[Section 9:1]

[1]See Sedona Principle 3 ("Parties should confer early in discovery regarding the preservation and production of electronically stored information when these matters are at issue in the litigation and seek to agree on the scope of each party's rights and responsibilities.").

be occasions when client systems are so complicated that it may be necessary to consult with a systems person from the company. That systems person can speak to information technology issues, which databases are proprietary, which are not, etc.

Those systems whose electronically stored information is not relevant to the proceeding should be excluded from a preservation mandate. Proper preparation means routine business processes including archiving, and destruction, will not be hampered and the day-to-day processes and procedures will remain.

§ 9:3 Attendance at the conference

Rule 26(f) of the Federal Rules of Civil Procedure does not require that the conference be conducted in person. The conference can be conducted by telephone. The Advisory Committee's Note to the 2006 Amendment of Rule 26(f) expresses a preference for in-person meeting, but recognizes the distances some counsel would have to travel and that the resulting expenses may outweigh the benefits of an in person meeting. The court may order that the parties or attorneys attend the conference in person.

§ 9:4 Topics for the conference—Generally

Rule 26(f) of the Federal Rules of Civil Procedure provides for the following topics of discussion during the conference:

- A plan for discovery
- Disclosure of electronically stored information and preservation of that information.
- Sources of electronically stored information from which the clients are and are not producing information.
- What electronically stored information will be included in the search for relevant documents.
- What electronically stored information the clients have that will not be searched.
- The form of production to opposing counsel (e.g., na-

tive file vs. another format and the load file specifications for eventual use).

- Issues dealing with privilege, such as the prospect of including a clawback agreement in a court order.
- The type of case and the amount at risk.

Conferring requirements are not satisfied by requesting or demanding compliance with the requests for discovery. The parties must determine precisely what the requesting party is actually seeking, what responsive documents or information the discovering party is reasonably capable of producing, and what specific, genuine objections or other issues, if any, cannot be resolved without judicial intervention.[1]

§ 9:5 Topics for the conference—Form of production

Because of the importance of specifying the appropriate format of electronically stored information in a request for production, it is important to the form for production of electronically stored information. While metadata is generally of more significance with respect to database applications, it is of less importance with respect to word processing applications. Caution should be exercised in demanding that electronically stored information be produced in native form with metadata intact, as the other party may then insist upon the same.

§ 9:6 Topics for the conference—Privilege

Problems of privilege waiver can be addressed at the conference. Rule 26(b)(5)(B) provides a procedure for addressing accidental production of privileged information. In addition, clawback agreements should be given serious consideration. Clawbacks can be used in those circum-

---

[Section 9:4]

[1]Williams v. Sprint/United Management Co., 245 F.R.D. 660 (D. Kan. 2007). Cf. Verigy US, Inc. v. Mayder, 2007 WL 3144577 (N.D. Cal. 2007) (plaintiff's previous request for a search of all documents containing the letter "V" strikes this court as being patently overbroad).

stances where information that is actually privileged is produced. A clawback agreement would include a mechanism returning, sequestering, and destroying the privileged information. In the event that the receiving party has disclosed the information before receiving notice from the producing party, the receiving party must take reasonable steps to retrieve the disclosure. It is prudent to incorporate a clawback agreement in a court order to mitigate the risk of waiver.[1]

§ 9:7 Topics for the conference—Accessibility

The question of accessibility of electronically stored information should be discussed at the conference. Under Rule 26(b)(2)(B) of the Federal Rules of civil Procedure, electronically stored information that is not reasonable accessible because of cost and undue burden does not normally have to be produced. Electronically stored information that is not reasonably accessible may involve hardware or software that is dated or obsolete, and restoring the information would entail undue burden or cost.

§ 9:8 Failure to resolve issues

If, at the end of the discovery conference and after good faith efforts are undertaken by counsel on both sides, the parties cannot within a reasonable time resolve the issues around electronically stored information that is claimed not to be reasonably accessible, the party resisting production can seek a protective order barring production. The burden is then on the movant to prove the information is not reasonably accessible. The party seeking the information, despite the fact that the information is inaccessible, may then show good cause that the evidence should be produced considering the limitations of Rule 26(b)(2)(C).

[Section 9:6]

[1]See Hopson v. Mayor and City Council of Baltimore, 232 F.R.D. 228, 240, 97 Fair Empl. Prac. Cas. (BNA) 617, 63 Fed. R. Serv. 3d 582 (D. Md. 2005).

§ 9:9 Failing to participate in framing discovery plan

Under Rule 37(g) of the Federal Rules of Civil Procedure, if a party or a party's attorney fails to participate in good faith in the development and submission of a discovery plan, the court may require the party or attorney to pay to any other party the reasonable expenses, including attorney fees caused by the failure. The court must give the party or attorney an opportunity for a hearing.

§ 9:10 Scheduling conferences

In federal court, after receiving the discovery report required under Rule 26(f) of the Federal Rules of Civil Procedure or after conducting a scheduling conference under Rule 16(a), the court issues a scheduling ordering setting timetables for pretrial matters.[1] The scheduling order must be issued within 90 days after the appearance of a defendant and within 120 days of the service of the complaint.

Rule 16(b) requires the court's order to include time limits for completing discovery. At the court's discretion the scheduling order may include provisions governing the disclosure or discovery of electronically stored information and provisions for recalling privileged documents after production.

II. CHECKLISTS

§ 9:11 Checklist for preparing for conference

- ☐ If client has received a preservation order, confirm its dissemination, monitoring and fulfillment. Follow up to ensure its compliance.
- ☐ If client has not received a preservation order, draft and disseminate a preservation letter to client. Follow up to assure its compliance.

[Section 9:10]

[1]Fed.R.Civ.P. 16(b).

☐ Identify persons knowledgeable about the client's electronically stored information with the ability to facilitate reasonably anticipated discovery.

☐ Contact and involve the organization's information technology personnel early in the process.

☐ Identify the personnel in the information technology department; specifically, which personnel control which electronically stored information—including the records management program.

☐ Investigate how client's electronically stored information is stored and how it can be retrieved.

☐ Identify sources of potentially responsive electronically stored information including desktops, laptops, removable media, file and e-mail servers, databases, systems for document and enterprise resource management, and backup tapes. This requires talking with key players and support staff, including IT personnel.

☐ Ascertain which electronically stored information the client deems accessible and the reasons why a client deems certain electronically stored information not reasonably inaccessible.

☐ Determine which electronically stored information is active and which electronically stored information is inactive.

☐ Review client's electronically stored information (including active and passive files) to determine whether the information may be used to support claims or defenses.

☐ Produce accurate inventories of electronically stored information to the opposing side.

☐ Discuss scope and cost with the client. This includes discussing the volume of electronically stored information, approaches to discovery, use of vendors and consultants, and costs associated with preservation, collection, processing, searching, reviewing and producing the information.

☐ Prepare a negotiation strategy. In preparing the negotiation strategy, it is essential to determine the time and cost of implications of the process. This may include a list of custodians of electronically stored information, date ranges, potentially inaccessible sources, search technology, form of production, and timing.

- ☐ Prepare a disclosure strategy This may include a list of custodians, a list of preserved sources of electronically stored information, sources that have been evaluated and not preserved (including reasons why it was determined the sources did not include potentially responsive information), search and review considerations, and timing.
- ☐ Prepare a request strategy. This may include a description of what you want from the opposing party and the form of production desired. It may also be appropriate to consider scheduling future conferences.

§ 9:12 Checklist for discovery conference

- ☐ Send preservation letter to opposing party as soon as possible.
- ☐ Let the opposing side know what you will and will not be searching.
- ☐ Determine production schedule.
- ☐ Draft an agreement regarding the inadvertent production of privileged documents including electronically stored information.
- ☐ Determine whether restoration of deleted electronically stored information is necessary
- ☐ Determine whether back-up or archived electronically stored information is within the scope of discovery
- ☐ Determine media format.
- ☐ Determine procedures for production.
- ☐ Determine who will bear costs of preservation, production, and restoration of electronically stored information, if necessary.
- ☐ Come to an agreement that will be incorporated into an updated discovery plan requiring a description of

the process of production for electronically stored information.

- ☐ Document efforts to reach an accord regarding discovery and efforts to work out an agreement when disputes arise.

§ 9:13 Questions for conference

- ☐ What is the case about?
- ☐ Who are the key players?
- ☐ What period of time are pertinent?
- ☐ When does the duty to preserve electronically stored information begin and end?
- ☐ What electronically stored information is at greatest risk of alteration or destruction?
- ☐ What nonparties have information that must be preserved?
- ☐ What data requires forensically sound preservation?
- ☐ What metadata are relevant?
- ☐ If metadata are relevant, how will it be preserved, extracted, and produced?
- ☐ What are the other party's data retention policies and practices?
- ☐ Are legacy systems involved?
- ☐ What are the current e-mail applications?
- ☐ Are there any earlier e-mail applications? If so, what are they?
- ☐ How will voice mail be handled?
- ☐ How will instant messaging be handled?
- ☐ Are there relevant databases? If so, how will their contents be produced?
- ☐ Are there attorney-client or work product issues unique to the electronically stored information?
- ☐ What search techniques will be used to identify responsive electronically stored information?
- ☐ What search techniques will be used to identify privileged electronically stored information?
- ☐ What keywords should be used for searching?
- ☐ How will duplicate documents be handled?

☐ In what form or forms will electronically stored information be produced?

☐ Who will the redaction of privileged, irrelevant, or confidential content be handled?

☐ What sources of electronically stored information are claimed not to be reasonably accessible?

Comment

This form is adapted from Ball, Piecing Together the E-Discovery Plan, Trial, June 2008.

III. FORMS

§ 9:14 Report of parties planning meeting

[Caption]

Report of Parties' Planning Meeting

1. Pursuant to *[rule]*, a meeting was held on *[date]*, at *[place]* and was attended by:

[name] for plaintiff(s)
[name] for defendant(s) *[party name]*
[name] for defendant(s) *[party name]*

2. Pre-Discovery Disclosures. The parties *[have exchanged] [will exchange by [date]]* the information required by *[rule]*.

3. Discovery Plan. The parties jointly propose to the court the following discovery plan: *[Use separate paragraphs or subparagraphs as necessary if parties disagree.]*

Discovery will be needed on the following subjects: *[brief description of subjects on which discovery will be needed]*.

Disclosure or discovery of electronically stored information should be handled as follows: *[brief description of parties' proposals]*.

The parties have agreed to an order regarding claims of privilege or of protection as trial-preparation material asserted after production, as follows: *[brief description of provisions of proposed order]*.

All discovery commenced in time to be completed by

[date]. [Discovery on [issue for early discovery] to be completed by [date].]

Maximum of interrogatories by each party to any other party. *[Responses due days after service.]*

Maximum of requests for admission by each party to any other party. *[Responses due days after service.]*

Maximum of depositions by plaintiff(s) and by defendant(s).

Each deposition *[other than of]* limited to maximum of hours unless extended by agreement of parties.

Reports from retained experts under *[rule]* due:
from plaintiff(s) by *[date]*
from defendant(s) by *[date]*

Supplementations under *[rule]* due *[time(s) or interval(s)]*.

4. Other Items. *[Use separate paragraphs or subparagraphs as necessary if parties disagree.]*

The parties *[request]/[do not request]* a conference with the court before entry of the scheduling order.

The parties request a pretrial conference in *[month and year]*.

Plaintiff(s) should be allowed until *[date]* to join additional parties and until *[date]* to amend the pleadings.

Defendant(s) should be allowed until *[date]* to join additional parties and until *[date]* to amend the pleadings.

All potentially dispositive motions should be filed by *[date]*.

Settlement *[is likely]/ [is unlikely] [cannot be evaluated prior to [date]] [may be enhanced by use of the following alternative dispute resolution procedure: [date]*.

Final lists of witnesses and exhibits under *[rule]* should be due
from plaintiff(s) by *[date]*
from defendant(s) by *[date]*

Parties should have ____ days after service of final lists of witnesses and exhibits to list objections under *[rule]*.

The case should be ready for trial by *[date] [and at this time is expected to take approximately [length of time]]*.

[Other matters.]

Dated: ________

[signature, etc.]

Dated: ________

[signature, etc.]

Comment

This form is adapted from Official Form 35 approved by the U.S. Supreme Court.

§ 9:15 Stipulation and order regarding discovery conference discussions

[Caption]

STIPULATION AND ORDER REGARDING DISCOVERY CONFERENCE DISCUSSIONS

WHEREAS, the parties have reached agreement on a date for their first discovery conference discussions regarding the production of digital or electronic documents as well as certain ground rules for such discussions generally;

NOW THEREFORE, the parties, through their respective counsel of record, hereby stipulate as follows:

A. On *[date]*, the parties shall engage in discussions regarding the production of electronic documents in this case. The discussions will be attended by an electronic document consultant retained by *[party]* who will have sufficient knowledge of *[party]*'s electronic documents to enable *[party]* to participate in a good faith effort to resolve all issues regarding the production of electronic documents without court action. The discussions also will be attended by an electronic document consultant retained by the *[opposing party]* who will have sufficient knowledge of the *[opposing party]*'s electronic documents to enable the *[opposing party]* to participate in a good faith effort to resolve all issues regarding the production of electronic documents without court action.

B. Except as set forth in the next sentence, any electronic document consultant who personally attends any conference regarding the production of electronic documents in this case shall not be subject to discovery requests, including requests for depositions, until such time as the parties otherwise agree or this Court orders that such discovery may be taken. If any such digital or electronic document consultant provides testimony on an issue or issues in this case, whether by affidavit, declaration, deposition, or otherwise, the consultant may be subject to discovery requests, including requests for depositions, limited to the issue or issues that are the subject of the consultant's testimony.

Dated: ________

[signature, etc.]

Dated: ________

[signature, etc.]

PURSUANT TO STIPULATION, IT IS SO ORDERED.

Dated: ________

____

Judge

§ 9:16 Interim order to confer and to preserve electronically stored information

[Caption]

Interim Order Regarding Preservation

1. Order to Confer

In order to further the just, speedy, efficient, and economical management of discovery, the parties are ORDERED to confer as soon as practicable, no later than 30 days after the date of this order, to develop a plan for the preservation of documents, data, and tangible things reasonably anticipated to be subject to discovery in this action.

The parties may conduct this conference as part of the Federal Rules of Civil Procedure Rule 26(f) conference if the conference is scheduled to take place within 30 days of the date of this order. The resulting preservation plan may be submitted to this Court as a proposed order under Federal Rules of Civil Procedure Rule 16(e).

2. Subjects for Consideration

The parties should attempt to reach agreement on all issues regarding the preservation of documents data, and tangible things. These issues include, but are not necessarily limited to:

(a) the extent of the preservation obligation, identifying the types of material to be preserved, the subject matter, time frame, the authors and addressees, and key words to be used in identifying responsive materials;

(b) the identification of persons responsible for carrying out preservation obligations on behalf of each party;

(c) the form and method of providing notice of the duty to preserve to persons identified as custodian: of documents, data, and tangible things;

(d) mechanisms for monitoring, certifying, or auditing custodian compliance with preservation obligations;

(e) whether preservation will require suspending or modifying any routine business processes of procedures, with special attention to document-management programs and the recycling of computer data storage media;

(f) the methods to preserve any volatile but potentially discoverable material, such as voicemail active data in databases, or electronic messages;

(g) the anticipated costs of preservation and ways to reduce or share these costs; and

(h) a mechanism to review and modify the preservation obligation as discovery proceeds, eliminating or adding particular categories of documents, data, and tangible things.

3. Duty to Preserve

(a) Until the parties reach agreement on a preservation plan, all parties and their counsel are reminder of their duty to preserve evidence that may be relevant to this action. The duty extends to documents, data, and tangible things in the possession, custody and control of the parties to this action, and any employees, agents, contractors, carriers, bailees, or other nonparties possessing materials reasonably anticipated to be subject to discovery in this action. Counsel is under an obligation to exercise reasonable efforts to identify and notify such nonparties, including employees of corporate or institutional parties.

(b) The term "documents, data, and tangible things" is to be interpreted broadly to include writings, records, files, correspondence, reports, memoranda, calendars, diaries, minutes, electronic messages, voicemail, e-mail; telephone message records or logs, computer and network activity logs, hard drives; backup data, removable computer storage media such as tapes, disks, and cards, printouts document image files, Web pages, databases, spreadsheets, software, books, ledgers, journals, orders, invoices, bills, vouchers, checks, statements, worksheets, summaries, compilations, computations, charts, diagrams, graphic presentations, drawings, films, charts, digital or chemical process photographs, video, phonographic, tape, or digital recordings or transcripts, drafts, jottings, and notes. Information serving to identify, locate, or link such material, such as file inventories, file folders, indices, and metadata, is also included in this definition.

(c) "Preservation" is to be interpreted broadly to accomplish the goal of maintaining the integrity of all documents, data, and tangible things reasonably anticipated to be subject to discovery under Rules 26, 45, and 56(e) of the Federal Rules of Civil Procedure in this action. Preservation includes taking reasonable steps to prevent the partial or full destruction, alteration, testing, deletion, shredding, incineration, wiping relocation, migration, theft, or mutation of such material, as well as negligent or intentional handling that would make material incomplete or inaccessible.

(d) If the business practices of any party involve the routine destruction, recycling, relocation, of mutation of such materials, the party must, to the extent practicable for the pendency of this order either
 (1) halt such business processes;
 (2) sequester or remove such material from the business process; or
 (3) arrange for the preservation of complete and accurate duplicates or copies of such material suitable for later discovery if requested.

(e) A party may apply to the court for further instructions regarding the duty to preserve specific categories of documents, data, or tangible things before the conference to develop a preservation plan. A party may seek permission to resume routine business processes relating to the storage or destruction of specific categories of documents, data, or tangible things, upon a showing c undue cost, burden, or overbreadth.

4. Procedure in the Event No Agreement Is Reached

If, after conferring to develop a preservation plan, counsel do not reach agreement on the subjects listed under paragraph 2 of this order or on other material aspects of preservation, the parties are to submit to the Court within three days of the conference a statement of the unresolved issues together with each party's proposal for their resolution of the issues. In framing an order regarding the preservation of documents, data, and tangible things, the court will consider those statements as well as any statements made in an applications under paragraph 3(e) of this order.

Dated: ________

____

Judge

Comment

The primary purpose of this order is to encourage the parties to confer in order to develop their own preservation plan. The form may be modified to serve as a stand-alone preservation order. The rule references in the form are to the Federal Rules of Civil Procedure. If the action is in a state court, the rule references should be modified accordingly.

This form is adapted from Form 40.25 in the Manual for Complex Litigation Fourth. When adapting for use in state court, the references to Federal Rules of Civil Procedure should be replaced by reference to applicable state rules.

§ 9:17 Case management report

[Caption]

Case Management Report

The parties have agreed on the following dates and discovery plan pursuant to *[rule]*:

DEADLINE OR EVENT		AGREED DATE
Mandatory Initial Disclosures (pursuant to *[rule]*)		*[date]*
Certificate of Interested Persons and Corporate Disclosure Statement		
Motions to Add Parties or to Amend Pleadings		*[date]*
Disclosure of Expert Reports	Plaintiff:	**Plaintiff's deadline to disclose expert—*[date]***
		Plaintiff's deadline to disclose expert report—*[date]*
	Defendant:	**Defendant's deadline to disclose expert—*[date]***
		Defendant's deadline to disclose expert report—*[date]*
Dispositive Motions		*[date]*
Meeting *In Person* to Prepare Joint Final Pretrial		*[date]*
Statement		
Joint Final Pretrial Statement (Including a Single Set of Jointly-Proposed Jury Instructions and Verdict Form (with diskette), Voir Dire Questions, Witness Lists, Exhibit Lists with Objections on Approved Form)		*[date]*

All Other Motions Including Motions in Limine, Trial Brief	*[date]*
Final Pretrial Conference	*[date]*
Trial Term Begins	*[date]*
Estimated Length of Trial	___ days
Jury/Non-Jury	
Mediation Deadline:	*[date]*
Mediator:	*[name]*
Address:	*[address]*
Telephone:	______________
All Parties Consent to Proceed Before Magistrate Judge	______________

I. Meeting of Parties in Person

Pursuant to *[rule]*, a meeting was held in person on *[date]*, at *[place]* and was attended by

Name	*Trial Counsel for*:
[name]	Plaintiff
[name]	Defendant

II. Pre-Discovery Initial Disclosures of Core Information *[rule]* Disclosures

The parties

☐ have exchanged
☐ agree to exchange information described in *[rule]* by *[date]*.

III. Agreed Discovery Plan for Plaintiff and Defendant

A. Certificate of Interested Persons and Corporate Disclosure Statement

Every party that has appeared in this action to date has filed and served or will file and serve a Certificate of Interested Persons and Corporate Disclosure Statement, which remains current:

Plaintiff filed a Certificate of Interested Persons and Corporate Disclosure Statement on *[date]*.

Defendant filed a Certificate of Interested Persons and Corporate Disclosure Statement on *[date]*.

B. Discovery Not Filed

The parties shall not file discovery materials with the Clerk except as provided in *[rule]*. The Court encourages the exchange of discovery requests on diskette. See *[rule]*. The parties further agree as follows:

i. The parties will try to furnish all discovery requests on diskette using Microsoft Word.
ii. Responses to interrogatories will include both the question posed followed by the response.
iii. Service of discovery requests by facsimile is sufficient.
iv. Documents, including electronic discovery will be produced in PDF format or by printing the electronic documents. Electronic discovery does not have to be produced in its natural form, unless the authenticity of a particular document becomes an issue in the case.

C. Limits on Discovery

Absent leave of Court, the parties may take no more

than ___ depositions per side (not per party). *[rule].* Absent leave of Court, the parties may serve no more than ___ interrogatories, including sub-parts. *[rule].* Absent leave of Court or stipulation of the parties each deposition is limited to ___ day(s) of ___ hours. The parties may agree by stipulation on other limits on discovery. The Court will consider the parties' agreed dates, deadlines, and other limits in entering the scheduling order. In addition to the deadlines in the above table, the parties have agreed to further limit discovery as follows:

1. Depositions: no additional agreements, but they are not waiving any rights to request additional time consistent with *[rule].*
2. Interrogatories: parties agree to a limit of ___ interrogatories
3. Document Requests:
4. Request to Admit:
5. Supplementation of Discovery:

D. Discovery Deadline

Each party shall timely serve discovery requests so that the rules allow for a response prior to the discovery deadline. The Court may deny as untimely all motions to compel filed after the discovery deadline, hi addition, the parties agree as follows:

E. Disclosure of Expert Testimony

On or before the dates set forth in the above table for the disclosure of expert reports, the parties agree to fully comply with *[rules].* Expert testimony on direct examination at trial will be limited to the opinions, basis, reasons, data and other information disclosed in the written expert report disclosed pursuant to this order. Failure to disclose such information may result in the exclusion of all or part of the testimony of the expert witness. The parties agree on the following additional matters pertaining to the disclosure of expert testimony:

The parties may agree to submission of videotaped expert testimony.

F. Confidentiality Agreements

Whether documents filed in a case may be filed under seal is a separate issue from whether the parties may agree that produced documents are confidential. The Court is a public forum, and disfavors motions to file under seal. The Court will permit the parties to file documents under seal only upon a finding of extraordinary circumstances and particularized need. A party seeking to file a document under seal must file a motion to file under seal requesting such Court action, together with memorandum of law in support. The motion, whether granted or denied, will remain in the public record.

The parties may reach their own agreement regarding the designation of materials as "confidential." There is no need for the Court to endorse the confidentiality agreement. The Court discourages unnecessary stipulated motions for a protective order. The Court will enforce appropriate stipulated and signed confidentiality agreements. Each confidentiality agreement or order shall provide, or shall be deemed to provide, that "no party shall file a document under seal without first having obtained an order granting leave to file under seal on showing of particularized need." With respect to confidentiality agreements the parties agree as follows: The parties agree that they will seek to protect confidential documents and information through confidentiality agreements entered into between counsel, as necessary.

G. Other Matters Regarding Discovery

Counsel for either party may appear telephonically for depositions and depositions may be videotaped.

Unless otherwise agreed, depositions will occur at *[place]*.

IV. Settlement and Alternative Dispute Resolution

A. Settlement

The parties agree that settlement is

☐ Likely
☐ Unlikely

The parties request a settlement conference before a United States Magistrate Judge.

☐ Likely
☐ Unlikely

B. Arbitration

[Rule] defines those civil actions that will be referred to arbitration automatically. Does this case fall within the scope of Local Rule 8.02(a)?

☐ Yes
☐ No

For cases not falling within the scope of Local Rule 8.02(a), the parties consent to arbitration pursuant to *[rule]*:

☐ Yes
☐ No
☐ Likely to agree in future

In any civil case subject to arbitration, the Court may substitute mediation for arbitration upon a determination that the case is susceptible to resolution through mediation. The parties agree that the case is susceptible to resolution through mediation, and therefore jointly request mediation in place of arbitration.

☐ Yes
☐ No
☐ Likely to agree in future

C. Mediation

The parties have agreed to select a mediator from the Court's approved list of mediators as provided by the

Clerk of Court or will seek approval of another mediator, and have agreed to the date stated in the table above as the last date for mediation.

D. Other Alternative Dispute Resolution

The parties intend to pursue the following other methods of alternative dispute resolution:

Dated: ________

[signature, etc.]

Dated: ________

[signature, etc.]

§ 9:18 Joint case management statement and proposed case scheduling order

[Caption]

Joint Case Management Statement and Proposed Case Scheduling Order

I. INTRODUCTION

Pursuant to *[rule]*, a conference was held on *[date]*, in Case No. ________, and was attended by *[names]*. The parties attended the Initial Case Management Conference for this matter on *[date]*, but since the parties could not agree as to the form of production of electronically stored information, the Court declined to issue a Scheduling Order, rather, it referred the parties to a discovery conference with Magistrate Judge *[name]* on *[date]*. The parties now appear for this Continued Case Management Conference to set the Scheduling Order in this matter.

A. Jurisdiction and Service

This case is brought under the *[statute]*. The Court has subject matter jurisdiction under *[statute]*.

Service has been effected on all named parties. Plaintiff may add additional individual defendants after the completion of initial discovery; Plaintiff will do so no later than *[date]*.

B. Facts

Plaintiff alleges that Defendant violated *[statute]* when Plaintiff *[describe]*.

C. Legal Issues

D. Motions

The parties have filed no motions and there are no motions pending before this Court. Defendant intends to file a motion for summary judgment once discovery is completed.

E. Amendment of Pleadings

The parties may amend their pleadings. A party needing to amend must do so on or before *[date]*.

F. Evidence Preservation

Defendant suspended the routine destruction of electronically stored information to preserve evidence relevant to the issues reasonably evident in this action and has preserved the information for production to Plaintiff, if necessary.

G. Disclosures

Pre-discovery Disclosures: The parties have exchanged initial disclosures required by *[rule]* on *[date]*.

H. Discovery

Defendant served its first set of Special Interrogatories and Request for Production of Documents on Plaintiff on *[date]*.

The parties propose to the court the following discovery plan:

1. Plaintiff's Discovery Plan. Plaintiff believes that discovery will be needed on the following subjects:
   a. Defendant's motivation for the selection of Plaintiffs reemployment position and its relationship to eventual termination.
   b. Discovery of electronically stored documents.
   c. Willful nature of Defendant's termination of Plaintiff.
   d. Defendant's financials.
   e. Reemployment of Plaintiff following military service.
   f. Relocation of Defendant's District managerial staff.
   g. Retraining schedule of Plaintiff following his reemployment.
2. Defendant's Discovery Plan. Defendant believes that discovery will be needed on the following subjects:
   a. Plaintiff's performance.
   b. Plaintiff's mitigation efforts.
   c. All issues raised in Defendant's answer and affirmative defenses.
3. Plaintiff requests a maximum of ____ interrogatories by each party to any other party. Defendant objects to the propounding of any interrogatories over the limits imposed by *[rule]*.
4. No limitation on requests for admission by each party to any other party.
5. Maximum of 10 depositions by Plaintiff and by Defendant.
6. Each deposition shall be limited to a maximum of 7 hours within one day unless extended by agreement of the parties. Defendant anticipates that it may need more than seven (7) hours to complete

the deposition of Plaintiff, and requests that the Court grant additional time.

7. Electronic Discovery: Defendant has agreed to provide Plaintiff with electronically stored information in its native format. Defendant will also provide a separate production in.TIP or.PDF format with Bates numbers allowing the parties to track the documents. Defendant will produce any partially privileged documents, and documents that contain confidential or proprietary information in native format and in.TIP or.PDF form along with any associated non-privileged metadata. Plaintiff does not agree to the production of any electronically stored information in any format other than the native format of the information.

Although the parties cannot agree on the form of production of privileged, confidential, or proprietary information, Magistrate Judge *[name]* deferred ruling or issuing a discovery order until an issue actually arose. Plaintiff has stated plaintiff will not intentionally seek discovery of privileged information from Defendant. The parties have filed a stipulated protective order that will govern the use of Defendant's designated confidential information.

I. Related Cases

There are no related cases.

J. Relief

In any action under *[statute]*, the court may award relief as follows: *[describe]*.

K. Settlement Alternative Dispute Resolution

The parties have filed a Stipulation and Proposed Order Selecting an ADR process: Settlement Conference with a Magistrate Judge to occur after initial discovery has been completed.

L. Consent to Magistrate Judge for All Purposes

The parties do not consent to the assignment of this case to a Magistrate Judge for trial.

M. Other References

This case is not suitable for reference to binding arbitration, a special master, or the Judicial Panel on Multidistrict Litigation.

N. Narrowing of Issues

The issues in this case cannot be narrowed by agreement. The parties will confer prior to trial to attempt to expedite the admission of evidence through stipulation. Defendant intends to file a motion to bifurcate the liability phase of trial from any trial on the issue of liquidated damages.

O. Expedited Schedule

Due to the inevitable issues surrounding the production of electronically stored information, the parties do not believe this case is suitable for an expedited schedule.

P. Scheduling

(1) All non-expert discovery shall cut off on *[date]*.

(2) Disclosure of and production of initial report from retained experts for the parties under *[rule]* are to be served on or before *[date]*.

(3) Supplementary expert disclosure and expert reports are to be served by *[date]*. Expert discovery shall cut-off on *[date]*.

(4) All dispositive motions shall be filed on or before *[date]*.

(5) The parties request a trial date of *[date]*.

Q. Trial

The parties estimate the length of trial at ____ days. Plaintiff has requested a jury.

R. Disclosure of Non-Party Interested Entities or Persons

Defendant has filed its "Certification of Interested Entities or Persons" as required by *[rule]*. Defendant restates that the following entities have either: (i) a financial interest in the subject matter in controversy or in a party to the proceeding; or (ii) any other kind of interest that could be substantially affected by the outcome of the proceeding: *[names]*.

Dated: ________

[signature, etc.]

Dated: ________

[signature, etc.]

§ 9:19 Scheduling order

[Caption]

Joint Scheduling Report

Plaintiffs, *[names]*, and Defendants, *[names]*, through respective undersigned counsel, submit their Joint Scheduling Report as follows:

1. Description of the Case

a. Attorneys:

For the Plaintiffs:

[names, addresses, and telephone numbers]

For the Defendants:

[names, addresses, and telephone numbers]

b. Plaintiffs allege Federal jurisdiction is based on *[statute].*

c. Plaintiffs are *[describe]* who seek *[describe].*

d. Major legal and factual issues:

Plaintiffs contend that *[describe].* Plaintiff see damages in the amount of $________, plus interest and costs.

Defendants contend that *[describe].*

2. Proposed case management plan

a) Pending motions: ________

b) Deadline for joinder of additional parties: *[date]*

c) Deadline for amendments to pleadings: *[date]*

d) (i) Rule 26 (a) (1) Disclosure shall be served by *[date]* (assuming confidentiality stipulation is in place).

(ii) Factual discovery shall be completed by November 1, 2007

(iii) Plaintiffs Expert Disclosure (including reports) shall be made by *[date].* Defendants Expert Disclosure (including reports) shall be made by *[date].*

(iv) Expert discovery shall be completed by *[date].*

e) Final prctrial order shall be filled by *[date].*

f) The parties estimate that a jury trial will last two weeks. The case will be trial ready on *[date].*

g) Motions related to limitations of liability shall be filed by *[date].*

h) The last filing date for dispositive motions is *[date].*

i) The parties agree that service of papers can also be made by e-mail or fax.

3. The parties do not unanimously consent to trial before magistrate.

4. Status of settlement discussions

The parties agree to discuss settlement and request a settlement conference in *[date].*

5. Privilege

a) The parties shall agree on a date to exchange privilege logs.

b) Assertions of privilege and work product shall be permitted for documents produced for a period of up to 60 days after production.

6. Electronic Discovery

a) Counsel shall request that their clients place a litigation hold on documents related to *[describe]*.

b) E-mails and other electronic data shall be produced either on disks or printed out as if they were hard copy documents. E-mails shall be searched under terms identifying *[describe]* in question or as otherwise reasonably demanded. Data contained in backup logs or tapes need not be produced unless shown by circumstances to be necessary. No party shall intentionally erase any relevant data or intentionally move any relevant data to backup logs.

Dated: ________

____

Judge

Chapter 10

Depositions

I. GUIDELINES

II. CHECKLISTS

III. FORMS

Research References

Additional References

ABA Discovery Standards, http://www.abanet.org/litigation/discoverystandards/2005civildiscoverystandards.pdf
Federal Judicial Center, http://www.fjc.gov
Llewellyn, Electronic Discovery Best Practices, 10 Rich. J.L. & Tech. 51 (2004)
The Sedona Conference, http://www.thesedonaconference.org
Waxse, "Do I Really Have to Do That?" Rule 26(a)(1) Disclosures and Electronic Information, 10 Rich.J.L. & Tech. 50 (2004)

Treatises and Practice Aids

eDiscovery & Digital Evidence § 7:13
Grenig and Kinsler, Federal Civil Discovery and Disclosure §§ 5.1 to 7.44 (2d ed.)

Trial Strategy

Recovery and Reconstruction of Electronic Mail as Evidence, 41 Am. Jur Proof of Facts 3d 1
Computer Technology in Civil Litigation, 71 Am. Jur Trials 111

KeyCite®: Cases and other legal materials listed in KeyCite Scope can be researched through the KeyCite service on Westlaw®. Use KeyCite to check citations for form, parallel references, prior and later history, and comprehensive citator information, including citations to other decisions and secondary materials.

I. GUIDELINES

§ 10:1 Generally

A deposition is testimony taken prior to trial before an officer authorized to administer oaths, subject to cross-examination, and preserved in writing. Under certain circumstances, deposition testimony may be admissible at trial. Depositions may be taken either upon oral examination or upon written questions. Depositions are almost always taken orally rather than in writing.

§ 10:2 Advantages and disadvantages of depositions upon oral examination

The major advantage of a deposition upon oral examination over any other discovery device is that oral examination permits more effective questioning. If the deponent's answers are evasive, incomplete, or non-responsive, the examiner can follow up with additional questions. In addition, the deponent's credibility and memory can be tested by questions about related matters that tend to confirm or disprove earlier answers. There is also a much better possibility of obtaining spontaneous admissions in depositions upon oral examination than with other discovery devices, such as interrogatories where the answers are usually prepared by opposing counsel. A deposition upon oral examination allows the examiner to determine the impression that a witness is likely to make on the jury if the case goes to trial.

A deposition upon oral examination may be more efficient than other discovery devices because a deposition usually can be set on just a few days' notice to the opposing party. In addition, documents can be inspected and answers can be obtained to oral questions at the time of the deposition.

§ 10:3 Whose deposition may be taken—Generally

The deposition of any person, including a party or nonparty witness, may be taken. A party may take the deposition of any other party—whether an adverse party or a coparty. A party may even take its own deposition. The person deposed may be a natural person, an organization such as a public or private corporation, a partnership, an association, or a governmental agency. Party deponents are not entitled to witness fees. However, a nonparty deponent may be entitled to witness fees.

§ 10:4 Whose deposition may be taken—Expert witnesses

Under Rule 26(b)(4)(A) of the Federal Rules of Civil Procedure, a party may depose any person who has been identified as an expert and whose opinions may be presented at trial.[1] Unless manifest injustice would result, the court must require the party seeking discovery to pay the expert a reasonable fee for the time spent in responding to discovery.[2]

An expert witness who is not expected to testify at trial may not be deposed except as provided by Rule 35(b) upon a motion showing that exceptional circumstances exist under which it is impracticable for the party seeking discovery to obtain facts or opinions on the same subject by other means.

§ 10:5 Whose deposition may be taken—Organizations—Generally

Because it is not literally possible to take the deposition of a corporation or other organization, when an organization is involved, the information must be obtained from a natural person who can speak for the organization.[1] Since the deposition of any person can be taken, the deposition of any person associated with the organization and acquainted with the facts can be taken. A Rule 36(b)(6) deposition can be effective way of deposing the person in an organization responsible for computer systems or electronically stored information.

Rule 30(b)(6) permits the discovering party to name in the notice of deposition a public or private corporation, a partnership, an association, or a governmental agency. The notice must describe with reasonable particularity the matters on which the examination is requested. It is then

---

[Section 10:4]

[1]Cf. Roberts v. Canadian Pacific Ry. Ltd., 2007 WL 118901 (D. Minn. 2007) (plaintiff could take deposition of defendant's computer forensics expert after an e-mail was discovered indicating a policy of destroying electronically stored information).

[2]Fed. R. Civ. P. 26(b)(4)(C).

[Section 1C:5]

[1]Fed. R. Civ. P. 36(b)(6).

the duty of the corporation to name one or more officers, directors, or managing agents, or other persons who consent to testify on its behalf and these persons must testify. A corporate party is not absolutely bound to its deposition designee's recollection.

The corporation's duty to name persons who will testify on its behalf relieves the party seeking discovery of the burden of ascertaining the appropriate individual to depose while relieving the other party of the inconvenience of having an unnecessarily large number of its officers deposed. Rule 30(b)(6) also assists organizations that find an unnecessarily large number of their officers and agents are being deposed by a party uncertain of who in the organization has knowledge. When a witness is designated by a corporation to speak on its behalf, producing an unprepared witness is tantamount to a failure to appear that is sanctionable.

Rule 30(b)(6) does not preclude a party from taking the deposition of a specific individual associated with a corporation or organization. But when a party utilizes Rule 30(b)(6), it has no right to insist that the organization choose a specific person, unless the person designated is an officer, director, or managing agent whom the corporation may be required to produce under Rule 30(b)(1).

§ 10:6 Whose deposition may be taken—Organizations—Employees

Except where the employee of an organization has been designated by the organization under Rule 30(b)(6) or the employee is an officer, director, or managing agent of the organization, the employee is treated the same as any other witness and the employee's presence must be obtained by subpoena rather than by notice. The deposition is not considered to be that of the organization and is usable only under the same circumstances as that of any other non-party witness.

§ 10:7 Specific individuals associated with organization—Officers and managing agents

If the deponent is an officer, director, or managing agent of an organization that is a party to the suit, the corporation is responsible for producing that person for the taking of the person's deposition after being served with a proper notice; a subpoena for their attendance is unnecessary. The question of whether a particular person is a "managing agent" is determined pragmatically on a case-by-case basis.

The deposition of "anyone who at the time of taking the deposition was an officer, director, or managing agent, or a person designated under Rule 30(b)(6) or Rule 31(a) to testify on behalf of a public or private corporation, partnership or association or governmental agency which is a party may be used by an adverse party for any purpose." The determination of whether a particular person is an officer, director, or managing agent is made by the trial court when the deposition is sought to be introduced or when sanctions are asked for the individual's failure to appear for the taking of his or her deposition. In determining whether an individual is an officer, director, or managing agent of an organization, courts consider the following:

- Whether the individual involved is invested by the organization with general powers to exercise his or her discretion and judgment in dealing with organization.
- Whether the individual can be depended upon to carry out the organization's direction to give testimony at the demand of a party engaged in litigation with the employer.
- Whether the individual can be expected to identify with the interests of the corporation rather than with those of the other parties.

§ 10:8 When depositions may be taken—Generally

Except when authorized by the Federal Rules of Civil Procedure, by local rule or order, or the agreement of the parties, the taking of a deposition under Rule 30 normally cannot be noticed until the parties have conferred as required by Rule 26(f). A showing of good cause is necessary to justify an expedited discovery order before the Rule 26(f) discovery conference. For an ex parte motion for expedited discovery to be justified, the evidence must show: (1) that the moving party's cause will be irreparably prejudiced if the underlying motion is heard according to the regular noticed motion procedures, and (2) the moving party is without fault in creating the crisis that requires ex parte relief or that the crisis is the result excusable neglect. A deposition may be taken before the commencement of an action in accordance with the procedures set forth in Rule 27 of the Federal Rules of Civil Procedure.

If the time for the deposition is inconvenient, the court has the power under Rule 26(c) to issue a protective order specifying the time or place on which discovery can be had. If the court changes the time, a second notice of taking the deposition is not necessary.

§ 10:9 When depositions may be taken—Sequence

Depositions may be taken in any sequence, unless the court upon motion, for the convenience of the parties and witnesses and in the interests of justice, orders otherwise.[1] The fact that one party is conducting discovery, by deposition or otherwise, does not operate to delay another party's right to discovery. It is appropriate to discuss the sequence of depositions at the discovery conference and the scheduling conference.

§ 10:10 Notice of deposition—Generally

A party desiring to take the deposition of any person must give reasonable written notice to every other party to the action. Service of the notice must be made upon all parties. The notice must be filed either before service or within a reasonable time afterwards.

[Section 10:9]

[1] Fed. R. Civ. P. 26(d).

The notice must be in writing and it must state the time and place of the taking of the deposition. Additionally, the notice must state the name and address of each person to be examined, if known. If the name is not known, a general description is sufficient to identify the person or the particular class or group to which the person belongs. A list of any materials the deponent is compelled to produce at the deposition must also be attached to or included in the notice. Any subpoena directing a witness to appear at the deposition should be attached to the notice.

§ 10:11 Notice of deposition—Time of notice

Under Rule 30(b)(1) of the Federal Rules of Civil Procedure, notice of the deposition must be given within a reasonable time before the deposition. Courts have upheld notice of six days and eight days. Rule 32(a) provides that a deposition cannot used against a party that has received less than 11 days' notice of the deposition, has promptly filed a motion for a protective order requesting that the deposition not be held or be held at a different time, and the motion is pending at the time the deposition is held.

§ 10:12 Notice of deposition—Party deponent

The deposition of a party may be taken by notice; a subpoena is not required.[1] The notice to a party deponent may be accompanied by a request made in compliance with Rule 34 for the production of documents and tangible things at the taking of the deposition. The attendance of an officer, director, or managing agent of an entity that is a party may be compelled by notice addressed to the named person. On the other hand, an individual employee of a party-entity who is not an officer, director, or managing agent of the party-entity may be compelled to attend a deposition only by subpoena.

[Section 10:12]

[1]See Fed. R. Civ. P. 30(b)(1).

§ 10:13 Notice of deposition—Organizational parties

A party may name as a party-deponent in the notice a public or private corporation, a partnership, an association, or a governmental agency.[1] The notice must designate with reasonable particularity the matters on which the examination is requested. An organization cannot be expected to designate an appropriate representative at a deposition if it does not know the subject matter of the testimony.

Once the deponent has satisfied his or her minimum obligation by responding to questions on matters set forth in the notice of deposition, then the scope of the deposition is determined solely by relevance. If the organization has objections to either questions outside the scope of the Rule 30(b)(6) designation, counsel for the organization should state the objection on the record and the witness should answer the question, to the best of the witness' ability.

§ 10:14 Notice of deposition—Objection to notice

Objections to the notice of deposition are waived unless a written objection is promptly served upon the party giving notice. Possible errors or irregularities include the wrong name, an incorrect date, incorrect location, improper service, lack of timely notice, or failure to include a list of compelled materials. Whenever possible, the objection should be made before the deposition.

§ 10:15 Compelling production of documents at deposition

The procedure for compelling production of documents at a deposition depends on whether the deponent is or is not a party. If a party seeks to compel another party deponent to bring with it documents and other tangible things, the notice of taking of the deposition must be ac-

---

[Section 10:13]

[1]See Fed. R. Civ. P. 30(b)(6).

companied with a request for the production of documents and things in compliance with the procedural requirements of for a request for production. If the deponent is not a party, production of the documents can be compelled only by a subpoena duces tecum. Witnesses may be compelled to produce documents that they control even though they do not have possession of them.

§ 10:16 Place of examination

Rules 45(d)(2) and 26(c)(2) of the Federal Rules of Civil Procedure control the taking of a deposition. Generally, the examining party may set the place for the deposition of another party wherever the examining party wishes, subject to the court's power to grant a protective order under Rule 26(c)(2) designating a different place. In the alternative, the parties may agree to a deposition location.

Courts usually permit an individual defendant to be deposed in the district of his or her residence, or, if an organizational party, at its principal place of business. However, corporate defendants are frequently deposed in places other than the location of the principal place of business, especially in the forum, for the convenience of all parties and in the general interests of judicial economy.

Factors that serve to dissipate the presumption that a corporate party's deposition should be held at its principal place of business and may persuade the court to require the deposition be conducted in the forum district or in some other place include:

- Location of counsel for the parties.
- Number of corporate representatives a party is seeking to depose.
- Likelihood of significant discovery disputes arising that would necessitate resolution by the forum court.
- Whether persons sought to be deposed often engage in travel for business purposes.
- Equities with regard to the nature of the claim and the parties' relationship.

If the deponent is an officer, director or managing agent of a corporate party, or other person designated under

Rule 30(b)(6), the place of examination is determined as if the deponent's place of residence, employment, or transacting business in person were that of the party.

An individual plaintiff must usually submit to deposition in the district where the plaintiff commenced the litigation. A plaintiff should not be able to complain of his or her chosen forum, while defendants have no similar choice.

Unless otherwise ordered by a court, party deponents are normally required to pay their own transportation costs. These rules are subject to modification based on certain factors, such as:

- Which party is better able to absorb the deponent's transportation costs.
- The location of documents necessary at the deposition.
- The convenience of the deponent, parties, and counsel.
- The location of documents or physical evidence.
- Which court is best suited to supervise the deposition.
- The deponent's physical well-being.
- The counsels' location.
- The location of prior depositions.

II. CHECKLISTS

§ 10:17 Checklist of matters to consider in selecting deponent

The deponent should be the person most knowledgeable about:

- ☐ Number, types, and locations of computers in use and no longer in use
- ☐ Operating systems and application software in use
- ☐ File-naming and location-saving conventions
- ☐ Disk- or tape-labeling conventions
- ☐ Backup and archival disk or tape inventories or schedules
- ☐ Most likely locations of digital records relevant to the subject matter of the case
- ☐ Most likely locations of digital records relevant to the subject matter of the case

- ☐ Backup rotation schedules and archiving procedures, including backup programs in use at any relevant time
- ☐ Digital records management policies and procedures
- ☐ Corporate policies regarding employee use of company computers and data
- ☐ Identities of all current and former employees who have or had access to network administration, backup, archiving, or other system operations during the relevant period

§ 10:18 Checklist for deponent's attorney

Before the deposition, the deponent's attorney should:

- ☐ Instruct the deponent not to answer questions they do not understand.
- ☐ Advise the deponent not speculate or guess. The deponent should be told that if the deponent speculates in favor of the deponent, it will be disregarded; if the deponent speculates with unfavorable results for the deponent it will be used against the deponent.
- ☐ Tell the deponent not to volunteer information.

§ 10:19 Checklist for commencing deposition

The examining attorney may begin the deposition by stating a series of rules, establishing the framework for the deposition. These rules may include the following:

- ☐ I'm going to ask you a series of questions regarding the incident that is the subject of the lawsuit and which happened on *[date]*.
- ☐ If at any time you do not understand one of my questions, please say so and I will repeat or restate the question.
- ☐ All of your answers must be made in words, since the court reporter cannot take down gestures.
- ☐ If you do not know the answer to a question, simply state that you do not know. I do not want you to guess or to speculate as to your answers.
- ☐ Please state your answers clearly for the record so

that the court reporter can accurately transcribe each of your words.

- ☐ Please wait until I finish each of my questions before answering and I will wait until you finish each of your answers before asking another questions.
- ☐ We will take a break about every hour to give the court reporter and all of us a chance to refresh ourselves. If you need a break before then, please ask and we will take one.
- ☐ Do you understand that the deposition will be transcribed by the court reporter and that everything said here today will be recorded?
- ☐ Do you understand that, at the trial, all the testimony given here today will be available in written form and if I ask you a question at trial that I ask you today, you may be asked to explain any differences that may occur in your answers?
- ☐ Do you understand that your testimony today is being given under oath, as if you were in a court of law?

§ 10:20 Checklist of objections

- ☐ Oath or affirmation
- ☐ Conduct of the parties
- ☐ Manner of taking the deposition
- ☐ Form of the questions or answers
  - ☐ Leading or suggestive question
  - ☐ Ambiguous or uncertain question
  - ☐ Compound questions
  - ☐ Question assumes a fact not in evidence
  - ☐ Question calls for narrative answer
  - ☐ Question calls for speculation or conjecture
  - ☐ Question is argumentative
- ☐ Any kind of error that might have been corrected had a timely objection been made

§ 10:21 Witness interview checklist

- ☐ Name

- ☐ Department or Business unit
- ☐ Address
- ☐ Telephone
- ☐ Cell Phone
- ☐ Administrative Assistant if any
- ☐ E-mail address/es
- ☐ Best way to reach witness

☐ Record Retention

- ☐ Knowledge of litigation hold
- ☐ Knowledge of organization's retention program
- ☐ Knowledge of backup procedures

☐ Employment History

- ☐ Tenure with company
- ☐ Brief description of current duties and responsibilities
- ☐ Changes over time
- ☐ Brief description of prior duties and responsibilities

☐ Reporting chain

- ☐ Who do you report to?
- ☐ Who reports to you?

☐ Computer use

- ☐ What computers do you have access to?
  - ☐ Laptop
  - ☐ Desktop
  - ☐ Network
  - ☐ PDAs
  - ☐ Home
  - ☐ Other
- ☐ Preservations steps
  - ☐ Did you receive the litigation hold for this matter?
  - ☐ What steps did you take to comply?
  - ☐ Have you destroyed any data called for in the hold?
  - ☐ Where do you maintain data that relates to the issues in this matter?

        - ☐ Hard copy
        - ☐ Computer
- ☐ Where do you store your data?
    - ☐ Active files on computer
        - ☐ Estimated volume of relevant data (Note: 1 GB = approximately 75,000 pages)
    - ☐ Software programs used in connection with duties
    - ☐ Back-ups
        - ☐ Official
        - ☐ Unofficial—diskettes, other portable media
        - ☐ Media used
            - ☐ CDs, DVDs
            - ☐ Internet based backups
            - ☐ Thumb drives
            - ☐ Zip Drives
            - ☐ Replaced or removed drives
            - ☐ Any other archiving techniques/media
    - ☐ Location of backups
    - ☐ Any materials associated with the issues that you keep off-site?
        - ☐ At home
        - ☐ Elsewhere
- ☐ Any password protected files
    - ☐ Which files?
    - ☐ Passwords
    - ☐ Any encrypted files?
        - ☐ If encrypted, why?
- ☐ E-mail accounts
    - ☐ Company
        - ☐ Which e-mail software in use?
        - ☐ Changes over time
    - ☐ Particular folders associated with issues
    - ☐ Any use of personal accounts such as Gmail

or Yahoo in connection with duties for company?

- ☐ Hard copy files
  - ☐ Where located?
  - ☐ Who can provide access?
  - ☐ Any desk files or informal files related to the issues?
  - ☐ Estimated volume in pages (Note: Average bankers box contains approximately 2,500 pages)
- ☐ Location of other data
  - ☐ Any sources of data that we have not discussed?
    - ☐ Elaborate
- ☐ Other knowledgeable witnesses
  - ☐ Who else might have knowledge of the issues?
  - ☐ Who do you think knows the most about the issues?
  - ☐ Did you have any contact with any representative of the other side?
    - ☐ Details
- ☐ Interviewer Input
  - ☐ Key witness
  - ☐ Significant witness
  - ☐ Peripheral
- ☐ Any reason to do forensic work regarding this interviewee?

☐ Yes ☐ No

Comment

The checklist can be used for interviewing a client's IT personnel, preparing for trial, and for conducting a deposition.

III. FORMS

§ 10:22 Notice of deposition upon oral examination

[Caption]

To: *[name]*
Attorney for *[name]*
[Address]

PLEASE TAKE NOTICE that *[defendant] [plaintiff] [name]* will take the deposition upon oral examination of *[defendant] [plaintiff]*, *[name and address of deponent]*, before a person authorized by law to administer oaths at *[place]*, on *[date]*, at *[time]*.

[Defendant] [Plaintiff] hereby requests *[name of deponent]* to appear before this oral examination at the above time and place.

The deposition will continue from day to day until completed. You are at liberty to appear and examine the witness.

Dated: ________

[signature etc.]

§ 10:23 Notice of deposition upon oral examination—Organization

[Caption]

To: *[name]*
[address]

PLEASE TAKE NOTICE that the deposition of *[plaintiff name 1 corporation] [defendant name 2 corporation]*, will be taken upon oral examination by *[defendant name 2] [plaintiff name 1]* on *[date]*, at *[time]*, before a qualified notary public. The deposition will continue thereafter until adjournment. Pursuant to *[rule]*, *[plaintiff name 1] [defen-*

dant name 2 corporation] shall designate one or more officers, directors, or managing agents, or other persons who consent to testify on its behalf regarding the following subjects:

1. The number, types, and locations of computers, including but not limited to desktops, laptops, personal digital Assistants (PDAs), and cellular telephones, currently in use and no longer in use.
2. Past and present operating system and application software, including dates of use and number of users.
3. Name and version of network operating system currently in use and in use at any relevant time, including size in terms of storage capacity, number of users supported, and dates and descriptions of system upgrades.
4. File-naming and location-saving conventions.
5. Disk and tape labeling conventions.
6. Backup and archival disk or tape inventories and schedules/logs.
7. Most likely locations of electronic records relevant to the subject matter of the action.
8. Backup rotation schedules and archiving procedures, including any automatic data recycling programs in use at any relevant time.
9. Electronic records management policies and procedures.
10. Corporate policies regarding employee use of company computers, data, and other technology;
11. Identities of all current and former personnel who have or had access to network administration, backup, archiving, or other system operations during any relevant time period.

Dated: ________

[signature]

§ 10:24 Notice of deposition upon oral examination—Organization—Another Form

[Caption]

To: All Parties and to Their Attorneys of Record:

NOTICE OF DEPOSITION OF *[NAME OF ORGANIZATION]'S* PERSON MOST KNOWLEDGEABLE CONCERNING ELECTRONICALLY STORED INFORMATION SYSTEMS AND STORAGE

TO ALL PARTIES AND TO THEIR ATTORNEYS OF RECORD:

PLEASE TAKE NOTICE that *[name of party]* will take the deposition upon oral examination of *[name of organization]* on *[date]*, commencing at *[time]* at *[place]*, which deposition shall continue thereafter, Saturdays, Sundays and holidays excepted, until completed. The deposition will be taken before a certified court reporter authorized to administer oaths

Pursuant to *[rule]*, *[name of organization]* shall designate and produce at the deposition or more of its officers, directors, managing agents, employees, or agents most qualified to testify on its behalf as to the matters described in Exhibit 1.

Dated: ________

[signature, etc.]

EXHIBIT 1

I. GENERAL DEFINITIONS

1. The terms "document" and "documents" mean and refer to a writing and/or recording as defined in *[rule]*, including, without limitation, any printed, written, recorded (in any audio, video, digital or any other electronic or electromagnetic medium), graphic, or other

tangible matter from whatever source, however produced or reproduced, whether sent, received, or neither, including, without limitation, the original, all drafts, and any non-identical copies (whether different from the original because of notes made on or attached to the copy or otherwise) thereof.

2. The terms "you," "your" and *"[name of organization]"* mean and refer to *[name of organization]*, and include all of its affiliates, subsidiaries, and parents, and any person acting under the control or on behalf of *[name of organization]* and/or its affiliates, subsidiaries, and/or parents, including their directors, officers, partners, employees, representatives, agents, attorneys and investigators.

3. The term *"[party]"* means and refers to *[name of parties]*, conjunctively or disjunctively.

4. The term "complaint" *[or "answer"]* means and refers to the complaint filed by *[party]* in this action on or about *[date]*.

5. The term *"[name of organization]"* means *[name]*.

6. The term "subject matters" refers to all allegations of the complaint *[or defenses raised in the answer]* and to all factual and legal assertions or claims made in the complaint.

II. TECHNICAL DEFINITIONS

7. The term "active file" means and refers to any file of electronically stored information that can be utilized by a computer in any manner without modification and/or re-construction. An active file is any file of electronically stored information that has not been erased or otherwise destroyed and/or damaged and which is readily visible to the operating system and/or the software with which it was created.

8. The terms "archive" and/or "backup" mean and refer to any processes for copying and storage, whether temporary or permanent, of electronically stored information in a computer or a network, other than active files in on-line storage. The term "backup" means and refers to all processes used with the purpose of maintain-

ing a copy of electronically stored information so that such data can be restored if the primary copies of it are lost or damaged, or with the purpose of keeping a record of electronically stored information on a computer or a network at a given point or several given points in time. The terms "archive" and "archiving" mean and refer to any process for maintaining electronically stored information off-line, whether referred to as an archive, dump, purge or any other terms, and also to any process or procedure for storage of electronic media which is not in current use on a computer or a network.

9. The term "computer" includes, but is not limited to, microcomputers (also known as personal computers), laptop computers, portable computers, notebook computers, palmtop computers, personal digital assistants, minicomputers and mainframe computers.

10. The term "configuration" means and refers to the elements and relationships which make up a computer or a network, including, but not limited to, the following information:

a. Computer type, brand, model and serial number
b. Brand, model, capacity, technical specifications and arrangement of all devices capable of storing and/or retrieving electronically stored information in magnetic and/or optical form, including, but not limited to, hard disk drives, floppy diskette drives, Bernoulli Box devices, fixed and portable tape and tape cartridge drives, magneto-optical disks, CD-ROM drives, DVD devices and other such drives (rewritable or WORM), flash memory, and arrays or combination of such devices
c. Brand and version of all software, including operating system, private and custom developed applications, commercial applications, shareware and/or work-in-progress.
d. Communications capability, whether asynchronous and/or synchronous, including, but not limited to, terminal to mainframe emulation, data download and/or upload capability to mainframe, and com-

puter to computer connections via network modem and/or direct connect.

11. The term "data" is equivalent to the term "electronically stored information."

12. The term "deleted file" means and refers to any file of electronically stored information that has been erased or deleted from the electronic media on which it resided. A deleted file includes any file of electronically stored information whose File Allocation Table (FAT) entry has been modified to indicate such information as being deleted and/or that is not readily visible to the operating system and/or the software with which it was created.

13. The term "documentation," when used in reference to computers, operating systems and utilities, application software and/or hardware devices, shall mean and refer to all documents and files of electronically stored information containing written and/or on-line information provided by the manufacturer or seller of the item and/or by in-house sources, including all manuals, guides, instructions, programming notes, protocols, policies, procedures and other sources of information about technical specifications, installation, usage and functioning of the computer, operating systems and utilities, application software and/or hardware devices.

14. The term "electronically stored information" means information of all kinds created, maintained and/or utilized by computers and/or networks, including all non-identical copies of such information. electronically information includes, but is not limited to, software (whether private, commercial or work-in-progress), programming notes or instructions, and input and/or output used or produced by any software or utility (including electronic mail messages and all information referencing or relating to such messages anywhere on a computer or a network, word processing documents and all information stored in connection with such documents, electronic spreadsheets, databases including all records and fields and structural information, charts, graphs and outlines, arrays of information and all other

information used or produced by any software), operating systems, source code of all types, programming languages, linkers and compilers, peripheral drivers, batch files, any and all ASCII files, and any and all miscellaneous files and/or file fragments, regardless of the media on which they reside and regardless of whether such electronically stored information consists of an active file, deleted file or file fragment. electronically stored information includes any and all information stored on computer memories, hard disks, floppy disks, CD-ROM drives, Bernoulli Box drives and their equivalent, magnetic tape of all types, microfiche, punched cards, punched tape, computer chips, including, but not limited to, EPROM, PROM, RAM and ROM, or on or in any other vehicle for digital data storage and/or transmittal. Electronically stored information also includes the file, folder tabs and/or containers and labels appended to, or associated with, any physical storage device associated with the information described above.

15. The terms "electronic media" and "media" mean and refer to any magnetic, optical or other storage device used to record electronically stored information. Electronic media storage devices may include, but are not limited to, computer memories, hard disk drives, floppy diskettes, CD-ROM disks, Bernoulli Box drives and their equivalent, magnetic tape of all types, microfiche, punched cards, punched tape, computer chips, including, but not limited to, EPROM, PROM, RAM and ROM, or on or in any other vehicle for digital data storage and/or transmittal.

16. The terms "file fragment" and "fragmentary file" mean and refer to any file of electronically stored information existing as a subset of an original active file. A file fragment may be an active file or deleted file. The cause of fragmentation resulting in the fragmentary file can include, but is not limited to, manual intervention, electronic surges, and/or physical defects on electronic media.

17. "Identify," when used in reference to any electronically stored information, means to provide information

specifying the software and/or operating system under which the electronically stored information was created; the type of electronically stored information (for example, word processing document, spreadsheet, database, application program.); and all other means of describing it with sufficient particularity to meet the requirements for its inclusion in a request for production of documents pursuant to the *[rules]*.

18. The term "layout" means and refers to the interconnections and relationships between computers and electronic media in a computer system. The term "layout" includes, but is not limited to:

a. The physical locations and relationships of all computers and/or their peripherals, of all sorts, whether physically attached or not to a given computer
b. The nature and type of any sort of Local Area, Wide Area or any other type of network, whether consisting of physical connections between nodes or not, including the functional and physical relationships of servers, workstations and terminals in each such network and the brand, name and version of all operating systems in use on the network as well as the brand, name and version of all application software available through the network
c. The nature, type and functions of all software and/or hardware or devices which operate in a capacity to share or exchange electronically stored information between two or more computers, especially any e-mail, database or executive information system.

19. The term "network" means and refers to any hardware and/or software combination that connects two or more computers together and which allows such computers to share and/or transfer digital signals between them. For the purposes of this definition, the connection between or among the computers need not be either physical or direct (Len, wireless networks utilizing radio frequencies and data sharing via indirect routes utilizing modems and phone company facilities). In ad-

dition, there need not be a central file or data server nor a central network operating system in place (i.e. peer-to-peer networks and networks utilizing a mainframe host to facility transfer of electronically stored information). The ability to share electronically stored information is the key factor.

20. The term "rotation" means and refers to any plan, policy, or scheme involving the reuse of electronic media after it has been used for backup, archive, or other electronically stored information storage purposes, particularly if such use results in the alternation and/or destruction of electronically stored information residing on such device before or in connection with its reuse.

21. The term "support" means and refers to any help or assistance provided to a user of a computer by another individual, whether as an official job function or not. Such help or assistance may take the form of, but is not limited to, answering questions, whether in person or by mechanical means, direct intervention, training, software troubleshooting, hardware troubleshooting, programming, systems consulting, maintenance, repair and/or user forums. Providers of support may be employees, contractors, and/or third-party providers.

27. The term "encryption" means and refers to any system program or device utilized to obtain, impart or maintain security to electronically stored information transmitted or stored in or by means of your computers.

III. MATTERS ON WHICH EXAMINATION IS REQUESTED

23. The configuration documentation and layout of the computers and/or networks used by *[name of organization]* to create, process and/or store electronically stored information referencing or relating to the subject matters.

24. Archiving and backup systems and procedures available on computers and/or networks used by *[name or organization]* to create, process, and/or store electronically stored information referencing or relating to the subject matters, including, but not limited to:

a. The names and version number of all software used for archiving and/or backup purposes
b. Documentation of the archiving and/or backup systems and procedures, both on line and in paper form
c. The criteria used to classify and move sets of electronically stored information for archiving
d. Backup schedules and protocols
e. The manner in which archive and backup sets of electronically stored information are organized, and tracking and logging of such information
f. Storage of and access to archive and backup sets of electronically stored information, including the manner in which such information is written and retrieved and use of compression routines
g. Storage media used for archive and backup purposes, including the manufacturer, model and type of such media
h. Records of the existence, location and custodianship of archive and backup media, including inventories, databases, catalogs, logs, lists, and indexes of such media
i. Media labeling conventions and all other codes and abbreviations used for archive and backup purposes.

25. Record retention plans, policies and procedures of *[name of organization]* applicable to electronically stored information referencing or relating to the subject matters, including, but not limited to:

a. The contents of your retention plans, policies and procedures;
b. Implementation of your retention plans, policies and procedures;
c. Documentation, whether on line or in paper form, of your retention plans, policies and procedures; and
d. Whether any changes have been made in your retention fields, headings, and other subdivisions appearing in e-mail messages, including, but not limited to, message numbers, message trails and/or

sequences, message titles and subject matter lines, locations of senders and recipients, dates of sending and receipt of messages;

26. All steps taken by you to preserve electronically stored information as evidence in connection with this action, including all steps taken to prevent or stop deletion, overwriting or modification of electronically stored information that may be relevant to this action.

27. Deletion, erasure and/or destruction of storage media including backup and/or archive sets of electronically stored information referencing or relating to the subject matters; damage to and/or destruction of media containing such electronically stored information, and logs and records of such activity.

28. The system utilities and application software programs available on computers and networks used by *[name of organization]* that have the capability of searching, retrieving, copying, writing, offloading, and/or exporting electronically stored information referencing or relating to the subject matters.

29. The e-mail and/or messaging systems used by *[name of organization]* to transmit or receive electronically stored information or other information referencing or relating to the subject matters, including, but not limited to, internal e-mail and external e-mail communications. (For the purpose of this item, "messaging systems" include paging systems, groupware, and other systems for which one of the primary purposes is transmission of documents or messages among users of your computers and/or network or between users of your computer and/or network and other such systems.) The deponent(s) should have knowledge regarding all aspects of your e-mail system(s), including, but not limited to, the following:

a. Hardware and software used for e-mail and messaging functions

b. Documentation for the e-mail and messaging system and its usage

c. The nature and the location of directories and/or lists of e-mail or messaging system users, and all systems, codes and numbers identifying users
d. Fields, headings and other subdivisions appearing in e-mail messages, including, but not limited to, message numbers, message trails and or sequences, message title and subject matter lines, locations of senders and recipients, dates of sending and receipt of messages
e. Technical specifications for the creation, transmission and storage of messages, including, but not limited to, specifications as to host systems, gateways and routers, and electronically stored information files or sets in which messages are stored and the location of such information on the system
f. Message logging functions
g. Electronically stored information storage, backup and archiving activity specifically relating to e-mail and other messaging systems, including retention plans, guidelines, rules, standards, protocols, policies and procedures;
h. Backup and/or archive media specifically relating to e-mail and other messaging systems, including inventories, databases, catalogs, logs, lists, indexes, and other documentation
i. Format and character sets used to write messages, and encoding, encryption, decoding and decryption of messages; and
j. Outside services for electronic mail and/or for information transmission and retrieval with which your computers and/or network is interconnected, including the name of the service, the time period during which your computers and/or network has been connected to it, the purposes for which the outside services are used, and which users of your computers and/or network are able to use such services.

30. Policies, procedures, guidelines, rules, standards, and protocols relating to the functioning and use of personal computers and local area networks which may

have been used to create or process electronically stored information referencing or relating to the Subject: matters, including, but not limited to:

a. Availability and usage of particular application software to users

b. Directory organization access, and naming conventions

c. Storage of files of electronically stored information at local workstations and/or on network servers

d. Codes, abbreviations and naming conventions applicable to file and extension names

e. Diskette storage and labeling

f. Logging and recording user and file activity.

31. Systems for storing and retrieving recordings of telephone calls.

32. Any other information needed to identify, access, copy and read electronically stored information referred to in the above items.

33. Any other information needed to identify, access, copy and read electronically stored information reflecting electronically-facilitated communications (via e-mail or otherwise) among *[name of organization]* personnel concerning *[name of party]*, or any of them, or the events and transactions encompassed within the allegations of the complaint.

Comment

This form can be adapted to the specific requirements of a particular case.

§ 10:25 Stipulation to take deposition upon oral examination

Stipulation to take deposition upon oral examination

[Caption]

[Plaintiff] and *[defendant]* stipulate and agree that the deposition upon oral examination of *[name of deponent]* shall be taken by *[plaintiff/defendant]* at *[place]*, on *[date]*,

at *[time]*. Notice of the time and place of this deposition as required by *[rule]* is waived.

Dated: ________

[signature etc.]

Dated: ________

[signature etc.]

§ 10:26 Deposition outline

A. Computer-related experience of deponent
   1. Formal training (degrees, certificate programs, continuing education)
   2. Positions held
   3. Descriptions of job functions
   4. Length of employment
   5. Reasons for leaving prior employers

B. Description of computer system
   1. General description of network topology (network operating system, type of file server, client computer operating system)
   2. Recent instances of hardware failures
   3. Existence of dial-up access to the network

C. Security of computer system
   1. Physical security measures (access control systems, such as passwords and key cards)
   2. Electronic protection (firewalls, virus software, intrusion detection software)
   3. Instances of attempted unauthorized access
   4. Prior instances of data loss
   5. Security policies

D. Backup Procedures
   1. Identify systems that are backed up

2. Frequency of backups
3. Location of backup tapes
4. Instances of loss of backup data
5. Software used to create backups
6. Internet backups
7. Backup policies
8. Changes in backup procedures in the last twelve months

E. Software used to create relevant data
1. Name of vendor and program
2. Version number of program
3. Service/maintenance updates
4. Any custom modifications to the program
5. Procedures for ensuring accurate entry of data
6. Procedures for ensuring accuracy of output
7. File format for data storage

Chapter 11

Interrogatories

I. GUIDELINES

II. CHECKLISTS

III. FORMS

Research References

Additional References

ABA Discovery Standards, http://www.abanet.org/litigation/discoverystandards/2005civildiscoverystandards.pdf

Federal Judicial Center, http://www.fjc.gov

Llewellyn, Electronic Discovery Best Practices, 10 Rich. J.L. & Tech. 51 (2004)

The Sedona Conference, http://www.thesedonaconference.org

Waxse, "Do I Really Have to Do That?" Rule 26(a)(1) Disclosures and Electronic Information, 10 Rich.J.L. & Tech. 50 (2004)

Treatises and Practice Aids

eDiscovery & Digital Evidence § 7:13

Grenig and Kinsler, Federal Civil Discovery and Disclosure §§ 8.1 to 8.31 (2d ed.)

Trial Strategy

Recovery and Reconstruction of Electronic Mail as Evidence, 41 Am. Jur Proof of Facts 3d 1

Computer Technology in Civil Litigation, 71 Am. Jur Trials 111

KeyCite®: Cases and other legal materials listed in KeyCite Scope can be researched through the KeyCite service on Westlaw®. Use KeyCite to check citations for form, parallel references, prior and later history, and comprehensive citator information, including citations to other decisions and secondary materials.

I. GUIDELINES

§ 11:1 Generally

Interrogatories are written questions served by one party on another party in a civil action. Any party may serve interrogatories on any other party without leave of court. Interrogatories are not available for nonparty discovery. Interrogatories must be answered in writing and under oath by the respondent within a specified time.

Interrogatories provide a simple and inexpensive means

of supplementing generalized pleadings with sworn statements of a party with respect to the facts of the party's claim or defense. Interrogatories may be very helpful in obtaining information about another party's computer systems and electronically stored information. Interrogatories may also be helpful in obtaining the names and addresses of witnesses, officers, or employees. Interrogatories, document production requests and requests for admission may all be contained in a single document.

Rule 33(d) of the Federal Rules of Civil Procedure was amended effective December 1, 2006, to allow parties to produce electronically stored information in response to interrogatories.

§ 11:2 Comparison with other discovery devices—Generally

Interrogatories are one of the four major discovery devices—depositions upon oral questions, interrogatories, document production requests, and requests for admission. These methods of discovery are complementary, not alternative or exclusive. Normally, a party may use any or all of these devices and may do so in any order, as long as there is no attempt to harass or oppress the responding party. There is no required sequence of discovery. Typically, parties start with interrogatories and document production requests, followed by depositions and requests for admission, but no particular sequence is mandated.

§ 11:3 Comparison with other discovery devices—Depositions

Although depositions and interrogatories are designed to gather and narrow facts, they differ in several respects. Depositions may be taken of any person, but interrogatories may only be directed to parties. The rationale for this limitation is that a party who is called upon to answers interrogatories will consult with counsel before doing so and will be careful to answer with precision, while a non-party, who has nothing at stake in the case, could be easily led into making misleading statements in response to one-sided or leading questions. When information is sought from a party, either interrogatories or depositions, or both, may be used.

One obvious advantage of interrogatories over depositions is that interrogatories are often less expensive. Interrogatories are simpler to use because there are none of the details that must be taken care of in arranging for a deposition, such as obtaining a court reporter and fixing the time and place for the examination. Depositions, on the other hand, are more effective at uncovering facts. Deposition questions are answered by the witness whereas interrogatories are usually answered by the party's attorney. Deposition answers are spontaneous, allowing for immediate follow-up questions. Follow-up questions in interrogatories must await the written answers of the responding party. The lack of spontaneous follow-up questions, combined with the fact that attorneys prepare the answers, makes interrogatories easy to evade.

§ 11:4 Comparison with other discovery devices—Requests for production

Interrogatories seek information while requests for production of documents seek tangible objects. Often, parties serve interrogatories and requests for production simultaneously. In some cases, it may be best to serve the interrogatories before the document production request. In such cases, the interrogatories should ask the answering party to identify specific documents or types of documents. After the answers to interrogatories are received, a document production request should be served on the answering party requesting production of the documents identified in the answers to interrogatories.

§ 11:5 Parties to whom interrogatories may be directed

Interrogatories may only be directed to parties; nonparties are subject to deposition, but not interrogatories. Interrogatories must be addressed to parties of record in the litigation. Any party may serve interrogatories on any other party in the action; there is no requirement of adversity.

Interrogatories may not be directed to officers, directors or employees of a corporate party (unless such individuals are themselves parties). If a party is a corporation, the interrogatories must be addressed to the corporation and it is obligated to designate who will answer for it. Interrogatories may not be directed to the attorney for the party

§ 11:6 Service of interrogatories

Interrogatories may be served by delivering a copy to the party or mailing the interrogatories to the party's last known address.[1] Once a party has appeared by counsel, the interrogatories are served upon the attorney. A copy of the interrogatories should also be served on all other parties to the action.

Rule 33(a) of the Federal Rules of Civil Procedure precludes the service of interrogatories before the time specified in Rule 26(d), absent a court order or written stipulation. Rule 26(d) provides that, except when authorized by local rule, order or stipulation, a party may not seek discovery from any source before the parties have conferred as required by Rule 26(f). State rules and local rules should be consulted with respect to when interrogatories may be served.

§ 11:7 Number of interrogatories

Rule 33(a) of the Federal Rules of Civil Procedure limits the number of interrogatories one party may serve upon another party to 25, including discrete subparts, absent leave of court or written stipulation. State rules or local rules may also limit the number of interrogatories. Written stipulation to serve more than 25 interrogatories should be employed when all parties to the stipulation wish to serve excess interrogatories.

[Section 11:6]

[1] See Fed. R. Civ. P. 5.

Subparts are those questions that are logically or factually subsumed within and necessarily related to the primary question. Subparts are secondary to the primary question and cannot stand alone. Subparts do not have to be separately numbered to count as separate interrogatories. An interrogatory that asks about multiple projects or events does not necessarily constitute multiple interrogatories.[1]

Leave to serve additional interrogatories should be allowed when the additional interrogatories would not cause undue burden or expense to the responding party. In many cases, it may be appropriate for the court to permit a larger number of interrogatories in the scheduling order.

§ 11:8 Propounding interrogatories—Generally

Interrogatories may relate to any matters that can be inquired into under the applicable scope of discovery. This includes the existence and location of tangible things and the identity and location of persons having knowledge of any discoverable matter. It also includes the names and addresses of persons interviewed by or on behalf of the responding party.

It is improper to object to interrogatories on the ground that the information sought is within the knowledge of the interrogating party. It is also improper to object to interrogatories on the basis that the information sought relates to evidence the responding party intends to introduce at trial, as all facts, both evidentiary and ultimate, are subject to discovery. Interrogatories may not be used, however, to force a responding party to reveal its trial strategy during the early stages of discovery.

An interrogatory may not inquire into privileged matters or matters protected by the work product doctrine. The burden of proving the existence and application of a privilege rests with the party asserting it. When a party

---

[Section 11:7]

[1] Banks v. Office of Senate Sergeant-at-Arms, 222 F.R.D. 7 (D.D.C. 2004).

withholds information on the ground of privilege or work product protection, it must make the claim expressly and describe the nature of the information withheld in such a manner that, without revealing the information itself privileged or protected, will enable other parties to assess the applicability of the privilege or protection. A mere claim of privilege or work product protection, unaccompanied by factual support, is insufficient. In appropriate cases, a protective order may be obtained by the responding party to limit the scope of discovery.

§ 11:9 Propounding interrogatories—Legal opinions and contentions

An interrogatory otherwise proper is not necessarily objectionable merely because an answer thereto involves an opinion or contention that relates to fact or the application of law to fact. However interrogatories asking for legal opinions are improper.

§ 11:10 Propounding interrogatories—Form of interrogatories

Interrogatories should be drafted so they are simple, concise and relevant to matters involved in the litigation. Each interrogatory should be a single direct question phrased in a fashion informing the other party what is requested of it. General language is permitted so long as the interrogatory gives the other party a reasonably clear indication of the information to be included in its answer.

The interrogatory should be clear and unambiguous; overbroad interrogatories lead to useless answers. Responding parties are not required to decipher poorly drafted interrogatories. If the interrogatory is vague or ambiguous, the responding party may qualify its answer, but usually will not object to the interrogatory. However, it is easy for the responding party to evade compound or complex interrogatories. The responding party has no obligation to attempt to decipher vague or compound interrogatories.

Interrogatories should be drafted in such a fashion as to

leave sufficient space following each interrogatory to enable the responding party to answer, and interrogatories should be numbered consecutively with no headings or subheadings to interrupt the flow. Local rules should be consulted to determine specific requirements for preparation of interrogatories and responses.

§ 11:11 Propounding interrogatories—Definitions

It is advisable, particularly in complex cases, to include definition and instruction sections in the interrogatories. Definitions are particularly important in cases involving multiple parties, multiple claims, or uncommon items of property. If inclusive definitions are used, the drafting party will find it much easier to draft the interrogatories and the responding party will find it much more difficult to give evasive answers. The longer the list of definitions, however, the less likely the responding party will read them and consequently the more likely the responding party will inadvertently evade an otherwise clear and concise interrogatory. More importantly, an unnecessarily long list of instructions and definitions may render the interrogatories unduly burdensome, enabling the responding party to obtain a protective order.

The initial interrogatories seeking information about a computer system are only as good as the definitional section of the interrogatories. Definitions are always important in interrogatories, because if used properly they can make it possible to craft very specific queries with a great deal of economy, thus avoiding problems with the requirement in many jurisdictions that a party can only ask a limited number of interrogatories without approval of a court. However, in discovering electronically stored information definitions are of greater importance.

When creating the definitions section of interrogatories, it is important to remember that the interrogatories are intended to uncover information about the architecture of the responding party's system and the definitions must be comprehensive enough to cover all of the possible sources where electronically stored information may reside.

§ 11:12 Propounding interrogatories—Questions

The interrogatories should include questions about the responding party's computer system and also the names, addresses, and other information about those who are responsible for managing the various parts of the system (e.g., the Webmaster, the network administrator, the e-mail administrator). The interrogatories should ask the responding party to identify the specific databases it maintains on various subjects.

The interrogatories should also ask the responding party to identify personnel, employee, and consultants or contractors, who work on and know its databases and information-management system. Because production of a database alone may not fully explain how it is used, it is a good idea to request "datamaps" or "schema." System documentation and database policies and procedures should also be requested.

In preparing interrogatories seeking information about a computer system, it should be recognized that there may be a number of things counsel does not know about the responding party's computer system. Counsel cannot begin to ask intelligent questions regarding electronically stored information until counsel has become educated about the responding party's computer system. Therefore, it is crucial that the discovering party request user and administrator manuals used by the responding party in administering its computer system.

The discovering party should be certain to request that the responding party specifically state which interrogatory is answered by which piece of electronically stored information. It is not sufficient to speculate that an answer may be available from a mass production of business records. A party seeking information about electronically stored information should request details about the responding party's use of backup software. Backup files can be useful in detecting whether there have been deletions or modifications.

II. CHECKLISTS

§ 11:13 Checklist of topics for interrogatories

- ☐ Identity of party's agents, and employees.
- ☐ Identity of witnesses.
- ☐ Identity of documents and tangible things.
- ☐ Identify personnel, employees, and consultants or contractors who work on or manage party's computer system or part of system.
- ☐ Specific databases party maintains on various subjects
- ☐ With respect to computer backup systems, the schedule for making backup copies, the type of software used, and location of storage of backup copies.
- ☐ Identity of experts, facts, and opinions.
- ☐ Details and sequences of events and transactions.
- ☐ Damages information and insurance coverage.
- ☐ Identity of persons who prepared answers and sources used.
- ☐ Positions on issues and opinions of fact.

§ 11:14 Checklist for drafting interrogatories

- ☐ **Begin with Form Interrogatories.** Use official form interrogatories initially, and then follow up with your own specially prepared interrogatories.
- ☐ **Use Your Discovery Plan.** Constantly refer to discovery plan.
    - ☐ What are the elements of proof issues?
    - ☐ How do the facts that must be gathered go to those elements?
- ☐ **Establish a List of Targets.** From discovery plan, develop a list of targets for interrogatories.
- ☐ **Create an Outline.** Develop a structured outline before drafting. Generally, a case-history structure works best. Consider using an issue-based or document-based structure. Build the interrogatory questions around the case chronology.
- ☐ **Chart the Outline.** Consider making a chart show-

ing a flow-chart outline of anticipated responses. Each question will have alternative responses that may then generate new questions.

☐ **Draft the Questions.** Once this structure is in place, fill in the blanks with interrogatory questions.

☐ **Check the Number of Questions.** Rules may limit the number of questions that may be asked. Consult local rules.

☐ **Check Drafting.** Questions and responses are open to interpretation by opposing counsel. The jury may see the interrogatory as well. For these two reasons, questions must be concise and precise. Avoid conflicts of verb tense. Avoid questions containing negatives ("no," "not," or "never").

☐ **Seek the Discovery Source.** Be sure question requires the indication of a source.

  ☐ Is the reply referring to a document that should be part of your discovery?

  ☐ Is there a potential witness who should be deposed?

III. FORMS

§ 11:15 Definitions for use in interrogatories seeking information about responding party's computer system

1. "Computer or computer equipment" means all data processing equipment, including but not limited to, central processing units (CPUs), whether contained in a server or free standing computer or laptop, and all parts of a server, computer or laptop that may contain data storage capabilities including, but not limited to hard disk drives, optical disk drives, removable media, such as floppy disk drives, CD-ROM and DVD drives, Zip drives, Jaz drives, Maxtor drives or snap drives. "Computer or computer equipment" also refers to any data processing cards or computer magnetic tapes, backup tapes, drum and disk storage devices or any other electronic storage media or system of whatever description. "Computer or computer equipment" also refers to any type of hardware used to store or manip-

ulate electronic images, including but not limited to microfilm, microfiche and their repositories and readers.

2. "Computer system" refers to free standing servers, computers and laptops, and also refers to the network infrastructure and computer support systems of the *[responding party]*, its subsidiaries (in this country or throughout the world), predecessors, successors, assigns, joint venturers, partners, parents, agents or affiliates, including but not limited to the following:

a. *[Responding party]*'s LAN and WAN network systems, including methods of connectivity (e.g., by T1, T3 or optical lines), domains (including PDCs, network OS and protocols), backup and disaster recovery hardware and media and the physical location of all electronic storage systems.

b. *[Responding party]*'s IS system of administration, including, backup and disaster recovery restoration plans, electronically stored information retention plans, purge plans, training plans, and libraries of hardcopy and online training and operation manuals.

c. All offsite technical and service bureau support, including but not limited to application service provider (ASP) support, scanning or data conversion support, offsite data storage or archive support.

d. Web hosting and administration services, including intranet and extranet sites, regardless of whether they exist in English, or some other language.

3. "Database" refers to any software program application (such as Microsoft Access, Lotus Approach, Borland's Paradox, Summation 5.21 or Summation's Iblaze, Concordance, or some other proprietary software) used to accumulate, manage, search and retrieve large amounts of electronic data. "Database" also refers to any collection of electronic data that is the subject of such a software application. When used to refer to such a collection of electronic data, "database" means any and all electronic information, or metadata, that has been saved to the database, regardless of format. When used in these interrogatories or requests to admit, a request related to a "Database" includes by definition the following implicit requests:

a. A full description of the method by which electronically stored information was retrieved, including the search terms and search methodology (e.g., word search or Boolean search) employed, the search engine settings used and the data set searched to retrieve the information;

b. The name of the operator(s) who conducted the search of the database;

c. The configuration and settings of the database at the time of the search;

d. The precise physical location of the database at *[responding party]*'s facility or facilities; and

e. A complete copy of the operating manual used in connection with the database.

4. "Data Collections not included in a database" refers to any raw accumulation of data in a computer system, such as Word or PDF documents stored only in a Windows directory. "Data Collections not included in a database" also refers to any electronic text that is not identified with a particular computer program, such as for example "ASCII." Whenever a request in these interrogatories and requests to produce elicit by necessity the identification of "Data Collections not included in a database" that request by definition implicitly requires the identification of where the "Data Collections not included in a database" is physically located on *[responding party]*'s computer system.

5. "Database field" refers to a specific area of a record in a database used for a particular category of electronically stored information. For example, all data relating to the phone numbers of customers might be stored in a field called "phone#." Whenever a request for a search of a database is made in these interrogatories and requests to produce, that request includes by definition

a) the identification of the number of fields that can be searched in a database and

b) the identification of the fields that were actually searched in supplying an answer.

6. "Database record" refers to the smallest convenient block of data in a database, and usually consists of infor-

mation that relates a single person, incident or document. For the purposes of these interrogatories and requests to produce, "database record" includes both the information directly saved to that record as metadata and any scanned image attached to the record (as is done in Summation).

7. "Data set" refers to the number of records that are initially the subject of a database query. "Data set" also refers to any "subset" of data that is accumulated in response to a search.

Comment

These definitions are intended to be used in initial discovery seeking information about a responding party's computer system. The definitions must be modified to fit each individual circumstance.

§ 11:16 Definitions for use in interrogatories and requests to produce

"Computer or computer equipment" means all data processing equipment, including but not limited to, central processing units (CPUs), whether contained in a server or free standing computer or laptop or PDA or similar device that may contain data storage capabilities, and also including any equipment where computer files, hidden system files or metadata presently reside such as hard disk drives, optical disk drives, removable media, such as floppy disk drives, CD-ROM and DVD drives, Zip drives, Jaz drives, Maxtor drives or snap drives, data processing cards, computer magnetic tapes, backup tapes, drum and disk storage devices or any other similar electronic storage media or system of whatever name or description.

"Computer or computer equipment" also means all digital image evidence that may be stored on any type of hardware used to store or manipulate electronic images, including but not limited to microfilm, microfiche and their repositories and readers, or design or engineering computer systems and regardless of any digital image's format, including.jpg, .bmp, or some other advanced or proprietary form of digital image format, such as CAD layered drawings.

"Computer or computer equipment" also refers to sources of digital evidence that may not presently be in use by your company or may have been deleted from your active systems, whether the source is a backup tape or disk, some other data retention system or some form of disaster recovery system.

"Computer or computer equipment" also refers to places where digital evidence may reside that may have been deleted from your active files and which may not be readily recoverable from a backup medium, such as metadata.

"Computer system" refers to free standing servers, computers and laptops, and also refers to the network infrastructure and computer support systems of the defendant or subject to the defendant's control, such as its subsidiaries, predecessors, successors, assigns, joint venturers, partners, parents, agents or affiliates (in this country or throughout the world), including but not limited to the following:

1. Defendant's LAN, WAN or other network systems, regardless of methods of connectivity (e.g., by T1, T3 or optical lines), domains, including PDCs, network OS (such as Novell, Microsoft, UNIX, Citrix or some other similar type) or protocols, backup and disaster recovery hardware and media, regardless of the physical location of those electronic storage systems.
2. Defendant's e-mail servers and any repository of e-mail (including within the inbox, sent box, deleted box or some similar file of the computers of employees or management), or in any backup form whatsoever, regardless of whether you use Microsoft Exchange, Outlook, Outlook Express, Lotus Notes or some combination of e-mail management software or some alternative commercial or proprietary e-mail management software.
3. Defendant's IS administrative offices, including backup and disaster recovery restoration plans and repositories, data retention plans and repositories, purge plans and repositories, training plans and repositories, and libraries of hardcopy materials of any description (regardless of where located) and online training and operation manuals that have been scanned to disk.

4. All offsite technical and service bureau support systems, including but not limited to application service provider (ASP) support, scanning or data conversion support, offsite data storage or archive support.
5. Web hosting and administration services, including intranet and extranet sites, regardless of whether they are now publicly posted or exist in English, or some other language.

"Database" refers to any software program application (such as Microsoft Access, Lotus Approach, Borland's Paradox, Summation or Summation's Iblaze, Concordance, or some other proprietary software) used to accumulate, manage, search and retrieve large amounts of electronic data. "Database" also refers to any collection of electronic data that is the subject of such a software application. When used to refer to such a collection of electronic data, "database" means any and all electronic information, or metadata, that has been saved to the database, regardless of format. When used in these interrogatories or requests to admit, a request related to a "Database" includes by definition the following implicit requests:

1. A full description of the method by which data was retrieved, including the search terms and search methodology (e.g., word search or Boolean search) that was employed, the search engine settings that were used and the data set that was searched to retrieve the information.
2. The name of the operator(s) who conducted the search of the database.
3. The configuration and settings of the database at the time of the search.
4. The precise physical location of the database at Defendant's facility or facilities.
5. A complete copy of the operating manual that is used in connection with the database.

"Data Collections not included in a database" refers to any raw accumulation of data in a computer system, such as Word or PDF documents stored only in a Windows directory. "Data Collections not included in a database" also refers to any electronic text that is not identified with a particular computer program, such as for example ASCII. Whenever a request in these interrogatories and requests to produce elicit by necessity the identification of "Data Collections not included in a database," that request, by definition, implicitly requires the identification of where the "Data Collections not included in a database" is physically located on Defendant's computer system.

"Database field" refers to a specific area of a record in a database used for a particular category of data; for example, all data relating to the phone numbers of customers might be stored in a field called "phone#." Whenever a request for a search of a database is made in these interrogatories and requests to produce, that request includes by definition a) the identification of the number of fields that can be searched in a database and b) the identification of the fields that were actually searched in supplying an answer.

"Database record" refers to the smallest convenient block of data in a database, and usually consists of information that relates a single person, incident or document. For the purposes of these interrogatories and requests to produce, "database record" includes both the information directly saved to that record as metadata and any scanned image attached to the record (as is done in Summation).

"Data set" refers to the number of records that are initially the subject of a database query. "Data set" also refers to any "subset" of data that is accumulated in response to a search.

CD or DVD production of discovery is acceptable however the following is required when discovery production is thus produced. Each image on the CD or DVD must be Bates stamped with a unique alpha-numeric identifier (taking care not to obscure in any way any of the information contained in the image).

A. Clearly Marked and Easily Identifiable File. This index must contain the following information as to each document contained on the CD or DVD in columnar display as follows:

i. In column one, the Bates stamp number of each electronic document on the CD or DVD;
ii. In column two, a brief but reasonably descriptive word description of the contents of each electronic document on the CD or DVD that clearly identifies what that electronic document contains;
iii. In column three, a clear reference to just what interrogatory or request is satisfied by the production of each electronic document on the CD or DVD;
iv. In column four, the format of each electronic document on the CD or DVD, and how and where the original or best copy of each such document is stored on the defendant's computer system, or if located elsewhere then on the defendant's primary computer system, its location on the computer system of subsidiaries (in this country or throughout the world), predecessors, successors, assigns, joint venturers, partners, parents, agents or affiliates; and
v. In column five, a statement as to whether each electronic document contained on the CD or DVD is a first, second, third or a later generation copy of the original document located on the defendant's computer system.

B. If the images on a CD or DVD exist in an off the shelve metadata environment, then the images must be produced with all accompanying metadata, unless privileged, and the database management system used to produce and house that metadata must be identified by application name and version type.

C. If the images on a CD or DVD exist in a proprietary metadata environment, then it is required that a working copy of the proprietary software, together with any user manuals or help files and the search engine used to search for and retrieve the data, must be provided that will work with each CD or DVD.

D. All data on a CD or DVD that is in text (regardless of format), must be OCRed before production.

Comment

These definitions can be used in interrogatories and requests for production. Not all definitions will be appropriate in all cases; it is necessary to select the definitions that are appropriate under the circumstances.

§ 11:17 Interrogatories

[Caption]

INTERROGATORIES TO *[NAME]*

To: *[name of party]*

You are notified to answer under oath the following interrogatories within ____ days of the time service is made on you.

1. Identify all e-mail systems in use, including but not limited to the following:
   (a) List all e-mail software and versions presently and previously used by you and the dates of use.
   (b) Identify all hardware that has been used or is currently in use as a server for the e-mail system, including its name;
   (c) Identify the specific type of hardware used as terminals into the e-mail system, including but not limited to home PCs, laptops, desktops, cellular telephones, personal digital assistants (PDAs) and its current location.
   (d) State how many users have been on each e-mail system, distinguishing between past and current users.
   (e) State whether the e-mail is encrypted in any way and list the passwords for all users.
   (f) Identify all users you know of who have generated e-mail related to the subject matter of this litigation.
   (g) Identify all e-mail you know of, including the creation date, the recipient, and the sender, relating to, referencing or relevant to the subject matter of this litigation.

2. Identify and describe each computer that has been or is currently in use by you or your employees, including but not limited to desktop computers, PDAs, portable

computers, laptop computers, notebook computers, and cellular telephones, including but not limited to the following:

(a) Computer type, brand and model number.

(b) Computers that have been re-formatted, had the operating system reinstalled or been overwritten, identifying the date of each event.

(c) The present location of each identified computer in your response to this interrogatory.

(d) The brand and version of all software, including operating systems, private and custom-developed applications, commercial applications and shareware for each identified computer.

(e) The communications and connectivity for each computer, including but not limited to terminal-to-mainframe emulation, data download and/or upload capability to mainframe, and computer-to-computer connections via network, modem and/or direct connection.

(f) All computers that have been used to store, receive or generate data related to the subject matter of this litigation.

3. As to each computer network, identify the following:

(a) Brand and version number of the network operating system currently or previously in use, including dates of all upgrades.

(b) Quantity and configuration of all network servers and workstations.

(c) Past and present persons, listing dates, responsible for the ongoing operations, maintenance, expansion, archiving and upkeep of the network.

(d) Brand name and version number of all applications and other software residing on each network in use, including but not limited to electronic mail and applications.

4. Describe in detail all inter-connectivity between the computer system at *[place 1]* the computer system at *[place 2]*, including a description of the following:

(a) All possible ways in which electronic data is shared between locations.

(b) The method of transmission.
(c) The type(s) of data transferred.
(d) The names of all individuals possessing the capability for such transfer, including list and names of authorized outside users of *[name's]* electronic mail system.
(e) The individual responsible for supervising interconnectivity.

5. With respect to data backups performed on all computer systems currently or previously in use, identify the following:

(a) All procedures and devices used to back up the software and the data, including but not limited to names of backup software used, the frequency of the backup process, and type of tape backup drives, including name and version number, type of media. State the capacity (bytes) and total amount of information (gigabytes) stored on each tape.
(b) Describe the tape or backup rotation and explain how backup data is maintained and state whether the backups are full or incremental, attaching a copy of all rotation schedules.
(c) State whether backup storage media is kept off-site or on-site. Include the location of such backup and a description of the process for archiving and retrieving on-site media.
(d) The individuals who conduct the backup and the individual who supervises this process.
(e) Provide a detailed list of all backup sets, regardless of the magnetic media on which they reside, showing current location, custodian, date of backup, a description of backup content and a full inventory of all archives.

6. Identify all extra-routine backups applicable for any servers identified in response to these interrogatories, such as quarterly archival backup, and yearly backup, and identify the current location of any such backups.

7. For any server, workstation, laptop, or home PC that has been "wiped clean" or reformatted so that you

claim that the information on the hard drive is permanently destroyed, identify the following:

(a) The date on which each drive was wiped.

(b) The method or program used.

8. Identify and attach any and all versions of document or data retention policies used by *[name]* and identify documents or classes of documents that were subject to scheduled destruction. Attach copies of document destruction inventories, logs, or schedules containing documents relevant to this action. Attach a copy of any disaster recovery plan. Also state:

(a) The date, if any, of the suspension of this policy in total or any aspect of the policy in response to this litigation.

(b) A description by topic, creation date, user or bytes of any and all data deleted or in any way destroyed after the commencement of this litigation. State whether the deletion or destruction of any data pursuant to the data retention policy occurred through automation or by user action.

(c) Whether any company-wide instruction regarding the suspension of the data retention or destruction policy occurred after or related to the commencement of this litigation and if so, identify the individual responsible for enforcing said suspension.

9. Identify any users who had backup systems in their PCs and describe the nature of the backup.

10. Identify the persons responsible for maintaining any schedule of redeployment or circulation of existing equipment and describe the system or process for redeployment.

11. Identify any data deleted, physically destroyed, discarded, damaged, physically or logically, or overwritten, whether pursuant to a document retention policy or otherwise, since the commencement of this litigation. Specifically identify those documents that relate to or reference the subject matter of this litigation.

12. Identify any user who has downloaded any files in excess of ten megabytes on any computer identified above since the commencement of this litigation.

13. Identify and describe all backup tapes in your possession including:

(a) Types and number of tapes in your possession.

(b) Capacity (bytes) and total amount of information (gigabytes) stored on each tape.

(c) All tapes re-initialized or overwritten since commencement of this litigation and state the date of the occurrence.

Dated: ________

[signature, etc.]

Comment

This form is adapted from Paroff et al., *Electronic Discovery in Technology Litigation*, 734 PLI/Pat 297 (2003).

§ 11:18 Interrogatories—Another form

[Caption]

INTERROGATORIES TO *[NAME OF PARTY]*

To: *[name of party]*

You are notified to answer under oath the following interrogatories within ____ days of the time service is made on you.

DEFINITIONS

A. The word "person" means all entities and, without limiting the generality of the foregoing, includes natural persons, joint owners, associations, companies, partnerships, joint ventures, corporations, trusts, and estates.

B. The word "document" means all written, printed, recorded, graphic, or photographic matter or sound reproductions, however produced or reproduced, pertaining to the subject matter indicated.

C. The words "identify," "identity," or "identification,"

when used with respect to a person or persons, require a statement of the full name and present or last known residence and business address of such person or persons and, if a natural person, his or her present or last known job title, and the name and address of his or her present or last known employer.

D. The words "identify," "identity," or "identification," when used with respect to a document or documents, requires a description of the document or documents by date, subject matter, name of the addressee, and the name and address of each person or persons having possession, custody, or control of such document or documents. If any such document was, but is no longer, in your possession, custody, or control, or in existence, state the date and manner of its disposition.

E. The word "identify," when used with respect to an act (including an alleged offense), occurrence, statement, or conduct (hereinafter collectively called "act"), means:

(1) to describe the substance of the event or events constituting such acts, and state the date when such act occurred;
(2) to identify each and every person or persons participating in such act;
(3) to identify all other persons (if any) present when such act occurred;
(4) to state whether any minutes, notes, memorandum, or other record of such act was made;
(5) to state whether such record now exists; and
(6) to identify the person or persons presently having possession, custody, or control of each such record.

F. The word "blocking" means either "logical blocking" or "physical blocking." "Logical blocking" means the location of fields within one record, sometimes referred to as record format. "Physical blocking" means the number of logical records written together on a storage device. In the case of unformatted records, "physical blocking" is the largest physical record that can be applied to the logical blocking factor to give the physical blocking factor.

G. The phrase "data set," although it may have a

slightly different meaning as to different computer installations, means "file" in reference to any collection of data.

H. The word "equipment" means all data processing equipment, including, but not limited to, central processing units, tape drives, drum and disk storage devices, control units, and printers; all unit record equipment, including, but not limited to, accumulators, calculators, and sorters; all record storage and retrieval equipment, including, but not limited to, microfilm storage and retrieval apparatus, and audio/visual storage and retrieval apparatus.

I. The word "field" means a specific area of a record used for a particular category of data; for example, a group of card columns used to represent a wage rate, or a set of locations used to express the address of the operand.

J. The word "file" means a collection of related records treated as a unit and, in a general sense, any collection of informational items similar to one another in purpose, form, and content.

K. The word "information" means data presented in various forms related to various topics, herein used to describe one topic's data.

L. The phrase "operating system" means an organized collection of techniques and procedures for operating a computer, usually part of a software package defined to simplify housekeeping, such as input/output procedures, sort/merge generators, and the like.

M. The word "program" means a set of instructions or steps, usually in symbolic form, that generates machine instructions and tells the computer how to handle a problem.

N. The word "record" means a group of related facts or fields of information treated as a unit. A record need not be a block in length.

O. The word "system" means an assembly of operations and procedures, men, and machines united by some form of regulated interaction to form an organized whole.

P. The words "used," "use," and "uses," when used with respect to files or programs, mean access, retrieved from, changed, updated, referenced, or in any other way referred to by name, directly or indirectly.

Q. The word "output" means information that is generated by a computer to an outside source, such as a printer.

INTERROGATORIES

1. Identify by unit all equipment used in creating, processing, retrieving, or updating information relating to *[specify]*. Identify all such equipment associated with any unit, and designate with which units such equipment is associated.

2. State the location of each unit of equipment identified in your answer to Interrogatory No. 1.

3. Describe fully the operating system used for all programmable equipment identified by your answer to Interrogatory No. 1.

4. Identify all files used by any system that creates, produces, or uses any information concerning *[describe]*. Identify each such file by name so that each file is uniquely defined and can be so referred to in subsequent discovery.

5. Identify the storage media used for each file identified in your answer to Interrogatory No. 4. If more than one medium is used for any one file, state the type of each such medium.

6. State the amount of storage media used (allocation) and the number of records for each file identified in your answer to Interrogatory No. 4.

7. Identify the organization (for example, sequential, indexed sequential, direct access) for each file identified in your answer to Interrogatory No. 4.

8. State whether each file identified in your answer to Interrogatory No. 4 is blocked or unblocked, and its physical blocking factor.

9. Identify the logical blocking for every unique record layout for each file identified in your answer to In-

terrogatory No. 4 that has a nonsequential organization. Identify the field or fields used as keys.

10. State the retention time for each file identified in your answer to Interrogatory No. 4.

11. If the retention period stated in your answer to Interrogatory No. 10 has changed since *[date]*, state the date or dates of each such change or changes and the previous retention period or periods.

12. State the earliest available date for each file identified in your answer to Interrogatory No. 4.

13. Identify any safe storage (off-premises storage) used by *[party]*.

14. Identify all files that are kept in safe storage. State the retention period or periods for each such file.

15. Identify all programs that use the files identified in your answer to Interrogatory No. 4. Identify each such program by name so that all programs are uniquely defined and can be so referred to in later discovery.

16. Identify which equipment units identified in your answer to Interrogatory No. 1 are used for each program identified in your answer to Interrogatory No. 15.

17. For each program identified in your answer to Interrogatory No. 15, identify the language used. If more than one language is used, identify which modules or subroutines utilize which language, and the function of each such module or subroutine.

18. For each program identified in your answer to Interrogatory No. 15, identify the schedule for running. If there is no predetermined calendar schedule, state the frequency of running during *[time frame]*.

19. For each program identified in your answer to Interrogatory No. 15, state the frequency of running during *[year]*.

20. For each program identified in your answer to Interrogatory No. 15, describe fully or identify all other output produced, but not limited to, permanent files, work files, description files, and the like.

21. Identify all output described or identified in your answer to Interrogatory No. 20 that is presently avail-

able, and the age of such output (this applies to hardcopy produced less frequently than monthly, or hardcopy not produced on a calendar schedule).

22. For each program identified in your answer to Interrogatory No. 15, describe fully or identify what variations of the standard production can be accomplished with changes in parameter cards.

23. Identify each program that can produce, as output in any form or media, the [describe particular information desired].

24. State the number of hours required to write a program that would produce the output described in Interrogatory No. 23, if such a program is not available.

25. Identify each program that is now, or has since *[date]* been used to calculate *[describe information required]*.

26. As to each program identified in your answer to Interrogatory No. 25, identify the period of time during which each such program was in use in a production mode.

27. Identify each person who is now, or was, a programmer, analyst, or supervisor of the programs identified in your answer to Interrogatory No. 25, and the period of time during which each such person was associated with each such program.

Dated: ________

[signature, etc.]

Comment

One judge has suggested that in conducting discovery with interrogatories, the parties' counsel should exchange computer disks on which the questions are written. Vincent v. Seaman, 142 Misc. 2d 196, 536 N.Y.S.2d 677 (County Ct. 1989). The recipient of a disk would upload it into the recipient's computer, write the answers to the disk following their respective questions, copy the disk for file storage, and then return the original disk to the proponent of the interrogatories.

§ 11:19 Interrogatories—Another form

[Caption]

INTERROGATORIES TO [*PARTY*]

To: *[name of party]*

You are notified to answer under oath the following interrogatories within ____ days of the time service is made on you.

DEFINITIONS

For purposes of these Interrogatories, certain terms have the following definitions:

A. The term "computer system" refers to all file servers, stand alone computers, workstations, and laptops owned or leased by *[name of party]* or physically located at *[place]*.

B. The term "your" refers to *[name of party]*.

C. T term "e-mail" refers to the exchange of text messages and computer files over a communications network, such as a local area network, intranet, extranet, or public network like the Internet or other online service provider.

INTERROGATORIES

1. Identify each authorized user of your computer system.

2. Describe all hardware modifications to the computer system in the past twelve months.

Software Applications

3. Describe the software (e.g., version, manufacturer, any custom modifications) used to create *[describe]*.

4. Describe each of the software applications (e.g., version, manufacturer, any custom modifications) installed on *[specify computer]*.

5. Describe any and all utility programs (e.g., disk maintenance programs, file recovery programs, network

maintenance programs) used to maintain the following computer(s): *[identify computer].*

6. Describe the software (e.g., version, manufacturer, any custom modifications) used to remotely access the computer system.

7. Describe all upgrades made to any software on the computer system during *[specify period].*

8. Describe any software that has been installed on the computer system during *[specify period].*

9. Describe any document management software used by *[name of party]* during *[specify period].*

10. Identify all escrow agents/services who may have copies of the source code for *[specify software].*

11. Identify all customers who self-escrowed the source code for *[specify software].*

12. Describe the file format used to store information created by *[specify software].*

Security

13. Describe each instance during the last five years in which an unauthorized party gained access to the computer system.

14. Describe each instance during the last five years in which a virus or other destructive program caused any data loss on the computer system.

15. Describe any disaster recovery plans for the computer system, which were in effect during *[specify time period].*

16. Describe all security measures relating to employee desktop computers.

17. Describe any methods used during *[specify period]* to monitor employee use of the computer system.

18. Describe any methods used during *[specify period]* to monitor employee use of the Internet.

19. Describe any methods used during *[specify period]* to monitor employee use of the e-mail.

20. Describe your procedures, if any, for deleting files from the computer system.

21. Describe all methods of accessing the computer system from outside *[name of organization]* (i.e., remote access procedures).

22. Describe all methods used to restrict access to the *[specify name of database]* database.

Computer Backups

23. Identify each computer in the computer system that is backed up.

24. Describe the backup schedule, if any, for each computer in the computer system.

25. Describe the backup procedures, if any, for each computer in the computer system.

26. Identify the backup software (e.g., version, manufacturer, any custom modifications) used, if any, for each computer in the computer system.

27. Identify the storage location for your archival backups.

28. Describe the types of files routinely backed up from the computer system.

29. Describe the procedures followed by *[name or party]* during *[specify time period]* for backing up information stored on its computer system(s), including, but not limited to, the frequency of backups, the software used to accomplish the backups, the type of media backups are stored on, and the location where backups are stored.

30. Describe any and all changes to your backup procedures in the last twelve months.

Miscellaneous

31. Describe the computer system(s) used by *[specify individual]*.

32. Describe any methods used to verify the accuracy of information input into the *[identify software application]*.

33. Identify all e-mail addresses used by *[specify individual's name or business name]*, including the

complete address and the dates during which the address was used.

34. Identify any computers on which a disk maintenance program (e.g., de-fragment, optimize, or compression software) has been run in the last six months.

35. Identify the person(s) responsible for the ongoing operation and maintenance of the computer system.

36. Identify each employee in your Information Systems Department.

Dated: ________

[signature, etc.]

§ 11:20 Interrogatories—Sex discrimination

[Caption]

INTERROGATORIES TO *[NAME OF PARTY]*

To: *[name of party]*

You are notified to answer under oath the following interrogatories within ____ days of the time service is made on you.

DEFINITIONS

A. PLAINTIFF means *[name]*.

B. DEFENDANT means *[name]*.

C. USER means a person who has access to a computer or in any manner uses or directs another to use any information stored in or generated by a computer.

D. COMPUTER OR COMPUTER EQUIPMENT means all data processing equipment, including but not limited to, central processing units, tape drives, drum and disk storage devices, control units, input devices, and output devices; all unit record equipment, including but not limited to, accumulators, calculators, and sorters; all record storage and retrieval equipment, including but not limited to, microfilm storage and retrieval apparatus, and audio/visual storage and retrieval apparatus.

E. COMPUTER SYSTEM means an assembly of computer operations and procedures, persons, equipment, and hardware and software, united by some form of regulated interaction to form an organized whole.

F. COMPUTER OR ELECTRONIC INFORMATION OR DATA OR DATABASE means all written or numerical information or data that is inputted, processed, or contained in the COMPUTER SYSTEM for any purpose.

G. IDENTIFY a document means to describe briefly the form of the document; describe generally the subject of its contents; state the date and place of preparation or mailing; and identify the person or firm who prepared the document, the person or firm who received it, and the person, or firm who had possession or control of the original of the document.

H. IDENTIFY an act, occurrence, statement, or conduct (hereinafter collectively referred to as "act") means to describe the substance of the event or events constituting such acts, and state the date when such act occurred; to identify each person participating in such act; to identify all other persons present when such act occurred; to state whether any minutes, notes, memoranda or other record of such act was made; to state whether such record now exists; and to identify the person presently having possession, custody, or control of each such record.

I. DOCUMENT means all written, printed, recorded, electronic, or graphic matter, photographic matter, sound reproductions, or electronically stored information however produced or reproduced, pertaining in any manner to the subject matter indicated.

J. YOU AND YOUR refer to DEFENDANT. The words YOU and YOUR shall be taken to include all officers, directors, agents, employees, attorneys, investigators, consultants, and anyone else acting on your or their behalf.

K. COMPUTER PROGRAM means a set of instructions or steps, usually in symbolic form, that generates machine instructions and tells the computer how to handle a problem or sort information.

L. COMPUTER APPLICATION means a program that performs a specific task or function including, e-mail messaging, word processing, or spread sheets.

M. DEFENDANT'S COMPUTER SYSTEM means any and all COMPUTER EQUIPMENT or COMPUTER SYSTEMS located at the defendant's premises or accessible for use by defendant.

N. E-MAIL means an electronic messaging application that provides for the receipt and sending of messages among users of a computer system and possibly to and from remote users.

O. OPERATING SYSTEM means an organized collection of programs for operating a computer, usually part of a software package defined to simplify housekeeping such as input/output procedures, sort merge generators, and so on.

P. BACK-UP TAPES means magnetic tape storage or archiving of ELECTRONIC INFORMATION originally contained on a COMPUTER SYSTEM.

Q. COMPUTER LOG means COMPUTER SYSTEM usage records such as a listing of electronically stored information, and may include title, subject matter, or first line of the document information and the date of the document.

R. COMPUTER SYSTEM MEDIA means the type of material used for storage of electronic information and includes floppy disks, hard drives, and magnetic tapes.

S. PURGE means to periodically or randomly delete or take off of the COMPUTER SYSTEM E-MAIL messages and transfer this information to BACK-UP TAPES to restore or make usable computer memory.

INTERROGATORIES

1. IDENTIFY yourself.

2. IDENTIFY all persons who assisted in preparing responses to these interrogatories.

3. Identify by name, manufacturer's model number, or serial number and unit type all COMPUTER EQUIPMENT defendant uses as part of its COMPUTER SYSTEM, and include a listing of all peripheral EQUIPMENT associated with any unit and designating with which units such EQUIPMENT is associated.

4. State the location of each unit of EQUIPMENT identified in your answer to Interrogatory 3.

5. Describe fully or identify the OPERATING SYSTEM used for all programmable EQUIPMENT identified in your answer to Interrogatories 3 and 4.

6. During the period *[date]* to *[date]*, did you discuss or engage in communications concerning the consequences to PLAINTIFF of PLAINTIFF'S departure from the company, including oral, written, or electronic discussions and communications?

7. If your answer to Interrogatory 6 is yes, describe fully the substance of each non-privileged discussion or communication.

8. If your answer to Interrogatory 6 is yes, state the date, time, place, and form of each such discussion or communication.

9. If your answer to Interrogatory 6 is yes, IDENTIFY every person who was present at each such discussion or communication, including the recipients and sender of the communication and any person to whom the communication was directed.

10. If your answer to Interrogatory 6 is yes, IDENTIFY all DOCUMENTS, including electronically stored information, that contain the discussions or communications.

11. For the period *[date]* to *[date]*, state whether BACK-UP TAPES were made of any COMPUTER SYSTEM E-MAIL messages, electronically stored information, word processing documents, or correspondence.

12. If YOUR answer to Interrogatory 11 is yes, state:

(a) The custodian of those tapes;

(b) Identification numbers or the system for identification for those tapes;

(c) The location of those tapes; and

(d) For what period of time those tapes are stored before being reused or discarded.

13. For the period *[date]* to *[date]*, state whether a periodic or random PURGE of E-MAIL messaging was performed.

14. If YOUR answer to Interrogatory 13 is yes, state when that PURGE occurred and identify the BACK-UP TAPE the electronic information was transferred to.

15. State how YOUR COMPUTER SYSTEM handles the deletion or "trash" disposal of E-MAIL messages by a computer user.

16. State whether a COMPUTER LOG is maintained listing E-MAIL messages that have been deleted or "trashed" from the COMPUTER SYSTEM.

17. If YOUR answer to Interrogatory 16 is yes, state the computer location of the COMPUTER LOG for deleted or "trashed" E-MAIL.

18. State whether YOU deleted or "trashed" E-MAIL messages regarding PLAINTIFF'S firing during the period *[date]* to *[date]*.

19. If YOUR answer to Interrogatory 18 is yes, state:

(a) The substance of those deleted or "trashed" E-MAIL messages;

(b) The sender and recipients of those messages, and

(c) The date and time of those messages.

20. State whether similar lawsuits have been commenced or filed against YOU regarding sex discrimination.

21. If YOUR answer to Interrogatory 20 is yes, state when and in which jurisdiction those lawsuits were commenced or filed.

22. If YOUR answer to Interrogatory 20 is yes, IDENTIFY the plaintiff in those lawsuits.

23. List all persons who participated in the decision to fire the PLAINTIFF.

24. State all explanations for the YOUR firing of the PLAINTIFF.

25. Do you contend that you did not discriminate, on the basis of PLAINTIFF'S gender, against the PLAINTIFF?

26. If your answer to Interrogatory 25 is yes, please state every fact that supports your contention.

27. If your answer to Interrogatory 25 is yes, please identify every document that supports your contention.

28. If your answer to Interrogatory 25 is yes, describe every tangible item of evidence and every document, including electronically stored information, that support your contention.

29. Do you contend there is no other electronically stored information that evinces discussions or communications concerning:

(a) The PLAINTIFF'S work performance;

(b) *[Name]*'s departure from the company, and

(c) The firing of the PLAINTIFF?

30. Do you contend the PLAINTIFF was fired for good cause?

31. Do you contend that no officer or director of the company insisted the PLAINTIFF be fired because the PLAINTIFF is a *[woman] [man]*?

32. Do you contend *[name]* did not send E-MAIL to officers and directors of the company stating the PLAINTIFF should be fired?

33. Do you contend that no officer or director of the company received an E-MAIL message stating the PLAINTIFF should be fired?

34. Do you contend that *[name]* did not intentionally delete or "trash"an E-MAIL message stating the PLAINTIFF should be fired?

35. Do you contend that there is another reason the PLAINTIFF was fired?

36. Do you contend the PLAINTIFF was fired for performance reasons?

Dated: ________

[signature, etc.]

Comment

These interrogatories are based on a hypothetical case involving a claim of sex discrimination in employment evidenced by an e-mail message. The interrogatories are designed to elicit information the plaintiff will need to know for preparation of the case, including the circumstances of the plaintiff's firing and the defenses that will be argued. The interrogatories emphasize questions seeking information about data within or exchanged through the defendant's computer system. Accordingly, they do not represent a complete set of questions regarding a claim of sex discrimination.

§ 11:21 Interrogatories combined with requests to produce information about computer system

[Caption]

Interrogatories

To: *[name of party]*

You are notified to answer under oath the following interrogatories within ____ days of the time service is made on you.

Each of the following interrogatories in this section refers ONLY to the *[name of party]*'s computer system, and not to the computer system of any of *[name of party]*'s counsel. In particular, the following interrogatories DO NOT inquire of the computer system maintained or managed by the *[name of party]*'s law firm, or any of that firm's personnel or agents.

1. Please identify the person or persons who have contributed to answering the interrogatories in this section.

2. Please identify by name, physical location, manufacturer's model number or serial number all of the computer equipment containing an installed copy of the database program.

3. Please state if there is any other location where hardcopy or electronic information regarding customer complaints resides other than within the database.

4. Is the database available in other languages besides English and, if so, what are those languages?

5. If the database is available in other languages, is there a master or main database that contains all records, regardless of language?

6. Please identify by name, physical location, manufacturer's model number or serial number all of the computer equipment physically containing actual copies of records.

7. Please identify by name, physical location, manufacturer's model number or serial number all of the computer equipment containing copies of any of the scanned electronic documents referred to in some of the records.

8. Please identify the location on your computer system where the master or main copy of the database resides.

9. Please provide the "version number" of the program currently being used at *[name of party]*, and state whether the program has been specially modified in any way by *[name of party]* computer system personnel to accommodate a) the database or b) the company's e-mail system.

10. Do any engineers or members of engineer departments at *[name of party]* use an e-mail system other than that provided by the program and, if so, what are the names of the other e-mail systems?

11. How do users of *[name of party]'s* e-mail system in the United States communicate with e-mail users in other parts of the world?

12. If there is a translation module or program used for automatically effecting a translation of e-mail from, for example, German to English, what is the name of that module or the program that effects translations?

13. Please identify by name, physical location, manufacturer's model number or serial number all of the computer equipment that is used to back up a) generally the files located on *[name of party]'s* computer system and b) specifically the e-mail system or systems used by the engineers and engineering departments at *[defendant] [plaintiff]*, its

subsidiaries (in this country or throughout the world), predecessors, successors, assigns, joint venturers, partners, parents, agents and affiliates.

14. Regardless of whether it is for security purposes or for some other purpose, is e-mail use at *[name of party]'s* monitored in any way?

15. If e-mail used at *[name of party]* is monitored, where are the monitoring logs or other information concerning such monitoring information stored?

16. Regardless of the date or where in the world they may be located, please state the location or locations where all archived copies of *[name of party]* computer system files are kept, housed or stored.

17. What purchase, merger or related documents exist concerning the acquisition of *[describe]* by *[name of party]*, whether in hardcopy or in electronic format and regardless of who possesses or controls them?

18. What engineering documents originally belonging to exist, regardless of type and whether in hardcopy or in electronic format and regardless of who possesses or controls them?

19. Regardless of the date or where in the world they may be located, please state the location or locations where archived copies of engineering documents originally belonging to *[specify]* are kept, housed or stored.

Requests to Produce

20. Please provide us with unabridged copies of the *[specify]* user's manuals for each version of that program that is currently running anywhere on your computer system.

21. Please provide us with copies of all manuals, electronic or hardcopy, a) furnished to any users of the database, or b) used by the administrators or intranet Web masters responsible for the maintenance and management of the database anywhere in the world and regardless of whether those manuals are written in English or some other language.

22. Please provide us with copies of all manuals,

electronic or hardcopy, a) furnished to any users of *[name of party]*'s e-mail system, or b) used by the administrators or intranet Web masters responsible for the maintenance and management of *[name of party]*'s e-mail system anywhere in the world and regardless of whether those manuals are written in English or in some other language.

23. Please provide us with copies of all manuals, electronic or hardcopy, used by the information systems personnel responsible for maintaining, backing up, restoring or purging generally the computer files located on the computer system of *[name of party]* anywhere in the world and regardless of whether those manuals are written in English or some other language.

24. Please provide us with copies of all manuals, electronic or hardcopy, used by the information systems personnel responsible for maintaining, backing up, restoring or purging the e-mail systems of *[name of party]* anywhere in the world and regardless of whether those manuals are written in English or some other language.

25. Please provide us with all policies or policy statements issued to engineer or engineer department users of *[name of party]*'s e-mail system, regardless of the date of same.

26. Please provide us with copies of any purchase, merger or related documents, whether in hardcopy or in electronic format, concerning the acquisition of by *[name of party]*.

Dated: ________

[signature, etc.]

Comment

These interrogatories and requests to produce can be adapted for use after information is discovered regarding the responding party's computer system.

§ 11:22 Order granting party leave to serve additional interrogatories

[Caption]

This cause comes before the Court on the plaintiff's motion for leave of the Court to serve additional interrogatories on defendant and on defendant's response.

Having considered the motion and the tendered interrogatories, this Court determines that, while relevant, the number of interrogatories tendered for a case of this nature is burdensome. This is particularly so in light of the fact that plaintiff intends to depose the defendant.

Accordingly, the Court now grants plaintiff leave to serve an additional ___ interrogatories on defendant. Plaintiff may designate ___ interrogatories from those tendered. Plaintiff may delay its designation until after plaintiff has completed defendant's depositions. In the alternative, plaintiff may compose a new set of ___ or fewer interrogatories consistent with this order.
Dated: ________

____

Judge

Comment

Some court rules (including Fed. R. Civ. P. 33) limit the number of interrogatories. In such cases, the court may give permission for more interrogatories than the number permitted in the rule. In this form, the judge allows more interrogatories than the number permitted by rule, but refuses to give permission for the plaintiff to ask as many as requested. The form can be modified if the court grants the entire request.

§ 11:23 Motion to compel answers to interrogatories

[Caption]

MOTION TO COMPEL ANSWERS TO INTERROGATORIES

[Party 1] moves the Court as follows:

1. On *[date]*, *[party 1]*, after commencement of the above-entitled action, served on the *[party 2]* ___ interrogatories in writing pursuant to *[rule]*, which interrogatories are attached to this motion.

2. *[Party 2]* answered interrogatories *[numbers of interrogatories]*, but did not answer such interrogatories under oath as required by *[rule]*.

3. *[Party 2]* failed to answer interrogatories *[numbers of unanswered interrogatories]*.

4. The undersigned certifies that the undersigned has in good faith attempted to confer with the attorney for *[party 2]* in an unsuccessful effort to secure the requested information without court action.

Wherefore, *[party 1]* moves that this Court enter an order directing and requiring *[party 2]* to answer all of these interrogatories under oath.

[Party 1] further moves the court for an order awarding *[party 1]* the reasonable expenses, including attorney fees incurred on this motion.

Dated: ________

[signature etc.]

§ 11:24 Order to compel answers to interrogatories

[Caption]

ORDER TO COMPEL ANSWERS TO INTERROGATORIES

This cause was heard on *[plaintiff's] [defendant's]* motion to compel *[defendant] [plaintiff]* to answer interrogatories served by *[plaintiff] [defendant]*, and upon due consideration it is

ORDERED that *[defendant] [plaintiff]* shall answer interrogatories numbers *[specify]*, and under oath, and it is

FURTHER ORDERED that the *[defendant] [plaintiff]* shall answer under oath interrogatory number except insofar as this interrogatory asks *[defendant] [plaintiff]* to state *[describe]*.

IT IS FURTHER ORDERED that *[defendant] [plaintiff]* pay *[plaintiff] [defendant]* the sum of $____ as reasonable expenses in obtaining this order and $ as reasonable attorney fees.

Dated: ________

____

Judge

Chapter 12

Requests for Production and Inspection

I. GUIDELINES

II. CHECKLISTS

III. FORMS

Research References

Treatises and Practice Aids

eDiscovery & Digital Evidence § 7:14

Grenig and Kinsler, Federal Civil Discovery and Disclosure §§ 11.1 to 11.73 (2d ed.)

Danner & Varn, Pattern Deposition Checklists §§ 10:01 to 10:231 (4th ed.)

Trial Strategy

Recovery and Reconstruction of Electronic Mail as Evidence, 41 Am. Jur Proof of Facts 3d 1

Computer Technology in Civil Litigation, 71 Am. Jur Trials 111

Law Reviews and Other Periodicals

Allman & Brady, Can Random Access Memory Make Good Law, Nat'l L.J., Dec. 10, 2007, at E1

Goldberg, Discovery and the Reluctant Host: The Federal Rules Sometimes Allow an Opponent to Poke Around in a Company's IT Closet, Nat'l L.J., March 10, 2008, at S1

Kerr, Turbulence Ahead: Adjusting for E-Discovery in Aviation Litigation, 72 J. Air L. & Com. 465 (2007)

Llewellyn, Electronic Discovery Best Practices, 10 Rich. J.L. & Tech. 51 (2004)

Meyer & Wraspir, eDiscovery: Preparing Clients for (and Protecting Them Against) Discovery in the Electronic Information Age, 26 Wm. Mitchell L.Rev. 939 (2000)

Note, Default Production of Electronically Stored Information Under the Federal Rules of Civil Procedure: The Requirements of Rule 34(b), 59 Hastings L.J. 221 (2007)

Philipp, Strategy Plays a Key Role in Computer Forensics: Finding the Right Hidden Data Can Make All the Difference, Nat'l L.J., March 19, 2007, at S8

Waxse, "Do I Really Have to Do That?" Rule 26(a)(1) Disclosures and Electronic Information, 10 Rich. J.L. & Tech. 50 (2004)

Additional References

Flaming, If You Don't Ask, You Won't Receive: Form of Production Under the New Rules, e-Discovery, 2007, at 16

Frickleton, Get a Handle on Electronic Hospital Data: Hospital Patient Data Can Reside in a Simple Database or in a Fully Integrated Electronic System, Trial, May 2006, at 44

Gable, Eight Tips for Working with a Consultant, Information Mgt. J., July/Aug. 2007, at 42

Jacoby et al., Finding the Right Format of Production for Electronic Information, Elec. Discovery & Records Mgt. Q., Summer 2007, at 28

Larson, The Other Side of Civil Discovery: Disclosure and Production of Electronic Records, in Casey, Handbook of Computer Crime Investigation: Forensic Tools and Technology (2002)

Socha, On Forms of Production, Elec. Disc. & Records Mgt. Q., winter 2007, at 22

ABA Discovery Standards, http://www.abanet.org/litigation/discoverystandards/2005civildiscoverystandards.pdf

Electronic Discovery Reference Model Project, http://www.edrm.net

Federal Judicial Center, http://www.fjc.gov

The Sedona Conference, http://www.thesedonaconference.org

KeyCite®: Cases and other legal materials listed in KeyCite Scope can be researched through the KeyCite service on Westlaw®. Use KeyCite to check citations for form, parallel references, prior and later history, and comprehensive citator information, including citations to other decisions and secondary materials.

I. GUIDELINES

§ 12:1 Generally

Once information is obtained regarding the responding party's electronically stored information, discovery requests can be refined to obtain relevant electronically stored information from the locations and systems identified in the interrogatories and depositions. If the discovering party believes that there is relevant electronically stored information, the discovering party should not hesitate to seek its production just because the discovering party has already been provided with hardcopy versions.

Procedural rules, such as Rule 34 of the Federal Rules of Civil Procedure, set forth the procedures for making and responding to requests for the production of documents and tangible things and entry upon land for inspection and other purposes. The rules are normally designed to operate extrajudicially, and may be used only against parties.

Under Rule 34, the party wishing to inspect documents or tangible things or to enter upon the property of another merely serves on the other party a request that this be permitted, setting forth what it is the party wishes to see and when, where, and how the party wishes to examine it. The opponent serves a response, either saying that the request will be granted or stating objections to the request. If the request is granted, the inspection takes places without court involvement. If the request is objected to, the discovering party decides whether to pursue the matter further. If the discovering party decides to pursue the matter further, the party makes a motion to compel, and the court may compel the requested inspection.

§ 12:2 Comparison with other discovery tools

Document production requests are one of the four major discovery devices—depositions, interrogatories, document production requests and requests for admission. These methods of discovery are complementary, not alternative or exclusive. A party may use any or all of these devices and may do so in any order, as long as there is no attempt to harass or oppress the responding party.

Document requests call for the production of documents and other tangible things and for entry upon land. As such, it is fundamentally different than depositions and interrogatories, which seek answers to questions. Production requests seek production of tangible things (such as documents or photographs) or the entry upon real property, while depositions and interrogatories seek information relating to the identity and location of such tangible and real property. Document production requests can only be used to inspect or copy things in existence at the time the request is served. They cannot be used to force another party to prepare documents or writings.

§ 12:3 Freedom of Information Act

The Freedom of Information Act[1] and rules of civil procedure, such as Rule 34 of the Federal Rules of Civil Procedure, provide separate mechanisms for obtaining disclosure of government documents. Many states have similar public records provisions. Although the FOIA is designed to inform the public about government action and not to benefit private litigants, any person, including a party to a lawsuit, may obtain records from the government unless the records fall within one of the exemptions to the FOIA. The FOIA requests may be used as a substitute to Rule 34 when the federal government is a party to an action or the federal government has information that may be helpful in other litigation.

[Section 12:3]

[1] 5 U.S.C.A. § 552.

The FOIA has several procedural advantages over civil discovery. FOIA requests are often quicker; initial decisions are required within 10 days. In addition, the FOIA provides for an immediate de novo review of adverse rulings, and the FOIA also provides for the recovery of fees and costs upon reversal in some cases. Rule 34 has some advantages over the FOIA: (1) document requests under Rule 34 are normally free of charge; (2) other discovery devices, such as interrogatories and depositions, may be used to locate relevant documents under the civil discovery rules; and (3) severe sanctions may be imposed on a recalcitrant party under Rule 37.

If the government refuses to release documents under the FOIA, the requesting party is entitled to seek redress in the courts. An issue that occasionally arises in FOIA actions is whether a party who makes a FOIA may use Rule 34 to obtain the same documents from the government defendant that the plaintiff sought in the FOIA request. One court prohibited such disclosure on the ground that:

> A request for production of documents is inappropriate in a Freedom of Information Act case which itself is premised upon a request for documents. If information encompassed by plaintiff's FOIA request is contained in the documents he requests production of, he is not entitled to those documents under Rule 34 because to give him that information would be to accord him final relief in the case. To the extent that plaintiff's production request does not involve documents within the scope of his FOIA request, production is objectionable because it would allow plaintiff to expand his request without going through the administrative procedures which are a prerequisite to an action for information under the Freedom of Information Act.[2]

§ 12:4 Actions in which production is available

Requests for production may be used in most civil ac-

---

[2]Stern v. United States, 29 Fed. R. Serv. 2d 1062 (D. Mass. 1980). See Robbins v. U.S. Bureau of Land Management, 219 F.R.D. 685, 58 Fed. R. Serv. 3d 219 (D. Wyo. 2004) (requesting party may not use Rule 34 to discover the very same documents sought in FOIA enforcement action).

tions. Rule 34 of the Federal Rules of Civil Procedure applies only to pending actions. However, in a proceeding to perpetuate testimony under Rule 27, the court may make orders of the nature provided for in Rule 34.

§ 12:5 Persons to whom production requests may be directed—Generally

Rule 34 of the Federal Rules of Civil Procedure and similar state rules may be used only against parties to the action. It applies only to parties in the pending action. Document production requests may not be directed to the attorney for a party or to a witness who is not a party. Although production requests may not be directed to a party's attorney, requests directed to represented parties should be served on their attorneys.

Because Rule 34 covers all documents and electronically stored information that are in the possession, custody or control of a party, a party must produce documents in the possession of its agents. As a result, a party cannot immunize a document from inspection by turning it over to a nonparty so long as it remains in the party's control. A document does not become privileged merely because a party gives it to the party's attorney. One exception to this rule is statements prepared by a client at the behest of their attorneys.

If an entity, typically a parent corporation, has been found to be the alter ego of a party, that entity may be subject to Rule 34. This issue arises most frequently when the alleged alter ego is a foreign corporation outside the jurisdictional limitations of Rule 45

§ 12:6 Persons to whom production requests may be directed—Custody or control

Rule 34(a) of the Federal Rules of Civil Procedure permits any party to serve on any other party a request to produce and allow the party making the request, or someone acting on the party's behalf, to inspect and copy any designated electronically stored information, documents, or things that contain matters within the scope of discovery in the possession, custody, or control of the party upon whom the request is served. Legal ownership or actual possession is not determinative. The test is whether the party has the legal right to control or obtain the items requested. The responding party cannot provide only those electronically stored information, documents, and things within its immediate possession; it must provide all electronically stored information, documents, and things to which it has a legal right to control or may obtain upon demand.

Whether electronically stored information and documents in the possession of a party's attorney are under the control of the party is resolved by discerning their origin.[1] If the items were originally produced by the party or its agents and then turned over to the attorney, they are considered under the party's control. Documents and electronically stored information that the responding party may obtain from a third party by written request are within the responding party's control. If documents and electronically stored information in the possession of a third party are controlled by the responding party, the responding party may not object to a production request on the ground that the requesting party may obtain the information directly from the third party with a subpoena.

A party may be required to produce electronically stored information, documents, and things in the party's possession, although they belong to a third person who is not a party to the action. If a party has possession, custody, or control, it must produce the information even though the items themselves are beyond the jurisdiction of the court. And, even if a party lacks possession, custody or control, it may be compelled to produce such information if it fails to interpose this objection in a timely fashion.

[Section 12:6]

[1]See Phillips v. Netblue, Inc., 2007 WL 174459 (N.D. Cal. 2007) (party producing e-mails containing hyperlinks to other third-party servers was not under duty to download and preserve hyperlinked images, as such images were not within producing party's possession, custody, or control).

§ 12:7 Making production requests—Generally

To inspect electronically stored information, documents, or tangible things or to enter upon property of another party, a party merely must serve on the other party a request that this be permitted. A request may be served on a party without first obtaining an admission from that party that the documents or things exist. The written request must:

- Designate what items the requesting party wishes to see.
- Specify a reasonable time, place and manner for the inspection and related acts.[1]

What constitutes a reasonable time, place and manner is within the court's discretion.

§ 12:8 Making production requests—Timing

Rule 34(b) of the Federal Rules of Civil Procedure precludes the service of production requests before the time specified in Rule 26(d), absent a court order or written stipulation. Rule 26(d) provides that, except when authorized by local rule, order or stipulation, a party may not seek discovery from any source before the parties have met and conferred as required by Rule 26(f). Rule 26(f) requires that the parties meet to develop, among other things, a discovery plan. This meeting must take place as soon as practicable in the litigation process but, in any event, at least 14 days before a scheduling conference is held or a scheduling order is due under Rule 16(b). Rule 16(b) requires that a scheduling order be entered within 90 days after the first appearance of a defendant or 120 days after the complaint has been served on any defendant, whichever occurs earlier.

Rule 34(b) is silent on how late in the litigation process a party may serve production requests. Trial courts have considerable discretion in determining the timeliness of

---

[Section 12:7]

[1]See Fed. R. Civ. P. 34(b).

discovery. Some courts have local rules governing discovery cut-off dates. Where no such rules exist, scheduling orders and pretrial orders may set a time limit for the completion of discovery, including service of or response to production requests.

Production requests should be served to allow sufficient time to complete the process before the discovery cut-off or trial deadline. Ideally, the discovery order should specify whether the discovery deadline is the deadline for service of electronically stored information and document production requests or for responses to such requests. If it is the latter, then requests must be served no less than 30 days before the discovery cut-off date.

The request must specify a reasonable time for making the inspection and performing the related acts. It must provide at least 30 days to allow for the written response. The court has the authority to shorten or lengthen the time to respond. The parties also may stipulate in writing to an extension. The request may simply call for inspection "at a time and place convenient to" the party to whom it is directed, allowing that party to designate the time and place. The actual time, place and manner of inspection is usually arranged by an informal agreement between the attorneys.

§ 12:9 Making production requests—Number of requests

There is no limit on the frequency of use of production requests, unless the court orders otherwise. There is also no required sequence of discovery. Typically, parties start the discovery process with interrogatories and production requests, followed by depositions and requests for admission, but no particular sequence is mandated. A request for production by one party does not prevent any other party from making its own request for production.

§ 12:10 Making production requests—Form and contents

Rule 34(b) of the Federal Rules of Civil Procedure

requires that each production request designate, either by individual item or by category, the item to be inspected and describe each with reasonable particularity.[1] Particularity in designation, of course, is a matter of degree, and depends on the circumstances of each case. If temporary information not routinely retained is desired, the requesting party must take effective affirmative action, including, when necessary, seeking a preservation order requiring a producing party to place transitory information into a form from which production can later be made.[2]

The request may specify the form or forms in which electronically stored information is to be produced. In making the discovery request, it is essential that the requesting party have an understanding of the responding party's digital information systems and how people interact with the system. The requesting party must determine which format will be best for the requesting party's case.

Native format files are original computer files in their original application or software forms.[3] Accordingly, it is necessary for the requesting party to understand fully what the native format is for the particular discovery sought in the case. This includes how the documents were kept, what software programs were used, how files were

---

[Section 12:10]

[1]See Sedona Principle 4 ("Discovery requests for electronically stored information should he as clear as possible, while responses and objections to discovery should disclose the scope and limits of the production.").

[2]See Healthcare Advocates, Inc. v. Harding, Earley, Follmer & Frailey, 497 F. Supp. 2d 627 (E.D. Pa. 2007) (no duty to preserve images automatically retained in and later deleted from temporary cache files where producing party was not aware of duty to do so); Columbia Pictures, Inc. v. Bunnell, 245 F.R.D. 443, 69 Fed. R. Serv. 3d 173 (C.D. Cal. 2007) (server log data was discoverable although it had existed only temporarily in computer's random access memory (RAM).

[3]See Wyeth v. Impax Laboratories, Inc., 248 F.R.D. 169 (D. Del. 2006) (plaintiff not required to produce electronic documents in their native format, complete with metadata, where plaintiff produced documents as image files and defendant failed to demonstrate particularized need for metadata).

named, and whether there was any electronic backup or overwriting of the documents.[4]

In deciding which format to request, the following factors should be considered:

- **Alterability and Spoliation.** Files converted to TIFF images cannot be altered. On the other hand, native files can normally be changed easily.
- **Bates Numbering.** It can be costly to track document in native format. Native file productions may make it impossible to Bates number the documents, prevent an effective audit trail of the documents produced. (Bates numbers can be added to the header or footer of a native document, but this modifies the document.) In contrast, a TIFF production allows for Bates number and accurate tracking of produced documents.
- **Redactions.** A TIFF review and production allows parties to redact confidential or privileged information. When documents are produced in native format, there is no effective way to place a redaction on the native file. Native file production can undermine a defendant's efforts to protect proprietary or privileged information.
- **Metadata.** If native files are produced, all associated metadata, embedded data, and hidden information will be included. Production of TIFF and PDF files with selected metadata fields allows a producing party greater control over what it is giving.[5] Metadata may be especially relevant in cases where the integrity of dates entered facially on documents.[6]

A responding party is not required to reproduce elec-

---

[4]Gonzalez & Montoya, Ten Tips Leading to Efficient and Effective eDiscovery for the Small Law Firm, GP/Solo, Apr. 2007

[5]Gonzalez & Montoya, Ten Tips Leading to Efficient and Effective eDiscovery for the Small Law Firm, GP/Solo, Apr. 2007

[6]See, e.g., Ryan v. Gifford, 2007 WL 4259557 (Del. Ch. 2007) (award of stock options). See also Wyeth v. Impax Laboratories, Inc., 248 F.R.D. 169 (D. Del. 2006) (most metadata is of limited evidentiary value, and reviewing it can waste litigation resources); Kentucky

tronically stored information in more than one form.[7] Accordingly, it is important for a requesting party to consider carefully the form in which it wishes to receive the information before requesting that it be produced.[8]

When seeking electronically stored information, the discovering party should:

- Provide a very specific and detailed request that includes a statement of why it is important to the discovering party's case. In the case of electronically stored information, failure to do so can have serious consequences.
- Not be too specific. If the request is too specific, certain critical information may not be provided; if the request is too broad, the producing party may object to the request.
- Expressly request digital documents by type.
- Specify the production format sought. Despite the fact that one should seek electronically stored information in its native format, counsel may wish to

---

Speedway, LLC v. NASCAR, Inc., 2006 WL 5097354 (Dec. 18, 2006) (in most cases and for most documents, metadata does not provide relevant information).

[7]See Williams v. Sprint/United Management Co., 99 Fair Empl. Prac. Cas. (BNA) 1502, 2006 WL 3691604 (D. Kan. 2006). See, e.g., Autotech Technologies Ltd. Partnership v. Automationdirect.com, Inc., 248 F.R.D. 556 (N.D. Ill. 2008) (party that sought metadata after production in PDF not entitled to native production); Schmidt v. Levi Strauss & Co., 2007 WL 2688467 (N.D. Cal. 2007) (where plaintiff's original document requests (served prior to December 1, 2006) did not specify form in which documents were to be produced, defendant who produced document as hard copy not required to reproduce documents in native format); Michigan First Credit Union v. Cumis Ins. Society, Inc., 2007 WL 4098213 (E.D. Mich. 2007) (sanctions not warranted for failure to produce data in native format with intact metadata where production order did not address native format files).

[8]See, e.g., D'Onofrio v. SFX Sports Group, Inc., 247 F.R.D. 43, 102 Fair Empl. Prac. Cas. (BNA) 1499 (D.D.C. 2008) (plaintiff's instruction in request for production directing that document be produced in such manner as to preserve and identify file from which they were taken did not constitute request that defendant produce electronic data in their original form with metadata, and defendant could not be compelled to do so).

obtain it in PDF or TIFF format for a number of reasons. For example, if counsel is using Summation it may make sense to obtain TIFF images because it will be easier to load into older versions of that program. However, the convenience of receiving electronically stored information in PDF or TIFF format is probably at the expense of receiving the total picture provided by receiving electronically stored information in its native format. Evidence provided in its native format can always be converted to PDF or TIFF.

It is prudent to seek to obtain electronically stored information in its native format. The discovering party can expect resistance when seeking to obtain electronically stored information in its native format (as opposed to PDF or TIFF format). Responding parties will frequently claim that it is burdensome for them to review all productions for privileged information or metadata, even claiming that they have an ethical duty not to disclose information in native format. That is why the discovering party's counsel must go to considerable pains to review the information furnished in hardcopy, PDF, or TIFF formats before seeking a native format production.

It is not always possible to obtain electronically stored information evidence in its native format in the first instance. However, after carefully reviewing the electronically stored information by the responding party, if it appears suspicious or incomplete, it is time for the discovering party to demand that the evidence be produced in its native format just as it exists in the responding party's computer systems.

Counsel should consider requesting production of the printout of a database (remembering that metadata may not be disclosed), the programs used to produce it, and the data from which the printout was derived. Counsel should also ask for the source listing with any explanatory documentation, and give consideration to obtaining source codes in order to perform tests on the program. Counsel should ask for an intelligible listing of the data the program used to generate the printout and a machine-readable copy of the data, together with an explanation of the format in which the data is recorded.

Counsel should not overlook relevant data that live outside documents and databases (e.g., system access logs, server logs). Most corporate information technology departments overwrite logs very frequently—timeliness will be important to preserve these.

CD or DVD productions are likely to be a responding party's preferred method of production, but such productions can be very problematic. They will certainly contain less interesting information than a mirrored drive because slack space and deleted files will not show up on data copied to an optical drive. The digital age will not change the tendency of responding parties to make matters difficult for a discovering party. This is especially the case when it comes to the production of digital evidence on CD or DVD. It is prudent to specify in the definitional section of interrogatories seeking the production of digital evidence what a discovering party will accept when that evidence is produced on CD or DVD. If the images do not exist in a database, then a detailed index of the contents of each CD or DVD should be provided on each CD or DVD.

If the producing party maintains the electronically stored information in a searchable format, it is helpful to get an agreement or court order requiring that the information be produced in that format. If the electronically stored information is produced in a format that is not readable, searchable, or usable, the requesting party should meet with the producing party before filing a motion to compel. If agreement cannot be reached, then the requesting party should seek an order compelling production of the electronically stored information in a searchable format.

§ 12:11 Making production requests—Service

In federal court, service of production requests is governed by Rule 5 of the Federal Rules of Civil Procedure. Requests may be served by delivering a copy to the party or mailing the request to the party's last known address.

Once a party has appeared by counsel, the requests are served upon the attorney. A copy of the requests should also be served on all other parties to the action. Rule 5(d) provides that requests and responses must not be filed until they are used in the proceeding or the court orders filing.

§ 12:12 Production requests—E-mail

E-mail has become one of the most popular means of communication in the workplace. Frequently, e-mail users fail to exercise care and use common sense when creating e-mail messages. Many e-mail users do not realize e-mail messages are more permanent than paper letters. E-mail is also very easy to duplicate and forward with the result that it can easily end up in the possession of an unintended recipient. In addition, if an organization runs periodic backups of its network, e-mail messages are backed up and stored on backup tapes.

An important difference between the discovery of e-mail and the discovery of paper documents is the sheer volume of e-mail. Additionally, computers have the ability to capture several copies (or drafts) of the same e-mail, multiplying the volume of documents. All of these e-mails must be scanned for both relevance and privilege.[1]

Archived e-mails typically lack a coherent filing system. Dated archival systems commonly store information on magnetic tapes that have become obsolete. Thus, parties incur additional costs in translating the data from the tapes into useable form.

[Section 12:12]

[1]Compare Zakre v. Norddeutsche Landesbank Girozentrale, 2004 WL 764895 (S.D. N.Y. 2004) (providing over 200,000 e-mails on two CD-ROMs in a text-searchable format was responsive to discovery request), with Hagemeyer North America, Inc. v. Gateway Data Sciences Corp., 222 F.R.D. 594 (E.D. Wis. 2004) (when producing documents in response to discovery request, responding party may not mingle responsive documents with large numbers of nonresponsive documents; however, responding party has no duty to organize and label documents if it has produced them as they are kept in usual course of business).

E-mail does not appear as a set of files as one might see in a Windows directory. E-mail lives within an environment rich with metadata that cannot easily be split into small parts.[2] In many computers, e-mail will be contained in Microsoft Outlook. To obtain and search all of the e-mails of a responding party using Outlook, it is necessary to seek production of what is called a PST file. A PST file is a Microsoft proprietary file containing the entire Outlook e-mail database. When viewed from Windows Explorer, it can appear as a single file or a grouping of a small number of files. A PST file cannot be opened correctly except with Outlook. A single PST file can house tens of thousands of e-mails in numerous directories, together with address books, and can grow very large (a two gigabyte PST is not uncommon).

After the discovering party has reviewed the e-mails furnished in hardcopy or in PDF format, and finds several that are particularly interesting, the discovering party may wish to consider asking to see just those e-mails in their native format so counsel can inspect their metadata. With the help of a forensic computer expert, the discovering party can instruct the responding party to segregate selected e-mail into separate folders and then export them to removable media.

§ 12:13 Production requests—Videoconferencing and voicemail

Voicemail and videoconferencing systems can preserve data about who participated in an exchange, and the date, time and length of the exchange. Videoconferencing and voicemail systems may archive copies of incoming and outgoing messages. Some videoconferencing equipment makes digital records of each conference.

Many voicemail systems archive copies of incoming and outgoing messages. Although voicemail has always been

[2]See Berman and Zerkier, Recognizing Import of E-Mail Headers in Discovery: Litigators May Use Embedded Data to Follow an "Information Trail," Nat'l L.J., Apr. 24, 2006, at S8.

subject to discovery, discovery respondents have, for the most part, successfully resisted turning over voicemails, citing expense and burden. However, the use of Unified Messaging Systems (UMS) may be changing this. UMS do not distinguish between e-mail, voicemail, and other forms of messaging. Because of the nature of UMS technology, the arguments of cost and burden will probably be less persuasive.

§ 12:14 Requests to produce—Databases

While discovery frequently centers on e-mail messages and digital versions of documents, in many cases electronic discovery requests include databases. A digital database is a collection of data in computers organized for rapid search and retrieval. A database program stores and organizes information on a variety of subjects in a variety of ways and provides access to information in all of its files quickly and easily. The organization of the data facilitates the rapid search and retrieval of data.

A database can include a table in a word processing program or a spreadsheet. A database also includes litigation support databases such as Summation and Concordance. These latter types of databases are sometimes referred to as "flat-file" databases—they have a single layer of data in which every record is equal in form to every other record. A table in a flat-file database cannot be related to other database tables.

A "relational" database is more complex than a flat file database. A relational database uses multiple tables to form a single database. Tables in a relational database can be related for business or information purposes. When a relational database is searched, the database matches information from a field in one table with information in a corresponding field of another table to produce a third table combining requested data from both tables. A relational database may be created using software such as Microsoft Access, Paradox, or FoxPro.

"Enterprise" databases are the most complex databases. An enterprise database can be created using Oracle,

Informix, or Microsoft SQL server software. These databases are used by organizations to manage large volumes of data across large distributed networks.

Discovery of databases may be necessary in order to uncover all of the pieces of data that can be vital evidence in a trial. However, database discovery raises difficult issues, as databases are not made up of discrete documents, but are constantly changing, being updated, and being linked together from multiple sources. It is not a simple matter for the responding party simply to produce a database, especially a relational or enterprise database.

It is not possible to import all databases into a single system for review. Issues can arise involving such matters as to how the database is configured, its size, functionality, reporting forms, and search methodology. However, because databases are considered documents, they must be produced if a proper discovery request is made.

Because the field properties of a database are considered metadata, a database discovery request should include a request for copies of operating instructions, user manuals, database design manual, and other information that may disclose the database field properties. In *Dunn v. Midwestern Indemnity*,[1] the court acknowledged that in many instances it will be essential for the discovering party to know the underlying theory and the procedures employed in preparing and storing machine-readable records. When this is true, the court said litigants should be allowed to discover any materials relating to the record holder's computer hardware, the programming techniques employed, the principles governing structure of the stored data, and the operation of the data processing system. The court went on to say that, when statistical analyses have been developed from more traditional records with the assistance of computer techniques, the underlying data used to compose the statistical computer input, the methods used to select, categorize, and evaluate the data for analy-

---

[Section 12:14]

[1]Dunn v. Midwestern Indem., 88 F.R.D. 191 (S.D. Ohio 1980).

sis, and all the computer outputs are normally proper subjects for discovery.

When making a request for production of a database, the requesting party should attempt do the following:

- Seek to determine the nature of the database requested.
- Determine the size of the database.
- Seek to determine the content of the database.

Courts have limited or denied requests for direct access to databases. For example, *In re Ford Motor Co.*[2] involved a plaintiff's claim that, because of defective design, her seat belt had come unbuckled during an accident. Arguing that Ford had not been forthcoming with information, the plaintiff requested direct access to Ford's database to determine what complaints Ford had received regarding seat belts. Recognizing that direct access to a database may be permissible in some circumstances, the Eleventh Circuit denied the plaintiff access because it found that she had not shown discovery abuses by Ford. The court also noted that the district court had given the plaintiff unlimited, direct access to Ford's databases without establishing protocols for the search. It pointed out that the court did not even designate search terms to restrict the search.

When dealing with a simple database, a database viewer can alleviate concerns about direct access to databases. A database viewer is software that allows a person to look at data and manipulate it in limited ways, but without the full functionality of the database. Relatively uncomplicated database files can also be presented in a format maintaining as much metadata and original formatting as possible. A third option, is the appointment of a special master appointed by the court.

§ 12:15 Requests to inspect—Generally

There are many types of evidence that can only be

---

[2]In re Ford Motor Co., 345 F.3d 1315, 56 Fed. R. Serv. 3d 438 (11th Cir. 2003).

recovered if one has access to a computer system. If there is a concern that the responding party's search of its computer was not thorough, and that the documents or information produced represents only a portion of the electronically stored information that actually exists, or if there is a reasonable basis to believe electronically stored information has been deleted, the requesting party should request that it be allowed to physically examine the responding party's computer system.[1] The discovering party must be in a position to make a credible argument to the court that there may be hidden information or other metadata that can only be discovered by seeing the data in its native format. A very high threshold will have to be cleared in order to conduct such discovery.[2]

[Section 12:15]

[1]See, e.g., G.D. v. Monarch Plastic Surgery, P.A., 239 F.R.D. 641, 67 Fed. R. Serv. 3d 352 (D. Kan. 2007) (patients who sued health care providers for wrongful disclosure of their confidential medical information stored on computer hard drive in discarded computer permitted to inspect, test, and evaluate computer itself).

[2]See, e.g., Bro-Tech Corp. v. Thermax, Inc., 2008 WL 724627 (E.D. Pa. 2008) (no evidence of intentional violation of order by producers as would warrant full disclosure of forensic copies of hard drives); Scotts Co. LLC v. Liberty Mut. Ins. Co., 2007 WL 1723509 (S.D. Ohio 2007) (Federal Rules of Civil Procedure do not require forensic computer search as a matter of course); Orrell v. Motorcarparts of America, Inc., 2007 WL 4287750 (W.D. N.C. 2007) (former employer entitled to inspect plaintiff's home computer where plaintiff claimed she had forwarded offensive e-mails from co-workers to her home computer); Benton v. Dlorah, Inc., 2007 WL 2225946 (D. Kan. 2007) (finding that defendants did not sustain burden of showing that plaintiff had failed to comply with requests for production, plaintiff's hard drive contained any additional information subject to discovery, or that plaintiff had spoliated evidence and denying motion that plaintiff produce hard drive); Balfour Beatty Rail, Inc. v. Vaccarello, 2007 WL 169628 (M.D. Fla. 2007) (plaintiff's request for defendants' computer hard drives denied, where plaintiff did not provide any information regarding what it sought to discover from the hard drives or make any contention that defendants had failed to provide requested information contained on hard drives); Williams v. Massachusetts Mut. Life Ins. Co., 226 F.R.D. 144, 146 (D. Mass. 2005) (plaintiff in employment discrimination suit not allowed to conduct forensic study of employer's electronically stored information

If requested access is sought to obtain information that is central to the matters at issue, courts are more likely to grant some form of access or review.[3] In *Hedenburg v. Aramark Food Services*,[4] the court was asked whether the

---

in attempt to locate e-mail between company officials allegedly reflecting discriminatory practice and policy, where employer had already undertaken its own search and forensic analysis and had sworn to its accuracy, and employee provided no reliable or competent information to show employer's representations were misleading or substantively inaccurate); Menke v. Broward County School Bd., 916 So. 2d 8, 205 Ed. Law Rep. 541, 23 I.E.R. Cas. (BNA) 936 (Fla. Dist. Ct. App. 4th Dist. 2005) (school district's expert denied right to inspect computers in home of suspended teacher to look for pornographic material); Ukiah Automotive Investments v. Mitsubishi Motors of North America, Inc., 2006 WL 1348562 (N.D. Cal. 2006) (where numerous financial statements were missing from responding party's computer records, court ordered responding party to produce computer on its own using an agreed-upon neutral inspector with expenses paid by producing party unless producing party produced information on its own).

[3]See, e.g., Frees, Inc. v. McMillian, 2007 WL 184889 (W.D. La. 2007), aff'd, 2007 WL 1308388 (W.D. La. 2007) (plaintiff allowed to inspect defendant's computer in action under Computer Fraud and Abuse Act, where plaintiff sought to show that alleged proprietary electronically stored information that was removed from plaintiff's laptop may have been downloaded to defendant's); Thielen v. Buongiorno USA, Inc., 2007 WL 465680 (W.D. Mich. 2007) (in suit under Telephone Consumer Protection Act of 1991 for allegedly sending text message to plaintiff's cellphone without plaintiff's permission, court allowed defendant to conduct a forensic examination of an image of plaintiff's computer with restrictions on scope of examination); Ukiah Automotive Investments v. Mitsubishi Motors of North America, Inc., 2006 WL 1348562 (N.D. Cal. 2006) (where numerous financial statements were missing from responding party's computer records, court ordered responding party to produce computer on its own using an agreed-upon neutral inspector with expenses paid by producing party unless producing party produced information on its own).

[4]Hedenburg v. Aramark American Food Services, 2007 WL 162716 (W.D. Wash. 2007). See also Balfour Beatty Rail, Inc. v. Vaccarello, 2007 WL 169628 (M.D. Fla. 2007) (in trade secrets case, access to computers denied because plaintiff's requests simply sought computer hard drives, and plaintiff did not provide any information regarding what it sought to discover from hard drives or make any content that defendants failed to provide requested information contained on hard drives).

defendant could make an image of the plaintiff's computer "[i]n an effort to probe the veracity of Plaintiff's claims." In denying access to the computer, the court commented that a thorough search of an adversary's computer is sometimes permitted where the contents of the computer go to the heart of the case. However, the court denied the defendant's requests, finding that the claims at issue were wholly unrelated to the contents of the plaintiff's computer.

A discovering party should not ignore alternatives to actually going on site to search a responding party's system, such as acquiring mirror images of hard drives or having the computer system searched by a neutral court-appointed experts (usually at the requesting party's expense).[5]

§ 12:16 Requests to inspect—Requirement of expert assistance

Lawyers are not capable of conducting forensic computer investigations alone, or even making a case for forensic investigations. First, lawyers do not want to become their own experts. Second, most lawyers cannot begin to articulate the reasons for conducting a forensic investigation without the assistance of qualified experts. Whether counsel represents the discovering or producing party in a lawsuit, marshaling and discovering electronically stored information will very probably require the assistance of competent forensic experts. Because electronically stored information is changed every time it is viewed, in order to avoid a claim of tampering of spoliation, it may be prudent to request that a court-appointed computer expert or technical employee of the opposing party participate in the inspection.

---

[5]See Eugene J. Strasser, M.D., P.A. v. Bose Yalamanchi, M.D., P.A., 669 So. 2d 1142, 1145 (Fla. Dist. Ct. App. 4th Dist. 1996) (where there has been no evidence to establish any likelihood that purged documents can be retrieved, one alternative might be for producing party's representative to physically access the computer system in the presence of requesting party's representative under an agreed-upon set of procedures to test plaintiff's theory that it is possible to retrieve the purged data).

II. CHECKLISTS

§ 12:17 Electronically stored information

- ☐ E-mails, including those sent, received, or drafted
- ☐ PowerPoint or similar presentations
- ☐ Tables
- ☐ Charts
- ☐ Graphs, and
- ☐ Database files
- ☐ Digital calendars
- ☐ Proprietary software files
- ☐ Internet browsing applications, including bookmarks, cookies, and history log
- ☐ Cellular telephone logs

§ 12:18 Electronic media checklist

- ☐ E-mail transmitted through company networks.
- ☐ Messages transmitted through external networks (e.g., Yahoo, Google, AOL)
- ☐ Hand-held electronic personal organizers.
- ☐ Databases of personal-information from computer-based contact managers.
- ☐ Databases used by the sales staff (e.g., contact-manager software, telemarketing data).
- ☐ Computer vendors (e.g., repair shop may have hard drive)
- ☐ All previous versions of word processing and spreadsheet documents, in addition to the current version. This should include data backups.
- ☐ Complete copy of all data on a hard drive. (Note that application software is protected from duplication by copyright.)
- ☐ Central computer or server data.
- ☐ Consider requesting paper file copies of electronic information, if they exist. Penciled margin notes often yield good information.
- ☐ Request electronic media in a form that can be read

by your equipment or software, or make arrangements for the material to be converted.

§ 12:19 Document production checklist

- ☐ **Coordinate with Opposing Counsel.** Before noticing the document production request, confer with opposing counsel regarding the volume of documents, including electronically stored information, and their accessibility. This will dictate the location of the production, which must be listed in the notice. From this response, determine how many people will be required to attend the production to review the documents, or if you are doing it yourself, how much time to budget.
- ☐ **Key Document Request.** Make sure key documents in the discovery plan have been included in the document request.
- ☐ **Agree on Document Numbering Approach.** Discuss a standardized document numbering conventions with all counsel.
- ☐ **Alpha-Numeric Numbering.** Documents should be numbered before copying in an alpha-numeric configuration, with the alpha portion indicating the source of the document. The documents should be numbered prior to the production for effective document control.
- ☐ **Number Everything.** All documents, including sticky notes on top of pages, should be numbered separately. In addition, if there is information on both sides of a page, give each side its own number.
- ☐ **Review All Case Background.** Prior to the production of documents review all case background material including the actual request for documents or subpoena to be certain you know what items to expect at the document production site. Know the parameters of privilege that specifically apply to your case.
- ☐ **Check For Numbering Gaps.** If the documents produced are numbered sequentially, make certain there are no gaps in the numbering. If there are gaps, determine if the gaps are due to missing documents or documents removed for privilege.

☐ **Document Privilege Log.** Opposing counsel must provide an item-by-item specific description of documents being withheld for privilege. This should be in the form of a privileged document log.

☐ **Document Inventory Log.** Make a document inventory log of all documents by file-folder title, document number range, if possible, and a brief description of the contents of each folder. This initial log or index can be done by hand, with a tape recorder or by using a laptop computer.

☐ **Document Production Record/Cover Sheet.** In addition to the inventory log, create a cover sheet that gives general information about the production, including location and those attending.

☐ **Guard Against Disclosures About Your Case.** Do not get chatty. At the production do not offer any information about your case to those producing the documents.

☐ **Quality Control For Legibility.** Check for document legibility, size and double-sided sheets.

☐ **Copy Everything.** Instruct the copying vendor to copy everything. That includes both sides of two-sided documents, sticky notes or any other notes stapled or otherwise attached to documents. Always make sure there is a quality control check for number and legibility.

☐ **Index Documents.** After receiving the documents you chose at the inspection, or after getting the documents back to your office from the production, they must be indexed. A paralegal should index each document by document number (or number range), date, author, recipient, people or companies mentioned. The index should also include a short description. Include remarks concerning handwritten or special notations on the documents.

III. FORMS

§ 12:20 Requests to produce

[Caption]

[PARTY'S] REQUESTS FOR PRODUCTION

In accordance with *[rule]*, *[plaintiff] [defendant] [name 1]* request *[defendant] [plaintiff] [name 2]* to produce the documents specified below, within thirty (30) days of service, or at such other time and place, or in such other manner, as may be mutually agreed upon by the parties. *[Name 2's]* production of documents must be in accordance with the Instructions and Definitions set forth below and *[rule]*.

INSTRUCTIONS AND DEFINITIONS

A. Whenever reference is made to a person, it includes any and all of that person's principals, employees, agents, attorneys, consultants and other representatives.

B. When production of any document in *[name 2's]* possession is requested, the request includes documents subject to the *[name 2's]* possession, custody or control. In the event that *[name 2]* is able to provide only part of the document or documents called for in any particular Request for Production, *[name 2]* must provide all document or documents that *[name 2]* is able to provide and state the reason, if any, for the inability to provide the remainder.

C. "Document" or "documents" means all materials within the full scope of *[rule]*, including but not limited to all writings and recordings, including the originals and all non-identical copies, whether different from the original by reason of any notation made on such copies or otherwise (including but without limitation to, e-mail and attachments, correspondence, memoranda, notes, diaries, minutes, statistics, letters, telegrams, minutes, contracts, reports, studies, checks, statements, tags, labels, invoices, brochures, periodicals, telegrams, receipts, returns, summaries, pamphlets, books, interoffice and intraoffice communications, offers, notations of any sort of conversations, working papers, applications, permits, file wrappers, indices, telephone calls, meetings or printouts, teletypes, telefax, invoices, worksheets, and all drafts, alterations, modifications, changes and amendments of any of the foregoing), graphic or aural representations of any kind (including without limitation, photographs, charts, microfiche, microfilm, videotape, recordings, motion pictures, plans, drawings, surveys), and electronic, mechanical, magnetic, optical or electric records or representations of any kind (including without limitation, computer files and programs, tapes, cassettes, discs, recordings), including metadata.

D. If any document is withheld from production under a claim of privilege or other exemption from discovery, state the title and nature of the document, and furnish a list signed by the attorney of record giving the following information with respect to each document withheld:

(1) the name and title of the author or sender, or both, and the name and title of the recipient;

(2) the date of the document's origination;

(3) the name of each person or persons, other than stenographic or clerical assistants, participating in the preparation of the document;

(4) the name and position, if any, of each person to whom the contents of the documents have previously been communicated by copy, exhibition, reading or substantial summarization;

(5) a statement of the specific basis on which privilege is claimed and whether or not the subject matter or the contents of the document is limited to legal advice or information provided for the purpose of securing legal advice; and

(6) the identity and position, if any, of the person or persons supplying the attorney signing the list with the information requested in subparagraphs above.

E. "Relate(s) to," "related to" or "relating to" means to refer to, reflect, concern, pertain to or in any manner be connected with the matter discussed.

F. Every Request for Production herein must be deemed a continuing Request for Production and Defendant is to supplement its answers promptly if and when Defendant obtains responsive documents which add to or are in any way inconsistent with *[name 2's]* initial production.

G. These discovery requests are not intended to be

duplicative. All requests should be responded to fully and to the extent not covered by other requests. If there are documents that are responsive to more than one request, then please so note and produce each such document first in response to the request that is more specifically directed to the subject matter of the particular document.

H. Any word written in the singular must be construed as plural or vice versa when necessary to facilitate the response to any request.

I. "And" as well as "or" must be construed disjunctively or conjunctively as necessary in order to bring within the scope of the request all responses which otherwise might be construed to be outside its scope.

DOCUMENT REQUESTS

1. All documents with reference to or written policies, procedures and guidelines related to Defendant's computers, computer systems, electronic data and electronic media including, but not limited to, the following:

a. Backup tape rotation schedules;

b. Electronic data retention, preservation and destruction schedules;

c. Employee use policies of company computers, data, and other technology;

d. File naming conventions and standards,

e. Password, encryption, and other security protocols;

f. Diskette, CD, DVD, and other removable media labeling standards;

g. E-mail storage conventions (such as limitations on mailbox sizes/storage locations; schedule and logs for storage);

h. Electronic media deployment, allocation, and maintenance procedures for new employees, current employees, or departed employees;

i. Software and hardware upgrades (including patches) for *[time]*, indicating who and what organization conducted such upgrades; and

j. Personal or home computer usage for work-related activities.

2. Organization charts for all Information Technology or Information Services departments or divisions from [relevant time period].

3. Backup tapes containing e-mail and other electronic data related to this action from *[date]*.

4. Exact copies (i.e., bit-by-bit copies) of all hard drives on the desktop computers, laptop computers, notebook computers, personal digital assistant computers, servers, and other electronic media related to this action from *[date]*.

5. Exact copies of all relevant disks, CDs, DVDs and other removable media related to this action from *[date]*.

6. For each interrogatory set forth in *[name 1's]* First Interrogatories, produce all documents that *[name 2]* referred to, relied upon, consulted or used in any way in answering such interrogatory.

7. All documents that contain or otherwise relate to the facts or information that *[name 2]* contends refute, in any way, the allegations contained in the *[Complaint] [Answer]* in this action.

8. All reports, including drafts, submitted by any expert witness or potential expert witness retained or consulted by any *[name 2]* with respect to the issues raised in this case.

Dated: ________

[signature, etc.]

§ 12:21 Requests to produce and to inspect

[Caption]

The *[requesting party]* requests that the *[producing party]* respond within ____ days to the following requests:

1. To produce and permit the plaintiff to inspect and copy and to test or sample the following documents, including electronically stored information:

[Describe each document and the electronically stored information, either individually or by category.]

[State the time, place, and manner of the inspection and any related acts.]

2. To produce and permit the plaintiff to inspect and copy, and to test or sample, the following tangible things:

[Describe each thing, either individually or by category.]

[State the time, place, and manner of the inspection and any related acts.]

3. To permit the plaintiff to enter onto the following land to inspect, photograph, test, or sample the property or an object or operation on the property.

[Describe the property and each object or operation.]

[State the time and manner of the inspection and any related acts.]

Dated: ________

[signature, etc.]

Comment

This form is adapted from Official Form 50 approved by the U.S. Supreme Court.

§ 12:22 Plaintiff's request for production of documents

[Caption]

PLAINTIFF'S REQUEST FOR PRODUCTION OF DOCUMENTS

Pursuant to *[rule]*, the Defendant *[name]* is requested to identify the documents set forth below in its possession, custody, or control or in the possession, custody, or control of the Defendant's agents, attorneys, employees, and/or representatives.

The documents are to be produced for inspection on the date and time and at the location specified above. The Defendant may satisfy this Demand for Production of Documents by mailing copies of the documents requested to the Plaintiff's attorney and making the originals available on reasonable notice.

INSTRUCTIONS

A. Copies of writings.

If there are several copies of a writing, and if any of the copies are not identical or are no longer identical because they have been written on or modified in any way, front or back, then each of the nonidentical copies is considered a separate writing and must be produced.

B. Withholding documents under a claim of privilege.

If any document is withheld under a claim of privilege, please identify the writing by providing the following information: the basis for the claim of privilege, the date of the document, the subject of the document, the author, the addressee(s) and all other persons who received the writing or copies of the document, as well as all those to whom the document or copies became available at any time, together with each person's job title and address. A privilege log must be included with your written response.

C. Documents no longer in the Responding Party's possession or control.

If any writing to be produced is no longer in the

Defendant's possession or control or is no longer in existence, please state whether the writing is missing or lost, destroyed, transferred voluntarily or involuntarily to others (and if so, to whom), or otherwise disposed of. In each instance, explain the circumstances surrounding the authorization for the disposition and the date of the disposition.

D. Documents stored electronically.

Pursuant to *[rule]*, electronically stored information shall be reduced to hardcopy form.

DEFINITIONS

For purposes of this Request certain terms are defined as follows:

1. The term "writing" is defined as in *[rule]* and includes, but is not limited to, all originals and duplicates of correspondence, memoranda, records, data sheets, purchase orders, tabulations, reports, evaluations, work papers, summaries, opinions, journals, calendars, diaries, statistical records, checks, notes, transcriptions, telegrams, teletypes, telex messages, telefaxes, recordings of telephone calls, electronically stored information, and other communications, including but not limited to notes, notations, memoranda, and other writings of or relating to telephone conversations and conferences, minutes and notes of transcriptions of all meetings and other communications of any type, microfiche, microfilms, tapes or other records, logs and any other information stored or carried electronically, by means of computer equipment or otherwise, and which can be retrieved in printed, graphic, or audio form, including, but not limited to, information stored in the memory of a computer, data stored on removable magnetic or optical media (for example, magnetic tape, floppy disks, removable cartridge disks, and optical disks), e-mail, data used for electronic data interchange, audit trails, digitized pictures and audio (for example,

data stored in MPEG, JPEG, and GIF), digitized audio, and voice mail.

2. The term "original" is defined as in *[rule]* and includes the writing itself or any counterpart intended to have the same effect by a person executing or issuing it. An original of a photograph includes the negative or any print therefrom. If data are stored in a computer or similar device, any printout or other output readable by sight, shown to reflect the data accurately, is an original.

2. The term "duplicate" is defined as in *[rule]* and includes a counterpart produced by the same impression as the original, or from the same matrix, or by means of photography, including enlargements and miniatures, or by mechanical or electronic rerecording, or by chemical reproduction, or by equivalent technique accurately reproducing the original.

3. The term "person" is defined as in *[rule]* and includes a natural person, firm, association, organization, partnership, business trust, corporation, limited liability company, or public entity.

4. The term "relating to" includes referring to, embodying, in connection with, referencing, evidencing, commenting on, corresponding to, sharing, describing, concerning, analyzing, reflecting, or constituting.

5. The terms "you" or "your" refer to Defendant and its agents, employees, representatives, and attorneys.

6. The term "computer" includes, but is not limited to, personal computers, microcomputers, laptop computers, portable computers, notebook computers, palmtop computers, personal digital assistants, file servers, application servers, workstations, network computers (sometimes called "thin clients"), minicomputers, and mainframes.

7. The term "computer system" refers to all file servers, stand alone computers, workstations, laptops, and personal digital assistants owned or leased by Defendant or physically located at *[place]*.

8. The term "network" refers to the local area network located at *[place]*, including, but not limited to, all files servers, client computers, workstations, firewalls, rout-

ers, proxy servers, Internet servers, mail servers, application servers.

9. The term "log file" refers to the information automatically collected by Web sites on the Internet. Such information includes, but is not limited to, the Internet address of each visitor, the date and time of the visit to the Web site, the particular pages of the site viewed, prior Web sites visited, and whether the visit was successful or whether a failure resulted (that is, an error occurred on the Web site).

10. The term "Web site" refers to the World Wide Web site located at *[address]*, the hypertext markup language (HTML) pages making up the site, and all information collected and stored by the site, including all log files relating to the usage of the site.

11. The term "e-mail" refers to the exchange of text messages and computer files over a communications network, such as a local area network, intranet, extranet, or public network like the Internet or other online service provider.

DOCUMENTS REQUESTED

The documents or writings to be identified and produced pursuant to this Demand are as follows:

Requests Relating to Corporate Policies and Guidelines

12. All writings relating to guidelines and policies governing employee use of the computer system prepared or adopted within the last five years, including, but not limited to, drafts of all such guidelines and policies.

13. All writings relating to guidelines and policies governing maintenance of hard disks on the computer system, including, but not limited to, guidelines and policies regarding the use of utility software to scan the disks for errors, to optimize disks, and to conduct low and high level formatting of disks.

14. All writings relating to guidelines and policies governing employee use of e-mail prepared or adopted

within the last five years, including, but not limited to, drafts of all such guidelines and policies.

15. All writings relating to guidelines and policies governing employee use of the Internet prepared or adopted within the last five years, including, but not limited to, drafts of all such guidelines and policies.

16. All writings relating to guidelines and policies governing when files are deleted from the computer system.

Requests Relating to Use of the Computer System

17. All writings relating to instances in which an employee has been disciplined in any way for misusing or abusing the computer system.

18. All writings relating to instances in which an employee has been disciplined in any way during the past five years for sending harassing, offensive, or sexually explicit e-mail to another employee.

19. Copies of all e-mail sent or received by [*specify individual*] relating to *[describe]*.

20. Copies of all e-mail during *[specify period]* sent or received by *[specify first individual]* in which *[specify second individual]* was also a recipient, including e-mail in which *[specify second individual]* was copied or blind-copied.

21. Copies of all e-mail sent or received by account name *[specify account name]*.

Requests Relating to Security

22. All writings relating to procedures and policies you followed during *[specify period]* for backing up files and other data from your computer.

23. All writings relating to procedures and policies you followed during *[specify period]* concerning the security of the computer system, including, but not limited to, all training materials for employees.

23. All writings relating to any security reviews or analyses of the computer system prepared within the last five years, including, but not limited to, reports,

memoranda, and correspondence prepared by or sent to third party security consultants.

24. All writings relating to any instances in the last five years in which an unauthorized party gained access to the computer system.

25. All writings relating to any instances in the last five years in which a virus or other destructive program caused any data loss on the computer system.

26. All writings relating to any instances in the last five years in which an equipment or software malfunction caused data loss on the computer system.

27. All writings relating to any instances in the last five years in which a hard disk has been replaced in any computer on the network.

28. All writings relating to any disaster recovery plans established during [*specify period*] for the network.

29. All writings relating to methods of accessing the network from outside Defendant (that is, remote access procedures).

Employee Monitoring

30. All writings relating to your efforts to monitor employee use of the network.

31. All writings relating to your efforts to monitor employee use of the Internet.

32. All writings relating to your efforts to monitor employee use of e-mail.

Requests Relating to the Web Site

31. All writings relating to the design and development of the Web site, including, but not limited to, copies of the executed development agreement and all drafts of the agreement with *[specify developer]*.

32. All writings relating to orders for merchandise made through the Web site during *[specify period]*.

33. All writings relating to instances in which an unauthorized party attempted to gain access to the Web site during *[specify period]*.

34. All writings relating to any instances in the last five years in which an equipment or software malfunction caused data loss on the Web site.

35. Copies of all log files generated by the Web site from *[specify beginning date]* to *[specify ending date]*, including, but not limited to, log files generated by duplicate or mirror Web sites.

36. All e-mail relating to *[describe]*, including, but not limited to, e-mail stored on desktop computer hard disks, floppy disks and other removable electronic storage media, file servers, workstations, laptops, handheld organizers, backup tapes, and Internet e-mail servers.

Requests Relating to Trading Partner Agreements

37. A copy of the trading partner agreement between Defendant and *[trading partner]*, dated *[specify date]*.

38. All writings relating to the negotiation of the trading partner agreement between Defendant and *[trading partner]*, including, but not limited to, drafts of the agreement, negotiation notes, and correspondence.

39. All writings relating to the trading partner agreement between *[trading partner]* and Defendant, dated *[date]*, including, but not limited to, confirmations of orders, acknowledgements of receipt, and tracking information.

40. All writings relating to communications with *[specify value added network]* regarding electronic data interchange transactions with *[specify trading partner]*.

Miscellaneous Requests

41. An organizational chart for your Information Systems Department.

42. A list of all authorized users of the computer system.

43. A copy of the network map.

44. All writings relating to source code escrow agreements for *[specify software]*.

45. Copies of any and all source code escrow agreements for *[specify software]*, including, but not limited to, copies of all drafts of such agreements.

Dated: ________

[signature, etc.]

§ 12:23 Request to produce information from databases

[Caption]

REQUESTS TO PRODUCE

To: *[name]*

In accordance with *[rule]*, *[discovering party] [name 1]* requests *[responding party] [name 2]* to produce the documents specified below, within thirty (30) days of service, or at such other time and place, or in such other manner, as may be mutually agreed upon by the parties. *[Name 2's]* production of documents must be in accordance with the Instructions and Definitions set forth below and *[rule]*.

INSTRUCTIONS AND DEFINITIONS

A. Whenever reference is made to a person, it includes any and all of that person's principals, employees, agents, attorneys, consultants and other representatives.

B. When production of any document in *[name 2's]* possession is requested, the request includes documents subject to the *[name 2's]* possession, custody or control. In the event that *[name 2]* is able to provide only part of the document or documents called for in any particular Request for Production, *[name 2]* must provide all document or documents that *[name 2]* is able to provide and state the reason, if any, for the inability to provide the remainder.

C. "Document" or "documents" means all materials within the full scope of *[rule]*, including but not limited to all electronically stored information, writings and recordings, including the originals and all non-identical copies, whether different from the original by reason of any notation made on such copies or otherwise (including but without limitation to, e-mail and attachments, correspondence, memoranda, notes, diaries, minutes, statistics, letters, telegrams, minutes, contracts, reports, studies, checks, statements, tags, labels, invoices, brochures, periodicals, telegrams, receipts, returns, summaries, pamphlets, books, interoffice and intraoffice communications, offers, notations of any sort of conversations, working papers, applications, permits, file wrappers, indices, telephone calls, meetings or printouts, teletypes, telefax, invoices, worksheets, and all drafts, alterations, modifications, changes and amendments of any of the foregoing), graphic or aural representations of any kind (including without limitation, photographs, charts, microfiche, microfilm, videotape, recordings, motion pictures, plans, drawings, surveys), and electronic, mechanical, magnetic, optical or electric records or representations of any kind (including without limitation, computer files and programs, tapes, cassettes, discs, recordings), including metadata.

D. If any document is withheld from production under a claim of privilege or other exemption from discovery, state the title and nature of the document, and furnish a list signed by the attorney of record giving the following information with respect to each document withheld:

(1) the name and title of the author or sender, or both, and the name and title of the recipient;

(2) the date of the document's origination;

(3) the name of each person or persons, other than stenographic or clerical assistants, participating in the preparation of the document;

(4) the name and position, if any, of each person to whom the contents of the documents have previously been communicated by copy, exhibition, reading or substantial summarization;

(5) a statement of the specific basis on which privilege is claimed and whether or not the subject matter or the contents of the document is limited to legal advice or information provided for the purpose of securing legal advice; and

(6) the identity and position, if any, of the person or persons supplying the attorney signing the list with the information requested in subparagraphs above.

E. "Relate(s) to," "related to" or "relating to" means to refer to, reflect, concern, pertain to or in any manner be connected with the matter discussed.

F. Every Request for Production herein must be deemed a continuing Request for Production and *[name 2]* is to supplement its answers promptly if and when *[name 2]* obtains responsive documents which add to or are in any way inconsistent with *[name 2's]* initial production.

G. These discovery requests are not intended to be duplicative. All requests should be responded to fully and to the extent not covered by other requests. If there are documents that are responsive to more than one request, then please so note and produce each such document first in response to the request that is more specifically directed to the subject matter of the particular document.

H. Any word written in the singular must be construed as plural or vice versa when necessary to facilitate the response to any request.

I. "And" as well as "or" must be construed disjunctively or conjunctively as necessary in order to bring within the scope of the request all responses which otherwise might be construed to be outside its scope.

REQUEST

Each of the following requests to produce in this section are directed toward eliciting database searches of actual *[name 2]* databases or other electronic data collections located at *[name 2]*. In particular, the following interrogatories ARE NOT to be answered from any data collections maintained or managed by the law firm, or any of that firm's personnel or agents.

1. Please search the master or main database residing on the *[defendant] [plaintiff]* computer system and produce search results based on the following requests for information:

a. Any records, of whatever date or from whatever region of the world, containing complaints about *[describe].*

b. Any records, of whatever date or from whatever region of the world, containing complaints about any *[describe]*, regardless of *[specify].*

c. Any records, of whatever date or from whatever region of the world, containing complaints about *[describe].*

2. Please search the master or main database residing on the *[defendant's] [plaintiff's]* computer system and produce search results based on the following requests for information:

a. Any records, of whatever date or from whatever region of the world, discussing or referring to *[describe].*

b. Any records, of whatever date or from whatever region of the world, discussing or referring to *[describe]*, regardless of *[specify].*

c. Any records, of whatever date or from whatever region of the world, discussing or referring to *[describe]*, as that term is defined above, of any *[defendant] [plaintiff] [describe].*

d. Any records, of whatever date or from whatever region of the world, discussing or referring to possible, recommended, planned or actual design improvements, as that term is defined above, of any *[describe]*, regardless of *[specify].*

e. Any records, of whatever date or from whatever region of the world, discussing or referring to possible, recommended, planned or actual design improvements, as that term is defined above, of *[describe]* manufactured at any time.

3. With regard to each and all of the preceding search results, and recalling that the definition of above includes every database that is referred to in any record, please produce any database records from any other *[defendant] [plaintiff]* databases referred to in the records that comprise the preceding search results.

4. Please search the main or master database residing on the *[defendant's] [plaintiff's]* computer system, and any data collections not included in a database (as that term is defined above) but residing on the *[defendant] [plaintiff]* computer system, and produce database search results or other documents based on the following requests for information:

a. Any records, or other documents from any data collections not included in a database (as that term is defined above), of whatever date or from whatever region of the world, discussing or referring to possible, recommended, planned or actual design improvements, as that term is defined above, of any *[describe]* manufactured at any time based on studies conducted by any *[defendant] [plaintiff]* committee charged with the responsibility of conducting competitive tear down, as that latter term is defined above.

b. Any records, or other documents from any data collections not included in a database (as that term is defined above), of whatever date or from whatever region of the world, discussing or referring to possible, recommended, planned or actual design improvements, as that term is defined above, of any *[defendant] [plaintiff] [describe]* manufactured at any time, regardless of who authored the record or document.

c. Any records, or other documents from any data collections not included in a database (as that term is defined above), of whatever date or from whatever region of the world, discussing or referring to the advisability of making design improvements (as that term is defined above) to *[defendant's] [plaintiff's] [describe]* manufactured at any time, regardless of who authored the record or document.

5. With regard to each and all of the preceding search

results that include *[describe]* records, and recalling that the definition of *[specify]* includes every database referred to in any *[describe]* record, please produce any database records from any other *[defendant] [plaintiff]* databases referred to in the *[describe]* records that comprise the preceding search results.

6. Please search the e-mail databases, whether active databases or stored or archived databases, residing on the *[defendant] [plaintiff]* computer system and produce search results based on the following requests for information:

a. Any e-mail, of whatever date or from whatever region of the world, discussing or referring to possible, recommended, planned or actual design improvements, as that term is defined above, of any *[defendant] [plaintiff] [describe]* manufactured at any time, regardless of who authored the e-mail.

b. Any e-mail, of whatever date or from whatever region of the world, discussing or referring to the advisability of making design improvements, as that term is defined above, to *[defendant] [plaintiff] [describe]* manufactured at any time, regardless of who authored the e-mail.

Dated: ________

[signature, etc.]

§ 12:24 Instructions where production on CDs or DVDs is anticipated

CD or DVD production of discovery is acceptable however the following is required when discovery production is thus produced:

(1) Each image on the CD or DVD must be Bates stamped with a unique alpha-numeric identifier (taking care not to obscure in any way any of the information contained in the image).

(2) If the images do not exist in a metadata database,

then a detailed index of the contents of each CD or DVD must be provided on each CD or DVD in a clearly marked and easily identifiable file.

(3) This index must contain the following information as to each document contained on a CD or DVD in columnar display as follows:

a) In column one, the Bates stamp number of each electronic document on a CD or DVD;

b) In column two, a word description of the contents of each electronic document on a CD or DVD clearly identifying what that electronic document contains;

c) In column three, a clear reference to just what interrogatory or request is satisfied by the production of each electronic document on a CD or DVD;

d) In column four, the format of each electronic document on a CD or DVD, and how and where the original or best copy of each such document is stored on the defendant's computer system, or if located elsewhere then on the *[responding party's]* primary computer system, its location on the computer system of subsidiaries (in this country or throughout the world), predecessors, successors, assigns, joint venturers, partners, parents, agents or affiliates; and

e) In column five, a statement as to whether each electronic document contained on a CD or DVD is a first, second, third or a later generation copy of the original document located on the *[responding party's]* computer system.

(4) If the images on a CD or DVD exist in an off the shelve metadata environment, then the images must be produced with all accompanying metadata, unless privileged, and the database management system used to produce and house that metadata must be identified by application name and version type. If the images on a CD or DVD exist in a proprietary metadata environment, then it is required that a working copy of proprietary software, together with any user manuals or help files and the search engine used to search for and retrieve the data, must be provided on each CD. In addition, When the data

on a CD or DVD is in text (regardless of format), it is required that the documents be OCRed before production.

Comment

This form can be used with a request to produce or even with interrogatories where it is anticipated that the information requested may be provided on a CD or DVD.

§ 12:25 General definitions and instructions

Definitions

1. For the purposes of these document requests, the term "document" means a writing of any kind, whether produced manually or by mechanical, chemical, electrical, or other artificial process, or by any combination of these methods, and whether visible to the unaided human eye or only with the aid of some devise, machine, or process. The term "document" includes but is not limited to:

(a) the original (or identical copy when the original is not available) of all:

(1) letters, notes, and all other correspondence, including but not limited to:

(aa) handwritten notes,

(bb) electronic or other transcriptions or taping of telephone or personal conversations or conferences,

(cc) taped correspondence,

(dd) electronic mail,

(ee) all original telephone logs, memoranda, telephone bills reflecting calls between the parties at issue during the relevant time period,

(ff) internal memoranda;

(2) reports, tabulations, analyses, opinions, summaries, and studies;

(3) financial documents;

(4) telegrams, cables, and teletype messages;

(5) messages, including reports, summaries, and minutes of telephone conversations, meetings, speeches, and all other oral communications;

(6) meeting minutes;

(7) transcripts and their digests, summaries, and analyses;

(8) purchase orders, bills, contracts, agreements, invoices, records of purchase or sale, purchase orders, leases, estimates, appraisals, valuations, releases, and other similar commercial documents;

(9) questionnaires and surveys;

(10) information stored in a computer, floppy disk, CD-ROM, or other storage device;

(11) diaries;

(12) computer printouts, printout summaries, and programs;

(13) audio recordings;

(14) still photographs and their negatives;

(15) motion picture film and its negative;

(16) audio and video tapes;

(17) graphs, charts, maps, plans, instructions, blueprints, diagrams, sketches, and drawings;

(18) tabulations, tallies, and other data compilations;

(19) books, pamphlets, periodicals, magazines, circulars, and bulletins;

(b) non-identical copies of original documents, whether different from their originals by reason of notations made on such copies, or otherwise;

(c) all attachments and enclosures to any requested item which are not separated;

(d) drafts and all revisions of any documents that are in the possession, custody, or control of, or known to the party answering these document requests. This definition applies to any document:

(1) prepared by the answering party for its own use,

(2) prepared by the answering party for transmittal to any other person, including a wholly or partially owned subsidiary, whether or not the document was actually transmitted,

(3) prepared by another person, including a

wholly or partially owned subsidiary of the answering party, for transmittal to or reception by the answering party, whether or not the document was actually transmitted or received;

(e) all documents must be sequential, organized in file folders, and identified by department and location.

2. For the purposes of these document requests, "financial documents" include but are not limited to:

(a) documents related to all of *[name's]* assets;

(b) documents related to all of *[name's]* expenditures, including but not limited to those for business, travel, entertainment, and other expense accounts;

(c) canceled checks, bank statements, and checkbooks for all checking accounts in which *[name]* has or has had an interest;

(d) federal and state individual income tax returns, with all schedules;

(e) books, records, financial statements, profit and loss statements, journal ledgers, and annual reports;

(f) vouchers or statements submitted by all of *[name's]* credit card companies;

(g) correspondence with bookkeepers, accountants, or auditors regarding *[name's]* operations and financial condition;

(h) documents evidencing gifts or inheritances;

(i) appraisals, insurance policies, pension plans, veteran's benefit plans, profit sharing, or retirement plans, in which *[name]* has a present, future, or potential future interest of any kind;

(j) financial or personal statements of financial condition given to any bank, savings and loan, mortgage company, credit union, credit bureau, financial company, business, or financial institution of any kind;

(k) all available budgets or projections;

(l) employment contracts, which are pertinent to *[name's]* assets, debts and liabilities, and income;

(m) deeds, mortgages, agreements of sale, and other documents pertaining to the assets owned by *[name]*;

(n) documents related to any financial loss, debts, and liabilities, including but not limited to

(1) documents related to unsatisfactory past loans,

(2) any filing for bankruptcy or any document discussing or considering it,

(3) documents related to any cessation of *[name's]* work or business.

3. For the purposes of these document requests, the term "person" means:

(a) natural persons,

(b) non-natural persons, including but not limited to:

(1) associations,

(2) bid depositories

(3) clubs,

(4) companies,

(5) cooperatives,

(6) corporations,

(7) estates,

(8) foundations,

(9) institutes,

(10) joint owners,

(11) joint ventures,

(12) limited partnerships,

(13) nonprofit organizations,

(14) partnerships,

(15) professional corporations,

(16) service corporations,

(17) sole proprietorships,

(18) societies,

(19) syndicates,

(20) trade associations,

(21) unions, whether or not formally incorporated under the laws of any political jurisdiction,

(22) domestic and foreign federal, state, departmental, regional, and local governments and their divisions, departments, agencies, and other governmental subdivisions.

4. For the purposes of these document requests, the term "personnel files" refers to any documents pertaining to an individual's employment history. Personnel files include but are not limited to:

(a) resumes and curriculum vitae,

(b) certificates or licenses,

(c) job applications,

(d) job descriptions,

(e) job duties and responsibilities,

(f) contracts and terms and conditions of employment,

(g) length of employment,

(h) performance evaluations, including reprimands,

(i) any investigations regarding complaints about job performance,

(j) prior occupations,

(k) attendance records,

(l) agreements with any labor union,

(m) collective bargaining agreements,

(n) physical or mental examinations, including drug tests,

(o) qualifications,

(p) termination notices,

(q) all other correspondence.

5. For the purposes of these document requests, the term "policy" means any rule, regulation, standard operating procedure, or other principle formally or informally adopted for the purpose of guiding or otherwise conducting the business operations of the answering party. The term "policy" also means any normal, frequent, or habitual course of conduct in which the answering party actually engages or has actually engaged during the relevant time period.

6. For the purposes of these document requests, the terms "you" and "your" mean:

(a) the party producing the documents from this request,

(b) its wholly or partially owned domestic and foreign subsidiaries,

(c) its merged or acquired predecessors,

(d) its successors by merger or acquisition,

(e) its present and foreign directors, trustees, officers, partners, consultants, agents and representatives,

(f) all other persons acting or purporting to act on behalf of those persons in paragraphs (a) through (e) above,

(g) all past and present employees exercising non-clerical or discretionary decision-making or policy-making authority on behalf of the answering party,

(h) divisions, departments, profit centers, and other corporate subdivisions of the answering party.

7. For the purposes of these document requests, the terms "defendant" and "plaintiff" mean:

(a) the party producing the documents from this request,

(b) its wholly or partially owned domestic and foreign subsidiaries,

(c) its merged or acquired predecessors,

(d) its successors by merger or acquisition,

(e) its present and foreign directors, trustees, officers, partners, consultants, agents and representatives,

(f) all other persons acting or purporting to act on behalf of those persons in paragraphs (a) through (e) above,

(g) all past and present employees exercising non-clerical or discretionary decision-making or policy-making authority on behalf of the answering party,

(h) divisions, departments, profit centers, and other corporate subdivisions of the answering party.

8. For the purposes of these document requests, the words "corporate documents" refer to all documents describing the structure, function, and maintenance of a business or corporation. "Corporate documents" include but are not limited to all documents consisting of or pertaining to:

(a) documents filed with any state or other governmental agency related to the incorporation of any entity,

(b) articles of incorporation,

(c) by-laws,

(d) each department and division and their functions,

(e) lists of each branch office,

(f) the list of directors and shareholders,

(g) stock registers,

(h) personnel files for all employees,

(i) annual reports,

(j) partnership agreements,

(k) minute books,

(l) stock tender offers,

(m) poison pills adopted,

(n) merger agreements,

(o) any takeover documents,

(p) company sales information, including but not limited to:

(1) receivables and payables lists,

(2) lists of the largest customers with the amount of sales to each, and

(3) lists of the largest suppliers with the amount of purchases from each.

9. For the purposes of these documents requests, words in the masculine gender shall be construed to include the feminine and the neuter; words in the feminine gender shall be construed to include the masculine and the neuter; and neutral words shall be construed to include the masculine and the feminine.

10. For the purposes of these document requests, words importing the singular shall be construed to include the plural, and words importing the plural shall be construed to include the singular.

11. For the purposes of these document requests, anything that is "related to" the subject matter requested is meant to include but is not limited to anything that constitutes, contains, embodies, reflects, identifies, states, refers to, alludes to, responds to, deals with, comments on, is in any way pertinent to, in connection with, in response to, about, regarding, announc-

ing, explaining, discussing, showing, describing, studying, reflecting, analyzing, or constituting.

12. For the purposes of these document requests, the word "and" also means "and/or."

13. For the purposes of these document requests, the word "all" also means "any and all."

14. For the purposes of these document requests, the word "any" also means "any and all."

15. For the purposes of these document requests, the word "between" also means "between and among."

16. For the purposes of these document requests, the word "including" also means "including but not limited to."

17. For the purposes of these document requests, the term "relevant time period" shall mean the period of time (choose only one):

(a) from a date five years before the alleged occurrence until the date of the filing of the complaint in this action,

(b) beginning with *[date]* and ending with the filing of the complaint in this action,

(c) beginning with the first date of the occurrence as alleged in the complaint and ending with the filing of the complaint in this action.

18. For the purposes of these document requests, the term "identify" means when used in reference to:

(a) a document, to state separately:

(1) its description (e.g., letter, report, memorandum, etc.),

(2) its date,

(3) its subject matter,

(4) the identity of each author or signer,

(5) its present location and the identity of its custodian,

(b) an oral statement, communication, conference or conversation, to state separately:

(1) its date and the place where it occurred,

(2) its substance,

(3) the identity of each person participating in the communication or conversation,

(4) the identity of all notes, memoranda or other documents memorializing, referring to or relating to the subject matter of the statement,

(c) a natural person or persons, to state separately:

(1) the full name of each such person,

(2) his or her present or last known business address and his or her present or last known residential address,

(3) the employer of the person at the time to which the request is directed and the person's title or position at that time,

(d) an organization or entity other than a natural person (e.g., a company, corporation, firm, association, or partnership), to state separately:

(1) the full name and type of organization or entity,

(2) the date and state of organization or incorporation,

(3) the address of each of its principal places of businesses,

(4) the nature of the business conducted.

19. For the purpose of these document requests, the term "communication" shall mean any transmission of information, the information transmitted, and any process by which information is transmitted, and shall include written communications and oral communications.

20. For the purposes of these document requests, the term "claim" means a demand or assertion, whether oral or written, formal or informal, by any person for monetary payment, the undertaking of action, or the cessation of action.

21. For the purposes of these document requests, the terms "consulted" or "contracted" means any form of communication, e.g., oral statements, telephone conversations or other mechanical communications or any other type of communication including written letters or documents.

22. For the purposes of these document requests, the terms "management" and "manage" includes any act of directing, conducting, administering, controlling, or handling an identified function or duty.

Instructions for Answering

1. You are required, in responding to this request to obtain and furnish all information available to you and any of your representatives, employees, agents, brokers, servants, or attorneys and to obtain and furnish all information, that is in your possession or under your control, or in the possession or under the control of any of your representatives, employees, agents, servants, or attorneys.

2. Each request which seeks information relating in any way to communications, to, from, or within a business and/or corporate entity, is hereby designated to demand, and should be construed to include, all communications by and between representatives, employees, agents of the business and/or corporate entity.

3. Each request should be responded to separately. However, a document which is the response to more than one request may, if the relevant portion is marked or indexed, be produced and referred to in a later response.

4. All documents produced shall be segregated and identified by the paragraphs to which they are primarily responsive. Where required by a particular paragraph of this Request, documents produced shall be further segregated and identified as indicated in this paragraph. For any documents that are stored or maintained in files for the normal course of business, such documents shall be procured in such files, or in such a manner as to preserve and identify the file from which such documents were taken.

5. If you object to part of any request, please furnish documents responsive to the remainder of the request.

6. Each request refers to all documents that are either known by the party to exist or that can be located or discovered by reasonably diligent efforts of the party.

7. The documents produced in response to this Request shall include all attachments and enclosures.

8. The documents requested for production include those in the possession, custody, or control of the party and the party's agents, representatives, or attorneys.

9. References to the singular include the plural.

10. The use of any tense of any verb shall be considered also to include within its meaning all other tenses of the verb so used.

11. *[If under Federal Rules of Civil Procedure]* Please note that the party, pursuant to Fed.R.Civ.P. 26(e), is under a continuing duty to seasonably supplement the production with documents obtained after the preparation and filing of a response to each request.

12. All documents called for by this request or related to this request, for which the party claims a privilege or statutory authority as a ground for nonproduction shall be listed chronologically as follows:

(a) the place, date, and manner of recording or otherwise preparing the document,

(b) the name and title of the sender,

(c) the identity of each person or persons (other than stenographic or clerical assistants) participating in the preparation of the document,

(d) the identity and title with the party, if any, of the person or persons supplying the party's attorneys with the information requested above,

(e) the identity of each person to whom the contents of the document have heretofore been communicated by copy, exhibition, sketch, reading or substantial summarization, the date of said communication, and the employer and title of said person at the time of said communication,

(f) type of document,

(g) subject matter (without revealing the relevant information for which privilege or statutory authority is claimed), and

(h) factual and legal basis for claim, privilege or specific statutory or regulatory authority which provides the claimed ground for nonproduction.

13. Each request to produce a document or documents shall be deemed to call for the production of the original document or documents to the extent that they are in, or subject to, directly or indirectly, the control of the party to whom this request is addressed. In addition, each request should be considered as including a request for separate production of all copies and, to the extent applicable, preliminary drafts of documents that differ in any respect from the original or final draft, or from each other (e.g., by reason of differences in form, or content, or by reason of handwritten notes, or comments having been added to one copy of a document, but not to the original or other copies thereof).

14. All documents produced in response to this Request shall be produced *in toto* notwithstanding the fact that portions thereof may contain information not requested.

15. If any documents requested herein have been lost or destroyed, the documents so lost or destroyed shall be identified by author, date, and subject matter.

16. Where exact information cannot be furnished, estimated information is to be supplied to the extent possible. Where estimation is used, it should be so indicated, and an explanation should be given as to the basis on which the statement was made and the reason exact information cannot be furnished.

17. With respect to any document requested which was once in the party's possession, custody or control, but no longer is, please indicate the date and the manner in which the document ceased to be in the party's possession, custody, or control and the name and address of its present custodian.

18. Unless otherwise indicated, each request is to be construed as encompassing all documents which pertain to the stated subject matter and to events which transpired between *[date]* up to the present.

Comment

This form contains many more definitions than will be needed in any single case. It can be adapted to the specific requests for production.

§ 12:26 Request for physical inspection of computer

[Caption]

To: Defendant and its attorneys of record

Pursuant to *[rule]*, Plaintiff requests that Defendant permit Plaintiff, Plaintiff's attorneys, and consultants to enter onto the premises located at *[specify address]* and inspect the computer described as: *[specify computer to be examined, e.g., serial number, type and model]*.

Such entry and inspection shall include, but will not necessarily be limited to, the following activities: photographing, physical inspection of network topography, preparation of a network map, and creation of a mirror copy of the hard disk(s).

Dated: ________

[signature, etc.]

Comment

Courts have become less inclined in recent years to grant inspection rights of a party's computers based merely on a suspicion the systems contain relevant evidence. See, e.g., Bethea v. Comcast, 218 F.R.D. 328, 57 Fed. R. Serv. 3d 428 (D.D.C. 2003) (former employee's request for an inspection order for her employer's computer systems based only on a mere suspicion the former employer had failed to produce all relevant documents rejected by court).

§ 12:27 Procedure for reviewing computer's hardware, software, and operating system

[Caption]

Procedure for Reviewing Computer Hardware, Software, and Operating System

A. This procedure shall apply to the following stated purposes of *[requesting party]* as outlined in the Motion to Compel:

(1) Inspect the computer to determine its operating system and applicable software applications

(2) Inspect the computer to explore how the files are kept on the computer and how they are identified
(3) Determine what actions *[producing party]* took to protect confidential information on the computer
(4) Determine the actions that were taken to allow confidential information to be accessed by the *[name]*
(5) Determine how the software that opens images functions
(6) Review registries and logs in the computer's operating system to determine, if possible, the people who have logged on to the computer as well as what files were opened after *[date]*

B. Procedure

(1) The court hereby appoints *[name]* as an expert to conduct an examination of defendants' computer.
(2) The parties shall submit a Protective Order for the court's approval, which will subsequently be entered, and signed by the Expert.
(3) Once a Protective Order is entered, *[producing party]* shall make available to the Expert, at *[producing party's]* place of business, and at a mutually agreeable time, the computer at issue in this litigation.
(4) The Expert will use its best efforts to avoid unnecessarily disrupting the normal business activities or business operations of the *[producing party]* while inspecting *[producing party's]* computer
(5) The computer at all times shall be maintained on *[producing party's]* premises.
(6) The only persons authorized to inspect or otherwise handle the computer are the Expert and employees of the Expert assigned to this project.
(7) No employee of *[requesting party]*, *[requesting party's]*, or *[requesting party]*, will inspect or otherwise handle the computer produced.
(8) The Expert will maintain all information in the strictest confidence;
(9) Once the computer is produced, the Expert shall attempt to recover a "mirror image," or forensic image, of the hard drive, in the presence of only the *[pro-*

ducing party] or *[producing party's]* counsel, and at the *[producing party's]* convenience. After a forensic copy is made, one copy shall be transmitted to the court and one copy shall be transmitted to the *[producing party]*.

(10) On the forensic copy, the Expert shall identify the computer's operating system and software applications related to the creation, storage, and viewing of files—Including images—on the computer;

(11) The Expert shall identify the internal hardware components of the computer, including the existing RAM card in the computer, and any other matters that the Expert deems relevant.

(12) The Expert shall then inspect the computer to determine its operating system and all software applications installed on the computer.

(13) The Expert shall inspect the computer and identify how individual files are organized on the computer and how files may be identified;

(14) The Expert shall inspect the computer to determine what actions defendants took to protect confidential information on the computer.

(15) The Expert shall inspect the computer to determine what, if any, actions were taken that specifically allowed *[name]* to access confidential information on the computer;

(16) The Expert shall inspect the computer to determine how the software that opens image files functions.

(17) If the file system permits, the Expert shall review the computer's registries and logs in the computer's operating system to determine the people who have logged on to the computer after it was discarded as well as what files were opened after the computer had been discarded; and

(18) The Expert shall provide a summary of the above information to plaintiffs and defendants.

Dated: ________

____

Judge

Comment

This form is adapted from the record in G.D. v. Monarch Plastic Surgery, P.A., 239 F.R.D. 641, 67 Fed. R. Serv. 3d 352 (D. Kan. 2007). The case involved the claim that the defendant health care providers wrongfully disclosed plaintiffs' medical information stored on a computer hard drive by placing the computer on the curb for trash disposal. After the computer was placed on the curb, plaintiffs allege a collector removed the computer and took it to a computer repair shop. Plaintiffs claim the repair shop employees were able to make the computer operable, and the collector was then able to view the confidential medical files.

§ 12:28 Procedure for reviewing information stored on producing party's computer

[Caption]

Procedure for Reviewing Information Stored on Computer

A. This procedure shall apply to the following stated purposes of *[requesting party]*:

(1) Search for all documents that concern the *[requesting party]* in this case

(2) Review the metadata concerning each file that concerns the *[requesting party]*

(3) Search the computer for deleted documents concerning the *[requesting party]*.

B. Procedure

(1) The court hereby appoints *[name]* as an expert to conduct an examination of defendants' computer.

(2) The parties shall submit a Protective Order for the court's approval, which will subsequently be entered, and signed by the Expert.

(3) Once a Protective Order is entered, *[producing party]* shall make available to the Expert, at *[producing party's]* place of business, and at a mutually agreeable time, the computer at issue in this litigation.

(4) The Expert will use its best efforts to avoid unnecessarily disrupting the normal business activities or business operations of the *[producing party]* while inspecting *[producing party's]* computer

(5) The computer at all times shall be maintained on *[producing party's]* premises.

(6) The only persons authorized to inspect or otherwise handle the computer are the Expert and employees of the Expert assigned to this project.

(7) No employee of *[requesting party]*, *[requesting party's]*, or *[requesting party]*, will inspect or otherwise handle the computer produced.

(8) The Expert will maintain all information in the strictest confidence;

(9) Once the computer is produced, the Expert shall attempt to recover a "mirror image," or forensic image, of the hard drive, in the presence of only the *[producing party]* or *[producing party's]* counsel, and at the *[producing party's]* convenience. After a forensic copy is made, one copy shall be transmitted to the court and one copy shall be transmitted to the *[producing party]*.

(10) *[Producing party]* shall review such mirror image copy in collaboration with the Expert, and shall produce to *[requesting party]* all responsive documents *[requesting party]* seek in their Motion to Compel for which the court has granted production Specifically, *[producing party]* shall provide to *[requesting party]* in hard-copy format:

a. All documents that concern *[requesting party]* in this case;
b. All metadata related to the documents that concern *[requesting party]* in this case; and
c. All recovered deleted documents concerning the *[requesting party]* in this case.

(11) In addition to the aforementioned responsive documents, *[producing party]* shall also provide a privilege log to *[requesting party]*, describing the nature of any privileged documents or communications in a manner that, without revealing information that is privileged

or protected, will enable *[requesting party]* to assess the applicability of the privilege or protection claimed;

(12) *[Producing party]* shall forward a copy of the privilege log to the court for potential in camera review;

(13) Once *[requesting party]* has reviewed the documents produced by *[producing party]*, as well as the privilege log, if the *[requesting party]* raises a dispute as to any of the documents, by providing a cogent basis for doubting the claim of privilege, or for believing that there are further relevant documents, the court will conduct an in camera review, limited to the issues raised.

Comment

This form is adapted from the record in G.D. v. Monarch Plastic Surgery, P.A., 239 F.R.D. 641, 67 Fed. R. Serv. 3d 352 (D. Kan. 2007). The case involved the claim that the defendant health care providers wrongfully disclosed plaintiffs' medical information stored on a computer hard drive by placing the computer on the curb for trash disposal. After the computer was placed on the curb, plaintiffs allege a collector removed the computer and took it to a computer repair shop. Plaintiffs claim the repair shop employees were able to make the computer operable, and the collector was then able to view the confidential medical files.

§ 12:29 Motion for default judgment against defendant for failure to comply with order for production of documents

[Caption]

Plaintiff moves the Court that judgment be rendered in favor of plaintiff and against defendant by default, as provided for by *[rule]*, for failure of defendant to comply with the order of this Court entered on *[date]*, requiring defendant to produce certain enumerated books and writings for inspection by plaintiff.

The undersigned certifies that the undersigned has in good faith attempted to confer with the *[defendant's]* attorney in an unsuccessful effort to secure the requested information without court action.

The attached *[affidavit] [declaration]* of *[name]* will be relied upon in support of this motion.

Dated: ________

[signature etc.]

§ 12:30 Motion for dismissal of action for plaintiff's failure to comply with order for production of documents

[Caption]

MOTION FOR DISMISSAL OF ACTION

Defendant moves the Court that the above-entitled action against defendant be dismissed as provided for by *[rule]*, for failure of plaintiff to comply with the order of this court entered on *[date]*, requiring plaintiff to produce certain enumerated books and writings for inspection by defendant.

The undersigned certifies that the undersigned has in good faith attempted to confer with the *[party's]* attorney in an unsuccessful effort to secure the requested information without court action.

The attached *[affidavit] [declaration]* of *[name]* will be relied upon in support of this motion.

Dated: ________

[signature etc.]

§ 12:31 Order for default judgment or dismissal of action for failure to comply with order for production of documents

[Caption]

ORDER

On the motion of *[plaintiff for a default judgment] [defendant for an order dismissing the action]*, for failure of *[defendant] [plaintiff]* to comply with the order of *[date]*, granting *[plaintiff] [defendant]* leave to examine certain documents pertinent to the issues in this action and in the possession of *[defendant] [plaintiff]*, it is

ORDERED that pursuant to *[rule] [judgment be entered for the plaintiff for such damages as plaintiff has sustained as alleged in the complaint] [the action be dismissed]*, and *[[plaintiff] be forbidden to support plaintiff's claim] [[defendant] be forbidden to oppose the plaintiff's claim] [[defendant's] defense is stricken] [[defendant is forbidden to introduce in evidence the following documents: [specify]]*.

Dated: ________

____
Judge

§ 12:32 Plaintiff's emergency motion to prevent the further destruction of evidence and for sanctions for spoliation of evidence

[Caption]

Plaintiff's Emergency Motion to Prevent the Further Destruction of Evidence and for Sanctions for Spoliation of Evidence

Plaintiff, for the reasons more fully set forth in the accompanying memorandum, respectfully requests this Court to enter an Order:

1. Requiring defendant to retain all electronic evidence, including e-mails, and cease deleting e-mails immediately;
2. Sanctioning defendant for spoliation of evidence, including but not limited to the entry of a default or, at a minimum, an adverse jury instruction at trial and an order barring defendant from claiming that its male employees did not circulate or show pornographic, lewd and inappropriate e-mail to members of the putative class;
3. Requiring defendant to cooperate with and provide ac-

cess to plaintiff's forensic data recovery experts to perform data recovery and to pay the costs of these services; and

4. For such other and further relief as this Court deems appropriate.

Dated: ________

[signature,etc.]

Comment

This motion is adapted from the record in *Wiginton v. Ellis*, (N.D. Ill. 2003).

§ 12:33 Order requiring production

[Caption]

ORDER

This is a *[describe]* action involving *[describe]*. *[Name 1]* has moved the Court for an order compelling *[name 2]* to produce the documents listed in a document entitled *[specify] [and otherwise to produce the initial disclosures required under [rule]]*. *[Name 2]* has responded and moved for a protective order.

The scheduling order of *[date]*, required the parties to make all disclosures required by *[rule]* on or before the discovery meeting, which took place on *[date]*. *[Name 1]* made its disclosures on *[date]*. *[Name 2]* made no disclosures under *[rule]* until *[date]*, when a document entitled *[specify]* was faxed to *[name 2]*'s counsel. Section of this disclosure statement consisted of a listing of the documents identified by *[name 2]* as being relevant under *[rule]*. *[Name 2]* indicated the documents would be produced "after entry of an appropriate protective order." No *[name 2]* documents were produced at that time or subsequently. Further, *[name 2]* indicated in the "disclosure statement" that it was self-insured and also carried "aggregate excess liability insurance coverage" but did not identify the insurer(s) or produce copies of the insurance agreements, as required by *[rule]*.

At the hearing held in this matter on *[date]*, the parties advised the Court that they had agreed upon a protective order. From a review of the record, it appears the protective order was entered on *[date]*. Thus, that request by *[name 2]* is considered moot. *[Name 2]* is otherwise ORDERED to produce by *[date]*, any outstanding documentation mandated by *[rule]*. *[Name 1]*'s request for sanctions, expenses and attorney fees will be taken under further advisement at this time. Thus, *[name 1]*'s motion to compel is GRANTED IN PART AS MODIFIED. *[Name 2]* is forewarned that a failure to cooperate fully in discovery will lead to sanctions.

[Name 1] has moved for sanctions under Rule 37(d) for *[name 2]*'s failure to respond to both interrogatories and requests to produce. *[Name 2]* has responded.

[Name 1] asserts that *[name 2]* has engaged in a clear, discernable pattern of conduct that, taken as a whole, constitutes a calculated, deliberate, systematic and flagrant abuse of discovery. Pursuant to Rule 37(d), plaintiffs request an order entering sanctions against *[name 2]*, including the sanction of Rule 37(b)(2) (B) of striking DCC's affirmative defenses, on the grounds that *[name 2]* has without cause or justification refused to produce witnesses in response to timely and appropriate *[rule]* notices of examination. *[Name 1]* also seeks an order entering sanctions on the grounds that *[name 2]* has provided only partial and incomplete responses to *[name 1]*'s first set of requests to produce, which responses consist of tens of thousands of unindexed, incomplete or illegible written materials in violation of *[rule]*.

[Name 1] contends those responses, contained mainly on CDs, constitute sham responses to *[name 1]*'s requests to produce and have been provided in an attempt to inundate the *[name 1]* without providing any substantive factual material responsive to *[name 1]*'s requests to produce. *[Name 1]* argues the CD responses occasioned considerable unnecessary effort and expense on the part of *[name 1]*'s counsel.

[Name 2] states the CDs it produced contained files that were clearly a listing of the documents being provided. Each file name included the word " "and most contained the word "list." Upon opening these files, lists are found, setting forth the contents of the remainder of the folder. *[Name 2]* claims it has gone to obvious lengths to satisfy what are, in many cases, overly broad and unduly burdensome requests.

In addition to other orders of this court, *[name 2]* is ORDERED to produce the following by *[date]*: legible and properly scanned documents to replace the illegible ones previously provided on the CDs; the 5,000 graphical images claimed to be undecipherable by *[name 1]*; all documents requested concerning *[describe]*; unredacted versions of all documents requested unless privilege is claimed; and any appendices it may have neglected to produce; any cross-referenced documents concerning *[describe]*.

Within the relevant time frame, *[name 2]* is also ORDERED to allow *[name 1]* access to any available searchable databases that may contain relevant discovery material. *[Name 1]* shall have unrestricted right to use and examine the databases subject to the protective order currently in place in this case. *[Name 2]* must also provide information as to how documents are organized on *[name 2]*'s main database and further explain the information divulged on the CDs.

[Name 1]'s motion for sanctions is taken under further advisement at this time. *[Name 2]* is again forewarned that failure to fully and completely cooperate in discovery will lead to sanctions.

Dated: ________

____
Judge

§ 12:34 Order for production—Another form

[Caption]

ORDER CONCERNING ELECTRONIC DISCOVERY HEARING

Purpose and Areas of Discussion

My responsibilities as the discovery Judge in this case are to insure that all significantly relevant and discoverable materials are preserved and produced, to expedite the discovery process, to minimize costs, and to achieve a reasonable balance between the legitimate discovery needs of the parties and the corresponding burden on the producing party. Because of the nature of the litigation, it is probable that the most significant discovery problems will arise in connection with Plaintiffs' discovery of Defendant's materials.

To carry out these responsibilities, a hearing on electronic discovery has been scheduled for *[date]*. The parties and I can make every attempt to tie down issues now, in an effort to head off problems and to facilitate discovery.

Defendant acknowledges the existence of a significant amount of discoverable electronic data. As the parties know, preservation, discovery, and production of electronic materials presents special problems.

I am interested in learning about the following:

1. Defendant's electronic document depository. A presentation and demonstration will be welcome.
2. Defendant's corporate structure and operations, including which departments or divisions would be involved in research and development, government approval, marketing, and monitoring the involved product.
3. The identities of the key individuals within each of the above areas of responsibility that would have been involved with the product.
4. The time frame during which relevant electronic or other discoverable information may have been created.
5. Basic information about the process of obtaining government approval for the product in question, including citations to regulations covering retention of research and other materials involved in the approval process.

6. Basic information about necessary record-keeping and reporting to the government during the time the product is marketed.
7. Defendant's computer systems, including servers, networks, e-mail systems, voice mail systems, data bases, desktop or laptop computers, PDAs, and backup or archival tapes or other similar storage media.
8. Changes made in Defendant's systems during the relevant period and any information as to the existence of any relevant and discoverable electronic data which is not located on currently used electronic devices (legacy data).
9. Whether relevant and discoverable electronic data may exist in third party storage or processing entities, such as internet storage or servicing facilities.
10. Any steps taken to insure preservation of relevant and discoverable materials—in addition to in-house counsel's memorandum to employees dated *[date]*, directing the preservation of hard copy and electronic documents. Whether any individuals have been given the responsibility of monitoring the process, and, if so, their names and positions.
11. Whether the parties anticipate special problems with discovery by Defendant of the various Plaintiffs' medical and other relevant and discoverable information.

No later than *[date]*, Defendant must submit information about its basic corporate structure, as listed in items 2 and 3 above, and information about the government approval and monitoring process as mentioned in paragraph 5 above. The Court needs somewhat more detailed information than that listing "management, medical affairs, regulatory affairs and labeling, and marketing," which appeared in *[name's]* Statement Regarding Document Preservation, Collection and Production filed *[date]*. Perhaps the organizational charts listed in the proposed order, if not too extensive, would be helpful.

Defendant must also have present for the hearing the individual or individuals most knowledgeable about its computer system. Any additional information bearing on the above categories that the parties could submit prior to the hearing would be welcome.

Preservation of Data

One concern I have with the proposed document depository is that the documents are being produced in Tagged Image File Format (.tif). Thus, although the documents would be in electronic form, it appears the production is the functional equivalent of a "hard copy" production and no "metadata" such as document history, earlier or deleted versions, electronic marginal comments, etc., would be available. Of further concern is 'Defendant's statement that after a document is scanned and the ".tiff' image created, Wyeth is "returning the original documents needed for ongoing business to the files."' As to electronic documents, this may result in destruction or alteration of relevant data. Therefore, all parties and their counsel are reminded of their duty to preserve evidence that may be relevant to this action. The duty extends to documents, data, and tangible things in the possession, custody, and control of the parties to this action, and any employees, agents, contractors, carriers, bailees, or other non-parties who possess materials reasonably anticipated to be subject to discovery in this action. Counsel is under an obligation to exercise reasonable efforts to identify and notify such non-parties, including employees of corporate or institutional parties.

"Documents, data, and tangible things" are to be interpreted broadly to include writings; records; files; correspondence; reports; memoranda; calendars; diaries; minutes; electronic messages; voicemail; e-mail; telephone message records or logs; computer and network activity logs; hard drives; backup data; removable computer storage media such as tapes, disks, and cards; printouts; document image files; Web pages; databases; spreadsheets; software; books; ledgers; journals; orders; invoices; bills; vouchers; checks; statements; worksheets; summaries; compilations; computations; charts; diagrams; graphic presentations; drawings; films; charts; digital or chemical process photographs; video, phonographic, tape, or digital recordings or transcripts thereof; drafts; jottings; and notes. Information that serves to identify, locate, or link such material, such as file inventories, file folders, indices, and metadata, is also included in this definition.

"Preservation" is to be interpreted broadly to accomplish the goal of maintaining the integrity of all documents, data, and tangible things reasonably anticipated to be subject to discovery under [rule] in this action. Preservation includes taking reasonable steps to prevent the partial or full destruction, alteration, testing, deletion, shredding, incineration, wiping, relocation, migration, theft, or mutation of such material, as well as negligent or intentional handling that would make material incomplete or inaccessible.

If Defendant's business practices involve the routine destruction, recycling, relocation, or mutation of such materials, Defendant must, to the extent practicable for the pendency of this order, either (1) halt such business processes; (2) sequester or remove such material from the business process; or (3) arrange for the preservation of complete and accurate duplicates or copies of such material, suitable for later discovery if requested.

Before or after the hearing, Defendant may apply to the court for further instructions regarding the duty to preserve specific categories of documents, data, or tangible things. Defendant may seek permission to resume routine business processes relating to the storage or destruction of specific categories of documents, data, or tangible things, upon a showing of undue cost, burden, or overbreadth.

IT IS SO ORDERED this *[date].*

____

Judge

Comment

This form is adapted from an order in a case involving a consumer action against a manufacturer of prescription drugs.

§ 12:35 Freedom of Information Act request

[Date]

Attn: Freedom of Information Act Officer

Re: Freedom of Information Act Request

Dear Sir or Madam:

This request is made pursuant to the Freedom of Information Act (5 U.S.C.A. § 552).

I respectfully request that a copy of the following documents: *[Provide reasonable description of the documents to be produced, e.g., all agency related e-mail sent by or addressed to (specify individual) from (specify start date) to (specify end date).]*

In furtherance of your obligations under 5 U.S.C.A. § 552, we request that you provide a written response to this request within twenty business days of receipt. For purposes of assessing any applicable fees, this request is made by a *[provide description of requesting entity, e.g., a private corporation for its business purposes, a non-profit educational institution, or news organization as part of its news gathering efforts and not for commercial use]*.

Please notify me immediately if the total fees for responding to this request will exceed $____.

If you have any questions regarding the foregoing, please do not hesitate to call me. Thank you for your assistance in this matter.

Sincerely,

[signature]

[If required by the agency's applicable rules, include the following declaration]

I declare under penalty of perjury under the laws of the State of *[state]* that the foregoing is true and correct.

[signature]

§ 12:36 Order for expedited forensic imaging

[Caption]

ORDER

1. The Forensic Examiner's costs shall be borne by the *[party]*.

2. Computer forensic analysis will be performed by *[specify]*..

3. All Forensic Examiners utilized must agree in writing to be bound by the terms of this Order prior to the commencement of their services.

4. Within two days of this Order or at such other time agreed to by the parties, *[party]* shall make its Computer(s), Server(s), and any other electronic storage devices located at *[party's]* place of business at *[address]*, *[including but not limited to [name's] laptop, which may be located at a different location,]* available to the Forensic Examiner to make mirror images of those devices as set out below:

a. Imaging of the Computer(s), Server(s), any other electronic storage devices in *[party's]* possession, custody, or control, [and *[name's]* laptop] shall be created using Encase or a similar hardware or software tool that creates a forensically sound, bit-for-bit, mirror image of the original hard drives. A bit-stream mirror image copy of the media item(s) will be captured and will include all file slack and unallocated space.

b. *[Party's]* Computers may include, but are not limited to, computers named *[describe]*. This Order does not limit imaging to one server if *[party]* possesses or has custody or control of additional servers, each of which shall be imaged pursuant to this Order.

c. All images and copies of images shall be authenticated by generating an MD5 hash value verification for comparison to the original hard drive.

d. The forensic images shall be copied and retained by the Forensic Examiner until such time the court or both parties request the destruction of the forensic image files.

5. The Forensic Examiner will maintain all mirrored images and do so in the strictest confidence, and not disclose any information obtained to unauthorized persons.

6. The Forensic Examiner will use its best efforts to avoid unnecessarily disrupting the normal activities or business operations of the defendants while inspecting, copying, and imaging the computers and storage devices.

IT IS SO ORDERED this *[date]*.

____

Judge

Comment

This form is adapted from an order in Xpel Technologies Corp. v. American Filter Film Distributors, 2008 WL 744837 (W.D. Tex. 2008).

§ 12:37 Order for forensic search of party's computer systems

[Caption]

ORDER

1. Within seven days of the date of this Opinion and Order, *[producing party's]* forensic computer expert shall mirror image both of *[producing party's]* computer systems' hard drives and *[producing party]* shall preserve this mirror image.

2. *[Producing party's]* forensic computer expert shall then remove only *[producing party's]* confidential personal information from the mirror image of *[producing party's]* computer systems' hard drives. *[Producing party's]* expert shall provide *[receiving party]* with the protocol he utilized to remove the confidential information.

3. *[Producing party]* shall then provide *[receiving party's]* computer forensic expert access to *[producing party's]* computer systems' hard drives.

4. *[Receiving party's]* forensic computer expert shall mirror image *[producing party's]* computer systems' hard drives in approximately four to eight hours for each system. If the expert finds that this is not enough time, *[producing party]* is expected to be reasonable in allowing some additional time. *[Receiving party]* is expected to be considerate with regard to scheduling times that are less intrusive to *[producing party]* and *[producing party's]* business.

5. *[Receiving party's]* expert shall review the expert's findings in confidence with *[producing party]* prior to making any findings available to *[receiving party]*.

6. *[Producing party]* shall identify for deletion any information that is irrelevant and create a specific privilege log of any relevant information for which *[producing party]* claims privilege. The computer forensic expert shall remove the information claimed as privileged and provide all other information to *[receiving party]*.

7. *[Receiving party's]* expert shall provide *[producing party]* with the protocol the expert utilized to remove the privileged information.

8. Forensic computer experts *[names]* shall act as officers of this Court. *[Receiving party]* shall be responsible for remunerating *[name]* and *[producing party]* shall be responsible for remunerating *[name]*.

IT IS SO ORDERED this *[date]*.

____

Judge

Comment

This form is adapted from an order in Ferron v. Search Cactus, L.L.C., 2008 WL 1902499 (S.D. Ohio 2008).

§ 12:38 Order for forensic search with clawback provision

[Caption]

ORDER

1. *[Producing party]* will conduct, at a minimum,

searches of its e-mail database using following terms: *[specify]*

2. These searches will create a universe of presumptively responsive documents. From those presumptively responsive documents, *[producing party]* may search for and preliminarily withhold as presumptively privileged any communications between counsel and corporate principals or upper management, provided however that the presumption of privilege shall not apply to any communications also disclosed to opposing counsel in any litigation, or where any other action has been taken with respect to those communications which would result in the waiver of any claim of attorney-client privilege or work product protection. The Court will leave it to *[producing party]* to design the protocol it wishes to use to identify presumptively privileged documents. However, *[producing party]* shall provide *[receiving party]* with a complete description of the protocol utilized.

3. *[Producing party]* shall produce to party all presumptively responsive documents, less any presumptively privileged documents, not later than thirty (30) days from the entry of this Order. *[Producing party]* may, however, review for privilege any presumptively responsive documents prior to their production. If, after conducting that review, *[producing party]* should believe that the attorney-client privilege or work product protection applies to any document, then *[producing party]* may withhold that document subject to *[producing party's]* obligation to provide a privilege log complying fully with the requirements of Rule 26(b)(5)(A).

4. *[Producing party]* shall review all presumptively privileged documents and produce, on a rolling basis, any documents within this category to which the attorney-client privilege or work product protection does not apply. For any presumptively privileged documents not so produced, *[producing party]* shall provide a privilege log complying fully with the requirements of Rule 26(b)(5)(A). *[Producing party's]* production of such documents shall be completed no later than forty-five (45) days from the entry of this Order.

5. Any documents produced pursuant to this Order shall be considered confidential and subject to the Protective Order ________ governing this case. Paragraph ____ of that Order is hereby modified to apply to any documents or communications produced pursuant to this Order.

6. Any documents produced pursuant to this Order shall be subject to the "clawback provision" set forth in this Order.

7. *[Producing party]* shall not refuse to produce any document returned by the searches stated above on the basis of relevancy, undue burden, or any other ground not specifically provided herein without first obtaining a protective order from this Court.

8. All documents produced pursuant to this Order shall be made available to *[receiving party]* in a searchable, electronic form.

9. The parties may, by mutual agreement, develop and employ search protocols which vary from those set forth above. In the absence of such agreement, however, production shall proceed in the manner described above.

10. If, upon completion of the production described above, *[receiving party]* believes that an additional search of *[producing party's]* e-mail database is warranted, *[receiving party]* may raise that issue with the Court at the appropriate time.

Inadvertent Production of Documents Clawback Provision

1. The inadvertent production of any document or other information during discovery in this action shall be without prejudice to any claim that such material is protected by any legally cognizable privilege or evidentiary protection including, but not limited to, the attorney-client privilege or the work product doctrine, and no party shall be held to have waived any rights by such inadvertent production.

2. Upon written notice of an unintentional production by the producing party or oral notice if notice must be delivered at a deposition, the receiving party must

promptly return or destroy the specified document and any hard copies the receiving party has and may not use or disclose the information until the privilege claim has been resolved. To the extent that the producing party insists on the return or destruction of electronic copies, rather than disabling the documents from further use or otherwise rendering them inaccessible to the receiving party, the producing party shall bear the costs of the return or destruction of such electronic copies.

3. To the extent that the information contained in a document subject to a claim has already been used in or described in other documents generated or maintained by the receiving party, then the receiving party will sequester such documents until the claim has been resolved. If the receiving party disclosed the specified information before being notified of its inadvertent production, it must take reasonable steps to retrieve it. The producing party shall preserve the specified information until the claim is resolved.

4. The receiving party shall have ten (10) days from receipt of notification of the inadvertent production to determine in good faith whether to contest such claim and to notify the producing party in writing of an objection to the claim of privilege and the grounds for that objection.

5. The producing party will then have ten (10) days from the receipt of the objection notice to submit the specified information to the Court under seal for a determination of the claim and will provide the Court with the grounds for the asserted privilege or protection. Any party may request expedited treatment of any request for the Court's determination of the claim.

6. Upon a determination by the Court that the specified information is protected by the applicable privilege, and if the specified information has been sequestered rather than returned or destroyed, the specified information shall be returned or destroyed.

7. Upon a determination by the Court that the specified information is not protected by the applicable privilege, the producing party shall bear the costs of placing

the information into any programs or databases from which it was removed or destroyed and render accessible any documents that were disabled or rendered inaccessible, unless otherwise ordered by the Court.

IT IS SO ORDERED this *[date].*

____

Judge

Comment

This form is adapted from an order in Williams v. Taser Int'l, Inc., 2007 WL 1630875 (N.D. Ga. 2007).

Chapter 13

Requests for Admissions

I. GUIDELINES

II. CHECKLISTS

III. FORMS

Research References

Additional References

ABA Discovery Standards, http://www.abanet.org/litigation/discoverystandards/2005civildiscoverystandards.pdf

Federal Judicial Center, http://www.fjc.gov
The Sedona Conference, http://www.thesedonaconference.org

Treatises and Practice Aids

eDiscovery and Digital Evidence § 7:14
Grenig and Kinsler, Federal Civil Discovery and Disclosure §§ 11.1 to 11.73 (2d ed.)

Trial Strategy

Recovery and Reconstruction of Electronic Mail as Evidence, 41 Am. Jur Proof of Facts 3d 1
Computer Technology in Civil Litigation, 71 Am. Jur Trials 111

KeyCite®: Cases and other legal materials listed in KeyCite Scope can be researched through the KeyCite service on Westlaw®. Use KeyCite to check citations for form, parallel references, prior and later history, and comprehensive citator information, including citations to other decisions and secondary materials.

I. GUIDELINES

§ 13:1 Generally

A request for admission is a device by which a litigant may request that an adversary admit, for the purposes of the pending action only, the truth of any matters relevant to the action, including statements of fact, opinions of fact, the application of law to fact, or the genuineness of documents.[1] Requests for admissions may be useful in establishing the following types of facts:

- The creator of a particular document.
- The owner of an e-mail address or domain name.
- The date a specified file was created or deleted.

A party served with a request for admission has several options:

- Admit the matter in full.
- Deny the matter in full setting forth in detail the reasons for such denial.

[Section 13:1]

[1]See Fed. R. Civ. P. 36.

- Admit part and deny part.
- Object to the request setting for the reasons therefor.
- State that after making a reasonable inquiry the information known or readily obtainable by the answering party is insufficient to enable the party to admit or deny.
- Seek a protective order.
- Move the court for an extension of time to answer.
- Seek a stipulation from the requesting party extending the time to answer.

Once the time period prescribed for answering expires (including any authorized extensions), the requesting party has several options:

- Accept the answer or objection.
- Move the court to determine the sufficiency of the answer or objection; if the court finds that the answer or objection is incomplete or insufficient, it may order that the request be re-answered.
- If the answering party denies the request and the proposition is proved during trial, and if the court in a post-trial hearing finds that the refusal was improper, the costs of proof may be imposed on the answering party.
- If the answering party fails to answer or object within the time specified in the applicable rule, the request will be deemed admitted.

§ 13:2 Role of requests for admissions

Unlike other discovery devices, requests for admission are not designed to discover facts. Because of the form in which requests for admission are submitted, it is assumed that the requesting party knows the facts before asking an adverse party to admit that the statement is true. Requests for admission ask the answering party to "admit that so-and-so" is true. Requests for admission are not substitutes for interrogatories. As a result, requests for admission may not be used to "gather" information after a party has exhausted the numerical limit on interrogatories.

Requests for admission serve two vital purposes. Admissions are sought, first, to facilitate proof with respect to issues that cannot be eliminated from the case, and secondly, to narrow the issues by eliminating those that can be. Thus, requests for admission can be used to define the issues involved in the case and to resolve some or all of the conflicts prior to trial.

§ 13:3 Disadvantages of requests for admissions

There are few disadvantages to using requests for admission. Answers to requests are only binding on the party who made them. Neither the requests nor the answers are binding on the party who propounded the requests for admission. A litigant does not bind itself to the truth of an admission by another party by submitting the request for admission. The requesting party may disregard an answer, even though it chooses to offer other answers from the same request into evidence.

There are, however, some minor disadvantages in propounding requests for admission. First, if requests are drawn too narrowly, they may reveal the drafting attorney's trial strategy. Second, unless drafted carefully and precisely, a denial will probably be upheld by the court, resulting in wasted time and money.

The ease with which answering parties effectively dodge requests for admission may be their greatest disadvantage. Often the answering party will respond to a request by stating that further discovery and investigation is necessary before it can give an intelligent response. In all likelihood, this response will be acceptable to the courts, especially early in the litigation. Another disadvantage of utilizing requests for admission is that the process of drafting requests may take substantially more time than the process of answering them. This is particularly true if the answering party can simply deny the requests.

§ 13:4 Actions in which requests for admissions may be used

Requests for admission may be made by any party upon

any other party in an action. Information required from a non-party may be obtained by oral deposition or by a deposition upon written questions. In addition, documents and tangible things may be obtained from non-parties by subpoena.

§ 13:5 Timing

Rule 26(f) of the Federal Rules of Civil Procedure requires that the parties meet to develop, among other things, a discovery plan. This meeting must take place as soon as practicable in the litigation process but, in any event, at least 21 days before a scheduling conference is held or a scheduling order is due under Rule 16(b). Rule 16(b) requires that a scheduling order be entered within 90 days after the first appearance of a defendant or 120 days after the complaint has been served on any defendant, whichever occurs earlier. Together, Rules 26 and 36 preclude the service of requests for admission until after the parties meet to develop a discovery plan, which may occur two or three months after the complaint is filed.

Rule 36(a) is silent on how late in the litigation process a party may serve requests for admission. Trial courts have considerable discretion in determining the timeliness of discovery. Some courts have local rules governing discovery cut-off dates. Where no such rules exist, scheduling orders and pretrial orders may set a time limit for the completion of discovery, including service of or response to requests for admission.

Requests should be served to allow sufficient time to complete the process before the discovery cut-off or trial deadline. Ideally, the discovery order should specify whether the discovery deadline is the deadline for service of requests for admission or for responses to such requests. If it is the latter, then requests must be served no less than 30 days before the discovery cut-off date.

Discovery requests served on the eve of trial may be stricken by the court, but the fact that a party has waited a considerable time before making a discovery request is no bar in itself to the discovery. Of course, the parties can stipulate to extend the time in which requests for admission may be served, provided they do not extend it beyond any discovery cut-off date imposed by the court. The fact that a motion for summary judgment has been filed, or that an evidentiary hearing has been conducted does not preclude the service of requests for admission.

§ 13:6 Number of requests

Rule 33 of the Federal Rules of Civil Procedure limits the number of interrogatories a party may serve on an adversary without leave of court. No similar limits are placed on requests for admission. There is also no limit on the number of times a party may serve requests for admission on an adversary. A party may serve multiple requests for admission as it learns more about the case.

Once the answers to the interrogatories are received, requests to produce electronically stored information and documents should be served on all parties. The requests to produce should seek all relevant documents, records, photographs and other tangible evidence, including any such evidence identified in the answer to interrogatories. The requesting party may also demand access to an adversary's computer to inspect and analyze electronically stored information. This would also be the time to serve document subpoenas on non-parties.

After the requesting party has received the electronically stored information, documents, and other tangible items, depositions should be taken of the opposing party and all essential witnesses. Depositions are designed to obtain detailed information from parties and non-parties, and to tie down each of them to a particular account of the relevant events. Depositions are also useful for obtaining admissions and other impeachment material. In cases where a party's physical or mental condition is at issue, a physical or mental examination of the party may be warranted at this point in the discovery process. In such cases, the requesting party must seek an order from the court requiring an adversary to appear for examination. After all other discovery has been completed, requests for admission should be served on the answering party.

§ 13:7 Service of requests

Requests may be served by delivering a copy to the party or mailing the requests to the party's last known address.[1] Once a party has appeared by counsel, the requests are served upon the attorney. A copy of the requests should also be served on all other parties to the action. Under Rule 5(d), requests for admission must not be filed with the court until they are used in the proceeding or the court orders the filing.

§ 13:8 Form of requests

Each matter for which an admission is requested must be separately set forth in short, numbered paragraphs. Requests should be simple and direct statements containing a single proposition. A request should be phrased so it can be admitted or denied without explanation. A request should not be argumentative in tone.

Except when documents are sought to be authenticated, requests for admission should not incorporate outside material, such as pleadings, motions or deposition transcripts. Incorporation by reference is improper because it unjustly casts upon the answering party the burden of determining at its peril what portions of the incorporated material contain relevant matters of fact that must be either admitted or denied. Facts admitted in response to a request for admission should be ascertainable merely by examination of the request and of the answer. The requests for admission and the answers should be in such a form so as to be read to the jury, without reference to extraneous materials. Incorporation by reference also gives the answering party too much room to evade the admission. In complex cases, drafting attorneys should also consider defining terms that will be used in more than one request. An instruction section may also be appropriate in complicated cases.

[Section 13:7]

[1]See Fed. R. Civ. P. 5.

§ 13:9 Scope of requests

According to Rule 36(a) of the Federal Rules of Civil Procedure, a party may serve upon any other party a written request for admission of the truth of any matters within the scope of Rule 26(b)(1). Essentially, Rule 36(a) entitles a party to require any other party to admit or deny the truthfulness of opinions or facts; the application of law to fact; or the genuineness of documents. Requests for admission, in other words, may pertain to any fact or fact-based issue in the litigation.

Rule 36 is not limited to matters known to the responding party. Rule 36 requests may be directed to undisputed facts or to facts crucial to the case. The Advisory Committee explained the scope of Rule 36 as follows:

> [Rule 36] provides that a request may be made to admit any matters within the scope of Rule 26(b) that relate to statements or opinions of fact or of the application of law to fact. It thereby eliminates the requirement that the matter be "of fact." This change resolves conflicts in the court decisions as to whether a request to admit matters of "opinion" and matters involving "mixed law and fact" is proper under the rule.

§ 13:10 Effect of admission

Any matter admitted is conclusively established unless the court on motion permits withdrawal or amendment of the admission. Such admissions, however, may be used only in the pending action.

§ 13:11 Authentication of documents and electronically stored information

Requests for admission are best suited for establishing the necessary foundation for real and documentary evidence at trial. Admissions may be used to obviate the need for authenticating a document or electronically stored information at trial. Being able to authenticate electronic documents by means of a request for admission is particularly useful. Using admissions for this purpose is common practice in state and federal courts.

It is not enough to ask the answering party to admit that a document or electronically stored information is genuine; rather, the requesting party must ensure that all foundational questions are included in the requests for admission. If a request asks the respondent to admit the genuineness of a document or electronically stored information, the document or a copy of the electronically stored information should be attached to the request and incorporated by reference.

The proper foundation for documents or electronically stored information can be established well in advance of trial, saving both time and money. In addition, a request may ask the answering party to admit the genuineness of documents belonging to someone other than the answering party, as long as the answering party has reasonable access to such documents or electronically stored information.

Rule 36 of the Federal Rules of Civil Procedure does not require that the document or electronically stored information be attached to a request for admission. Rather it provides that "[c]opies of the documents shall be served with the request unless they have been or are otherwise furnished or made available for inspection and copying." If a document has already been identified in discovery, such as an exhibit in a prior deposition, it need not be attached to the requests for admission, so long as there is no question about which document the requesting party is referring to.

Because questions may arise as to how a party may admit the authenticity of electronically stored information, it may be helpful to print a hardcopy version of the file in question along with information relating to its creation date, author, etc. For example, when an e-mail is printed, the printout usually contains the original sender's name, the recipient, date of transmission, and other relevant information. All of this can be included on the document for which authentication is being requested.

If the proponent of the discovery desires to have an electronic file, itself, authenticated, this can be done by copying the file to WORM (write-once, read many) media. Certain types of writeable CDs are WORM. The party desiring authentication need only copy the relevant files to the CD. Thereafter, the files cannot be modified or changed in any way. The responding party can then be requested to admit the authenticity of the files indelibly stored on the CD.

II. CHECKLISTS

§ 13:12 Requests for admissions drafting checklist

- ☐ Review any interrogatories or depositions for damaging testimony and draft requests for admissions based on that information.
- ☐ When drafting, use an evolving discovery plan to focus firmly on proving your case (or disproving that of your opponent).
- ☐ Since requests for admissions are generally based on issues raised by the pleadings, they work best when they are constructed on a framework using the language of that pleading. Use the pleading as a form, adding or demanding specifics as needed, depending on the level of disputed information.
- ☐ Draft with an extremely narrow focus. Any vagueness will provide grounds for denial.
- ☐ Keep requests for admissions simple. Complex or ambiguous requests will probably be objected to and not admitted.
- ☐ Stick to factual areas only. Avoid attempting to draw conclusions on issues of law.

III. FORMS

§ 13:13 Requests for admissions

[Caption]

The *[requesting party]* asks the *[responding party]* to respond within 30 days to these requests by admitting, for purposes of this action only and subject to objections to admissibility at trial:

1. The genuineness of the following documents, copies of which *[are attached] [are or have been furnished or made available for inspection and copying]*.

[List each document.]

The truth of each of the following statements: *[List each statement.]*

Dated: ________

[signature, etc.]

Comment

This form is adapted from Official Form 51 approved by the U.S. Supreme Court.

§ 13:14 Requests for admissions—Another form

[Caption]

To: *[name]*

[Party 1], by counsel, pursuant to *[rule]*, hereby submits the following request for admissions.

You must file and serve a written response to this request within 30 days following service these requests. Your response to each matter may be in the form of an admission, a specific denial, an objection (with reasons clearly stated), or a statement that the matter cannot be admitted or denied. You may not give lack of information or knowledge as a reason for failure to admit or deny unless you state that you have made reasonable inquiry and the information known or readily available to you is insufficient to enable you to admit or deny.

TRUTHFULNESS OF FACTS

1. Each of the following documents exhibited with this request is genuine.

[List the documents, including electronically stored information, and describe each document.]

2. Each of the following statements is true.

[List the statements.]

Dated: ________

[signature etc.]

§ 13:15 Requests for admissions—Alternate form

[Caption]

To: *[name]*

[Party 1], by counsel, pursuant to *[rule]*, hereby submits the following request for admissions.

You must file and serve a written response to this request within 30 days following service these requests. Your response to each matter may be in the form of an admission, a specific denial, an objection (with reasons clearly stated), or a statement that the matter cannot be admitted or denied. You may not give lack of information or knowledge as a reason for failure to admit or deny unless you state that you have made reasonable inquiry and the information known or readily available to you is insufficient to enable you to admit or deny.

TRUTHFULNESS OF FACTS

Please admit the truthfulness of each of the facts set forth below.

REQUEST FOR ADMISSION NO. 1:

Admit that *[specify employee name]* was assigned the following e-mail address: *[specify e-mail address]*.

REQUEST FOR ADMISSION NO. 2:

Admit that *[specify company name]* is the registered owner of the following domain name: *[specify domain name]*.

REQUEST FOR ADMISSION NO. 3:

Admit that on or about *[specify date]* the following files were deleted from *[specify user name]*'s desktop computer.

REQUEST FOR ADMISSION NO. 4:

Admit that *[name]* had no disaster recovery plan in effect for the network as of *[date]*. For purposes of these Requests for Admissions, certain terms have the following definitions: The term "network" refers to the local area network located at, including, but not limited to, all files servers, client computers, workstations, firewalls, routers, proxy servers, Internet servers, mail servers, and application servers.

GENUINENESS OF DOCUMENTS

Please admit the genuineness of each of the documents described below; copies of the documents are attached to this Request.

REQUEST FOR ADMISSION RE GENUINENESS OF DOCUMENT NO. 1:

Admit that the e-mail dated *[specify date]* from *[specify sender]* to *[specify recipient]* is genuine. A copy of the e-mail is attached as Exhibit A.

REQUEST FOR ADMISSION RE GENUINENESS OF DOCUMENT NO. 2:

Admit that the audit trail, with a printout date of *[date]*, is genuine. A copy of the audit trail is attached as Exhibit B.

REQUEST FOR ADMISSION RE GENUINENESS OF DOCUMENT NO. 3:

Admit that the printout, dated *[date]*, of the files and directories residing on the hard disk of *[name's]* computer is genuine. A copy of the file and directory printout is attached as Exhibit C.

REQUEST FOR ADMISSION RE GENUINENESS OF DOCUMENT NO. 4:

Admit that the Employee Computer Use Policy, dated *[date]*, is genuine. A copy of the Policy is attached as Exhibit D.

REQUEST FOR ADMISSION RE GENUINENESS OF DOCUMENT NO. 5:

Admit that the Disaster Recovery Plan, dated *[date]*, is genuine. A copy of the Disaster Recovery Plan is attached as Exhibit E.

Dated: ________

[signature, etc.]

§ 13:16 Requests for admissions—Genuineness of documents

[Caption]

To: *[name]*

[Party 1], by counsel, pursuant to *[rule]*, hereby submits the following requests for admissions.

You must file and serve a written response to this request within 30 days following service these requests. Your response to each matter may be in the form of an admission, a specific denial, an objection (with reasons clearly stated), or a statement that the matter cannot be admitted or denied. You may not give lack of information or knowledge as a reason for failure to admit or deny unless you state that you have made reasonable inquiry and the information known or readily available to you is insufficient to enable you to admit or deny.

You are hereby requested to admit the genuineness of the following described documents:

1. The printout, dated *[date]*, of the files and directories residing on the hard disk of *[name's]* computer is genuine. A copy of the file and directory printout is attached as Exhibit D.

[Describe additional documents with specificity.]

Dated: ________

[signature, etc.]

§ 13:17 Motion for order that matter is admitted on grounds of insufficiency of answer or objection

[Caption]

MOTION FOR ORDER THAT MATTER IS ADMITTED

[Requesting party] moves the Court for an order that the answer of *[responding party]* to *[requesting party's* requests for admissions, as set forth below, does not comply with the requirements of *[rule]*, and that the facts as set forth below in *[responding party's]* requests for admissions be deemed admitted, and for an award of expenses in this matter pursuant to *[rule]*.

The grounds for this motion are as follows:

1. *[Requesting party]* served on *[responding party]* on *[date]*, requests for admissions of the following facts: *[include specific requests for admissions]*.

2. *[Responding party]* served on *[requesting party]* on *[date]*, a response to the requests for admissions as follows: *[include responding party's response verbatim]*.

3. *[Responding party's]* response does not contain a specific answer to *[requesting party's]* requests for admissions and does not comply with the requirements of *[rule]*, nor does it state any objection to *[requesting party's]* requests for admissions.

Dated: ________

[signature etc.]

§ 13:18 Motion for award of expenses incurred to prove matter opponent failed to admit

[Caption]

MOTION FOR AWARD OF EXPENSES

[Requesting party] moves the Court for an order requiring *[responding party]* to pay *[requesting party's]* reasonable expenses incurred in making proof, at the trial of the above-entitled action, of the matters of substantial importance listed below on the following grounds:

1. On *[date]*, *[requesting party]* served upon *[responding party]* and filed a request *[for the admission of the following facts: [number and list requests] [for the admission of the genuineness of the following documents: [number and list requests]*.

2. In response to *[requesting party's]* request for admissions, *[responding party]* served a response upon *[requesting party]* on *[date]*, *[in which [responding party] denied the following facts [list the fact statements denied] [in which plaintiff denied the genuineness of the following documents and here list the documents as in the request]*.

3. At the trial of the above-entitled action, *[requesting party]*t proved the truth of the facts so denied by *[responding party]* by prove of the genuineness of the documents by the following evidence *[describe]*, which evidence was not controverted by *[responding party]*.

The reasonable expenses incurred in the proof of the above-described facts were $________, as more fully appears by the attached *[affidavit] [declaration]*.

Dated: ________

[signature etc.]

Chapter 14

Discovery from Non-Parties of Electronically Stored Information

I. GUIDELINES

II. CHECKLISTS

III. FORMS

Research References

Treatises and Practice Aids

eDiscovery & Digital Evidence §§ 7:10, 10:2 to 10:7

Grenig and Kinsler, Federal Civil Discovery and Disclosure § 5.10 (2d ed.)

Trial Strategy

Recovery and Reconstruction of Electronic Mail as Evidence, 41 Am. Jur Proof of Facts 3d 1

Computer Technology in Civil Litigation, 71 Am. Jur Trials 111

Law Reviews and Other Periodicals

Llewellyn, Electronic Discovery Best Practices, 10 Rich. J.L. & Tech. 51 (2004)

Additional References

Feldman, Essentials of Electronic Discovery: Finding and Using Cyber Evidence (2003)

Grenig, Discovery from Non-Parties of Electronically Stored Information, Elec. Disc. & Records Mgt. Q., fall 2007, at 24

Grenig, West's Federal Forms: District Court (4th ed.)

ABA Discovery Standards, http://www.abanet.org/litigation/discoverystandards/2005civildiscoverystandards.pdf

Federal Judicial Center, http://www.fjc.gov

The Sedona Conference, http://www.thesedonaconference.org

KeyCite®: Cases and other legal materials listed in KeyCite Scope can be researched through the KeyCite service on Westlaw®. Use KeyCite to check citations for form, parallel references, prior and later history, and comprehensive citator information, including citations to other decisions and secondary materials.

I. GUIDELINES

§ 14:1 Generally

Rules of civil procedure, including the Federal Rules of Civil Procedure, authorize the following formal methods for obtaining discovery:

- Depositions upon oral examination or written questions
- Written interrogatories

- Production of documents or things or permission to enter upon land or other property for inspection
- Physical or mental examination
- Requests for admission

Of these methods, only depositions can be used with respect to non-parties. In order to obtain documents or permission to inspect with respect to a non-party, the subpoena process must be used. Even the taking of a deposition of a non-party requires use of a subpoena.

Under the Federal Rules of Civil Procedure, Rules 45(a) and (b) apply to the issuance of subpoenas for the attendance of witnesses and for the production of documents at the trial or hearing. Rule 45(c) provides for the service of a subpoena. Rule 45(d) contains provisions relating to deposition subpoenas. Rule 45(e) contains provisions relating to the issuance and service of subpoenas.

§ 14:2 Subpoenas—Generally

There are two types of subpoenas:

- A subpoena ad testificandum compels the attendance of a witness.
- A subpoena duces tecum calls for the production of documents and things.

§ 14:3 Subpoenas—Issuance

In many jurisdictions, the clerk of the court may issue the subpoena in blank to a party requesting it. Local rules may require a written request for subpoena. Rule 45(a)(3) empowers an attorney to issue a subpoena, so long as the attorney is admitted in the district in which the action is pending. The attorney must sign the subpoena, but the seal of the court is no longer required. The attorney must specify the district court "from" which the subpoena is issued. The clerk will still issue the subpoena when a party itself applies for it.

In federal proceedings, a subpoena for attendance at a deposition is issued by the court for the district in which the deposition is to occur and bears the same case name and number as the case in the court where the trial is to occur. If a separate subpoena is issued commanding the production of documents or an inspection, the subpoena issues from the court for the district in which the production or inspection is to occur.

Rule 45(c)(3)(A)(ii) provides that the subpoena may not be effective if it purports to require the witness to travel more than 100 miles from the witness's residence or place of employment or business. If the witness's residence or employment is more than 100 miles from the place of trial, but within the state in which the trial court sits, the court can command the witness by a court order to appear for the trial. In determining whether a subpoena exceeds the 100-mile travel limit, the proper measure is the length of a straight line connecting the two points and not a calculation of the distance over actual highways and roads.

§ 14:4 Subpoenas—Service

Rule 45(b) of the Federal Rules of Civil Procedure sets forth the requirements for serving a subpoena in federal cases. State and local rules should be consulted for other jurisdictions.

Rule 45(b)(2) permits a pretrial subpoena (e.g., a deposition subpoena or a subpoena seeking the pretrial production of documents) to be served in any of the following areas:

- Anywhere within the district of the court "by which" it is issued
- Anywhere within a 100-mile radius of the site selected for the deposition, production, or inspection
- Anywhere within the state containing that site.

It is necessary to issue the subpoena in the name of a district (from the place of trial) court whenever the witness from whom testimony or a document or other tangible is sought cannot be reached within any of the three enumerated areas as measured from the trial court. In seeking the proper district from which to issue a pretrial subpoena when the witness is not amenable to service within the stated areas measured from the trial court, the attorney should be careful to choose a district whose geography fully satisfies not only Rule 45(b)(2), but also Rules 45(c)(3)(A)(ii) and 45(e), if that is possible.

Rule 45(e)(1) also allows service "at a place within the state where a state statute or rule of court permits service of a subpoena issued by a state court of general jurisdiction sitting in the place where the district court is held." When a statute of the United States so provides and upon proper application and cause, a court may authorize a subpoena for trial to be served outside the district or beyond 100 miles from the place of hearing or trial.

Under Rule 45(c), the summons may be served by any non-party age 18 or over. Reference to the marshal as a server has been omitted. No change was made in the method of service of a subpoena. The subpoena is served by "delivering" the subpoena to the person to be served. The subpoena must be personally served. It is not sufficient to leave a copy of the subpoena at the dwelling place of the witness. Service on a person's lawyer will not suffice.

Service of the subpoena must be accompanied by tendering to the witness the fees for one day's attendance and the mileage allowed by law. Fees and mileage need not be tendered if the subpoena is issued on behalf of the United States or an officer or agency of the United States.

Whenever a subpoena under Rule 45 is served on a person and sets up a deposition, Rule 45(b)(1) requires that notice of the subpoena be given to parties before the subpoena is served on the person commanded to produce or permit inspection. Notice should be served in accordance with Rule 5.

§ 14:5 Depositions

A non-party witness can be compelled to give deposition testimony only by service of a subpoena and the payment or tendering of a witness fee. An individual employee of a party who is not an officer, director, or managing agent of the party-entity may only be compelled to attend a deposition by subpoena.

In federal court, subpoenas for the attendance of a witness at a deposition are issued pursuant to Rule 45(a)(2). These subpoenas must be issued from the court for the district in which the deposition is to be taken. Rules 45(a)(2) and Rule 45(c) limit the places at which a deposition may be taken. Rule 45(a)(2) provides that a deposition subpoena must state the method of recording the testimony.

If a corporation, partnership, association, or governmental unit is a non-party, the subpoena must notify the entity of its duty to designate the person or persons to testify for it. If a subpoena is issued to a person not a party calling upon that person to produce documents but not to appear for the taking of a deposition or to testify, there is authority that the subpoena is irregular and must be quashed.

§ 14:6 Production of documents and electronically stored information—Generally

Document and electronically stored information requests under Rule 34 of the Federal Rules of Civil Procedure may be used only against parties to the action. There are several ways to circumvent Rule 34's party-only restriction, for the courts have shown a tendency to liberally construe the term "parties" for purposes of production. First, federal courts have permitted document production requests to be directed to persons who, though not technically parties to the action, are sufficiently similar to parties to allow the request.

Second, because Rule 34 covers all documents and electronically stored information in the possession, custody, or control of a party, a party must produce documents and electronically stored information in the possession of its agents. As a result, a party cannot immunize documents and electronically stored information from inspection by turning it over to a non-party so long as it remains in the party's control.

Third, although Rule 34 may not be used to discover materials from a non-party, Rule 34(c) expressly provides that a person not a party to the action may be compelled to produce documents and things or to submit to an inspection as provided in Rule 45. Rule 45 authorizes a party to inspect the documents of non-parties by a subpoena duces tecum.

Fourth, if an entity, typically a parent corporation, has been found to be the alter ego of a party, that entity may be subject to Rule 34.

A subpoena duces tecum compels the production of documents and electronically stored information or things possessed or controlled by a non-party. If a subpoena duces tecum is served on one who has custody of records that belong to another person, formal notice should be served on the owner of the records before production will be required. A subpoena duces tecum may not be used to obtain privileged documents.

The form of a subpoena duces tecum is the same as a subpoena for the attendance of witnesses with the addition of language commanding the person to whom it is directed to produce the documents or things designated in the subpoena. The subpoena should designate with reasonable particularity the documents and electronically stored information that are to be produced. If a party does not know exactly what documents and electronically stored information it wishes produced, the party may require the production of all documents and electronically stored information relating to a certain specified matter or issue. If the documents and electronically stored information are to be produced at the taking of a deposition, the scope of the documents electronically stored information sought may be the same as the scope of discovery under the applicable rule of civil procedure

A subpoena duces tecum seeking the production of electronically stored information or documents from a non-party may be used independently of the regular testimonial subpoena. A subpoena duces tecum may be used to obtain electronically stored information or documents from a non-party without any scheduling of a deposition of the non-party. The party who seeks a pretrial production of electronically stored information or documents from a non-party through use of a subpoena duces tecum must serve notice on all the other parties, including the time and place of the examination and all related particulars. If testimony is also sought from the custodian of the electronically stored information or documents, the subpoena served on the custodian can include both testimonial and document production clauses. The scope of a subpoena duces tecum is as broad against a non-party as against a party.

Under Rule 45(c)(1)(A), a person commanded to produce documents, electronically stored information, or tangible things, or to permit the inspection of premises, need not appear in person at the place of production or inspection unless also commanded to appear for a deposition, hearing, or trial.

Rule 45(a)(1)(B) provides that a subpoena is available to permit testing and sampling as well as inspection and copying. Courts must vigilantly protect non-parties under Rule 45(c) when testing and sampling are requested.

§ 14:7 Production of documents and electronically stored information—Form of production

Rule 45(a)(1) provides that a subpoena can designate a form or forms for production of electronically stored information. Rule 45(c)(2) authorizes the person served with a subpoena to object to the requested form or forms. Rule 45(d)(1)(B) provides that, if the subpoena does not specify the form or forms for electronically stored information, the person served with the subpoena must produce electronically stored information in a form or forms in which it is usually maintained or in a form that is reasonably usable.[1]

One court has concluded that production of native format in response to a subpoena was the least burden-

[Section 14:7]

[1]See Auto Club Family Ins. Co. v. Ahner, 2007 WL 2480322 (E.D. La. 2007) (third-party producer ordered to produce information in electronic format).

some form for production.[2] However, because electronically stored information is frequently voluminous and setting up the necessary security protocols to protect the information may be time consuming, disruptive, and expensive, native format should not be considered presumptively the least burdensome form.

§ 14:8 Objections

The proper procedure for challenging a subpoena requiring personal attendance is by motion to quash. The court can modify or quash the subpoena if it is unreasonable or oppressive.

Rule 45(c)(2)(B) of the Federal Rules of Civil Procedure provides that a person commanded to produce documents or tangible things or to permit inspection may serve on the party or attorney designated in the subpoena a written objection to inspecting, copying, testing or sampling any or all of the materials or to inspecting the premises—or to producing electronically stored information in the form or forms requested. The objection must be served before the earlier of the time specified for compliance or 14 days after the subpoena is served.

If an objection is made, at any time, on notice to the commanded person, the serving party may move the issuing court for an order compelling production or inspection. These acts may be required only as directed in the order, and the order must protect a person who is neither a party nor a party's officer from significant expense resulting from compliance.[1] An order requiring compliance must protect a person who is neither a party nor a party's officer from significant expense resulting from compliance.[2]

---

[2]In re Honeywell Intern., Inc. Securities Litigation, 230 F.R.D. 293 (S.D. N.Y. 2003).

[Section 14:8]

[1]Rule 45(c)(1)(A).

[2]Rule 45(c)(2)(B).

Under the Electronic Communications Privacy Act[3] an Internet service provider cannot be required to produce witness e-mails.[4] The Privacy Act does not provide an exception for civil discovery subpoenas from non-governmental parties.

§ 14:9 Protecting privileges or work product

The recipient of a subpoena duces tecum may refuse to produce privileged documents. If the issuing party contests the asserted privilege, the court can be requested to conduct an in camera inspection of the documents.

Rule 45(d)(2) adds a procedure for asserting a privilege or protecting trial-preparation materials after production. If a non-party produces electronically stored information subject to a claim of privilege, Rule 45(d)(2) require that, once notified, the receiving party promptly return, sequester, or destroy the specified information and not make any use of it until the privilege issue is resolved.

§ 14:10 Protection from undue burden or expenses

Rule 45(c)(1) requires a party or attorney responsible for issuing and serving a subpoena to take reasonable steps to avoid imposing undue burden or expense on a person subject to the subpoena. The issuing court must enforce this duty and impose an appropriate sanction—which may include lost earnings and reasonable attorney fees—on a party or attorney who fails to comply.

Under Rule 45(c), third parties enjoy more protection from burdensome and costly discovery than parties. Rule 45(d)(1)(D) permits the responding person to refuse to provide discovery of electronically stored information from sources the party identifies as not reasonably accessible,

---

[3]18 U.S.C.A. §§ 2510 to 2521, 18 U.S.C.A. §§ 2701 to 2710.

[4]In re Subpoena Duces Tecum to AOL, LLC, 550 F. Supp. 2d 606 (E.D. Va. 2008).

unless the court orders such discovery for good cause.[1] A third-party seeking a protective order must make a particular and specific demonstration of fact in support of its motion.[2]

II. CHECKLISTS

§ 14:11 Deposition subpoena checklist

- ☐ Check local rules of the applicable jurisdiction regarding subpoenas.
- ☐ Use the jurisdiction's form for a deposition subpoena, or use that form as a model for your own form.
- ☐ If you are requesting documents at the deposition, draft a subpoena duces tecum.
- ☐ Serve the notice of deposition on all parties.
- ☐ In many jurisdictions you will need to have the court issue the subpoena. You will need proof of service of the notice of deposition, along with the notice and the subpoena itself. In some jurisdictions, California for example, any attorney of record may issue a subpoena. Submit duplicate copies of all items so they may be file-stamped and returned to you for your files.
- ☐ After checking jurisdiction rules for witness fees, at-

[Section 14:10]

[1]Auto Club Family Ins. Co. v. Ahner, 2007 WL 2480322 (E.D. La. 2007) (lawyer's statement in memorandum in support of motion for protective order that electronically stored information is not reasonably accessible or that it would be unduly burdensome to comply with request was not evidence). See, e.g., Bank of America Corp. v. SR Intern. Business Ins. Co., Ltd., 2006 NCBC 15, 2006 WL 3093174 (N.C. Super. Ct. 2006) (subpoena requesting production of e-mails from eight persons over a two-year period from 350 to 400 backup tapes was found to be undue burden on a non-party); U.S. v. Amerigroup Illinois, Inc., 2005 WL 3111972 (N.D. Ill. 2005) (subpoena seeking production was undue burden where it was difficult and time consuming for non-party to restore deleted e-mails, and backup tapes were by their very nature highly inaccessible)

[2]Auto Club Family Ins. Co. v. Ahner, 2007 WL 2480322 (E.D. La. 2007) (rejecting motion for protective order permitting movant to provide hard copy of files rather than electronic version).

tach a check for the witness fee to a photocopy of the subpoena. A copy is left with the deponent, and the original is simply displayed at the time of service.

- ☐ Hire a process server to complete service and provide the server with the witness fee check, the original and a copy of the subpoena and any information that will help locate the deponent for efficient and accurate service.

III. FORMS

§ 14:12 Deposition subpoena

[Caption]

To: *[name]*

Greeting:

We command you, that all business and excuses being laid aside, you and each of you attend before an officer authorized by law to take deposition at *[address]*, on *[date]*, at *[time]*, to testify and give evidence on behalf of the *[party]* in a case pending and undetermined in the *[court]* in which *[name 1]* is plaintiff and *[name 2]* is one of the defendants, No. ________.

And this you shall in no way omit, under the penalty of the law in that case made and provided, and you also are to diligently and carefully search for and bring with you and produce at the time and place stated above the documents described in Attachment A.

The testimony shall be recorded by *[sound] [sound and visual] [videotape] [stenographic means]*.

Dated ________

[signature etc.]

ATTACHMENT A TO SUBPOENA

Instructions

Documents to be produced include all documents in the possession, custody or control of *[organization]*, wherever located, including documents in the possession, custody or control of its directors, officers, employees, representatives or agents. As used in this subpoena, the term "document" means any written, recorded, or graphic material of any kind, whether prepared by a director, officer, employee, representative, or agent of *[organization]* or by any other person, that is in *[organization's]* possession, custody, or control. Without limitation on the term "control," a document is deemed to be in *[organization's]* control if you have the right to secure that document or a copy thereof from another person.

The terms "documents" and "records," as used in this subpoena include any relevant electronic files, stored on file servers, e-mail servers, hard drives, or other electronic storage media within *[organization's]* control. The terms "documents" and "records" refer to and include every document, report, summary, bulletin, manual, purchase order, purchase contract, release, map, policy statement, notation, worksheet, memorandum, letter or other written record reflecting the indicated information. Any such electronic documents or records are to be produced in usable form, along with instructions for reading such data.

Documents to Be Produced

[List of documents]

§ 14:13 Deposition subpoena—Another form

[Caption]

To: *[name]*

YOU ARE HEREBY COMMANDED to appear in the office of *[attorney's office and address]* to give testimony in the above-entitled cause on *[date]*, at *[time]*, to bring with you the documents described in the attached Addendum, and not to depart without leave.

The testimony shall be recorded by *[sound] [sound and visual] [videotape] [stenographic means].*

Dated: ________

[signature etc.]

ADDENDUM TO CIVIL SUBPOENA TO ______

(a) all documents, upon which you intend to rely in your testimony;

(b) all documents referring in any way, either directly or indirectly, to communications between you *[or anyone else associated with [describe]]* and *[describe]* relating to: *[describe with particularity subject matter of deposition].*

§ 14:14 Deposition subpoena—Corporate officer

[Caption]

To: *[name]*

Greeting:

We Command You, that all business and excuses being laid aside, you and each of you attend at *[address]*, on *[date]*, at *[time]*, to testify and give evidence in a certain cause now pending and undetermined in the Court, in which *[name 1]* is plaintiff and *[name 2]*, on the part of *[defendant] [name 2].*

And you also are to diligently and carefully search for, examine, and inquire after and bring with you, and produce at the above time and place, the documents described in the attached schedule and made a part of this subpoena which are in the possession, custody or control of *[name 1]*, or any of its subsidiaries or controlled companies, or the officers, directors, agents, representatives, employees or counsel of any of them.

The testimony shall be recorded by *[sound] [sound and visual] [videotape] [stenographic means].*

Definitions

The term "documents" includes all writings, or records of any kind, including, but not limited to, the originals and all copies and drafts of contracts, agreements, and amendments to them, correspondence, e-mail, text messages, memoranda, reports, recordings and other transcription of telephone or other conversations, conferences or meetings, affidavits, books of account, transcripts of testimony in judicial or administrative proceedings, minutes of meetings, including directors' meetings and committee meetings, diaries, intra-office communications, logs, advertisements, scrap-books, press and publicity releases, reports to stockholders or to governmental bodies, records, reports, or summaries of negotiations and all other writings of every kind, including documents passing from or to or between *[name 1]* or its domestic or foreign subsidiaries or affiliated or controlled companies, or the officers, or representatives or any of them, and any documents passing from or to or between those companies and foreign companies, or the officers, directors, agents, representatives, employees or counsel of any of them.

The term "*[name 1]*" as used here includes *[specify]* and any and all domestic or foreign subsidiaries and affiliated companies under the control of *[name 1]*.

The term "patent" as used here means any patent usable in the manufacture or sale of radio and television apparatus or any constituent part.

Subpoena Duces Tecum

1. All documents referring or relating to foreign patents or foreign patent licenses or rights of any kind covering any invention which is the subject of any United States patent licensed under the standard license agreements issued or proffered by *[name 1]* to any licensee or prospective licensee in the United States at any time during the life of the patent in suit.

2. All communications between *[name 1]* and any

company or person having licensing rights under foreign patents of *[name 1]*, referring to or relating to the actual or proposed licensing of any foreign patent on inventions which are the subject of any United States patent licensed under any *[name 1]* standard license agreement issued or proffered in the United States at any time during the life of the patent in suit.

3. All documents referring or relating to the following foreign patent licensing organizations or any of their patent pooling or licensing activities: *[list]* Any other foreign patent pool or company or organization having licensing rights under any of the patents of *[name 1]* and any other patentee and all communications between *[name 1]* or any of its officers, agents, representatives or counsel and any of the foreign patent licensing organizations, or any of the officers, agents, representatives or counsel of any of the organizations.

4. All documents concerning the creation, administration, operation, purposes or policies of any and all patent pools or licensing organizations having rights in respect of patents of *[name 1]* or foreign patents covering inventions of *[name 1]*, including without limiting the generality of the foregoing, *[list]*.

5. All documents referring or relating to the issuance or denial of any license to import or export under any foreign patent of *[name 1]*.

6. All documents relating to the assertion against *[name 2]* or others engaged in the manufacture or sale of *[describe]* in the United States of America, Canada or any other country of any foreign or domestic patents or patent rights owned or licensed by *[name 1]*.

7. All documents relating or referring to policies or practices of *[name 1]* or of any person having a right to extend licenses under any patent rights of *[name 1]* in the United States of America or any foreign country in respect of any actual or proposed license of the export or import of *[describe]*.

8. All documents relating or referring to any request or inquiry, by any person or company manufacturing or selling *[describe]*, for a license under some but less than all of

the patent rights owned by *[name 1]* or in which *[name 1]* has, or at any time during the life of the patent in suit has had, a beneficial interest.

9. All documents relating or referring to package licensing of *[name 1]* patent rights, together with all copies, drafts, and vouchers relating to the documents, and all other documents, letters, and paper writings whatsoever, that can or may afford any information or evidence in this cause. And this you shall not omit, under the penalty of the law in that case made and provided.

Dated: ________

[signature etc.]

§ 14:15 Request for subpoena

[Caption]

To: Clerk of the Court:

Please issue a Subpoena for *[name 1]* to appear as witness on behalf of *[name of party]* [at a deposition scheduled for *[time]* on *[date]*.

Dated: ________

[signature etc.]

Comment

Local rules may require a request for a subpoena. This form may be modified to conform to local requirements. Rule 45 permits the attorney for a party to issue a subpoena.

§ 14:16 Notice of taking deposition upon oral examination—Naming and describing person not a party

[Caption]

To: *[names]*

Please take notice that at *[time]* on *[date]*, at *[address]*, *[defendant] [plaintiff] [name 1]* will take the deposition upon oral examination of *[name 2]* before *[name 3]*, a notary public, or before some other officer authorized by law to take depositions. The oral examination will continue from day-to-day until completed. You are invited to attend and cross-examine.

The testimony will be recorded by *[sound] [sound and visual] [videotape] [stenographic means]*.

Dated: ________

[signature etc.]

§ 14:17 Notice of taking of deposition of witness—Including designation of materials in related subpoena duces tecum

[Caption]

To: *[names]*

Please take notice that at *[time]* on *[date]*, at *[address]*, *[defendant] [plaintiff] [name 1]* will take the deposition of *[name 2]*, of *[address]*, upon oral examination before *[name 3]*, a notary public, or before some other officer authorized by law to take depositions. The oral examination will continue from day-to-day until completed. You are invited to attend and cross-examine.

Attached is a designation of the materials to be produced upon the oral examination of *[name 2]*, pursuant to a subpoena duces tecum to be served upon that person.

The testimony will be recorded by *[sound] [sound and visual] [videotape] [stenographic means]*.

Dated: ________

[signature etc.]

§ 14:18 Notice of taking deposition of witness—Including reference to materials designated in attached subpoena

[Caption]

To: *[names]*

PLEASE TAKE NOTICE that pursuant to Rule 30 of the Federal Rules of Civil Procedure, *[defendant] [plaintiff] [name 1]* will take the deposition upon oral examination of *[name 2]* before a notary public on *[date]*, at *[time]*, and thereafter from day-to-day until completed, at *[address]*.

[Defendant] [Plaintiff] [name 1] requests that deponent bring to this deposition all documents described in the attached Addendum to Civil Subpoena.

The testimony will be recorded by *[sound] [sound and visual] [videotape] [stenographic means]*.

Dated: ________

[signature etc.]

Part IV

RESPONDING TO DISCOVERY OF ELECTRONICALLY STORED INFORMATION

Chapter 15

Responding to Discovery*

I. GUIDELINES

*(This chapter relies extensively on the Electronic Discovery Reference Model prepared by the Electronic Discovery Reference Model Project (http://www.edrm.net). Content is available free under the GNU Free Documentation License 1.2. Launched in May 2005, the Electronic Discovery Reference Model (EDRM) Project was created to address the lack of standards and guidelines in the electronic discovery market—a problem identified in the 2003 and 2004 Socha-Gelbmann Electronic Discovery surveys as a major concern for vendors and consumers alike. The completed reference model will provide a common, flexible and extensible framework for the development, selection, evaluation and use of electronic discovery products and services. The completed model was placed in the public domain in May 2006. Copyright 2005–2006. Socha Consulting LLC and Gelbmann & Associates. All rights reserved.

II. CHECKLISTS

III. FORMS

Research References

Treatises and Practice Aids

eDiscovery & Digital Evidence §§ 8:1 to 8:20

Trial Strategy

Recovery and Reconstruction of Electronic Mail as Evidence, 41 Am. Jur Proof of Facts 3d 1

Computer Technology in Civil Litigation, 71 Am. Jur Trials 111

Law Reviews and Other Periodicals

Allman & Brady, Can Random Access Memory Make Good Law, Nat'l L.J., Dec. 10, 2007, at E1

Boehning & Toal, Courts Consider When Cost-Shifting Is Appropriate, Nat'l L.J., Aug. 20, 2007, at S3

Kwuon & Wan, Stakes Higher than Ever for Attorney Missteps, Nat'l L.J., Dec. 10, 2007, at E2

Losey, Hash: The New Bates Stamp, 12 J. of Tech. L. & Policy 1 (2007).

Meyer & Wraspir, eDiscovery: Preparing Clients for (and Protecting Them Against) Discovery in the Electronic Information Age, 26 Wm. Mitchell L. Rev. 939 (2000)

Schwartz & Walden, Attorneys Should Never Forget Who Is Responsible: Vendors Can Take the Anxiety Out of Discovery, but Need Supervision, Nat'l L.J., Aug. 20, 2007, at S2

Additional References

Arnold, e-Discovery and Recovery for Microsoft Exchange, Elec. Disc. & Records Mgt. Q., winter 2007, at 10

Berman, Solving the Lotus Notes Discovery Puzzle, Elec. Disc. & Records Mgt. Q., spring 2008, at 8

Carpenter, Why Automated First Pass Review? Just Do the Math, Elec. Disc. & Records Mgt. Q., winter 2007, at 36

Feldman, Top Things to Do When Collecting Electronic Evidence, GP/Solo, March 2008, at 28

Gibbs, et al., The Data Preservation Data Collection Continuum, Elec. Disc. & Records Mgt. Q., winter 2007, at 5

Greenwood, Manhattan Work at Mumbai Prices, ABA J, Oct. 2007

Jacoby & Rogers, Melding Electronic and Hardcopy Documents into a Single Document Review, Elec. Disc. & Records Mgt. Q., winter 2007, at 30

Jenks, Globalization and Automated Discovery, Elec. Disc. & Records Mgt. Q., fall 2007, at 8

Karls, On the Digital Paper Trail: Using E-mail Analysis & Other Best Practices for Preliminary Internal Investigations, Elec. Disc. & Records Mgt. Q., summer 2007, at 5

Kassis, Prepare to Hear More Discovery Requests for Audio, Elec. Disc. & Records Mgt. Q., winter 2007, at 28

Mansperger, 10 Steps to Prepare for E-Discovery, AIIM-E-Doc Magazine, July/Aug. 2007, at 14

Paskach, Predictability and Consistency in eDiscovery, Metro. Corp. Counsel, Mar. 2007

Schleuter, Defusing the Audio Content Time Bomb—Audio Electronic Discovery Considerations, Elec. Disc. & Records Mgt. Q., fall 2007, at 5

Scholtes, How to Make E-Discovery and E-Disclosure Easier, AIIM E-Doc Magazine, July/Aug. 2007, at 24

Socha, E-Discovery Metrics: What They Are, Why They Matter, and What You Can Do with Them, Elec. Disc. & Records Mgt. Q., spring 2008, at 34

ABA Discovery Standards, http://www.abanet.org/litigation/discoverystandards/2005civildiscoverystandards.pdf
eDirect Impact, Inc., http://www.edirectimpact.com
Electronic Discovery Reference Model Project, http://www.edrm.net
Federal Judicial Center, http://www.fjc.gov
The Sedona Conference, http://www.thesedonaconference.org

KeyCite®: Cases and other legal materials listed in KeyCite Scope can be researched through the KeyCite service on Westlaw®. Use KeyCite to check citations for form, parallel references, prior and later history, and comprehensive citator information, including citations to other decisions and secondary materials.

I. GUIDELINES

§ 15:1 Generally

A response to an electronic discovery request is not that different from a response to a standard document request. The responding party must identify key internal personnel who may have relevant information, the types of documents or information that may be relevant, and the potentially relevant time period. Rule 34(a) allows the responding to search its records to produce the required, relevant data. Rule 34(a) does not give the requesting party the right to conduct the actual search.[1]

However, lawyers involved in producing their client's digital records in discovery may find the process daunting for any number of good reasons. Legal issues aside, unfamiliar technical terms and potential traps dominate the whole arena of electronic discovery. Even the most mundane aspects of electronic discovery appear to be the province of technical experts, often leaving the attorney's role seemingly subordinate to that of a technical consultant.

[Section 15:1]

[1]In re Ford Motor Co., 345 F.3d 1315, 56 Fed. R. Serv. 3d 438 (11th Cir. 2003); Palgut v. City of Colorado Springs, 2007 WL 4277564 (D. Colo. 2007).

In most productions of electronically stored information, the process of gathering and producing the information can be broken down into five basic procedural steps. The eight steps are as follows:

1. **Identifying.** Identify potentially relevant sources of electronically stored information, as well as legal, technical, or practical issues (including time and cost) that might impact the production.
2. **Preserving.** Preserve source media containing responsive electronically stored information.
3. **Collecting**
4. **Processing.** Process the electronically stored information from the preserved media to collect potentially responsive files, separate them from the "grossly" irrelevant and privileged materials, and otherwise prepare the electronically stored information for an organized, efficient review by counsel.
5. **Reviewing.** Review the electronically stored information resulting from the processing to determine the electronically stored information responsive material to the discovery request.
6. **Analyzing.**
7. **Producing.** Produce responsive electronically stored information and privilege logs.
8. **Presenting.**

While electronic discovery involves special problems, it should be kept in mind that the rules of civil discovery apply to electronic discovery as well as paper discovery. Accordingly, this chapter includes some forms applicable to electronic discovery and paper discovery.

§ 15:2 Using vendors and consultants

In selecting a vendor, the following matters should be considered

- Length of time vendor has been involved with applicable technology
- If vendor is selling technology, does the vendor own it or is owned by another source

- The vendor's training, education, certification, and professional memberships
- The vendor's policy on subcontracting and partnering
- Size of the vendor, including number of employees
- Client references
- Prior expert testimony experience and court opinions involving the vendor
- Warranties and errors and omissions insurance
- Physical location of the vendor
- Which of the vendor's personnel will be working on the project
- Experience with maintaining document integrity
- Amenability to escrowing any software code to guard against problems in the event the vendor is unable to perform

While vendors can take out some of the anxiety of discovery, they still need supervision. Demonstrating the accuracy and completeness of the process used by a vendor to collect and review the electronically stored information is critical in any litigation or investigation. The attorneys should never forget who is ultimately responsible.[1]

While there has been an increase in the use of off-shore (foreign) lawyers and organizations to assist with discovery of electronically stored information, the use is not without critics. An action was filed in the U.S. District Court for the District of Columbia seeking declaratory and injunctive relief in order to obtain a ruling about whether the electronic transmission of data from the United States to a foreign legal services provider waives Fourth Amendment protection with respect to data that are electroni-

[Section 15:2]

[1]Cf. Qualcomm Inc. v. Broadcom Corp., 2008 WL 66932 (S.D. Cal. 2008), vacated in part, 2008 WL 638108 (S.D. Cal. 2008); Rafael Town Center Investors, LLC v. The Weitz Company, LLC, 2007 WL 2261376 (N.D. Cal. 2007).

cally transmitted.[2] Contending that "foreign nationals who reside overseas lack Fourth Amendment protections" and that "the United States Government engages in pervasive surveillance of electronically transmitted data wherein one party to the transmission is a foreign national residing overseas," the action seeks declarations as to whether:

- A law firm's electronic transmission of client data will result in a waiver of Fourth Amendment protection;
- The electronic transmission of non-client data, such as data produced during discovery, will save Fourth Amendment protections to such data;
- Off-shore providers of legal services have an obligation to disclose the likelihood of Fourth Amendment waiver with respect to data electronically transmitted to foreign national residing overseas; and
- The president has an obligation to establish intelligence gathering protocols for the purpose of safeguarding Fourth Amendment rights regarding attorney communications to and from foreign nationals residing overseas.

Three bar committees (New York City, San Diego County, and Los Angeles County) have determined that lawyers may contract with foreign lawyers not admitted to practice in any jurisdiction in the United States, or with nonlawyers outside the United States, to perform legal work for U.S. clients. The opinions indicate that foreign legal outsourcing should be subject to the same ethical requirements as domestic use of nonlawyers. A U.S. lawyer must supervise the foreign lawyers' work, preserve client confidences, avoid conflicts, normally bill only for the direct cost of outsourcing, and obtain advance client consent in certain circumstances.

§ 15:3 Identifying—Generally

The identifying phase is used to determine the scope,

---

[2]Newman McIntosh & Hennessey, LLP v. Bush, Civil Action 1:08-cv-00787-CKK (D.D.C. 2008).

breadth, and depth of electronically stored information that can be pursued during discovery. Identification takes into consideration any claims and defenses, preservation demands, disclosure requirements, and discovery demands.

Electronically stored information should be identified and preserved as soon as possible after litigation is reasonably foreseeable, discovery has been initiated, or a preservation letter has been received.[1] Electronically stored information has tenuous grip on life. Such routine business practices as recycling backup tapes, purging old e-mail, or even turning computers on and off can alter or extinguish digital data. The tasks associated with identification are therefore those that should start immediately.

Identification involves a series of inquiries to assist in determining not only sources of potentially responsive records, but also to identify legal, technical, and practical issues that might impact the production of records—such things as nondisclosure agreements, or problems associated with electronically stored information that is not reasonably accessible. Finally, identification involves making an early determination of costs, which can be instrumental in limiting the scope of discovery or supporting efforts to share or shift costs of discovery.

Unlike paper records, which tend to be organized into files and stored in file cabinets, electronically stored information may be stored in a number of places—geographically and virtually, across different computers, network shares, and backup media. Determining just what electronically stored information may be responsive to discovery generally requires considering what sorts of records should or could exist. A useful way of to go about this is to consider potential sources from two directions:

[Section 15:3]

[1]See Sedona Principle 11 ("A responding party may satisfy its good faith obligation to preserve and produce relevant electronically stored information by using electronic tools and processes, such as data sampling, searching, or the use of selection criteria, to identify data reasonably likely to contain relevant information.").

1. What records does the organization produce (a business-function centered view); and
2. What records the organization's technology can produce (a technology-centered view).

The two views are complementary and together force a more complete analysis than either approach alone. In addition to the hard copy document search, at a minimum the following should be done to search for potentially relevant digital information:

It is insufficient to simply claim the organization has done a thorough search for electronically stored information in response to discovery requests. Producing counsel should have the person conducting the search execute an affidavit:

- stating that after diligent search there is no responsive electronically stored information in the organization's possession, custody or control;
- describing efforts to locate electronically stored information responsive to the requests at issue; and
- articulating the efforts the organization has taken to locate, retrieve, and restore the responsive electronic electronically stored information.

§ 15:4 Identifying—Business function

The business-function analysis focuses on the categories of electronically stored information the client generates or maintains in the ordinary course of business. When attempting to determine what responsive records the client has under the business function approach, the person conducting the identification might look for people analogous to traditional records custodians, but with respect to electronically stored information.

If it is known that certain employees could be key to litigation, or the discovery requests have focused on certain people, then inquiry should focus on how those individuals use computers. The following questions may be helpful in determining potentially responsive electronically stored information:

- What kind of work do you do?
- Do you use a computer for this work?
- Describe how you use your computer at work.
- How many computers do you use for your work?
- Do you use any home or personal computers for work?
- What is your level of computer expertise?

The questions are rather broad to encourage the employee to think about what records the employee may have and where the employee may have them.

§ 15:5 Identifying—Technology

The technological side of identification looks beyond the business function to consider the computer resources available to those within the organization or enterprise for the creation and storage of digital records. In this step of the process, the person conducting the identification attempts to understand the kinds of electronically stored information the client is capable of producing. Whereas the business function analysis asks what should have been created or stored digitally. For example, an office suite almost always contains programs permitting employees to create records not typically associated with a job function.

The technological analysis also encompasses considerations such as network capabilities and topology. It is important to understand that networks also can store information far from the source of the records. It is quite possible that the employees creating or maintaining records have no idea where the records might physically exist, since network storage can often appear as local hard drives to the person using the computers. Finally, the technology phase of identification requires consideration of the backup systems used by the organization.

§ 15:6 Identifying—Possible impediments to production

Having identified the potentially responsive electronically stored information, the organization party should begin to identify legal, technical, or practical issues that could complicate the production effort. Legal issues may include protection of trade secrets or third-party confidentiality agreements, such as non-disclosure agreements. Technical issues often include password protected files and legacy data on archaic computer platforms—issues that can make production prohibitively costly, and in some instances, even impossible. The organization should be prepared to justify in technical terms why it will be burdensome or technically infeasible to produce such electronically stored information.

Finally, simple practical issues, such as missing backup tapes or electronically stored information on home computers of recently terminated employees, can severely impede production or cause costs to creep up. By attending to such issues while identifying responsive electronically stored information, the organization can be prepared to address these issues.

§ 15:7 Identifying—Costs and time to complete production

The final task in the identification procedures is identifying the probable time and cost required to satisfy the discovery requests. Before actually working with the electronically stored information—restoring and reviewing data—it is unlikely the organization will know enough to anticipate every factor that might weigh in on cost and time. Nonetheless, making reasonable estimates of cost and time as soon as possible allows for timely discussion with the propounding party, or for motions, if necessary, before expending substantial costs or time.

§ 15:8 Preserving—Generally

Preservation refers to taking protective custody of electronically stored information for potential evidentiary purposes. Preservation ensures that electronically stored information is protected from destruction or alteration. It is a complicated, multi-faceted concept. It begins with the determination of when the duty to preserve arises and continues into the litigation hold process. Assessment of the preservation task involves identification of those groups of potentially relevant materials that will be most critical or most difficult to preserve or collect. Those will be driven by the issues and priorities of the individual case.

Preservation can take many forms, from evidentiary copies prepared by a forensic professional to simply taking custody of a laptop or backup tapes. Typically preservation should focus on preserving media—hard drives, floppy disks, and backup tapes, for example—rather than particular files, folders, or other forms of electronically stored information. Preserving media, as opposed to preserving just the electronically stored information that appears responsive initially, preserves not only the potentially responsive electronically stored information, but also files and other information that could become important as discovery progresses. Preserving media also preserves other data, such as metadata or deleted material, that could be used later to corroborate or authenticate the electronically stored information produced.

The burden of preservation can be ameliorated if full opportunity is taken to discuss the matter during the discovery conference. A collaborative approach to discovery, and preservation in particular, can reduce the costs of electronic discovery for the benefit of all parties.

Preservation does not mean an organization must later agree to produce evidence. By preserving electronically stored information, the organization is only insuring the information will be available if it is later determined it is relevant or discoverable. If it is later determined the organization should have preserved the information but did not, sanctions could be imposed for spoliation.

§ 15:9 Preserving—Technical assistance

Some preservation issues may require an immediate implementation of hard drive mirror imaging for key players by a forensic expert. Other issues may involve isolation of access from certain segments of the organization's systems until collection can occur. The assistance of the information technology department may be needed to suspend some operations or re-route certain tasks to different servers. Failing to engage the needed technical support can be a costly mistake.

§ 15:10 Preserving—Archive media

Special consideration should be given to archive media, such as backup tapes. Typically, system administrators will only maintain a limited quantity of backup tapes, and then reuse them on a scheduled cycle—known as tape rotation. When discovery demands request electronically stored information that may be on backup tapes, the organization should ensure that all relevant backup tapes are pulled out of service and stored in a safe place, preferably in the custody of someone who can later establish a chain of custody for authentication purposes.

§ 15:11 Collecting—Generally

Collecting involves gathering potentially relevant electronically stored information from various sources, such as tapes, dries, portable storage devices, and networks before reviewing the information. The preserving and collecting phases can sometimes overlap. In addition, the collecting of electronically stored information will provide feedback for the identification function which may effect and expand identified content.

Electronically stored information should be collected in a manner that is comprehensive, maintains its content integrity, and preserves its form. Metadata should be collected and maintained during the collection process. In addition, information regarding chain of custody and authentication is frequently required.

§ 15:12 Collecting—Planning

Proper planning of the search strategy is essential to the overall effectiveness of collection. In planning, it is necessary to first determine where the electronically stored information is. All knowledgeable persons must be included in the planning process.

§ 15:13 Collecting--Security

At the beginning of the collection effort, appropriate steps must be taken to preserve the content of electronically stored information. This includes ensuring that procedures are in place to preserve privileged or work product from other information collected and produced. All electronically stored information collected must be secured by the collection agent in a manner that prohibits unauthorized access to the information, and tracks all attempts to access the information.

§ 15:14 Collecting—Scope

Relevant electronically stored information must be collected from each person or custodian deemed part of the appropriate collection. Costs and benefits must be weighed to determine what is appropriate and reasonable for the litigation. The three primary categories of electronically stored information capable of being collected are: fixed storage, portable storages, and third-party hosted storage environments not under direct control of the information owner.

§ 15:15 Collecting—Methodology

Each type of data storage requires a different strategy and approach. For example fixed storage may use manual copying. This involves copying selected files and/or directories, then pasting them to a network folder or CD. The quality of data from the manual copy method is completely dependent on the operator performing the search. Active data copying may be used to capture all the "active data" on a media. However, this method fails to capture "inactive data." The forensic image process creates a mirror image copy of a medium so that both active and inactive data sets are maintained.

The most commonly used search methodology is the

keyword search. A keyword search is a set-based search using simple words or word combinations, with or without Boolean and related operators. Courts have generally accepted keyword searches.[1] However, because of the difficulty of doing a proper keyword search, an electronic evidence expert should be involved throughout the process. Statistical sampling can be used to determine the validity of keywords and the accuracy of the search. Because of the cost and volume of may searches, it is prudent for the parties to discuss in advance the parameters of the search and the set of keywords to be used.[2]

A keyword search is particularly appropriate where the inquiry focuses on finding particular documents and the use of language is relatively predictable. However, keyword searches do not reflect context. They can also miss documents containing a word that has the same meaning as the term used in the query but is not specified. Misspelled words may be missed in a keyword search.

Conceptual search methods relying on semantic relations between words and using a thesaurus to capture documents that would be missed in keyword searching. A concept search attempts to locate information relating to a desired concept without the presence of a particular word or phrase.

§ 15:16 Processing—Generally

The processing of electronically stored information involves the accommodation of a wide variety of unstructured data. It must handle each form in a manner appropriate to its file type, and generate output that is

---

[Section 15:15]

[1]See, e. g., Zubulake v. UBS Warburg LLC, 229 F.R.D. 422, 94 Fair Empl. Prac. Cas. (BNA) 1, 85 Empl. Prac. Dec. (CCH) P 41728 (S.D. N.Y. 2004).

[2]See Treppel v. Biovail Corp., 233 F.R.D. 363 (S.D. N.Y. 2006) (where plaintiff would not agree to keyword search terms, defendant was justified in using keyword search terms to find responsive documents and should have proceeded unilaterally).

structured in accordance with review requirements often varying with client needs and review technology specifications. The principal objective is preparing relevant files for efficient and expedient review, production, and subsequent use.

Processing reduces the overall set of data collected by setting aside files that are duplicates or not relevant. Processing involves culling the potentially relevant electronically stored information that may be on a hard drive or backup tape from the vast amount of irrelevant information, such as the thousands of files that make up modern operating systems and applications. The purpose of processing is to reduce the amount of information that will have to be reviewed for privilege or responsiveness. Typically processing pays for itself many times over in reducing the amount of electronically stored information reviewers will have to look at before producing the information.

Processing also includes identifying duplicate files, creating records of MD5 Hash values, which are unique numerical values calculated for each record and can be used to quickly determine whether files are exactly identical or whether a particular file has changed over time. Finally, processing includes segregating files based on categories of type—such as documents, e-mail, presentation, accounting data, as well as eliminating all file types known to be irrelevant, such as executables, or music files.

By inserting Bates numbers, files can be more easily tracked over time and movement—it is not unusual for files to have similar, if not identical, names but different content. Digital Bates numbering guarantees that the numbered files can be accurately identified not only as they move through processing, facilitating auditing, but also as they are produced in discovery and later used in pretrial proceedings and in trial.

It may be help to convert electronically stored information from the form in which it is found to one allowing a more effective and efficient review to be conducted. An organization may retain electronic evidence or forensics computing consultants to conduct the processing. However, unlike the preservation stage, the processing phase can be done by competent technical staff using commercially available software.

§ 15:17 Processing—Pre-planning

Pre-planning is an important part of managing processing of electronically stored information. Decisions made in identifying, preserving, and collecting electronically stored information dictate some of the requirements and activities that must be conducted during the processing phase. The schedule for review and the technologies used to review the electronically stored information influence the way the information must be processed.

§ 15:18 Processing—Specifications

Processing specifications drive the scope and therefore the timeframe and cost of processing and reviewing electronically stored information. At the discovery conference, agreement should be reached not only on what electronically stored information is to be processed, but also on what the input and output format of that information will be.

Options for output from files include the following:

- Metadata associated with the file
- Searchable text contained in the file
- The native file itself
- A rendering or image of the file

Processing specifications can aid reviewers by providing fielded information that can be used as a first pass at tagging and coding data. Appropriate specifications can save the review time, and consequently costs.

Technological solutions assist in the culling data through suppression of duplicates (deduplication), filtering of documents based on their attributes (metadata) such as date ranges, file types, and key words, phrases, and concepts. The choice of culling options to be used will direct assumptions regarding how much of the electronically stored information collected will be segregated before review, affecting later processing and reviewing costs.

§ 15:19 Processing—Stages

Electronically stored information can be received by an electronic discovery processing team in a number of forms, including various media or electronic transmissions. Because electronically stored information may be used as evidence, it must be authenticated before being admitted at trial, making a carefully documented chain of custody essential. Upon receipt, the electronically stored information must be tracked and managed on both a physical and a file level.

Once the electronically stored information is received, properly accounted for, and document, the information must be restored to a computer system environment for processing. It is important to isolate the source data before putting it onto an active network or processing platform until the viability of the data has been determined.

§ 15:20 Processing—Quality control

Quality control must occur throughout the entire processing phase. To ensure both technical correct result as well as deliver the review teams expected result, it is best to employ a combination of automated and manual quality controls.

Automated controls provide a consistently applied methodology to check for many important aspects of electronic discovery. Automation tools can be used to flag files containing a disproportionately high number of binary characters or size thresholds. Once the files are flagged, they can be subject to visual inspection as the remainder of the collection is processed, then integrated back into the collection. Automation can also be used for file count checks at each stage of the process to account for all data, and to check that fielded information I in conformity with field types.

Manual controls are important to ensure a review team receives an appropriate result. Visual inspection is an example of a manual control. Other manual controls include exception handling. Because source data is unstructured data and not all electronic files run through an automated process, there is some level of exception handling. Exception handling includes password cracking or manipulation of the file to ensure proper rendering of the file as an image. In data collections with a larger percentage of corrupted data, more visual inspection may be needed to ensure that the imaged data is a faithful representation of the original data.

§ 15:21 Processing—Data conversion

After the search strategies have been implemented, the documents may be staged for review in accordance with the instructions of the legal team. An organization has a number of options available, ranging from reviewing electronically stored information in its original native format to review materials in quasi-paper forms such as TIFF or PDF.

Instead of converting electronic documents to images before review, the initial review can be conducted in the native format of the electronically stored information. In order to accommodate native review, many service and software processing providers have developed technologies to provide reviewers the ability to review native files after the metadata has been preserved and linked to the document.

§ 15:22 Processing—Reporting

Reporting is an important control that can be exercised throughout the processing phase. Information about processing can be extremely valuable in establishing a review strategy. If a service provided is used, the provider should be asked:

- What reports or information is available from the system in place?
- How frequently are those reports produced?
- Does the organization or its lawyers have immediate access to important project information?

Reports will provide both the organization and the service provider with the information necessary to communicate effectively and to manage the project.

Media analysis reports typically include information regarding the number of files contained on a given piece of media, the type of files contained on the media, and the size of the electronically stored information contained on the media. Custodian level reports provide data volume by custodian. Chain of custody reports begin at the time the information is collected. Once the information on the media has been uploaded to the computer network, file level reporting begins.

When files are not returned to the organization, data culling reports provide a means for the organization to ensure that all electronically stored information has been handled properly. Deduplication reports include the name of the file, the location path of the file, as well as information regarding other instances of the same file. Search and filter reports contain similar file level information as name and path location, and they also contain specific information regarding the reason the file was segregated, as well as to which search term or piece of metadata information the file was responsive. Search reports can also contain analysis regarding the search terms, the number of files responsive to the search, and the number of times those terms were contained within the files.

Status reports provide information regarding how quickly data collect is progressing through the automated process. They are a good way to track the progress of the data set being processed, so that if any anomalies arise requiring a change in the delivery schedule, all the appropriate parties are informed as soon as possible. Status reports can also be used to refine cost estimates.

Exception reports provide file name and location information regarding files that cannot be rendered to image or viewed as a native file, or files containing passwords that could not be overcome. Custom reports on the electronically stored information may be necessary to validate or refute different theories.

§ 15:23 Processing—Evaluating

Once the actual review of the electronically stored information commences, the organization begins to get a real sense for what issues and topics are revealed within the information. The review team may consider it appropriate to request additional documents from the existing custodian list or may add custodians to the list. The changing parameters of custodian lists and priorities based one valuations of reviewed material can have a significant effect on the processing phase.

The purpose of evaluation is to provide an understanding of the information requested for processing. The evaluation report should clearly describe what and how much media and/or files were evaluated and provide the context and purpose behind the evaluation. It should clearly detail the methodology used to perform the evaluation by describing the process steps taken to create the evaluation. Any conclusions reached in the evaluation should be justified.

§ 15:24 Processing—Audit and chain of custody

An effective chain of custody requires a set of procedures that are actually followed. The procedures should be in writing and the steps should be documented. The entire process must be taken into consideration. Restricting the number of persons who touch the evidence helps avoid handling errors and mistakes. In addition, the software used to handle the electronically stored information to handle the data should have appropriate reporting and audit capabilities.

The collection team should be trained in computer forensics in or to insure that the collection process is done according to forensic protocols so that all electronically stored information collected is properly preserved and no harm is done to the computer.

As soon after collection as is practicable, the electronic discovery provider must take physical custody of the evidence. Following its written procedure, the person responsible for logging the evidence collection should be given custody of it immediately, and the evidence logged in. Whenever the original evidence is accessed, it should only be accessed by the team in charge of logging and securing the evidence. Any activities involving the original evidence should be logged.

When the evidence is physically collected, the collection should be documented by having the collector sign a form indicating:

- The date
- The time
- The name of the person from whom the evidence was collected
- A description of the items collected including unique identifiers

A copy of the form should be provided as a receipt to the person or organization from whom the evidence was collected.

As soon as practicable after logging it, the original evidence should be forensically copied using a copying tool that does not change the electronically stored information in any way. It is important to use only software and hardware tools certified for non-intrusive duplication.

As soon as possible after collection, using a non-destructive hashing tool, an MD5 hash should be obtained from the media. This hash is a unique electronic fingerprint allowing others to verify that the original evidence was not altered from that point forward and that duplicates of the media are truly identical.

§ 15:25 Processing—Culling, prioritizing, and triage

Culling and searching occur throughout the discovery process. Culling is the process of programmatically removing irrelevant content while searching is the process of identifying content that is most likely relevant and will require review. When developing a culling and searching strategy, the objective should be to identify the most relevant content first and move it to the review team. Even after collection and culling, the volume and types of electronically stored information can be overwhelming.

Even with excellent culling techniques, the electronically stored information needs to be further evaluated to further understand the information to further eliminate the electronically stored information, identify future challenges, and process certain electronically stored information. A critical analysis of the types of files in the collection can aid in understanding even the largest collections.

§ 15:26 Processing—Searching

Searching may be used to determine what electronically stored information is collected. It may be used within a review tool to prioritize workflow, and used during processing as a means to both cull and flag electronically stored information before review. Search terms to be applied to a given collection of electronically stored information are typically determined by the legal term with approval of the opposing party. The goal of the list of search terms is to narrow the dataset to include all relevant documents and segregate documents that are not responsive. Searches may be conducted using keywords, Boolean terms, proximity operators, and concepts.

When documents are removed during the culling phase based on criteria established by the review team or negotiated with the opposing party, they should only be suppressed from review. They should still be accessible if needed later.

§ 15:27 Processing—Cost drivers

Because the cost of processing electronically stored information for electronic discovery can be tremendous, determining which party should bear this cost can be very important. The volume and composition of the dataset is a driving element in the cost of electronic discovery. The discovery team should be cautioned about the impact decisions made in the preservation, identification, and collection phases of electronic discovery have on processing and reviewing documents.

§ 15:28 Reviewing—Generally

Reviewing involves evaluating the electronically stored information for such matters as relevance and privilege. The quantity of electronically stored information makes reviewing printouts of the information largely impractical. Organizations can save time and actually achieve greater accuracy by using computers to review electronically stored information. Unfortunately, relying on the computer is not without problems—the most frequently encountered problem is the lack of programs to open electronically stored information.

This problem is often easily addressed by installing what is known as viewing software—software allowing one to open a large number of data files from most of the common applications. Improving on the simple file viewing approach, an indexing search utility application can be added. A number of vendors are marketing products combining the viewer and index search tools, and including a database to maintain information regarding the reviewers' notes and decisions about whether to produce or withhold particular records.

§ 15:29 Reviewing—Planning

At early as practicable a determination should be made of what is to be reviewed, how it is to be reviewed, and what is the intended outcome. A discovery conference can be very helpful in making these decisions. In addition, the discovery order may direct what electronically stored information is to be collected and reviewed.

While the scope of the review is usually dictated by the discovery request or order, a helpful strategy is to control the scope of review through the use of technology or other aids. These techniques should be discussed at the discovery conference. There should be clear documentation of the key issues and a distinction between issues of fact and issues of law.

A coding manual may be prepared to define not only the objectives of the review, but the rules for the review team. A coding manual may include rules for addition additional bibliographic information to the data base, publication of a look-up table to assist in identifying key players and known entities, rules for identifying and coding privilege documents, and rules for identifying and tagging nonresponsive documents.

Determining the form for the review should also be established during the initial planning stages. A review may take many forms and utilize several different formats: manual paper review; internal review using an in-house review system; internal review using a hosted online system; external review using temp attorneys set-up in a war room with the necessary review tools. The nature and needs of the matter as well as the following factors will help determine the format of the review:

- Agreements made by counsel during the discovery conference, or ordered by the court
- Time and cost constraints for the project
- How the documents were collected
- Training required by each member of the review team
- Available resources to support different formats

A paralegal or junior level attorney may go through the repository to identify records known not to be relevant to the matter, suppressing them from further review, or deleting them from the database altogether. They may engage the help of a litigation support specialist or electronic discovery vendor to automate the identification of known irrelevant documents so that the reviewers do not have to examine every single document having all the attributes as those previously identified as irrelevant.

After culling, suppressing irrelevant documents, and providing the necessary indexing to the document repository, the review team addresses the task of reviewing documents that need to be produced, (or that have been produced by opposing parties). In a large repository with several reviewers, this task is often divided in a logical way in order to meet case management deadlines.

If information on key issues and players has been developed, the review team can capture documents relating to key players and known issues in the case. Look-up tables can be developed to aid the reviewer to quickly pick from a list of options. Key players may also be identified by the bibliographic coding staff if they are asked to capture all names in a document.

Regardless of who conducts the review or the review techniques, the goal of the review is a consistent result in which responsive or privileged documents are correctly assigned. Constant sampling and quality control review during the process is essential.

§ 15:30 Reviewing—Selecting a vendor

There are many factors that need to be considered when selecting a third-party vendor for the review portion of electronic discovery. The vendor requirements should be determined during the initial planning phases of the project. Considerations when selecting a vendor include the financial condition and longevity of the firm to the breadth of their services, the methodologies behind their technical processing and the experience of their project managers. The first and foremost consideration when selecting a vendor is to assure that you have a clear understanding of the goals and objectives of the review:

A critical decision in the vendor selection process is determining whether to perform an in-house review, that is, using an application that is loaded and supported within the organization's internal network, or if using an online or Web-based review tool with hosting provided by a third-party vendor. Software vendors have developed off-the-shelf solutions that litigation firms can leverage instead of trying to build the solutions themselves. The top in-house litigation support systems all have their pros and cons. It is essential that each firm carefully select the system best suited for the type of litigation the firm handles the most.

Most electronic discovery vendors provide the ability to perform your review in a TIFF or PDF format, and several vendors also provide a review platform that allows you to convert the data to an image (TIFF/PDF), but also keep a link to the data in its native format, if native format review is desired. Vendors who offer review within the native format must retain the integrity of the native file so that the review does not cause any spoliation of the underlying native file.

The features and functionality provided by the review platform is probably the most important factor when selecting a vendor. Frequently, a matrix defining the essential requirements can be used when comparing vendors and can greatly simplify the decision making process.

The vendor must be able to meet the production requirements as determined by the organization's overall strategy. Most vendors can produce TIFFs or PDFs, but some productions now require native productions or load files for litigation support databases such as Concordance or Summation. If that is the case, it is necessary to fully understand the capabilities of the vendor around generating native documents.

§ 15:31 Reviewing—Managing the process

The review system should allow the organization effectively to manage and report on the review team and document set. The reports should be produced daily, or even better, a dynamic report generated through the administrative function in the system.

The first step is to designation of a lead attorney to manage the review. Choosing an attorney to act as the project manager responsible for the day-to-day review process is critical to the success of the review. The lead attorney must be knowledgeable about the facts and issues of the matter and should have experience with similar types of review projects. In addition, the lead attorney must be comfortable with the technology to be used on the project.

A number of variables determine the makeup of the review team, such as the volume of data, the time in which the review must be completed, and the budget allotted to the review by the client. Additionally, logistical issues often will require consideration. Some firms are able to maintain standing review facilities for large projects. Others rely on outsourced facilities to be able to staff larger projects. Finally, the complexity of the matter may play a role in how a firm decides to staff an electronic document review.

Training the review team probably is the most important component of a successful review. Coordinated, well thought out training of the team with regard to both the specifics of the matter and the technology being used is critical to ensuring efficiency and accuracy. Unless all members of the review team fully understand the expectations, the technology and the overall goals of the project, the review likely will be inefficient or even incomplete.

The lead attorney should conduct a team meeting as soon as possible to discuss case issues, explain in detail the information to be captured or coded during the review, and provide a brief overview of the technology that will be used. A coding manual that can be used as a reference tool by the team throughout the project should be distributed and reviewed at the meeting. This document must be updated throughout the course of the review as new issues arise, or the requirements of the review shift.

Some of the information discussed at the initial meeting and covered n the manual includes:

- Specifics of the document request
- Facts or issues at issue in the matter
- Codes being used to define issues in the matter
- Privilege
- Confidentiality
- Hot or key documents that may need to be identified
- Documents requiring redaction based on privileges or confidentiality that may apply

Technical training must be specific to the technology and tools being used and should include detailed information about the interface design and functionality. The vendor or consultant retained often will provide a day or two of onsite training. If not, Web-based training sessions can be conducted by the provider of the review platform. If an in-house solution is to be used, the law firm should be prepared to provide adequate training on the use and functionality of that tool. The lead attorney should use all of the tools that are available to make the review as efficient and effective as possible and make sure the review team is adequately trained to take advantage of these tools.

Depending on the needs of the case, a centralized location for the review may be set-up. It is equally acceptable for the review team to work remotely or within their individual offices although this may require a greater need for internal communication protocols. In any case, the review environment should be well lit, be free of distracting outside noise, and be positioned so that no unrelated foot traffic runs through the area.

The review environment also should include appropriate computer technology that allows the review to be completed with a minimum of technical distractions, such as slow connections or software glitches. In order to ensure that technology supports the workflow and does not distract from it, it is helpful if the lead attorney identify and designate a lead technology support person early in the planning process. Additionally, vendor/consultant contact information for technology support should be obtained and disseminated to the review team.

The technology lead should be involved in the initial planning process, ensure that the hardware and software needed for the review are correctly installed, and that all systems have been tested before the review begins. In this age of increasingly managed computing environments at law firms, the technology lead should work to ensure during the planning process that the review team will be able to access the full functionality of the review tool from the firm's computing environment. Once these issues are addressed and the review has started, the technology lead should be readily available to address any hardware or software problems that may occur as the review progresses. The technology lead also may act as the primary liaison between the review team, the firm's IT department and the vendor/consultant if technology issues arise.

Even though the review may be conducted on-line, the

reviewer still needs an adequate work space with appropriate desk area to spread out reference material, sample documents, etc. Reference material all should be contained in a three ring notebook to keep the information consolidated and allow for easy updates. Similarly, if a centralized location is used, a white board should be available in the room to allow for posting of new rules, items of interest and other hot topics to facilitate communication.

As reviewers become more familiar with the document set, each will begin to see emerging patterns in the collection that may affect the determination of relevance and privilege. It is important that knowledge gained by one reviewer be shared as quickly and easily as possible with the entire team. While this can be done via e-mail, instant messaging and with daily team meetings, an easy way to facilitate effective information sharing is to locate the entire team (or as much of it as possible) in a single work area. In that way, team members can freely discuss and review not only new insights into the document collection, but also unexpected problems that arise as the review progresses.

It is important to determine as early as possible whether after hours technical support will be needed. The review team may need to work multiple shifts or extra hours in order to complete a review that has a short timeframe for completion. If this is the case, then the technical lead should establish a contact protocol that allows the review team to obtain support as quickly as possible after normal business hours. Depending upon the specific needs of the review team, this protocol might include a cell phone or pager number to provide more immediate access to the project or technical lead. The specific limits of after hour support should be established in writing and understood by all involved.

Monitoring and measuring the productivity of the review process and the review team itself is another critical factor in assuring that the team is progressing in a timely and effective manner. Reporting requirements for which metrics are tracked and how they are tracked should be determined before the review begins.

The review platform should allow reviewers to mark a document for further review when they are unsure about how to code it. This ensures that reviewers are not forced to make an uninformed decision. They also should be able to easily revisit a document and change the coding in the event that it becomes clear that their original decision was not correct, although sometimes the review tool and/or workflow make this difficult.

The review platform should also be customizable enough to allow for quality control restrictions that can be applied to families of documents such as threaded e-mails and attachments. For example, the protocol of the review might be that if any e-mail attachment is considered privileged, then that makes the whole family group (e-mail and attachments) privileged. If such protocols do exist they should be captured and executed automatically by the software to ensure consistency.

To guarantee uniform results from the review team and ensure that deadlines can be met, some form of quality control monitoring and reporting will be needed throughout the entire review lifecycle. Quality control monitoring may include a second-level review of all or a percentage of the documents in the review collection. Second-level review is performed by more experienced attorneys who are very familiar with the matter under review. This typically is done with regard to documents coded as privileged. In many law firms, all documents initially deemed privileged are reviewed by at least one, if not two, highly experienced attorneys.

In addition to or in lieu of a second-level review, the lead attorney may randomly review the team's coding to check for inconsistent application of the review protocol. Both of these steps provide for validation of coding decisions and can bring to light inconsistent coding patterns that then can be addressed with the entire review team. Both should be done on a daily basis in order to identify problems with the review process or with an individual reviewer's understanding of the process.

Electronic discovery costs can carry enormous consequences for clients regardless of their size. A large publicly traded corporation may face negative investor reaction if such costs are large enough to become a reportable event on an SEC Form 10-Q or Form 10-K filing. Small start-up companies may face a loss of venture capitalist funding and risk the ability to continue business operations. The consequences for an individual facing an expensive electronic discovery project may include bankruptcy or, in the event of a criminal prosecution, the need to weigh personal finances against the potential for prison time.

It is incumbent on counsel to maintain tight control of costs at every step of the discovery process, including the review phase. It also is appropriate for counsel to expect and demand that the electronic discovery vendors and consultants retained on behalf of the client play an active and responsible role in cost containment. In many cases, the vendor/consultant has the most immediate view into the progress and costs related to a project.

If the review is dynamic such that new data is being processed and uploaded into the review tool over time, or if productions are taking place on a rolling basis, a schedule should be established with the vendor/consultant to provide periodic reports of costs to date. It also is important to obtain immediate notification of any unanticipated costs even before the work is done. It often can be the case that an unexpected cost will require rethinking the parameters of the project. One of the most important things to avoid is the surprise bill to the client.

§ 15:32 Reviewing—Technologies

A well-planned, thoughtful approach to the review process, a careful and thorough examination of an appropriate vendor, and efficient management can result in overall time and cost savings. Utilizing technologies that group like documents together can also enable a more targeted, accurate and efficient review—all of which can ultimately translate into significant cost savings to the responding party.

Document review platforms have undergone many

technological enhancements over the past several years. New technologies to improve the efficiency and accuracy of the review process are appearing everyday from fuzzy searching to concept searching, near-dupes, visualization and social network analysis.

§ 15:33 Reviewing—Privileges

To assist in privilege review, searches can be conducted for names of attorneys or law firms, indicating a high probability of the result set being privileged communications. The documents meeting the privileged search criteria may be assigned to an attorney whose responsibility it is to review for privilege and mark the documents.

In order to reduce the scope and cost of discovery and reduce the cost of privilege review, Fed. R. Civ. P. 26(b)(5) was amended in 2006 to expressly allow "quick peek" agreements. A quick peek agreement involves the purposeful disclosure of information, without intending to waive a claim of privilege, with an express reservation of rights to assert privilege at a later point in the discovery process. Properly handled a quick peek can:

- Protect electronically stored information from being altered or destroyed
- Control what metadata the opposing party can examine
- Mark electronically stored information for further review and production
- Protect electronically stored information from inappropriate use

§ 15:34 Analyzing—Generally

Analysis involves evaluation collected electronically stored information to determine relevant summary information, such as key topics, important people, specific vocabulary and jargon, and important individual documents. The information may be useful before a detailed review is conducted to help with important early decisions and to improve the productivity of all remaining electronic discovery activities. Analysis is performed throughout the process as new information is uncovered and issues of the case evolve.

§ 15:35 Analyzing—Techniques and tools

The most basic and commonly available tool of analysis is search, which is used to find documents according to various selection criteria. In general a good search tool should have most or all of these capabilities:

- Multiple fields
- A complete set of query operators
- Relevance ranking
- Exhaustive queries
- Sorting
- Stemming or lemmatization
- Performance
- Derived metadata

§ 15:36 Analyzing—Pitfalls

It is critical that electronic discovery be viewed as an iterative process. Simply performing search and collection once or twice up front seldom proves sufficient, and further collections are generally warranted throughout the discovery effort. Assumptions concerning date ranges made early in the analysis phase can be wrong, in that certain key dates may have been unknown or incorrect. Assumptions made concerning keywords, phrases and concepts of interest may have been incomplete. As analysis yields results, new keywords, phrases and concepts, and in some cases new custodians of interest are added to the scope of the investigation, requiring re-searching of the original (or a subset thereof) dataset. Failure to employ an iterative process can lead to an incomplete set of evidence which could, of course, jeopardize the case.

When processing, analyzing and reviewing documents from a variety of data sources and representing e-mail, spreadsheets, documents, database content and the like, it is very easy to make invalid assumptions that metadata types are consistent across all electronically stored information.

Any time technology is used for electronic discovery purposes, understanding what is happening 'behind the scenes' is critical. Operators need to understand each tool extremely well. Moreover, operators need to understand the complement of analytical tools that they are using as a whole. Failure to understand the tools in use could lead to loss of data; corruption or alteration of data; missed data and overall risk to your case.

§ 15:37 Producing—Generally

Production can occur in a number of situations:

- Delivering electronically stored information to various recipients, such as law firms, corporate legal departments, and service providers.
- Delivering electronically stored information for use in other systems, such as automated litigation support systems, and Web-based repositories.
- Delivering electronically stored information on various media, such as CDs, DVDs, tape, hard drives, portable storage devices, and paper.

At one time it was common for the producing party to print and Bates number all electronically stored information—thus producing the records on printout forms. A number of factors now make this a less acceptable procedure. Most notably, one faces the challenge of the sheer quantity of electronically stored information. It simply is not economical to print out millions upon millions of pages.

Another factor that weighs against the printed-out production is that electronically stored information may not print-out satisfactorily. E-mail is a good example: while it is quite easy to print out a message, it becomes more problematic to print-out an e-mail with attachments. On the other hand, the producing party may prefer to produce in a mode that does not disclose metadata.

In general, it is far more economical to produce electronically stored information in digital form. In some instances that parties may prefer to convert the electronically stored information to a common format, such as TIFF or PDF. The alternative, and usually more cost effective, as well as accurate, mode of production is to produce in native format. Producing electronically stored information digitally may give the producing party a technical, rather than legal, basis to share costs with the party seeking discovery.

§ 15:38 Producing—Negotiation considerations

Negotiations about the form in which the production of documents by all parties will be made should have taken place by the time documents are being prepared to be produced. The intent of the Federal Rules of Civil Procedure is that parties will discuss and plan for the production of documents in the initial stages of the litigation. From a practical standpoint, the determination or agreement about the form of production must be made at the initial stages of the electronic discovery process to ensure the chosen form is still an option after the collection, processing, and review is complete.

In order to successfully negotiate the form of production, a few factors should be considered. Questions to consider during negotiations include:

- How will paper documents be produced?
- What types of electronic documents make up the data set?
- What formats for the production documents provide access to the electronically stored information necessary to best address issues in the case?
- What types of media should be used to produce and receive production documents?

While negotiating with other parties about how electronically stored information will be produced, there are factors that must be considered by each party's internal legal team that will impact the negotiations with other parties, including:

- Will a third party service provider, outside counsel's

litigation support department or the in-house litigation support department handle the technical work?
- What technical formats for the electronically stored information will be needed by each party?

Unless there is an expectation of and vehicle for communication between the parties about production issues, each party will be reacting to the unexpected throughout the discovery process, rather than planning for and managing the production and receipt of electronically stored information. During negotiations and throughout the discovery process, communication between representatives from each party with technical knowledge about the electronically stored information of the party they represent will make the production process more efficient and, therefore, less costly in time and money.

If metadata is an issue in the lawsuit, the organization should consider consulting with a forensics expert as early as possible in the lawsuit. Experts will most likely be called upon to validate and interpret the metadata and the earlier the expert is involved the better to prevent the loss or oversight of vital data. If the nature of the litigation makes specific metadata fields important, there should be a conference to identify all the possible metadata fields based on the actual data, determine the factors that may influence the content of that metadata.

One of the key issues to determine and negotiate early in a case is whether the documents' metadata is considered an integral part of the case. This will impact how the documents are collected and reviewed. However, if the documents have been collected or reviewed in a manner that altered metadata, the form of the production may be impacted.

If metadata is considered an issue in the case then two forms of production are options—native file or image format with extracted data, including metadata and the full text of the file. If metadata is not an issue in the case, then there may be more options as to the form of production and whether any of the metadata fields will be produced. Typically, a party should be prepared to produce in the same format in which the party requests to receive documents.

A rolling production is a negotiated schedule for producing data in stages rather than all at once. It should be negotiated in circumstances where a party has a lot of information that has to be reviewed and produced in a short timeframe.

Negotiations should address production media types including, CD, DVD, hard drive, and Web hosted. A Web-hosted production is one in which the documents are hosted by either a third party or an extranet site that is negotiated between the parties. This may be a good option to provide security and control of all the documents (e.g. production to a regulatory agency) or in a class action with multiple parties receiving the same data. Another benefit is that costs for hosting the documents could be shared between parties. In this scenario, the documents can be hosted, each party has secure and separate log-in access to the data sets being produced to them, and the receiving parties can review and designate the documents they want and the format in which they will receive the documents.

§ 15:39 Producing—Form

Absent party agreement or court order specifying the form or forms of production, production should be made in the form or forms in which the information is ordinarily maintained or in a reasonably usable form, taking into account the need to produce reasonably accessible metadata enabling the receiving party to have the same ability to access, search, and display the information as the producing party where appropriate or necessary in light of the nature of the information and the needs of the case.[1] There are four basic forms of production for electronically stored information:

[Section 15:39]

[1]Sedona Principle 12.

- Paper
- Quasi-paper, which is essentially paper in electronic form, such as TIF files and PDF files, often with associated metadata and full text
- Quasi-native form, such as an IBM AS400 database produced as an ASCII, comma-delimited file with associated file and field structural information
- Native, where the electronic information is produced as it is maintained and used

Producing data in its native format has certain limitations and risks that should be considered. These include the inability to individually number or endorse "pages" for document control, inability to redact—leading to privilege problems, issues with reviewing the production. For some file types the native format may be the only way to adequately produce the documents.

If producing in native format it is important to take precautions to protect the documents from alteration. Annotations with Bates numbers, confidentiality designations, and redacting is not possible without altering the native document. Therefore, it is important to work off a copy of the file, to ensure the original file remains unaltered.

Under Rule 34(b) of the Federal Rules of Civil Procedure, a requesting party may specify the form of production. If it fails to do so or if the responding party objects to the requested form of production, the responding party must state its intended form of production in its response to discovery requests. If a request does not specify a form for producing electronically stored information, a party is required to produce it in a form or forms in which it is ordinarily maintained or in a reasonably usable form or forms.[2]

---

[2]See Williams v. Sprint/United Management Co., 230 F.R.D. 640, 96 Fair Empl. Prac. Cas. (BNA) 1775, 62 Fed. R. Serv. 3d 1052, 29 A.L.R.6th 701 (D. Kan. 2005) (metadata ordinarily visible to users of Excel spreadsheets should presumptively be treated as part of the document and should thus be discoverable). But see In re Payment Card

§ 15:40 Presenting

Presentation involves consideration of how an organization can present most effectively the electronically stored information at depositions, hearings, and trials. While this phase is last on the list, it should be thought of as the first in making appropriate decisions.

In presenting e-mails, it is important not to separate the attachments from the e-mails.[1]

II. CHECKLISTS

§ 15:41 Checklist for searching for electronically stored information

- ☐ Search each key person's:
  - ☐ office computer hard drive
  - ☐ home computer (if used for business purposes)
  - ☐ personal digital assistants
  - ☐ network files
- ☐ Search each key person's assistant's or staff member's:

Interchange Fee and Merchant Discount, 2007 WL 121426 (E.D. N.Y. 2007): (finding defendants waited too long to complain of metadata-stripped production and suggesting there had been a waiver); Wyeth v. Impax Laboratories, Inc., 248 F.R.D. 169 (D. Del. 2006) (plaintiff not required to produce electronic documents in their native format, complete with metadata, where plaintiff produced documents as image files and defendant failed to demonstrate particularized need for metadata); Kentucky Speedway, LLC v. NASCAR, Inc., 2006 WL 5097354 (Dec. 18, 2006) (in most cases and for most documents, metadata does not provide relevant information).

[Section 15:40]

[1]See PSEG Power N.Y., Inc. v. Alberici Constructors, Inc., 2007 WL 2687670 (N.D. N.Y. 2007) (observing that defendant was entitled to receive e-mails with related attachments, plaintiff ordered to re-produce e-mails at its expense (over $200,000) with attachments); CP Solutions PTE, Ltd. v. General Elec. Co., 2006 WL 1272615 (D. Conn. 2006) (where thousands of e-mails were produced commingled and separated from their attachments, court ordered producing party to provide requesting party with information necessary for matching e-mails and attachments).

- ☐ office computer hard drive
- ☐ home computer (if used for business purposes)
- ☐ personal digital assistants
- ☐ network files
- ☐ Intranet, extranet, or e-mail depositories

☐ Search any individual easily accessible backup data, such as floppy disks, thumb drives, CD-ROMs or DVDs

☐ Understand the technical architecture of the organization's computer infrastructure and be prepared to discuss all locations where digital data may reside

☐ Search any backup repositories that are not maintained for the purpose of disaster recovery (such as remote servers designed to make data available across an enterprise, ASPs, data warehouses, offsite storage sites, intranet, or extranet servers)

☐ Consider searching for metadata and relevant deleted data and be prepared to justify why such searches are burdensome or technically infeasible

§ 15:42 Critical Decisions

Collection Choices

☐ **Are e-mail files part of the anticipated or requested discovery? If so, do any key people maintain Internet e-mail accounts in addition to their organization account?** Large e-mail providers frequently retain their e-mail logs for no longer than 30 days. If a case potentially requires exploration of e-mail from Internet accounts, the discovery team must promptly request the records before they are lost. Normally this requires a subpoena.

☐ **Is it possible illegal activity may be uncovered?** Cases involving electronically stored information may uncover wrongdoing involving a member of the IT department. Terminating the responsible employee is not necessarily the best course of action. The employee may be the only person who knows how to access the files, find the problem, or fix it. The employee may also have the ability to access the files remotely. Unless remote access is eliminated before the employee's termination, the employee could access the network and damage it. It may be more prudent to restrict an employee's complete access privileges. The employee can then be notified of management's knowledge of the situation and given an opportunity to cooperate to mitigate the damage. If the situation involves possible criminal activity, law enforcement should be involved as early as possible.

☐ **May deleted or hidden files play a significant role in the case?** Electronic files can be collected using three methods: (1) forensically (capturing all the information contained on a specific electronic device by using either a forensic copy technique or by making an image of all or part of the device), (2) semi-forensically (using nonvalidated methods and applications to capture files), or (3) Non-forensically (using cut-and-paste copy methods to move copies of files from one location to another). Determining whether contextual information or only the content of electronic documents must be produced must be done before any data are captured. Once semi- or non-forensic methods are used, the records cannot be returned to their original state.

☐ **Are backup tapes involved?** Where backup tapes may be part of the information required to be produced, it is necessary to stop any rotation schedule.

Processing Choices

☐ **Who are the key people?** It is essential to identify people important to the case. Key individuals may include executives as well as assistants and support personnel from technology, accounting, sales and marketing, operations, and human resources.

☐ **Where are the files?** Electronically stored information can be in numerous locations. All potential locations of electronically stored information must be identified, including home computers, laptops, smart phones, MP3 players, and thumbdrives.

☐ **How can the number of files collected be limited?** Methods for limiting the number of files (and the cost of collection) include collecting only those in a certain date range, or only those containing selected key words.

☐ **How should protected files be handled?** Encrypted files or files with passwords may not be easily or quickly accessed. It may be necessary to access a subpoena to obtain a password.

☐ **How should duplicate documents be handled?** Electronically stored information almost always includes duplicate files. For example, numerous individuals may have received the same e-mail with the same attachments. Key documents may have been reviewed by several people who saved them on their hard drives. In collecting documents, it is possible to identify exact duplicate documents, limiting the number of documents requiring review. De-duping involves identifying files that are exact duplicates and eliminating them. If anything has changed in a document such as formatting, it is not an exact duplicate and is not de-duped. It is important that all parties agree on what is meant by "de-duping" Some electronic discovery tools delete duplicate files so they are gone from the collection, while others do not delete the duplicates but merely identify them for future use if needed.

☐ **How should near-duplicate documents be handled?** Near duplicates are files that have been significantly altered or contain only a portion of the main document. The volume of documents may require that near duplicates be identified and reviewed as a group to reduce review time and costs. Identifying near duplicates requires comparing each document to every other document or using sophisticated software applications requiring additional processing time.

☐ **What should be the form of the collection?** The Federal Rules of Civil Procedure require the parties to meet and determine the format in which they wish to receive electronically stored information. If there is no agreement, the format is that in which the documents are ordinarily maintained or a reasonably usable format. The form requested may depend upon the litigation review system used. Native files with extracted metadata reflect the exact original file, but cannot be Bates numbered and are subject to inadvertent change. Converting native files to TIF or PDF is time consuming and expensive. Frequently, files are processed in native format, reviewed for relevancy, and choosing only those that may be produced or used extensively for conversion.

Comment

This checklist is adapted from Unger, 10 Critical Decisions for Successful E-discovery, Information Mgt. J., Sept./Oct. 2007, at 70.

§ 15:43 Business function checklist

☐ What records do the employees in the department or business produce in the course of business?

☐ What records do the employees in the department or business generate or maintain for accounting, regulatory or legal reasons?

☐ Which types of records are prepared, even in draft form, using computers?

☐ What records are stored on computer?

☐ What are your backup and retention policies and are they in writing?

☐ What type of backup repositories exist that are not maintained for the purpose of disaster recovery (such as remote server designed to make data available across an enterprise)?

- ☐ Does the organization use ASPs, data warehouses, offsite storage sites, intranet or extranet servers?
- ☐ What computer programs exist that create records without any or regular intervention of human operators (such as automatic audit or monitoring software)?

§ 15:44 Technology checklist

- ☐ Whether the backup uses media that is reused
- ☐ Identification of what electronically stored information is typically backed up
- ☐ Whether any backups are maintained for long periods of time for archival purposes
- ☐ What the backup schedule is
- ☐ What type of backup repositories exist that are not maintained for the purpose of disaster recovery (such as remote servers designed to make electronically stored information available across an enterprise)

§ 15:45 Checklist for review process

- ☐ Determine the relevancy of the information or documents collected or produced.
- ☐ Bibliographically code database fields to facilitate improved search and retrieval of the documents collected or produced.
- ☐ Determine whether or not any privilege applies to the documents subject to be produced.
- ☐ Determine which requests for production the documents are responsive to.
- ☐ Identify documents that should be marked as "confidential" or have portions redacted.
- ☐ Relate key documents to alleged facts or legal issues previously outlined in the case.
- ☐ Relate key documents to key players who may testify about the documents.
- ☐ Identify other subjective information.

§ 15:46 Processing checklist

- ☐ Capture and preserve the body of electronically stored information.
- ☐ Associate document collections with particular users.
- ☐ Capture and preserve metadata associated with the electronically stored information.
- ☐ Establish relationship between various source data files.
- ☐ Automate identification and elimination of redundant duplicate data with the given data set.
- ☐ Provide a means to suppress programmatically material that is irrelevant to review based on criteria such as keywords, date ranges, or other available metadata.
- ☐ Unprotect and reveal information within files.
- ☐ Accomplish all process goals in a manner that is both defensible with respect to organization's legal obligations and appropriately cost effective and expedient.

§ 15:47 Checklist for logging electronically stored information

- ☐ Electronic discovery identification and inventory number (we strongly recommend using a barcode labeling system)
- ☐ Date received
- ☐ Matter name
- ☐ Client name
- ☐ Client/matter number
- ☐ Name of person/company/shipper delivering evidence
- ☐ Description of items, including manufacturer name, model number and unique identifier/serial number whenever possible
- ☐ MD5 Hash of each piece of media where possible (electronic fingerprint)
- ☐ Name of person receiving evidence (Logged by)
- ☐ Check Out
    - ☐ If Yes

- ☐ Date
- ☐ Reason
- ☐ Custodian name
  - ☐ Name of recipient (when evidence shipped from electronic discovery provider to anyone)
  - ☐ Name of shipper
  - ☐ Shipper's tracking number
  - ☐ Date of shipment
  - ☐ Date of receipt
- ☐ Check-in date

§ 15:48 Database checklist

- ☐ Ask that the production request be specific, providing information regarding field definitions, query forms, and reports to help refine the request.
- ☐ Produce the requested information in a form usable to the requesting party, although it may vary from database to database.
- ☐ Where no existing single report gives a full view of the data, advise the requesting party whether it is possible to create such a report and what it would cost to develop a custom report.
- ☐ Only allow onsite access to databases for purposes of defining queries where no other alternative information regarding structure is available.

§ 15:49 Checklist for selecting a vendor

- ☐ How many years of experience does the vendor have and how many of those years were spent doing electronic discovery?
- ☐ What is the vendor's financial stability?
- ☐ What are the skills and knowledge the vendor's project management
- ☐ Is the vendor flexible and does it have a formalized change process in place to track and record changes made to the original specifications?

- ☐ What level of support will your receive from the vendor?
- ☐ What training does the vendor provide?
  - ☐ Does the vendor charge for training?
  - ☐ Does the vendor provide separate administrator training from reviewer training?
  - ☐ Does the vendor provide onsite training?
  - ☐ Does the vendor provide ongoing training for new employees?
  - ☐ How often does the vendor release new versions of its software and does it provide training on the new features? Is there a charge?
  - ☐ Does the vendor provide training manuals covering all aspects of its system?
- ☐ What are the costs of the vendor's services and what is included and excluded?
- ☐ What are the project-management fees?

§ 15:50 Checklist for quality check

QUALITY CHECK

- ☐ **Redacted text are not produced.** An image can be redacted, but unless the corresponding text file and metadata are redacted, the client's privileged information will be disclosed.
- ☐ **Privileged documents are not produced.** Privileged documents must not be produced. Using red labels for DVDs containing a client's privileged documents make it less likely that the wrong disk will be given to opposing counsel.
- ☐ **Text is extracted rather than OCRed.** Many vendors OCR text without anyone else knowing it. While extracting the text of a document for use in keyword filters is 100% accurate, OCR is at best only 70% to 80% accurate, meaning that this process overlooks 20% to 30% of the documents.
- ☐ **Metadata are not altered by opening difficult documents instead of simply viewing**

them. Many documents are TIFFed by using QuickView Plus, which does not actually open the document, it simply views it. QuickView Plus cannot TIFF all documents. For these problem documents, vendors sometimes load them onto one of their computers to open before TIFFing it. In so doing, they change the metadata so it reflects information from the electronic discovery vendor's computer—including the file path, custodian, and last accessed date—not the true custodian's computer.

☐ **All file types are collected.** Some people create their own file extension names for their own unique naming convention. Instead of using ".doc" for a word processing document, they may use ".ltr" to denote a letter, or ".mem" for a memo. If the vendor only processes the main file extension types, the vendor may be missing many documents. There are software programs that do not rely on the file extension alone to identify file types.

☐ **Spreadsheets columns are opened to widest cell and show hidden cells.** When an image of a spreadsheet is created, it is very easy to miss data if each column is not expanded to the width of the widest cell in the column. While data in the native file can still be seen, it will be missing in the TIFF if every column is not expanded.

☐ **Spreadsheet formulas are produced.** Typically the numbers in a spreadsheet are not nearly as important as how the numbers are calculated. Simply printing out a spreadsheet to PDF loses the formulas.

☐ **"Current dates" are not altered.** Sometimes memoranda, letters, or other documents will have fields that will automatically display the current date. This practice can be good to make sure a one does not misdate a letter one intends to write, but bad if one later wants to determine

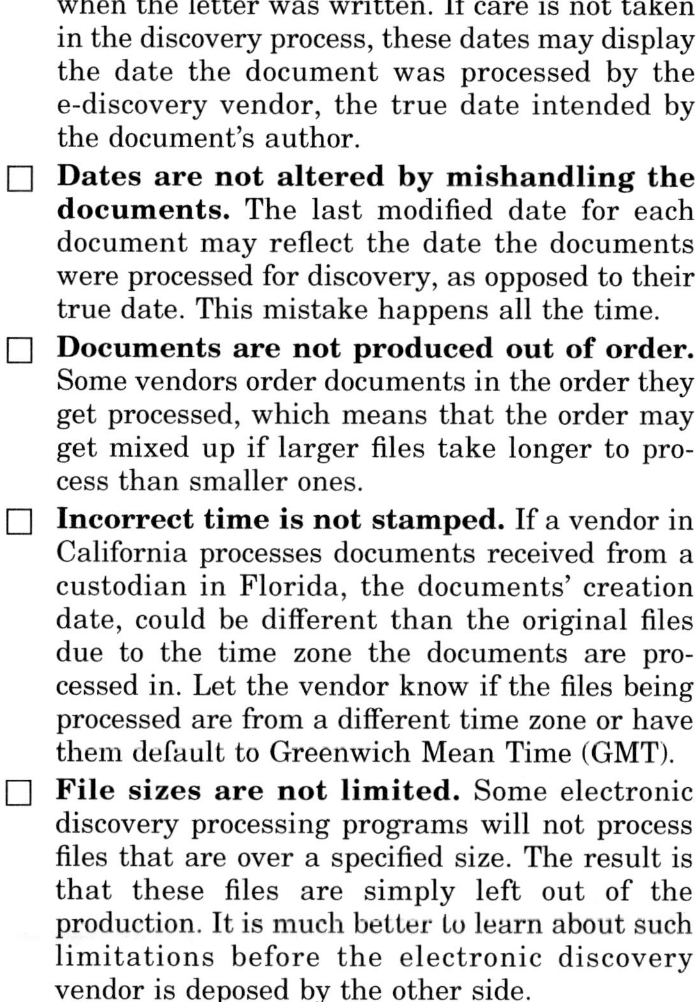

when the letter was written. If care is not taken in the discovery process, these dates may display the date the document was processed by the e-discovery vendor, the true date intended by the document's author.

- ☐ **Dates are not altered by mishandling the documents.** The last modified date for each document may reflect the date the documents were processed for discovery, as opposed to their true date. This mistake happens all the time.
- ☐ **Documents are not produced out of order.** Some vendors order documents in the order they get processed, which means that the order may get mixed up if larger files take longer to process than smaller ones.
- ☐ **Incorrect time is not stamped.** If a vendor in California processes documents received from a custodian in Florida, the documents' creation date, could be different than the original files due to the time zone the documents are processed in. Let the vendor know if the files being processed are from a different time zone or have them default to Greenwich Mean Time (GMT).
- ☐ **File sizes are not limited.** Some electronic discovery processing programs will not process files that are over a specified size. The result is that these files are simply left out of the production. It is much better to learn about such limitations before the electronic discovery vendor is deposed by the other side.

Comment

This checklist is adapted from a list compiled by Attorney Kenton Hutcherson of Dallas, Texas.

III. FORMS

§ 15:51 Sample electronic budgeting tool

Document Review Budget Estimate				
Matter Name:				
Date:				
Total Cost Estimate		**$7,796,741**	**$3,503,070**	**$1,182,802**
		Large	**Medium**	**Small**
E-File Collection		***Scenario 1***	***Senario 2***	***Scenario 3***
Key Custodians		10	6	2
GB/Key Custodian		10	10	10
Tier 2 Custodians		25	9	3
GB/Tier 2 Custodians		7.5	7.5	7.5
GB Shared Server Data		15	7.5	2
Estimated GB Collected		302.5	135	44.5
Estimated Pages/GB		75,000	75,000	75,000
Page equivalent		22,687,500	10,125,000	3,337,500
Yield after Pre-Processing as %		0.3	0.3	0.3
Yield after Pre-Processing GB		90.75	40.5	13.35
Estimated # pages		6,806,250	3,037,500	1,001,250
Box Equivalent (2,500pp/box)		2,723	1,215	401
Estimated % Responsive		0.25	0.25	0.25
Estimated # Responsive Pages		1,701,563	759,375	250,313
Collection Costs				

Document Review Budget Estimate				
Matter Name:				
Date:				
Collection Costs (1 hour/custodian @ $300/hr)		$10,500	$4,500	$1,500
DeDup and Cull Cost/GB		1250	1250	1250
Estimate GB Collected		302.5	135	44.5
Total Collection, DeDup and Cull Costs		$388,625	$173,250	$57,125
EDD Processing Costs				
EDD Processing Cost/GB		$1,750	$1,750	$1,750
Total GB to be Processed		90.75	40.5	13.35
Total EDD Processing Costs		**$158,813**	**$70,875**	**$23,363**
Paper Collection and Processing				
Pages/Key Custodians (Assume 5000 pages/ custodian)		50,000	30,000	10,000
Pages Tier 2 Custodians (Assume 2500 pages/ custodian)		62,500	22,500	7,500
Total Pages		112,500	52,500	17,500
Scan/OCR/page		0.2	0.2	0.2
Processing costs		$22,500	$10,500	$3,500
Vendor Load Fee/ page		0	0	0
Load Fees		$5,625	$2,625	$875
Total Paper Processing Costs		**$28,125**	**$13,125**	**$4,375**
Total Pre-Review Costs		**$575,563**	**$257,250**	**$84,863**

Document Review Budget Estimate				
Matter Name:				
Date:				
Phase 1 Review				
GB to be reviewed		90.75	40.5	13.35
Pages to be reviewed		6,806,250	3,037,500	1,001,250
Attorney review rate (pp/hour)		175	175	175
Attorney hours needed to complete review		38893	17357	5721
Cost per hour of attorney review		$65	$65	$65
Review attorney cost of Phase 1 review		$2,528,036	$1,128,214	$371,893
Supervisory billable time for training, project management, etc. (˜10% Rev Atty Cost)		$252,804	$112,821	$37,189
Total Cost of Phase 1 Review		**$2,780,839**	**$1,241,036**	**$409,082**
Phase 2 Review				
Yield from Phase 1 Review		0.4	0.4	0.4
Pages to be Reviewed in Phase 2		2,722,500	1,215,000	400,500
Attorney review rate (pp/hr)		200	200	200
Attorney hours needed to complete review		13,613	6,075	2,003
Cost per hour of attorney review		$250	$250	$250
Review attorney cost of Phase 2 review		$3,403,125	$1,518,750	$500,625

Document Review Budget Estimate				
Matter Name:				
Date:				
Supervisory billable time for training, project management, etc. (10% Rev Atty Cost)		$340,313	$151,875	$50,063
Total Cost of Phase 2 Review		**$3,743,438**	**$1,670,625**	**$550,688**
Review of Materials Received from Opposition				
Assume Equal Amount of Data Received as Produced		0	0	0
Attorney review rate (pp/hr)		200	200	200
Attorney hours needed to complete review		0	0	0
Cost per hour of attorney review		$250	$250	$250
Review attorney cost of Phase 2 review		$0	$0	$0
Supervisory billable time for training, project management, etc. (~10% Rev Atty Cost)		$0	$0	$0
Total Cost of Reviewing Opposition Production		**$0**	**$0**	**$0**
Production				
Responsive Pages		1,701,563	759,375	250,313
Production Costs/ Page @ $0.10		$170,156	$75,938	$25,031

Document Review Budget Estimate				
Matter Name:				
Date:				
Total Costs of Production		**$170,156**	**$75,938**	**$25,031**
Privilege Log				
Privileged Pages (Assume 10% of Responsive Documents are Privileged)		170,156	75,938	25,031
Privileged Documents (Assume 5pp/doc)		34,031	15,188	5,006
Percent Reduced during Phase 2 Review		0.6	0.6	0.6
Privileged Documents to be Logged		13,613	6,075	2,003
Logging Pace docs/hr		8	8	8
Logging Hours Needed		1,702	759	250
Hours/day		8	8	8
Logging days needed		213	95	31
Loggers (Staff attorneys)		5	5	5
Project Days needed		43	19	6
Avg Hourly Billing Rate		$275	$275	$275
Personnel Costs		$467,930	$208,828	$68,836
Export cost/page @ $0.10		$17,016	$7,594	$2,503
Total Privilege Log Costs		**$484,945**	**$216,422**	**$71,339**
ASP Costs				

Document Review Budget Estimate				
Matter Name:				
Date:				
Database Set-Up Fees (Includes Initial Upload)		$1,000	$1,000	$1,000
User Set Up Fees (Assume $100/ User; 20 Users)		$2,000	$2,000	$2,000
Monthly Mainentance (Assume $200/Mo; 24 Month Life of Case)		$4,800	$4,800	$4,800
Image Storage (TBD)				
Log In/Month (Assume 20 Users @ $100/user/ month/24 months)		$24,000	$24,000	$24,000
Additional Uploads (TBD)				
Project Management (Assume 50 hours @ $200/ hour)		$10,000	$10,000	$10,000
Total ASP Costs		**$41,800**	**$41,800**	**$41,800**
Total Cost Estimate		**$7,796,741**	**$3,503,070**	**$1,182,802**

Comment

The form can be used for internal budgeting purposes and it can also be used to support a motion shifting costs. The numbers and categories are examples of the costs of electronic discovery and will vary from case to case.

§ 15:52 Chain-of-custody log

Chain-of-Custody Log

Name of Individual Receiving Information: ______________

Date of collection or receipt: ______________________

Time of collection or receipt: ______________________

Place of collection or receipt: ______________________

Name of custodian: ______________________

Electronically stored information obtained, including media:

Media Type: ______________________
Media Standard: ______________________
Media Manufacturer: ______________________
Media Serial Numbers and/or Volume Names: __________
____

Writing on Labels: ______________________
Characterization of data: ______________________
Amount of data: ______________________
Type of data: ______________________
Write-Protection Status: ______________________

Data Collection Procedures

Tools Used for Each Procedure: ______________________
____

Name of Individual Conducting Each Procedure: ________
____

Outcome of Procedures: ______________________
Problems Encountered: ______________________

Additional Documentation

Movement of Evidence: ______________________
Purpose of Movement: ______________________
Date of Media Check In: ______________________
Time of Media Check In: ______________________

Date of Media Check Out from Secured Storage: ______
Time of Media Check Out from Secure Storage: ______
Physical Inspection of Information: ______
Description of Analysis: ______

______

Comment

A chain-of-custody log is intended to prove the integrity of the information produced has been maintained from its production through introduction court. A chain-of-custody log should document how the information was gathered, analyzed, and preserved. Because electronically stored information can be easily altered if proper precautions are not taken, a chain-of-custody log for electronically stored information must demonstrate the following: (1) the information has been properly copied, transported, and stored; (2) the information has not been altered in any way; and (3) all media has been secured throughout the process.

Documentation must be maintained throughout the life of the information and should be ready for review at any time. Every of contact with the information must be documented during the discovery process. A complete and accurate logging procedure will help assure that electronically stored information can be authenticated in court.

§ 15:53 Interrogatories and responses to interrogatories

[Caption]

Responses to interrogatories

INTERROGATORY NO. 1

[Set forth interrogatory, e.g., "State every fact upon which you base your allegation contained in paragraph of the Complaint. . ..."]

RESPONSE TO INTERROGATORY NO. 1

[Set forth any objections, e.g., ". . .objects to this interrogatory on the ground that it is overbroad in that . . .." Answer the interrogatory if objection is not dispositive of the obligation to respond]

INTERROGATORY NO. 2

[Set forth interrogatory, e.g., "State every fact upon which you base your allegation contained in paragraph of the Complaint. . .."]

RESPONSE TO INTERROGATORY NO. 2

[Set forth any objections, e.g., ". . . objects to this interrogatory on the ground that it is overbroad in that. . .." Answer the interrogatory if objection is not dispositive of the obligation to respond]

State of)
) ss.
County of)

[Name], being duly sworn upon his/her oath, deposes and says:
I am the *[plaintiff/defendant]* in the above-entitled action and have read the interrogatories served upon me by the *[plaintiff/defendant] [name]*; and the foregoing answers to those interrogatories are true according to the best of my knowledge, information, and belief.

[Signed]

Subscribed and sworn to be before me a Notary Public for ________, this *[date]*.

[seal]

____

My commission expires *[date]*.

Comment

It is important to check local rules with respect to format of responses to interrogatories. Some rules may permit oath to be by declaration under penalty of perjury.

§ 15:54 Motion for extension of time within which to file answers or objections to interrogatories

[Caption]

[Plaintiff] [Defendant] moves the Court for a ____-day extension until *[date]* within which to file objections to interrogatories or within which to answer interrogatories for the following reasons:

1. Interrogatories under *[rule]* were served on *[name]*, attorney for *[plaintiff] [defendant]*, on *[date]*. There were interrogatories, seeking such detailed information that it is impossible, if the interrogatories were answered without objection, to answer them within thirty days after service. The information sought in most of the interrogatories is not within the knowledge of the local counsel and, in order to answer these interrogatories or to file pertinent objections to them, it will be necessary to have considerable correspondence with *[plaintiff] [defendant]*. The time for service of the answers is not sufficient in which to accomplish this.

2. Because of the numerous interrogatories, the wide scope of information sought, and the nature of the interrogatories, it is apparent that many, if not all, are not pertinent to the issues in the proceedings, and that it will require preparation and study to object to the answering of any of the interrogatories.

3. It will most likely be necessary that the *[plaintiff] [defendant]* seek an order limiting the scope of inquiry. An affidavit is attached and made a part of this motion.

Dated: ________

[signature etc.]

Comment

It is prudent to request a time extension for both answering and objecting to interrogatories. The request for a time extension should be made before the time to answer expires.

§ 15:55 Order enlarging time to file answers or object to interrogatories

[Caption]

This cause was heard upon the motion of the *[plaintiff] [defendant]* for an enlargement of time within which to file objections to interrogatories propounded to the *[plaintiff] [defendant]* under *[rule]* and for an enlargement of time within which to answer interrogatories that may not be objected to. For good cause shown, it is, therefore,

ORDERED AND ADJUDGED, that the *[plaintiff] [defendant]* are granted until *[date]*, in which to file objections to such interrogatories and in which to file answers to interrogatories to which there may be no objections made.

Dated: ________

____

Judge

§ 15:56 Motion to seal answers to interrogatories

[Caption]

[Plaintiff] [Defendant] moves the Court to seal its answers to the interrogatories recently filed and to admonish *[defendant] [plaintiff]* and *[defendant's] [plaintiff's]* counsel not to disclose to anyone the contents of the answers to the interrogatories.

[Defendant] [Plaintiff] has been informed and believes that a person or persons unknown are publishing or making use of the answers for purposes unauthorized and unconnected with this action to the detriment of *[plaintiff] [defendant]*.

Dated: ________

[signature etc.]

§ 15:57 Response to request for production of documents

[Caption]

REQUEST NUMBER ONE:

[Set forth terms of response.]

RESPONSE TO REQUEST NUMBER ONE:

[Set forth any objections, then indicate whether such documents will be produced.]

Dated: ________

[signature etc.]

§ 15:58 Response to request for production-another form

[Caption]

To:

Attorney for *[name]*
[Address]

In response to *[plaintiff's] [defendant's]* request to produce and for inspection in the above-entitled action, served upon *[defendant] [plaintiff]* on *[date]*, the inspection and related activities requested will be permitted with respect to each item or category as requested *[with the exception of Items and, to which inspection [defendant] [plaintiff] objects on the ground that [describe]]*.

Dated: ________

[signature etc.]

§ 15:59 Response to requests for admissions

[Caption]

[Responding party], by its attorney, hereby respond to *[requesting party's]* Requests for Admissions served on it by *[requesting party]* as follows:

REQUEST NO. 1:

Each of the following documents, exhibited with this request is genuine: *[specify]*.

RESPONSE NO. 1:

Admit.

REQUEST NO. 2:

Each of the following statements is true: *[list statements]*:

RESPONSE NO. 2:

[Responding party] cannot truthfully admit or deny these statements for the reason that, although *[responding party]* has made reasonably inquiry, *[responding party]* has been unable to locate the source or verify the accuracy of the statements and, therefore, the information known to *[responding party]* is insufficient to admit or deny the request.

Dated: ________

[signature etc.]

§ 15:60 Motion for leave to amend or withdraw response to requests for admissions

[Caption]

[Responding party] moves the Court for an order for leave to make the following amended responses to the requests for admissions served by *[requesting party]* upon *[responding party]* on *[date]*, and answered by *[responding party]* by service of responses on *[date]*: *[include the letter or number of requests and the amended responses] [for leave to withdraw the following responses, etc.]*.

This motion is made on the ground that *[include grounds for motion]*, all of which more fully appears from the affidavit or declaration of *[name]* attached as Exhibit A.

Dated: ________

[signature etc.]

§ 15:61 Motion for extension of time within which to answer requests for admissions

[Caption]

The *[responding party]* states that the Requests for Admission under *[rule]* did not reach or come to the attention of the *[responding party's]* attorney, *[name]*, until *[date]*, since which time *[responding party's]* attorney has been engaged continuously in the trial of cases in *[court]*, with the exception of *[dates]*, and has not had sufficient opportunity to ascertain the information with which to answer the Request for Admissions under *[rule]*.

Wherefore, the *[responding party]* moves the Court to allow it additional time, through *[date]*, within which to answer or object to *[requesting party's]* Requests for Admission.

Dated: ________

[signature etc.]

Comment

The request for a time extension should be made before the time to answer expires.

§ 15:62 Quick peek agreement

1. *[Name of responding party]* agrees to make relevant information requested by *[name of requesting party]* available for inspection.

2. *[Name of requesting]* shall review the information and designate the information it believes is responsive to its requests.

3. *[Name of responding party]* shall then review the designated information for privilege and work-product protection.

4. Following the review *[name of responding party]* shall produce the information it believes is relevant and not protected by privilege or the work-product doctrine.

Comment

This is an excerpt from a quick peek agreement, containing the essentials. The agreement could also provide for such things as who will be allowed to see the documents. In order to prevent a claim of waiver of privilege made by a third-party, it is appropriate to have the agreement incorporated into a court order.

§ 15:63 Chain of custody log

Name of individual who received evidence:

Date of collection or receipt:

Time of collection or receipt:

Place of collection or receipt:

Name of custodian:

Description of data obtained, including media-specific information:

Media type, standard, and manufacturer

Serial numbers and/or volume names

Writing on labels

Characterization of data

Amount of data

Type of data

Write-protection status

Description of data collection procedures

List of tools used for each procedure

Name of the individual conducting each procedure

Outcome of procedures

Problems encountered, if any

Movement of evidence, including purpose of transfer

Date and time of media check-in

Date and time of media check-out from secure storage

Physical (visual) inspection of data

Description of data analysis

Dated:

[signature]

Comment

The purpose of a chain of custody log is to prove the integrity of evidence has been maintained from the time of its seizure through production in court. A chain of custody log documents how the electronically stored information was gathered, analyzed, and preserved for production. A chain of custody log for electronically stored information must demonstrate the data has been properly copied, transported, and stored. It must also show the information has not been altered, and that all media has been secured throughout the process. Every instance of contact with the data must be documented throughout the entire discovery process.

The chain of custody log must be maintained throughout the life of the evidence and must be available for review at any time.

Chapter 16

Privilege and Privacy

I. GUIDELINES

II. CHECKLISTS

III. FORMS

Research References

Treatises and Practice Aids

eDiscovery & Digital Evidence §§ 10:8 to 10:19

Trial Strategy

Recovery and Reconstruction of Electronic Mail as Evidence, 41 Am. Jur Proof of Facts 3d 1

Computer Technology in Civil Litigation, 71 Am. Jur Trials 111

Law Reviews and Other Periodicals

Carroll, Developments in the Law of Electronic Discovery, 27 Am. J. Trial Advoc. 357 (2003)

Coyle, "Metadata" Mining Vexes Lawyers, Bars—Invisible Document Data a Big Problem, Nat'l L.J., Feb. 18, 2008, at 1

MacLean, Erasing E-Mails Brings Liabilities: Deleting E-Mail from a Single Laptop Can Trigger U.S. Anti-Hacking Law, Nat'l L. J., March 20, 2006, at 9

Note, Look Before You Leap: A guide to the Law of Inadvertent Disclosure of Privileged Information in the Era of E-Discovery, 93 Iowa L. Rev. 627 (2008)

Note, The Requirement for Metadata Production Under Williams v. Sprint/United Management Co.: An Unnecessary Burden for Litigants Engaged in Electronic Discovery, 93 Cornell L. Rev. 221 (2007)

Additional References

Farrar & McClellan, Metadata Management in Microsoft Office: How Firms Can Protect Themselves against Unintentional Disclosure and Misuse of Metadata, GP/Solo, May 2006

Franks & Kunde, Why Metadata Matters, Information Mgt. J., Sept./Oct. 2006, at 55

Grenig, Clawback Agreement Doesn't Protect from Deliberate Disclosure of Privileged Information, Elec. Disc. & Records Mgt. Q., fall 2007, at 34

Protecting Privacy and Security of Electronically Stored Information, Elec. Disc. & Records Mgt. Q., summer 2007, at 22

Jacoby et al., Finding the Right Format of Production for Electronic Information, Elec. Disc. & Records Mgt. Q., summer 2007, at 28

Rossick, Protecting Against Inadvertent Waiver of the Attorney-Client Privilege, Elec. Disc. & Records Mgt. Q., fall 2007, at 18

Spahn, Metadata: A Case Study in the Nature of Ethics Rules, Experience, summer 2007, at 44

ABA Discovery Standards, http://www.abanet.org/litigation/discoverystandards/2005civildiscoverystandards.pdf

eDirect Impact, Inc., http://www.edirectimpact.com

Electronic Discovery Reference Model Project, http://www.edrm.net.

Federal Judicial Center, http://www.fjc.gov

The Sedona Conference, http://www.thesedonaconference.org

I. GUIDELINES

§ 16:1 Generally

Although a person's or an organization's confidential information may become subject to discovery once litigation commences, some confidential information may be protected by federal or state statutes, common law privileges, or the attorney work product doctrine. In addition, parties frequently agree at the beginning of litigation on appropriate restrictions regarding the discovering party's right to use or disseminate confidential discovery material.

It is important to protect confidential or private information from formal and informal discovery.[1] Even during the most contentious litigation, serious consideration must be given to implementing appropriate procedures to protect digital information from inadvertent disclosure as well as intentional interception or tampering.

§ 16:2 Statutes protecting electronically stored information—Health Insurance Portability and Accountability Act

The Health Insurance Portability and Accountability Act[1] ("HIPAA") was enacted in 1996 to address various issues related to health insurance and medical care. One of the purposes of HIPAA is to provide uniform privacy protection for health care records. Title II of HIPAA provides extensive rules regarding the secure storage and exchange of electronic data transactions and requirements promoting the confidentiality and privacy of individually identifiable health information. The Secretary of Health and Human Services has issued HIPAA regulations limiting disclosure of protected healthcare information.[2]

HIPAA generally applies only to:[3]

- health plans,

[Section 16:1]

[1]See Sedona Principle 10 ("A responding party should follow reasonable procedures to protect privileges and objections in connection with the production of electronically stored information.").

[Section 16:2]

[1]Pub. L. No. 104-191.

[2]45 C.F.R. § 164.512.

[3]45 C.F.R. § 160.102.

- health care clearinghouses, and
- health care providers ("providers").

HIPAA also obligates providers to enter into contracts with "business associates" (a term including any person or entity that has access to the provider's medical records or information) requiring the business associates to comply with HIPAA. HIPAA applies only to "protected health information," broadly defined to include any individually identifiable health information. This includes any records or information that identifies an individual or could reasonably be used to identify an individual.[4]

HIPAA regulates the methods by which a health care provider may release a patient's health information, including oral medical records. Thus, an attorney must comply with HIPAA before communicating (whether informally or through discovery) with a patient's treating physician. HIPAA provides three mechanisms for discovery of health care information in civil litigation. These are:

- Patient authorization
- Court order
- Certain types of subpoenas or discovery requests

Probably the easiest and least expensive method of obtaining a patient's health care records or information is to have the patient execute a HIPAA authorization. A health care provider may release a patient's protected health information to an attorney or litigant upon receipt of a HIPAA authorization executed by the patient. To be effective, a HIPAA authorization must include a long list of criteria spelled out in 45 C.F.R. § 164.508. These criteria must be tailored to each case. It is also advisable to attach a cover letter to any patient authorization explaining that the authorization complies with HIPAA.

The second method for discovering protected health care records and information is by order of a court or adminis-

[4]45 C.F.R. § 160.103.

trative tribunal.[5] The health care provider may only disclose the health care information expressly authorized by the order. Thus, the parties and the court must ensure that the order is prepared with precision. The order may result from a contested motion or by agreement of the parties. A court may also order a party to sign a HIPAA patient authorization. A subpoena signed by a judge should suffice as a HIPAA order.

Protected health information may be discovered by subpoena, discovery request, or other lawful process if the health care provider receives satisfactory assurance, as described below, from the discovering party that reasonable efforts have been made by the discovering party to:

- Ensure that the individual who is the subject of the protected health information that has been requested (i.e., the patient) has been given notice of the request; or
- Secure a qualified protective order that meets the requirements set forth below.[6]

Satisfactory assurance that the discovering party has given notice to the patient exists where the health care provider receives from the discovering party a written statement and accompanying documentation demonstrating that:

- The discovering party has made a good faith attempt to provide written notice to the patient (or, if the patient's location is unknown, to mail notice to the patient's last known address);
- The notice includes sufficient information about the litigation or proceeding in which the protected health information is requested to permit the patient to raise an objection to the court or administrative tribunal; and
- The time (probably a minimum of 10 days) for the

[5]45 C.F.R. § 164.512(e). See, e.g., A Helping Hand, LLC v. Baltimore County, Md., 295 F. Supp. 2d 585, 592 (D. Md. 2003) (noting that courts may order disclosure of protected health information).

[6]45 C.F.R. § 164.512(e)(1)(ii).

patient to raise objections has elapsed and no objections were filed or all objections were resolved in favor of the discovering party.

The subpoena should not be served on the health care provider until the time for objections has expired.

Satisfactory assurance that the discovering party has made reasonable efforts to secure a qualified protective order exists where the health care provider receives from the discovering party a written statement and accompanying documentation demonstrating that:

- The parties to the dispute giving rise to the request for information have agreed to a qualified protective order and have presented it to the court or administrative tribunal with jurisdiction over the dispute;[7] or
- The discovering party has requested a qualified protective order from such court or administrative tribunal.[8] HIPAA does not require the entry of a protective order; it merely requires the discovering party to make reasonable efforts to secure a qualified protective order.

A "qualified protective order" is an order of a court or of an administrative tribunal or a stipulation by the parties that: (1) prohibits the parties from using or disclosing the protected health information for any purpose other than the litigation or proceeding for which such information was requested; and (2) requires the return to the covered entity or destruction of the protected health information (including all copies made) at the end of the litigation or proceeding.[9]

---

[7]45 C.F.R. § 164.512(e)(1)(iii) to (iv). See, e.g., Hutton v. City of Martinez, 219 F.R.D. 164, 57 Fed. R. Serv. 3d 850 (N.D. Cal. 2003) (health care provider ordered to release records where the parties had agreed to a qualified protective order).

[8]45 C.F.R. § 164.512(e)(1)(iv).

[9]45 C.F.R. § 164.512(e)(1)(iii) and (vi).

§ 16:3 Statutes protecting electronically stored information—Federal Wiretap Act

The Federal Wiretap Act[1] prohibits the unauthorized interception and disclosure of wire, oral or electronic communications.[2] "Electronic communication" includes e-mail, voice mail, cellular telephones, and satellite communications.[3] Online communications are covered by the Act.[4]

Federal courts have consistently held that, in order to be intercepted, electronic communications must be acquired contemporaneously with transmission and that electronic communications are not intercepted within the meaning of the Act if they are retrieved from storage.[5]

Producing counsel normally will not be justified under

[Section 16:3]

[1]18 U.S.C.A. §§ 2510 et seq. The Act is Title III of the Omnibus Crime Control and Safe Streets Act of 1968.

[2]18 U.S.C.A. § 2511.

[3]18 U.S.C.A. § 2510(12).

[4]18 U.S.C.A. § 2510(1). See, e.g., In re Pharmatrak, Inc., 329 F.3d 9, 18 (1st Cir. 2003) (transmissions of completed online forms constitute electronic communications under Act); U.S. v. Kennedy, 81 F. Supp. 2d 1103 (D. Kan. 2000) (applying Act to collection and disclosure of Internet subscriber information); U.S. v. Hambrick, 225 F.3d 656 (4th Cir. 2000) (analyzing Internet service's providing customer information under Act).

[5]See In re Pharmatrak, Inc., 329 F.3d 9, 22 (1st Cir. 2003) (contemporaneous aspect of interception clearly present where Web traffic monitoring service's computer code was effectively an automatic routing program because it automatically duplicated part of the communication between a user and a pharmaceutical site employing the service, and set this information to the third-party service); Theofel v. Farey-Jones, 359 F.3d 1066, 1077 (9th Cir. 2004) (no "interception" occurred in violation of Wiretap Act when defendant allegedly gained unauthorized access to plaintiff's e-mails that were already delivered to recipients and stored electronically by plaintiff's Internet service provider). See also U.S. v. Steiger, 318 F.3d 1039, 1050 (11th Cir. 2003), explaining there is only a narrow window during which an e-mail interception may occur—the seconds or mili-seconds before which a newly composed message is saved to any temporary location following a send command. Therefore, unless some type of automatic routing

the Act in refusing to produce e-mail or other digital evidence contained on a discovery target's computer system on the theory that it is protected from disclosure as a form of communication. In almost every instance, e-mail sought during discovery will be on some type of storage media, and thus "interception" within the meaning of the Act will not be a valid concern.

However, applying state law, a Florida court barred introduction of chat room conversations. Relying on the Florida Security of Communications Act,[6] a Florida state court barred an estranged wife from introducing records of her husband's communications on a private online chat room that the wife had secretly recorded on his computer.[7] The court found the wife had illegally "intercepted" the husband's electronic communications via e-mail and instant messaging within the meaning of the Act, when she installed a spyware program on a computer that simultaneously copies electronic communications as they were being transmitted.[8]

---

software is used (for example, a duplicate of all of an employee's messages are automatically sent to the employee's boss), interception of e-mail within the prohibition of the Wiretap Act is virtually impossible).

[6]F.S.A. § 934.03.

[7]O'Brien v. O'Brien, 899 So. 2d 1133 (Fla. Dist. Ct. App. 5th Dist. 2005).

[8]But cf. White v. White, 344 N.J. Super. 211, 781 A.2d 85 (Ch. Div. 2001) (in a divorce action, wife did not unlawfully access husband's stored electronic communications in violation of New Jersey Wiretap Act and did not intrude on his seclusion by accessing those e-mails, where wife had legitimate reason for being in files, and she had a right to seize evidence she believed showed her husband was being unfaithful).

§ 16:4 Statutes protecting electronically stored information—Electronic Communications Privacy Act

The Electronic Communications Privacy Act[1] ("ECPA") extensively amended the Federal Wiretap Act.[2] It prohibits the interception of wire, oral, or electronic communications, or the use of electronic means to intercept oral communications, or the use of electronic means to intercept oral communications or to disclose or use any communications that were illegally intercepted.[3]

The ECPA provides a broad, functional definition of electronic communications, including any transfer of signs, signals, writing, images, sounds, data, or intelligence of any nature transmitted in whole or in part by a wire, radio, electromagnetic, photoelectric, or photo-optical system that affects interstate or foreign commerce, with certain exceptions. Title II of the ECPA limits access to stored electronic communications.

ECPA restrictions regarding disclosure of stored e-mail information facially applies only to public systems and e-mails stored within such systems. In *Anderson Consulting LLP v. UOP*,[4] the court held that a proprietary system operated by an employer was not a public system, although during a project an accounting firm was allowed to use the system.[5]

Online commerce uses various methods to collect infor-

[Section 16:4]

[1]Pub. L. No. 99-508, 100 Stat. 1848 (1986), codified as 18 U.S.C.A. §§ 2510 to 2521, 2701 to 2710.

[2]18 U.S.C.A. §§ 2510 et seq.

[3]18 U.S.C.A. § 2701(a).

[4]Andersen Consulting LLP v. UOP, 991 F. Supp. 1041 (N.D. Ill. 1998).

[5]See Freeman v. DirecTV, Inc., 457 F.3d 1001 (9th Cir. 2006) (provisions of ECPA imposing civil liability on providers of electronic communication services that knowingly divulged the contents of those communications while being stored by that provider did not create secondary liability for aiding and abetting or conspiracy to violate those provisions).

mation about system users and their online behavior patterns, in order to tailor advertising or other responses to mesh with those patterns. This frequently involves the use of "cookies." Cookies are computer programs commonly used by Web sites to store useful information such as usernames, passwords, and preferences, making it easier for users to access Web pages in an efficient manner.

The use of cookies, their ability to capture and retain data about individual users without necessarily requiring the system user's assent raises a number of privacy issues. The ECPA was the basis for privacy claims in *In re DoubleClick, Inc. Privacy Litigation*,[6] The court rejected three federal statutory bases for objecting to the use of cookies to track the use of computers. However, in *In re Intuit Privacy Litigation*,[7] the court refused to dismiss a claim under the ECPA dealing with cookies.

Producing counsel will want to consider whether the rights of individuals in information or e-mails stored on a computer system are protected under the ECPA because the system is in effect public. In light of *Anderson Consulting LLP v. UOP*,[8] it is unlikely that any but the most clearly public system will be subject to the ECPA, but caution is definitely appropriate.

§ 16:5 Statutes protecting electronically stored information—Stored Communications and Transactional Records Act

The Stored Communications and Transactional Records Act,[1] created as part of the Electronic Communications Privacy Act of 1986, prohibits certain access to electronic

---

[6]In re DoubleClick Inc. Privacy Litigation, 154 F. Supp. 2d 497 (S.D. N.Y. 2001).

[7]*In re Intuit Privacy Litigation, 138 F. Supp. 2d 1272 (C.D. Cal. 2001).

[8]Andersen Consulting LLP v. UOP, 991 F. Supp. 1041 (N.D. Ill. 1998).

[Section 16:5]

[1]18 U.S.C.A. §§ 2701 to 2711.

communications service facilities, as well as disclosure by such services of information contained on those facilities. It permits private plaintiffs to bring a private civil action against those who knowingly or intentionally violate the Act.[2] The Act is useful for protecting the privacy of e-mail and other Internet communications.

The Act prohibits service providers from knowingly disclosing the contents of a communication to any person or entity while in electronic storage by that service.[3] It also prohibits the service provider from knowingly disclosing to any governmental agency any record or other information pertaining to a subscriber of the service.[4] Accordingly, most service providers will not disclose such information without a subpoena. However, the Ninth Circuit found that disclosure by an internet service provider of a customer's e-mail messages pursuant to an invalid and overly broad civil subpoena did not constitute an "authorized" disclosure by the provider, as would allow the defendant to avoid liability under the Act.[5]

In *Jessup-Morgan v. America Online, Inc.*,[6] a subscriber sued AOL, alleging a violation of the Act, invasion of privacy, and other claims arising out of the provider's disclosure of her identity pursuant to a subpoena. The plaintiff had posted messages inviting users to see sexual liaisons with her paramour's wife. The court held that disclosure of the subscriber's identity did not violate the ECPA because the ECPA specifically authorizes such disclosures of subscriber information to private parties.[7]

---

[2]18 U.S.C.A. § 2707(a).

[3]18 U.S.C.A. § 2701(a).

[4]18 U.S.C.A. § 2701(a).

[5]Theofel v. Farey-Jones, 359 F.3d 1066, 1073 (9th Cir. 2004).

[6]Jessup-Morgan v. America Online, Inc., 20 F. Supp. 2d 1105, 26 Media L. Rep. (BNA) 2426 (E.D. Mich. 1998).

[7]See O'Grady v. Superior Court, 139 Cal. App. 4th 1423, 44 Cal. Rptr. 3d 72, 34 Media L. Rep. (BNA) 2089, 79 U.S.P.Q.2d 1398 (6th Dist. 2006), as modified (disclosure of identity of author of stored message not permitted by Act, but Act authorizes disclosure of a record or

§ 16:6 Statutes protecting electronically stored information—Computer Fraud and Abuse Act

The Computer Abuse and Fraud Act[1] makes it illegal to access a "protected" computer under certain circumstances, including computers operated by or on behalf of financial institutions.[2] The Act also makes it a crime to intentionally access a computer without authorization or to exceed authorized access, and obtain information from any "protected computer" if the conduct involved an interstate or foreign communication.[3] A "protected computer" is a computer:

- Used exclusively for the use of a financial institution; or
- Used by or for a financial institution, and the conduct constituting the offense affects that use by or for the financial institution; or
- Used in interstate or foreign commerce or communication.[4]

§ 16:7 Judicial privacy policy

Unless sealed or otherwise subject to restricted access by statute, federal rule, or policy, judicial records are

---

other information pertaining to a subscriber to or customer of the service, not including the contents of communications). See also 18 U.S.C.A. § 2703(c)(1)(A).

[Section 16:6]

[1]18 U.S.C.A. §§ 1030 et seq.

[2]See 18 U.S.C.A. § 1030(a)(2)(A). See, e.g., International Airport Centers, L.L.C. v. Citrin, 440 F.3d 418, 24 I.E.R. Cas. (BNA) 129 (7th Cir. 2006) (former employee's installation and use of a secure-erasure program to delete files on his employer-issued laptop prior to leaving that job was sufficient for employer to state a claim under Computer Fraud and Abuse Act).

[3]18 U.S.C.A. § 1030(a)(2)(C).

[4]18 U.S.C.A. § 1030(e)(2)(A) and (B).

presumed available for public inspection and copying.[1] The privacy policy of the Judicial Conference of the United States sets forth requirements relating to privacy and public access to electronic case files.[2] The policy recognizes that certain types of cases, categories of information, and specific documents may require special protection from unlimited public access.[3] The policy observes that the federal courts are not required to provide electronic access to case files, assuming a paper file is maintained.

§ 16:8 European Data Protection Directive

In 1998 the European Union enacted the European Data Protection Directive.[1] The Directive prohibits transferring "personal data" to countries where private protection is inadequate. It also can have an impact on Web sites utilizing cookies to collect data about customers.

§ 16:9 Trade secrets and proprietary information

Rule 26(c)(7) of the Federal Rules of Civil Procedure provides protection for trade secrets. The owner of a trade secret generally may keep the information confidential so long as there is no attempt to conceal fraud or otherwise

---

[Section 16:7]

[1]See, e.g., Richmond Newspapers, Inc. v. Virginia, 448 U.S. 555, 575–78, 100 S. Ct. 2814, 2826, 65 L. Ed. 2d 973, 6 Media L. Rep. (BNA) 1833 (1980) (tradition of public access to case files is also rooted in constitutional principles); Nixon v. Warner Communications, Inc., 435 U.S. 589, 597, 98 S. Ct. 1306, 1312, 55 L. Ed. 2d 570, 3 Media L. Rep. (BNA) 2074 (1978) (there is a common law right to inspect and copy public records and documents, including judicial records and documents).

[2]See http://www.privacy.uscourts.gov/b4amend.htm.

[3]See, e.g., U.S. Dept. of Justice v. Reporters Committee For Freedom of Press, 489 U.S. 749, 761, 109 S. Ct. 1468, 1476, 103 L. Ed. 2d 774, 16 Media L. Rep. (BNA) 1545 (1989) (technology may affect the balance between access rights and privacy and security interests).

[Section 16:8]

[1]Council Directive 97/66/EC at http://www.bioheathmatics.com/heathinformatics/eudir.aspx.

work an injustice. "Trade secret" is defined as information including a formula, pattern, compilation, program, device, method, technique or process that:

i. Derives independent economic value, actual or potential from not being generally known to, and not being readily ascertainable by proper means by, other persons who can obtain economic benefit from its disclosure or use, and
ii. Is the subject of efforts to maintain its secrecy that are reasonable under the circumstances.[1]

In order to obtain a protective order, the moving party must demonstrate that disclosure of the allegedly confidential information will work a clearly defined and very serious injury to the movant's business and put the holder of the trade secret at a competitive disadvantage. If the information is not currently confidential or difficult to acquire, or if it was obtained before litigation, it will not constitute a trade secret under Rule 26(c)(7).

§ 16:10 Work product

In *Hickman v. Taylor*,[1] the U.S. Supreme Court recognized that certain trial preparation materials are protected from discovery under the work product doctrine. *Hickman* established three important principles. First, items gathered by counsel when preparing for trial are protected from disclosure. Second, this protection is not absolute and opposing counsel may obtain materials by showing a need for them. Third, protection from discovery is greatest for materials that demonstrate the attorney's thought process.

The work product doctrine is not a "privilege" within the meaning of the Federal Rules of Evidence; it is a tool of

[Section 16:9]

[1] Unif.Trade Secrets Act § 1(4).

[Section 16:10]

[1] Hickman v. Taylor, 329 U.S. 495, 67 S. Ct. 385, 91 L. Ed. 451, 1947 A.M.C. 1 (1947).

judicial administration to safeguard the adversarial process. The work product doctrine protects trial preparation materials that reveal an attorney's strategy, intended lines of proof, evaluation of strengths and weaknesses, and inferences drawn from interviews. The work product doctrine is designed to preserve the privacy of attorneys' thought processes and to prevent parties from "borrowing the wits of their adversaries."

The holding of *Hickman* can be summarized as follows:

- Information as to facts and witnesses' statements obtained by the adverse party's attorney is not within the common law attorney-client privilege.
- The broader policy against invasion of a lawyer's files does not make them absolutely immune from discovery.
- The party asking for disclosure of information protected by the work product doctrine must show special circumstances in order to obtain it.
- When the proponent of discovery can obtain the desired information elsewhere, the proponent has not met the burden of showing such special circumstances.

In 1970 Fed. R. Civ. P. 26 was amended to provide express protection of work product. The work product doctrine, as a federal right derived from the Federal Rules of Civil Procedure, is resolved according to federal law in a diversity suit. Rule 26(b)(3) provides work product with qualified protection from discovery. Rules 26(b)(3) does the following:

- It defines the class of materials protected as work product.
- It describes the showing required to obtain discovery of work product material.
- It protects an attorney's mental impressions, conclusions, opinions, or legal theories concerning the litigation.

Rule 26(b)(3) provides a qualified protection for documents and tangible things otherwise discoverable and prepared in anticipation of litigation or for trial by or for another party. In order to come within the qualified immunity from discovery created by Rule 26(b)(3), three tests must be satisfied. The material must be:

- Documents and tangible things
- Prepared in anticipation of litigation or for trial
- By or for another party or by or for that other party's representative

A party asserting work product protection has the burden of establishing that the protection applies. To carry that burden, the party must make a clear showing that the asserted protection applies. The party must describe in detail the documents or information sought to be protected and provide precise reasons for the objection to discovery. The information provided must be sufficient to enable the court to determine whether each element of the asserted protection is satisfied. A blanket claim as to the applicability of work product protection does not satisfy the burden of proof.

§ 16:11 Privileges—Generally

If a party claims privilege, Fed. R. Civ. P. Rule 26(b)(5) provides that the party must "make the claim expressly and shall describe the nature of the documents, communications, or things not produced or disclosed in a manner that, without revealing information itself privileged or protected, will enable other parties to assess the applicability of the privilege or protection." This provision does not attempt to define for each case what information must be provided when a party asserts a claim of privilege.

A party invoking the attorney-client privilege must show:[1]

- a communication between a client and the client's attorney that
- was intended to be and was in fact kept confidential, and

[Section 16:11]

[1]In re County of Erie, 473 F.3d 413 (2d Cir. 2007).

- was made for the purpose of obtaining or providing legal advice.

Confidential communication between client and attorney are protected only if the predominant purpose of the communication was to render or solicit legal advice.[2] Once established, the attorney-client privilege can be waived if the communication is shared with corporate employees who are not directly concerned with or did not have primary responsibility for the subject matter of the communication.[3]

When information is withheld on the basis of a privilege, the party claiming the privilege should:

- Expressly claim the privilege; and
- Describe the nature of the documents, communications or things not produced or disclosed in a manner that will enable other parties to assess the applicability of the privilege or protection.

Failure to claim a privilege in a timely manner may constitute waiver of the privilege.[4]

§ 16:12 Privileges—Metadata

Unless the creator of an electronic document removes the metadata or sends an image file, such as a PDF, when sharing electronic documents with others, recipients of the document will be able to access this information. Because of the potential of metadata to reveal confidential client information, confidences, and strategies, ethics opinions have emphasized the sending attorney's responsibility to ensure that metadata are not transmitted inadvertently.

Lawyers frequently prepare documents and electroni-

---

[2]In re County of Erie, 473 F.3d 413 (2d Cir. 2007) (e-mails between assistant county attorney and county officials proposing changes to existing strip search policy were protected by attorney-client privilege).

[3]Muro v. Target Corp., 2007 WL 1630407 (N.D. Ill. 2007).

[4]See Ritacca v. Abbott Laboratories, 203 F.R.D. 332, 334–35, 49 Fed. R. Serv. 3d 1052 (N.D. Ill. 2001) (parties asserting objection to discovery on ground of privilege must present objection in timely and proper manner).

cally circulate drafts among other lawyers in the firm for their review and comment. The other lawyers may insert their suggested revisions and comments, some may address the strengths and weaknesses of the client's position. If the final version of such a document is electronically transmitted to opposing counsel, it may be possible for opposing counsel to discover the comments and revisions The sender of the document may not be aware of the metadata embedded within the document, or that the metadata remain in the electronic document despite the sender's good faith belief that it was "deleted."

All the state bars that have addressed the issue of metadata have agreed that a sending lawyer has a duty to protect confidential or privileged information from being disclosed, but they split on the duty of an opposing party. The American Bar Association says that a lawyer who is concerned about the possibility of sending, producing, or providing to opposing counsel a document containing, or that might contain, metadata, or who wishes to take some action to reduce or remove the potentially harmful consequences of its dissemination, may be able to limit the likelihood of its transmission by scrubbing metadata from documents, or by sending a different version of the document without the embedded information.[1] The Florida Bar Association and the New York State Bar Association have concluded that a lawyer's failure to ensure that metadata has been scrubbed from a document before transmitting it constitutes a failure to safeguard client confidences.[2]

[Section 16:12]

[1]ABA Formal Ethics Opinion 06-442 (Aug. 5, 2006). Contra Prof. Ethics of the Fla. Bar Opinion 06-2 (Sept. 15, 2006) (lawyer receiving electronic document should not try to obtain information from metadata that lawyer knows or should know is not intended for receiving lawyer); New York State Bar Ass'n Committee on Prof. Ethics Opinion 749 (Dec. 14, 2001) (lawyer may not intentionally use computer technology to surreptitiously obtain privileged or otherwise confidential information of an opposing party).

[2]New York State Bar Ass'n Committee on Prof. Ethics Opinions 749 and 782; Prof. Ethics of the Fla. Bar Opinion 06-2 (Sept. 15, 2006).

However, scrubbing metadata in discovery could be considered spoliation.[3]

The New York State Bar Association has concluded that lawyers may not intentionally use computer technology to surreptitiously obtain privileged or other confidential information of an opposing party.[4] The bars in Florida, Alabama, and Arizona have joined New York in holding that the recipient has a duty not to "mine" the document for metadata or otherwise engage in conduct amounting to an unjustified intrusion into the client-lawyer relationship that exists between the opposing party and the party's counsel.[5] The District of Columbia Bar has declared that a receiving lawyer is prohibited from reviewing metadata sent by an adversary only when the lawyer has actual knowledge that the metadata were sent inadvertently.[6]

The American Bar Association and the Maryland State Bar Associations have determined that there is not a specific prohibition against a lawyer's reviewing and using embedded information in electronic documents, whether received from opposing counsel, an adverse party, or an agent of an adverse party.[7] The Pennsylvania Bar Association says that each attorney must determine whether to use the metadata contained in electronic files based upon

---

[3]See Williams v. Sprint/United Management Co., 230 F.R.D. 640, 96 Fair Empl. Prac. Cas. (BNA) 1775, 62 Fed. R. Serv. 3d 1052, 29 A.L.R.6th 701 (D. Kan. 2005).

[4]New York State Bar Ass'n Committee on Prof. Ethics Opinions 749 and 782.

[5]Alabama Opinion No. 2007-02; Arizona Ethics Opinion 07-03; Prof. Ethics of the Fla. Bar Opinion 06-2 (Sept. 15, 2006) (reserving ruling on documents produced in response to discovery request).

[6]District of Columbia Bar, Opinion 341.

[7]ABA Formal Ethics Opinion 06-442 (Aug. 5, 2006); Maryland Opinion 2007 09 (2007). Contra Prof. Ethics of the Fla. Bar Opinion 06-2 (Sept. 15, 2006) (lawyer receiving electronic document should not try to obtain information from metadata that lawyer knows or should know is not intended for receiving lawyer); New York State Bar Ass'n Committee on Prof. Ethics Opinion 749 (Dec. 14, 2001) (lawyer may not intentionally use computer technology to surreptitiously obtain privileged or otherwise confidential information of an opposing party).

the attorney's judgment and the particular factual situation. Factors to be considered include the nature of the information received, how and from whom the information was received, attorney-client privilege, work-product rules, common sense, reciprocity, and professional courtesy.

§ 16:13 Privileges—Privilege log

Under Rule 26(b)(5) of the Federal Rules of Civil Procedure and many state rules of civil procedure, a party asserting a privilege must specifically identify each document or communication and the type of privilege or protection being asserted in a privilege log. To properly demonstrate that a privilege exists, the privilege log should contain a brief description or summary of the contents of the document, the date the document was prepared, the person or persons who prepared the document, the person to whom the document was directed, or for whom the document was prepared, the purpose in preparing the document, the privilege or privileges asserted with respect to the document, and how each element of the privilege is met as to that document. The summary should be specific enough to permit the court or opposing counsel to determine whether the privilege asserted applies to that document.

The summary should be specific enough to permit the court or opposing counsel to determine whether the privilege asserted applies to that document. In a privilege log concerning a string of e-mail communications, only the privileged communication identified by the date, time, and participants in the communication may be withheld; every other part of the string not so-identified must be produced.[1]

While a party claiming a privilege should provide reasonable specifics, the party should not be required to expend undue effort in preparing privilege logs or similar listings of withheld materials. In some cases, the burden

[Section 16:13]

[1]Muro v. Target Corp., 2007 WL 1630407 (N.D. Ill. 2007).

of specifying the withheld materials may justify a protective order. Where the number of documents is extremely voluminous, the court may permit the preparation of a privilege log on a categorical basis.

Generally, a party may not file a privilege log under seal absent court order. Even when stipulated to by adverse parties, the court must weigh any interests in confidentiality against that of the public to open records.[2] Moreover, by not providing a copy to the opposing party, a party negates the very purpose of a privilege log, which is to enable other parties to assess the applicability of the privilege log or protection.

§ 16:14 Privileges—Reviewing documents

The costs of reviewing electronically stored information for privilege and confidentiality can be enormous. However, it may be possible to protect a producing party's documents at much lower cost by enforcement of a confidential order and a protocol requiring that e-mails be reviewed on an attorneys' eyes-only basis and that review of privileged documents not be deemed a waiver of the privilege.[1]

Even with such protections, disclosure of privileged documents cannot be compelled. Accordingly, it may still

---

[2]Carty v. Government of Virgin Islands, 203 F.R.D. 229, 230 (D.V.I. 2001). Cf. Leucadia, Inc. v. Applied Extrusion Technologies, Inc., 998 F.2d 157, 165, 21 Media L. Rep. (BNA) 1737, 25 Fed. R. Serv. 3d 1315 (3d Cir. 1993); Citizens First Nat. Bank of Princeton v. Cincinnati Ins. Co., 178 F.3d 943, 944, 51 U.S.P.Q.2d 1218 (7th Cir. 1999).

[Section 16:14]

[1]Rowe Entertainment, Inc. v. William Morris Agency, Inc., 205 F.R.D. 421, 2002-1 Trade Cas. (CCH) P 73567, 51 Fed. R. Serv. 3d 1106 (S.D. N.Y. 2002). See Playboy Enterprises, Inc. v. Welles, 60 F. Supp. 2d 1050, 45 Fed. R. Serv. 3d 981 (S.D. Cal. 1999) (use of protective order and provision precluding waiver of attorney-client privilege sufficient); Anti-Monopoly, Inc. v. Hasbro, Inc., 1996-1 Trade Cas. (CCH) P 71294, 1996 WL 22976 (S.D. N.Y. 1996) (notwithstanding confidentiality order, business data should not be viewed by competitors).) However, in the absence of such an agreement or protocol, knowing disclosure of a privileged e-mail waives the privilege.)

be necessary to determine who should bear the costs if, notwithstanding the implementation of precautions, the producing party chooses to conduct a complete review before production.

§ 16:15 Privileges—Inadvertent production—Generally

Because of the volume of digital materials that may be produced, a privilege review of the materials may be incredibly expensive and time consuming. Additionally, there is always the possibility that some privileged documents may be missed during an extensive privilege review.

Courts differ with respect to the consequences to a producing party if, despite reasonable precautions, privileged material is inadvertently disclosed. Some courts have held that a mere inadvertent production of attorney-client privileged documents does not waive the privilege.[1] Other courts have held that once a document has been turned over to opposing counsel, the confidentiality of the document has been breached, destroying the basis for the

[Section 16:15]

[1]See Georgetown Manor, Inc. v. Ethan Allen, Inc., 753 F. Supp. 936, 18 Fed. R. Serv. 3d 1218 (S.D. Fla. 1991). See also McCafferty's, Inc. v. The Bank of Glen Burnie, 179 F.R.D. 163, 49 Fed. R. Evid. Serv. 808, 41 Fed. R. Serv. 3d 1011 (D. Md. 1998) (Where employee of attorney's client tore a confidential memorandum into 16 pieces and threw it into trash can, investigator for the plaintiff found the torn-up memorandum in the dumpster. Court held that attorney-client privilege had not been waived because the memorandum had not been disclosed. Court explained it was reasonable for the employee to have concluded that by tearing up the memo and throwing it away in a private location she was continuing to preserve confidentiality.) Sampson Fire Sales, Inc. v. Oaks, 201 F.R.D. 351, 359–62, 50 Fed. R. Serv. 3d 647 (M.D. Pa. 2001) (inadvertent disclosure of letter from plaintiff's attorney to plaintiff that occurred when it was faxed to wrong number did not waive attorney-client privilege). But see Gragg v. International Management Group, 2007 WL 1074894 (N.D. N.Y. 2007) (legal counsel's "nonchalant review" of electronic records acted to waive attorney-client privilege as to four inadvertently disclosed e-mails).

continued existence of the privilege.[2] Some courts have taken a middle ground, examining the adequacy of the precautions taken by the party who inadvertently produced the document in determining whether waiver should be found.[3]

Model Rule of Professional Conduct 4.4(b) was adopted by the American Bar Association in August 2002. The rule provides that a "lawyer who receives a document relating to the representation of the lawyer's client and knows or reasonably should know that the document was inadvertently sent shall promptly notify the sender." The rule requires only that the receiving attorney notify the sender; it does not require return of the document. Although a lawyer is not obligated to return a document unread if the lawyer notices that it was sent inadvertently, the decision to do so voluntarily is a "matter of professional judgment ordinarily reserved to the lawyer."[4] After notification, the comments to Rule 4.4(b) indicate that the next step is to

---

[2]See, e.g., International Digital Systems Corp. v. Digital Equipment Corp., 120 F.R.D. 445, 12 Fed. R. Serv. 3d 1151 (D. Mass. 1988). See also Koch Materials Co. v. Shore Slurry Seal, Inc., 208 F.R.D. 109, 118–19, 59 Fed. R. Evid. Serv. 249 (D.N.J. 2002) (inadvertent disclosure of handwritten unsigned documents authored by plaintiff's in-house counsel waived attorney-client privilege with respect to documents); Lifewise Master Funding v. Telebank, 206 F.R.D. 298, 303–04 (D. Utah 2002) (party that produces privileged documents in response to discovery request thereby waives attorney-client and work product privileges if it intended to disclose documents, but was merely unaware of legal consequences or nature of document produced).

[3]See, e.g., Koch Materials Co. v. Shore Slurry Seal, Inc., 208 F.R.D. 109, 118–19, 59 Fed. R. Evid. Serv. 249 (D.N.J. 2002); Sampson Fire Sales, Inc. v. Oaks, 201 F.R.D. 351, 359–62, 50 Fed. R. Serv. 3d 647 (M.D. Pa. 2001); Transamerica Computer Co., Inc. v. International Business Machines Corp., 573 F.2d 646, 1978-1 Trade Cas. (CCH) P 62031, 25 Fed. R. Serv. 2d 604 (9th Cir. 1978). Generally, the burden of proving inadvertent disclosure is on the party asserting the privilege. In re Sulfuric Acid Antitrust Litigation, 235 F.R.D. 407, 417-19, 2006-1 Trade Cas. (CCH) P 75315 (N.D. Ill. 2006), supplemented, 432 F. Supp. 2d 794, 2006-1 Trade Cas. (CCH) P 75316 (N.D. Ill. 2006).

[4]Model Rule of Prof. Conduct 4.4(b), comment [3].

determine whether the disclosure has waived the privileged status of the document.[5]

§ 16:16 Privileges—Inadvertent production—Recovery of produced material

Rule 26(b)(5)(B) of the Federal Rules of Civil Procedure provides a procedure for a party to assert a claim of privilege or trial-preparation material protection after information is produced in discovery. If the claim is contested, the rule permits any party that received the information to present the matter to the court for resolution. Rule 26(b)(5) does not address whether the privilege or protection that is asserted after production was waived by the production.

Problems of recovery can be ameliorated if the parties discuss the privilege issues during the discovery conference. Rule 26(f) directs the parties to discuss privilege issues in preparing their discovery plan. A court may incorporate any party agreement concerning privileged matters into a scheduling order.[1]

§ 16:17 Privileges—Inadvertent production—Recovery of produced material—Rule 502 of the Federal Rules of Evidence

The 2006 amendments to the Federal Rules of Civil Procedure do not address whether privilege is waived when privileged material is inadvertently produced during discovery.[1] A proposed new Rule 502 of the Federal Rules Evidence attempts to provide some certainly and restraint on costs associated with inadvertent disclosure. As As

---

[5]Model Rule of Prof. Conduct 4.4(b), comment [2].

[Section 16:16]

[1]Fed.R.Civ.P. 16(b)(4).

[Section 16:17]

[1]See Hopson v. Mayor and City Council of Baltimore, 232 F.R.D. 228, 235, 97 Fair Empl. Prac. Cas. (BNA) 617, 63 Fed. R. Serv. 3d 582 (D. Md. 2005) (although federal amendments encourage prudent counsel to utilize "quick peek" or "clawback" agreements, they are certainly not risk free, particularly with regard to third parties).

passed by the Senate in February 2008 (S2450), the proposed Rule 502 provides:

Rule 502 Attorney-Client Privilege and Work Product; Limitations on Waiver

The following provisions apply, in the circumstances set out, to disclosure of a communication or information covered by the attorney-client privilege or work-product protection.

(a) Disclosure Made in a Federal Proceeding or to a Federal Office or Agency; Scope of a Waiver. When the disclosure is made in a Federal proceeding or to a Federal office or agency and waives the attorney-client privilege or work-product protection, the waiver extends to an undisclosed communication or information in a Federal or State proceeding only if:

(1) the waiver is intentional;

(2) the disclosed and undisclosed communications or information concern the same subject matter; and

(3) they ought in fairness to be considered together.

(b) Inadvertent Disclosure. When made in a Federal proceeding or to a Federal office or agency, the disclosure does not operate as a waiver in a Federal or State proceeding if:

(1) the disclosure is inadvertent;

(2) the holder of the privilege or protection took reasonable steps to prevent disclosure; and

(3) the holder promptly took reasonable steps to rectify the error, including (if applicable) following Federal Rule of Civil Procedure 26(b)(5)(B).

(c) Disclosure Made in a State Proceeding. When the disclosure is made in a State proceeding and is not the subject of a State-court order concerning waiver, the disclosure does not operate as a waiver in a Federal proceeding if the disclosure:

(1) would not be a waiver under this rule if it had been made in a Federal proceeding; or

(2) is not a waiver under the law of the State where the disclosure occurred.

(d) Controlling Effect of a Court Order. A Federal court may order that the privilege or protection is not waived by disclosure connected with the litigation pending before the court in which event the disclosure is also not a waiver in any other Federal or State proceeding.

(e) Controlling Effect of a Party Agreement. An agreement on the effect of disclosure in a Federal proceeding is binding only on the parties to the agreement, unless it is incorporated into a court order.

(f) Controlling Effect of This Rule. Notwithstanding Rules 101 and 1101, this rule applies to State proceedings and to Federal court-annexed and Federal court-mandated arbitration proceedings, in the circumstances set out in the rule. And notwithstanding Rule 501, this rule applies even if State law provides the rule of decision.

(g) Definitions. In this rule:

(1) 'attorney-client privilege' means the protection that applicable law provides for confidential attorney-client communications; and

(2) 'work-product protection' means the protection that applicable law provides for tangible material (or its intangible equivalent) prepared in anticipation of litigation or for trial.

Explanatory Note on Evidence Rule 502

Prepared by the Judicial Conference

Advisory Committee Evidence Rules

(revised 11/28/2007)

This new rule has two major purposes:

1) It resolves some longstanding disputes in the courts about the effect of certain disclosures of material protected by the attorney-client privilege or the work product doctrine—specifically those disputes involving inadvertent disclosure and selective waiver.

2) It responds to the widespread complaint that litigation costs necessary to protect against waiver of attorney-client privilege or work product have become prohibitive due to the concern that any disclosure of protected information in the course of discovery (however innocent or

minimal) will operate as a subject matter waiver of all protected communications or information. This concern is especially troubling in cases involving electronic discovery. *See, e.g.*, Hopson v. Mayor and City Council of Baltimore, 232 F.R.D. 228, 244, 97 Fair Empl. Prac. Cas. (BNA) 617, 63 Fed. R. Serv. 3d 582 (D. Md. 2005) (electronic discovery may encompass "millions of documents" and to insist upon "record-by-record pre-production privilege review, on pain of subject matter waiver, would impose upon parties costs of production that bear no proportionality to what is at stake in the litigation.").

The rule seeks to provide a predictable, uniform set of standards under which parties can determine the consequences of a disclosure of communications or information covered by the attorney-client privilege or work product protection. Parties to litigation need to know, for example, that if they exchange privileged information pursuant to a confidentiality order, the court's order will be enforceable. For example, if a federal court's confidentiality order is not enforceable in a state court then the burdensome costs of privilege review and retention are unlikely to be reduced.

The rule makes no attempt to alter federal or state law on whether a communication or information is protected as attorney-client privilege or work product as an initial matter. Moreover, while establishing some exceptions to waiver, the rule does not purport to supplant applicable waiver doctrine generally.

The rule governs only certain waivers by disclosure. Other common-law waiver doctrines may result in a finding of waiver even where there is no disclosure of privileged information or work product. *See, e.g.*, Nguyen v. Excel Corp., 197 F.3d 200, 5 Wage & Hour Cas. 2d (BNA) 1352, 45 Fed. R. Serv. 3d 1298 (5th Cir. 1999) (reliance on an advice of counsel defense waives the privilege with respect to attorney-client communications pertinent to that defense); Byers v. Burleson, 100 F.R.D. 436, 38 Fed. R. Serv. 2d 403 (D.D.C. 1983) (allegation of lawyer malpractice constituted a waiver of confidential communications under the circumstances). The rule is not intended to displace or modify federal common law concerning waiver of privilege or work product where no disclosure has been made.

Subdivision (a). The rule provides that a voluntary disclosure in a federal proceeding or to a federal office or agency, if a waiver, generally results in a waiver only of the communication or information disclosed; a subject matter waiver (of either privilege or work product) is reserved for those unusual situations in which fairness requires a further disclosure of related, protected information, in order to protect against a selective and misleading presentation of evidence to the disadvantage of the adversary. *See, e.g.*, In re United Mine Workers of America Employee Ben. Plans Litigation, 159 F.R.D. 307, 312 (D.D.C. 1994) (waiver of work product limited to materials actually disclosed, because the party did not deliberately disclose documents in an attempt to gain a tactical advantage). Thus, subject matter waiver is limited to situations in which a party intentionally puts protected information into the litigation in a selective, misleading and unfair manner. It follows that an inadvertent disclosure of protected information can never result in a subject matter waiver. The rule rejects the result in In re Sealed Case, 877 F.2d 976, 28 Fed. R. Evid. Serv. 358 (D.C. Cir. 1989), which held that inadvertent disclosure of documents during discovery automatically constituted a subject matter waiver.

The language concerning subject matter waiver—"ought in fairness"—is taken from Rule 1206, because the animating principle is the same. Under both Rules, a party that makes a selective, misleading presentation that is unfair to the adversary opens itself to a more complete and accurate presentation.

To assure protection and predictability, the rule provides that if a disclosure is made at the federal level, the federal rule on subject matter waiver governs subsequent state court determinations on the scope of the waiver by that disclosure.

Subdivision (b). Courts are in conflict over whether an inadvertent disclosure of privileged information or work product constitutes a waiver. A few courts find that a disclosure must be intentional to be a waiver. Most courts find a waiver only if the disclosing party acted carelessly in disclosing the communication or information and failed to request its return in a timely manner. And a few courts hold that any mistaken disclosure of protected information constitutes waiver without regard to the protections taken to avoid such a disclosure. *See generally* Hopson v. Mayor and City Council of Baltimore, 232 F.R.D. 228, 97 Fair Empl. Prac. Cas. (BNA) 617, 63 Fed. R. Serv. 3d 582 (D. Md. 2005) for a discussion of this case law.

The rule opts for the middle ground: inadvertent disclosure of privileged or protected information in connection with a federal proceeding or to a federal office or agency does not constitute a waiver if the holder took reasonable steps to prevent disclosure and also promptly took reasonable steps to prevent disclosure.. This position is in accord with the majority view on whether inadvertent disclosure is a waiver.

Cases such as Lois Sportswear, U.S.A., Inc. v. Levi Strauss & Co., 104 F.R.D. 103, 105, 17 Fed. R. Evid. Serv. 1440 (S.D. N.Y. 1985) and Hartford Fire Ins. Co. v. Garvey, 109 F.R.D. 323, 332 (N.D. Cal. 1985), set out a multi-factor test for determining whether inadvertent disclosure is a waiver. The stated factors (none of which is dispositive) are the reasonableness of precautions taken, the time taken to rectify the error, the scope of discovery, the extent of disclosure and the overriding issue of fairness. The rules does not explicitly codify that test, because it is really a set of non-determinative guidelines that vary from case to case. The rule is flexible enough to accommodate any of those listed factors. Other considerations bearing on the reasonableness of a producing party's efforts include the number of documents to be reviewed and the time constraints for production. Depending on the circumstances, a party that uses advanced analytical software applications and linguistic tools in a screening for privilege and work product may be found to have taken "reasonable steps" to prevent inadvertent disclosure. The implementation of an efficient system of records management before litigation may also be relevant.

The rule does not require the producing party to engage in a post-production review to determine whether any protected communication or information has been produced by mistake. But the rules does require the producing party to follow up on any obvious indications that a protected communication or information has been produced inadvertently.

The rule applies to inadvertent disclosures made to a federal office or agency, including but not limited to an office or agency that is acting in the course of its regulatory, investigative or enforcement authority. The consequences of waiver, and the concomitant costs of pre-production privilege review can be as great with respect to disclosures to offices and agencies as they are in litigation.

Subdivision (c). Difficult questions can arise when 1) a disclosure of a communication or information protected by the attorney-client privilege or as work product is made in a state proceeding, 2) the communication or information is offered in a subsequent federal proceeding on the ground that the disclosure waived the privilege or protection, and 3) the state and federal laws are in conflict on the question of waiver. The Committee determined that the proper solution for the federal court is to apply the law that is most protective of privilege and work product. If the state law is more protective (such as where the state law is that an inadvertent disclosure can never be a waiver), the holder of the privilege or protection may well have relied on that law when making the disclosure in the state proceeding. Moreover, applying a more restrictive federal law of waiver could impair the state objective of preserving the privilege or work-product protection for disclosures made in state proceedings. On the other hand, if the federal law is more protective, applying the state law of waiver to determine admissibility in federal court is likely to undermine the federal objective of limiting the costs of production.

The rule does not address the enforceability of a state court confidentiality order in a federal proceeding, as that question is covered both by statutory law and principles of federalism and comity. *See* 28 U.S.C. § 1738 (providing that state judicial proceedings "shall have the same full faith and credit in every court within the United States . . . as they have by law or usage in the courts of such State . . . from which they are taken"). *See also* Tucker v. Ohtsu Tire & Rubber Co., Ltd., 191 F.R.D. 495, 499 (D. Md. 2000) (noting that a federal court considering the enforceability of a state confidentiality order is "constrained by principles of comity, courtesy, and . . . federalism"). Thus, a state court order finding no waiver in connection with a disclosure made in a state court proceeding is enforceable under existing law in subsequent federal proceedings.

Subdivision (d). Confidentiality orders are becoming increasingly important in limiting the costs of privilege review and retention, especially in cases involving electronic discovery. But the utility of a confidentiality order in reducing discovery costs is substantially diminished if it provides no protection outside the particular litigation in which the order is entered. Parties are unlikely to be able to reduce the costs of pre-production review for privilege and work product if the consequence of disclosure is that the communications or information could be used by non-parties to the litigation.

There is some dispute on whether a confidentiality order entered in one case is enforceable in other proceedings. *See generally* Hopson v. Mayor and City Council of Baltimore, 232 F.R.D. 228, 97 Fair Empl. Prac. Cas. (BNA) 617, 63 Fed. R. Serv. 3d 582 (D. Md. 2005), for a discussion of this case law. The rule provides that when a confidentiality order governing the consequences of disclosure in that case is entered in a federal proceeding, its terms are enforceable against non-parties in any federal or state proceeding. For example, the court order may provide for return of documents without waiver irrespective of the care taken by the disclosing party; the rule contemplates enforcement of "claw-back" and "quick peek" arrangements as a way to avoid the excessive costs of pre-production review for privilege and work product. *See* Zubulake v. UBS Warburg LLC, 216 F.R.D. 280, 290, 92 Fair Empl. Prac. Cas. (BNA) 684, 56 Fed. R. Serv. 3d 326 (S.D. N.Y. 2003) (noting that parties may enter into "so-called 'claw-back' agreements that allow the parties to forego privilege review altogether in favor of an agreement to return inadvertently produced privilege documents"). The rule provides a party with a predictable protection from a court order — predictability that is needed to allow the party to plan in advance to limit the prohibitive costs of privilege and work product review and retention.

Under the rule, a confidentiality order is enforceable whether or not it memorializes an agreement among the parties to the litigation. Party agreement should not be a condition of enforceability of a federal court's order.

Under subdivision (d), a federal court may order that disclosure of privileged or protected information "in connection with" a federal proceeding does not result in a waiver. But subdivision d) does not allow the federal court to enter an order determining the waiver effects of a separate disclosure of the same information in other proceedings, state or federal. If a disclosure has been made in a state proceeding (and is not the subject of a state-court order on waiver), then subdivision (d) is inapplicable. Subdivision (c) would govern the federal court's determination whether the state-court disclosure waived the privilege or protection in the federal proceeding.

Subdivision (e). Subdivision (e) codifies the well-established proposition that parties can enter an agreement to limit the effect of waiver by disclosure between or among them. Of course such an agreement can bind only the parties to the agreement. The rule makes clear that if parties want protection against non-parties from a finding of waiver by disclosure, the agreement must be made part of a court order.

Subdivision (f). The protections against waiver provided by Rule 502 must be applicable when protected communications or information disclosed in federal proceedings are subsequently offered in state proceedings. Otherwise the holders of protected communications and information, and their lawyers, could not rely on the protections provided by the Rule, and the goal of limiting costs in discovery would be substantially undermined. Rule 502(f) is intended to resolve any potential tension between the provisions of Rule 502 that apply to state proceedings and the possible limitations on the applicability of the Federal Rules of Evidence otherwise provided by Rules 101 and 1101.

The rule is intended to apply in all federal court proceedings, including court-annexed and court-ordered arbitrations, without regard to any possible limitations of Rules 101 and 1101. This provision is not intended to raise an inference about the applicability of any other rule of evidence in arbitration proceedings more generally.

The costs of discovery can be equally high for state and federal causes of action, and the rule seeks to limit those costs in all federal proceedings, regardless of whether the claim arises under state or federal law. Accordingly, the rule applies to state law causes of action brought in federal court.

Subdivision (g). The rule's coverage is limited to attorney- client privilege and work product. The operation of waiver by disclosure, as applied to other evidentiary privileges, remains a question of federal common law. Nor does the rule purport to apply to the Fifth Amendment privilege against compelled self- incrimination.

The definition of work product "materials" is intended to include both tangible and intangible information. *See* In re Cendant Corp. Securities Litigation, 343 F.3d 658, 662, 62 Fed. R. Evid. Serv. 577, 56 Fed. R. Serv. 3d 710 (3d Cir. 2003) ("work product protection extends to both tangible and intangible work product").

II. CHECKLISTS

§ 16:18 Privilege log checklist

☐ A brief description of the document explaining whether it is a memorandum, letter, e-mail, etc.

☐ The date the document was prepared

☐ The date of the document, if different from the preparation date

☐ The identity of the person or persons who prepared the document

☐ The identity of the persons for whom the document was prepared, including a showing based on competent evidence supporting any assertion the document was created by or under the supervision of an attorney

☐ The identity of the persons to whom the document and any copies were sent

☐ The purpose for preparing the document, including an evidentiary showing supporting any assertion that the document was prepared in the course of adversarial litigation or I anticipation of a threat of adversarial litigation that was real and imminent; a similar evidentiary showing that the subject of the communications within the document relates to seeking or giving advice; and a showing that the documents do not contain or incorporate non-privileged underlying facts

- ☐ The number of pages in the document
- ☐ The privilege or privileges asserted with respect to the document
- ☐ How each element of the privilege is met as to that document
- ☐ Any other pertinent information necessary to establish the elements of each asserted privilege

Comment

This form is adapted from Blaser v. Mt. Carmel Regional Medical Center, Inc., 2007 WL 1452993 (D. Kan. 2007).

§ 16:19 Checklist for determining whether information is a trade secret

- ☐ The extent to which the information is known outside the business
- ☐ The extent to which it is known by employees and others involved in the business
- ☐ The extent of measures taken by the employer to guard the secrecy of the information
- ☐ The value of the information to the employer and to the employer's competitors
- ☐ The amount of effort or money expended by the employer in developing the information
- ☐ The ease or difficulty with which the information could be properly acquired or duplicated by others

Comment

See Restatement (First) of Torts § 757 comment b. See, e.g., Jet Spray Cooler, Inc. v. Crampton, 361 Mass. 835, 840, 282 N.E.2d 921, 925, 174 U.S.P.Q. 272 (1972).

§ 16:20 Checklist for determining whether conduct of business implies desire that information be kept secret

- ☐ The existence of absence of an express agreement restricting disclosure
- ☐ The nature and extent of security precautions taken by the possessor to prevent acquisition of the information by unauthorized third parties
- ☐ The circumstances under which the information was disclosed to any employee to the extent they give rise to a reasonable inference that further disclosure, without the consent of the possessor, is prohibited
- ☐ The degree to which the information has been placed in the public domain or rendered readily ascertainable by third parties through patent applications or unrestricted product marketing

Comment

See Trent Partners and Associates, Inc. v. Digital Equipment Corp., 120 F. Supp. 2d 84, 111 (D. Mass. 1999).

III. FORMS

§ 16:21 Privilege log

LOG NUMBER	DISCOVERY REFERENCE OR EXHIBIT NUMBER
Identity and Position of Author	
Identity and Position of Recipients	
Privilege Claimed	
Present Location	

LOG NUMBER	DISCOVERY REFERENCE OR EXHIBIT NUMBER
Identity and Position of Author	

Identity and Position of Recipients
Privilege Claimed
Present Location

§ 16:22 Privilege log—Another form

Doc. Number	Type of Doc.	Date	Author	Recipient/ Addressee	Other Re-cipients	Description	Applicable Privileges

§ 16:23 Written authorization by patient for release of protected health information

AUTHORIZATION BY PATIENT FOR RELEASE OF PROTECTED HEALTH INFORMATION

Patient Name: Medical Record #:
Date of Birth: Social Security #:
I hereby authorize the use or disclosure of the Protected Health Information ("PHI") described below to be provided to or obtained by the following:

Name of Individual/ Facility/Company to Receive PHI	Name of Individual/Facility to Disclose PHI
Address:	Address:

Information authorized for use or disclosure or to be obtained:

☐ All medical information concerning this patient.
☐ Medical information of this patient compiled from ________ to ________.
☐ Only: ________
Dates of Treatment, if known:

The information will be obtained, used, or disclosed for the **following purpose(s) only**:

☐ Insurance
☐ Continued treatment
☐ Legal
☐ At the request of the patient or patient's representative
☐ Other (specify)

I understand:

I may revoke this authorization at any time, in writing, except revocation will not apply to information already used or disclosed in response to this authorization. I may revoke this document by presenting my written revocation as provided in the Notice of Privacy Practices of *[Name of Health Care Facility or Health Care Provider].* Unless revoked or otherwise indicated, the automatic expiration date will be one year from the date of signature or upon occurrence of the following event:

I release the entities listed above, their agents and employees from any liability in connection with the use or disclosure of the protected health information covered by this authorization. The entity authorized to disclose the information will not be compensated by the recipient for the disclosure, except for the cost of copying and mailing as authorized by law.

Information used or disclosed pursuant to this authorization may be subject to redisclosure by the recipient and no longer protected by federal law. However, the recipient may be prohibited from disclosing substance abuse information under the Federal Substance Abuse Confidentiality Requirements.

I have the right to inspect the health information to be released and I may refuse to sign this authorization.

Unless the purpose of this authorization is to determine payment of a claim for benefits, the requesting entity will not condition the provision of treatment or payment for my care on my signing this authorization.

Signature of Patient or Legal Representative	Date
Description of Legal Representative's Authority	Expiration Date of Authorization

§ 16:24 Motion to authorize disclosure of protected health information

[Caption]

MOTION TO AUTHORIZE DISCLOSURE OF PROTECTED HEALTH INFORMATION

Defendant *[name]*, moves the Court for an order authorizing disclosure of protected health information of Plaintiff *[name]* from *[health care facility or provider from whom discovery is sought]* pursuant to 45 C.F.R. § 164.512(e)(1)(i).

1. This motion is made on the grounds that Plaintiff *[name]* has sued the Defendant, *[name]*, for *[describe]* and Plaintiff *[name]* is relying on Plaintiff's *[physical] [mental] [emotional]* condition in this action as an element of Plaintiff's claim.

2. Under *[statute]*, Plaintiff has waived any privilege granted by law concerning any communication made with a physician or health care provider relevant to that *[physical] [mental] [emotional]* condition.

3. Defendant is seeking from *[health care facility or provider from whom discovery is sought]* all *[describe medical records sought]* relevant to the *[physical] [mental] [emotional]* condition of Plaintiff.

4. Plaintiff has refused to provide Defendant with a written authorization for release of protected health information.

5. This Motion is supported by the accompanying brief.

Dated: ________

[signature, etc.]

§ 16:25 Subpoena duces tecum to produce documents or other things—Attendance of witness not required

[Caption]

SUBPOENA DUCES TECUM TO HEALTH CARE PROVIDER
SEEKING PROTECTED HEALTH INFORMATION

TO: *[Name of Health Care Provider]*

You are commanded to produce and permit inspection and copying of the following described protected health information at the offices of *[name 1]*, attorney for Defendant *[name 2]*, located at *[address]*, on *[date]*, at *[time]*. *[Describe protected health information with reasonable particularity.]*

In order to allow objections to be filed to the production of documents and things that have been requested, you should not produce any of them until the date specified in this subpoena, and if an objection is filed, until the court rules on the objection.

In addition, you may not release these records until you are provided with a written statement from the undersigned attorney of satisfactory assurance of reasonable efforts to *[provide notice to [name 3][secure a qualified protective order]]*.

Dated: ________

[signature, etc.]

§ 16:26 Written statement of satisfactory assurance of notice to patient

WRITTEN STATEMENT OF SATISFACTORY ASSURANCE OF NOTICE TO PATIENT

TO: *[List health care facilities and providers from whom discovery of protected health information is sought.]*

PATIENT NAME:

SUBJECT: *[Identify type of records sought]*

Defendant *[name 1]* is a party in the action entitled pending before the Hon. *[name 2]* of the Court. *[Specify Court]*. Pursuant to 45 C.F.R. § 164.512(e)(1)(ii)(A), Defendant is seeking the protected health information described above of *[name 3]*. Defendant has made a good faith effort to provide written notice to *[name 3]*.

The Notice to Patient informed *[name 3]* Defendant was seeking protected health information for purposes of the above-described litigation and provided *[name 3]* with ten days to make an objection to the disclosure to the Court. Attached is a copy of the Notice to Patient and a registered mail receipt showing that the Notice to Patient was mailed to the last known address for *[name 3]* on *[date]*.

The time for *[name 3]* to make an objection to the disclosure to the Court has expired and no objection has been filed.

or

[Name 2] filed an objection to the disclosure, and the Court ruled on the objection by an Order authorizing disclosure of the protected health information. A copy of the Order is attached.

Dated: ________

[signature, etc.]

§ 16:27 Notice to patient of intent to discover protected health information

NOTICE TO PATIENT OF INTENT TO DISCOVER PROTECTED HEALTH INFORMATION

TO: *[Name of Patient]*

SUBJECT: *[Identify type of records sought]*

PLEASE TAKE NOTICE that Defendant *[name 1]* has *[prepared a subpoena for the production of records from] [issued subpoena for a deposition of] [identify health care facility or provider]* in connection with the action entitled pending before the Hon. *[name 2]* of the Court. Defendant is seeking the following protected health information concerning you pursuant to 45 C.F.R. § 164.512(e)(1)(ii)(A): *[Describe protected health information with reasonable particularity.]*

If you object to this discovery, you must file an objection in the above-described action by *[date]*. If you do not file an objection, Defendant will proceed with this discovery.

Dated: ________

[signature, etc.]

§ 16:28 Written statement of satisfactory assurance of reasonable efforts to secure a qualified protective order

WRITTEN STATEMENT OF SATISFACTORY ASSURANCE
OF REASONABLE EFFORTS TO SECURE A QUALIFIED PROTECTIVE ORDER

TO: *[List Health Care Facilities and Providers From Whom Discovery of Protected Health Information Is Sought]*

PATIENT NAME: *[name 3]*

SUBJECT: *[Identify type of records sought]*

Defendant *[name 1]* is a party in the action entitled pending before the Hon. *[name 2]* of the Court. *[Defendant]* is seeking the protected health information of *[name 3]* described above pursuant to 45 C.F.R. § 164.512(e)(1)(ii)(B).

Defendant has requested a qualified protective order from the court in the litigation described above.

or

[Name 3] and Defendant have agreed to a qualified protective order and have presented it to the court in the litigation described above.

A copy of the *[Motion for a Qualified Protective Order]* *[Agreed Qualified Protective Order]* is attached.

Dated: ________

[signature, etc.]

§ 16:29 Agreed qualified protective order (HIPAA)

[Caption]

AGREED QUALIFIED PROTECTIVE ORDER

This matter is before the Court on the Agreement of Plaintiff *[name 1]* and Defendant *[name 2]* for a Qualified Protective Order complying with 45 C.F.R. § 164.512(e)(1)(v)(A) and (B) and authorizing disclosure of protected health information pursuant to 45 C.F.R. § 164.512(e)(1)(iv)(A).

Based on the agreement of the parties, this Court finds that:

1. Plaintiff *[name 1]* has relied on plaintiff's *[physical] [mental] [emotional]* condition in this action as an element of Plaintiff's claim and under *[statute]* has waived any privilege granted by law concerning any communication made with a physician or health care provider relevant to that *[physical] [mental] [emotional]* condition; and

2. Defendant is seeking all *[identify type of medical records sought]* from *[identify health care facility or provider from whom discovery is sought]* that are relevant to the *[physical] [mental] [emotional]* condition of Plaintiff.

IT IS THEREFORE ORDERED that:

1. Plaintiff's protected health information may be obtained by Defendant *[name 2]* pursuant to discovery;

2. *[Identify health care facility or provider from whom discovery is sought]* is authorized to disclose, in response to any discovery request from Defendant *[name 2]* any and all protected health information relevant to the physical/mental/emotional condition of Plaintiff *[name 1]* to Counsel for Defendant *[name 2]*;

3. Defendant *[name 2]* is prohibited from using or disclosing the protected health information for any purpose other than this litigation; and

4. At the end of this litigation Defendant *[name 2]* is ordered to destroy all protected health information, including any copies made of the information.

Dated: ________

____
Judge

Approved As to Form:

Dated: ________

[signature, etc.]

§ 16:30 Confidentiality agreement

NO WAIVER OF PRIVILEGE

1. Inspection or production of documents (including physical objects) shall not constitute a waiver of the attorney-client privilege or work product immunity or any other applicable privilege if, as soon as reasonably possible after the producing party becomes aware of any inadvertent or unintentional disclosure, the producing party designates any such documents as protected from disclosure by attorney-client privilege or work product protection or any other applicable privilege and requests return of such documents to the producing party.

2. Upon request by the producing party, the receiving party immediately shall return to the producing party all copies of such inadvertently produced document(s), all copies thereof and any materials derived from or based thereon to the producing party. Notwithstanding this provision, outside litigation counsel of record are not required to delete information that may reside on their respective firm's electronic back-up systems that are over-written in the normal course of business.

§ 16:31 Confidentiality agreement—Another form

CONFIDENTIALITY AGREEMENT

The parties have agreed to produce all documents deemed discoverable under the *[rules]*, including electronically stored information, that are responsive to the discovery requests and not privileged or otherwise exempted from discovery under the *[rules]*, or other applicable source of law.

A. Some of the electronically stored information as well as other documents produced in this matter may contain communications or other information protected by the attorney-client privilege or work-production doctrine and not subject to discovery under *[rules]*.

B. Some of the produced electronically stored information and other documents in this matter may contain protected work-product material prepared or compiled in anticipation of litigation and not subject to discovery under *[rules]*.

C. The parties acknowledge that, despite each party's best efforts to conduct a thorough pre-production review of all electronically stored information and other documents, some material protected by the work-product doctrine or attorney-client privilege may be inadvertently disclosed to the other party during the course of this litigation;

D. The volume of potentially discoverable electronically stored information may substantially increase the total volume of documents that will be produced by the parties, thereby increasing the risk of inadvertent disclosure of material protected by the attorney-client privilege or the work-product doctrine.

E. In the course of this litigation, the parties may, either inadvertently or knowingly, produce information that is of a confidential, private, personal, trade secret, or proprietary nature ("confidential information").

F. The undersigned parties desire to establish a mechanism to avoid waiver of privilege or any other applicable protective evidentiary doctrine as a result of the inadvertently disclosure of material protected by the attorney-client privilege or work-product doctrine or confidential information.

G. The parties agree that this Agreement governs the disclosure of sensitive material and material protected by the attorney-client privilege or work-product doctrine in this action.

NON-WAIVER OF PRIVILEGE OR OTHER PROTECTIVE DOCTRINE BY INADVERTENT DISCLOSURE

1. The inadvertent disclosure of any document subject to a legitimate claim that the document should have been withheld from disclosure as protected by the attorney-client privilege or-work product doctrine does not waive any protection for that document or for the subject matter of the inadvertently disclosed document if the producing party, upon becoming aware of the disclosure, promptly requests its return and takes reasonable precautions to avoid such inadvertent disclosure.

2. Unless the requesting party disputes the claim, any documents the producing party deems to contain inadvertently disclosed material protected by attorney-client privilege or work-product doctrine must be upon written request promptly returned to the producing party or destroyed at the producing party's option. This includes all copies, electronic or otherwise, of any such documents. In the event that the producing party requests destruction, the requesting party must provide written certification of compliance within thirty (30) days of the written request. In the event that the requesting party disputes the producing party's claim as to the protected nature of the inadvertently disclosed material, a single set of copies may be sequestered and retained by and under the control of requesting party for the sole purpose of seeking court determination of the issue pursuant to Federal Rule of Civil Procedure 26(b)(5)(B).

3. Any such material protected by the attorney-client privilege or work-product doctrine inadvertently disclosed by the producing party to the requesting party pursuant to this Agreement, must be and remain the property of the producing property.

4. To the extent there may be inconsistency between this Agreement and *[rules]*, the *[rules]* control.

CONFIDENTIAL TREATMENT OF CONFIDENTIAL MATERIAL

5. Any material protected by the attorney-client privilege or work-product doctrine or confidential material disclosed in this litigation is to be considered confidential and proprietary to the producing party and the requesting party must hold it in confidence and must not use any such material other than for the purposes of this litigation. To that end, the parties limit the disclosure of all such material only to those persons with a need to know the information for purposes of supporting their position in this litigation. In addition, such material must not be disclosed, published or otherwise revealed to any other party in this litigation except with the specific prior written authorization of the producing party.

6. If any material protected by the attorney-client privilege or work-product doctrine or confidential material is disclosed through inadvertence or otherwise to any person not authorized under this Agreement, the party causing the disclosure must inform the person receiving such material that the information is covered by this Agreement, make its best efforts to retrieve such material, and promptly inform the producing party of the disclosure.

7. The requesting party has no confidentiality obligations with respect to any information that:

a. is already known to the requesting party without restriction;
b. is or becomes publicly known otherwise than by the requesting party's breach of this Agreement;
c. is received by the requesting party without restriction from a third-party who is not under an obligation of confidentiality;
d. is independently developed by the requesting party;
e. is approved for release by written authorization of the producing party; or
f. is disclosed by the requesting party pursuant to judicial action, provided that producing party is notified at the time such action is initiated.

8. Any material protected by the attorney-client privilege or work-product doctrine or confidential material disclosed by the producing party to the requesting party pursuant to this Agreement is and remains the property of the producing property.

GENERAL PROVISIONS

9. This Agreement terminates and supersedes all prior understandings or agreements on the subject matter hereof.

10. This Agreement is binding on the parties to the Agreement when signed regardless of whether or when the court enters its Order on it.

11. Nothing in this Agreement prevents any party from applying to the court for a modification of this Agreement should the moving party believe the Agreement, as originally agreed upon, is hampering its efforts to prepare for trial; or from applying to the court for further or additional protective Agreements; or from an Agreement between the parties to any modification of this Agreement, subject to the approval of the court.

12. This Agreement shall survive the final termination of this case regarding any retained documents or contents thereof.

13. The effective date of this Agreement is *[date]*.

Dated: ________

[signature, etc.]

Dated: ________

[signature, etc.]

§ 16:32 Stipulation for protective order

[Caption]

STIPULATED PROTECTIVE ORDER

Upon the stipulation of counsel and for good cause appearing:

IT IS HEREBY ORDERED that the following Protective Order be entered:

1. *[Rule]* Good Faith Designation. In responding to a discovery request, counsel for a party may in good faith designate any document containing "protected health information" under the Health Insurance Portability and Accountability Act of 1996 ("HIPAA") as "CONFIDENTIAL" by labeling the item with the mark "CONFIDENTIAL" or otherwise including that designation on an appropriate cover letter or document sufficient to advise the document's recipient of the designation.

2. "Document" Defined. The word "document" or "documents" as used herein means all paper and any other tangible thing, including, but not limited to, electronic files, produced in response to a formal or informal discovery request herein.

3. Inadvertence/Oversight. Inadvertent production of protected document(s) shall not constitute a waiver of the right to make an after-the-fact good faith designation. Upon the discovery of such inadvertent production, the producing party shall notify the parties in receipt of the document that it is designated "CONFIDENTIAL." An after-the-fact designation may be made orally on the record in any deposition, together with any explanation relative to inadvertence or oversight, and shall be honored by all present in the same manner as if originally designated "CONFIDENTIAL."

4. Disagreement Over Designation. In the event a recipient of a document declared "CONFIDENTIAL" disagrees with the designation, the proponent of confidentiality shall be so advised in writing by the objecting party and the producing party shall have 10 days within which to withdraw the confidential designation or move the Court to make a determination of confidentiality of any document in dispute. Pending such determination by the Court, any document in issue shall continue to be protected pursuant to the provisions of this Order.

5. General Use of CONFIDENTIAL Documents. Pursuant to 45 C.F.R. § 164.512(e)(1)(v), documents identified as "CONFIDENTIAL" and the confidential information contained therein may be used only for purposes of this litigation.

6. Disclosure to Others. "CONFIDENTIAL" information shall only be produced, revealed or disclosed to:

a. the Court, its staff, court reporters, jury and witnesses at trial;

b. attorneys in this action and employees of such counsel to whom it is necessary that the material be shown for purposes of the prosecution or defense of this action;

c. the parties to this action;

d. consultants or experts unrelated to the parties to this action and retained by them in order to assist in the prosecution or defense of this action, provided such persons are first given a copy of this Order and advised of the obligation to maintain the confidentiality of the information;

e. a deponent at the time of deposition, provided that such persons are first given a copy of this Order and advised of the obligation to maintain the confidentiality of the information; and

f. any other person by the parties' mutual written agreement or order of the Court after notice to all parties. Any such person who is given access to protected information shall be given a copy of this Order and advised of the obligation to maintain the confidentiality of the information.

7. Filing of CONFIDENTIAL Documents. In the event a party seeks to use "CONFIDENTIAL" documents as part of any court filing, the party shall comply with the procedures set forth in the *[rule]*. The Clerk of the Court is authorized, pursuant to *[rule]*, to accept materials submitted by the parties for filing under seal without further order of this Court. Documents filed under seal pursuant to the terms of this Protective Order shall be excluded, as provided by *[rule]*, from both the public case file and the electronic docket.

8. Use of CONFIDENTIAL Documents in Deposition. In the event a party seeks to use "CONFIDENTIAL" documents in a deposition, those portions of the deposition transcripts describing or incorporating any protected materials shall be deemed designated as "CONFIDENTIAL."

9. Admissibility. The provisions of this Order shall not determine whether and to what extent any document or information is admissible into evidence.

10. HIPAA. This Order is intended to comply with the HIPAA requirements of 45 C.F.R. § 164.512(e)(1)(v).

11. Return at Close of Litigation. Within 30 days of the final resolution of this litigation, a party that has received "Confidential" documents containing "protected health information" under HIPAA must either destroy or return such documents to the producing party.

IT IS SO STIPULATED:

Dated:

[signature etc.]

Dated:

[signature etc.]

IT IS SO ORDERED.

Dated: ________

____

Judge

Commentary

This form is adapted from the record in Abbott v. Good Shepherd Medical Center, 2005 WL 318575 (D. Or. 2005).

§ 16:33 Confidentiality order

[Caption]

CONFIDENTIALITY ORDER

To expedite the flow of discovery material, facilitate the prompt resolution of disputes over confidentiality, protect adequately material entitled to be kept confidential, and ensure that protection is afforded only to material so entitled, it is, pursuant to the court's authority under *[rule]* and with the consent of the parties, ORDERED:

1. Nondisclosure of Stamped Confidential Documents

Except with the prior written consent of the party or other person originally designating a document to be stamped as a confidential document, or as hereinafter provided under this order, no stamped confidential document may be disclosed to any person.

[A "stamped confidential document" means any document that bears the legend (or that must otherwise have had the legend recorded upon it in a way that brings it to the attention of a reasonable examiner) "Confidential-Subject to Protective Order in Civil Action No. ________, [court] "to signify that it contains information believed to be subject to protection under [rule]. For purposes of this order, the term "document" means all written, recorded, or graphic material, whether produced or created by a party or another person, whether produced pursuant to Rule 34, subpoena, by agreement, or otherwise. Interrogatory answers, responses to requests for admission, deposition transcripts and exhibits, pleadings, motions, affidavits, and briefs that quote, summarize, or contain materials entitled to protection may be accorded status as a stamped confidential document, but, to the extent feasible, must be prepared in such a manner that the confidential informa-

tion is bound separately from that not entitled to protection.]

2. Permissible Disclosures

Notwithstanding paragraph 1, stamped confidential documents may be disclosed to counsel for the parties in this action who are actively engaged in the conduct of this litigation; to the partners, associates, secretaries, paralegal assistants, and employees of such counsel to the extent reasonably necessary to render professional services in the litigation; to persons with prior knowledge of the documents or the confidential information contained therein, and their agents; and to court officials involved in this litigation (including court reporters, persons operating video recording equipment at depositions, and any special master appointed by the court). Subject to the provisions of subparagraph (c), such documents may also be disclosed—

(a) to any person designated by the court in the interest of justice, upon such terms as the court may deem proper; and

(b) to persons noticed for depositions or designated as trial witnesses to the extent reasonably necessary in preparing to testify; to outside consultants or experts retained for the purpose of assisting counsel in the litigation; to employees of parties involved solely in one or more aspects of organizing, filing, coding, converting, storing, or retrieving data or designing programs for handling data connected with these actions, including the performance of such duties in relation to a computerized litigation support system; and to employees of third-party contractors performing one or more of these functions; provided, however, that in all such cases the individual to whom disclosure is to be made has signed and filed with the court a form containing—

(1) a recital that the signatory has read and understands this order;

(2) a recital that the signatory understands that unauthorized disclosures of the stamped confidential documents constitute contempt of court; and

(3) a statement that the signatory consents to the exercise of personal jurisdiction by this court.

(c) Before disclosing a stamped confidential document to any person listed in subparagraph (a) or (b) who is a competitor (or an employee of a competitor) of the party that so designated the document, the party wishing to make such disclosure must give at least 10 days' advance notice in writing to the counsel who designated such information as confidential, stating the names and addresses of the person(s) to whom the disclosure will be made, identifying with particularity the documents to be disclosed, and stating the purposes of such disclosure. If, within the 10-day period, a motion is filed objecting to the proposed disclosure, disclosure is not permissible until the court has denied such motion. The court will deny the motion unless the objecting party shows good cause why the proposed disclosure should not be permitted.

3. Declassification

A party (or aggrieved entity permitted by the court to intervene for such purpose) may apply to the court for a ruling that a document (or category of documents) stamped as confidential is not entitled to such status and protection. The party or other person that designated the document as confidential must be given notice of the application and an opportunity to respond. To maintain confidential status, the proponent of confidentiality must show by a preponderance of the evidence that there is good cause for the document to have such protection.

4. Confidential Information in Depositions

(a) A deponent may during the deposition be shown and examined about stamped confidential documents if the deponent already knows the confidential information contained therein or if the provisions of paragraph 2(c) are complied with. Deponents must not retain or copy portions of the transcript of their depositions that contain confidential information not provided by them or the entities they represent unless they sign the form prescribed in paragraph 2(b). A deponent who is not a party or a representative of a party must be furnished a copy of this order before being examined about, or asked to produce, potentially confidential documents.

(b) Parties (and deponents) may, within 15 days after receiving a deposition, designate pages of the transcript (and exhibits thereto) as confidential. Confidential information within the deposition transcript may be designated by underlining the portions of the pages that are confidential and marking such pages with the following legend: "Confidential-Subject to Protection Pursuant to Court Order." Until expiration of the 15-day period, the entire deposition will be treated as subject to protection against disclosure under this order. If no party or deponent timely designates confidential information in a deposition, then none of the transcript or its exhibits will be treated as confidential; if a timely designation is made, the confidential portions and exhibits must be filed under seal separate from the portions and exhibits not so marked.

5. Confidential Information at Trial

Subject to the *[rules]*, stamped confidential documents and other confidential information may be offered in evidence at trial or any court hearing, provided that the proponent of the evidence gives five days' advance notice to counsel for any party or other person that designated the information as confidential. Any party may move the court for an order that the evidence be received in camera or under other conditions to prevent unnecessary disclosure. The court will then determine whether the proffered evidence should continue to be treated as confidential information and, if so, what protection, if any, may be afforded to such information at the trial.

6. Subpoena by Other Courts or Agencies

If another court or an administrative agency subpoenas

or orders production of stamped confidential documents that a party has obtained under the terms of this order, such party must promptly notify the party or other person who designated the document as confidential of the pendency of such subpoena or order.

7. Filing

Stamped confidential documents need not be filed with the clerk except when required in connection with motions under *[rules]* or other matters pending before the court. If filed, they must be filed under seal and must remain sealed while in the office of the clerk so long as they retain their status as stamped confidential documents.

8. Client Consultation

Nothing in this order must prevent or otherwise restrict counsel from rendering advice to their clients and, in the course thereof, relying generally on examination of stamped confidential documents; provided, however, that in rendering such advice and otherwise communicating with such clients, counsel must not make specific disclosure of any item so designated except pursuant to the procedures of paragraphs 2(b) and (c).

9. Prohibited Copying

If a document contains information so sensitive that it should not be copied by anyone, it must bear the additional legend "Copying Prohibited." Application for relief from this restriction against copying may be made to the court, with notice to counsel so designating the document.

10. Use

Persons obtaining access to stamped confidential documents under this order must use the information only for preparation and trial of this litigation (including appeals and retrials), and must not use such information for any other purpose, including business, governmental, commercial, administrative, or judicial proceedings. *[For purposes of this paragraph, the term "this litigation" includes other related litigation in which the producing person or company is a party.]*

11. Non-Termination

The provisions of this order must not terminate at the conclusion of these actions. Within 120 days after final conclusion of all aspects of this litigation, stamped confidential documents and all copies of same (other than exhibits of record) must be returned to the party or person that produced such documents or, at the option of the producer (if it retains at least one copy of the same), destroyed. All counsel of record must make certification of compliance herewith and must deliver the same to counsel for the party who produced the documents and not more than 150 days after final termination of this litigation.

12. Modification Permitted

Nothing in this order must prevent any party or other person from seeking modification of this order or from objecting to discovery that it believes to be otherwise improper.

13. Responsibility of Attorneys

The attorneys of record are responsible for employing reasonable measures, consistent with this order, to control duplication of, access to, and distribution of copies of stamped confidential documents. Parties must not duplicate any stamped confidential document except working copies and for filing in court under seal.

14. No Waiver

(a) Review of the confidential documents and information by counsel, experts, or consultants for the litigants in the litigation must not waive the confidentiality of the documents or objections to production.

(b) The inadvertent, unintentional, or in camera disclosure of confidential document and information must not, under any circumstances, be deemed a waiver, in whole or in part, of any party's claims of confidentiality.

15. Nothing contained in this protective order and no action taken pursuant to it shall prejudice the right of any party to contest the alleged relevancy, admissibility, or discoverability of the confidential documents and information sought.

Dated: ________

____
Judge

Comment

The order may indicate whether disclosure may be made to in-house counsel actively involved in the conduct of the litigation and to attorneys involved in related litigation in other courts.

Chapter 17

Spoliation

I. GUIDELINES

II. CHECKLISTS

III. FORMS

§ 17:23 Adverse inference instruction

Research References

Treatises and Practice Aids

eDiscovery & Digital Evidence §§ 11:1 to 11:19

Grenig and Kinsler, Federal Civil Discovery and Disclosure §§ 16.1 to 16.22 (2d ed.)

O'Malley, Grenig, & Lee, Federal Jury Practice and Instructions (5th ed.)

Trial Strategy

Recovery and Reconstruction of Electronic Mail as Evidence, 41 Am. Jur Proof of Facts 3d 1

Computer Technology in Civil Litigation, 71 Am. Jur Trials 111

Law Reviews and Other Periodicals

Brownstone et al., It's Not Purely a Civil Matter: Criminal Penalties May Apply to Destruction of Electronic Evidence under Sarbanes-Oxley, Nat'l L.J., March 10, 2008, at S1

Carroll, Developments in the Law of Electronic Discovery, 27 Am.J.Trial Advoc. 357 (2003)

Comment, Paper or Plastic?: Electronic Discovery and Spoliation in the Digital Age, 42 Hous. L. Rev. 1163 (2005)

Additional References

Isaza. Determining the Scope of Legal Holds: Waypoints for Navigating the Road Ahead, Information Mgt. J., March/Apr. 2007

Pass, Safe Harbor and Sanctions Under Rule 37, e-Discovery, 2007, at 34

Van Buskirk, Practical Strategies for Digital Discovery, The Brief, Spring 2003, at 50

ABA Discovery Standards, http://www.abanet.org/litigation/discoverystandards/2005civildiscoverystandards.pdf

Federal Judicial Center, http://www.fjc.gov

The Sedona Conference, http://www.thesedonaconference.org

KeyCite®: Cases and other legal materials listed in KeyCite Scope can be researched through the KeyCite service on Westlaw®. Use KeyCite to check citations for form, parallel references, prior and later history, and comprehensive citator information, including citations to other decisions and secondary materials.

I. GUIDELINES

§ 17:1 Generally

Persons and organizations are free to develop their own document retention and destruction policies so long as they are consistent with legislation, court rules, and court decisions, and they are reasonably tailored to the needs of the person or organization. However, there are times when the normal document destruction policy must be suspended, and documents must be retained and protected. The failure to take such action may have serious consequences.

§ 17:2 Spoliation

Spoliation is the destruction, significant alteration, or non-preservation of evidence relevant to pending or reasonably foreseeable litigation.[1] Spoliation "can occur as the result of actions by parties or by nonparties. It can be inadvertent or intentional. It can be the product of absolute good faith, the result of negligence or the exercise of consummate evil." Regardless of who destroys or conceals evidence, spoliation interferes with the proper administration of justice by giving one party an unfair advantage over an adversary. In the most egregious instances, spoliation amounts to a form of cheating that blatantly compromises the ideal of the trial as a search for truth and expropriates an injured party's legal remedy.

[Section 17:2]

[1]See Silvestri v. General Motors Corp., 271 F.3d 583, 590, 51 Fed. R. Serv. 3d 694 (4th Cir. 2001); Zubulake v. UBS Warburg LLC, 220 F.R.D. 212, 216, 92 Fair Empl. Prac. Cas. (BNA) 1539 (S.D. N.Y. 2003); Barsoum v. NYC Housing Authority, 202 F.R.D. 396, 399, 50 Fed. R. Serv. 3d 26 (S.D. N.Y. 2001).

If a party cannot fulfill the duty to preserve because the party does not own or control the evidence, the party still has an obligation to give the opposing party notice of the possible destruction of the evidence, and access to the evidence if it is within the party's power to do so, where the party anticipates litigation involving that evidence.[2]

Digital realities increase the risk that a party or its counsel may be charged with spoliation. There are many reasons for this. For example, not all clients take the threat of harm due to spoliation seriously, since it seems so easy to delete, alter, or eliminate a digital file.[3] Those who are responsible for advising targets of discovery must recognize the very real danger that an anxious or overly defensive client will engage in efforts to delete or "sanitize" sources of digital information. To avoid criticism, counsel must take all reasonable steps to prevent it from happening and to set up procedures designed to police the preservation of digital evidence.[4]

Spoliation of digital evidence can have very severe consequences and the act of spoliation is actually easier to establish in the case of electronically stored information evidence than it is in the case of paper evidence. Courts have made it clear that they take the preservation of digital evidence very seriously. If advised of a threat in advance, a

---

[2]Silvestri v. General Motors Corp., 271 F.3d 583, 591, 51 Fed. R. Serv. 3d 694 (4th Cir. 2001).

[3]Munshani v. Signal Lake Venture Fund II, LP, 60 Mass. App. Ct. 714, 805 N.E.2d 998 (2004).

[4]See In re Old Banc One Shareholders Securities Litigation, 2005 WL 3372783 (N.D. Ill. 2005) (referring to party's duty to properly preserve evidence upon notice of probable litigation). National Ass'n of Radiation Survivors v. Turnage, 115 F.R.D. 543, 557 (N.D. Cal. 1987); In re Prudential Ins. Co. of America Sales Practices Litigation, 169 F.R.D. 598, 36 Fed. R. Serv. 3d 767 (D.N.J. 1997); U.S. v. Koch Industries, Inc., 197 F.R.D. 463 (N.D. Okla. 1998).

court may well order the preservation of computerized data during the pendency of a lawsuit.[5]

There are many consequences that can flow from a failure to preserve digital data. These consequences include charges of malpractice, discipline for ethical violations, contempt citations, and significant monetary sanctions. In *United States v. Philip Morris*,[6] the court found that a significant number of e-mails had been lost and that defendants' employees were not following the company's own internal procedures for document preservation. The court imposed a sanction of $2,750,000 on the defendant.

In another case, a plaintiff discovered ten months into a lawsuit that the defendant was deleting e-mails in the normal course of business after thirty days. The court ordered the defendant to recover the deleted e-mail and invited the plaintiff to seek the appointment of a forensic computer expert to perform the recovery at the defendant's expense.[7] In yet another case a defendant claimed e-mail did not exist but it was later shown that it was in fact saved on backup tapes. The court ordered the defendant to restore the backup tapes at a cost of over $1,000,000.[8]

It is not enough to recognize the need to avoid spoliation and warn against it; counsel must aggressively take steps to ensure the protection of digital evidence. Complicating matters is the fact that in a digital environment a host of problems that did not exist in a paper universe must be faced by today's counsel. Addressing these problems imposes both new legal and ethical obligations on the practitioner. Unfortunately, the boundary line between law and ethics in this area is often unclear.

---

[5]See, e.g., In re Cell Pathways, Inc., Securities Litigation, II, 203 F.R.D. 189, Fed. Sec. L. Rep. (CCH) P 91507 (E.D. Pa. 2001); In re Bridgestone/Firestone, Inc., ATX, 129 F. Supp.2d 1207 (S.D.Ind. 2001).

[6]U.S. v. Philip Morris USA, Inc., 327 F. Supp. 2d 21 (D.D.C. 2004).

[7]Aero Products Intern., Inc. v. Intex Recreation Corp., 2004 WL 417193 (N.D. Ill. 2004).

[8]Linnen v. A.H. Robins Co., Inc., 10 Mass. L. Rptr. 189, 1999 WL 462015 (Mass. Super. Ct. 1999).

§ 17:3 Duty to preserve

Determining the boundaries of the duty to preserve involves two related inquiries:

- When does the duty to preserve attach?
- What evidence must be preserved?

A person or organization must preserve all documents discoverable in litigation that is pending or in probable litigation of which the person or organization has notice.[1] In the absence of actual notice, a person must preserve documents that the person knows or should know will be discoverable in "reasonably foreseeable" litigation. "Reasonable foreseeability" is determined on a fact-specific basis. If litigation is pending or reasonably foreseeable, the legal standard for the retention of documents is their discoverability in the litigation.[2]

Unlike paper documents, which require an overt act like shredding to be destroyed, electronically stored information can be and often is destroyed by routine computer use. Simply turning on a personal computer can destroy "slack" and "temporary" files, cause data to be overwritten, or alter metadata (for example, data showing when a file was created or modified). Just clicking on a file can

---

[Section 17:3]

[1]Vela v. Wagner & Brown, Ltd., 203 S.W.3d 37 (Tex. App. San Antonio 2006) (expert is required to preserve expert's work product and party who retained expert may be sanction if expert destroys work product). See also Fujitsu Ltd. v. Federal Exp. Corp., 247 F.3d 423, 436 (2d Cir. 2001). See Sedona Principle 5 ("The obligation to preserve electronically stored information requires reasonable and good faith efforts to retain information that may be relevant to pending or threatened litigation. However, it is unreasonable to expect parties to take every conceivable step to preserve all potentially relevant electronically stored information.").

[2]Fujitsu Ltd. v. Federal Exp. Corp., 247 F.3d 423, 436 (2d Cir. 2001).

change its "last-accessed" date, inviting a suggestion that it has been altered.[3]

While a litigant is under no duty to keep or retain every paper or digital document in the litigant's possession once a complaint is filed, a litigant is under a duty to preserve what it knows, or reasonably should know, is relevant in the action, is reasonably calculated to lead to discovery of admissible evidence, is reasonably likely to be requested during discovery, and/or is the subject of a pending discovery request.

A person's exposure to spoliation liability in discarding records under a routine procedure depends primarily on: (1) the relevance of the documents to pending or reasonably foreseeable litigation; and (2) the nature of the person's document retention policy. Even if a person were to inadvertently dispose of documents discoverable in reasonably foreseeable litigation, pursuant to its formal policy, the person would not necessarily be sanctioned for spoliation.[4]

§ 17:4 Foreseeability of future litigation

Absent actual notice, all forms of spoliation liability turn on foreseeability.[1] When a complaint has not yet been filed and there is no specific statutory or other legal duty

---

[3]Gates Rubber Co. v. Bando Chemical Industries, Ltd., 167 F.R.D. 90 (D. Colo. 1996).

[4]See Williams v. Sprint/United Management Co., 230 F.R.D. 640, 652, 96 Fair Empl. Prac. Cas. (BNA) 1775, 62 Fed. R. Serv. 3d 1052 (D. Kan. 2005) (when party is ordered to disclose electronic documents as they are maintained in ordinary course of business, producing party should produce electronic documents with metadata intact, unless that party timely objects to production of metadata, parties agree that metadata should not be produced, or producing party requests protective order).

[Section 17:4]

[1]See, e.g., Computer Associates Intern., Inc. v. American Fundware, Inc., 133 F.R.D. 166, 169, 18 U.S.P.Q.2d 1649 (D. Colo. 1990) (prelitigation correspondence constitutes actual notice of litigation). But see Getty Properties Corp. v. Raceway Petroleum, Inc., 2005 WL 1412134 (D.N.J. 2005) (failure to retain interim or transitory information not

between the parties, the question is whether it is "reasonably foreseeable" that a lawsuit will ensue and that the evidence will be discoverable in connection with that suit. The majority of jurisdictions endorse the "reasonable foreseeability" test.

Thus, the duty to preserve evidence before the filing of a lawsuit typically arises when the party is on notice that the litigation is "likely to be commenced." This notice usually occurs when a person is served with either a judicial or administrative complaint, but it also may occur as a result of prelitigation communication with the plaintiff.

There appear to be no cases extending the foreseeability requirement to a remote possibility of future litigation. In *Willard v. Caterpillar, Inc.*,[2] the defendant destroyed documents in the ordinary course of business relating to a 35-year-old product over which it had never been sued. The destruction was held not to constitute spoliation of evidence because, in the court's view, the mere possibility of future litigation was not enough.

Another way in which courts have determined the existence of such notice is through consideration of prior complaints or lawsuits filed against the company over similar or related matters.[3] There are very few reported cases that treat the issues of "related litigation" or "similar products" in the context of spoliation, and there is not

---

required for business purposes is not kind of willful action that discovery sanctions are intended to redress).

[2]Willard v. Caterpillar, Inc., 40 Cal. App. 4th 892, 48 Cal. Rptr. 2d 607, 620–21 (5th Dist. 1995) (disapproved of on other grounds by, Cedars-Sinai Medical Center v. Superior Court, 18 Cal. 4th 1, 74 Cal. Rptr. 2d 248, 954 P.2d 511 (1998)).

[3]Cf. Stevenson v. Union Pacific R. Co., 354 F.3d 739, 63 Fed. R. Evid. Serv. 166, 57 Fed. R. Serv. 3d 617 (8th Cir. 2004) (declaring that there must be some indication of an intent to destroy the evidence for the purpose of obstructing or suppressing truth in order to impose sanction of adverse inference instruction, court upheld sanctions against defendant, because defendant had been careful to preserve a voice tape in other cases where tape proved to be beneficial to defendant and had made immediate effort to preserve other types of evidence but not voice tape in this case).

enough detail in the available cases to define these terms for purposes of determining when additional litigation is reasonably foreseeable.

The leading case is *Lewy v. Remington Arms Co.*,[4] a products liability action relating to a rifle that fired upon the release of its safety. The manufacturer's record retention policy provided for the destruction of complaints and gun examination reports after three years, absent any action concerning a particular record. Since other complaints had been filed against the manufacturer with respect to the rifle model in question, the court remanded the case for a determination regarding the propriety of destroying the plaintiff's records under the circumstances. The court suggested that frequent discovery requests for a specific type of document in litigation over the same product may establish the reasonable foreseeability of the relevance and probably materiality of other documents of that type in future litigation.

Remington suggests limits on what courts will consider "similar products." The *Remington* court did not rule that complaints about the defective firing pin meant that the defendant should foresee lawsuits involving all of its firing pins, let alone all of its rifles. Rather, it announced the common-sense rule that there was an issue as to whether destruction of documents involving a specific model was appropriate, where the company had received a series of complaints about that model. There is apparently no additional authority to assist in determining when products are sufficiently "similar" to assume that complaints about one create foreseeable litigation involving another.

Additional facts surrounding the document retention policy may also indicate the reasonable foreseeability of litigation. The *Remington* court suggested that a three-year retention period might be appropriate for some types of documents but not others, including possibly customer complaints. Finally, the court thought it relevant whether lawsuits concerning the complaint or related complaints

---

[4]Lewy v. Remington Arms Co., Inc., 836 F.2d 1104, Prod. Liab. Rep. (CCH) P 11662, 24 Fed. R. Evid. Serv. 516 (8th Cir. 1988).

have been filed, the frequency of such complaints, and the magnitude of the complaints. In *Remington*, lawsuits concerning the complaint and related complaints would appear to refer to lawsuits or complaints pertaining to the firing controls of the specific rifle model in question.

The issue of whether a company must maintain documents prior to actual notice of litigation arose in *Scott v. IBM Corp.*[5] In that case, an employee brought an action against his former employer for discrimination. The suit arose out of IBM's decision to layoff Scott as part of a company-wide reduction-in-force (RIF). Before the suit, IBM destroyed documents related to the RIF. The court held that the destruction warranted sanctions because the detailed nature of the destroyed documents themselves demonstrated that IBM was on notice of the sensitive nature of the layoff. Moreover, the court concluded:

> [W]hile litigation was not guaranteed, it could be viewed as reasonably foreseeable. IBM managers knew that Mr. Scott, if not others included in the RIF, were protected by federal employment discrimination laws. Mr. Scott had made previous claims of race discrimination within IBM, and thus IBM had ample notice that it was discharging a litigious employee when it fired him. Common sense would dictate preserving all helpful documentation when dealing with the discharge of an employee with a litigious history.[6]

In *Sanchez v. Stanley-Bostich, Inc.*,[7] as amended, the court approved an adverse inference instruction against the plaintiff (Sanchez) based on spoliation. Sanchez claimed that he was injured while using the defendant's (Stanley's) staple gun. After the accident, Sanchez's lawyer instructed him to take photographs of the staple gun at issue, but neither Sanchez nor his lawyer did anything to preserve the gun itself. The court was asked to determine

---

[5]Scott v. IBM Corp., 196 F.R.D. 233, 12 A.D. Cas. (BNA) 99 (D.N.J. 2000), as amended, (Nov. 29, 2000).

[6]Scott v. IBM Corp., 196 F.R.D. 233, 249, 12 A.D. Cas. (BNA) 99 (D.N.J. 2000), as amended, (Nov. 29, 2000).

[7]Sanchez v. Stanley-Bostich, Inc., Prod. Liab. Rep. (CCH) P 15635, 1999 WL 639703 (S.D. N.Y. 1999).

whether Sanchez "had an obligation to preserve the gun for Stanley's use." Answering this question affirmatively, the court stated:

> The obligation to preserve evidence may arise before the filing of a complaint where a party is on notice that litigation will likely be commenced. Here, at the time the photographs were taken Sanchez had already retained counsel, and indeed was acting at his direction. Clearly, the photographs were taken in preparation of a possible lawsuit. Yet, Stanley was not informed of the anticipated claim.[8]

§ 17:5 What must be preserved

Once a person has notice of potential litigation, the person has a duty to act reasonably in preserving documents. Although a litigant is not under a duty to keep or retain every document in its possession once a complaint is filed, a litigant is under a duty to preserve what it knows, or reasonably should know, is relevant in the action, is reasonably calculated to lead to the discovery of admissible evidence, is reasonably likely to be requested during discovery, and/or is the subject of a pending discovery request.[1]

One of the biggest problems with preserving electronically stored information is finding and identifying it. Generally, data management systems are developed to satisfy daily business practices, not to accommodate discovery needs. An additional problem is created by the volatility of digital information. Electronically stored information can be altered, overwritten, or destroyed simply by running conflicting software or by conducting routine maintenance.

In federal court, a first look at what documents should be retained normally revolves around the persons named in the disclosures made pursuant to Rule 26(a)(1)(a) of the Federal Rules of Civil Procedure. If a person is named in

---

[8]Sanchez v. Stanley-Bostich, Inc., Prod. Liab. Rep. (CCH) P 15635, 1999 WL 639703 (S.D. N.Y. 1999).

[Section 17:5]

[1]Zubulake v. UBS Warburg LLC, 220 F.R.D. 212, 217–18, 92 Fair Empl. Prac. Cas. (BNA) 1539 (S.D. N.Y. 2003).

those disclosures, documents made by or for that person must be saved.[2] Other documents that should be retained are those involving persons in the organization likely to have relevant information as that term is defined by Rule 26(b)(1) of the federal rules of civil procedure.[3]

Once the persons whose documents should be retained are identified, those persons "must retain all relevant documents (but not multiple identical copies) in existence at the time the duty to preserve attaches, and any relevant documents created thereafter."[4] Beyond taking these initial steps, there is no magic way to fulfill the preservation obligation. Rather, the touchstone should be reasonableness—whether the party has taken all reasonable steps necessary to preserve the relevant or potentially relevant documents.[5]

Zubulake contains a practical summary of the duty to preserve:

> The scope of a party's preservation obligation can be described as follows: Once a party reasonably anticipates litigation, it must suspend its routine document retention/destruction policy and put in place a "litigation hold" to ensure the preservation of relevant documents. As a general rule, that litigation hold does not apply to inaccessible backup tapes (e.g., those typically maintained solely for the purpose of disaster recovery), which may continue to be recycled on the schedule set forth in the company's policy. On the other hand, if backup tapes are accessible (i.e., actively used for information retrieval), then such tapes would likely be subject to the litigation hold.
>
> However, it does make sense to create one exception to this general rule. If a company can identify where particular employee documents are stored on backup tapes, then

[2]Zubulake v. UBS Warburg LLC, 220 F.R.D. 212, 218, 92 Fair Empl. Prac. Cas. (BNA) 1539 (S.D. N.Y. 2003).

[3]Zubulake v. UBS Warburg LLC, 220 F.R.D. 212, 218, 92 Fair Empl. Prac. Cas. (BNA) 1539 (S.D. N.Y. 2003).

[4]Zubulake v. UBS Warburg LLC, 220 F.R.D. 212, 218, 92 Fair Empl. Prac. Cas. (BNA) 1539 (S.D. N.Y. 2003).

[5]See Zubulake v. UBS Warburg LLC, 220 F.R.D. 212, 92 Fair Empl. Prac. Cas. (BNA) 1539 (S.D. N.Y. 2003).

> the tapes storing the documents of "key players" to the existing or threatened litigation should be preserved if the information contained on those tapes is not otherwise available. This exception applies to all backup tapes.[6]

This articulation of the duty to preserve strikes a reasonable balance between a party's right to discover relevant evidence and an organization's need to operate without undue burden or expense. It also emphasizes the necessity of having a written, reasonable, need-based, and transparent document retention and destruction policy so that a court can understand what documents are being preserved or destroyed and why that action is being taken. Without such a policy, the duty to preserve will be, by necessity, much broader than it need be.

One of the most common preservation mistakes is failing to cease document destruction procedures upon notice of suit or the likelihood of suit. The Court in *Zubulake v. UBS Warburg LLC*[7] described the obligation of a party who anticipates litigation to preserve digital evidence in the following terms:

> A party or anticipated party must retain all relevant documents (but not multiple identical copies) in existence at the time the duty to preserve attaches, and any relevant documents created thereafter. In recognition of the fact that there are many ways to manage electronic data, litigants are free to choose how this task is accomplished. For example, a litigant could choose to retain all then-existing backup tapes for the relevant personnel (if such tapes store data by individual or the contents can be identified in good faith and through reasonable effort), and to catalog any

---

[6]Zubulake v. UBS Warburg LLC, 220 F.R.D. 212, 92 Fair Empl. Prac. Cas. (BNA) 1539 (S.D. N.Y. 2003). See Consolidated Aluminum Corp. v. Alcoa, Inc., 244 F.R.D. 335 (M.D. La. 2006) (as general rule, party's duty to place a litigation hold on evidence does not apply to inaccessible backup tapes for electronic evidence—those typically maintained solely for purpose of disaster recovery, which may continue to be recycled on the schedule set forth in party's policy, but if backup tapes are accessible (actively used for information retrieval), then such tapes would likely be subject to litigation hold).

[7]Zubulake v. UBS Warburg LLC, 220 F.R.D. 212, 92 Fair Empl. Prac. Cas. (BNA) 1539 (S.D. N.Y. 2003).

later-created documents in a separate electronic file. That, along with a mirror-image of the computer system taken at the time the duty to preserve attaches (to preserve documents in the state they existed at that time), creates a complete set of relevant documents. Presumably there are a multitude of other ways to achieve the same result.

The scope of a party's preservation obligation can be described as follows: Once a party reasonably anticipates litigation, it must suspend its routine document retention/destruction policy and put in place a "litigation hold" to ensure the preservation of relevant documents. As a general rule, that litigation hold does not apply to inaccessible backup tapes (e.g., those typically maintained solely for the purpose of disaster recovery), which may continue to be recycled on the schedule set forth in the company's policy. On the other hand, if backup tapes are accessible (i.e., actively used for information retrieval), then such tapes *would* likely be subject to the litigation hold.[8]

Counsel face a number of important considerations when it comes to deciding what to preserve and how. The *Zubulake* decision only touches on some of the issues. In deciding what electronically stored information to preserve, counsel should carefully research the subject. Counsel should not rely on his or her own understanding of what constitutes electronically stored information or how it can be preserved. Counsel does not want to be in the position of becoming a technical witness if and when the question of digital data preservation becomes an issue in litigation. Moreover, most counsel are not in a strong position to determine:

- What metadata are and how they ought to be preserved, if at all.
- What the distinction is between backup and disaster tape systems.
- What backup or data storage sequences should be suspended.
- What steps should be taken to "image" hard drives.
- What steps should be taken to segregate business

[8]Zubulake v. UBS Warburg LLC, 220 F.R.D. 212, 218, 92 Fair Empl. Prac. Cas. (BNA) 1539 (S.D. N.Y. 2003) (italics in original).

e-mail from personal e-mail or otherwise protect employee privacy or trade secret privileges.

- What must be done to distinguish between unique and duplicate digital data.
- What steps should be taken to preserve Web pages, intranet systems, or ASP data depositories.

§ 17:6 Written preservation plans

A written preservation plan focuses on preserving electronically stored information once litigation is foreseeable. Counsel must evaluate the extent to which retention policies must be suspended because of the impending litigation. Before adoption of a plan, evidence generally may be legitimately destroyed when done pursuant to a document retention policy that is reasonable and evenly applied.

The success of a preservation plan depends to a very large degree on an intimate knowledge on the part of producing counsel of the administrative controls and architecture of a defendant's computer system. For most attorneys, such knowledge can only be acquired by retaining technical assistance, and this is especially important when it comes to devising workable preservation plans.

Retention polices are not the same as preservation plans. It may be necessary to suspend retention policies in order to insure that relevant evidence is not destroyed in the course of the routine reuse of backup tapes. The destruction of electronically stored information pursuant to a bona fide retention policy where no litigation is anticipated will normally be acceptable.

Still, counsel should approach existing or planned retention policies with a degree of skepticism. The issue often becomes whether an organization in adopting a retention policy knew or should have known that litigation was imminent. In *Lewy v. Remington Arms Co.,*[1] the Eighth Circuit ruled:

> In cases where a document retention policy is instituted in order to limit damaging evidence available to potential plaintiffs, it may be proper to give an [adverse inference] instruction similar to the one requested by the Lewys. Similarly, even if the court finds the policy to be reasonable given the nature of the documents subject to the policy, the court may find that under the particular circumstances certain documents should have been retained notwithstanding the policy. For example, if the corporation knew or should have known that the documents would become material at some point in the future then such documents should have been preserved. Thus, a corporation cannot blindly destroy documents and expect to be shielded by a seemingly innocuous document retention policy.

§ 17:7 Ethical considerations

Lawyers who aid the deliberate concealment or destruction of evidence may be disciplined under relevant ethical codes or rules of court.[1] For example, the American Bar Association's Model Code of Professional Conduct may be violated when evidence is concealed or destroyed by a lawyer. Under Model Rule 3.4(a), a lawyer must not "unlawfully obstruct another party's access to evidence or unlawfully alter, destroy or conceal a document or other material having potential evidentiary value."

The Model Code of Professional Responsibility states that a lawyer must not "conceal or knowingly fail to disclose that which he is required by law to reveal," during representation of a client. (ABA Code DR 7-102(A)(3).) DR 7-109(A) adds that "[a] lawyer shall not suppress any evi-

---

[Section 17:6]

[1] Lewy v. Remington Arms Co., Inc., 836 F.2d 1104, 1112, Prod. Liab. Rep. (CCH) P 11662, 24 Fed. R. Evid. Serv. 516 (8th Cir. 1988).

[Section 17:7]

[1] See Donato v. Fitzgibbons, 172 F.R.D. 75, 79, 38 Fed. R. Serv. 3d 1086 (S.D. N.Y. 1997) (obligation to preserve evidence runs first to counsel, who has duty to advise client of type of information potentially relevant to lawsuit and of the necessity of preventing its destruction).

dence that he or his client has a legal obligation to reveal or produce." Spoliation performed by the client at the lawyer's direction may also violate the Model Rules. (See ABA Code DR 7-102(A)(7) ("In his representation of a client, a lawyer shall not counsel or assist his client in conduct that the lawyer knows to be illegal or fraudulent."); Model Rule of Professional Conduct 3.4(a) (same).) This prohibition may embrace document retention policies designed in bad faith at the behest of the lawyer.

Counsel should carefully monitor their clients' document production, as many clients may not appreciate the implications of hiding or destroying damaging evidence.[2] Additionally, counsel must monitor experts. Many tests require destruction of the evidence itself and could lead to spoliation claims. Constant vigilance by a lawyer may avoid costly litigation or sanctions, as well as prevent ethical conflicts from arising.

§ 17:8 Consequences of preservation

It should be stressed that preservation does not mean that counsel must later agree to produce evidence. By preserving data, counsel is only insuring that the data will be available if the data are later determined to be relevant or discoverable. If it is later determined that counsel should have preserved data but did not, counsel could face charges of complicity in evidence spoliation that could subject counsel and the client to serious penalties.

---

[2]See, e.g., Board of Regents of University of Nebraska v. BASF Corp., 2007 WL 3342423 (D. Neb. 2007) (when responding to request for production of documents, counsel are required to direct conduct of thorough search for responsive documents with due diligence and ensure all responsive documents under the "custody or control" of the client unless protected from discovery, are produced); In re September 11th Liability Insurance Coverage Cases, 243 F.R.D. 114, 68 Fed. R. Serv. 3d 526 (S.D. N.Y. 2007) (imposition of sanctions of $500,000 against insurer and its attorneys jointly and severally in insurance coverage litigation appropriate for discovery violations).

§ 17:9 Sanctions—Generally

If a court determines a person or organization disposed of or failed to preserve discoverable documents, including electronically stored information, in the face of reasonably foreseeable litigation, the court has considerable discretion in deciding whether the person's actions should be punished.[1] In determining whether sanctions for prelitigation document destruction are appropriate, courts often balance the competing interests of the parties.[2] The authority to sanction litigants for spoliation arises under the applicable rules of civil procedure and a court's inherent power.[3]

The alleged spoliator's state of mind and any prejudice that results to the complaining party from the absence of evidence are two factors frequently considered by the courts. For example, the more critical the missing evidence and the greater the resulting prejudice to the complaining party, the more heavily the state of mind factor weighs in the complaining party's favor. If the complaining party's case is not impaired, no tort liability will result and sanctions are unlikely, especially if there is no evidence of bad faith.

With few exceptions, courts tend not to find liability

[Section 17:9]

[1]See Fujitsu Ltd. v. Federal Exp. Corp., 247 F.3d 423, 436 (2d Cir. 2001) (determination of appropriate sanction is confined to sound discretion of trial judge and is assessed on a case-by-case basis). See, e.g., United Medical Supply Co. v. United States, 77 Fed. Cl. 257 (2007) (government's reckless disregard of preservation duty warranted spoliation sanctions).

[2]See, e.g., Alliance to End Repression v. Rochford, 75 F.R.D. 438, 441 (N.D. Ill. 1976). See Sedona Principle 14 ("Sanctions, including spoliation findings, should be considered by the court only if it finds that there was a clear duty to preserve, a culpable failure to preserve and produce relevant electronically stored information, and a reasonable probability that the loss of the evidence has materially prejudiced the adverse party.").

[3]Zubulake v. UBS Warburg LLC, 229 F.R.D. 422, 94 Fair Empl. Prac. Cas. (BNA) 1, 85 Empl. Prac. Dec. (CCH) P 41728 (S.D. N.Y. 2004).

where organizations dispose of records and meet all three of the following criteria:

- Disposal was done pursuant to formal policies.
- The disposal was in the ordinary course of business.
- Disposal was not made in bad faith.[4]

Generally, courts apply a balancing test to determine whether a party will be held liable for intentional spoliation of evidence for the systematic destruction of its internal records. The test consists of four factors:

- the nature and seriousness of the harm to the injured party;
- the nature and significance of the interests promoted by the actor's conduct (was it unfair or immoral);
- the character of the means used by the actor; and
- the actor's motive (was the destruction of the records primarily to prevent their use in litigation).[5]

Others suggest a three-pronged inquiry:

- the party having control over the evidence had an obligation to preserve it at the time it was destroyed;
- the records were destroyed with a culpable state of mind; and
- the destroyed evidence was relevant to the party's claim or defense such that a reasonable trier of fact could find that the evidence would support that claim or defense.[6]

In *Willard*, several factors weighed in the defendant's

---

[4]See, e.g., Smith v. New York City Health & Hospitals Corp., 284 A.D.2d 121, 726 N.Y.S.2d 89 (1st Dep't 2001) (hospital that destroyed records as part of business routine prior to time it was notified of plaintiff's claim is not subject to sanctions). See Fed. R. Civ. P. 37(f).

[5]Willard v. Caterpillar, Inc., 40 Cal. App. 4th 892, 48 Cal. Rptr. 2d 607, 621 (5th Dist. 1995) (disapproved of on other grounds by, Cedars-Sinai Medical Center v. Superior Court, 18 Cal. 4th 1, 74 Cal. Rptr. 2d 248, 954 P.2d 511 (1998)).

[6]See Kronisch v. U.S., 150 F.3d 112, 127 (2d Cir. 1998); Byrnie v. Town of Cromwell, Bd. of Educ., 243 F.3d 93, 107–12, 151 Ed. Law Rep. 776, 85 Fair Empl. Prac. Cas. (BNA) 323, 82 Empl. Prac. Dec. (CCH) P 40939 (2d Cir. 2001).

favor. No secondary evidence suggested that the contents of the missing documents would be particularly helpful to the plaintiff's case; the company had never been sued over the allegedly defective tractor in 35 years; and remote prelitigation document destruction in the ordinary course of business was not unfair or immoral. However, the court did conclude that the defendant's motive in destroying the documents was to prevent their use in future litigation. With only one factor against the defendant, the court declined to find the defendant liable for spoliation of evidence.[7]

This judicial balancing suggests that the greater the ability of a spoliator to predict the interference its behavior will cause, the greater the sanctions a court is likely to apply, and vice versa. In most jurisdictions, prejudice to the complaining party's case is a prerequisite for spoliation sanctions.[8] Whether sanctions are appropriate and the level of sanctions warranted turn on three key factors:

- the degree of fault of the party who altered or destroyed the evidence;
- the degree of prejudice suffered by the opposing party; and
- whether there is a lesser sanction that will avoid substantial unfairness to the opposing party, and,

---

[7]Willard v. Caterpillar, Inc., 40 Cal. App. 4th 892, 923, 48 Cal. Rptr. 2d 607, 626 (5th Dist. 1995) (disapproved of on other grounds by, Cedars-Sinai Medical Center v. Superior Court, 18 Cal. 4th 1, 74 Cal. Rptr. 2d 248, 954 P.2d 511 (1998)).

[8]See, e.g., Groves v. Cost Planning and Management Intern., Inc., 372 F.3d 1008, 1010, 93 Fair Empl. Prac. Cas. (BNA) 1769, 85 Empl. Prac. Dec. (CCH) P 41691 (8th Cir. 2004) (spoliation inference denied where plaintiff was unable to show that destroyed documents would have helped her case); Himes v. Woodings-Verona Tool Works, Inc., 565 N.W.2d 469, 470 (Minn. Ct. App. 1997) (decision on sanctions for spoliation of evidence focuses on prejudice to opposing party, even where evidence was destroyed through inadvertence or negligence, as opposed to willful action).

where the offending party is seriously at fault, will serve to deter such conduct in the future.[9]

As a result, there is less risk that a person or organization will be penalized for disposing of discoverable but not material evidence, despite the fact that discoverability is the articulated standard for document retention. As long as there is no evidence of bad faith, courts are highly unlikely to sanction the spoliator of noncritical evidence because there is little or no prejudice to the complaining party.[10]

However, bad faith spoliation is strongly disfavored by the courts, and may tip the scales back in favor of the complaining party, even where the party is only slightly prejudiced by the absence of the evidence.[11] Courts do not often find bad faith when faced with document disposal by large organizations with formal record retention policies; yet, when the courts find bad faith, the spoliator is invariably sanctioned.

The more litigated situation is that involving the alleged spoliation of centrally relevant evidence. In that scenario, the courts are split about the appropriate standard. While in many jurisdictions bad faith is a prerequisite to at least the more severe spoliation sanctions, a growing number of states recognize and punish negligent

---

[9]See Paramount Pictures Corp. v. Davis, 234 F.R.D. 102, 111–13, 77 U.S.P.Q.2d 1933 (E.D. Pa. 2005) (defendant's wiping his home computer's memory clean after learning of producer's suit warranted application of spoliation inference). See also Parkinson v. Guidant Corp., 315 F. Supp. 2d 760, 762 (W.D. Pa. 2004); Blandin Paper Co. v. J&J Indus. Sales, Inc., 65 Fed.R.Evid.Serv. 279 (D.Minn. 2004) (spoliation sanctions denied where nonspoliating party was not prejudiced).

[10]See, e.g., Ratliff v. City of Gainesville, Tex., 256 F.3d 355, 363–64, 86 Fair Empl. Prac. Cas. (BNA) 472 (5th Cir. 2001).

[11]See, e.g., Collazo-Santiago v. Toyota Motor Corp., 149 F.3d 23, 29, Prod. Liab. Rep. (CCH) P 15280 (1st Cir. 1998) (of particular importance when considering appropriateness of sanctions is prejudice to nonoffending party and degree of fault of offending party); Troup v. Tri-County Confinement Systems, Inc., 708 A.2d 825, 827, Prod. Liab. Rep. (CCH) P 15251 (Pa. Super. Ct. 1998) (even where defendants do not suffer serious prejudice, plaintiff's willful and knowing destruction of evidence is sufficient to warrant sanctions).

spoliation.[12] The availability of an independent cause of action for spoliation is not necessary; some courts will allow an adverse inference to be drawn, under certain circumstances, even when the spoliator acts without bad faith.

This means there is a second prong to the spoliation analysis. The critical legal question is whether the litigation was reasonably foreseeable at the time the discoverable documents were destroyed. The existence of a legal duty depends on the answer to this first question. Yet, if the answer to the question is yes, then a second and more practical question may arise: Were the missing documents discoverable, relevant or material? The answer to this second question appears to affect the likelihood that sanctions will be applied against the spoliator.

If the evidence is highly prejudicial but there is no evidence of bad faith, some courts have employed negligence theories to justify sanctioning the spoliator. The clearest conclusion that can be derived from the varying cases in the numerous jurisdictions is that the fact-specific balancing approach provides courts with the necessary flexibility for results-oriented analyses.

A court is not required to hold an evidentiary hearing to determine the validity of spoliation allegations.[13] Appellate courts will not hear spoliation claims unless the claims were raised at the district court.[14]

§ 17:10 Sanctions—Penalties for spoliation

State and federal courts do not approach remedies for spoliation of evidence with any degree of uniformity. To begin with, federal courts in diversity actions are split on

---

[12]See Elwell v. Conair, Inc., 145 F. Supp.2d 79, 88 (D.Me. 2001) (bad faith is not prerequisite for imposition of sanctions for spoliation); Millsap v. McDonnell Douglas Corp., 162 F. Supp.2d 1262, 1308 (N.D.Okla. 2001) (depending on severity of sanction sought, law in this circuit requires showing of bad faith).

[13]Busch v. Dyno Nobel, Inc., 40 Fed. Appx. 947, 48 U.C.C. Rep. Serv. 2d 874 (6th Cir. 2002).

[14]Ridgeway v. O'Bryan, 88 Fed. Appx. 259 (9th Cir. 2004).

whether spoliation is a procedural or substantive matter, so different remedies might apply to the same facts.[1] In addition, state courts differ widely as to available remedies and the severity with which they are to be applied. Depending on the jurisdiction, a spoliation claim may be brought during the course of litigation or as a separate cause of action. Spoliation may occur "along a continuum of fault," ranging from innocent behavior to negligence to willful violation of the law.[2]

A court may employ a variety of sanctions to reestablish a level playing field, including unfavorable evidentiary

---

[Section 17:10]

[1]Compare Fakhro v. Mayo Clinic Rochester, 2004 WL 909740 (D. Minn. 2004) (federal law applies to spoliation sanctions in diversity actions); Silvestri v. General Motors Corp., 271 F.3d 583, 590, 51 Fed. R. Serv. 3d 694 (4th Cir. 2001) (spoliation is governed by federal law); Townsend v. American Insulated Panel Co., Inc., 174 F.R.D. 1, 4, 37 Fed. R. Serv. 3d 1166 (D. Mass. 1997) (in diversity actions, sanctions for spoliation controlled by federal law, not state law), with State Farm Fire & Cas. Co. v. Frigidaire, a Div. of General Motors Corp., 146 F.R.D. 160, 161–62, 26 Fed. R. Serv. 3d 95 (N.D. Ill. 1992) (spoliation sanctions are substantive rather than procedural and the relevant state's law should be applied); Warden v. Cross, 94 Fed. Appx. 474 (9th Cir.2004) (applying California law); Ward v. Texas Steak Ltd., 2004 WL 1280776 (W.D. Va. 2004) (recognizing it is a court of limited jurisdiction and concluding that, when spoliation of evidence does not occur in the course of pending federal litigation, a federal court exercising diversity jurisdiction in which the rule of decision is supplied by state law is required to apply those spoliation principles the forum state would apply).

[2]Beil v. Lakewood Engineering and Mfg. Co., 15 F.3d 546, 552, 27 Fed. R. Serv. 3d 1453, 1994 FED App. 0024P (6th Cir. 1994); Welsh v. U.S., 844 F.2d 1239, 1246, 25 Fed. R. Evid. Serv. 979 (6th Cir. 1988). Willfulness is generally not a prerequisite to such sanctions. Kansas-Nebraska Natural Gas Co., Inc. v. Marathon Oil Co., 109 F.R.D. 12, 17 (D. Neb. 1983). But see Independent Petrochemical Corp. v. Aetna Cas. and Sur. Co., 654 F. Supp. 1334, 1364, 27 Env't. Rep. Cas. (BNA) 1735, 27 Env't. Rep. Cas. (BNA) 1745 (D.D.C. 1986), on reconsideration, 672 F. Supp. 1 (D.D.C. 1986) and order aff'd, 944 F.2d 940, 33 Env't. Rep. Cas. (BNA) 1984, 21 Envtl. L. Rep. 21483 (D.C. Cir. 1991).

presumptions, discovery sanctions and criminal penalties.[3] Remedies for spoliation include:

- Criminal penalties[4]
- Unfavorable evidentiary presumptions[5]
- Discovery sanctions[6]
- Dismissal of law suits[7]
- An action in tort for damages for spoliation of evidence[8]
- An adverse inference instruction[9]

---

[3]Silvestri v. General Motors Corp., 271 F.3d 583, 590, 51 Fed. R. Serv. 3d 694 (4th Cir. 2001); Costello v. City of Brigantine, 17 I.E.R. Cas. (BNA) 1225, 2001 WL 732402 (D.N.J. 2001).

[4]See, e.g., U.S. v. Lundwall, 1 F. Supp. 2d 249 (S.D. N.Y. 1998) (withholding and subsequent destruction of documents of defendant held to be criminal obstruction of justice under 18 U.S.C.A. § 1503). But see In re E.I. DuPont De Nemours & Company-Benlate Litigation, 99 F.3d 363, 36 Fed. R. Serv. 3d 427, 27 Envtl. L. Rep. 20432 (11th Cir. 1996) ($100 million sanctions ordered payable to civil court were overturned as primarily criminal in nature; however, separate criminal investigation was initiated).

[5]Dillon v. Nissan Motor Co., Ltd., 986 F.2d 263, 268, 38 Fed. R. Evid. Serv. 82, 25 Fed. R. Serv. 3d 304 (8th Cir. 1993) (expert testimony excluded as sanction for destroying evidence); BTO Logging, Inc. v. Deere & Co., 174 F.R.D. 690, 692–93, 39 Fed. R. Serv. 3d 637 (D. Or. 1997) (same).

[6]In re Prudential Ins. Co. of America Sales Practices Litigation, 169 F.R.D. 598, 36 Fed. R. Serv. 3d 767 (D.N.J. 1997); Edwards v. Louisville Ladder Co., 796 F. Supp. 966, 971 (W.D. La. 1992).

[7]See, e.g., Walters ex rel. Walters v. General Motors Corp., 209 F. Supp. 2d 481, Prod. Liab. Rep. (CCH) P 16408 (W.D. Pa. 2002) (summary judgment entered against spoliator); Elwell v. Conair, Inc., 145 F. Supp. 2d 79, 88 (D. Me. 2001) (dismissal is the most severe sanction and should be reserved for cases where a party has maliciously destroyed relevant evidence); Barsoum v. NYC Housing Authority, 202 F.R.D. 396, 399, 50 Fed. R. Serv. 3d 26 (S.D. N.Y. 2001) (outright dismissal is a harsh remedy to be used only in extreme cases).

[8]Hazen v. Municipality of Anchorage, 718 P.2d 456 (Alaska 1986) (rejected by, City of Gladewater v. Pike, 727 S.W.2d 514 (Tex. 1987)).

[9]Cf. McDowell v. Government of Dist. of Columbia, 233 F.R.D. 192, 202–03, 63 Fed. R. Serv. 3d 1233 (D.D.C. 2006) (proposing negative inference sanction jury instruction be given if defendants failed to

- Other sanctions including reimbursement of attorney fees, monetary penalties against the party or attorney; recovery of discovery costs; striking an answer; barring the presentation of evidence relating to the destroyed material; barring the filing of pleadings; and, in the most egregious instances, entry of default judgment or dismissal against the spoliator[10]

Most jurisdictions are careful to impose the least severe sanctions commensurate with the wrongdoing.[11] In cases where bad faith is not clear, for example, courts tend to favor a rebuttable presumption that the destroyed evidence was unfavorable to the party responsible for its absence. The burden-shifting presumption permits the defendant to submit a reasonable explanation for the destruction of the evidence, and thus is less severe than the "spoliation inference."

---

produce requested database); Stevenson v. Union Pacific R. Co., 354 F.3d 739, 747, 63 Fed. R. Evid. Serv. 166, 57 Fed. R. Serv. 3d 617 (8th Cir. 2004) (declaring that there must be some indication of an intent to destroy the evidence for the purpose of obstructing or suppressing truth in order to impose sanction of adverse inference instruction, court upheld sanctions against defendant, because defendant had been careful to preserve a voice tape in other cases where tape proved to be beneficial to defendant and had made immediate effort to preserve other types of evidence but not voice tape in this case).

[10]See Krumwiede v. Brighton Associates, L.L.C., 2006 WL 1308629 (N.D. Ill. 2006), subsequent determination, 2006 WL 2349985 (N.D. Ill. 2006) (default judgment entered against producing party because of intentional destruction of evidence).

[11]Webb v. District of Columbia, 146 F.3d 964, 971, 73 Empl. Prac. Dec. (CCH) P 45480, 41 Fed. R. Serv. 3d 120 (D.C. Cir. 1998) (default judgment not appropriate where less onerous remedies would have sufficed); ABC Home Health Services, Inc. v. International Business Machines Corp., 158 F.R.D. 180 (S.D. Ga. 1994); Turner v. Hudson Transit Lines, Inc., 142 F.R.D. 68 (S.D. N.Y. 1991); E.E.O.C. v. Jacksonville Shipyards, Inc., 690 F. Supp. 995, 998, 47 Fair Empl. Prac. Cas. (BNA) 267, 47 Empl. Prac. Dec. (CCH) P 38228 (M.D. Fla. 1988) (default judgment inappropriate where lesser sanctions may effectively remedy the prejudice suffered by the EEOC). However, courts are prepared to impose severe sanctions where spoliation is egregious. See U.S. v. Philip Morris USA, Inc., 327 F. Supp. 2d 21 (D.D.C. 2004) (spoliation ordered to pay $2,750,000 into court as a sanction).

Several factors influence whether a court will impose judicial sanctions for the destruction or loss of evidence. The most important factors are the culpability of the alleged spoliator and the resulting prejudice to the innocent party. Other factors include the degree of interference with the judicial process, whether a lesser sanction will remedy the harm, whether sanctions are necessary to deter similar conduct, and whether sanctions will unfairly punish an innocent party for spoliation committed by an attorney.

§ 17:11 Sanctions—When penalties likely to be applied

Courts can be aggressive against organizations instituting document retention programs in bad faith primarily for the purpose of destroying unfavorable records discoverable in litigation. In *Capellupo v. FMC Corp.*,[1] a senior official of the defendant employer was warned by an employee that she intended to file a class action gender discrimination suit. The official in turn informed others, and various memoranda were exchanged regarding the possible suit. Company management responded by implementing a broad policy of document destruction on the eve of the lawsuit, resulting in the destruction of material evidence. The court found the company was on notice once the information had filtered through upper management and immediately prior to the implemented policy of destruction. The court awarded monetary sanctions to the plaintiff, doubling the fees and costs.

Regardless of the reasons for its creation, a document retention policy may possess inherently suspicious characteristics. In *Reingold v. Wet N' Wild Nevada, Inc.*,[2] a Nevada court invoked the adverse inference against a

[Section 17:11]

[1]Capellupo v. FMC Corp., 126 F.R.D. 545, 50 Fair Empl. Prac. Cas. (BNA) 153, 51 Empl. Prac. Dec. (CCH) P 39441 (D. Minn. 1989).

[2]Reingold v. Wet 'N Wild Nevada, Inc., 113 Nev. 967, 944 P.2d 800 (1997) (overruled by, Bass-Davis v. Davis, 122 Nev. 442, 134 P.3d

water park found to have willfully destroyed documents relevant to potential litigation. The park's document retention policy provided for the routine destruction of first aid logs before the statute of limitations had even run on potential litigation for the season; the court concluded the policy was deliberately designed to prevent the production of such records in later litigation.

Even if the record retention policy is legitimate, courts may scrutinize the facts for bad faith management or application of the policy. Sanctions have been invoked where a company failed to make reasonable efforts to communicate the presence of pending or future litigation to employees who purge obsolete files or are responsible for implementing routine document destruction. In *Telectron, Inc. v. Overhead Door Corp.*,[3] the court found the defendant corporation had deliberately maintained internal secrecy regarding an antitrust suit. Not only was there an absence of a coherent document retention policy, but the court concluded that "a desired byproduct of the defendant's internal secrecy about the suit was a pervasive state of ignorance . . . about the sorts of documents which fell within the scope of [plaintiff's] discovery requests."

In *Blinzler v. Marriott International, Inc.*,[4] the defendant hotel destroyed its phone logs 30 days after the failure of one of its clerks to promptly call an ambulance that resulted in the death of a guest. The defendant contended that such destruction took place in the ordinary course of business and pursuant to an established practice. However, on the night in question, the decedent's wife had repeatedly inquired of Marriott personnel whether the ambulance had yet been called. The court viewed the requests as notice to the hotel that future litigation was likely and upheld the trial court's sanction.

---

103 (2006) (holding that the destruction of records was negligent and not willful destruction)).

[3]Telectron, Inc. v. Overhead Door Corp., 116 F.R.D. 107, 123, 1988-1 Trade Cas. (CCH) P 68061 (S.D. Fla. 1987).

[4]Blinzler v. Marriott Intern., Inc., 81 F.3d 1148, 1159 (1st Cir. 1996).

Computer Associates International, Inc. v. American Fundware, Inc.,[5] involved a defendant with a policy of destroying previous versions of software source codes, a policy the court did not find inherently wrongful. Under the circumstances, however, the court found the company was under a duty to suspend its policy and preserve the evidence. Destruction of the source code occurred after the filing of plaintiff's complaint, and even pre-litigation discussions had made clear the code would be critical evidence in upcoming litigation. The court granted a default judgment for the plaintiff on the issue of liability.

Another improper application of an otherwise reasonable document retention policy is the unusual or sporadic destruction of documents. Culpability or actual knowledge of likely litigation is frequently inferred from sporadic destruction, disposal of documents in a manner inconsistent with the requirements of an established policy, or any other kind of document disposal that is out of the ordinary. *Capellupo v. FMC Corp.*[6] is an of document destruction under circumstances strongly indicating the company was on notice of impending litigation and had acted in bad faith. In that case, the company instituted its document retention policy on the eve of major litigation.

In a growing number of jurisdictions, willfulness is no longer a necessary element for imposition of sanctions. For example, in the case of *In re Prudential Insurance Co. of America Sales Practices Litigation*,[7] an insurance company in ongoing litigation recognized its legal obligations to preserve evidence, yet because of poor management it failed to communicate the presence of critical court orders to personnel responsible for routine document disposal. As a result, uninformed employees continued to

---

[5]Computer Associates Intern., Inc. v. American Fundware, Inc., 133 F.R.D. 166, 170, 18 U.S.P.Q.2d 1649 (D. Colo. 1990).

[6]Capellupo v. FMC Corp., 126 F.R.D. 545, 552–53, 50 Fair Empl. Prac. Cas. (BNA) 153, 51 Empl. Prac. Dec. (CCH) P 39441 (D. Minn. 1989).

[7]In re Prudential Ins. Co. of America Sales Practices Litigation, 169 F.R.D. 598, 36 Fed. R. Serv. 3d 767 (D.N.J. 1997).

apply the company's policy, resulting in the destruction of a number of documents subject to preservation orders. The court sanctioned the company $1 million for its "grossly negligent" conduct.

§ 17:12 Sanctions—When penalties unlikely to be applied

In making determinations of foreseeability, courts recognize the unique problems faced by large organizations, criticizing unreasonably expansive duties to preserve evidence as immensely burdensome. Most courts require only that the would-be spoliator act reasonably under the circumstances. This means that, where litigation is merely possible, but not "reasonably foreseeable," routine document disposal is highly unlikely to result in spoliation sanctions.

A manufacturer is not required to preserve all documents for decades in the absence of reasonably foreseeable litigation simply because of the possibility that some documents might be relevant to future litigation.[1] Discovery sanctions for spoliation are warranted only if evidence was destroyed when a product liability action was contemplated, rather than merely possible.[2]

Courts routinely refuse to invoke sanctions against organizations that dispose of documents without bad faith and pursuant to a legitimate and uniformly applied record retention policy, sometimes even in the face of pending litigation. Regardless of the pendency of litigation, courts often stop short of sanctioning the spoliator where there is no evidence that the actions were taken in bad faith;

[Section 17:12]

[1] Willard v. Caterpillar, Inc., 40 Cal. App. 4th 892, 922, 48 Cal. Rptr. 2d 607 (5th Dist. 1995) (disapproved of on other grounds by, Cedars-Sinai Medical Center v. Superior Court, 18 Cal. 4th 1, 74 Cal. Rptr. 2d 248, 954 P.2d 511 (1998)).

[2] Willard v. Caterpillar, Inc., 40 Cal. App. 4th 892, 48 Cal. Rptr. 2d 607, 620–21 (5th Dist. 1995) (disapproved of on other grounds by, Cedars-Sinai Medical Center v. Superior Court, 18 Cal. 4th 1, 74 Cal. Rptr. 2d 248, 954 P.2d 511 (1998)).

compliance with routine company policy may serve as one indicator that bad faith was absent. For example, *Wright v. Illinois Central R.R.*,[3] involved track-inspection records destroyed pursuant to routine procedures by an employee unaware of the existing lawsuit. Although it was perhaps also true that the missing records were not centrally relevant to the plaintiff's claim of excessive speed, the court refused to invoke the adverse inference because there was no evidence of bad faith.

In *Coates v. Johnson & Johnson*,[4] the court reached a similar result. An employee who, upon inquiry, had been informed there was no need to keep certain employment records for a pending class action, destroyed them when a company plant closed. The lack of any evidence of bad faith prompted the court to refuse to invoke the adverse inference.

Courts do not require organizations to hold onto every piece of discoverable paper in their files, even under certain circumstances when litigation is foreseeable. Nor do the courts oblige frequently sued organizations to preserve all their records. Beyond this, however, not much is absolutely clear. It appears courts are least likely to impose sanctions where the following is true:

- Litigation is remote or foreseeability is otherwise attenuated
- Documents are disposed of pursuant to a routine, evenly applied, established policy
- There is no evidence of conscious effort to interfere with the litigation
- The evidence disposed of is not critical to the opponent's likelihood of success

§ 17:13 Sanctions—Adverse inference instruction

The preferred sanction in the event of negligent destruc-

---

[3]Wright By and Through Wright v. Illinois Central R. Co., 868 F. Supp. 183 (S.D. Miss. 1994).

[4]Coates v. Johnson & Johnson, 756 F.2d 524, 551, 37 Fair Empl. Prac. Cas. (BNA) 467, 36 Empl. Prac. Dec. (CCH) P 35073, 18 Fed. R. Evid. Serv. 498, 1 Fed. R. Serv. 3d 678 (7th Cir. 1985).

tion of evidence is the "spoliation inference"—instructing the jury to draw an adverse inference based on matters probably contained within the destroyed evidence.[1] In its strictest form, the "spoliation inference" establishes prima facie the elements of the injured party's claim that cannot be proven without the missing evidence.[2] Courts tend to consider the intent of the actor and the content of the missing evidence to be the two most important factors in determining whether the adverse inference is warranted.[3]

[Section 17:13]

[1]See Blinzler v. Marriott Intern., Inc., 81 F.3d 1148, 1159 (1st Cir. 1996) (when evidence indicates party is aware of circumstances likely to give rise to future litigation, and yet destroys potentially relevant records without particularized inquiry, fact finder may reasonably infer that party probably did so because records would harm its case).

[2]See, e.g., Nation-Wide Check Corp., Inc. v. Forest Hills Distributors, Inc., 692 F.2d 214, 218, 11 Fed. R. Evid. Serv. 1588 (1st Cir. 1982). See also Kelley v. United Airlines, Inc., 176 F.R.D. 422, 39 Fed. R. Serv. 3d 898 (D. Mass. 1997) (airline was negligent in failing to search for and preserve relevant documents thereby warranting adverse inference sanction). Zubulake v. UBS Warburg LLC, 229 F.R.D. 422, 94 Fair Empl. Prac. Cas. (BNA) 1, 85 Empl. Prac. Dec. (CCH) P 41728 (S.D. N.Y. 2004) (spoliation of evidence germane to proof of an issue at trial can support inference that evidence would have been unfavorable to party responsible for its destruction). Cf. Residential Funding Corp. v. Degeorge Financial Corp., 306 F.3d 99, 107, 53 Fed. R. Serv. 3d 1105 (2d Cir. 2002) (adverse inference instruction may be warranted in some circumstances for the untimely production of evidence).

[3]See Select Medical Corp. v. Hardaway, 2006 WL 859741 (E.D. Pa. 2006) (denying motion for spoliation inference because producing party had legitimate reason for erasing hard drive); Advantacare Health Partners v. Access IV, 2004 WL 1837997 (N.D. Cal. 2004) ("The evidentiary rationale applies here. The record clearly indicates that Defendants destroyed evidence in response to impending litigation. This behavior suggests that the evidence would have been threatening to the defense of the case and that it is therefore relevant in an evidentiary sense."); Zubulake v. UBS Warburg LLC, 229 F.R.D. 422, 94 Fair Empl. Prac. Cas. (BNA) 1, 85 Empl. Prac. Dec. (CCH) P 41728 (S.D. N.Y. 2004) (party seeking an adverse inference instruction based on spoliation must establish three elements: (1) party having control over evidence had an obligation to preserve it at the time it was destroyed, (2) records were destroyed with a "culpable state of mind," and (3)

Courts are split as to whether an intentional showing is necessary to merit the spoliation inference.[4]

An adverse inference charge serves two purposes—remediation and punishment.[5] The remedial purpose of the sanction serves to place the prejudiced party in the same position to prove its case as it would have been if the evidence had been preserved. The punitive purpose both deters parties from destroying relevant evidence and directly punishes the party responsible for spoliation.[6]

In the event of a spoliation inference, the fact finder is allowed to draw an unfavorable inference against the spoliator in a lawsuit because the spoliator is presumed to have been motivated by the concern that the material hidden, destroyed, or lost would have been unfavorable to its

destroyed evidence was relevant to party's claim or defense such that reasonable trier of fact could find it would support that claim or defense).

[4]Intent or bad faith required: Great American Ins. Co. of New York v. Lowry Development, LLC, 2007 WL 4268776 (S.D. Miss. 2007) (defendant's disposal of laptop and untruthful testimony of circumstances of disposal warranted adverse inference instruction); Greyhound Lines, Inc. v. Wade, 485 F.3d 1032 (8th Cir. 2007); Morgan v. U.S. Xpress, Inc., 2006 WL 1548029 (M.D. Ga. 2006) (mere negligence in losing or destroying evidence is not enough for adverse inference as it does not sustain an inference of consciousness of a weak case); DaimlerChrysler Motors v. Bill Davis Racing, Inc., 2005 WL 3502172 (E.D. Mich. 2005) (court must consider reasons for destruction of evidence to determine if they support inference of bad faith); Jinks-Umstead v. England, 68 Fed. R. Evid. Serv. 1200 (D.D.C. 2005); Hodge v. Wal-Mart Stores, Inc., 360 F.3d 446, 64 Fed. R. Evid. Serv. 200 (4th Cir. 2004). Negligence sufficient: Residential Funding Corp. v. Degeorge Financial Corp., 306 F.3d 99, 107, 53 Fed. R. Serv. 3d 1105 (2d Cir. 2002); World Courier v. Barone, 2007 WL 1119196 (N.D. Cal. 2007).

[5]Barsoum v. NYC Housing Authority, 202 F.R.D. 396, 399, 50 Fed. R. Serv. 3d 26 (S.D. N.Y. 2001) (purpose of sanctions is to deter future spoliation of evidence, shift risk of erroneous judgment onto party responsible for loss of evidence, and remedy prejudice suffered by nonspoliating party).

[6]Donato v. Fitzgibbons, 172 F.R.D. 75, 81–82, 38 Fed. R. Serv. 3d 1086 (S.D. N.Y. 1997).

position.[7] The Missouri Supreme Court, for example, posited that the authority to award negative presumptions and authority to grant inferences is inherent in the court's equitable power to presume all things against the wrongdoer.[8]

§ 17:14 Sanctions—Independent cause of action

No independent claim for spoliation of evidence exists under federal law.[1] Some states, however, recognize an independent tort of spoliation of evidence, destruction of evidence or a similar cause of action.[2] Other jurisdictions recognize essentially the same tort under traditional

[7]Byrnie v. Town of Cromwell, Bd. of Educ., 243 F.3d 93, 107, 151 Ed. Law Rep. 776, 85 Fair Empl. Prac. Cas. (BNA) 323, 82 Empl. Prac. Dec. (CCH) P 40939 (2d Cir. 2001). See also Zubulake v. UBS Warburg LLC, 229 F.R.D. 422, 94 Fair Empl. Prac. Cas. (BNA) 1, 85 Empl. Prac. Dec. (CCH) P 41728 (S.D. N.Y. 2004) (concept of "relevance" encompasses not only the ordinary meaning of the term, but also that the destroyed evidence would have been favorable to the movant).

[8]Brown v. Hamid, 856 S.W.2d 51, 56 (Mo. 1993). But see Brewer v. Dowling, 862 S.W.2d 156, 159 (Tex. App. Fort Worth 1993), writ denied (Jan. 26, 1994) (although intentional spoliation of evidence raises presumption that evidence would have been unfavorable to cause of spoliator, mere fact that evidence was missing did not entitle plaintiff to spoliation jury instruction).

[Section 17:14]

[1]See, e.g., Sterbenz v. Attina, 205 F. Supp. 2d 65, 54 Fed. R. Serv. 3d 348 (E.D. N.Y. 2002); Silvestri v. General Motors Corp., 271 F.3d 583, 590, 51 Fed. R. Serv. 3d 694 (4th Cir. 2001); Cloud v. ABC, Inc., 30 Media L. Rep. (BNA) 1402, 2001 WL 1622250 (S.D. N.Y. 2001); Tiano v. Jacobs, 2001 WL 225037 (S.D. N.Y. 2001); Lombard v. MCI Telecommunications Corp., 13 F. Supp. 2d 621 (N.D. Ohio 1998). See also Larison v. City of Trenton, 180 F.R.D. 261 (D.N.J. 1998) (existence of affirmative cause of action for spoliation determined by state law).

[2]Jurisdictions include Alaska (Hazen v. Municipality of Anchorage, 718 P.2d 456 (Alaska 1986) (rejected by, City of Gladewater v. Pike, 727 S.W.2d 514 (Tex. 1987))); Illinois (Rodgers v. St. Mary's Hosp. of Decatur, 149 Ill. 2d 302, 173 Ill. Dec. 642, 597 N.E.2d 616 (1992)); Indiana (Thompson ex rel. Thompson v. Owensby, 704 N.E.2d 134 (Ind. Ct. App. 1998)); Kansas (Foster v. Lawrence Memorial Hosp., 809 F. Supp. 831 (D. Kan. 1992)); New Jersey (Hirsch v. General Motors Corp., 266 N.J. Super. 222, 628 A.2d 1108 (Law Div. 1993) (holding modified

causes of actions, e.g., civil conspiracy, fraud, breach of contract, or breach of duty of good faith and fair dealing.[3] The basic tort, however, has yet to gain widespread acceptance among the various jurisdictions. Several states have explicitly refused to adopt the tort, most frequently citing the adequacy of existing remedies and the speculation of damages.[4] Other jurisdictions have expressly declined to rule on the existence of a separate tort, or the status of the tort is uncertain.[5]

---

by, Rosenblit v. Zimmerman, 166 N.J. 391, 766 A.2d 749 (2001))); North Carolina (Henry v. Deen, 310 N.C. 75, 310 S.E.2d 326 (1984)); Ohio (Smith v. Howard Johnson Co., Inc., 67 Ohio St. 3d 28, 1993-Ohio-229, 615 N.E.2d 1037 (1993)).

[3]At least one court has held that the tort of spoliation exists only when the spoliation is discovered after the entry of judgment. Costello v. City of Brigantine, 17 I.E.R. Cas. (BNA) 1225, 2001 WL 732402 (D.N.J. 2001).

[4]Including Connecticut (Reilly v. D'Errico, 12 Conn. L. Rptr. 457, 1994 WL 547671 (Conn. Super. Ct. 1994)); Kentucky (Monsanto Co. v. Reed, 950 S.W.2d 811, Prod. Liab. Rep. (CCH) P 14982 (Ky. 1997)); Maryland (Miller v. Montgomery County, 64 Md. App. 202, 494 A.2d 761 (1985)); Missouri (Baugher v. Gates Rubber Co., Inc., 863 S.W.2d 905 (Mo. Ct. App. E.D. 1993)); New York (Weigl v. Quincy Specialties Co., 158 Misc. 2d 753, 601 N.Y.S.2d 774, 85 Ed. Law Rep. 921 (Sup 1993)); Texas (Trevino v. Ortega, 969 S.W.2d 950 (Tex. 1998)); Washington (Henderson v. Tyrrell, 80 Wash. App. 592, 910 P.2d 522 (Div. 3 1996), as amended on denial of reconsideration, (Mar. 14, 1996)); West Virginia (Harrison v. Davis, 197 W. Va. 651, 478 S.E.2d 104 (1996)); Wisconsin (Ely v. St. Luke's Hosp., 182 Wis. 2d 510, 514 N.W.2d 878 (Ct. App. 1994)).

[5]Including Alabama (Christian v. Kenneth Chandler Const. Co., Inc., 658 So. 2d 408 (Ala. 1995)); Arizona (La Raia v. Superior Court In and For Maricopa County, 150 Ariz. 118, 722 P.2d 286 (1986)); Arkansas (Wilson v. Beloit Corp., 921 F.2d 765 (8th Cir. 1990)); Georgia (Gardner v. Blackston, 185 Ga. App. 754, 365 S.E.2d 545 (1988)); Idaho (Yoakum v. Hartford Fire Ins. Co., 129 Idaho 171, 923 P.2d 416 (1996)); Louisiana (Edwards v. Louisville Ladder Co., 796 F. Supp. 966 (W.D. La. 1992)); Michigan (Panich v. Iron Wood Products Corp., 179 Mich. App. 136, 445 N.W.2d 795 (1989)); Minnesota (Federated Mut. Ins. Co. v. Litchfield Precision Components, Inc., 456 N.W.2d 434 (Minn. 1990)); Pennsylvania (Olson v. Grutza, 428 Pa. Super. 378, 631 A.2d 191 (1993)).

There is no uniform body of case law concerning the elements of the tort of spoliation. In all cases, the elements of the tort have been derived from the standards applied to claims that preexisted the separate cause of action. The basic elements of intentional spoliation are:

- Pending or probable litigation involving the plaintiff
- Knowledge by the defendant of the existence or likelihood of the litigation
- Intentional "acts of spoliation" on the part of the defendant designed to disrupt the plaintiff's case
- Disruption of the plaintiff's case
- Damages proximately caused by the acts of the defendant[6]

§ 17:15 Sanctions—Rule 37 of the Federal Rules of Civil Procedure

Rule 37 of the Federal Rules of Civil Procedure gives federal courts wide discretion to structure the form of sanctions.[1] Courts have generally employed this discretion to provide a sanction commensurate with the measure of bad faith exhibited by the spoliator.[2] The sanction for spoliation, like any sanction, lies within the sound discretion of the court, and should be designed to deter spoliation and restore the prejudiced party to the same position he would have been in absent the destruction of evidence by

[6]Nix v. Hoke, 139 F. Supp. 2d 125, 136 n.10 (D.D.C. 2001). See Owca v. Federal Insurance Co., 95 Fed. Appx. 742 (6th Cir. 2004) (following elements are required for tort of intentional spoliation: (1) pending or probable litigation involving plaintiff; (2) knowledge on part of defendant that litigation exists or is probable; (3) willful destruction of evidence by defendant designed to disrupt plaintiff's case; (4) disruption of plaintiff's case; and (5) damages proximately caused by defendant's acts).

[Section 17:15]

[1]Ellicott Mach. Corp. Intern. v. Jesco Const. Corp., 199 F. Supp. 2d 290, 52 Fed. R. Serv. 3d 1239 (D. Md. 2002) (court has broad discretion to sanction spoliators).

[2]Carlucci v. Piper Aircraft Corp., Inc., 775 F.2d 1440, 1448, 3 Fed. R. Serv. 3d 325 (11th Cir. 1985).

the opposing party, as well as to shift the burden of an erroneous judgment to the spoliator.[3]

Although federal courts routinely state that Rule 37 sanctions may not be imposed as punishment, that is often the effect of the sanctions. The decision to impose sanctions for spoliation under Rule 37 requires consideration of three factors:

- the obligation of the party against whom sanctions are sought to preserve the evidence in issue;
- the spoliating party's intent; and
- the relevance of the evidence to the contested issues or the prejudice to the nonspoliating party.[4]

Rule 37(f) provides what is sometimes referred to as a "safe harbor." Under Rule 37(f), absent exceptional circumstances, a court may not impose sanctions "on a party for failing to provide electronically stored information lost as a result of the routine, good-faith operation of an electronic information system."

Rule 37(f) recognizes a distinctive feature of computer operations—the routine alteration and deletion of information that attends ordinary use of a computer. Rule 37(f) applies only to information lost because of the "routine operation of an electronic information system"—the ways in which such systems are generally designed, programmed, and implemented to meet the party's technical and business needs.[5]

The operation of the computer system resulting in

---

[3]See Electronic Funds Solutions v. Murphy, 134 Cal. App. 4th 1161, 1183, 36 Cal. Rptr. 3d 663 (4th Dist. 2005) (discovery sanction do not exist "to provide a weapon for punishment for past violations or penalty for past conduct but to secure compliance with orders of the court").

[4]Ellicott Mach. Corp. Intern. v. Jesco Const. Corp., 199 F. Supp. 2d 290, 52 Fed. R. Serv. 3d 1239 (D. Md. 2002); Barsoum v. NYC Housing Authority, 202 F.R.D. 396, 399–400, 50 Fed. R. Serv. 3d 26 (S.D. N.Y. 2001). Cf. Greyhound Lines, Inc. v. Wade, 485 F.3d 1032 (8th Cir. 2007).

[5]See Doe v. Norwalk Community College, 248 F.R.D. 372, 231 Ed. Law Rep. 292 (D. Conn. 2007) (safe-harbor provision requires routine system in place and some affirmative action by party to prevent system

alteration or deletion of information must have been in good faith. Good faith in the routine operation of a computer system may involve a party's intervention to modify or suspend certain features of that routine operation to prevent the loss of information, if that information is subject to a preservation obligation.[6]

According to the Advisory Committee, the good faith requirement of Rule 37(f) means that a party is not permitted to exploit the routine operation of an information system to thwart discovery obligations by allowing that operation to continue in order to destroy specific stored information that it is required to preserve. When a party is under a duty to preserve information because of pending or reasonably anticipated litigation, intervention in the routine operation of an information system is one aspect of what is often called a "litigation hold." Among the factors that bear on a party's good faith in the routine operation of an information system are the steps the party took to comply with a court order in the case or party agreement requiring preservation of specific electronically stored information.

The Advisory Committee states that, whether good faith would call for steps to prevent the loss of information on sources the party believes are not reasonably accessible under Rule 26(b)(2), depends on the circumstances of each case. One factor is whether the party reasonably believes that the information on such sources is likely to be discoverable and not available from reasonably accessible sources.

The protection provided by Rule 37(f) applies only to sanctions under the Federal Rules of Civil Procedure. It

---

from destroying or altering information); Disability Rights Council of Greater Washington v. Washington Metropolitan Transit Authority, 242 F.R.D. 139 (D.D.C. 2007) (safe harbor was not intended to apply to situation where defendant did not stop automatic destruction of e-mails following filing of law suit).

[6]See Arista Records, L.L.C. v. Tschirhart, 241 F.R.D. 462 (W.D. Tex. 2006) (default judgment against defendant was warranted for bad faith and willful destruction of evidence on computer in violation of discovery order).

does not affect other sources of authority to impose sanctions or rules of professional responsibility. Rule 37(f) does not prevent a court from making the kinds of adjustments frequently used in managing discovery if a party is unable to provide relevant responsive information. The Advisory Committee explains that, for example, a court could order the responding party to produce an additional witness for deposition, respond to additional interrogatories, or make similar attempts to provide substitutes or alternatives for some or all of the lost information.

II. CHECKLISTS

§ 17:16 Checklist of counsel's responsibilities

- ☐ **Counsel's Duty to Monitor Compliance.**
  - ☐ Once a party reasonably anticipates litigation, it must suspend its routine document retention or destruction policy and put in place a "litigation hold" to ensure the preservation of relevant documents.
  - ☐ Generally, the litigation hold does not apply to inaccessible backup tapes (those typically maintained solely for the purpose of disaster recovery), which may continue to be recycled on the schedule set forth in the party's policy.
  - ☐ Where back tapes are accessible (actively used for information retrieval, then such tapes likely are subject to the litigation hold.
  - ☐ Counsel must oversee compliance with the litigation hold, monitoring the party's efforts to retain and produce the relevant documents. Proper communications between a party and the party's counsel will ensure:
    - ☐ All relevant information or at least all sources of relevant information is discovered
    - ☐ Relevant information is retained on a continuing basis
    - ☐ Relevant non-privileged material is produced to the opposing party.

- ☐ **Counsel's Duty to Locate Relevant Information.**
  - ☐ After a "litigation hold" is in place, a party and the party's counsel must make certain all sources of potentially relevant information are identified placed on hold.
  - ☐ Counsel must become fully familiar with the client's document retention policies, as well as the client's data retention architecture.
    - ☐ This invariably involves speaking with information technology personnel who can explain system-wide backup procedures and the actual implementation of the party's recycling policy.
    - ☐ It involves communicating with the key players in the litigation in order to understand how they stored information.
    - ☐ Unless counsel interviews each employee, it is impossible to determine whether all potential sources of information have been inspected.
    - ☐ To the extent it is not feasible for counsel to speak with every key player, it may be possible to run a system-wide keyword search. Counsel should preserve a copy of each "hit."
  - ☐ It is not sufficient to notify all employees of a litigation hold and expect the party will retain and produce all relevant information.
  - ☐ Counsel must take affirmative steps to monitor compliance so that all sources of discoverable information are identified and searched.
- ☐ **Counsel's Continuing Duty to Ensure Preservation.**
  - ☐ Once a party and its counsel have identified all the sources of potentially relevant information, they are under a duty to retain that information and to produce information responsive to the opposing party's requests.
  - ☐ The duty to supplement responses under applicable rules of civil procedure, while nominally the party's, really falls on counsel.

- ☐ The continuing duty to supplement disclosures strongly suggests that parties also have a duty to be sure discoverable information is not lost.

☐ **There are a number of steps counsel can take to ensure compliance with this preservation obligation.**

- ☐ First, counsel must issue a litigation hold at the outset of litigation or whenever litigation is reasonably anticipated. Periodically the litigation hold should be re-issued so that new employees are aware of it, and so that the litigation hold is fresh in the minds of all employees.
- ☐ Second, counsel should communicate directly with the "key players" (people identified in a party's initial disclosure and any subsequent supplementation).
  - ☐ Because these persons are employees likely to have relevant information, it is important that the preservation duty be communicated clearly to them.
  - ☐ The key players should be periodically reminded that the litigation hold is still in place.
- ☐ Third, counsel should instruct all employees to produce digital copies of their relevant active files.
  - ☐ Counsel must also be sure that all backup media the party is required to retain is identified and stored in a safe place.
  - ☐ Where a small number of relevant backup tapes are involved, it is advisable for counsel to take physical possession of backup tapes or have the backup tapes segregated and placed in storage.

Comment

See Zubulake v. UBS Warburg LLC, 229 F.R.D. 422, 94 Fair Empl. Prac. Cas. (BNA) 1, 85 Empl. Prac. Dec. (CCH) P 41728 (S.D. N.Y. 2004).

§ 17:17 Checklist for determining whether destruction of documents pursuant to records retention policy constitutes spoliation of evidence

- ☐ Was the policy reasonable under the facts and circumstances?
- ☐ Had lawsuits concerning the current complaint or related complaints been filed?
- ☐ Was the policy instituted in bad faith (to limit damaging evidence available to plaintiffs)?
- ☐ Did the organization know, or should it have known, that the destroyed documents would become "material at some point in the future"?

Comment

See Lewy v. Remington Arms Co., Inc., 836 F.2d 1104, 1112, Prod. Liab. Rep. (CCH) P 11662, 24 Fed. R. Evid. Serv. 516 (8th Cir. 1988).

§ 17:18 Checklist for avoiding spoliation

- ☐ Timely suspend document retention policies when litigation is reasonably foreseeable.
- ☐ Honor preservation letters.
- ☐ Turn off digital devices only by unplugging in most cases.
- ☐ Request that information be preserved in native format whenever possible to preserve metadata.
- ☐ Quarantine digital media.
- ☐ Create bit-stream backups (imaging) of digital media.
- ☐ Avoid booting up suspect machines.
- ☐ Avoid redeploying machines unless the data they contain are irrelevant to imminent or ongoing litigation.
- ☐ Forbid forensically naive network administrators or other members of the information technology department from checking out or otherwise investigating relevant devices.

§ 17:19 Checklist for detecting potential spoliation

- ☐ Scrutinize the timing and sequence of the opponent's

documents. A clear indication of potential spoliation is a gap in routinely filed documents. Missing pages are another obvious red flag.

- ☐ Track down all drafts. If a document is labeled "fourth draft," make sure you also have drafts one, two, and three.
- ☐ Spot-check "cc" recipients. Tracing the path of every document through a large organization is a waste of resources, but trailing key documents can reveal changes or undisclosed drafts.
- ☐ Dissect drafts of important letters and memoranda. Important documents are usually preceded by one or more drafts. Check your opponent's word processing archives if drafts are not produced.
- ☐ Do not forget e-mail. E-mail is routinely ignored by attorneys gathering documents responsive to requests. If the opponent uses an e-mail system, insist that you receive any relevant messages in their native format. The informal language used in e-mails is often more damaging than carefully crafted documents.

Comment

See Conley & Seidman, *Identifying Spoliation in the 1990s*, FED.DISC. NEWS, May 1995, at 4.

III. FORMS

§ 17:20 Preservation policy

Preservation Policy
(Litigation Hold)

1. If an employee believes, or is informed by *[organization]* that certain records are relevant to litigation or potential litigation, the employee must preserve those records, including electronically stored information, until the *[organization's]* Legal Department determines the records are no longer needed. This duty to preserve supersedes any established destruction schedule for those records.

2. If an employee believe the duty to preserve may apply, or has any question regarding the possible applicability of the duty to preserve, the employee should contact the *[organization's]* Legal Department. An employee's failure to comply with this Document Retention Policy may result in disciplinary action, including suspension or termination. An employee should refer questions about this policy to *[name]*, at *[telephone number]* or *[e-mail address]*.

3. The duty to preserve extends to documents, data, and tangible things in the possession, custody and control of the parties to this action, and any employees, agents, contractors, carriers, bailees, or other nonparties possessing materials reasonably anticipated to be subject to discovery in this action. Counsel is under an obligation to exercise reasonable efforts to identify and notify such nonparties, including employees of corporate or institutional parties.

4. The term "documents, data, and tangible things" is to be interpreted broadly to include writings, records, files, electronically stored information, correspondence, reports, memoranda, calendars, diaries, minutes, electronic messages, voicemail, e-mail; telephone message records or logs, computer and network activity logs, hard drives; backup data, removable computer storage media such as tapes, disks, and cards, printouts document image files, Web pages, databases, spreadsheets, software, books, ledgers, journals, orders, invoices, bills, vouchers, checks, statements, worksheets, summaries, compilations, computations, charts, diagrams, graphic presentations, drawings, films, charts, digital or chemical process photographs, video, phonographic, tape, or digital recordings or transcripts, drafts, jottings, and notes. Information serving to identify, locate, or link such material, such as file inventories, file folders, indices, and metadata, is also included in this definition.

5. "Preservation" is to be interpreted broadly to accomplish the goal of maintaining the integrity of all documents, data, and tangible things reasonably anticipated to be subject to discovery under *[rules]* in this action. Preser-

vation includes taking reasonable steps to prevent the partial or full destruction, alteration, testing, deletion, shredding, incineration, wiping relocation, migration, theft, or mutation of such material, as well as negligent or intentional handling that would make material incomplete or inaccessible.

5. The following categories of electronically stored information are to be segregated and preserved: *[specify]*.

6. During this litigation hold there will be no deletion, modification, alteration of electronically stored information subject to the litigation hold.

7. Employees should advise whether specific categories of electronically stored information subject to the litigation hold require particular actions (e.g., printing paper copies of e-mail and attachments) or transfer into "read only" media.

8. Loading of new software that materially impacts electronically stored information subject to the hold may occur only upon prior written approval from *[name]*.

9. In order to preserve metadata, or data that has been deleted but not purged, the Information Technology Department shall *[describe]*.

10. Employees must reasonably safeguard and preserve all portable or removable electronic storage media containing potentially relevant electronically stored information.

11. Employees shall maintain hardware that has been removed from active production, if such hardware contains legacy systems with relevant electronically stored information and there is no reasonably available alternative that preserves access to the native files on such hardware.

12. *[Name]* is the contact person who will address questions regarding preservation duties.

13. *[Names]* have the responsibility to confirm that compliance requirements are met.

§ 17:21 Litigation hold letter—To client

[date]

[name 1]
[address]

Subject: *[Case Name]*

Data Preservation

Dear *[name 1]*:

Your assistance and cooperation are required with respect to preserving information in this case, including electronically stored information. Electronically stored information is an important and irreplaceable source of discovery and evidence.

This lawsuit requires that all employees preserve all information from *[organization's]* computer systems, removable electronic media, and other locations relating to *[describe]*. This includes, but is not limited to, e-mail and other electronic communication, word processing documents, spreadsheets, databases, calendars, telephone logs, contact manager information, Internet usage files, and network access information.

You must take every reasonable step to preserve this information until further notice from *[name 2]*. Failure to do so could result in extreme penalties against *[organization]* including dismissal of the case.

If you have any questions or need further information, please contact *[name 3]* at *[telephone number]*.

Sincerely,

[signature, etc.]

§ 17:22 Litigation hold letter—To client—Another form

[date]

[name 1]
[address]

Subject: *[Case Name]*
Preservation of Electronically Stored Information

Dear *[name 1]*:

The purpose of this letter is to inform you that the *[organization]* is involved in a litigation proceeding known as *[case name, case no., jurisdiction]* (the Case). As a result, *[organization]* may be required to produce certain documents, including electronically stored information, relating to the case. In an effort to ensure that *[organization]* is taking all reasonable steps to preserve and safeguard evidence relating to the case, the documents in the categories listed below, whether in hard copy or electronic form, cannot be altered, destroyed or discarded for any reason.

Documents subject to this requirement may be in paper or electronic form, including e-mails, instant text messages, memorandums, and all correspondence, whether in draft or final form. Documents also refer to handwritten and typewritten documents and nonidentical copies of the same documents.

Your failure to retain these documents or ignore the directive of this memorandum can result in severe consequences, including various forms of punishment imposed by a court of law.

Documents Covered:

Until further notice, please search for and then maintain any documents relating to the following topics: *[specify]*.

Any and all documents relating to the *[describe]*, including, without limitation: *[list all potentially relevant documents]*

Any and all communications relating to, or stemming from, the *[describe]*.

Instructions:

Please instruct all personnel within the *[organization]* not to alter, destroy, discard, interfile, annotate, remove, rearrange or modify any documents identified for production in the case. Please also inform all appropriate personnel who are responsible for handling, or who have access to, the documents of the instructions conveyed in this letter. Additionally, please instruct such personnel that they must segregate and label all documents that may be produced in the *[describe]*.

Questions:

Any questions or concerns about this memorandum should be directed to *[name]* at *[telephone number]*. Thank you for your cooperation in this matter.

Very truly yours,

[signature, etc.]

Please preserve all electronically stored information relating to *[describe]*, including hidden system files or metadata, presently located on or contained in a free standing computer or laptop, or on any part of a server, CPU or digital device that may contain data storage capabilities including, but not limited to hard disk drives, optical disk drives, removable media, such as floppy disk drives, CD-ROM and DVD drives, Zip drives, Jaz drives, Maxtor drives or snap drives, data processing cards, computer magnetic tapes, backup tapes, drum and disk storage devices or any other similar electronic storage media or system of whatever name or description.

Please also preserve all digital images relating to *[describe]* that may be stored on any type of hardware used to store or manipulate electronic images, including but not limited to microfilm, microfiche and their repositories and readers, or design or engineering computer systems and regardless of any digital image's format, including.jpg, .bmp, or some other advanced or proprietary form of digital image format, such as CAD layered drawings.

Please preserve all existing sources of electronically stored information relating to *[describe]* that may not presently be in use by your company or may have been deleted from your active systems, whether the source is a backup tape or disk, some other data retention system or some form of disaster recovery system.

Including the imaging of hard drives, please take all reasonable steps to preserve electronically stored information relating to *[describe]* that may have been deleted from your active files and which may not be readily recoverable from a backup medium, such as metadata.

Please also preserve electronically stored information relating to *[describe]* that is subject to your control regardless of where else it may be located on-site at your main offices, within the network infrastructure of your company or on or in one of your other computer support systems including those at your subsidiaries, predecessors, successors, assigns, joint venturers, partners, parents, agents or affiliates (in this country or throughout the world), including but not limited to the following locations:

a. Your LAN and WAN network systems, regardless of methods of connectivity (e.g., by T1, T3 or optical lines), domains, including PDCs, network OS (such as Novell, Microsoft, UNIX, Citrix or some other similar type) or protocols, or your backup and disaster recovery hardware and media, regardless of the physical location of those electronic storage systems.

b. Your e-mail servers and any repository of your e-mail (including within the inbox, sent box, deleted box or some similar file of the computers of employees or management), or in any backup form whatsoever, regardless of whether you use Microsoft Exchange, Outlook, Outlook Express, Lotus Notes or some combination of e-mail management software or some alternative commercial or proprietary e-mail management software.

c. Your IS administrative offices, including backup and disaster recovery restoration repositories, data retention repositories, purge repositories, training repositories, or libraries of hardcopy materials of any description (regardless of where located) and online training and operation manuals that have been scanned to disk.

d. Your offsite technical and service bureau support systems, including but not limited to ASP (application service provider) support, scanning or data conversion support, offsite data storage or archive support.

e. Your Web hosting and administration services, including intranet and extranet sites, regardless of whether they are now publicly posted or exist in English or some other language.

Please consider yourself under a continuing obligation to preserve electronically stored information relating to *[describe]* that may come into existence after the date of this letter, or that may exist now or in the future but of which you have no current knowledge.

Very truly yours,

[signature, etc.]

§ 17:23 Adverse inference instruction

If a party fails to produce evidence that is under that party's control and reasonably available to that party and not reasonably available to the adverse party, then you may infer that the evidence is unfavorable to the party who could have produced it and did not.

Comment

Under the "adverse inference rule," when a party has relevant evidence within its control that the party fails to produce, that failure gives rise to an inference that the evidence is unfavorable to it. International Union, United Auto., Aerospace and Agr. Implement Workers of America (UAW) v. N. L. R. B., 459 F.2d 1329, 1336, 79

L.R.R.M. (BNA) 2332, 67 Lab. Cas. (CCH) P 12374, 32 A.L.R. Fed. 807 (D.C. Cir. 1972); Rockingham Machine-Lunex Co. v. N.L.R.B., 665 F.2d 303, 304, 108 L.R.R.M. (BNA) 3228, 92 Lab. Cas. (CCH) P 13142 (8th Cir. 1981). See also Interstate Circuit v. U.S., 306 U.S. 208, 226, 59 S. Ct. 467, 474, 83 L. Ed. 610, 40 U.S.P.Q. 299 (1939) (production of weak evidence when strong is available can lead only to conclusion that strong evidence would have been adverse).

When a party has destroyed evidence relevant to the dispute being litigated, a "spoliation inference" arises to the effect that the destroyed evidence would have been unfavorable to the position of the offending party. Schmid v. Milwaukee Elec. Tool Corp., 13 F.3d 76 (3d Cir.1994).

No inference can be drawn from the failure to produce evidence not in a party's control. Savard v. Marine Contracting Inc., 471 F.2d 536, 541–42, 1973 A.M.C. 323 (2d Cir. 1972), cert. denied sub nom. Savard v. Perini Corp., 412 U.S. 943, 93 S. Ct. 2778, 37 L. Ed. 2d 404, 1973 A.M.C. 2163 (1973).

The rule that an unfavorable inference shall be drawn against a party that fails to introduce evidence known to be in its control does not apply where party has good reason to believe that its opponent has failed to meet its burden of proof. N.L.R.B. v. Chester Valley, Inc., 652 F.2d 263, 271, 107 L.R.R.M. (BNA) 3148, 91 Lab. Cas. (CCH) P 12861 (2d Cir. 1981). In such situations, there is a good faith belief that there is no need to offer further evidence, and therefore no inference can properly be drawn from nonproduction. The inference raised by nonproduction of material evidence in control of a party can be rebutted by adequate explanation for nonproduction. Fernandez v. Chios Shipping Co., Ltd., 542 F.2d 145, 155, 1976 A.M.C. 1780, 1 Fed. R. Evid. Serv. 355 (2d Cir. 1976); Tupman Thurlow Co., Inc. v. S. S. Cap Castillo, 490 F.2d 302, 308, 1974 A.M.C. 51, 18 Fed. R. Serv. 2d 36 (2d Cir. 1974).

In Zimmermann v. Associates First Capital Corp., 251 F.3d 376, 383, 85 Fair Empl. Prac. Cas. (BNA) 1505, 81 Empl. Prac. Dec. (CCH) P 40835 (2d Cir. 2001), the Second Circuit approved the following instruction where the employer failed to produce information critical to plaintiff's attempt to demonstrate disparate treatment:

> You have heard testimony about records which have not been produced. Counsel for plaintiff has argued that this evidence was in the defendant's control and would have proven facts material to the matter in controversy.
>
> If you find that the defendant could have produced these records were within their control and would have proven facts material to the matter in controversy.
>
> If you find that the defendant could have produced these records and that the records were within their control, and that these records would have been material in deciding facts in dispute in this case, then you are permitted, but not required to, infer that this evidence would have been unfavorable to the defendant.
>
> In deciding whether to draw this inference you should consider whether the evidence not produced would merely have duplicated other evidence already before you. You may also consider whether the defendant had a reason for not producing this evidence, which was explained to your satisfaction.

In Zubulake v. UBS Warburg LLC, 229 F.R.D. 422, 94 Fair Empl. Prac. Cas. (BNA) 1, 85 Empl. Prac. Dec. (CCH) P 41728 (S.D. N.Y. 2004), the court gave the following instruction regarding spoliation:

> If you find that UBS could have produced this evidence, and that the evidence was within its control, and that the evidence would have been material in deciding facts in dispute in this case, you are permitted, but not required, to infer that the evidence would have been unfavorable to UBS.

Chapter 18

Not Reasonably Accessible Electronically Stored Information

I. GUIDELINES

II. CHECKLISTS

III. FORMS

Research References

Trial Strategy

Recovery and Reconstruction of Electronic Mail as Evidence, 41 Am. Jur Proof of Facts 3d 1
Computer Technology in Civil Litigation, 71 Am. Jur Trials 111

Law Reviews and Other Periodicals

Boehning & Toal, Courts Consider When Cost-Shifting Is Appropriate: A Ruling Suggests It Is Called for only When Data Are Inaccessible, Nat'l L.J., Aug. 20, 2007, at S3

Noyes, Good Cause Is Bad Medicine for New E-Discovery Rules, 21 Harv. J.L. & Tech. 49 (2007)

Additional References

Babbitt & Termine, The New Reasonable Accessibility Standard: What's So Reasonable About It?, e-Discovery, 2007, at 42

ABA Discovery Standards, http://www.abanet.org/litigation/discoverystandards/2005civildiscoverystandards.pdf

eDirect Impact, Inc., http://www.edirectimpact.com

Electronic Discovery Reference Model Project, http://www.edrm.net

Federal Judicial Center, http://www.fjc.gov

The Sedona Conference, http://www.thesedonaconference.org

KeyCite®: Cases and other legal materials listed in KeyCite Scope can be researched through the KeyCite service on Westlaw®. Use KeyCite to check citations for form, parallel references, prior and later history, and comprehensive citator information, including citations to other decisions and secondary materials.

I. GUIDELINES

§ 18:1 Generally

It is often easier to locate and retrieve electronically stored information than paper-based information. However, some sources of electronically stored information can be accessed only with substantial burden and cost. That burden and cost may make the information on such sources not reasonably accessible.[1]

The responding party may be able to identify difficult-to-access sources that may contain responsive information, but that the responding party is not able to retrieve the information or even to determine whether any respon-

[Section 18:1]

[1]Advisory Committee Note to 2006 Amendment to Fed. R. Civ. P. 26.

sive information in fact is on the sources—without incurring substantial burden or cost[2]. Rule 26(b)(2)(B) of the Federal Rules of Civil Procedure addresses issues raised by difficulties in locating, retrieving, and providing discovery of some electronically stored information.

According to the Advisory Committee:

> The volume of—and the ability to search—much electronically stored information means that in many cases the responding party will be able to produce information from reasonably accessible sources that will fully satisfy the parties' discovery needs. In many circumstances the requesting party should obtain and evaluate the information from such sources before insisting that the responding party search and produce information contained on sources that are not reasonably accessible. If the requesting party continues to seek discovery of information from sources identified as not reasonably accessible, the parties should discuss the burdens and costs of accessing and retrieving the information, the needs that may establish good cause for requiring all or part of the requested discovery even if the information sought is not reasonably accessible, and conditions on obtaining and producing the information that may be appropriate.[3]

Sources that might be considered not reasonably accessible sources of electronically stored information include:

- Backup tapes intended for disaster recovery purposes
- Legacy data remaining from obsolete systems that is unintelligible on successor systems

---

[2]See Sedona Principle 8 ("The primary source of electronically stored information for production should be active data and information. Resort to disaster recovery backup tapes and other sources of electronically stored information that are not reasonably accessible requires the requesting party to demonstrate need and relevance that outweigh the costs and burdens of retrieving and processing the electronically stored information from such sources, including the disruption of business and information management activities."), and Sedona Principle 9 ("Absent a showing of special need and relevance, a responding party should not be required to preserve, review, or produce deleted, shadowed, fragmented, or residual electronically stored information.").

[3]Advisory Committee Note to 2006 Amendment to Fed. R. Civ. P. 26.

- Deleted electronically stored information that remains in a fragmented form requiring a forensics to restore and retrieve
- Electronically stored information in a database that was designed to create information in ways such that it would lose its significance when produced outside the database[4]

The Advisory Committee acknowledged that amended Rule 26(b)(2)(B) might encourage some to "bury" information in some inaccessible format in order to keep it from being discovered in litigation, but noted that this conduct would be subject to sanctions under both the present and the proposed rules.[5]

§ 18:2 Two-tiered analysis

Rule 26(b)(2)(B) of the Federal Rules of Civil Procedure creates what is frequently referred to as a "two-tier" system. Under Rule 26(b)(2)(B), a party is not required to provide discovery of electronically stored information from sources the party identifies as not reasonably accessible because of undue burden or cost. However, a court may nonetheless order discovery from sources identified as not reasonably accessible if the requesting party shows good cause, considering the limitations of Rule 26(b)(2)(C) applicable to all discovery.

In many circumstances, the two-tier approach will be

---

[4]Report of the Civil Rules Advisory Committee (May 27, 2005).

See W.E. Aubuchon Co., Inc. v. BeneFirst, LLC, 245 F.R.D. 38, 68 Fed. R. Serv. 3d 361 (D. Mass. 2007) (categories of sources of electronically stored information, from most to least accessible, are (1) active online data (e.g., hard drives), (2) near-line data (typically, robotic storage devices such as optical disks) and offline storage/archives (removable optical disks or magnetic tape media that can be labeled and stored in shelf or rack), (3) backup tapes (devices like tape records that read data from and write it onto a tape, sequential access devices that are not typically organized for retrieval of individual documents or files), and (4) erased, fragmented or damaged data, which can only be accessed after significant processing).

[5]Advisory Committee Note to Proposed Amendment to Fed. R. Civ. P 26(b)(2) (May 27, 2005).

worked out by negotiation. At the same time, more easily accessed sources—whether computer-based, paper, or human may yield all the reasonably useful information.[1] According to the Advisory Committee: "Lawyers sophisticated in these problems are developing a two-tier practice in which they first sort through the information that can be provided from easily accessed sources and then determine whether it is necessary to search the difficult-to-access sources."[2]

§ 18:3 Claim information not reasonably accessible—Responding party

Under Rule 26(b)(2)(B) of the Federal Rules of Civil Procedure, the responding party is required to identify, by category or type, the sources containing potentially responsive information that it is neither searching nor producing. The identification should provide enough detail to enable the requesting party to evaluate the burdens and costs of providing the discovery and the likelihood of finding responsive information on the identified sources.[1]

If the parties cannot agree on what terms the sources identified as not reasonably accessible should be searched and discoverable information produced, the issue may be raised either by a motion to compel discovery or by a

---

[Section 18:2]

[1]Advisory Committee Note to Proposed Amendment to Fed. R. Civ. P 26(b)(2) (May 27, 2005).

[2]Advisory Committee Note to Proposed Amendment to Fed. R. Civ. P 26(b)(2) (May 27, 2005).

[Section 18:3]

[1]See, e.g., City of Seattle v. Professional Basketball Club, LLC, 2008 WL 539809 (W.D. Wash. 2008) (bald assertions of burden insufficient); Parkdale America, LLC v. Travelers Cas. and Sur. Co. of America, Inc., 2007 WL 4165247 (W.D. N.C. 2007) (plaintiffs failed to establish e-mail in LotusNotes format was not reasonably accessible because of undue burden or cost). But see Best Buy Stores, L.P. v. Developers Diversified Realty Corp., 247 F.R.D. 567, 69 Fed. R. Serv. 3d 1035 (D. Minn. 2007) (plaintiff not required to produce database prepared in separate litigation).

motion. The responding party then has the burden to show that the identified sources are not reasonably accessible because of undue burden or cost.[2]

While Rule 26(b)(2)(B) relieves producing parties from the initial obligation of producing potentially discoverable information from sources the party identifies as not reasonably accessible because of undue burden or cost, it does not relieve the party of its common law or statutory duties to preserve evidence.[3] Whether the party is required to preserve unsearched sources of potentially responsive information it believes are not reasonably accessible depends on the circumstances of each case.[4] A responding party is entitled to conduct a cost-benefit analysis under Rule 26(b)(2)(C). If the burden of preservation is extraordinarily high and the potential benefit is low, there should be no need to preserve. If the cost of preservation is low and the risk of losing potentially relevant data is high, preservation is the prudent course.

A responding party may wish to resolve the issue by moving for a protective order.[5] By making a motion for a protective order, a responding party may be able to resolve whether, or the extent to which, it must preserve the information stored on the difficult-to-access sources until discoverability is resolved.[6]

---

[2]See Semsroth v. City of Wichita, 239 F.R.D. 630, 634, 27 A.L.R. 6th 705 (D. Kan. 2006) (relying on then proposed 2006 amendments of Fed. R. Civ. P. 26(2)(B).

[3]Advisory Committee Note to 2006 Amendment to Fed. R. Civ. P. 26.

[4]Advisory Committee Note to 2006 Amendment to Fed. R. Civ. P. 26. (the decision is left to the good judgment and risk tolerance of the organization's decision-maker).

[5]Advisory Committee Note to Proposed Amendment to Fed. R. Civ. P 26(b)(2) (May 27, 2005).

[6]Advisory Committee Note to Proposed Amendment to Fed. R. Civ. P 26(b)(2) (May 27, 2005).

§ 18:4 Order requiring discovery of information not reasonably accessible

A finding that the responding party has shown that a source of information is not reasonably accessible does not preclude discovery; the court may still order discovery for good cause.[1] In ordering discovery of information that is not reasonably accessible, the court may specify conditions for the discovery.[2]

In some cases a single proceeding may suffice both to find that a source is not reasonably accessible and also to determine whether good cause nonetheless justifies discover and to set any conditions that should be imposed.[3] Conditions include limits on the amount, type, or sources of information that must be accessed and produced. In addition, the court may require the requesting party to pay part or all of the reasonable costs of obtaining the information from inaccessible costs.

The proceedings may have to be staged if focused discovery is necessary to determine the costs and burdens in obtaining information from the sources identified as not reasonably accessible, the likelihood of finding responsive information on such sources, and the value of the information to the litigation.[4] A finding that a source is not reasonably accessible may lead to further proceedings to determine whether there is good cause to order limited or

---

[Section 18:4]

[1] Advisory Committee Note to Proposed Amendment to Fed. R. Civ. P 26(b)(2) (May 27, 2005).

[2] Peskoff v. Faber, 244 F.R.D. 54 (D.D.C. 2007) (it was appropriate to ascertain cost of forensic testing to see if it justified forensic search for relevant e-mails).

[3] Advisory Committee Note to Proposed Amendment to Fed. R. Civ. P 26(b)(2) (May 27, 2005).

[4] Advisory Committee Note to Proposed Amendment to Fed. R. Civ. P 26(b)(2) (May 27, 2005).

extensive searches and the production of information stored on such sources.[5]

In many cases, discovery obtained from accessible sources will be sufficient to meet the needs of the case.[6] If information from such sources does not satisfy the requesting party, Rule 26(b)(2)(B) allows that party to obtain additional discovery from sources identified as not reasonably accessible, subject to judicial supervision, on a showing of good cause.[7] One method of showing a need for discovery is by sampling the sources to determine what they contain and how difficult it would be obtain what they contain.[8]

In determining whether the requesting party has shown of good cause for obtaining discovery from a source of electronically stored information that is not reasonably accessible, consideration must be given to the limitations of Rule 26(b)(2)(C) that balance the costs and potential benefits of discovery.[9] A determination of good cause depends not only on the burdens and cost of discovery, but also whether those burdens and costs can be justified in

---

[5]Advisory Committee Note to Proposed Amendment to Fed. R. Civ. P 26(b)(2) (May 27, 2005).

[6]Advisory Committee Note to Proposed Amendment to Fed. R. Civ. P 26(b)(2) (May 27, 2005).

[7]Advisory Committee Note to Proposed Amendment to Fed. R. Civ. P 26(b)(2) (May 27, 2005).

[8]See, e.g., Hagemeyer North America, Inc. v. Gateway Data Sciences Corp., 222 F.R.D. 594 (E.D. Wis. 2004) (requiring defendant to restore sample of backup tapes and requiring parties to address whether expense of satisfying entire discovery request was proportionate to likely benefit); Zubulake v. UBS Warburg LLC, 217 F.R.D. 309, 91 Fair Empl. Prac. Cas. (BNA) 1574 (S.D. N.Y. 2003) (ordering that five backup tapes selected by plaintiff be restored by defendant and examined to determine whether they had responsive e-mail messages); McPeek v. Ashcroft, 202 F.R.D. 31, 50 Fed. R. Serv. 3d 528 (D.D.C. 2001) (ordering backup restoration of e-mails attributable to specified period).

[9]Fed. R. Civ. P. 26(b)(2)(B).

the circumstances of the case.[10] The test is based on the burden and cost of locating, restoring, and retrieving potentially responsive information from the sources in which it is stored.[11]

Rule 26(b)(2)(C) permits a court to limit discovery if it determines:

- the discovery sought is unreasonably cumulative or duplicative, or is obtainable from some other source that is more convenient, less burdensome or less expensive;
- the party seeking discovery has had ample opportunity by discovery in the action to obtain the information sought; or
- the burden or expense of the proposed discovery outweighs its likely benefit, taking into account the needs of the case, the amount in controversy, the parties' resources, the importance of the issues at stake in the litigation, and the importance of the proposed discovery in resolving the issues.

The ultimate question is whether the burden of complying with the discovery request outweighs the likely benefit of the proposed discovery.[12] The first inquiry should be to ask what the benefits to be derived from the discovery are.[13] This involves the following questions:

- What is the likelihood that the discovery will uncover relevant information?

---

[10]Advisory Committee Note to 2006 Amendment to Fed. R. Civ. P. 26.

[11]Advisory Committee Note to Proposed Amendment to Fed. R. Civ. P 26(b)(2) (May 27, 2005). But see Reidy & Baros, *Win the Battle for Access to E-data*, TRIAL, Dec. 2006, at 49, 52 ("because information deemed not reasonably accessible is specially protected (it need not be searched for responsive documents), the "undue burden or cost test" should be more demanding than the "unduly burdensome").

[12]Zubulake v. UBS Warburg LLC, 217 F.R.D. 309, 322–23, 91 Fair Empl. Prac. Cas. (BNA) 1574 (S.D. N.Y. 2003). Accord Semsroth v. City of Wichita, 239 F.R.D. 630, 638, 27 A.L.R.6th 705 (D. Kan. 2006).

[13]Semsroth v. City of Wichita, 239 F.R.D. 630, 638, 27 A.L.R.6th 705 (D. Kan. 2006).

- What is the potential value of that information in resolving the issues of the case?

Then, these benefits should be compared to the cost of burden resulting from the discovery.[14] The following questions should be asked:

- What is the total cost of production compared with the amount in controversy?
- What is the total cost of production compared to the resources available to each party?

These factors should be given such weight as may be justified by the individual case as they are all critical to the ultimate question of whether the costs outweigh the likely benefits of production.[15]

§ 18:5 Backup tapes

Backup tapes are a reasonable storage method for purpose of disaster recovery.[1] Backup tapes created as a disaster-recovery measure have been considered to be an inaccessible format because the electronically stored information is not organized for retrieval of individual documents, and it is usually more time consuming and expensive to restore the information due to the fact the information has been compressed.[2] Because organizations are increasingly opting for Internet or disc-based backups,

---

[14]Semsroth v. City of Wichita, 239 F.R.D. 630, 638, 27 A.L.R.6th 705 (D. Kan. 2006).

[15]Semsroth v. City of Wichita, 239 F.R.D. 630, 638, 27 A.L.R.6th 705 (D. Kan. 2006).

[Section 18:5]

[1]Advisory Committee Note to 2006 amendment to Fed. R. Civ. P. 26. See Semsroth v. City of Wichita, 239 F.R.D. 630, 635, 27 A.L.R.6th 705 (D. Kan. 2006) (applying then-proposed 2006 amendments of Fed. R. Civ. P. 26(2)(B)). But see Quinby v. WestLB AG, 245 F.R.D. 94 (S.D. N.Y. 2006), subsequent determination, 2007 WL 38230 (S.D. N.Y. 2007) (party converted data into an inaccessible format at a time when it should have reasonably anticipated litigation and should have anticipated that data would be discoverable in such litigation).

[2]Zubulake v. UBS Warburg LLC, 217 F.R.D. 309, 319, 91 Fair Empl. Prac. Cas. (BNA) 1574 (S.D. N.Y. 2003). Accord Semsroth v. City

rather than tape drives, these newer technologies overcome the sequential-access problem associated with tape drives.

Because backup tapes must be restored before they can be searched for relevant electronically stored information, this suggests the process of producing such information would constitute an unreasonable burden.[3] The more likely it is that the backup tape contains important, relevant to the requesting party's case, the fairer it is to require the responding party to search at its own expense.[4]

Generally backups are viewed as short-term retention copies of a file or record in case the original is lost or damaged. An archive is thought of as the means to meet a requirement to retain a record for future reference.

Archival data is information an organization maintains for maintains for long-term storage and record keeping purposes, but which is not immediately accessible to the computer system users. It may be written to removable media, tape, or other electronic storage devices. Some systems allow users to retrieve archival data directly while others require the intervention of a professional. Electronic archives preserve the content, prevent or track alterations, and control access to electronic records. Most archival data is reasonably accessible.

---

of Wichita, 239 F.R.D. 630, 636, 27 A.L.R.6th 705 (D. Kan. 2006). But see Treppel v. Biovail Corp., 249 F.R.D. 111 (S.D. N.Y. 2008) (inadequate preservation efforts necessitated restoration and production of e-mail from backup tapes).

[3]Petcou v. C.H. Robinson Worldwide, Inc., 2008 WL 542684 (N.D. Ga. 2008) (no duty to search backup tapes for e-mails of sexual nature-);Zubulake v. UBS Warburg LLC, 217 F.R.D. 309, 318, 91 Fair Empl. Prac. Cas. (BNA) 1574 (S.D. N.Y. 2003). Accord Semsroth v. City of Wichita, 239 F.R.D. 630, 637, 27 A.L.R.6th 705 (D. Kan. 2006). But see Reidy & Baros, *Win the Battle for Access to E-data*, TRIAL, Dec. 2006, at 49, 54 ("restoration is not necessarily burdensome or costly").

[4]Zubulake v. UBS Warburg LLC, 217 F.R.D. 309, 333, 91 Fair Empl. Prac. Cas. (BNA) 1574 (S.D. N.Y. 2003), citing McPeek v. Ashcroft, 202 F.R.D. 31, 34, 50 Fed. R. Serv. 3d 528 (D.D.C. 2001).

§ 18:6 Legacy systems

Many cases involve legacy databases that using outdated or obsolete technology, including outdated operating systems and hardware. Customized solutions are often required to collect potentially relevant data from legacy databases. The Advisory Committee has indicated that legacy data remaining from obsolete systems that is unintelligible on successor systems is considered information no reasonably accessible.[1]

Even when legacy data can be read and used, a database contains a large quantity of unformatted electronically stored information that becomes useful only when it is put into a report. Databases contain entries and complex table structures appear nonsensical if just providing the raw data. Many databases do not permit the creation of customized reports containing the information in the form that is deemed potentially relevant in the litigation. Therefore, a third party is frequently required to write customized software to extract electronically stored information from various locations in the database and to create a formatted document that can be reviewed.

Because of the costs, an organization may be tempted to make portions of a database available to the requesting party, forcing requesting party to pay the costs of securing the electronically stored information from the database. Great caution should be taken in agreeing to turn over unreviewed databases to opposing counsel. The courts are split over whether to grant access to the responding party's databases for the requesting party to run searches.[2]

When dealing with older technology, legacy systems or databases, it is important to describe the complexity of the

---

[Section 18:6]

[1]Advisory Committee Note to 2006 Amendment to Fed. R. Civ. P. 26.

[2]Compare In re Honeywell Intern., Inc. Securities Litigation, 230 F.R.D. 293 (S.D. N.Y. 2003) (providing access), with In re Ford Motor Co., 345 F.3d 1315, 56 Fed. R. Serv. 3d 438 (11th Cir. 2003) (not providing access).

collection and production of that information as early as possible. It may be necessary to use outside experts who can provide testimony regarding the complexity, time involved, and cost of obtaining legacy information. If the parties to the case cannot agree on a reasonable approach to this problem, a court may need to issue an order specifying the appropriateness and limits of collecting and producing the legacy data.

§ 18:7 Deleted information

While deleted electronically stored information is often retrievable, it may require considerable effort. While this does not put the information beyond discovery, the difficulty of accessing the information means the information is not reasonably accessible.

§ 18:8 Databases

A database contains a large quantity of electronically stored information that is typically unformatted and becomes useful only when it is put into a report. Databases appear nonsensical if just providing the raw data. Many database systems do not permit the creation of customized reports containing the information in the form that is deemed potentially relevant in the litigation. A third party is often needed to write customized software to extract data from various locations in the database and create a formatted document that can be reviewed.

Thus, according to the Advisory Committee, databases that "cannot readily create very different kinds or forms of information from the kind or form from which they were designed are a problem in discovery.[1] It may be possible to avoid this problem if the requesting party formulates the request to fit the design of the database.

[Section 18:8]

[1]Advisory Committee Note to 2006 Amendment to Fed. R. Civ. P. 26.

II. CHECKLISTS

§ 18:9 Checklist of considerations for determining whether to require discovery of electronically stored information that is not reasonably accessible

- ☐ The specificity of the discovery request
- ☐ The quantity of information available from other and more easily accessed sources
- ☐ The failure to produce relevant information that seems likely to have existed but is no longer available on more easily accessed sources
- ☐ The likelihood of finding relevant, responsive information that cannot be obtained from other, more easily accessed sources
- ☐ Predictions as to the importance and usefulness of the further information
- ☐ The importance of the issues at stake in the litigation
- ☐ The parties' resources

Comment

Adapted from Advisory Committee Note to 2006 Amendment to Rule 26.

III. FORMS

§ 18:10 Defendant's motion for protective order regarding re-creation of backup server tapes

[Caption]

Defendant *[Name's]* Motion for Protective Order Regarding Re-Creation of Backup Server Tapes

Defendant *[name]*, through its undersigned counsel and pursuant to *[rules]*, hereby moves the Court for the entry of a Protective Order with regard to the recreation of ____ backup server tapes. Defendant is filing the present motion in the abundance of caution in light of the impending close of discovery.

As required to do by *[rules]*, prior to filing the instant motion, Defendant disclosed to Plaintiff the issues addressed herein and since that time, the parties have been attempting to arrive at a resolution of the present dispute. Defendant will advise the Court immediately should the parties resolve the issues addressed in this motion.

Factual Background

1. On *[date]*, Plaintiff served Defendant with its First Request for Production of Documents ("First Request"). Defendant responded to the First Request on [*date*], and in connection with the First Request has produced over ________ pages of documents.

2. Prior to the *[date]*, pursuant to *[rule]*, both parties exchanged additional documents. As a result of such supplemental productions and in light of the forthcoming holiday, on *[date]*, Defendant filed a Motion for a Two-Week Enlargement of the Discovery Deadline of *[date]*, in order to confirm that all responsive documents, electronic or otherwise, had been produced in response to the First Request.

3. On *[date]*, the Court granted Defendant's Motion for a Two-Week Enlargement of the Discovery Deadline. Accordingly, the discovery period is now set to close on *[date]*.

4. In connection with the confirmation process that all responsive documents to the First Request had been produced, Defendant has recently learned of the existence of ____ backup server tapes which, after a reconstruction process, may possibly have responsive documents that may not have been previously produced in the instant action.

5. By way of background, shortly after being served with the lawsuit, Defendant's Law Department identified close to ____ individuals who were involved with Plaintiff's account. The Law Department sent each of the identified individuals who were still employed with the Defendant, a Notice to Preserve explicitly instructing them to preserve any documentation, including electronic documents, that had anything to do with

[name] Medical Center. Thereafter, the Law Department obtained responsive documents that have been produced to Plaintiff.

6. As part of its standard operating procedure, Defendant backs up approximately ____ servers on a weekly basis. The backup server tapes contain not just e-mails, but Defendant's entire computer network. Thus, each backup tape contains a possible mixture of e-mails and other data maintained on Defendant's computer network. The backed-up e-mails include the non-deleted e-mails for its current employees as well as the non-deleted e-mails for its former employees. If an user has deleted an e-mail prior to the end of the week backup date, such an e-mail will not be on the backup tape. (If person A sends an e-mail to person B and both users delete the exchange of e-mails prior to the weekly backup date, the e-mails will not be on the backup tapes regardless of whether the persons were still employed by the company at the time the Notice to Preserve was issued.) Thus, by the time the Notice to Preserve was issued, the e-mails for the former employees were already on the Defendant's backup server tapes.

7. Accordingly, along with the Notice to Preserve, the Law Department sent a simultaneous request to Defendant's IT Department that it extract from the backup server tapes any e-mail data related to Plaintiff generated by the close to thirty individuals previously identified as having had some involvement with Plaintiff's account. Unfortunately, Defendant has just recently confirmed to counsel that the IT Department inadvertently failed to undertake this step.

8. Defendant's IT Department still has the backup server tapes in its possession. The total number of backup tapes dating back to *[date]*, is ____. In order to determine which tape contains backup e-mails, the library for each tape must first be examined. Once a tape has been identified as having backup e-mails, the e-mails need to be restored and then reviewed for responsiveness to the discovery requests served in the underlying lawsuit. Moreover, without reviewing all of

the tapes and then reconstructing those which contain backups of the e-mail server, Defendant cannot determine which users' e-mails are on a particular tape. Thus, there is no manner by which to limit the recreation process to just those users who were no longer employed by the company at the time the lawsuit was filed.

9. After the possible responsive documents, if any, are identified and reconstructed, any previously produced e-mails would have to be removed in order to avoid duplicate production. Lastly, any responsive, but previously not produced, e-mails would have to be reviewed for privilege. At this juncture, Defendant cannot determine whether in fact there are any responsive documents on the backup server tapes and, if there are any such e-mails, whether they are merely duplicates of what has already been produced in the litigation. Only by examining, re-creating and reviewing the backup server tapes can this possibility be explored and laid to rest.

10. The processes described in the foregoing paragraphs are extremely expensive and time-consuming. The preliminary estimates that Defendant has received from outside data reconstruction vendors to review each of the ____ backup server tapes to determine which of the tapes contain backup e-mails, and thereafter re-create the e-mails, review the e-mails for possible responsiveness, and eliminate all previously produced e-mails all exceed $________, not including attorney and paralegal review time. Additionally, with the use of the outside vendors, completion of the foregoing processes would take between three to six weeks.

11. As soon as undersigned counsel received all of the foregoing information, the same was provided to Plaintiff's counsel. Indeed, on *[date]*, Defendant's counsel provided Plaintiff's counsel with detailed correspondence explaining the Notice to Preserve process, the IT Department's inadvertent oversight, and the costs involved with recreating the backup server tapes in the search for possible additional documents. On *[date]*, Plaintiff's counsel requested additional follow-up infor-

mation from Defendant as to the identity of the approximately ___ individuals identified as having some involvement with Plaintiff's account. Such information was provided to Plaintiff's counsel on the same date. Plaintiff has not yet advised whether it wishes to have the backup server tapes recreated and, if so, the exact scope of such a recreation. In light of the undue burden and extraordinary costs involved with such an undertaking, Defendant respectfully submits that, if Plaintiff does elect to insist on such a course of action, the costs involved with such a procedure should be borne by the Plaintiff, and not the Defendant.

Argument and Citation of Authority

I. Re-Creation of the Data on the Backup Sever Tapes Is Not Reasonably Accessible and, Therefore, an Undue Burden

Rule 26(b)(2)(B) of the Federal Rules of Civil Procedure provides that:

> A party need not provide discovery of electronically stored information from sources that the party identifies as not reasonably accessible because of undue burden or cost. On motion to compel discovery or for a protective order, the party from whom discovery is sought must show that the information is not reasonably accessible because of undue burden or cost. If that showing is made, the court may nonetheless order discovery from such sources if the requesting party shows good cause, considering the limitations of Rule 26(b)(2)(C). The court may specify conditions for the discovery.

The facts of the present situation are similar to those addressed by the Court in Cognex Corp. v. Electro Scientific Industries, Inc., 2002 WL 32309413 (D. Mass. 2002). At issue in *Cognex,* were 820 of the defendant's electronic backup tapes, covering a period from 1992 through 2001, which had not been searched yet by the defendant for relevant documents. *Id.* at * 1. The plaintiff not only sought to compel the recreation and search of the backup tapes but offered to bear the "full burden and costs of such a search." *Id.* at *3. Nevertheless, the Court denied the Motion to Compel. In deciding not to compel the defendant to search the 820 backup tapes, the *Cognex* Court emphasized the following factors:

- The defendant had already conducted an extensive search for relevant documents.
- There was no evidence that the defendant had consciously destructed documents or that there were serious discrepancies in the discovery.
- The fact that the defendant disclosed the backup tapes during this late stage of the case was not indicative of bad faith.
- The case was not one where one would expect the most relevant e-mails to be deleted and transferred to backup tapes.
- There was nothing inherently wrong with the defendant, which was a big corporation, adopting a backup policy; there was no suggestion of any improper action by the defendant in either the adoption or practice of such a policy.

Id. at *5.

All of the above factors are present in the instant case. First, as described above, Defendant identified the individuals who were involved with Plaintiff's account and sent a Notice to Preserve to those individuals who were still employed by the company. It then had its Law Department gather responsive documents. Subsequent to this process, as further individuals have been identified as having been involved with the case, the documents and e-mails of such individuals have been produced through supplemental productions. In this regard, to date, Defendant has produced over ____ pages of documents in connection with a single-count breach of contract claim.

Second, there is no evidence that Defendant has consciously destroyed documents. To the contrary, the backup server tapes are still in the Defendant's possession and the Defendant has voluntarily disclosed the existence of the same.

Third, although Defendant voluntarily disclosed the

existence of the backup tapes at the close of the discovery period; the timing of such a disclosure does not, in and of itself, indicate any bad faith by the Defendant. Moreover, the issue is not one that was created by virtue of the timing of the self-disclosure. Due to the costly and cumbersome process involved with examining and re-creating the backup tapes and the existence of the former employees' e-mails on the backup tapes since the inception of the lawsuit, the issue, by necessity, is one that would have had to be addressed at some point during the course of this litigation.

Fourth, this is not the type of case were one would expect the most relevant e-mails to be deleted and transferred to backup tapes. The sheer volume of e-mails and documents already produced vitiate any such possible inference.

Fifth, there is nothing inherently wrong with Defendant's policy with regard to its backup server tapes and, specifically, with regard to its policy of having its former employees' e-mails saved on backup server tapes. Indeed, most companies recycle backup tapes after a certain period of time; Defendant does not. Therefore, this is not the case where Defendant consciously set out to devise a process to conceal or frustrate Plaintiff's ability to obtain responsive documents in connection with its lawsuit. Rather, this is a case where possible additional responsive documents are, and from the inception of the case have been, inaccessible due to the undue burden and costs of recreating data from backup server tapes. As noted by the court in *Cognex,* "[t]here is certainly no controlling authority for the proposition that restoring all backup tapes is necessary in every case." *Id.* at *4. Here, Defendant has turned over data that was reasonably accessible at the time the lawsuit was filed and throughout the course of the litigation. It should not, however, be required to re-create and turn over data which was never in an accessible format in order to ensure that every possible relevant document has been disclosed. *Cognex,* 2002 WL at *5 ("[a]t some point, the adversary system needs to say 'enough is enough' and recognize that the costs of seeking every relevant piece of discovery is not reasonable"). Accordingly, Defendant respectfully submits that it should not be required to examine the ________ backup server tapes and recreate the e-mail date contained within such tapes.

II. If the Court Orders the Re-Creation of the Backup Server Tapes, the Costs Should Be Shifted to the Plaintiff

In the event that the Court concludes that the backup server tapes do have to be reexamined and re-created, Defendant respectfully submits that the costs of such an endeavor should be shifted to the Plaintiff. The factors to be considered by a court in a cost-shifting analysis were set forth by Judge Scheindlin in Zubulake v. UBS Warburg LLC, 217 F.R.D. 309, 91 Fair Empl. Prac. Cas. (BNA) 1574 (S.D. N.Y. 2003). They are as follows:

(1) The extent to which the request is specifically tailored to discover relevant information;
(2) The availability of such information from other sources;
(3) The total cost of production, compared to the amount in controversy;
(4) The total cost of production, compared to the resources available to each party;
(5) The relative ability of each party to control costs and its incentive to do so;
(6) The importance of the issues at stake in the litigation; and
(7) The relative benefits to the parties of obtaining the information.

217 F.R.D. at 322.

According to the court in *Zubulake,* the first two factors, known as the "marginal utility test," are the most important. The marginal utility test provides: "The more likely it is that the backup tape contains information that is relevant to a claim or defense, the fairer it is that the [responding party] search at its own expense.

The less likely it is, the more unjust it would be to make the [responding party] search at its own expense. The difference is 'at the margin.' "*Id.* The second group of factors addresses the cost issues." These factors include the total cost of production compared to the amount in controversy, the total cost of production compared to the resources available to each party, and the relative ability of each party to control costs and its incentive to do so. *Id.* at 323. The next factor is the importance of the litigation, which rarely comes into play. *Id.* The last, and least important, factor is the "relative benefits of production as between the requesting and producing parties . . . because it is fair to presume that the response to a discovery request generally benefits the requesting party." *Id.*

With regard to the first two factors, Defendant submits that a request for e-mails regarding all possible individuals involved with Plaintiff's account is not specifically tailored to the discovery of relevant information. Moreover, given the duplicative and repetitive nature of e-mail communications, it is highly likely that an e-mail from a former employee that that was sent to a current employee but presently resides in one of the ____ backup servers has already been produced as part of the e-mails retrieved and disclosed from the current employees. Therefore, the cost of re-creating the possible former employee to former employee e-mails in comparison to the amount in controversy becomes of utmost importance. As set forth above, the costs of reviewing the ____ backup tapes and re-creating the stored e-mails, not including any attorney and paralegal time, exceeds $________. The amount in controversy in this matter, according to Plaintiff's own Initial Disclosures and Interrogatory responses is in excess of $________, of which only approximately $________ constitute non-consequential, compensatory damages. Thus the backup server recreation costs could actually equal or exceed Plaintiff's claim for compensatory damages. Defendant therefore respectfully submits that the possible recreation costs are completely out of proportion with Plaintiff's possible recovery in the case. Accordingly, if Plaintiff wishes to have the backup server tapes recreated, this Court should require it to bear the cost of such a process.

That Defendant might have the financial resources to bear the recreation costs of more than $______ should be of minimal importance. No company, regardless of size, should be required to recreate inaccessible data when the cost of such an undertaking bears no resemblance to the compensatory damages in the case.

Defendant recognizes that the Court in *Zublake* emphasized the importance of an extensive factual analysis to support a cost-shifting conclusion and, in this regard, first ordered a sample recreation of a certain number of backup server tapes in order to make a factual-based determination as to all of the factors. Although Plaintiff has not, to date, offered such a suggestion, depending on the parameters of such a sample, Defendant might not be opposed to such a course of action.

Conclusion

For the reasons set forth above, Defendant submits that it should not be required to undertake the extraordinary costs of re-creating backup server tapes to eliminate the possibility of additionally relevant e-mails that may have not been previously produced in the litigation. To the extent the Court concludes otherwise, Defendant respectfully requests that, in light of the lack of proportionality between the recreation costs and the amount in controversy, the costs of the recreation process be borne by the Plaintiff.

Dated: ______

[signature, etc.]

Comment

This form is adapted from a motion in Mount Sinai Medical Center of Florida, Inc., a Florida not-for-profit corporation, Plaintiff, v. McKesson Medication Management, LLC, a foreign limited liability company,

Defendant., 2006 WL 4034460 (S.D. Fla. 2006).

§ 18:11 Order governing discovery of deleted data

[Caption]

Order Governing Discovery of Deleted Data

The following is a protocol for allowing discovery of deleted files and documents in computer memories. In general, the Court previously ordered *[plaintiff]* to select and to pay an expert in recovery of such information, and to have that expert serve as an officer of the court and to turn over the recovered information to *[defendant's]* counsel for appropriate review to supplement *[plaintiff's]* discovery responses. The court also set a further hearing on the matter for resolution of further details. *[Plaintiff]* has identified an appropriate expert to carry out the inspection of the relevant computers; *[defendant]* has identified the computer in question; and counsel for the parties conferred and drafted a proposed order. The court heard argument on several disputed details on *[date]*. Pursuant to the parties' draft and the arguments presented, the court now orders as follows:

1. This inspection process applies to the following computers: *[specify]*.

2. Pursuant to the *[plaintiff's]* designation and *[defendant's]* statement that it has no objections, *[expert]* is hereby appointed as an officer of the court to carry out the inspection and copying of data from *[defendant's]* designated computers. From the date of this order, all communications between *[expert]* and *[plaintiff's]* counsel shall take place either in the presence of *[defendant's]* counsel or through written or electronic communication with a copy to *[defendant's]* counsel.

3. Before carrying out any inspections pursuant to this order, *[expert]* shall sign a protective order in the form adopted previously by the court in this action. Execution of such order shall be deemed acceptance of appointment pursuant to this entry.

4. On or before *[date]*, *[expert]* shall inspect *[defendant's]* designated computers and create an exact copy or

"bit stream image" of the hard drives of those computers. The court intends that the inspection be carried out to minimize disruption of and interference with *[defendant's]* business, and that *[defendant]* and its counsel shall cooperate in providing access to the designated computers.

5. On or before *[date]*, *[expert]* shall recover from the designated computers all available word-processing documents, incoming and outgoing electronic mail messages, PowerPoint or similar presentations, spreadsheets, and other files, including but not limited to those files that were "deleted." Files making up operating systems and higher-level systems are not to be duplicated. The copying is to be limited to the types of files reasonably likely to contain material potentially relevant to this case.

6. On or before *[date]*, *[expert]* shall provide such documents in a reasonably convenient form to *[defendant's]* counsel, along with, to the extent possible, (a) information showing when any recovered "deleted" files were deleted, and (b) information about the deletion and the contents of deleted files that could not be recovered. The court shall also be provided with a copy of the information in (a) and (b).

7. On or before *[date]*, *[expert]* shall file a report with the court setting forth the scope of the work performed and describing in general terms (without disclosing the contents) the volume and types of records provided to *[defendant's]* counsel.

8. On or before *[date]*, *[defendant's]* counsel shall review the records for privilege and responsiveness, shall appropriately supplement *[defendant's]* response to discovery requests, and shall send by overnight delivery to *[plaintiff's]* counsel all responsive and non-privileged documents and a privilege log reflecting which documents were withheld pursuant to the attorney-client privilege or work product immunity.

9. On or before 30 days after either a judgment becomes final and non-appealable or a settlement agreement has been executed by both parties, *[expert]* shall destroy the records copied from the designated computers and shall confirm such destruction to the satisfaction of defendant.

10. In accepting appointment as officers of the court for purposes of this assignment, *[expert]* agrees that it shall be compensated for its time and expenses only by *[plaintiff]*, and that it shall have no right to seek reimbursement or compensation from *[defendant]* or the United States.

Dated: ________

____
Judge

Chapter 19

Motions and Protective Orders

I. GUIDELINES

II. CHECKLISTS

III. FORMS

Research References

Additional References

ABA Discovery Standards, http://www.abanet.org/litigation/discoverystandards/2005civildiscoverystandards.pdf
Barkett, Bytes, Bits and Bucks: Cost Shifting and Sanctions in eDiscovery, 71 Def. Couns. J. 334 (2004)
Carroll, Developments in the Law of Electronic Discovery, 27 Am.J. Trial Advoc. 357 (2003)
Ellsworth & Pass, Cost Shifting in Electronic Discovery, 5 Sedona Conf. J. 125 (2004)
Federal Judicial Center, http://www.fjc.gov
Heckman & Brydges, Winning Electronic Discovery Motions, 5 Sedona Conf. J., Fall 2004, at 151
Krause & Coggio, Electronic Discovery: Where We Are, and Where We're Headed, J. Proprietary Rts., Mar. 2004, at 16
Lange, Who Should Pay for Electronic Discovery, Boston B.J., Jan./Feb. 2004, at 14
Lewis & Kransdorf, Passing the Buck: Cost-Shifting Under the New e-Discovery Rules, e-Discovery, 2007, at 26
Redgrave & Bachmann, Ripples on the Shores of Zubulake: Practice Considerations from Recent Electronic Discovery Decisions, Fed.Law., Nov./Dec. 2003, at 31
Robichaud, Old Wine in New Bottles: Discovery Disputes and Cost-Shifting in the Digital Age, The Brief, Winter 2004, at 56
Ryan, 10 Ways to Beat eDiscovery Abuse, Trial, Sept. 2004, at 42
The Sedona Conference, http://www.thesedonaconference.org

Treatises and Practice Aids

eDiscovery & Digital Evidence §§ 7:1 to 7:4
Grenig and Kinsler, Federal Civil Discovery and Disclosure §§ 7.1 to 7.4 (2d ed.)

Trial Strategy

Recovery and Reconstruction of Electronic Mail as Evidence, 41 Am. Jur Proof of Facts 3d 1
Computer Technology in Civil Litigation, 71 Am. Jur Trials 111

I. GUIDELINES

§ 19:1 Generally

The importance of an evidentiary record on discovery motions cannot be overemphasized. An extensive record may be necessary to communicate the necessary facts to the court. Declarations or affidavits from information technology staff and consultants, as well as from vendors may be essential to address case-specific issues as well as general background information. A party's papers may need to include cost estimates from several vendors, as well as an itemized estimate of costs from the vendor of choice.

Depending on the judge's level of sophistication, it may be necessary for a party to educate the court with respect to discovery of electronically stored information. First, key terms and concepts should be defined. The court should be educated with respect to the nature of the evidence sought and its relevance.

It is important to remember that courts do not reward those who sleep on their rights or fail to take reasonable steps to protect their rights. A party wishing to seek sanctions because of a responding party's failure to permit discovery must be able to demonstrate that the discovering party has made the proper requests and sought the appropriate assistance of the court to compel discovery.[1]

§ 19:2 Protective orders—Generally

With many responding parties, the first response to any

[Section 19:1]

[1]See, e.g., Bryant v. Jones, 2006 WL 584762 (N.D. Ga. 2006), as amended, (Mar. 20, 2006) (denying sanctions where requesting party did not expressly raise issue in written discovery requests).

electronic discovery request is a demand for a protective order. Often sought as an effort by the defending party to protect claimed trade secrets or to reduce the burden and expense of the request, the goal is to limit the scope of discoverable information and to restrain the discovering party from sharing discovered information with other persons who have similar cases.

The purpose of the protective order is not to prevent full disclosure, but to minimize the disruption and inconvenience inherent in discovery. Protective orders provide a safeguard for parties and other persons in light of the otherwise broad reach of discovery. In order to further that objective, courts have broad discretionary powers to limit by protective orders the scope and manner of discovery and the procedures to be used.[1] Under extraordinary circumstances, a court may even prohibit discovery in any form at all.[2]

Rule 26(c) of the Federal Rules of Civil Procedure empowers a court to make a wide variety of orders for the protection of parties and witnesses in the discovery process. Protective orders are a necessary corollary to the scope of discovery permitted by Rule 26(b)(1). Rule 26(c) permits a court to issue orders protecting a party or person from annoyance, embarrassment, oppression, or undue burden or expense.

§ 19:3 Protective orders—Good cause

Where the discovery is relevant, the burden is on the

[Section 19:2]

[1]See, e.g., Chemical & Indus. Corp. v. Druffel, 301 F.2d 126, 129, 133 U.S.P.Q. 133 (6th Cir. 1962); Patrnogic v. U.S. Steel Corp., 43 F.R.D. 402, 403, 11 Fed. R. Serv. 2d 800 (S.D. N.Y. 1967); Textured Yarn Co. v. Burkart-Schier Chemical Co., 41 F.R.D. 158, 160, 10 Fed. R. Serv. 2d 843 (E.D. Tenn. 1966).

[2]See Salter v. Upjohn Co., 593 F.2d 649, 651, 27 Fed. R. Serv. 2d 822 (5th Cir. 1979) (very unusual for trial court to prohibit taking of deposition altogether, and, absent extraordinary circumstances, such order would likely be in error).

party seeking a protective order to show good cause.[1] Authorization to enter a protective order is not a blanket authorization for the court to prohibit disclosure of information whenever it deems it advisable to do so, but is rather a grant of power to impose conditions on discovery in order to prevent injury, harassment, or abuse of the court's process. A party seeking a protective order based on the undue burden or expense of complying with a discovery request must submit affidavits or declarations or other detailed explanations as to the nature and extent of the claimed burden or expense unless the request is unduly burdensome on its face.[2]

A motion for a protective order relieving a party of the obligation to respond to various interrogatories and requests for protection should not be granted on the ground they are overly broad, as overbreadth is not one of the grounds enumerated in Rule 26(c).[3] While it is an objection that may be asserted in responding to a discovery request, it is not a basis upon which a court may enter a Rule 26(c) protective order.

§ 19:4 Protective orders—Procedure for obtaining

Protective orders may be granted on motion of a party or the person from whom discovery is sought "for good cause shown" and "as justice requires."[1] A party may not ask for an order to protect the rights of another party or a witness if that party or witness does not claim protection for itself, but a party may seek an order if the party believes its own interest is jeopardized by discovery sought

---

[Section 19:3]

[1]Security Ins. Co. of Hartford v. Trustmark Ins. Co., 218 F.R.D. 24 (D. Conn. 2003).

[2]Aikens v. Deluxe Financial Services, Inc., 217 F.R.D. 533 (D. Kan. 2003).

[3]Aikens v. Deluxe Financial Services, Inc., 217 F.R.D. 533 (D. Kan. 2003).

[Section 19:4]

[1]See, e.g., Fed.R.Civ.P. 26(c).

from a third person.[2] While a party may not seek a protective order to protect the rights of another party, but a third party may be allowed to intervene to contest the issuance of a protective order.

When discovery is sought from third parties, a protective order may be more easily obtained.[3] There are strong considerations indicating that discovery may be more limited to protect third parties from harassment, inconvenience, or disclosure of confidential documents.[4]

Protective orders are ordinarily sought from the court in which the action is pending.[5] Rule 26(c) permits a motion on "matters relating to a deposition" to be made to the court in the district in which the deposition is to be taken.[6] If a deposition has begun, either the court in which the action is pending or the court in which the deposition is being taken may give relief under Rule 26(c).

Before moving for a protective order, a party normally must confer or attempt to confer in good faith with other affected parties in an effort to resolve the dispute without court action. Rules may require that the motion must be

---

[2]See American Rock Salt Co., LLC v. Norfolk Southern Corp., 228 F.R.D. 426, 466 (W.D. N.Y. 2004) (motion for protective order generally must be brought by individual whose interests are affected, and party may not move for protective order to protect interests of another, but may move to protect party's own interests when discovery is sought from another).

[3]See Dart Industries Co., Inc. v. Westwood Chemical Co., Inc., 649 F.2d 646, 648 (9th Cir. 1980).

[4]Collins & Aikman Corp. v. J. P. Stevens & Co., 51 F.R.D. 219, 221, 169 U.S.P.Q. 296 (D.S.C. 1971).

[5]See Kirshner v. Uniden Corp. of America, 842 F.2d 1074, 1081, 10 Fed. R. Serv. 3d 441, 10 Fed. R. Serv. 3d 921 (9th Cir. 1988).

[6]But see E. I. duPont de Nemours & Co. v. Deering Milliken Research Corp., 72 F.R.D. 440, 193 U.S.P.Q. 186, 22 Fed. R. Serv. 2d 1426 (D. Del. 1976) (local courts whose only connection with case is supervision of taking deposition should be especially hesitant to pass judgment on what constitutes relevant evidence).

accompanied by a certificate that the movant has met its obligation to meet and confer.[7]

Protective orders are often obtained by agreement, particularly with respect to confidential information and in litigation likely to involve a large volume of documents. Courts frequently have given pro forma approval to stipulations reached between the parties, even when the agreement constitutes an "umbrella protective order" shielding virtually all documents from review by third parties.[8] However, some courts are unwilling to sign a blanket protective order without a specific showing of need.[9]

With respect to interrogatories, requests for production of documents and requests for admissions, the normal procedure is for the responding party to object to the improper discovery demands. However, this should not preclude the responding party from seeking a protective order if it so desires.

Nonetheless, a party may not remain completely silent when it regards discovery as improper. If a responding party does not wish to appear or to respond, it must object properly or seek a protective order. If there are extenuating circumstances that explain a party's failure to object properly or to seek a protective order, the court should take these into account in determining what sanctions to impose, even where a deposition is involved.

---

[7]Fed.R.Civ.P. 26(c).

[8]See In re Alexander Grant & Co. Litigation, 820 F.2d 352, 356, 14 Media L. Rep. (BNA) 1370, 8 Fed. R. Serv. 3d 251 (11th Cir. 1987) (need to speed discovery was good cause for blanket order).

[9]See Public Citizen v. Liggett Group, Inc., 858 F.2d 775, 789, 15 Media L. Rep. (BNA) 2129, 12 Fed. R. Serv. 3d 1099 (1st Cir. 1988) (in deciding whether to issue a stipulated protective order, district court must independently determine if "good cause" exists); Cipollone v. Liggett Group, Inc., 822 F.2d 335, 7 Fed. R. Serv. 3d 1438 (3d Cir. 1987) (case management needs do not constitute good cause for protective order; court must consider specific harm to producing party); Citizens First Nat. Bank of Princeton v. Cincinnati Ins. Co., 178 F.3d 943, 944, 51 U.S.P.Q.2d 1218 (7th Cir. 1999) (district court could not delegate to parties authority to determine whether good cause existed to justify sealing of documents forming part of the record).

A motion for a protective order must be accompanied by a certification that the movant has in good faith conferred or attempted to confer with other affected parties in an effort to resolve the dispute without court action. Rule 26(c) of the Federal Rules of Civil Procedure does not state a time period within which a motion for a protective order must be sought, but the motion should be brought on or before the date the discovery in question is to take place.[10]

The standard of review of a trial court's granting or denying of a protective order is whether the trial court misused its discretion. It is insufficient merely to argue on appeal that no reason existed for the trial court not to enter an order.

§ 19:5 Protective orders—Good cause standard

Most rules of procedure, including Rule 26(c) of the Federal Rules of Civil Procedure require the movant to show good cause why the protective order should be granted. The application of the good cause standard varies depending upon the nature of the material sought to be protected and the method of discovery. Generally, the burden of establishing good cause for a protective order is on the party seeking the order.[1] It is not enough for the party seeking a protective order to argue that no reason exists not to enter the order; the movant must show a positive reason why the order should be entered.[2]

The moving party must make a clear showing of a par-

---

[10]See National Independent Theatre Exhibitors, Inc. v. Buena Vista Distribution Co., 748 F.2d 602, 609, 1984-2 Trade Cas. (CCH) P 66311, 40 Fed. R. Serv. 2d 954 (11th Cir. 1984) (untimely protective order granted on condition that opponent's costs be paid).

[Section 19:5]

[1]See In re Agent Orange Product Liability Litigation, 821 F.2d 139, 145, 7 Fed. R. Serv. 3d 1091 (2d Cir. 1987); Blankenship v. Hearst Corp., 519 F.2d 418, 429, 1975-2 Trade Cas. (CCH) P 60384 (9th Cir. 1975); Schorr v. Briarwood Estates Ltd. Partnership, 178 F.R.D. 488, 491 (N.D. Ohio 1998).

[2]See Lohrenz v. Donnelly, 187 F.R.D. 1 (D.D.C. 1999) (party seeking protective order against discovery bears burden of making showing

ticular and specific need for the order.[3] Even if good cause for a protective order is shown, the court must still balance the interests in allowing discovery against the relative burdens to the parties and nonparties.[4]

The likelihood that discovery will be time-consuming or costly is an insufficient basis for a protective order, unless the burden outweighs any possible benefit to the party propounding the discovery.[5] The moving party has the burden to show that responding to the discovery is unduly

---

of good cause sufficient to overcome defendant's legitimate and important interest in trial preparation); Pro Billiards Tour Ass'n, Inc. v. R.J. Reynolds Tobacco Co., 187 F.R.D. 229, 44 Fed. R. Serv. 3d 1269 (M.D. N.C. 1999) (burden of showing good cause for protective order rests on part requesting it); Gottstein v. National Ass'n for the Self Employed, 186 F.R.D. 654 (D. Kan. 1999) (party seeking protective order carries burden of persuasion to show good cause for it by submitting particular and specific demonstration of fact, as distinguished from stereotyped and conclusory statements); G-69 v. Degnan, 130 F.R.D. 326, 331 (D.N.J. 1990).

[3]See U.S. E.E.O.C. v. Caesars Entertainment, Inc., 237 F.R.D. 428, 432, 66 Fed. R. Serv. 3d 71 (D. Nev. 2006) (mere showing that discovery may involve some inconvenience or expense does not suffice to establish good cause for a protective order); Washington v. Thurgood Marshall Academy, 230 F.R.D. 18, 21 (D.D.C. 2005), on reconsideration, 232 F.R.D. 6, 203 Ed. Law Rep. 698, 63 Fed. R. Serv. 3d 754 (D.D.C. 2005) (when moving for protective order, movant must establish good cause by demonstrating the specific evidence of the harm that would result); Peskoff v. Faber, 230 F.R.D. 25, 28, 62 Fed. R. Serv. 3d 503 (D.D.C. 2005), order clarified, 233 F.R.D. 207 (D.D.C. 2006) (same).

[4]See In re Coordinated Pretrial Proceedings in Petroleum Products Antitrust Litigation, 669 F.2d 620, 623, 1982-1 Trade Cas. (CCH) P 64482, 33 Fed. R. Serv. 2d 717 (10th Cir. 1982). See also Swackhammer v. Sprint Corp. PCS, 225 F.R.D. 658, 666, 60 Fed. R. Serv. 3d 945 (D. Kan. 2004) (in ruling on an undue burden objection, a court must keep in mind that discovery should be allowed unless the claimed hardship is unreasonable in light of the benefits to be secured from the discovery).

[5]Beach v. City of Olathe, Kansas, 203 F.R.D. 489, 493 (D. Kan. 2001) (discovery should be allowed unless hardship is unreasonable compared to benefits to be secured from discovery).

burdensome.[6] A court may recognize the burdensome nature of discovery in considering a non-party's request for a protective order.[7]

A movant-defendant cannot establish good cause for a protective order by arguing that the plaintiff intends to share the information the defendant produces with others.[8] Some courts have found that, in the absence of bad faith intent or to create frivolous law suits, sharing the results of discovery promotes the efficient resolution of litigation.[9]

---

[6]See U.S. E.E.O.C. v. Caesars Entertainment, Inc., 237 F.R.D. 428, 432, 66 Fed. R. Serv. 3d 71 (D. Nev. 2006) (party seeking protective order must point to specific facts supporting the request, as opposed to conclusory or speculative statements about the need for a protective order and the harm that will be suffered without one); Cory v. Aztec Steel Bldg., Inc., 225 F.R.D. 667, 672 (D. Kan. 2005) (defendants statement that complying with plaintiff's request for production of documents would require "numerous man hours" did not establish that establish that request was unduly burdensome, absent sufficient details or information in terms of time, money, or procedure involved in complying with request); Culkin v. Pitney Bowes, Inc., 225 F.R.D. 69, 71 (D. Conn. 2004) (party objecting to discovery request on grounds of overbreadth or undue burden bears the burden of supporting the objection via affidavits or evidence); Swackhammer v. Sprint Corp. PCS, 225 F.R.D. 658, 666, 60 Fed. R. Serv. 3d 945 (D. Kan. 2004) (party objecting to interrogatory on ground of undue burden must provide an affidavit or other evidentiary proof of time or expense involved).

[7]See Anker v. G.D. Searle & Co., 126 F.R.D. 515, 519 (M.D. N.C. 1989) (burden on involuntary party expert should be mitigated by assessing costs on deposing party and by limited protective order).

[8]See In re Upjohn Co. Antibiotic Cleocin Products Liability Litigation, 81 F.R.D. 482, 27 Fed. R. Serv. 2d 389, 27 Fed. R. Serv. 2d 392 (E.D. Mich. 1979), order aff'd, 664 F.2d 114, 32 Fed. R. Serv. 2d 1441 (6th Cir. 1981) (plaintiff, with court review, could sell discovery materials to litigants in other actions against defendant). See also Patterson v. Ford Motor Co., 85 F.R.D. 152 (W.D. Tex. 1980). But see Scott v. Monsanto Co., 868 F.2d 786, 792, 13 Fed. R. Serv. 3d 650 (5th Cir. 1989) (plaintiff's claimed harm from the inability to share and compare information with other litigants in other cases did not render entry of protective order abuse of discretion).

[9]See Baker v. Liggett Group, Inc., 132 F.R.D. 123, 126 (D. Mass. 1990) (sharing discovery information with litigants in other action is

§ 19:6 Objecting to relevance

Rules of civil procedure regulate the scope of discovery.[1] Generally, any matter is discoverable, subject to the following specific limitations:

- The matter must be relevant to the claim or defense of any party.[2]
- The matter must not be privileged.
- The matter must not be protected by the work product doctrine.
- The matter is not protected information from non-testimonial experts.
- The matter is not protected by a recognized right to privacy.

Under most rules of procedure, a court can limit discovery if it determines, among other things, that discovery is:

- Unreasonably cumulative or duplicative
- Obtainable from another source that is more convenient
- Burden or expense of proposed discovery outweighs its likely benefit[3]

The burden of establishing relevancy is on the party

---

particularly appropriate in tobacco tort cases in which individual plaintiffs must litigate against large corporate defendants).

[Section 19:6]

[1]See Desert Orchid Partners, L.L.C. v. Transaction System Architects, Inc., 237 F.R.D. 215, 217 (D. Neb. 2006) (scope of discovery under a subpoena is the same as the scope of discovery under rules governing discovery scope and production of documents and is subject to the rules that apply to other methods of discovery); Schaaf v. SmithKline Beecham Corp., 233 F.R.D. 451, 63 Fed. R. Serv. 3d 1081 (E.D. N.C. 2005) (same).

[2]See Fed. R. Civ. P. 26(b)(1). The description of the scope of discovery may be different in state rules. See Bolton v. Sprint/United Management Co., 89 Empl. Prac. Dec. (CCH) P 42763, 2007 WL 756644 (D. Kan. 2007) (objection to production of metadata in native files as not relevant to plaintiff's claims).

[3]See In re Priceline.com Inc. Securities Litigation, 233 F.R.D. 83, 85 (D. Conn. 2005). Cf. Favale v. Roman Catholic Diocese of Bridgeport,

seeking the disclosure.[4] The requirement of relevancy with regard to discovery matters should be construed liberally and with common sense. Rule 26(b)(1) confines discovery to matters "relevant to the claim or defense of any party." For good cause, the court may order discovery of any matter relevant to the subject matter involved in the action. Accordingly, Rule 26 creates two categories of discovery: (1) discovery controlled or managed by the attorneys consisting of matters "relevant to the claim or defense of any party" and (2) discovery managed by the court encompassing the broader category of anything "relevant to the subject matter."

In addition to relevance, the information sought must be admissible or reasonably calculated to lead to the

---

233 F.R.D. 243, 245–46, 206 Ed. Law Rep. 929 (D. Conn. 2005) (court may limit discovery if it determines, among other things, that discovery is (1) unreasonably cumulative or duplicative, (2) obtainable from another source that is more convenient, less burdensome, or less expensive, or (3) that burden or expense of proposed discovery outweighs its likely benefit); Pointer v. DART, 417 F.3d 819, 821, 96 Fair Empl. Prac. Cas. (BNA) 285, 86 Empl. Prac. Dec. (CCH) P 42036 (8th Cir. 2005), cert. denied, 546 U.S. 1173, 126 S. Ct. 1338, 164 L. Ed. 2d 54, 97 Fair Empl. Prac. Cas. (BNA) 832 (2006) (appellate review of district court's relevancy determination on motion to quash a subpoena is for abuse of discretion).

[4]Lugosch v. Congel, 218 F.R.D. 41 (N.D. N.Y. 2003). See Sanyo Laser Products Inc. v. Arista Records, Inc., 214 F.R.D. 496 (S.D. Ind. 2003) (when discovery being sought appears relevant, party resisting discovery has burden to establish lack of relevance by demonstrating that requested discovery is of such marginal relevance that potential harm occasioned by discovery would outweigh ordinary presumption in favor of broad disclosure); General Elec. Capital Corp. v. Lear Corp., 215 F.R.D. 637 (D. Kan. 2003) (when discovery sought appears relevant, party resisting discovery has burden to establish lack of relevance by demonstrating that requested discovery (1) does not come within scope of relevance as defined under discovery rule, or (2) is of such marginal relevance that the potential harm occasioned by discovery would outweigh the ordinary presumption in favor of broad disclosure); Hammond v. Lowe's Home Centers, Inc., 216 F.R.D. 666 (D. Kan. 2003) (same).

discovery of admissible evidence.[5] Discovery cannot be objected to on the ground that the information sought will be inadmissible at trial.

§ 19:7 Objecting to frequency or extent of use

Rule 26(b)(2)(C) of the Federal Rules of Civil Procedure provides:

> On motion or on its own, the court must limit the frequency or extent of discovery otherwise allowed by these rules or by local rule if it determines that:
>
> (i) the discovery sought is unreasonably cumulative or duplicative or can be obtained from some other source that is more convenient, less burdensome, or less expensive;
>
> (ii) the party seeking discovery has had ample opportunity to obtain the information by discovery in the action; or
>
> (iii) the burden or expense of the proposed discovery outweighs its likely benefit, considering the needs of the case, the amount in controversy, the parties' resources, the importance of the issues at stake in the action, and the importance of the discovery in resolving the issues.

The Advisory Committee explained this language:

> Textual changes . . . are made in new paragraph (2) to enable the court to keep tighter rein on the extent of discovery. The information explosion of recent decades has greatly increased both the potential cost of wide-ranging discovery and the potential for discovery to be used as an instrument for delay or oppression.

State rules frequently contain similar provisions. In addition, state courts undoubtedly have the inherent power to limit the frequency or extent of use of discovery in order to avoid abuses.

---

[5]See In re Priceline.com Inc. Securities Litigation, 233 F.R.D. 83, 85 (D. Conn. 2005) (valid discovery request need only encompass any matter that bears on, or that reasonably could lead to other matter that could bear on, any issue that is or may be in case); Chavannes v. Protective Life Ins. Co., 232 F.R.D. 698 (S.D. Fla. 2006) (plaintiff-beneficiary required to produce video of insured's funeral in Haiti regardless of whether plaintiff intended to use video at trial, where plaintiff at various times had claimed video existed, did not exist, was missing or lost, or was protected by work product).

§ 19:8 Objecting to undue burden

Rules frequently impose a general limitation on the scope of discovery in the form of a proportionality test, protecting against redundant or disproportionate discovery.[1] Faced with an overly broad discovery request, a protective order can be sought limiting the scope of discovery. Where the requested discovery, whether electronic or paper, is unduly burdensome or expensive, the court may order an allocation of costs.[2] However, a party cannot avoid the production of electronically stored information merely by responding that the requests are unduly burdensome.[3]

In *Apsley v. Boeing Co.,*[4] an age discrimination case arising before the effective date of the 2006 amendments to the Federal Rules of Civil Procedure, the court was called

---

[Section 19:8]

[1]See Fed. R. Civ. P. § 26(b)(2)(C). See, e.g., McNally Tunneling Corp. v. City of Evanston, Illinois, 2001 WL 1568879 (N.D. Ill. 2001) (where responding party had already provided requesting party with all the information contained in its computer files in hard copy-form, requesting party has burden of establishing that the hard copies of the computer are insufficient). But see Public Citizen v. Carlin, 2 F. Supp. 2d 1, 13 (D.D.C. 1997), rev'd on other grounds, 184 F.3d 900 (D.C. Cir. 1999) (while exact duplicate of particular record might be discardable, electronic versions of records cannot categorically be regarded as valueless "extra copies" of paper versions). See Sedona Principle 2 ("When balancing the cost, burden, and need for electronically stored information, courts and parties should apply the proportionality standard embodied in Fed. R. Civ. P. 26(b)(2)(C) and its state equivalents, which require consideration of the technological feasibility and realistic costs of preserving, retrieving, reviewing, and producing electronically stored information, as well as the nature of the litigation and the amount in controversy.").

[2]See, e.g., City of Seattle v. Professional Basketball Club, LLC, 2008 WL 539809 (W.D. Wash. 2008) (bald assertions of burden insufficient to establish undue burden);Zubulake v. UBS Warburg LLC, 217 F.R.D. 309, 320–23, 91 Fair Empl. Prac. Cas. (BNA) 1574 (S.D. N.Y. 2003).

[3]See, e.g., Giardina v. Lockheed Martin Corp., 2003 WL 1338826 (E.D. La. 2003).

[4]Apsley v. Boeing Co., 2007 WL 163201 (D. Kan. 2007).

upon to determine whether a request for the defendants to produce e-mail was overly broad and unduly burdensome. The plaintiffs sought to compel the production of all the defendants' e-mails meeting specified criteria. The criteria included a description of the individuals whose e-mails should be targeted for screening, the time period during which the e-mails sought would have been sent, a description of the possible subject matters of the e-mails, and nineteen search terms.

The defendants responded that there were multiple servers located in different cities that could contain relevant e-mails, that the number of individuals likely to be subject to search was large, and that many of them had multiple e-mail addresses. Setting the matter for a hearing, the court directed the parties to address question regarding details of the discovery request and what responding to the request would entail.

§ 19:9 Cost shifting—Generally

It is typically presumed that a responding party bears its own costs of complying with discovery requests.[1] However, where producing the information is "unduly burdensome or expensive," a court may condition "discovery on the requesting party's payment of the costs of discovery." The normal and reasonable translation of electronically stored information into a form usable by the

[Section 19:9]

[1]Oppenheimer Fund, Inc. v. Sanders, 437 U.S. 340, 358, 98 S. Ct. 2380, 2393, 57 L. Ed. 2d 253, Fed. Sec. L. Rep. (CCH) P 96470, 25 Fed. R. Serv. 2d 541 (1978); OpenTV v. Liberate Technologies, 219 F.R.D. 474, 57 Fed. R. Serv. 3d 539 (N.D. Cal. 2003). See Sedona Principle 13 ("Absent a specific objection, party agreement or court order, the reasonable costs of retrieving and reviewing electronically stored information should be borne by the responding party, unless the information sought is not reasonably available to the responding party in the ordinary course of business. If the information sought is not reasonably available to the responding party in the ordinary course of business, then, absent special circumstances, the costs of retrieving and reviewing such electronic information may be shared by or shifted to the requesting party.").

discovering party should be the ordinary and foreseeable burden of a respondent in the absence of a showing of extraordinary hardship.[2]

Rules in some states impose some costs of discovery of electronically stored information on the requesting party. For example, in California, Cal.Code Civ.P. § 2031(g)(1) provides: "If necessary, the responding party at the reasonable expense of the demanding party shall, . . . translate any data compilations . . . into reasonably usable form."[3] In Texas, Tex.R.Civ.P. 196.4 provides: "The responding party must produce the electronic or magnetic data that is responsive to the request and is reasonably available to the responding party in its ordinary course of business. If the responding party cannot—through reasonable efforts—retrieve the data or information requested or produce it in the form requested, the responding party must state an objection complying with these rules. If the court orders the responding party to comply with the request, the court must also order the requesting party pay the reasonable expenses of any extraordinary steps required to retrieve and produce the information." While many rules of procedure do not explicitly refer to "cost-shifting," there is no doubt the courts may require a party requesting discovery to pay the costs that will be incurred by the responding party.

In determining whether cost shifting may be appropriate it is necessary to thoroughly understand the respond-

---

[2]See Daewoo Electronics Co., Ltd. v. U.S., 10 Ct. Int'l Trade 754, 650 F. Supp. 1003, 1006, 8 Int'l Trade Rep. (BNA) 1627 (1986); OpenTV v. Liberate Technologies, 219 F.R.D. 474, 57 Fed. R. Serv. 3d 539 (N.D. Cal. 2003) (cost shifting warranted where digital data in the form of source code was stored in an inaccessible format for purposes of discover, where process of extracting search code from its database took between 1.25 and 1.5 hours per source code, amounting to between 125–150 hours of work to complete extraction process for approximately 100 versions of source code requested by requesting party).

[3]See Toshiba America Electronic Components, Inc. v. Superior Court, 124 Cal. App. 4th 762, 21 Cal. Rptr. 3d 532 (6th Dist. 2004) (Cal.Code Civ.P. § 2031(g)(1) expressly shifted to demanding party cost of recovering usable information from tapes).

ing party's computer system, both with respect to active and stored data. For electronically stored information kept in an accessible format, the usual rules of discovery apply: the responding party should pay the costs of producing responsive electronically stored information. A court should consider cost-shifting only when electronically stored information is relatively inaccessible, such as in backup tapes.

Because the cost-shifting analysis is so fact-intensive, it is necessary to determine what electronically stored information may be found on the inaccessible media. Requiring the responding party to restore and produce responsive electronically stored information from a small sample of the requested backup tapes is a sensible approach in most cases.

§ 19:10 Cost shifting—Judicial responses

It is typically presumed that a responding party bears its own costs of complying with discovery requests.[1] However, where producing the information is "unduly burdensome or expensive," a court may condition "discovery on the requesting party's payment of the costs of discovery."[2] A court will order a cost-shifting protective order only upon motion of the responding party to a discovery

[Section 19:10]

[1]See Oppenheimer Fund, Inc. v. Sanders, 437 U.S. 340, 358, 98 S. Ct. 2380, 2393, 57 L. Ed. 2d 253, Fed. Sec. L. Rep. (CCH) P 96470, 25 Fed. R. Serv. 2d 541 (1978); OpenTV v. Liberate Technologies, 219 F.R.D. 474, 57 Fed. R. Serv. 3d 539 (N.D. Cal. 2003).

[2]See Okoumou v. Safe Horizon, 2005 WL 2431674 (S.D. N.Y. 2005) (if plaintiff wanted to pursue discovery of e-mails on a Lotus ccmail system, she was free to do so, but reserving extent to which e-mails are discoverable and allocation of cost of restoring those e-mails requires further analysis); OpenTV v. Liberate Technologies, 219 F.R.D. 474, 477, 57 Fed. R. Serv. 3d 539 (N.D. Cal. 2003) (cost shifting warranted where digital data in the form of source code was stored in an inaccessible format for purposes of discovery, where process of extracting search code from its database took between 1.25 and 1.5 hours per source code, amounting to between 125–150 hours of work to complete extraction process for approximately 100 versions of source code

request and for good cause shown.[3] The responding party has the burden of proof on a motion for cost-shifting.[4]

While Rule 26(b)(2)(B) provides that conditions, such as cost shifting, can be imposed when a party seeks discovery of electronically stored information that is not reasonably accessible. It is not quite so clear whether cost shifting can be imposed when requesting parties seek access to large amounts of accessible electronically stored information.[5]

§ 19:11 Cost shifting—Federal Rule amendments

Rule 26(b)(2)(B) of the Federal Rules of Civil Procedure permits a court to issue a protective order where the party from whom discovery is sought shows the information is not reasonably accessible because of undue burden or cost.[1] Rule 26(b)(2) provides that a party is not required to produce electronically stored information that is not "reason-

---

requested by requesting party); Daewoo Electronics Co., Ltd. v. U.S., 10 Ct. Int'l Trade 754, 650 F. Supp. 1003, 1006, 8 Int'l Trade Rep. (BNA) 1627 (1986) (normal and reasonable translation of electronic data into form usable by discovering party should be ordinary and foreseeable burden of a respondent in absence of a showing of extraordinary hardship).

[3]Zubulake v. UBS Warburg LLC, 216 F.R.D. 280, 283, 92 Fair Empl. Prac. Cas. (BNA) 684, 56 Fed. R. Serv. 3d 326 (S.D. N.Y. 2003).

[4]Zubulake v. UBS Warburg LLC, 216 F.R.D. 280, 283, 92 Fair Empl. Prac. Cas. (BNA) 684, 56 Fed. R. Serv. 3d 326 (S.D. N.Y. 2003). See Mikron Industries, Inc. v. Hurd Windows & Doors, Inc., 2008 WL 1805727 (W.D. Wash. 2008) (cost shifting rejected where moving party failed to meet and confer in good faith and conclusory characterization of ESI as "inaccessible" were insufficient).

[5]See, e.g., Peskoff v. Faber, 240 F.R.D. 26, 67 Fed. R. Serv. 3d 760 (D.D.C. 2007), subsequent determination, 244 F.R.D. 54 (D.D.C. 2007) (accessible data must be produced at cost of producing party; cost shifting does not become possibility unless there is first showing of inaccessibility). See Boehning & Toal, Courts Consider When Cost-Shifting Is Appropriate: A Ruling Suggests It Is Called for only When Data Are Inaccessible, Nat'l L.J., Aug. 20, 2007, at S3.

[Section 19:11]

[1]See Peskoff v. Faber, 240 F.R.D. 26, 67 Fed. R. Serv. 3d 760 (D.D.C. 2007) (accessible data must be produced at the cost of the pro-

ably accessible" because of "undue burden or cost." The amendment attempts to codify *Zubulake*[2] with respect to cost shifting.

The issue of cost shifting can also arise within the context of a subpoena to a third party who is not part of the litigation to which the subpoena relates. Where a subpoena to a third-party requested a broad range of documents, electronic files, and e-mails requiring contracting with information technology professionals, it may be appropriate for the requesting party to compensate the subpoenaed party for the costs of production.[3]

Rule 45 of the Federal Rules of Civil Procedure has been amended to provide protection from undue impositions on nonparties. Rule 45(c)(1) requires a party serving a subpoena to take reasonable steps to avoid imposing an undue burden or expense on a person subject to the subpoena. Rule 45(c)(2)(B) permits the persons served to object to the subpoena and directs that an order requiring compliance must protect a person who is neither a party nor a party's officer from significant expense resulting from compliance.

§ 19:12 Cost shifting—Not reasonably accessible

Electronically stored information is frequently cheaper and easier to produce than paper evidence as it can be searched automatically and key words can be run for privilege checks. Furthermore, production of electronically stored information can be made in electronic form eliminating the need for mass photocopying.

If electronically stored information is reasonably accessible, that may end the cost-shifting inquiry—the responding party should pay the costs of producing responsive

---

ducing party; cost shifting does not even become a possibility unless there is first a showing of inaccessibility).

[2]Zubulake v. UBS Warburg LLC, 216 F.R.D. 280, 283, 92 Fair Empl. Prac. Cas. (BNA) 684, 56 Fed. R. Serv. 3d 326 (S.D. N.Y. 2003).

[3]In re Automotive Refinishing Paint, 229 F.R.D. 482, 496–97, 2005-1 Trade Cas. (CCH) P 74861 (E.D. Pa. 2005).

data. If electronically stored information is not reasonably accessible, the cost-shifting analysis may focus on the scope of the discovery request and the ability of the requesting party to show that relevant information is contained in the unreasonably accessible storage media. The stronger the showing that electronically stored information contains relevant information, the better the position of a requesting party in the cost-shifting analysis.[1]

A court should consider cost-shifting only when digital data is relatively inaccessible, such as in backup tapes. A court should carefully consider the following in determining whether costs of discovery should be shifted:

- The extent to which the request is specifically tailored to discover relevant information.
- The availability of such information from other sources.
- The total cost of production, compared to the amount in controversy.
- The total cost of production, compared to the resources available to each party.
- The relative ability of each party to control costs and its incentive to do so.
- The importance of the issues at stake in the litigation.
- The relative benefits to the parties of obtaining the information.[2]

The seven factors should not be weighted equally. When evaluating cost-shifting, the central question must be, does the request impose an "undue burden or expense" on the responding party?[3] Weighing the factors in descending

---

[Section 19:12]

[1]See Byers v. Illinois State Police, 53 Fed. R. Serv. 3d 740 (N.D. Ill. 2002).

[2]Zubulake v. UBS Warburg LLC, 217 F.R.D. 309, 324, 91 Fair Empl. Prac. Cas. (BNA) 1574 (S.D. N.Y. 2003).

[3]Zubulake v. UBS Warburg LLC, 217 F.R.D. 309, 322–23, 91 Fair Empl. Prac. Cas. (BNA) 1574 (S.D. N.Y. 2003) ("Put another way, 'how

order of importance may solve the problem and avoid a mechanistic application of the test.[4]

The first two factors comprise the "marginal utility" test, the next four as addressing cost issues, and the last factor is "the least important because it is fair to presume that the response to a discovery request generally benefits the requesting party."[5] In the unusual case where production will provide a tangible or strategic benefit to the responding party, that factor may weigh against shifting costs.[6]

Requiring the responding party to restore and produce backup tapes may inform the cost-shifting analysis. When based on an actual sample, the marginal utility test will not be an exercise in speculation—there will be tangible evidence of what the backup tapes may have to offer.[7] There will also be tangible evidence of the time and cost required to restore the backup tapes, which in turn will inform the second group of cost-shifting factors.[8]

"Sampling" backup tapes and other media that are difficult to access may provide an effective means for deter-

---

important is the sought-after evidence in comparison to the cost of production?' ").

[4]Zubulake v. UBS Warburg LLC, 217 F.R.D. 309, 323, 91 Fair Empl. Prac. Cas. (BNA) 1574 (S.D. N.Y. 2003). See also McPeek v. Ashcroft, 202 F.R.D. 31, 34, 50 Fed. R. Serv. 3d 528 (D.D.C. 2001) ("The more likely it is that the backup tape contains information that is relevant to a claim or defense, the fairer it is that the [responding party] search at its own expense. The less likely it is, the more unjust it would be to make the [responding party] search at its own expense. The difference is 'at the margin.' ").

[5]Zubulake v. UBS Warburg LLC, 217 F.R.D. 309, 323, 91 Fair Empl. Prac. Cas. (BNA) 1574 (S.D. N.Y. 2003).

[6]Zubulake v. UBS Warburg LLC, 217 F.R.D. 309, 323, 91 Fair Empl. Prac. Cas. (BNA) 1574 (S.D. N.Y. 2003).

[7]Zubulake v. UBS Warburg LLC, 217 F.R.D. 309, 324, 91 Fair Empl. Prac. Cas. (BNA) 1574 (S.D. N.Y. 2003).

[8]Zubulake v. UBS Warburg LLC, 217 F.R.D. 309, 324 n.77, 91 Fair Empl. Prac. Cas. (BNA) 1574 (S.D. N.Y. 2003) ("Of course, where the cost of a sample restoration is significant compared to the value of the suit, or where the suit itself is patently frivolous, even this minor effort *may* be inappropriate.") (italics in original).

mining whether the records contain relevant information.[9] Requesting parties should attempt to identify which of their opponent's inaccessible data would most likely yield the largest amount of, and the most useful, evidence, and they should target the most promising subset for sampling. Once samples are identified, the parties should make convincing presentations as to why production should or should not be required, and, if required, why in fairness the other side should pay for it.[10]

§ 19:13 Cost shifting—Avoiding and resisting

A discovering party needs to be very aware of the risk that sloppy, imprecise, or overly broad discovery can result in substantial cost shifting expenses, and possibly sanctions. There was a time when a discovering party could issue broad discovery requests and then it became the obligation of the responding party to decide whether a particular request mandated the production of certain evidence. Those days are past. A solid understanding of an adversary's computing infrastructure will aid a targeted and well-considered discovery effort. Doing due diligence with the experts will help to formulate specific, justifiable requests.

Discovery requests not drafted with thoughtful specificity may carry a significant price tag for a careless counsel.

---

[9]Zubulake v. UBS Warburg LLC, 217 F.R.D. 309, 324, 91 Fair Empl. Prac. Cas. (BNA) 1574 (S.D. N.Y. 2003); Rowe Entertainment, Inc. v. William Morris Agency, Inc., 205 F.R.D. 421, 432, 2002-1 Trade Cas. (CCH) P 73567, 51 Fed. R. Serv. 3d 1106 (S.D. N.Y. 2002). Cf. Peskoff v. Faber, 244 F.R.D. 54 (D.D.C. 2007) (appropriate to ascertain cost of forensic testing of computers and server to see if it justified forensic search for relevant e-mails).

[10]See, e.g., Hagemeyer North America, Inc. v. Gateway Data Sciences Corp., 222 F.R.D. 594 (E.D. Wis. 2004) (defendant required to restore sample of backup tapes in question).

In the words of the court in *Rowe Entertainment, Inc. v. William Morris Agency, Inc.*[1]:

> The less specific the requesting party's discovery demands, the more appropriate it is to shift the costs of production to that party. Where a party multiplies litigation costs by seeking expansive rather than targeted discovery, that party should bear the expense.

Rowe teaches that a discovering party conducts fishing expeditions very much at that party's peril. Before searches of large amounts of electronically stored information will be permitted, a discovering party may be required to demonstrate that such searches are likely to result in the production of relevant evidence.[2] One way to do this is to require a discovering party to produce evidence from witnesses that there is important relevant electronically stored information on a responding party's computer system.[3] In the case of large amounts of unindexed electronically stored information, such as might be found on disaster recovery backup tapes, one might allow the discovering party to have searches conducted on a limited number of tapes, by means of a test run, looking for certain evidence. The more hits there are, the less likely costs of discovery will be shifted to the discovering party.[4]

Rowe also makes allowance for the fact that a discovering party who has received documents in one format may have the right to request them in a different format, but only if the plaintiff is prepared to pay the costs:

[Section 19:13]

[1]Rowe Entertainment, Inc. v. William Morris Agency, Inc., 205 F.R.D. 421, 429–30, 2002-1 Trade Cas. (CCH) P 73567, 51 Fed. R. Serv. 3d 1106 (S.D. N.Y. 2002).

[2]Rowe Entertainment, Inc. v. William Morris Agency, Inc., 205 F.R.D. 421, 430, 2002-1 Trade Cas. (CCH) P 73567, 51 Fed. R. Serv. 3d 1106 (S.D. N.Y. 2002).

[3]Rowe Entertainment, Inc. v. William Morris Agency, Inc., 205 F.R.D. 421, 430, 2002-1 Trade Cas. (CCH) P 73567, 51 Fed. R. Serv. 3d 1106 (S.D. N.Y. 2002).

[4]McPeek v. Ashcroft, 202 F.R.D. 31, 34, 50 Fed. R. Serv. 3d 528 (D.D.C. 2001).

Some cases that have denied discovery of electronic evidence or have shifted costs to the requesting party have done so because equivalent information either has already been made available or is accessible in a different format at less expense. In Anti-Monopoly, Inc. v. Hasbro, Inc., 1996 WL 22976 *1 (S.D.N.Y. 1996). the defendant had already produced the requested data in hard copy. However, the plaintiff sought the same information in electronic form, presumably to facilitate computerized analysis. While recognizing that prior production in one form did not foreclose the plaintiff's demand, the court held that "[if] plaintiff wants the computerized information, it will have to pay defendants' reasonable costs of creating computer programs to extract the requested data from defendants' computers."[5]

Rowe makes an important distinction between electronically stored information retained for the purposes of accessing it in the ordinary course of business and data that has been retained just for the purpose of disaster or emergency recovery. According to *Rowe*, no cost shifting is allowed where data that has been retained with an intention that it can be retrieved in the ordinary course of business, whereas the cost of retrieving data from emergency backup tapes may be shifted to the requesting party.[6]

The groundwork for resisting a motion to shift costs can be established by the discovering party's insisting on conferences, constructing reasonable and focused requests, seeking court assistance when the responding party resists discovery, and educating the court from the beginning about why the digital evidence sought will expedite the

---

[5]Rowe Entertainment, Inc. v. William Morris Agency, Inc., 205 F.R.D. 421, 430, 2002-1 Trade Cas. (CCH) P 73567, 51 Fed. R. Serv. 3d 1106 (S.D. N.Y. 2002).

[6]Rowe Entertainment, Inc. v. William Morris Agency, Inc., 205 F.R.D. 421, 430, 2002-1 Trade Cas. (CCH) P 73567, 51 Fed. R. Serv. 3d 1106 (S.D. N.Y. 2002).

litigation.[7] When seeking to avoid cost shifting, a requesting party should consider the following arguments:[8]

- The requesting party's need for the discovery
- The inability of the requesting party to pay the costs related to the discovery in comparison with the producing party's ability to pay
- The likelihood that the requested information will lead to the discovery of admissible evidence
- The difficulty the requesting party will encounter in finding information from any other source
- The ease with which the responding party can find and produce the information requested
- The specificity of the discovery request
- The quantity of information available from other and more easily accessed sources
- The failure of the responding party to produce relevant information that seems likely to have existed, but is no longer available on more easily accessible sources
- Predictions as to the importance and usefulness of the further information
- The importance of the issues at stake in the litigation
- The parties respective sources

II. CHECKLISTS

§ 19:14 Checklist of cost shifting factors

- ☐ The extent to which the request is specifically tailored to discover relevant information.
- ☐ The availability of such information from other sources.
- ☐ The total cost of production, compared to the amount in controversy.

---

[7]See, e.g., In re Livent, Inc. Noteholders Securities Litigation, 2003 WL 23254 (S.D. N.Y. 2003) (ordering parties to review *Rowe* and confer to reach an agreement on issues such as cost-shifting).

[8]Fed. R. Civ. P. 26(b)(2). See Gonzalez & Montoya, Ten Tips Leading to Efficient and Effective eDiscovery for the Small Law Firm, GPS/Solo, Apr. 2007.

☐ The total cost of production, compared to the resources available to each party.
☐ The relative ability of each party to control costs and its incentive to do so.
☐ The importance of the issues at stake in the litigation.
☐ The relative benefits to the parties of obtaining the information.

Comment

See Zubulake v. UBS Warburg LLC, 217 F.R.D. 309, 322, 91 Fair Empl. Prac. Cas. (BNA) 1574 (S.D. N.Y. 2003).

§ 19:15 Checklist of factors to consider in compelling disclosure of e-mail

☐ How many persons are covered by the requesting party's e-mail request?
☐ What is the estimate cost of complying with the request?
☐ What are the benefits of discovery that the requesting party is requesting?
☐ Do the search terms and their quantity materially increase the cost of discovery?
☐ Should the costs of discovery be shifted?
☐ What computer resources or expertise did the requesting party rely on in formulating a search protocol?
☐ If the information is produced, how will the requesting party process the information?
☐ Is there a more efficient method for discovering the information requested?

Comment

This form is adapted from the record in Apsley v. Boeing Co., 2007 WL 163201 (D. Kan. 2007).

III. FORMS

§ 19:16 Notice and motion for protective order

[Caption]

NOTICE AND MOTION FOR PROTECTIVE ORDER

To: *[name]*

Attorney for *[party]*

[Address]

Please take notice that on *[date]* at *[time]*, or as soon thereafter as counsel can be heard, the undersigned will move this court at *[location]* for an order forbidding the taking of the deposition of *[name]*, on the ground that the examination is sought for the sole purpose of annoying and embarrassing the defendant *[name]*.

At the hearing, the undersigned will rely upon the affidavit of *[name]*, a copy of which is attached as Exhibit A.

The undersigned will further move for the reasonable expenses incurred in obtaining the order sought by this motion, including reasonable attorney fees.

Dated: ________

[signature etc.]

§ 19:17 Motion to stay all discovery pending resolution of certain motions submitted pursuant to stipulation

[Caption]

MOTION TO STAY DISCOVERY

Pursuant to an agreement with plaintiff *[name]*, defendant *[name]* moves for entry of an order staying all discovery in this matter pending resolution by the Court of defendant's Motion for *[specify]* pursuant to *[rule]*. In support of this motion, defendant submits the attached stipulation of the parties.

Dated: ________

[signature etc.]

STIPULATION

The parties, by their counsel, hereby stipulated that all discovery in this cause should be stayed pending a resolution of the defendant's Motion for *[specify]*.

Dated: ________

[signature etc.]

Dated: ________

[signature etc.]

§ 19:18 Motion for return of computer backup tapes

[Caption]

Defendant's Motion for Return of Computer Backup Tapes

To: *[name]*
[address]

Defendant *[name 1]*, by its attorneys, respectfully moves this Court for an order requiring Plaintiffs to return to *[name 1]* a set of improperly-obtained computer backup tapes from *[name 1's]* office. In support of its motion, Defendant *[name 1]* states as follows:

1. Counsel for the parties held a case management conference on *[date]*. At that meeting, Plaintiffs' counsel advised Defendant's counsel for the first time that, on

[date], Plaintiffs' counsel had received an anonymous box of approximately backup tapes that appeared to belong to defendant *[name 1]*. Plaintiffs' counsel advised further that they sent the box of tapes to *[name 2]* (Plaintiffs' computer forensic vendor), along with another backup tape they had received from Plaintiff *[name 3]* (who had been the Defendant's information technology employee working with the tapes during *[name 3]*'s employment with Defendant).

2. At the request of Defendant's counsel, Plaintiffs' counsel subsequently provided an inventory of those tapes, which appear to be total tapes from Defendant's office.

3. On *[date]*, Defendant's counsel faxed a letter to Plaintiffs' counsel asking for immediate return of the tapes, along with the box and any packing materials in which they were received. See Exhibit A. In that letter, Defendant's counsel asked Plaintiffs' counsel to provide the following information regarding the delivery of these tapes, including: (a) the disposition of the box and any packing materials in which they were received; (b) the date and location identified on the postmark; (c) the approximate time they were received; (d) who at the law firm representing plaintiffs received and opened the box; (e) whether anything was removed from the box; (f) when the box was transferred to *[name 2]* and to whom at *[name 2]*; (g) the chain of custody for the transfer of the tapes from the law firm representing Plaintiffs to *[name 2]*; and (h) whether any tapes were reviewed or analyzed by anyone on Plaintiffs' legal team, any of the Plaintiffs, or anyone at *[name 2]*).

4. As of the time of this motion, Plaintiffs' counsel has not responded to Defendant's counsel's *[date]* letter. On *[date]*, Defendant's counsel telephoned Plaintiffs' counsel to follow up on the *[date]* letter. Plaintiffs' counsel represented that Plaintiffs would not turn over the tapes without a court order.

5. Defendant *[name 1]* keeps and uses the data on its computer backup tapes in the ordinary course of business. They are regularly used to restore lost data, e.g., when an employee's computer crashes. That is why Defendant *[name 1]* created the backup tapes in the first place.

6. The backup tapes received by Plaintiffs contain stolen data, and may even be stolen originals. Defendant *[name 1]* is attempting to ascertain whether Plaintiffs received the original backup tapes, but it may take months to make this determination.

7. Regardless of whether Plaintiffs received original or copied backup tapes, Plaintiffs have a duty to return the tapes to defendant.

8. Moreover, it is illegal for Plaintiffs to refuse to return the tapes to Defendant. *[Statute]* states that a person commits theft when the person knowingly obtains control over stolen property knowing the property to have been stolen or under such circumstances as would reasonably induce the person to believe the property was stolen. If it were not already apparent to Plaintiffs' counsel by their mysterious receipt of an anonymous box of tapes, Defendant's counsel's *[date]*, letter to Plaintiffs' counsel, and the *[date]*, conversation with Plaintiffs' counsel put Plaintiffs on notice that the data on the tapes, and perhaps the very tapes themselves, were stolen.

WHEREFORE, for the foregoing reasons, Defendant *[name 1]* respectfully moves this Court for an order requiring Plaintiffs to return to Defendant the improperly-obtained computer backup tapes from Defendant's office.

Dated: ________

[signature, etc.]

Comment

This form is adapted from a motion in Wiginton v. CB Richard Ellis, Inc., 229 F.R.D. 568, 94 Fair Empl. Prac. Cas. (BNA) 627 (N.D. Ill. 2004). While the motion involves the return of backup tapes, it can be adapted for use in seeking the return any electronic media.

§ 19:19 Motion to shift costs

[Caption]

Defendant's Memorandum in Support of Motion for Fair Apportionment of Electronic Discovery Costs

INTRODUCTION

Over the course of a few months, Defendants reviewed a total of 1,082,807 pages of e-mails and attachments based on Plaintiffs' requests for: (i) the restoration of 108 backup tapes from four different timeframes; and (ii) the search of those tapes with 39 different search terms and numerous variations thereof. The cost of this massive project exceeded several hundred thousand dollars. Nineteen people worked on the e-mail review, many on an almost full-time basis.

The size and complexity of this undertaking was staggering. Plaintiffs knew that their requests would require extraordinary time and effort, yet they took the position that they should contribute none of the costs, let alone a fair share, caused by their own overly broad document requests. Defendants undertook their review and production subject to their right to seek such a fair allocation, which is the purpose of this Motion.

Courts recognize that electronic discovery is qualitatively and quantitatively different than traditional paper discovery due to the ability of modern technology to store vast amounts of information. E-discovery can, and often does, impose substantial burdens and expenses on the responding party. Accordingly, many courts (including this Court) allocate an equitable distribution of the costs of e-discovery between the requesting and the producing parties in appropriate circumstances.

As discussed below, these circumstances clearly are present in this case. The first and most important factor applied by the courts—the extent to which the requests are specifically tailored to discover relevant information—clearly mandates an allocation of costs to Plaintiffs. Plaintiffs have requested broad and expansive restorations, searches, reviews and productions of e-mails from Defendants' backup tapes. On their face, Plaintiffs' search terms are vague, ambiguous, and disconnected to the specific issues raised in this litigation. For example, Plaintiffs' search terms include such common words as "cherry*," "pregnan*," "cancer," and "marketing," with the asterisks representing any prefix or suffix associated with those terms. Plaintiffs' demanded terms snag everything in their path, and catch e-mails about such irrelevant topics as recipes or baby showers. The proof, however, is in the tangible impacts of Plaintiffs' requests, which have required Defendants to review 151,315 e-mails and attachments, comprising a total of 1,082,807 pages. Out of this massive amount of documents, Defendants identified and produced only 26,324 responsive documents. The breadth and expansiveness of Plaintiffs' requests are demonstrated by this extraordinary disparity between the searches demanded by Plaintiffs and the e-mails that are even potentially relevant in this case.

Plaintiffs already have represented to the court that they intend to avoid shouldering their fair share of the costs by making baseless accusations about the production process, many of which contradict their own prior accusations. Plaintiffs even have asserted that Defendants, not Plaintiffs, are somehow responsible for the breadth and scope of Plaintiffs' own requests encompassing over 300 individuals, 39 search terms (and multiple variations thereof) and 108 backup tapes. Plaintiffs' mudslinging, however, fails to counter the facts that: (1) Plaintiffs requested and are responsible for the production, and instead of narrowing or focusing the review, actually expanded the process to include additional persons, search terms and dates; and (2) the production methods employed by Defendants, through their consultant (Consultant), are the most efficient and cost-effective methods available, especially considering the breadth and scope of Plaintiffs' requested searches and the tight deadlines under which the parties were operating.

For those reasons and others set forth below, Defendants hereby request that this Court apportion to Plaintiffs 50% of the costs caused by Plaintiffs' requests concerning the restoration, search, review, and production of e-mails from backup tapes.

BACKGROUND

A. Plaintiffs' Initial Requests Required A Relatively Focused Production Of E-mails In Their Native Format.

When Plaintiffs initially requested electronic versions of e-mails from Defendants, it was in connection with document requests to Defendant served on *[date]*, and a subpoena served on *[name]* on or about *[date]*. Prior to this time, Plaintiffs had not issued a formal request for the electronic production of e-mails. Defendants expended considerable time and effort in negotiating and reaching agreement with Plaintiffs concerning the search terms to be used and the scope of backup tapes to be reviewed. When all was said and done, very little time remained before the *[date]* fact discovery cut-off for Defendants to restore and produce the documents.

Because only two timeframes of backup tapes were implicated by Plaintiffs' requests, Defendants undertook the restoration process in-house and produced the documents in their native format (as they were stored on the Outlook system). Because the documents existed in their native format, they could not be bates-labeled without alteration, and Plaintiffs complained on a number of occasions about that inherent deficiency of a native production. The native format documents also could not be redacted electronically. Instead, documents requiring redaction had to printed, redacted, and produced in hard copy form. Once again, Plaintiffs complained. Plaintiffs even went so far as to seek an order from the Court compelling the production of these redacted documents electronically.

B. Plaintiffs Requested An Additional Restoration of A Multitude Of Backup Tapes and Demanded Searches With Overbroad Criteria.

One day after the Court entered an order on [*date*],

extending the fact-discovery deadline, Plaintiffs demanded a new restoration, search, review and production of backup e-mails. Plaintiffs then informed Defendants that Plaintiffs also demanded the production to be bates-labeled, that Plaintiffs demanded Boolean searches performed on the e-mails, and that Plaintiffs demanded additional persons to be added to the search list.

As Plaintiffs' demands accumulated, it became clear that Plaintiffs were insisting on the restoration and search of 108 backup tapes and the search of 327 individuals' e-mail accounts using 39 search terms (and multiple variations thereof). Subsequently, Plaintiffs insisted on the search of the e-mail accounts of several more individuals. Defendants, fully cognizant of *[date]*, Order and the need to avoid any delay in the production process, discussed and memorialized their "concerns . . . based on [the] burden" of Plaintiffs' requests, but agreed to proceed subject to all "rights and remedies with regard to the costs incurred in performing additional restorations and searches and undertaking the production." As Defendants made clear: "We are proceeding with the work so that we avoid any delay based on the parties' failure to agree regarding the allocation of costs. However, we intend to seek reimbursement for a fair portion of the costs associated with the extensive and expensive tasks necessitated by the backup e-mail production that Plaintiffs have requested."

C. Defendants Needed To Retain A Consultant To Restore and Search the Backup Tapes and Enable Defendants To Review The E-mails.

Defendants could not avoid incurring substantial costs in connection with this production in light of Plaintiffs' broad search demand, including the number of backup tapes requiring restoration and the nature and scope of the demanded search terms. Nevertheless, Defendants did select the most efficient and least costly method available to them. Defendants employed Consultant, one of the nation's leading providers of e-discovery services, to assist with the production. Defendants simply could not undertake a restoration, search and review of the size and complexity demanded by Plaintiffs without the assistance of a consultant like Consultant. Furthermore, after Consultant began the restoration process, it discovered that five of the 108 backups tapes contained corrupted information. It is unlikely that Amerigroup Illinois would have been able to restore these corrupted tapes without Consultant's technical expertise.

Specifically, Consultant performed the following work on the backup tapes:

a) *Restoration of media*—Consultant extracted all data on every tape (unless corrupt) onto a hard drive for further analysis;

b) *Header Scan*—Consultant included header information on all tapes to allow backup tapes to be properly ordered;

c) *Restoration of Exchange Databases*—Consultant attempted to locate and extract case-specific custodians as instructed by Defendants;

d) *Tape Copy and Recovery*—Consultant copied corrupt tapes in an attempt to recover corrupt data;

e) *Exchange Database Analysis*—Consultant analyzed the database to determine user names located on corrupt tapes;

f) *Exchange Database Repair*—Consultant attempted to obtain relevant data from the corrupt tape after users were located on corrupt media;

g) *Exchange Database Repair*—Level 2—Consultant employed repair processes for cases of more serious corruption; and

h) *Expedite Fees*—Consultant rescheduled other work in order to make this job a priority.

As part of the restoration procedure, Consultant processed the documents from their native application into PDF format, with text and metadata preserved and indexed for search accuracy. Consultant then uploaded the PDF documents onto its Online Review Application, which is an Internet-based system. This enabled multiple reviewers to examine the restored e-mails for responsiveness, another critical capability necessitated by the breadth of Plaintiffs' requests and the number of e-mails resulting therefrom. This is a standard method for conducting such a large volume e-mail production. *See* Wiginton v. CB Richard Ellis, Inc., 229 F.R.D. 568, 570, 94 Fair Empl. Prac. Cas. (BNA) 627 (N.D. Ill. 2004) (shifting 75% of e-discovery costs where outside vendor was hired to "restore and extract the user e-mails from the tapes, perform searches for keywords and file attachment types, and load the results of the searches onto [vendor's] Internet-based system, for review").

PDF processing was critical to this process for a number of reasons. First, native file review quickly becomes extremely complicated and expensive due to the variety of software programs, including outdated versions of the same program, that are often encountered. In this case, Consultant processed over 90 distinct file types. If this data were reviewed natively, each computer employed in the review process would require software compatible with all 90 of these file types.

Furthermore, Consultant's PDF processing made it feasible to review, search, categorize, redact, and produce e-mails on the scale necessitated by Plaintiffs' requests. If the documents remained in a native application, such as Microsoft Outlook, each attachment would have to be opened manually to check for relevant or privileged information. Duplicative e-mails and attachments would need to be reviewed separately, increasing the number of e-mails to be reviewed by tens of thousands and raising serious risks of inconsistent responsiveness and privilege determinations by different reviewers. Additionally, no redactions could electronically be made to documents in their native format. Nor could the documents be bates-labeled or marked "confidential."

Moreover, processing the documents into a PDF format avoids the potential for inadvertent changes to the native files. For example, a document created in a word-processing program typically stores a "date last modified" field in the document's metadata. The simple act of opening a file for review, even when no changes are made, can alter the document's modification history. Other changes, such as modifying the "create" date, can occur when native files are copied for review, before reviewers even begin their work. Without proper precautions, relevant and material information can be forever altered. These changes to the metadata can occur during the review process and/or after documents are produced to opposing counsel.

D. Plaintiffs' Overly Broad Requests Resulted in Substantial Costs to Defendants.

The total cost of work performed by Consultant in restoring the backup tapes, performing the specified searches, and uploading the data to the Online Review Application, which includes project management, software maintenance, software upgrades, hosting, database security and all functionality provided by the Online Review application, and performing additional necessary work is $238,508.66. This figure does not include the costs associated with the time spent by personnel in the course of the review and production, which far exceeds the total for the work performed by Consultant.

Since Defendants are seeking a fair allocation of the costs of the electronic discovery, Defendants are not seeking reimbursement for, and have redacted from the attached invoices, costs (i) that relate solely to the Defendants' production needs; and (ii) that relate to duplicate production resulting from the need to insure family groups of e- mails and their attachments remained together.

The bottom line is that the total costs incurred in connection with responding to Plaintiffs' e-discovery requests have exceeded several hundred thousands of dollars. Defendants therefore request a fair apportionment of these costs.

ARGUMENT

Courts agree that shifting the costs of e-discovery is appropriate under the *[rules]*, but they disagree about the standard to be used in determining when such cost-shifting should take place. Cost-shifting is implicit in the protective order provisions of *[rule]*, which authorizes "any order which justice requires to protect a party or person from . . . undue burden or expense." *See also* Advisory Committee Notes to 1970 Amendments to Rule 34 ("The courts have ample power under Rule 26(c) to protect respondent against undue burden or expense, either by restricting discovery or requiring that the discovering party pay costs."). Furthermore, as one court has noted, "the maturation of Rule 26(b)(2) over several decades allows judges to use the limitations of Rule 26(b)(2) with increasing frequency and with an eye toward equity . . . [which] undeniably, includes cost-shifting in discovery." United Parcel Service of America, Inc. v. The Net, Inc., 222 F.R.D. 69, 71 (E.D. N.Y. 2004).

The Northern District of Illinois, in particular, has embraced cost-shifting of electronic discovery expenses. *See, e.g.*, Portis v. City of Chicago, 2004 WL 2812084 (N.D. Ill. 2004) ("cost-shifting is not that unusual, particularly in cases involving discovery of electronic evidence"); *Wiginton*, 229 F.R.D. at 577 (shifting 75% of e-discovery costs to the requesting party); Byers v. Illinois State Police, 53 Fed. R. Serv. 3d 740 (N.D. Ill. 2002), at* 12 (N.D. Ill. June 3, 2002).

Of the three tests devised by the courts for determining the appropriateness of cost-shifting, the most recent test, announced in Zubulake v. UBS Warburg LLC, 217 F.R.D. 309, 91 Fair Empl. Prac. Cas. (BNA) 1574 (S.D. N.Y. 2003) ("*Zubulake I*"), now predominates. The *Zubulake I* court concluded that the following seven factors should be considered, in descending order of importance:

1. the extent to which the requested information is specifically tailored to discover relevant information;

2. the availability of such information from other sources;
3. the total cost of production, compared with the amount in controversy;
4. the total cost of production compared to the resources available to each party;
5. the relative ability of each party to control costs and its incentive to do so;
6. the importance of the issues at stake in the litigation; and
7. the relative benefits to the parties of obtaining the information.

217 F.R.D. at 322. As the *Zubulake I* test has been applied by this Court, Defendants focus on those factors for purposes of this Motion. *See Wiginton*, 229 F.R.D. at 573.

A. COST-SHIFTING IS NECESSARY AND APPROPRIATE BECAUSE THE E-MAILS ARE STORED ON BACKUP TAPES.

Under *Zubulake I*, the threshold test for determining whether cost-shifting may prove appropriate in any particular case is whether the data sought is "inaccessible." *Zubulake I*, 217 F.R.D. at 323 ("[a] court should consider cost-shifting *only* when electronic data is relatively inaccessible, such as in backup tapes") (emphasis in original). *Zubulake I* identifies two categories of electronic data that are considered "inaccessible" and thus appropriate for cost-shifting: (1) backup tapes, and (2) erased, fragmented or damaged data. *Id.* All of the e-mails at issue here are stored on 108 backup tapes. Furthermore, five of the 108 backup tapes contained corrupted data that had to be recovered and restored. Accordingly, the threshold test is met in this case, permitting this Court to allocate a portion of the e-discovery costs to Plaintiffs.

B. THE FACTORS WEIGH HEAVILY IN FAVOR OF COST-SHIFTING.

Taken together, Factors 1 and 2 restate what is better

known as the "marginal utility" test, which weighs the relative costs and benefits of the e-discovery requests. *See McPeek*, 202 F.R.D. at 34. These factors are the most important of the seven *Zubulake I* factors, and carry the greatest weight in determining whether e-discovery costs should be shifted. *Zubulake I*, 217 F.R.D. at 322. Here, the "marginal utility" test strongly weighs in favor of cost-shifting due to the overbroad and unduly burdensome nature of Plaintiffs' requests.

In Zubulake v. UBS Warburg LLC, 216 F.R.D. 280, 287, 92 Fair Empl. Prac. Cas. (BNA) 684, 56 Fed. R. Serv. 3d 326 (S.D. N.Y. 2003) ("*Zubulake III*"), the court found that cost-shifting was appropriate even though "the discovery request was narrowly tailored to discover relevant information." In sharp contrast to the present case, the *Zubulake* plaintiff *narrowed* her original request from communications with all employees to e-mails that were sent to or from *only five specified employees*. *Id.* at 285. This resulted in a mere 1,075 e-mails after duplicates were eliminated, 600 of which were responsive and were produced. *Id.* at 282.

Here, Plaintiffs expanded their initial e-discovery requests to encompass 108 backup tapes. Plaintiffs also expanded the scope of the search to include 327 persons and 39 different search terms and variations thereof. Compounding the breadth of their requests, Plaintiffs demanded that various search terms beginning or ending with asterisks must be searched for "all forms of a word that have characters where [each] asterisk is located." Plaintiffs' search terms included such common words as "cherry*," "pregnan*," "marketing," and "cancer." As an inevitable result of Plaintiffs' choice of these terms, Defendants were forced to review a multitude of irrelevant and unresponsive documents. The search terms, which would ordinarily serve to narrow and focus the documents to be reviewed, instead required Defendants to review everything from resumes and interview schedules to chain e-mails circulating among Defendants' employees.

The numbers demonstrate the overbreadth and

impropriety of Plaintiffs' requests including the search terms and methodology. Unlike the approximately 1,000 potentially responsive e-mails in *Zubulake III*, Plaintiffs' overly-broad requests flagged over 151,315 e- mails and attachments to be reviewed for potential production. Only 26,324 of the reviewed e- mails were produced, which amounts to a paltry 17.39%. By contrast, 55.8% of documents were responsive in *Zubulake III*, yet the court still held that 25% of the e-discovery costs should be shifted to the plaintiffs. In *Wiginton*, where the response rate was only 4.5 to 6.5%, the court shifted 75% of the costs of the discovery. 229 F.R.D. at 577. Here, where the response rate falls between these extremes, the marginal utility test weighs in favor of cost-shifting, and it would be both fair and equitable to shift 50% of the e-discovery costs to Plaintiffs.

The fact that the e-mails on the backup tapes were not readily available from other sources does not change this analysis. In *Wiginton*, for example, responsive and relevant documents were "only available through restoring and searching the backup tapes." 229 F.R.D. at 574. Nevertheless, the Court held that "because the search also revealed a significant number of unresponsive documents . . . the marginal utility test weigh[ed] slightly in favor of cost-shifting." *Id.* Here, similarly, the significant number of unresponsive documents resulting from Plaintiffs selection of broad search terms means the marginal utility test weighs in favor of cost-shifting.

The third *Zubulake I* factor—the total cost of the production compared with the amount in controversy—also weighs in favor of cost-shifting. As set forth above, the costs incurred in responding to Plaintiffs' e-discovery requests exceeded several hundred thousands of dollars. The amount in controversy, however, is entirely speculative at this point. While Plaintiffs will no doubt claim that there is the potential for a multi-million dollar recovery, a similar argument was unavailing in *Wiginton*. In *Wiginton*, the court found that this factor weighed in favor of cost-shifting despite Plaintiffs' claim that that their recovery could potentially be in the "tens of millions:"

Plaintiffs claim that should a class be certified, their class recovery could extend into the tens of millions of dollars. While the Court cannot completely accept Plaintiffs' speculative estimate of its potential damage award, neither can it accept that their claims are worthless . . .. Nevertheless, several hundred thousand dollars for one limited part of discovery is a substantial amount of actual dollars to pay for such a search. Therefore, this factor weighs in favor of cost-shifting. 229 F.R.D. at 575. The total cost of production in this case will meet or even exceed the total in *Wiginton*. Plaintiffs here should similarly bear their fair share of the e-discovery costs.

With respect to the fourth factor—the total cost of production compared to the resources available to each party—the *Zubulake* case recognizes that "it is not unheard of for plaintiff's firms to front huge expenses when multi-million dollar recoveries are in sight." *Zubulake III*, 216 F.R.D. at 288. Furthermore, Tyson is not the only plaintiff in this case. The State of Illinois elected to intervene, and in so doing brought with it all of the State's vast resources. The Illinois State Budget for fiscal year 2006, for example, provides for a total budget in excess of $70 million for the Office of the Attorney General. And the United States government also intervened in this case, providing even deeper pockets to fund the litigation. Plaintiffs' resources also show the need for cost-shifting.

The fifth factor—the relative ability of each party to control costs and its incentive to do so—also weighs in favor of allocating costs to Plaintiffs. The *Wiginton* court held that the scope of the search that a plaintiff requires is an important element in the costs of the production, because "[a] smaller search term list would result in less hits, and less documents that must be transferred to an electronic viewer." *Wiginton*, 229 F.R.D. at 576. *See also* Byers, 2002 WL 1264004, at *12 (noting that shifting a portion of the costs to a plaintiff provides an incentive for more focused requests). Here, Plaintiffs' demands encompassed over 300 individuals and 39 search terms, with multiple variations thereof.

In contrast, Defendants have done what they can to control the substantial costs caused by Plaintiffs' requests. The magnitude and complexity of the restoration process required the services of a large consultant, such as Consultant, with the resources and manpower to handle the task in a timely manner. Defendants, in conjunction with Consultant, then selected the most efficient and least costly restoration process available. As discussed above, converting the native files to PDF format, and then uploading them to Consultant's Online Review Application, resulted in substantial savings of both time and money. Indeed, this Court has recognized the need for such Internet-based systems in large-scale electronic discovery. *Wiginton*, 229 F.R.D. at 570. It was simply not feasible for Defendants to handle this document production in a less expensive manner.

The final two factors also support the need to allocate costs to Plaintiffs. Plaintiffs have demanded these restorations, searches, reviews and production in order to benefit their case. Indeed, Plaintiffs are touting and citing certain produced e-mails as supposedly supporting their allegations in this matter. Defendants undertook these processes at the requests of Plaintiffs, who should pay a fair proportion of the resulting costs.

CONCLUSION

For the reasons set forth above and in the Motion, this Court should allocate 50% of the $238,508.66 costs of the backup e-mail production process to Plaintiffs.

Dated: ________

[signature, etc.]

Comment

This form is adapted from a motion in U.S, ex rel. Tyson v. Amerigroup Illinois, Inc., 2006 WL 1782970 (N.D. Ill. 2006). Because the fact-intense nature of a cost-shifting motion, the basic facts have been left in the form to illustrate the amount of detail that may be necessary.

§ 19:20 Defendant's opposition to plaintiffs' motion to compel defendant to produce electronic documents in native format with metadata

[Caption]

Defendant's Opposition to Plaintiffs' Motion to Compel Defendant to Produce Electronic Documents in Native Format with Metadata

Defendant respectfully opposes Plaintiff's Motion to Compel Defendant to Produce Electronic Documents in Native Format with Metadata. Defendant respectfully requests that Plaintiffs' motion be denied. To the extent that Plaintiffs' motion is granted, Defendant respectfully requests that the associated costs be shifted to Plaintiffs.

INTRODUCTION

This is a patent case involving United States Patent No. 6,685,941 ("the '941 patent"). As Plaintiffs identified, this case involves a number of issues—invalidity of the '941 patent, unenforceability of the '941 patent due to inequitable conduct, a license granted by Plaintiffs to Defendant to practice the '941 patent, Bristol's ownership rights of the '941 patent pursuant to an agreement with UM, and alleged infringement of the '941 patent.

Plaintiffs have requested Defendant to produce paper and electronic documents. They are amendable to Defendant producing the paper documents converted to TIFF format with search capability. Yet, this same format is not acceptable to Plaintiffs for electronic files. They allege there may be hidden data or data about the documents that is relevant that will not be available in TIFF format (TIFF file images are similar to what an electronic document would look like if printed). Instead, Plaintiffs insist that native files and metadata be produced for every electronic document. However, information associated with native files and metadata for the vast majority of the documents will have marginal, if any, relevance to the claims and the defenses of this litigation. And, insisting upon the wholesale production of native files and metadata for every document is an unreasonable request that would result in an undue burden and undue expense on Defendant, without any likelihood of benefit to Plaintiffs. In fact, courts have held that a requesting party needs to make a showing of *a particularized need* before a motion to compel native files and metadata will be granted. In the spirit of compromise, Defendant proposed to provide Plaintiffs with native files and metadata for specific documents, following Plaintiffs review of the files in TIFF format, within reason. Not happy with this compromise, Plaintiffs filed the present motion, before even reviewing the TIFF versions of the electronic documents.

Plaintiffs state that Defendant "steadfastly has maintained that it will not produce native documents together with their metadata." This is simply not true, as is evidenced by Defendant's letters:

ARGUMENT

I. The Production of Native Files and/or Metadata Upon a Showing of a Particularized Need Is Consistent with Recent Case Law

Plaintiffs insist that native files and metadata be produced for each and every electronic document Defendant intends to produce. Defendant proposed to provide Plaintiffs with native files and metadata for specific documents following Plaintiffs review of the files in TIFF format, within reason. In practice, courts have not been as kind—requiring requesting parties to show *a particularized need* for the native files and/or metadata before ordering them produced.

The Sedona Conference, as one of its fourteen principles for electronic document production, states that "[u]nless it is material to resolving the dispute, there is no obligation to preserve or produce metadata absent agreement of the parties or order of the court." THE

SEDONA PRINCIPLES: *Best Practices Recommendations & Principles for Addressing Electronic Document Production* (The Sedona Conference Working Group Series, July 2005 Version). The Sedona Conference recognizes that information associated with native files and metadata is sometimes inaccurate, and that in most cases it need not be produced (*Id.* at 46–47).

II. The Information Contained in Native Files and/or Metadata Is Not Relevant in Most Cases

The fact that the information contained in native files and/or metadata is not relevant in most cases (and in fact is incorrect in many cases) militates against a wholesale production of native files and metadata. Plaintiffs argue that "whenever a document is relevant, it is almost certainty that the identity of the document's author and editors, the date of its creation and modification, the title of the document, and the directory location of the document would also be relevant or reasonably calculated to lead to the discovery of admissible evidence" (P. Br. at 5). This is contrary to what courts and The Sedona Conference have concluded. For example, the fact that a letter dated February 10, 1999 was actually created on February 8, 1999 or that a secretary was the typist is not relevant. However, should Plaintiffs identify a particular document where the creation date, author, or other issues of authenticity are legitimately subject to question, Defendant's proposal provides a remedy to this concern. Therefore, just because Defendant is producing a document in TIFF format does not make the native files or metadata of the document relevant to the claims or defenses of the litigation.

III. The Burden and Expense of Plaintiffs' Request Outweigh Its Likely Benefit

Plaintiffs' motion should be denied as the burden and expense that would be incurred by Defendant would be undue, particularly in light of the minimal, if any, benefit that would be conferred upon Plaintiffs by the production of native files and metadata for every electronic file produced.

Defendant is currently reviewing the electronic files in imaged (TIFF) format. This allows the attorneys to review the documents without opening a software application other than the image viewer. Based on the document review performed thus far, Defendant estimates that the review of the documents in imaged format will take approximately one to two minutes per document (that is, to determine whether or not the document is relevant, privileged, confidential, or highly confidential).

If documents are to be reviewed in their native format (the format requested by Plaintiffs), it is necessary to first open the appropriate software application (e.g., to review a Microsoft Word document, the reviewer first has to open the document in the Microsoft Word application). Then, if the next document happens to be a Microsoft Excel document, the reviewer would need to open the Microsoft Excel application. This alone would add a significant quantity of time to the document review process, as the review is expected to encompass approximately 6,500,000 pages (approximately 650,000 documents). After the correct software application is opened, then the reviewer needs to determine if there is information present that would not otherwise be printed. For example, with respect to a Microsoft Word application, the reviewer needs to turn on the feature that allows tracked changes to be viewed before being able review this information. Then, the reviewer would need to review the metadata associated with the document. Defendant expects the impact of reviewing the files in their native format along with the information available from the native files and metadata will increase the time to review each document from one to two minutes to two to three minutes. While this may seem insignificant, as Defendant expects to review approximately 650,000 documents, this equates to an estimated increase of 5,400 man-hours to the review process.

Defendant's outside counsel is attempting to minimize the cost of the review, but the additional man-hours are expected to yield an increase of at least approximately $500,000 to the document review process This does not include the additional costs associated with Defendant's counsel obtaining the native files and producing them to Plaintiffs, which is expected to exceed $100,000. It would be far less burdensome for the requesting party to identify the files for which it needs metadata or native files.

Plaintiffs argue that the production of native files and metadata for select documents "would not aid in searching and understanding the montage of Defendant's production." But, Plaintiffs have not identified a tangible benefit that understanding the montage of the production would provide them nor how the montage is relevant to the claims or defenses. They state that they would need to "attempt to divine—by complete guesswork those documents for which the original electronic file might contain relevant metadata or other printed information." But, Defendant is not suggesting divining or guesswork; rather, Defendant is suggesting that the Plaintiffs identify specific documents for which they would like to review the native files and metadata. To the extent that native files and metadata do exist, Defendant will provide it, within reason.

Plaintiffs also state that the identification of specific files for which they need the native files or metadata "reveals attorney work product about which documents plaintiffs are focusing on, which they may intend to use for deposition, and the like." But, this is nothing new—it is necessary to reveal such information throughout litigation. For example, the parties exchanged keyword search terms that they view as important for the case for the purpose of filtering electronic documents, and Plaintiffs have identified documents that they are focusing on for their infringement contentions.

In light of the fact that most of the information associated with the native files and metadata for the electronic documents is of limited evidentiary value and reviewing it can waste litigation resources, and in light of the fact that most of the information available from native files or metadata is not relevant, the burden and expense is undue. Moreover, as Defendant has agreed to provide Plaintiffs with the native files and metadata to the extent that they make a reasonably request after Plaintiffs review of the documents in imaged format, this undue expense is also unnecessary.

IV. Bristol Requests that Plaintiffs Be Asked to Bear the Cost Burden to the Extent that Bristol Is Compelled to Review and Produce the Native Files and Metadata

As illustrated above, it is Defendant's position that the burden and expense of producing native files and metadata for every electronic document outweighs the small, if any, benefit received by Plaintiffs. Therefore, to the extent that the Court grants Plaintiffs' motion, Bristol respectfully requests that Plaintiffs be asked to bear the financial burden associated with the Bristol's review and production of the information.

While this Court is not limited to performing the cost-shifting analysis based on a particular set of factors, the Southern District of New York has set forth a commonly-cited seven factor test to determining whether cost-shifting is appropriate, weighed more-or-less in the following order:

1. The extent to which the request is specifically tailored to discover relevant information;
2. The availability of such information from other sources;
3. The total cost of production, compared to the amount in controversy;
4. The total cost of production, compared to the resources available to each party;
5. The relative ability of each party to control costs and its incentive to do so;
6. The importance of the issues at stake in the litigation; and

7. The relative benefits to the parties of obtaining the information.

Zubulake v. UBS Warburg LLC, 217 F.R.D. 309, 322–24, 91 Fair Empl. Prac. Cas. (BNA) 1574 (S.D. N.Y. 2003). While *Zubulake* addressed the situation where the electronic data is not accessible, cost-shifting is not limited to situations where the electronic data is not accessible.

Regarding the first factor, Plaintiffs request is not specifically tailored to discover relevant information. The information associated with native files and metadata is rarely relevant (see above). And, Plaintiffs are requesting the information for every electronic file produced. This factor weighs in favor of cost-shifting.

Regarding the second factor, the relevant information will likely be available from other sources. For example, the author of a letter, date of the letter, and recipients are likely to be on the letter itself (which will be provided in TIFF format). This factor weighs in favor of cost-shifting.

Regarding the third factor, while the Plaintiffs have not identified an amount in controversy, the cost for the review and production of this information is not insignificant—expected to be at least approaching $500,000; with at least another $100,000 to obtain and produce the native files. Regarding the fourth factor, while Defendant has significant resources, these resources should not be wasted. These factors weigh in favor of cost shifting.

Regarding the fifth factor, Plaintiffs can control the cost by requesting native files or metadata for specified files, but they have no incentive to do so unless they bear the financial burden. To the contrary, during its document review, Defendant will be reviewing all of the information simultaneously and therefore has an incentive to control cost. This factor weighs in favor of cost-shifting.

Regarding the sixth factor, while the issues of this litigation are important, the production of native files and metadata is not expected to have any effect on the outcome of the litigation. Regarding the seventh factor, the benefit expected to be conferred upon either party by producing all of the native files and metadata is expected to be minimal. Therefore, these factors are neutral.

Looking at these factors as a whole, cost-shifting is appropriate.

CONCLUSION

Based on the foregoing, Defendant respectfully requests that Plaintiffs' motion be denied. In the alternative, Defendant respectfully requests that the cost associated with obtaining, reviewing, and producing the native files and metadata be shifted to the Plaintiffs.

Dated: ________

[signature, etc.]

Comment

This form is adapted from a motion in Repligen Corp. v. Bristol-Myers Squibb Co., 2007 WL 684265 (E.D. Tex. 2007).

§ 19:21 Order to quash notice to take depositions and subpoenas

[Caption]

This matter is pending on a motion by the *[party]* to quash certain of *[party's]* notice to take depositions. A memorandum filed this date is incorporated in and made a part of this order. Accordingly,

IT IS HEREBY ORDERED that the motion of the defendant is granted and the notice to take the deposition of *[name]* is quashed on the condition that *[for example]* an officer or managing agent of the *[party]* who has knowledge of the issues in controversy be directed to appear and have his/her deposition taken at the place indicated in *[party's]* motion within ten days from this date.

IT IS FURTHER ORDERED that the subpoena directed to *[name]* directing him/her to produce *[describe]* is also quashed.

Dated: ________

____

Judge

§ 19:22 Order extending time within which to answer requests for admissions

[Caption]

This cause was heard on the motion of the *[plaintiff] [defendant]* for additional time, through *[date]*, within which to answer the *[defendant's] [plaintiff's]* Requests for Admissions and the motion having been considered by the Court,

IT IS ORDERED that *[plaintiff's] [defendant's]* motion be and is hereby granted and *[plaintiff] [defendant]* is hereby allowed through *[date]*, within which to answer the *[defendant's [plaintiff's]* Requests for Admissions.

Dated: ________

____

Judge

[signature etc.]

§ 19:23 Order sealing answers to interrogatories

[Caption]

The answers to the interrogatories filed in this matter by *[plaintiff] [defendant]* on *[date]* are hereby sealed and the parties and parties' counsel are admonished not to disclose their contents to anyone.

Dated: ________

____
Judge

Index